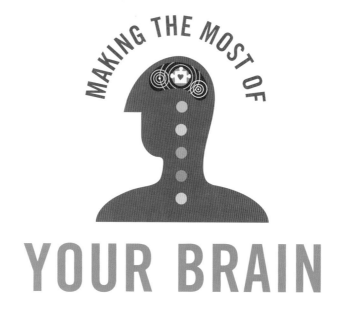

MAKING THE MOST OF YOUR BRAIN

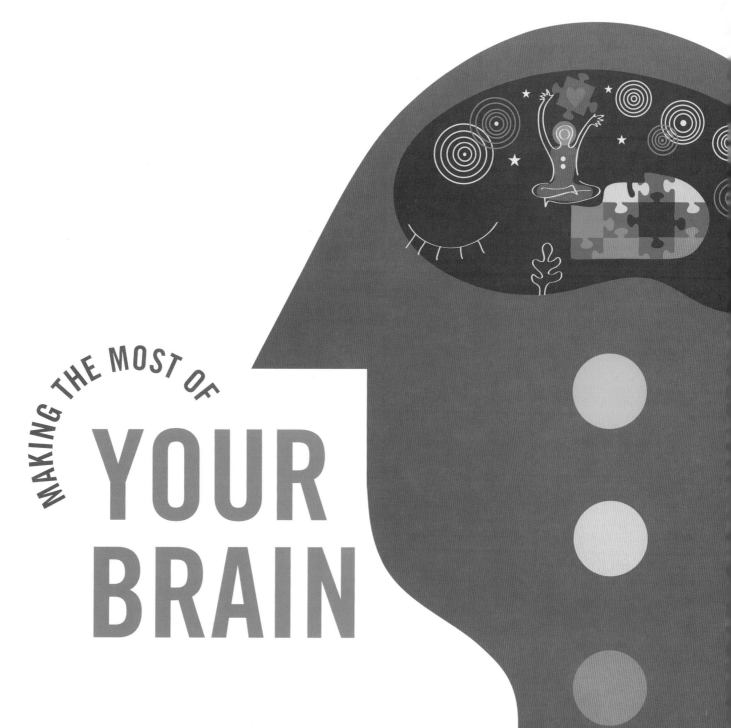

MAKING THE MOST OF
YOUR
BRAIN

THE READER'S DIGEST ASSOCIATION LIMITED   LONDON • NEW YORK • SYDNEY • MONTREAL

CONTENTS

3 THE CONSCIOUS & UNCONSCIOUS BRAIN

INTRODUCTION

Most of us never stretch our brain beyond a fraction of its vast potential. *Making the Most of Your Brain* aims to reveal that potential through a wealth of fascinating, up-to-date information, as well as practical exercises and tips that will help you to understand your brain and stretch its capabilities. Whatever your age, once you realise what your brain is capable of achieving, you will be able to use it to improve your memory, enhance your intelligence, increase your creativity and much more besides.

The human brain is the most complex and sophisticated system to be found anywhere on planet Earth. Its power and versatility are awesome – so much so that we will probably never succeed in understanding it fully. And if the brain is mysterious, even more so is the mind, the living experience of the human brain in action. The mind is intimately bound up with every aspect of being a person: identity, character, intelligence, creativity, empathy, emotions, action. To get some grasp of how astonishing the mind, and therefore the brain, truly is, consider just how much is going on and what exactly is happening when, for example, you remember how delicious yesterday's lunch was while listening to music on the radio, musing on where to go for your summer holiday, and making a cup of tea. Each of these things is essentially commonplace, yet reflects a different aspect of how the brain contributes to our lives – memory, pleasure, attention, anticipation, physical coordination – and can do them all at the same time. Such understanding can only go a certain way toward grasping

MAKING THE MOST OF YOUR BRAIN

the inner processes involved in these experiences. Even science can go only so far – although we are gradually learning more from scientists, thanks to discoveries that are partly the result of research and experiment and partly the result of chance.

The book is divided into three parts. Part One, **The Healing Brain**, focuses on the brain's ability to influence well-being and health. It reveals the mechanisms behind the brain's powers to promote self-healing, and explains how the brain can control pain and aid recovery from illness. It describes what can go wrong with the brain and what can be done about it. And it explores practical ways by which we can harness the healing capacity of our brains to benefit our lives and health.

Memory is the foundation for everything that we learn and do in life, and Part Two, **A Good Memory**, will help you to understand how your memory works and how to make the most of it. Here, you will discover what is known about the different types of memory and how they operate in all aspects of our lives. There are practical exercises and routines that can improve everyday memory power, and help to make sure memory does not fail with age. Also explained are techniques used by memory champions which, with practice, anyone can use to improve their memory performance.

Part Three, **The Conscious and Unconscious Brain**, explores the burning issue of brain science today: the quest to understand consciousness. It examines how the conscious and unconscious aspects of our minds work together to produce our thoughts and actions, and reveals some very recent discoveries about the workings of the brain. It also describes techniques that can enhance your conscious awareness and help you to achieve a more focused mind.

1

THE HEALING BRAIN

YOUR AMAZING BRAIN

The human brain is the most complex system in the known universe. Its 100 billion cells and intricate network of neural fibres give it immense processing power and incredible versatility that far outweighs that of any computer. Here are ten amazing facts about the brain that give an insight into what it is capable of and its incredible healing abilities.

THE BRAIN IS ABLE TO ALTER ALMOST ANY BODY FUNCTION

Heart rate can be slowed, the bowel relaxed and blood vessels opened or closed, just through thought. Imagining being warm, for example, can increase the temperature in a person's fingers by more than 1°C.

THE BRAIN HAS POWERS TO MEND THE DAMAGE AFTER STROKE

Although nerve cells affected by stroke usually die, connections between surviving cells can regrow, bypassing damaged areas. In this way, the brain can resculpture itself, often regaining some of the functions lost immediately after a stroke.

CUDDLING A BABY ENCOURAGES IT TO GROW

Physical affection causes the brain to secrete a chemical called dopamine which in turn triggers the release of growth hormones. Babies deprived of close physical contact with others may therefore be slower to develop, psychologically as well as physically.

IN REGULATING THE APPETITE THE BRAIN CAN MATCH CALORIE INPUT TO ENERGY OUTPUT ALMOST PERFECTLY

In practice, the region of the brain that controls food intake is frequently overridden by conscious desires for food created by social and other pressures. But left alone, the brain provokes hunger only when glucose levels fall below the optimum level. In this situation, a person's weight would vary less than 5 per cent during their entire adult life.

THE BRAIN IS THE FASTEST-GROWING ORGAN IN THE BODY

In a developing foetus, up to a quarter of a million brain cells are produced every minute. After birth, rapid growth continues. By the time a child is two years old, its brain is nearly as big as an adult's.

THE BRAIN CONSTANTLY MONITORS EVERYTHING HAPPENING AT THE BODY'S SURFACE, AND IN EVERY MUSCLE AND JOINT

By doing this, the brain keeps track of where the body begins and ends, and enables it to maintain balance and carry out automatic, as well as deliberate, movements. Most of this input is registered unconsciously, but if it is cut off – by brain injury or sensory deprivation – the body collapses.

DURING CHILDBIRTH, THE MOTHER'S BRAIN IS FLOODED WITH A HORMONE THAT HELPS BUILD THE MOTHER–CHILD BOND AND DULL THE MEMORY OF THE PAIN

Giving birth is painful – so much so that many women vow they will never put themselves through it again. Yet most do. One reason is that the memory of the pain is partly wiped out by the hormone oxytocin – leaving only an intellectual (rather than emotional) recollection of how bad the pain was.

THERE ARE MORE POTENTIAL CONNECTIONS BETWEEN THE CELLS IN A SINGLE BRAIN THAN ATOMS IN THE ENTIRE UNIVERSE

The brain has about 100 billion neurons, and each neuron has up to one thousand 'docking points' where it can connect with others. If all these connections were made, there would be 100 thousand billion information-exchanging links. In practice, of course, only a tiny fraction of these connections are ever established.

A 'HAPPY' BRAIN CAN HELP TO FIGHT OFF INFECTIONS

The body's immune system responds directly to changes in the brain. A sad event – such as losing a loved one – can produce a measurable depletion in the number of infection-fighting blood cells within four days.

NO TWO BRAINS ARE IDENTICAL

The brain is so sensitive to its environment that even identical twins have visible differences in brain structure by the time they are born. These are caused by the minute differences in nutrients and sensory stimuli that each foetus experiences.

1 MIND, BRAIN AND BODY

Any understanding of the role of the brain in healing rests on an understanding of its central position in the relationship between brain, body and mind. In exploring the human brain, our most astonishing asset, we probe the very fundamentals of human nature, collectively and as individuals. But as soon as we begin to do this we confront a problem: how does the brain, mere flesh and blood, give rise to our thoughts and experiences – the world of the mind?

In this chapter we touch on some of the more influential theories on the relationship of mind, brain and body – ideas that have steered the development of Western medicine and healing practices. There are many mysteries still to uncover, but modern computerised scanning technology is beginning to reveal the brain in action and to confirm the holistic view long held by Eastern traditions: that mind and body are inextricably linked. The brain, it seems, is where our physical and mental selves come together.

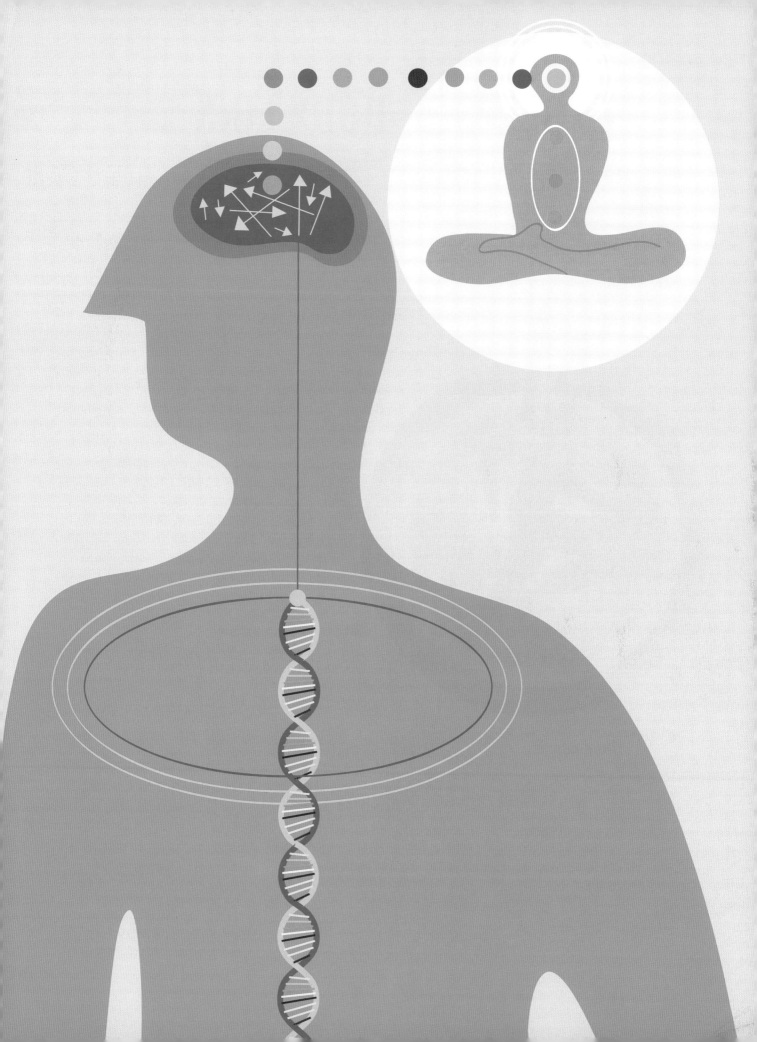

THE MIND–BODY LINK

The relationship between body and mind has occupied some of the world's greatest thinkers for centuries. Many Western philosophers concluded that mind and body were entirely separate, and this view had a strong influence on the development of scientific medicine and its practice. Today, a more integrated approach is increasingly being accepted across many areas, from medicine to religion.

It seems obvious that every person has a mind and a body, and that the brain is the place where all the activity that we call thinking occurs. But what exactly is the relationship between these three vital parts of ourselves – mind, brain and body? This may seem a simple question, but it is one that has puzzled thinkers through the ages, and they have come up with a variety of different answers. What is clear today, however, is that the interaction between mind and body is an important key to maintaining good health.

The idea that mind and body are intrinsically linked and therefore cannot be treated separately has a long history in healing. In ancient Greece, for example, people who were physically ill or emotionally troubled would visit one of the temples of the healing god Asclepius. Here, far removed from the stress of daily life, they would enjoy music, drama and philosophical discussion and focus on diet, fitness and self-examination to revive both mind and body.

Descartes and dualism

In 17th-century Europe, however, a radical new approach emerged. The French thinker, René Descartes, known as the father of modern philosophy, rejected the idea that mind and body are unified. Instead, he developed the concept of dualism in

---

THINK AGAIN! THE EMERGENCE OF THOUGHTS

In the epic poems of Homer, composed in the 8th century BC, the mind hardly gets a mention. Homer's characters do not 'think' or make decisions. Instead, they are instructed by voices ('my heart told me…'), driven by inner tensions, or coerced by a god. Emotions are also described very differently from today: rather than being something in the mind, an emotion was always located in the body. A gasp or pounding heart was a feeling.

As in other cultures without a tradition of writing, Homer's ancient contemporaries did not recognise the difference between a thought and the words that utter it. Mind and body were thus one and the same to them. However, as written language developed, later generations came to recognise a distinction between the symbols used and the ideas they represented. This distinction could be applied to spoken words, too, and writing and speech became understood as expressing pre-existing thoughts. In effect, 'the mind' was invented by the ancient Greeks as a place in which people kept their thoughts, intentions and desires before expressing them.

which mind and body are quite separate. Descartes was striving to set the knowledge and philosophy of his day on new, more solid foundations. To do this he started from scratch, discarding all preconceptions that could be doubted. He even speculated on whether his whole life was a dream or the deception of a malignant demon. But, by reflecting on his own thinking, he realised that this itself was sufficient to prove his existence. He concluded: 'I am, I exist, is necessarily true as often as I put it forward or conceive of it in my mind'. From this follows perhaps the best-known quotation in all philosophy: 'I think, therefore I am', or in Latin, 'cogito ergo sum'.

Descartes argued that a person, and indeed the whole world, consists of two radically different substances, mind and matter. The mind, which he saw as the real identity of a person, existed as a spiritual 'substance' in a spiritual sphere, while the body, a physical substance, was in a separate material universe. Descartes could not deny that the two substances interacted with each other, commenting that 'I am not merely present in my body as a sailor in a ship, but I am very closely united and as it were intermingled with it'. But this revealed the main problem with dualism: if body and mind are fundamentally different, how can they interact or affect each other? And what makes it possible for our minds to interact with the physical world around us?

Descartes never fully unravelled the 'intermingling' of mind and body. Indeed, the 'mind–body problem' has continued to intrigue philosophers ever since. Nevertheless, the philosophical separation of mind and body seemed to be the best theory available, and became very influential throughout Western thought. Like Descartes, Christianity has often suggested the separation of mind and body (and the inferiority of the latter), encouraging followers to purify their souls by winning control over their bodily impulses. In the context of religion, dualism remains popular today – perhaps because it can provide a basis for belief in life after death in the face of physical mortality, just as Descartes believed that after the body dies the mind continues to exist.

Meanwhile, alongside the scientific advances of Isaac Newton and his contemporaries, Western medical science was rapidly developing its knowledge of the human body along dualistic principles, analysing it much as a machine and focusing on its separate parts.

Reuniting mind and body

From the beginning of the 20th century, however, developments in science and philosophy began to move away from dualism, and it has become increasingly accepted throughout all areas of knowledge that mind and body are inextricably linked. The British philosopher Gilbert Ryle was

Restorative waters Popular in ancient civilisations as today, the spa combines physical therapy with mental relaxation, reflecting a unified approach to mind, health and body.

FOCUS ON

THE DOCTOR–PATIENT RELATIONSHIP

In hospital, patients may be surrounded by a frightening array of monitors, tubes and charts, and find themselves being spoken about rather than to, while experts debate their medical condition. This picture reflects the influence of dualism on healthcare: until recently, the treatment of the body dominated, while the patient's feelings were seen as unimportant. But this is now changing, with the growing awareness that the patient's mind is important to the recovery process. Acquiring an interactive bedside manner that respects the patient as an individual, rather than just a set of symptoms, has become an important aspect of a doctor's training.

18

All together Gilbert Ryle, the 20th-century philosopher, argued that the mind is not an entity independent of the body, but is integral to it. Mind is to body as team spirit is to a team of sports players.

THEORIES OF MIND AND BODY

Over the centuries, philosophers have tried to find a way of explaining mind and body that accounts for how different these two aspects of our selves seem, while revealing how they can still interact. These are some of the more influential attempts:

Occasionalism: Neither mind nor body affects the other; God is the one and only true cause. If someone wills to wiggle a toe, this act causes God to intervene to make the toe move.

Double-aspect theory: Mind and body are different aspects of the same underlying reality – typically either God or Nature.

Psychophysical parallelism: Mind and body are two distinct, independent entities that run in parallel like two perfectly synchronised clocks.

Immaterialism: There is no such thing as matter; what we think of as the body is just the perception of the mind.

Materialism: There is only one substance – matter; the mind can be explained on the basis of physical laws.

Epiphenomenalism: The workings of the mind are simply the effects of physical changes in the body.

Identity theory: Being in a certain state of consciousness and being in a corresponding physical state are just different descriptions of the same thing.

influential here: he attacked Descartes' ideas as fundamentally mis-taken, famously calling them 'the dogma of the ghost in the machine'.

Today, science is beginning to show just how intimate the mind–body relationship is. New imaging techniques are mapping the brain at work, revealing amazing discoveries about the physical neural processes that underlie mental states, emotions and even thinking itself.

In medicine, analysing the parts rather than the whole has paid off handsomely. It has enabled medical science to conquer many illnesses, and led to people generally leading longer, healthier lives. It has produced an understanding of the body and the diseases that affect it that is unrivalled in its detail and its success in diagnosis and treatment. Furthermore, the evidence-based approach to assessing the effectiveness of treatments is now agreed to be the ultimate test of any type of therapy, Western or otherwise. Nevertheless, there is a growing sense that something is missing, and that an integrated approach may be ultimately a more help-ful way to get to the bottom of many health problems.

Increasingly, therefore, medical methods regard the mind and the body as constantly interacting. For example, patients suffering mental illness are offered a range of therapies,

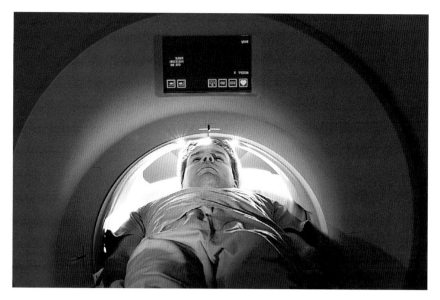

Scanning the brain New imaging techniques have revealed huge amounts of information about the workings of the brain and nervous system, but many questions about the mind and brain remain unanswered.

from physical treatments like drugs to psychological approaches, such as counselling or psychotherapy. Health psychologists study how biological, psychological and social factors affect health and illness, and health psychology practitioners help individuals to make lifestyle changes that can improve their health or enable them to cope more easily with chronic illness.

Drawing on alternatives

Eastern healing systems such as ayurvedic medicine have always assumed the interaction of mind and body. Ayurveda emphasises that everyone has self-healing potential, facilitated by factors such as good self-esteem, a realistic understanding of one's own nature, and the desire and will to be well, which encourages a healthy diet and lifestyle, as well as other self-care techniques such as massage and meditation.

Complementary and alternative medicine (CAM) has become increasingly popular in the Western world, possibly because of a greater general anxiety about health across society. CAM therapies such as osteopathy, chiropractic and herbal medicine have often fulfilled an important function in providing help and comfort to people who have not found effective treatments in conventional medicine. The potentially damaging side-effects of some potent drugs has also led people to turn to alternative medicine treatments.

Many Western medical scientists and practitioners now believe that the focus on technological approaches, including the use of drugs and surgery, needs to be balanced by more attention to the individual as a whole and the role of the mind in health. In the UK, some medical schools now give students basic information on complementary medicine, and some complementary therapies are available in doctors' surgeries. Complementary medicines are bringing Western and Eastern healing systems together, pointing towards a more holistic approach to medicine for the future.

> **"Health is … a state of complete physical, mental and social well-being, and not merely the absence of disease or infirmity."**
>
> World Health Organisation

Holistic approaches

While Western medicine excels in treating acute problems, the holistic approach, long favoured in Eastern healing traditions, aims to prevent problems before they cause illness. Holistic treatment focuses on the whole person, including lifestyle and mental state.

Eastern healing practices and complementary therapies have a long anecdotal history of health benefits. There has been little systematic research into their effectiveness, but what is accepted is that many of these therapies induce relaxation and a sense of well-being, both of which can have therapeutic effects.

Meditation

The mind is central to Eastern traditions of health and well-being, and an important aspect of some forms of Eastern medicine is meditation. Whereas in Christian spirituality meditation often means concentrating the mind on a particular topic, Eastern meditation aims to promote detachment from thoughts and images, opening up silent gaps between them to quieten the mind. Most traditional meditation has four basic requirements: a quiet place, a comfortable, poised posture, an object for the attention to dwell upon, and a passive attitude. Posture is vital. In most meditative techniques the spine is kept straight, which distributes weight evenly and reduces muscular tension. In Buddhist meditation, the focus of attention is often the rise and fall of the breath, and the gentle movement and rhythm of abdominal breathing promotes relaxation. Studies of brain wave patterns in meditation indicate that the deepest relaxation occurs when thoughts are few or absent.

> **"The mind is everything; what you think, you become."**
>
> Buddha, 563–483 BC

Yoga

Yoga is one of the most ancient health techniques of the East, dating back more than 5000 years. The name means 'yoke' or 'union' in Sanskrit and represents the binding of body and mind into one harmonious experience. In the practice of yoga, breathing techniques are important because breath is seen as the source of life. Physical exercises are designed to improve efficiency and overall health, and meditation brings inner silence and alleviates

ALEXANDER TECHNIQUE

As a young actor, Frederick Alexander (1869–1955) suffered from recurrent hoarseness, which his doctors failed to cure. He decided to try to tackle the problem himself and began by watching himself. He noticed that, as he started to recite, he pulled his head back and down towards his shoulders, raising his chest and hollowing his lower back. The resulting tension in his neck affected the relationship of all his other body parts: his voice problem was in his posture.

Alexander realised that he only had to think about reciting and his body reacted with its habitual pattern of tension. He began to practise 'directions' and what he called 'inhibition', in which he used mental control to stop himself from responding in his automatic, harmful way. His hoarseness disappeared and his health and well-being improved.

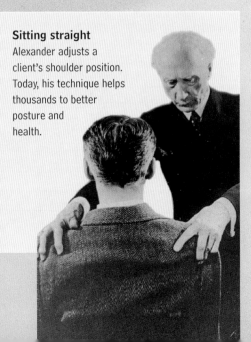

Sitting straight
Alexander adjusts a client's shoulder position. Today, his technique helps thousands to better posture and health.

BACH FLOWER REMEDIES

Bach flower remedies are infusions of flowers in water preserved in alcohol that can be either taken in drops on the tongue or diluted in water. They were devised by an English physician, Dr Edward Bach, who believed that the body has inherent powers to heal itself but that long-standing anxiety impairs a person's health. His remedies do not address physical complaints directly, but aim to help patients 'let go' of negative thoughts so that the 'life force' can flow freely, allowing the body to regain health. The theory is that the life force of the flowers contained in the remedies helps to revive the body.

stress. There is good evidence that yoga can improve fitness, flexibility, strength and stamina, and have beneficial effects on metabolic rate, lung capacity and blood pressure.

Ayurvedic medicine

This traditional Indian medical system has always recognised the power of the mind to heal. Diseases are believed to begin with imbalances in bodily energy, which create a chain effect of mental stress, unhealthy living and further ill health. These can be corrected by techniques that combine mental and physical practices.

Ayurvedic treatment includes diet and lifestyle changes, massage with oils, herbal remedies and therapies to promote internal cleansing and the removal of toxic waste. Breathing exercises and body postures derived from yoga aim to improve physical health, while meditation is considered essential to healing and disease prevention.

Western developments

Eastern medicine has influenced several holistic practices in the West. Autogenic training, sometimes referred to as Western yoga, is a system of relaxation exercises that increases control over physiological processes. It is particularly useful in chronic illnesses, such as high blood pressure. Other therapies include Alexander technique; Bach flower remedies; and biofeedback (see page 114), which improves health by teaching people to respond to signals from the body.

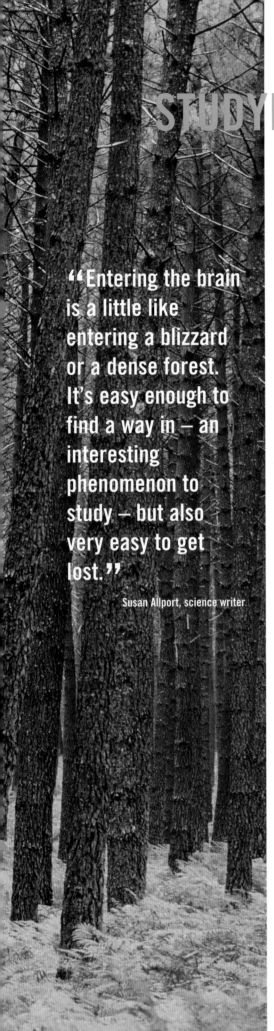

For much of history, the brain has been seen as a mysterious 'black box': the only clue to what went on inside was what came out of it. During the 20th century, a variety of approaches were used to explore how the mind functions. Today, brain imaging techniques are bringing us tantalisingly close to seeing the workings of the mind in action.

"Entering the brain is a little like entering a blizzard or a dense forest. It's easy enough to find a way in – an interesting phenomenon to study – but also very easy to get lost."

Susan Allport, science writer

It is difficult to understand how the physical tissue of the brain can produce an apparently non-physical thing like consciousness. Mind and body (of which the brain is a part) seem so different that it is tempting to agree with the 17th-century French philosopher Descartes, who concluded that they must be entirely separate kinds of substance. The first clues about the way the brain functions came through so-called 'natural experiments' – studies of people with brain damage caused by strokes or head injury. The ancient Greek physician Hippocrates had noted that an injury to the left side of the brain often disrupted speech; his finding was confirmed in 1861, when the French neurologist Paul Broca identified the brain area responsible for speech production through post-mortem examination of stroke patients.

Bumps on the surface

Many attempts have been made to find a systematic way to match brain and mind. The Austrian anatomist Franz Gall (1758–1828) was convinced that human characteristics such as 'amativeness' (amorousness), 'morality', 'acquisitiveness' and so on, were each produced by specific brain 'organs' in different areas of the cortex – the outer layer of the brain. Particularly well-developed characteristics supposedly caused bumps on the skull, which could be measured to give a character reading. Gall developed his theory of 'phrenology' by drawing up a detailed map showing the location of the various organs, and selling special devices to measure them. Head-measuring became a popular pastime in the 19th century, and many towns in the USA (and in Europe) had their own phrenology institute.

Phrenology was, of course, nonsense: no amount of normal brain development could cause detectable bulges on the skull. The discovery of brain areas genuinely responsible for certain functions – the two main language areas in the left hemisphere – began the discrediting of phrenology (although interest in it persisted), as they were nowhere near the brain 'organ' that Gall had claimed was responsible for language.

Mind theories

Another reason for the fall of phrenology was that, by 1900, Sigmund Freud had developed a far more sophisticated method of studying the mind – psychoanalysis. Freud focused on bringing suppressed conflicts and fears to the patient's consciousness. With its emphasis on unconscious motivation, the method caught the public imagination and for nearly half a century it was generally thought to offer the clearest model of the workings of the human mind. Unlike phrenology, psychoanalysis also offered the prospect of therapy to cure problems.

Freud's success encouraged others to seek an explanation of mind through systematic introspection. However, people's ability to report accurately and consistently on their own perceptions proved disappointing. One 'introspectionist laboratory' reported, for example, that people could have 12,000 sensual experiences; another claimed that it was 44,000. Psychologists became embarrassed by their confusing findings, and sought to put their work on a more scientific footing.

Behaviourism was a reaction to the pitfalls of psychoanalysis and introspection. The behaviourists regarded the mind as an input-output machine: in went a stimulus and out came behaviour. In describing the relationship between stimulus and behaviour, they ignored anything that was not observable or measurable. The behaviourist era reached its peak in the 1920s, around the time that early computers were being developed. Scientists could see how these worked: the machine was programmed with a few rules and then fed bits of information, which the computer manipulated according to the rules. It was plausible to assume that the mind functioned in a similar way.

In the 1950s and 60s, cognitive psychology took the behaviourist principle a step further by emphasising internal mental processes, such as decision-making, thinking and language. Cognitive psychologists were concerned with the rules the brain uses to interpret information, but not with the nature of the brain itself. While the approach made valuable advances in the study of the

Reading the brain
Phrenology aimed to give clues to personality by reading the bumps on people's skulls. A head map showing the supposed location of characteristics was used in conjunction with measuring devices, like the one above from the 1920s.

Real lives — THE REMARKABLE CASE OF PHINEAS GAGE

In 1848 a gang of labourers was clearing a new railway route through New England. Phineas Gage – a young man known for his sobriety, good sense and caution – had the dangerous task of laying explosive to blow up any large rocks in the way. One day, the iron bar he was using to pack a charge struck a spark, igniting the explosive and sending the bar flying up through his skull. The bar removed a large section of Gage's brain, but, astonishingly, he survived and made a near-complete physical recovery. Mentally, though, Gage was never the same again. His intelligence was not greatly affected, but his personality changed beyond recognition: he became an aggressive drunkard – boorish, careless and unable to concentrate. 'Gage', remarked his doctor, 'is no longer Gage.'

This extraordinary change in character provided one of the earliest clues that the normal human ability to inhibit base urges and generally behave correctly is dependent on the frontal lobes of the brain. The brain areas damaged in Gage's accident are precisely those now known to produce what we think of as the 'higher' human attributes of mind.

The iron bar passed right through Gage's skull, damaging the frontal lobe

24

Egas Moniz

In 1935, Egas Moniz, a Lisbon neurologist, heard a lecture by two Harvard researchers who reported changing an anxious, hyperactive chimpanzee into a seemingly serene animal by cutting the connections between the front and back of its brain. Without waiting for the lecture to end, he rushed back to his hospital and persuaded one of the surgeons there to try this surgery on some human patients. The results were profound: people who had been crippled by obsessions, anxiety and agitation became instantly calm.

Moniz's work prompted surgeons throughout the world to perform similar operations. Frontal leucotomy – and, later, the more extensive frontal lobotomy – were so popular that during the 1940s at least 20,000 people were treated in the USA alone. Only decades later did the drawbacks become clear, and these operations were eventually discarded in favour of new drugs.

Moniz, meanwhile, had to give up work when he was shot by one of his own leucotomy patients. If he had not been so impatient in 1935, he might have avoided this fate: the part of the lecture he didn't wait for reported a second experiment in which, rather than becoming calm after the operation, the chimp became inexplicably aggressive.

Wired for learning Babies have a natural instinct for language learning, which they use from a very early age. Artificial neural networks are now being built to mimic the way that human brains can learn without being taught.

thinking process, no direct link could be made to the increasing knowledge about the anatomy of the brain. Psychology was, in effect, split into two separate areas of knowledge.

Probing inside the brain

Meanwhile, some scientists continued to probe the brain physically. In the 1950s, the Canadian neurologist Wilder Penfield pinpointed areas of long-term memory by stimulating the brains of patients undergoing surgery. The brain has no pain receptors, so operations can be performed with the patient awake and thus able to report what happens when different parts of the brain are touched. Penfield discovered that placing electrodes on parts of the temporal cortex (at the side of the brain) triggered vivid descriptions of long-forgotten events.

In the last 20 years, the mapping of brain processes has leapt ahead with the development of techniques such as positron emission tomography (PET) and functional magnetic resonance imaging (fMRI). It is now possible to watch the workings of a normal, conscious brain on a computer monitor and match the ripples and flares of activity to the person's reports of perceptions, thoughts and emotions. At the same time, the development of drugs that alter behaviour by targeting particular regions of the brain has helped to fill in the details of what is happening at the molecular level.

The biological approach is being supplemented by insights from computer science. Self-learning computers that can adapt their own circuits have provided a powerful new 'neural network' model for investigating the brain. These models are tantamount to creating a 'virtual' brain that can be studied outside the body. Of course, they will never work precisely like real brains, but such systems are providing fascinating clues as to how brains develop over time.

LOOKING INSIDE THE BRAIN

Modern imaging techniques can reveal brain activity as well as structure. They allow doctors and scientists to observe the complex functioning of different regions of the brain, and to diagnose where damage has occurred. Some methods use X-rays, some measure brain activity, while others record brainwaves.

CT (computed tomography)

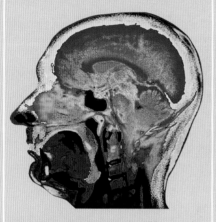

CT produces detailed cross-sectional images of the brain. The CT scanner sends out an X-ray beam as it rotates around the body, and uses its internal computer to create a high-quality image. CT scans can reveal tumours and other abnormalities.

EEG (electroencephalography)

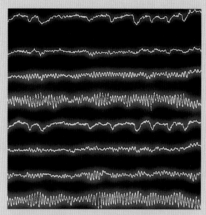

EEG measures brainwaves — the electrical activity created when large numbers of neurons fire. Each of the eight patterns above represents activity in a different part of the brain. EEG is used to study changes in brain activity, for example in epilepsy.

PET (positron emission tomography)

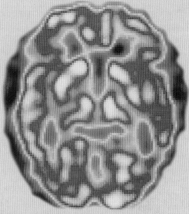

PET scans evaluate the amount of metabolic activity in brain tissue. The patient is injected with a radioactive substance that is absorbed into active cells. The radioactivity detected produces an image of active brain areas.

MEG (magnetoencephalography)

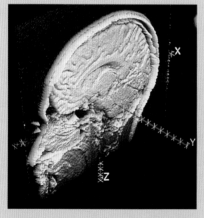

MEG, like EEG, measures brainwaves, but it does so by picking up the tiny magnetic pulses produced along with the brain's electrical activity. It is a faster scanning technique than PET or MRI.

MRI (magnetic resonance imaging)

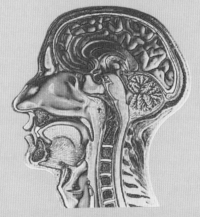

MRI scans use magnets and radiowaves to create brain images. The technique is radiation-free and one of the safest imaging methods available. It is used for imaging the spinal cord as well as the brain.

fMRI (functional magnetic resonance imaging)

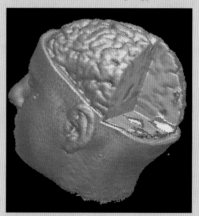

fMRI measures the amount of oxygen in different brain areas, which indicates the level of activity. Several pictures are taken every second, so that over time a 'film' of the brain's activity is created.

GENES AND THE MIND

Look at a collection of family photographs, and you can see the influence of genes in shared physical characteristics such as eye colour and the shape of facial features. Genes are also a known factor in certain illnesses, including heart disease and some cancers. But when it comes to personality and behaviour, the role played by our genetic inheritance is rather more difficult to unravel.

Genes are found inside the nucleus of every cell. They are the set of instructions for making enzymes – the proteins that enable cells to function properly. Although humans mostly inherit the same basic set of genes, the human genome, there are small variations in the structure of each gene. These inherited variations can result in considerable differences in the way the brains of different individuals function, because specific enzymes are needed for the production of neurotransmitters (messenger molecules by which brain cells communicate).

Inheriting characteristics

While personality is shaped by many different influences through life, the biological component of personality – known as temperament – is present from birth, and so is likely to be influenced by genes. If you have children, you probably find that they seem to develop unique personalities from a very early age, despite growing up in a very similar environment. But how much of an adult's personality is determined by the genes?

Physical characteristics, such as eye colour, are each determined by several genes, and the same is true of personality characteristics. So it is not simply a matter of inheriting a single gene 'for' a particular characteristic. In addition, for behavioural characteristics, environmental factors such as parenting, education, lifestyle and diet will probably have at least as strong an influence as genetic inheritance. For example, a person who inherits genes that make them susceptible to depression may indeed become depressed, but the influence of a stable family and friends, a good education and a fulfilling career may well protect the person. Similarly, someone who inherits genes that predispose them to antisocial behaviour might get into trouble in an environment with opportunities for crime, but might not in another environment

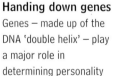

Handing down genes
Genes – made up of the DNA 'double helix' – play a major role in determining personality and health.

FACT: The Human Genome Project has established that a human being has only around 30,000 genes – about the same number as a mouse.

with more positive influences. In short, genes can predispose individuals to develop particular behavioural traits or psychological disorders, but whether they do go on to develop them is far from certain.

When the 'working draft' of the human genome was unveiled in 2001, scientists were surprised to learn that humans have less than a quarter of the 140,000 genes originally estimated, and the implications of this finding are still being considered. The low number of genes in the genome suggests that the role of environmental factors in behaviour may be even greater than previously thought. There simply aren't enough genes acting in the brain to determine the full range of human behaviour in all its subtlety and complexity. Instead, a relatively limited set of genes is interacting with myriad environmental influences.

Genes and destiny

While inherited temperament can play a major part in mental and physical health, there are probably as many ways that you can make your inherited behavioural characteristics work for you as against you. If you are born with genes that make you susceptible to stress, for example, you might take this into account when choosing a career. The thing to remember is that while genes may have a powerful influence on behaviour and health, they are by no means the whole story – lifestyle and environment are just as important.

2 BRAIN AND BODY CONNECTIONS

We readily associate the mind and brain with intelligence because we use our brains to learn new facts and to draw conclusions. However, the brain is very much more than a tool for thinking – it is the command centre of the body, and in this role it strongly influences our health and well-being.

The brain sits at the centre of the labyrinthine empire of the senses, keeping us in touch with the outside world through sight, sound, smell and touch. At the same time it constantly monitors the environment inside the body, sending instructions through the nervous system to keep body systems working properly. Every experience we have – from hunger to heartbreak, from pleasure to pain, from excitement to illness – is mediated through the brain and its nervous system. This chapter explores the brain-body connections that make this possible, revealing the routes through which the brain exerts its control over the body.

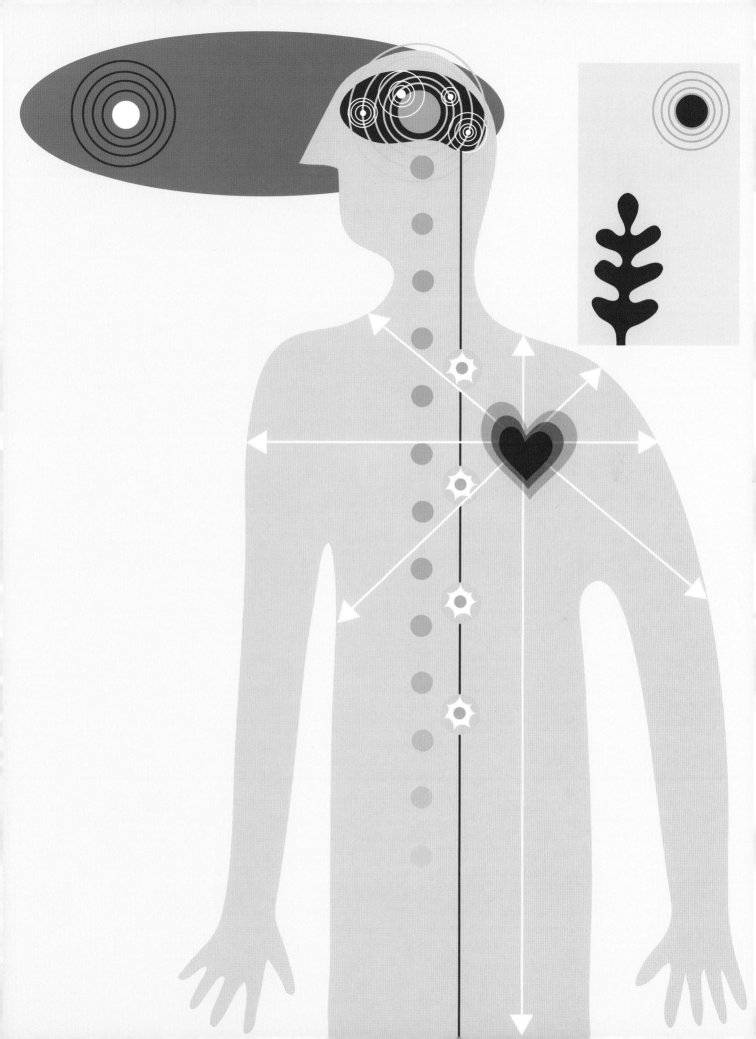

INSIDE THE CONTROL CENTRE

The brain is the control centre of the nervous system, a network that stretches to the tips of the toes and into every organ of the body. This system allows continuous, two-way communication between brain and body: anything that occurs in one inevitably affects the other.

The brain exists primarily to support the body, just like any other organ such as the liver or the heart. This primary function is often obscured, however, by the brain's dazzling capacity to generate something that at first glance seems to be quite removed from the body – the conscious mind. Yet even consciousness depends on, and serves, the body. Sights, sounds, sensations, thoughts and emotions are the consciously experienced elements of a vast and mainly unconscious system that keeps the body functioning and enables us to adapt to our environment. While each part of the brain has a specific function, none works alone.

Divisions of the brain

The structure of the brain reflects its evolution: the oldest part – the limbic system – lies deep inside the brain, while the most recently evolved areas form the grey, wrinkled surface known as the cerebral cortex, the outer layer of the cerebrum. The cerebral cortex in each hemisphere is made up of four lobes, with each lobe divided into hundreds of smaller areas. Some of these areas receive information from the sense organs and transform it into conscious perceptions. The body is continuously monitored by several cortical areas, which receive and convey information via the spinal cord and peripheral nerves. The somatosensory cortex, for example, functions as a 'body map' that corresponds to various parts of the body. Other cortical areas generate thoughts and language, and turn the bodily changes that underlie emotion into feelings.

The limbic system lies deep within the brain. This primitive part of the brain contains several distinct structures, including the thalamus, the hippocampus, the amygdala and the hypothalamus. These structures ensure that we react appropriately to any sort of stimulus, such as thirst or a fast-approaching object that we need to avoid. The limbic system also governs activities that are concerned with self-preservation, such as responding to danger, and the expression of emotion.

Beneath the limbic system is the brain stem, where the areas that regulate basic bodily functions such as heart rate and breathing are located; parts of the brain stem also stimulate emotion, attention and consciousness. Attached to the brain stem is the cerebellum – a minature version of the whole brain – which mainly controls movement and coordination.

THE WHOLE BRAIN

The three main divisions of the brain are the cerebrum (made up of the two hemispheres), the limbic system, and the brain stem and cerebellum.

● The outer layer of the cerebrum – the cortex – is responsible for all the brain's higher mental functions.

● The limbic system is the primitive, unconscious area of the brain.

● The brain stem and cerebellum form the lowest part of the brain, and regulate a wide range of bodily functions and movement.

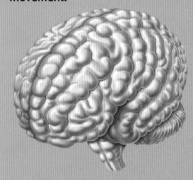

CROSS-SECTION OF THE BRAIN

Corpus callosum   Limbic system

Cerebellum

Cerebrum   Brain stem

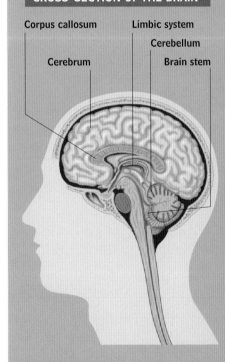

A LOOK INSIDE THE BRAIN

THE CEREBRUM

RIGHT HEMISPHERE

Anterior cingulate cortex
This switches attention either outwards, to what is happening outside the body, or inwards to thoughts and feelings.

Prefrontal cortex
This supports higher human faculties such as planning, creativity, and the inhibition of urges.

Motor cortex
Movement instructions are sent from here to every part of the body.

Somatosensory cortex
Nerves from every part of the body converge here, bringing sensory information. Each part of the body has its own 'slice' of this cortical area.

Corpus callosum
A band of tissue that links the two cerebral hemispheres.

LEFT HEMISPHERE

THE LIMBIC SYSTEM

Amygdala
'Tastes' incoming sensory information for threatening content, sending 'fight or flight' messages to the body and alerting areas of the cortex connected with fear, anger and sadness.

Hypothalamus
Registers and controls temperature, libido, hunger and aggression via endocrine (hormone-producing) glands throughout the body.

Thalamus
Relays sensory information to the appropriate part of cortex. It also directs attention and modulates levels of awareness.

Hippocampus
Lays down memories. It stores personal and important memories and shunts others to permanent storage places in the cortex.

THE BRAIN'S FOUR LOBES

Frontal lobe
The seat of conscious ideas – it draws images and memories together to form thoughts and plans.

Parietal lobe
Contains 'body maps' that respond to sensory information, and control movement and orientation.

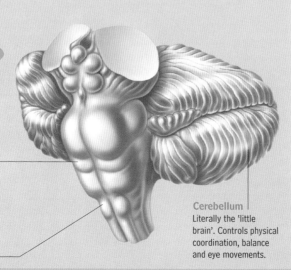

Temporal lobe
Encodes long-term factual memories. It also processes sound and language.

Occipital lobe
Receives stimuli from the eyes and translates them into perceptions.

THE BRAIN STEM AND CEREBELLUM

Pons
Links the medulla with the thalamus. Nerve tracts linking the spinal cord and the cerebral cortex pass through here.

Medulla
Extension of the spinal cord, forming the lowest part of the brain stem. Regulates heart beat rate, breathing and blood pressure.

Cerebellum
Literally the 'little brain'. Controls physical coordination, balance and eye movements.

Left brain, right brain

The brain's left and right hemispheres are almost mirror images, each controlling and responding to messages from the other side of the body. Yet the two hemispheres work in slightly different ways.

Imagine a pair of twins who have lived together all their lives, sharing every thought, sensation and emotion through continuous dialogue. Each of them is capable of doing nearly everything the other can do, but they also have individual strengths – when faced with a task, the one that is better at that sort of thing automatically takes the leading role.

The brain probably evolved as two similar halves so that there was a 'spare' brain to take over if one was damaged. However, as humans developed more skills, space started to run out. Nature found a way round this problem by placing some of the new-found abilities in just one hemisphere rather than doubling up.

Sensory information from each side of the body enters the brain, then crosses over to the opposite hemisphere. Similarly, signals from each hemisphere cross over to control the other side of the body – when you raise your right hand, it is your left hemisphere that controls it.

At birth, both hemispheres contain all that is required to develop every mental skill – a young child could lose an entire hemisphere and still develop normally because the remaining one will do the work of a whole brain. However, minor

differences between the hemispheres make each one best suited to particular tasks and, over time, the differences become so entrenched that the loss of a hemisphere in later life is catastrophic.

Left–right differences

On the whole, the right hemisphere is good at making out 'wholes', such as grasping an emotion, and the left is better at analysing things, such as tackling a maths problem. In practice, nearly everything in our minds is the result of both right and left-hemisphere processing. Understanding a joke, for example, involves following the plot (a left-hemisphere function) and 'getting' the point (a right-hemisphere speciality).

Enjoyment or terror?
During a roller coaster ride, the more emotional right hemisphere of the brain may transmit feelings of fear, which the left hemisphere interprets as excitement, because analytically it knows that you're perfectly safe.

Guitar genius Rock musician Jimi Hendrix played guitar left-handed using a right-handed guitar held upside down. Left-handed people are often thought to be particularly creative, perhaps because they are influenced more by the intuitive right hemisphere.

The most obvious difference between the hemispheres concerns language. In nearly all right-handed people, and some left-handers, language is processed entirely by the left hemisphere. Hence, a stroke in the left hemisphere may well cause language problems, while a right-hemisphere stroke is likely to affect the sense of where things are.

Language is crucial to our thoughts because most of our thinking is done in the form of words. While both hemispheres contribute to our perceptions, only the left hemisphere reports them. If you look at a picture, the right hemisphere will tend to interpret the content in an intuitive way – the colours may provoke a feeling not expressed in words. By contrast, the left hemisphere will recognise the colours as 'red', 'blue' and so on, but will not be so moved by them emotionally. Normally, the right hemisphere will transmit its feeling about the picture to the left hemisphere, which then incorporates this information into its own view, before turning the overall perception into words.

However, the left hemisphere may misinterpret what the right tells it, as the information received will be interpreted according to how the left hemisphere sees the situation. If the left hemisphere is not aware of a threat, for example, it may report 'fear' messages from the right hemisphere as 'excitement' instead. The two hemispheres work together to make the best judgements about the threats and opportunities that confront the person.

ARE YOU LEFT OR RIGHT-BRAINED?

Although we all use both hemispheres in our thinking, most people tend to favour one or the other. Try this test to see which plays the stronger role in determining your behaviour:

		YES	NO
1	Do you often have hunches?	☐	☐
2	Do you use your hands a lot when you talk?	☐	☐
3	Can you tell how much time has passed without a watch?	☐	☐
4	When you have hunches, do you often follow them?	☐	☐
5	Would you prefer to learn a new dance step by following the sequence in your head rather than by following a demonstration?	☐	☐
6	Do you find algebra easier than geometry?	☐	☐
7	Are you good at getting the gist of what people mean when they talk in a language you can't speak?	☐	☐
8	When you look at a picture in a book do you read the caption before you study the image?	☐	☐
9	Are you better at faces than names?	☐	☐
10	Do you like to complete one task before going on to the next?	☐	☐

Score:
For questions 1, 2, 4, 7 and 9, give yourself an 'R' for any yes answers and an 'L' for any no answers. For questions 3, 5, 6, 8 and 10, give yourself an 'L' for any yes answers and an 'R' for any no answers. Now add up your total number of Ls and Rs. More Rs than Ls overall suggests that you tend toward right-hemisphere thinking, while more Ls than Rs suggests left-hemisphere dominance. Most people have a mixture of both left and right styles of thinking.

MESSAGE SYSTEMS

Rapid reaction Top sportsmen and women rely on their bodies' message systems to keep them at the peak of their abilities.

The body has two major message networks – the nervous system and the endocrine system – which provide the main links between the brain and body. Understanding how these systems work is a key to understanding how the mind affects the health of the body.

The nervous system, with its control centre, the brain, produces all our conscious acts and thoughts, as well as maintaining our unconscious body operations. It keeps the heart beating and the digestion functioning, it prompts us to breathe, sleep, wake and eat, it enables us to walk and it brings us sights, sounds and sensations. The endocrine system distributes the body's hormones, controlled by the hypothalamus and the pituitary gland at the base of the brain, with far-reaching effects on our health.

A two-part structure

The nervous system consists of two interconnected parts: the central nervous system (CNS), made up of the brain and spinal cord; and the peripheral nervous system (PNS), a network of sensory and motor nerves that stretches throughout the body. Within the CNS, the brain has a dense network of some 100 billion nerve cells, or neurons. Most of these nerve cells communicate only with each other, carrying out the activity required to process thoughts, sensations, perceptions, and the unconscious functions that underlie them. The nerve cells form two-way communication pathways that keep each part of the brain informed about what is happening in the other parts.

FACT FILE   THE DEVELOPING BRAIN – FROM CONCEPTION TO CHILDHOOD

UP TO BIRTH
• Seven weeks after conception, the brain's main structures – hindbrain, cerebellum, midbrain and forebrain – are clearly visible. The primitive structures at the base of the human brain develop first, reflecting the order in which different parts of the brain evolved.
• After three months, the spinal cord has formed and the cerebellum and cerebral cortex are well developed, but still smooth.
• By six months, the cerebral cortex has outgrown the lower regions of the brain and starts to form the characteristic wrinkles on its surface. These ridges and furrows are known as gyri and sulci.
• At birth, a baby's brain contains as many nerve cells as it will have as an adult, but has relatively few connections between them. It looks similar to an adult's brain but the cortex is still smoother.

BIRTH ONWARDS
• From birth to three years of age, the brain develops neural connections at extraordinary speed.
• By the age of six, there are more connections between cells than there are in adulthood; unused neural connections then begin to die back.

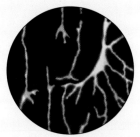

Neural connections at birth

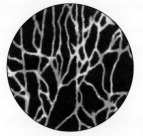

Neural connections at 3 years

In control The nervous and endocrine systems affect the whole body, regulating all our movements and bodily functions.

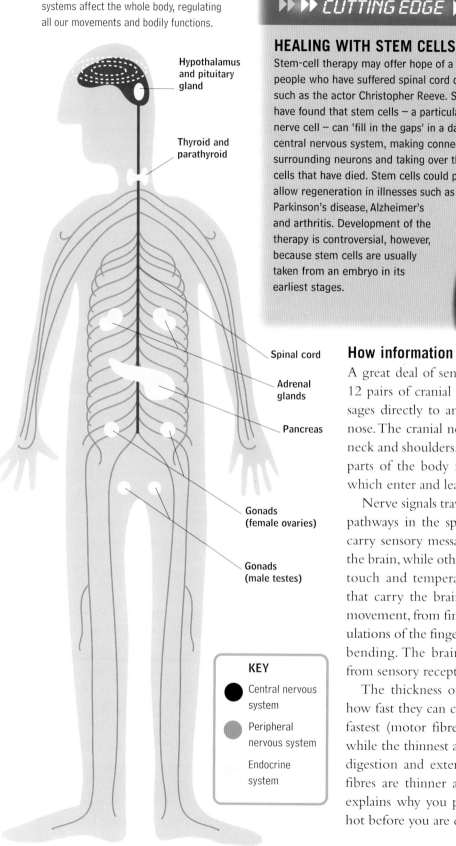

Hypothalamus and pituitary gland

Thyroid and parathyroid

Spinal cord

Adrenal glands

Pancreas

Gonads (female ovaries)

Gonads (male testes)

KEY

● Central nervous system

● Peripheral nervous system

Endocrine system

▶▶ ▶▶ *CUTTING EDGE* ▶▶ ▶▶ *CUTTING EDGE* ▶▶ ▶▶

HEALING WITH STEM CELLS

Stem-cell therapy may offer hope of a cure to people who have suffered spinal cord damage, such as the actor Christopher Reeve. Scientists have found that stem cells – a particular type of nerve cell – can 'fill in the gaps' in a damaged central nervous system, making connections with surrounding neurons and taking over the work of cells that have died. Stem cells could potentially allow regeneration in illnesses such as Parkinson's disease, Alzheimer's and arthritis. Development of the therapy is controversial, however, because stem cells are usually taken from an embryo in its earliest stages.

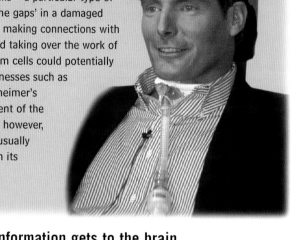

How information gets to the brain

A great deal of sensory information enters the brain via 12 pairs of cranial nerves in the head. These carry messages directly to and from the eyes, ears, taste buds and nose. The cranial nerves also control muscles in the face, neck and shoulders. Information to and from all the other parts of the body is carried by the peripheral nerves – which enter and leave the brain via the spinal cord.

Nerve signals travel along several major 'up' and 'down' pathways in the spinal cord. Some of the up pathways carry sensory messages on body position and posture to the brain, while others carry information about pain, basic touch and temperature. Down pathways include those that carry the brain's instructions for different types of movement, from fine movements such as delicate manipulations of the fingers, to large movements like turning or bending. The brain gathers information continuously from sensory receptors at the end of each nerve fibre.

The thickness of the peripheral nerve fibres dictates how fast they can conduct information. The thickest and fastest (motor fibres) connect to muscles and tendons, while the thinnest and slowest convey information about digestion and external temperature. Pain-sensing nerve fibres are thinner and slower than motor fibres, which explains why you pull your hand away from something hot before you are consciously aware of feeling pain.

CREATING EMOTION

That our emotions affect us physically is self-evident – we laugh, cry, tremble with fear or glow with pleasure, depending on what happens to us. What is less obvious is that the process also works in reverse. Your facial expressions and body posture send messages not just to other people but also to your own brain, and the brain responds by producing the emotion that the body is signalling.

• You can test this very simply if you clench your fists, glare and grimace for a few moments. Now relax your shoulders and muscles, and smile. Feel the difference?

We also respond to other people's emotions in this way. For example, brain scans have shown that when people look at photos of someone wrinkling their nose in disgust, the cells that produce disgust in their own brains become active.

The autonomic nervous system

Included in the peripheral nervous system is the autonomic nervous system (ANS), whose main role is to keep internal organs, glands and muscles working appropriately; for example, the ANS ensures that the heart rate is low when the body is at rest and speeds up during exertion. Most of the time we are unaware of the continuous, subtle changes produced by the ANS. However, if we are suddenly plunged into a new or challenging situation, we immediately become conscious of dramatic bodily changes, which register as feelings of fear, anger or anxiety.

The most familiar example of this is the 'fight or flight' response to fear. Fear stimulates the amygdala in the brain's limbic system, which triggers the neighbouring hypothalamus to send signals to endocrine glands all over the body. The glands release chemicals that activate the nervous system, which in turn speeds up the heartbeat, opens sweat glands and constricts some small blood vessels, typically draining the face of colour. Information about these events is then fed back to the brain, producing a cycle that may continue, with the sensation of fear building each time. The situation is usually resolved either by action or by the thinking parts of the brain sending signals to the amygdala to quieten its activity.

Neurons, axons and dendrites

All the activity in the nervous system relies on neurons. There are dozens of different types of neuron, but all have extensions – long, finger-like nerve fibres called axons and short, branching projections from the cell body called dendrites – that enable them to make contact with other neurons.

Contact between nerve cells takes place at 'docking points' on the surface of the dendrites, where axons from other cells connect with them. Most nerve cell have one axon, but often many dendrites and thousands of docking points. Axons

FACT: A single neuron can receive information from up to 100,000 other neurons, then distinguish which ones to react to and which to ignore.

actively seek out dendrites to connect with, growing towards their goal. Axons send out signals and dendrites receive them. A signal consists of a wave of electrical charge that starts at the cell body and travels along the axon. So that the charge does not dissipate along the way, axons are encased in an insulating covering called the myelin sheath. If this covering breaks down – as occurs in multiple sclerosis – the signals are interrupted and the nerves cannot convey correct instructions to the body. Each neuron works like a tiny computer, taking in and comparing signals from many other neurons before deciding whether, and at what strength, to 'fire' and send the signal on. Usually, they give priority to signals coming in from neurons with a history of sending 'reliable' information.

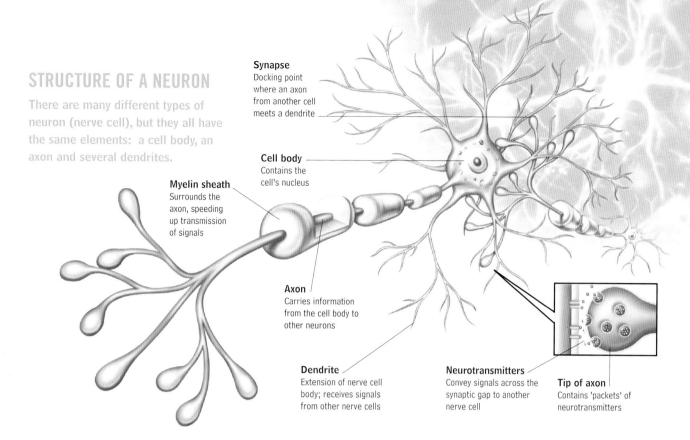

STRUCTURE OF A NEURON

There are many different types of
neuron (nerve cell), but they all have
the same elements: a cell body, an
axon and several dendrites.

Synapse
Docking point
where an axon
from another cell
meets a dendrite

Cell body
Contains the
cell's nucleus

Myelin sheath
Surrounds the
axon, speeding
up transmission
of signals

Axon
Carries information
from the cell body to
other neurons

Dendrite
Extension of nerve cell
body; receives signals
from other nerve cells

Neurotransmitters
Convey signals across the
synaptic gap to another
nerve cell

Tip of axon
Contains 'packets' of
neurotransmitters

Chemical messengers – neurotransmitters and hormones

An axon meets a dendrite at the synaptic gap. In most cases, signals are
transmitted across the gap by chemical messengers called neurotransmitters
contained in the tip of the axon. When a cell fires, neurotransmitter molecules are released into the synaptic gap and attach to receptors on the
neighbouring dendrite. If there are enough of them, they trigger a signal
in the body of the receiving cell that travels along its axon to repeat the
process. In this way, a signal can travel through a huge network of cells,
forming a neural firing pattern that may represent a thought, a feeling or
a perception. Some neurotransmitters, however, have a 'closing-down'
effect on neurons: GABA (gamma-aminobutyric acid), for example, prevents neighbouring cells from firing and stops other areas of the brain
from becoming active, so it produces a quietening effect on the body.
Tranquillisers and sleeping pills work by stimulating the neurons that produce GABA.

Neurotransmitters are not the only chemical messengers in the nervous
system. The hypothalamus regulates the ebb and flow of hormones that
stimulate growth, sexual development and egg or sperm production, and
this important area of the brain is also a link between the nervous system
and the endocrine system. Hormones released by the hypothalamus trigger the pituitary gland to release its own hormones, which travel to the
ovaries and prompt them to produce oestrogen, or to the testes to prompt
testosterone production. Most hormonal systems are circular: what happens in a gland is transmitted back to the brain, where it has a further
effect on the hypothalamus, which in turn regulates the gland. So although
the endocrine system is often described in textbooks as separate from the
nervous system, in reality the two systems are interdependent.

FACT FILE

NEUROTRANSMITTERS

The brain's main
neurotransmitters are:

• **Acetylcholine:** controls
activity in areas concerned with
attention, learning and memory.

• **Dopamine:** activates cells
involved in motivation and
pleasure. In Parkinson's disease,
there is a loss of dopamine cells
in the motor area of the brain.

• **Encephalins and
endorphins:** natural opioids
that reduce pain and stress.

• **Gamma-aminobutyric acid
(GABA):** inhibits brain activity
and has a sedating effect.

• **Glutamate:** the 'workhorse'
chemical that keeps the brain
ticking over.

• **Noradrenaline:** induces
physical and mental arousal and
heightens mood.

• **Serotonin:** the 'feel-good'
chemical. It produces feelings of
well-being and regulates sleep,
appetite and blood pressure.

INTERPRETING THE MESSAGES

The brain is constantly receiving information about conditions both inside and outside the body. It interprets and uses this information to maintain a stable environment inside the body, despite changes outside. This complex process – known as homeostasis – is essential for survival and for keeping the body's tissues in working order.

The human body, just like plants or bacteria, can only thrive in certain conditions. Our basic survival requirements are a minimum of warmth, oxygen, water and food, but we also have less obvious needs: mental stimulation, attachment to others, amusement and novelty. Deny us the basics and we will soon die; take away the other needs and our health – mental and physical – will be seriously undermined.

Homeostasis – keeping the body stable

However benign our environment, it does not give us the things we need at precisely the time we need them. For example, we cannot immediately match our energy output, calorie by calorie, to the food we eat, or replace every drop of sweat we lose with a sip of water. Nor can we ensure that we are always in an environment that is a comfortable temperature. Homeostasis ensures that the body's needs are met – that we maintain a store of nutrients to fuel action; that cells retain water even when none is available from outside; and that core body temperature remains at an optimum level, despite external fluctuations.

Homeostasis is a whole-body mechanism that works by the influence of automatic processes within certain organs and the controlling influence of conscious and unconscious areas of the brain. It combines information from the senses – the sight of water, say – with self-generated knowledge,

Accustomed to the cold Until the 20th century, the native people of Tierra del Fuego, at the southernmost tip of South America, lived almost entirely without clothes, despite being in a climate described as 'cold and inhospitable' by the naturalist Charles Darwin, who travelled there in 1832. This is a striking example of homeostasis in operation, enabling the human body to adapt to adverse conditions.

FOCUS ON

BONDING FOR SURVIVAL

Mothers and babies trigger behaviour in each other that helps them to bond. For example, an infant's crying prompts his mother to pick him up. The baby will then probably quieten down, open his eyes and follow her movements. When she touches the baby's cheek, he is likely to turn his head, looking for her nipple. Breast-feeding itself strengthens the bonding process.

Babies are born with a well-developed homeostasis mechanism already in place. A normal newborn baby, placed naked on her mother's chest and simply covered with a blanket, will maintain her body temperature just as efficiently as a baby in a high-tech incubator. Homeostasis, bonding and other survival mechanisms probably evolved millions of years ago, during much more dangerous times, to help the human infant's chances of survival.

APPETITE RESEARCH

For the first time in history, there are now more overfed people in the world than there are underfed. Surveys have shown that obesity is on the increase, including among children, and researchers have been trying to find drugs that might help to combat this new epidemic. At the other end of the scale, eating disorders such as bulimia and anorexia nervosa are also on the increase: studies in the 1990s showed that at least two per cent of females in the USA suffered from bulimia or anorexia – and the numbers are rising.

Controlling hunger signals

Research efforts to counteract some of these problems have focused mainly on examining the chemical messengers in the brain that signal hunger and satiety. Low serotonin levels are known to trigger binge-eating, and drugs that increase this brain chemical are sometimes prescribed for bulimia. Other molecules that control intake of food include the hormone leptin, which dampens appetite, and substances called orexins, which stimulate it. The search is on for drugs that will stimulate the appropriate brain chemicals to make disorders such as obesity and bulimia a thing of the past.

like feeling thirsty, to produce an appropriate response. Water levels in body cells, for example, are partly controlled by the kidneys, which absorb water from the blood, expelling it as urine when levels are high, and conserving it when they are low. A low water level in cells is signalled to the brain via nerve cells called osmoreceptors, which activate parts of the hypothalamus, producing feelings of thirst. The conscious areas of the brain then take over, directing you to find a drink. The same process occurs with food: when you have eaten a big meal, nerve endings in the stomach wall send signals to another part of the hypothalamus, which creates the feeling of being satisfied. And when blood sugar levels fall again, yet another part of the hypothalamus produces a feeling of hunger and prompts you to find food.

In cold blood
Unlike humans, lizards and other cold-blooded animals are unable to control their body temperature from within. Instead, they have to rely on their environment to keep them warm, by basking in the sun, for example.

Hormones and bonding

Similar processes ensure that our social, intellectual and emotional needs are fulfilled. Attachment and mental stimulation, for example, are essential for development and survival, especially in infancy, and the human need for contact with others continues throughout life. Intimate bonding behaviour (such as sex and breastfeeding) is associated with increased levels of a hormone called oxytocin, which creates feelings of satisfaction and serenity. These pleasant feelings in turn encourage us to seek out the people or situations that produce them, pulling us into ever-closer relationships with those we depend on, or who depend on us. However, perpetual cuddling would make us vulnerable, so oxytocin-induced relaxation is countered by bursts of exploratory, outward-looking behaviour mediated by neurotransmitters like noradrenaline. Hence the balance is maintained between the need for social bonding and the need to explore the wider environment.

FACT: Capsaican – the chemical in chilli peppers that makes them taste hot – interferes with the nerves that send 'feeling full' messages to the brain. So if you want to lose weight, lay off the chilli.

WHAT IS PAIN?

Pain is one of our most useful survival mechanisms. What you feel as pain, however, does not necessarily match up with what is happening to your body, because pain is – like everything we experience – 'all in the mind'.

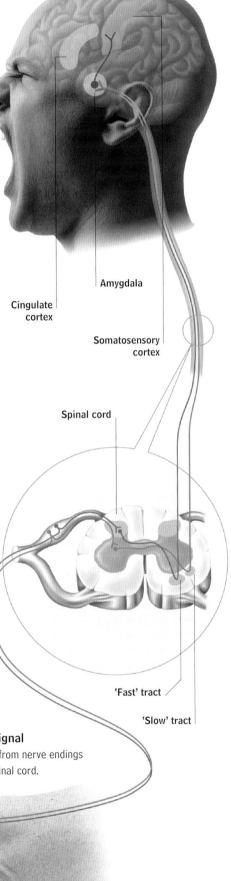

Sometimes, stubbing your toe lightly on a chair can make you cry out in pain, while at other times you can take a much harder knock and barely notice. When we are very busy or excited, even severe physical injuries may go unnoticed – in fact, just occupying yourself with some mental task or sinking into a pleasant daydream can reduce pain considerably.

The reason you don't notice pain when you are occupied is because you have to pay attention to information coming in from the senses in order to be conscious of it. Pain signals from nerves in the skin, joints and muscles enter the brain and are registered in the brain's 'body map' – the somatosensory cortex. But this does not automatically produce the experience of pain. For this to happen, another part of the brain must bring the signals to consciousness by directing attention to them. The area responsible is the frontal section of the cingulate cortex, which lies in the deep groove between the brain's two hemispheres.

This acts as a switch, directing attention either to the outside world or to what is happening within the body. When it is activated, we become conscious of information – such as pain – in the somatosensory cortex; when it is 'off' we are completely absorbed in whatever is happening in the world around us.

Neuropathic pain

Sometimes we experience pain even when there are no pain signals coming in. This type of pain, known as neuropathic pain, is 'all in the mind' – but it is not imaginary.

Cingulate cortex

Amygdala

Somatosensory cortex

Spinal cord

'Fast' tract

'Slow' tract

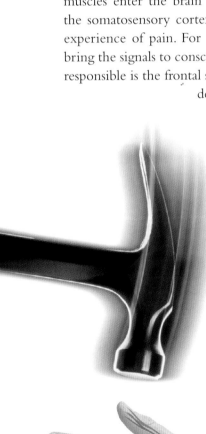

'Fast' pain fibres (red)

'Slow' pain fibres (blue)

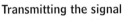

Transmitting the signal
Pain messages travel from nerve endings to the brain via the spinal cord.

Real lives   THE BOY WHO COULDN'T FEEL PAIN

James is one of a handful of children who do not have the capacity to feel pain. The cause of the condition remains mysterious – it may be due to failure of the pain receptors, or a 'disconnection' in the brain system that brings pain to consciousness. His mother, Ruth, fights a constant battle to keep him out of danger:

'Jim is very bright, and as sensible as any four-year-old. But I can't take my eye off him for a moment because he has no natural physical fear – he has never learnt that putting his hand in the fire will burn him or that tumbling downstairs may not be a good idea. By the time he was two, he had broken both legs, fractured his skull and burnt his arm severely. Once, he dislocated his wrist and I didn't know about it until I put him to bed and he complained that he couldn't cuddle his teddy. And because he doesn't feel pain himself, he finds it difficult to understand that other children do – so he tends to play roughly with them.

'The doctors can't do anything about it, so I just have to watch his every move and keep explaining to him that he must take care. I hope as he gets older, he will develop a better sense of danger.'

Rather, it is a form of memory. It usually occurs in people who continue to feel pain even after an injury has healed. In this case, the original pain signals cause certain brain cells to fire together and then, over time, to 'wire' together – the resulting firing pattern is the pain. Normally these links would fall apart when the pain signals stopped, but in neuropathic pain the links remain etched in the brain, like any other type of memory. This sort of pain is often distressing because it seems to have no physical cause.

How pain helps us

Compared to the complicated brain processes that control pain perception, the 'wiring' that sends pain signals to the brain is relatively simple. There are two main types of pain fibre, both of which end in receptors that react to damaging stimuli like pressure or heat. Thicker 'fast' fibres carry signals from the receptors to the brain at high speed, producing a sharp 'warning' stab of pain: this is the first thing you are aware of when you hurt yourself, and it alerts you to the injury. Narrower 'slow' fibres conduct signals at lower speed, and cause the aching, throbbing pain that follows an injury, lasting for hours or even days. Once pain signals arrive in the brain, they pass to the amygdala, which acts as a relay station directing pain signals on to other areas.

Although pain is a useful warning system, once it has done its job of alerting us to injury, it ceases to be beneficial. Fortunately, there is no need for most people to suffer: mild pain can be helped by paracetamol, aspirin or ibuprofen, while severe pain can usually be controlled with the use of drugs such as opioids.

> **"I had to run through a wall of fire – literally – to get out of the house. I felt the flames as I did it – but they didn't feel hot – more like little moist flicks of a tongue. When I arrived in hospital I had to have five skin grafts on my face. But I can honestly say I didn't feel it happen – not a thing."**
>
> Jeremy, survivor of a house fire.

Desires

A key function of the brain is to serve the needs of the body. The body signals its needs through urges, emotions and desires that provoke the brain into producing actions designed to satisfy them. But desires can be confusing and contradictory.

When our bodies want something, they let us know about it. An empty stomach makes itself known by producing feelings of hunger, dehydrated cells produce thirst, constricted muscles make us feel restless, and desire induces feelings of lust. These simple appetites and urgings, or 'basic' desires, are produced by body chemicals that act on the hypothalamus at the base of the brain, which in turn sends appropriate signals to the cerebral cortex.

'Higher' desires, like attraction to something beautiful, are also linked to changes within the brain. Certain images, for example, may provoke pleasant memories – not strongly enough to make them conscious, perhaps, but enough for them to produce a less intense version of the pleasurable feelings experienced when the event happened.

CHANGING DESIRES

Get out an old photo album and take a good look at the clothes you were wearing years ago. The chances are that you selected them with great care, possibly even longed for them and saved to buy them – but what do you think of them now? Would you wear them today?

Responding to influences

Our basic 'wants', such as hunger or the need for clothing to keep warm, are responses to bodily needs, but the way we choose to satisfy them with particular foods and clothing styles is often dictated by external factors, such as peer group pressure and fashion. Most of us laugh with embarrassment when we look at old photos, because the clothes that once seemed so attractive and stylish now look dull or rather ridiculous.

The same can often be said of the things we want to have in our homes, the foods and activities we enjoy, and even the people we find attractive. Our tastes are constantly influenced by changing trends, and we are often encouraged to hanker after the latest fashions.

However, human desires are often conflicting. Someone might crave chocolate – yet at the same time want to lose weight. Someone who hates the idea of being unfaithful to their partner might still be attracted to another person. Such conflicts arise because we can desire things on two levels: we feel basic, physical urges for things that offer immediate satisfaction, and we also have complex hopes and dreams that can lead us to put our instinctive urges on hold, or even suppress them altogether.

Dealing with conflicting desires

Most of the time it is fairly easy to cope with conflicting desires: for example, parents will patiently read a bedtime story to a child after a hard day's work, even though they might prefer to be relaxing in front of the television. The reward of the child's pleasure offsets any irritation caused by deferring the need to relax. But if a person becomes trapped in a situation where basic desires are constantly denied, it can create a chronic state of inner tension that may eventually take its toll on health.

This is particularly true of unconscious desires. For example, take someone who looks after an elderly relative and so cannot go on holiday. At a conscious level, the desire to take good care of the relative may outweigh the desire to have a break, but unconsciously the thought of a holiday may persist, unacknowledged. The result can be a seemingly inexplicable feeling of irritation that may come to influence the carer's behaviour. Over time, the slow build-up of stress hormones released as a result of the irritation could also lead to health problems.

For this reason, it is important to try to understand your desires at every level by attending to your feelings and questioning why they occur. Being conscious of a basic desire at least enables you to deal more effectively with the frustration it brings, and perhaps find some alternative way of satisfying it.

"**There are two tragedies in life. One is not to get your heart's desire. The other is to get it.**" George Bernard Shaw

SEXUAL ATTRACTION

Sexual desire occurs on two distinct levels: on one level it manifests as an 'approach and go-for-it' urge, while at the other it is gentle, romantic, admiring and usually focused on a particular individual. Brain imaging studies suggest these different types of desire occur in different regions of the brain, and that romantic desire evolved much later than the basic sexual urge.

In both men and women, the basic urge is created by clusters of cells within the hypothalamus, which is concerned with emotional activity. These clusters are moulded early in life by sex hormones, and those which are most developed have the greatest influence on the type of person you find attractive. The individual you choose, however, is decided by experiences encoded in the 'higher' regions of the brain in the cerebral cortex.

Differing responses

The two components of sexual desire are typically more separate in men than in women. When men experience 'pure lust', a primitive brain area called the claustrum is activated, whereas romantic interest results in more diffuse brain activation that takes place in parts of the cortex. In women, sexual desire is typically of this more diffuse kind, and this is more integrated with the basic urge.

BODY RHYTHMS

Our bodies are subject to hourly, daily and even longer natural rhythm cycles. These rhythms dictate when we are most vulnerable to illness, when a baby is most likely to be conceived and born, and how we respond to drugs. Developments in our understanding of the body's daily rhythm – the circadian cycle – have suggested new possibilities for improving health by getting in tune with our natural body clock.

Animal routines The migration of birds is determined by the seasonal rhythms that affect all animals. Humans are less influenced by seasons, but our internal body clock regulates our daily cycle of activity.

All bodily functions vary over time in a rhythmic fashion. Some regular body rhythms, such as the beating of the heart and the firing of neurons in the brain, have cycles of less than a second. Others are much longer: for example, there is a yearly cycle in sexual activity which leads to more babies being born in late summer than at any other time. Indeed, in the USA, government statistics show that over the last 60 years, more babies were born in August than in any other month. It is thought that the increased sexual activity in late autumn is due to men having higher testosterone levels then. No-one is quite sure why this is, although it may be linked to the changing amount of daylight. Seasonal cycles are most

FACT FILE TIME OF DAY AND YOUR BODY

| 06.00 | 07.00 | 08.00 | 09.00 | 10.00 | 11.00 | 12.00 | 13.00 | 14.00 | 15.00 | 16.00 | 17.00 |

Body weight at its lowest

Fastest reaction times

Migraine

Rheumatoid arthritis symptoms

Heart attacks and angina

Highest blood pressure

Sneezing and nasal allergy symptoms

pronounced in other animals, where the annual routine of hibernation, breeding, nurturing and migration dictate the essential activity patterns in an animal's life.

The circadian clock

In humans, by far the most pronounced body rhythm is the circadian cycle, which is controlled by the brain. Circadian means 'around a day' and describes how physiological properties, such as body temperature and blood pressure, change in a regular cycle of 24–25 hours. The circadian cycle runs (more or less) alongside our daily cycle of sleeping and waking. It is regulated by a 'biological clock', which responds to external cues, the most important of which is the level of light.

The circadian clock is situated in the suprachiasmic nuclei (SCN), a patch of around 100,000 cells located in the hypothalamus at the base of the brain. The SCN lies above the optic chiasma, a major nerve junction linking the eyes to the brain, and connections between the optic nerves and the SCN allow cells within the SCN to respond to rising or falling light levels. Onward connections between the SCN and the hypothalamus tune physiological functions accordingly. Thus, after dawn, rising light levels tell the SCN to wake up the body. At night, falling light levels cause

Daily events Because of the body's circadian (daily) cycle, specific body states and illnesses are more likely to occur at certain times of the day.

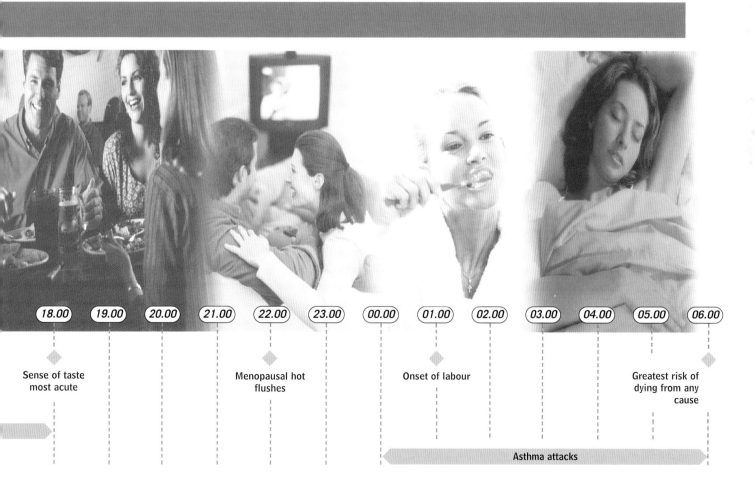

| 18.00 | 19.00 | 20.00 | 21.00 | 22.00 | 23.00 | 00.00 | 01.00 | 02.00 | 03.00 | 04.00 | 05.00 | 06.00 |

Sense of taste most acute

Menopausal hot flushes

Onset of labour

Greatest risk of dying from any cause

Asthma attacks

FIND YOUR TEMPERATURE RHYTHM

The common belief that 37° Celsius is normal body temperature is inaccurate – this figure is actually an average. Body temperature in fact ranges from about 36.5°C to 37.5°C throughout the day. It is at its lowest early in the morning two to three hours before you normally wake up, and rises through the morning and early afternoon to reach a plateau in mid-afternoon. Then it dips a little and increases again to peak at around 7pm. A temperature of, say, 37°C might indicate that you had a mild fever if measured at dawn, but would be considered normal later in the day.

• You can track your own daily temperature rhythm. Take your temperature first thing in the morning, before you

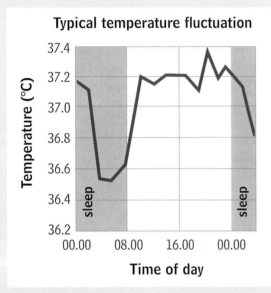

Typical temperature fluctuation

even get out of bed, and thereafter at two-hourly intervals throughout the day until bedtime. Do this for several days and plot the temperatures onto a graph like the one shown above to see if you can identify a regular pattern to the rhythm.

If you are unwell (with a bad cold or flu, for example) and find that your morning temperature is less than it was the evening before, remember that this may not necessarily mean that you are well again. It could just be the natural variation of your normal temperature rhythm – so you should carry on taking care of yourself until you are sure that you have recovered fully.

the SCN to activate the nearby pineal gland, resulting in the production of melatonin – the 'darkness hormone' – which helps prepare the body for sleep.

Rest and activity

The circadian rhythm also includes many shorter cycles. One of the most familiar is the rest–activity cycle, which lasts between 90 and 120 minutes. You may have noticed that although you start the day awake and finish it asleep, you don't just become gradually more tired as the day wears on. Many of us experience a dip in energy in the mid-afternoon period, and although you may feel worn out when you get home from work in the late afternoon or early evening, it is quite common to experience a 'second wind' between 8pm and 10pm – in fact, most people find it almost impossible to fall asleep at this time of the evening. The Israeli scientist Peretz Lavie demonstrated that there are sleep 'gates' that open every 90 minutes or so. In his experiments, he asked people to try to stay awake or fall asleep at 20-minute intervals over a 24-hour period and as a result found this marked rest–activity cycle in operation.

Blood pressure variation

Circadian rhythms have important implications for health and well-being. Blood pressure, for example, can be up to 20 per cent lower in the morning than in the afternoon. If you have high blood pressure, it may be missed if the doctor always measures your blood pressure in the morning. On the other hand, if it is measured in the afternoon, the doctor may think you have high blood pressure when in fact you do not. Also, if you are taking medication for high blood pressure, it is harder for your doctor to assess how well the treatment is working if the natural circadian variation is not taken into account.

The daily variation in physiological rhythms also means that many illnesses are at their worst – or are more likely to strike – at certain times of the day. For example, heart attacks are two to three times more likely to occur in the morning than later in the day, partly because blood pressure is rapidly rising then. Blood is thicker in the morning, making it more likely to form a clot in the blood vessels leading to the brain (causing a stroke) or the heart.

FOCUS ON   *SEASONAL AFFECTIVE DISORDER – SAD*

Every autumn, some people feel a familiar sense of dread. They find it increasingly difficult to get up in the morning, and often crave comfort foods, such as cheese on toast and chocolate. As a result they may start to gain weight, adding to their misery. By the middle of winter, they are feeling hassled and desperate.

These are all typical symptoms of seasonal affective disorder, also known as SAD, a form of depression triggered by falling light levels. However, in SAD

the pattern of symptoms is different from those in clinical depression, which may involve waking early and loss of appetite.

SAD depression usually lifts with the coming of spring. In the winter, the symptoms are treatable with antidepressants or light therapy, which involves being exposed to bright artificial light for several hours a day to make up for lack of sunlight. However, for some people, the only permanent solution to SAD is a move to a sunnier climate.

Body rhythms and medicine

Because the severity of an illness will vary during a 24-hour period, the need for medication varies too. What is more, the way the body handles drugs changes over the course of the day. In the case of medications taken orally, variations in blood flow and stomach acidity will affect the amount of drug that is absorbed, while the rhythms of kidney and liver activity determine how long the drug stays in the body before being excreted. This has implications for side effects as well as for the drug's effectiveness. For example, if you take aspirin in the morning, it is more likely to cause stomach irritation than aspirin taken at night.

When your doctor instructs you to take a medicine in three equal doses three times a day, this assumes that your body responses remain the same all day long. In fact you will probably absorb a different amount of the drug each time. Ideally, doses throughout the day should be adjusted to take account of your natural body rhythms – this is the principle behind chronomedicine.

❝In prescribing equal doses over the day, your doctor presumes that your need for medication is the same all day... this belief is wrong. In the future, doctors will make greater use of computers to determine the best timing and dose of medications.❞

Michael Smolensky, chronomedicine expert

▶▶ CUTTING EDGE ▶▶

CHRONOMEDICINE

Chronobiology (from the Greek 'chronos', meaning time) is the study of biological rhythms. Recently, chronobiology has given rise to chronomedicine, a new approach to making and prescribing drugs that takes into account the body's daily rhythms. Potentially, this means that people could be treated with smaller, better-timed drug doses for the same effect. In some cases, however, chronomedicine could even be life-saving. For example, the drug 5-fluorouracil – used to treat breast and digestive system cancers – has fewer side effects if taken at night, while adriamycin (used for ovarian and bladder cancer), is better tolerated in the morning. With the correct timing, a patient may be able to cope with a bigger dose of chemotherapy, which is likely to be more effective at killing tumours.

Pavlov and conditioning

Pavlov's discovery of 'conditioning' – a process by which the brain forms associations between events that occur together – has given fascinating insights into our ability to learn new behaviour patterns.

The Russian scientist Ivan Pavlov never considered himself a psychologist, but he has had a huge influence on the science of psychology, which was still in its infancy when he began his landmark experiments in the late 19th century.

As far as Pavlov was concerned, he was always a physiologist. His main research interests were the function of the nerves of the heart, the activity of the digestive glands and the workings of the higher nervous centres in the brain. It was Pavlov's research into digestion that originally brought him worldwide recognition, but he is now best known as the discoverer of Pavlovian or 'classical' conditioning. This is the process by which we come to automatically associate events that have occurred together. In fact, this work came out of his research into digestion.

Ivan Pavlov (1849–1936) was the archetypal 'absent-minded professor', focused on his work at the expense of everything else, including his family.

Conditioning in action

Working at the University of St Petersburg in Russia, Pavlov began to observe certain digestive irregularities in the dogs on which he was experimenting, which he attributed to 'psychic' (that is, psychological) causes. He noticed that some of the dogs would begin to secrete digestive juices simply at the sight of the man who usually fed them, before any food was actually given. Pavlov decided to try to determine the cause of these 'psychic secretions' by studying what kind of stimulus (that is, a noticeable event or object) caused a dog to salivate –

a secretion that was much easier to detect than digestive juices.

This led to his most famous set of experiments. A bell would be repeatedly sounded just before food was placed in the mouth of a dog, which was held immobile in a frame in order to ensure that the bell was the only stimulus. The food would naturally make the dog salivate, but Pavlov found that, with enough pairings of bell and food, the sound of the bell on its own would cause the dog to salivate without any

food being presented. This he called a 'conditional response', as it was conditional on the bell having been paired with the food beforehand. (The effect is now known as a 'conditioned response', due to an error in the original translation into English of Pavlov's research paper.)

We now know that Pavlovian conditioning is one of the simplest and most effective ways in which the brain adapts to its environment. It is the most basic form of learning: even in very primitive animals, if a stimulus such as food is repeatedly paired with a neutral stimulus (like the bell in Pavlov's experiment), a response to the neutral stimulus will eventually result. Pavlov went on to explore in detail the characteristics of classical conditioning, experimenting with varying time intervals and different types of stimuli.

Pavlov's legacy

Pavlov's ideas have stood the test of time and his approach to the study of behaviour has been hugely influential, setting the new science of psychology on the road to an increasingly 'objective' approach, rather than relying on speculation about hidden mental processes or people's subjective reports of their own experiences. His ideas have played an important role in helping us to understand many aspects of human behaviour. While most forms of thinking involve complex brain processes, such as language and reasoning, our brains and bodies are also working together at an unconscious level all the time. Sometimes this process can allow habits, anxieties and even physical problems whose origins seem hidden to develop, and Pavlov's work has provided insights into why this happens.

Psychological techniques developed from classical conditioning have been used to treat disorders such as depression, anxiety and phobias. Exposure therapy, where the patient learns to live through the unpleasant feelings associated with the confrontation with a phobic object or situation, has been shown to be highly successful.

PAVLOV IN FICTION

Pavlovian conditioning features prominently in the disturbing novel *A Clockwork Orange* by Anthony Burgess, made into a famously controversial film by Stanley Kubrick in 1971.

Treated for violence

Set in the near future, the story centres on a young thug, Alex, who goes on regular rampages of rape and violence. He is eventually arrested and compelled to undergo a radical form of treatment, based on Pavlovian conditioning. Under the technique, Alex is made to feel physically sick while being forced to watch scenes of sex and brutality. When he is finally released, Alex is unable to perform any violent acts because he becomes paralysed by sickness whenever he tries – he has been conditioned against violence.

While the story is fictional, a similar aversion technique based on Pavlovian conditioning is sometimes used in real life in an attempt to alter some types of inappropriate behaviour.

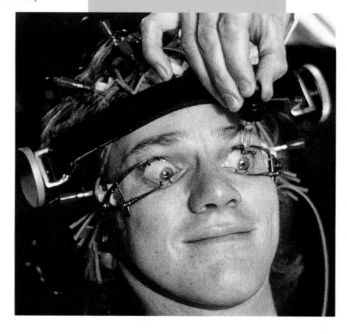

THE CONDITIONED RESPONSE

Whenever your mouth waters at the mention of chocolate, or you find yourself working harder after a few words of praise, you are demonstrating conditioned responses in the way you react to the world. Learning by simple association, or 'conditioning', was once thought by psychologists to be the mechanism that explained most human behaviour. Now, however, we know that human responses are more complex.

FOCUS ON

REWARD VERSUS PUNISHMENT

Behavioural psychologists have studied the way praise, punishment and attention affect behaviour and can be used to modify it. Disruptive behaviour in children is often a way of seeking attention – and parents can be taught to tackle the problem by ignoring (that is, withdrawing attention from) the worst behaviour and rewarding all reasonable behaviour. These tactics often produce results in a very short time. Punishment may seem a more obvious option, but reward has been shown to be a much more powerful conditioner.

Similarly, if people with minor health symptoms are 'rewarded' with too much attention or sympathy, they can become more prone to repeated symptoms and ill health generally. Indeed, doctors are not always brief just because they are pressed for time.

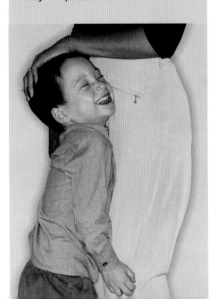

We may not feel that we have much in common with Ivan Pavlov's dogs, which became conditioned to associate food with the sound of a bell, but we all have our own learned responses to our environment that produce certain bodily reactions and behaviours. A lot of conditioning in humans happens unconsciously and involves aspects of memory that we cannot verbally described.

Conditioning through experience

Most people have had the experience of being sick after eating something unpleasant – perhaps a suspect mussel in a plate of moules marinière or something fatty or green forced on them in childhood – and then had recurrent feelings of queasiness when exposed to that food again. Humans, as well as other animals, can form a strong unconscious link between sensory characteristics, such as the smell and taste of a particular food, and the physical consequences of eating it – especially if that consequence is to feel sick, and the food has an unusual or novel flavour. The merest whiff of the offending food can bring back a wave of nausea that it is almost impossible to overcome by conscious effort.

Now known as conditioned taste aversion, this kind of response probably developed in mankind's early evolution as a way of avoiding eating foods such as berries and fungi that might be poisonous. The body and brain are so strongly 'programmed' to respond in this way that conditioned taste aversion can be triggered even when the bout of illness has no actual connection to the food. This can have unforeseen consequences. For example, chemotherapy treatments tend to be followed by unpleasant attacks of nausea and sickness. After a number of treatments, some cancer patients begin to experience these symptoms simply by entering the treatment room. Children have sometimes been given ice-cream to cheer them up before chemotherapy sessions – with the unfortunate result that they become conditioned to feel nauseous in response to ice-cream and it ceases to be a treat.

Similarly, our emotional responses to things, people and places are conditioned by previous experiences. After being stung by a wasp, someone might become fearful at the mere sight of a wasp or bee; conversely, if the sting was less painful than previously imagined, the experience might lessen the fear. Likewise, someone who has had painful dental treatment may begin to feel anxiety as soon as they set foot in a dental surgery –

Real lives   *TOO MUCH OF A GOOD THING*

Many people have a strong aversion to a specific kind of alcoholic drink – perhaps whisky or brandy. Usually, they assume this is because they simply dislike the flavour – but very often it is a result of conditioned taste aversion, dating back to over-indulgence as a young adult. Naomi, now 38, had such an experience:

'At the end of my first term at university, my boyfriend and I decided on the spur of the moment to hitch-hike to Scotland and stay with an aunt of his there. We arrived in mid-evening, exhausted and chilled after travelling through freezing weather in just city

clothes. Our hostess was very hospitable and poured us each a large Scotch whisky, which I had never tasted before – and then another. As fast as I could drink, my glass would be topped up again – and, being young and shy, I had no idea how to decline politely. I got horrendously drunk, with predictable consequences. Although I like brandy and other spirits, I've never been able to face whisky again – in fact, I've wondered how other people could drink it with any pleasure. Then last year I took a psychology course and learned about conditioned taste aversion, and it dawned on me that this

was the cause of my dislike of whisky. Knowing this has meant I've now tried the occasional sip of the stuff – otherwise, I'm sure my aversion would have lasted my whole life, from just one experience.'

a response that can diminish if they find a dentist they trust. Anyone trying to give up smoking may have as much trouble trying to break free from the conditioned response of smoking in certain situations as they have beating the physical addiction.

Unlearning learned responses

A common feature of depression is the belief that escape from misery or unhappiness is impossible. Such 'learned helplessness' is a conditioned response, developing from a succession of unpleasant events that seem unavoidable and uncontrollable. Experiences accumulate to produce a sense of defeat and passivity, even in situations that can in fact be dealt with. Children (and adults) can be affected by this type of conditioning in their education, if minor learning failures are handled insensitively and produce the feeling that trying to learn is pointless. Similarly, people who are consistently discouraged by a spouse or partner – even in trivial issues such as parking a car correctly – may suffer recurrent feelings of helplessness, with consequences for physical as well as mental health. Cognitive behavioural therapy techniques try to reverse the effects of such conditioning by rewarding positive thinking and behaviour and questioning the validity of defeatist thought patterns.

Temper tantrum By not rewarding children's tantrums with attention, parents can develop an effective conditioning process that punishes bad behaviour and helps to instil reasonable behaviour.

UNDERSTAND YOUR HABITS

The brain's susceptibility to conditioning means that, over the years, we all build up patterns of behaviour – responses that may have been appropriate at one point in our lives but may no longer be beneficial. Many of these 'habits' are unconscious, so the first step to changing them is to discover what they are. Of course, some habits become a recurring cycle: if you avoid talking to people at parties because you view yourself as a poor conversationalist, you'll get no practice, so when you do find yourself in a position to have a chat you will probably be tongue-tied. But you can learn new habits – once you have a clear aim. So take a look at your habits and decide which to live with and which to change. Here are five ways to get you started on a programme of self-awareness and change.

BE A MIRROR

Have you ever caught sight of yourself in a mirror and been surprised at some aspect of your appearance – perhaps a slouch or a tense facial expression? Such glimpses tend to be caught in mirrors in public places, or in reflective surfaces like shop windows, rather than in any mirrors we have at home. But often we might have an intuition about what we would see in a mirror if there were a convenient one nearby – and this is why we may sometimes deliberately avoid seeing our own reflection. Ask yourself 'what would a mirror tell me about my habits of posture or expression that I do not really wish to know?' Then ask 'how can I change my habits to make me feel better about myself – and more comfortable within my own skin?' This exercise can be particularly self-revealing.

USE HABIT TO BEAT HABIT

Habits can catch us unawares – we notice our own pattern of behaviour after, rather than during, the event. One way to be more conscious of habitual responses, and more likely to put energy into changing them, is to cultivate the 'habit' of flagging them as they happen. Use physical 'props' to help bring invisible habits to the foreground of your attention. For example, if you want to cut down on smoking, resolve to put on a glove every time you pick up a cigarette for a few days. The act of doing this will make your habit seem more of an aberration and give you time to change your mind. Even if you opt to break your resolve, you will remember this transgression against your self-imposed rule. And this in turn will highlight your behaviour and make you more eager to change it.

SCAN THE ALTERNATIVES

Does every day seem to follow the same stale pattern? Are you stuck in a rut? A 'habit audit' can give you a clearer picture of your habits and their consequences for your life. Keeping a diary is immensely valuable for this. But you may also find it helpful to observe other people's lifestyles. Look closely and open-mindedly at the ways in which others carry themselves in different situations – doing the shopping, playing with their children, and so on. Admit that your own life is not a fixed norm from which everyone else is deviating: it is merely one variation among many. Learn from other people. Try their behaviour patterns for a change, instead of your own. You may find unexpected rewards.

CHANGE HABITS OF FEELING

Habits can invade our patterns of thinking and feeling as well as our actions. Quickly make a random list of adjectives referring to qualities you find admirable in other people – it might include, for example, 'ambitious', 'thoughtful', 'sensitive', 'mature', 'meticulous', 'funny'. Then consider how far these characteristics apply to you. If you admire a quality that you believe you lack, does that not immediately suggest a pathway for personal development?

Imagine the growing fulfilment you would derive from being able gradually to change yourself into a more admirable person through your own efforts. Bear in mind that an effective way to mature your feelings is to start by changing the behavioural responses associated with them. For example, let us say you are reluctant to give up a leisure activity to visit a friend who needs a shoulder to cry on. You might think of yourself, shame-faced, as inconsiderate or even selfish. But to change this feeling you do not have to work at changing your character – all that's needed is to reschedule your golf, call and tell your friend when to expect you.

OBSERVE YOURSELF

Recruit a close friend or family member to act as your secret recorder. Brief him or her to capture you unawares on video at a party – or to record you on audio cassette. Then study the recordings and watch for recurrent patterns. Are you usually the one to initiate conversations or do you follow others' leads? Do you give people time to reply when you are chatting? Do you use meaningless phrases like 'you know' or 'sort of' all the time? If you want to change a verbal habit, try thinking through what you want to say before you begin to speak – many verbal tics are unconsciously intended to give extra thinking time. Ask a friend to give you a secret signal if you start to repeat your habit – whether it is talking too loudly or too quickly, or tending to stare at people.

THE NEW SCIENCE OF PNI

PNI stands for psychoneuroimmunology – where 'psycho' means the mind, 'neuro' the nervous system and 'immunology' the body's immune defences. This new medical discipline focuses on the mechanisms by which the mind is able to affect the body, and takes a whole-body approach to these systems, rather than looking at them separately.

PNI began with the surprising discovery that the body's immune system can be conditioned to react to things that would normally have no effect on it. The finding was made by US researcher Robert Ader when he was working on conditioning in mice. One experiment involved giving the mice cyclophosphamide – an immune suppressant that severely reduced their ability to produce anti-bodies to invading organisms – in a saccharin-flavoured drink. What Ader discovered was that similar effects on the immune system occurred in conditioned mice when they were given the sweet drink on its own, without the drug. Their immune systems had 'learned' to respond to the drink as if it were the drug associated with it.

Researchers began to wonder if they could pair a drug that boosts the immune system with another substance and use the learned response to achieve beneficial effects using lower drug doses. In a later experiment they did just that. A woman with lupus, an immune disorder that damages joints, skin and internal organs, at first took all her doses of medicine together with cod-liver oil and rose perfume. Over a 12-month period, she came to need only half as many doses of medication as expected if the doses were alternated with cod-liver oil and perfume; she continued this regime for five years, and her condition improved.

Mind and the immune system
Emotions, moods and thoughts can have a physical effect on the brain, in turn affecting the body's response to stress and illness.

Influencing immunity

Not so long ago, this phenomenon would have seemed baffling because the immune system and the nervous system were thought to be quite sep-arate. Immunology was based on cells and molecules fighting invading organisms and the idea that these apparently automatic chemical processes could be learned seemed absurd.

When you feel a cold coming on, the two things you are least likely to feel like are having a good laugh and getting romantic with your partner. But it may be well worth making the effort as both these activities can help to ward off infections by boosting the activity of your immune system.

Laughter works by reducing the levels of stress hormones in the blood, which slow down the immune cells responsible for searching out and destroying viruses. Having a cuddle may also benefit the immune system by raising levels of the 'attachment' hormone, oxytocin. This hormone is produced when people show affection (as well as during orgasm), and it is the foundation of the mother–child bond. Babies who do not get enough physical affection in the weeks after birth fail to produce normal amounts of oxytocin, and that may be one reason why they tend not to thrive and succumb more easily to infections.

Recently, however, biologists have discovered numerous bridges that effectively bind the nervous and immune systems into one complex, interactive whole. Things that happen at the very 'highest' level of the nervous system – our thoughts, beliefs and perceptions – can affect individual molecules in the furthest reaches of the body, and vice versa. Although it seems hard to imagine how difficult periods in our lives could affect our ability to fight illness at cell level, research shows that this is indeed the case. In one study, 40 medical students were assessed six weeks before their final exams and again during the exams. Their levels of distress increased between the first and second assessment, and the number and activity of a particular type of immune cell were significantly lower during the exam period. PNI is the science of discovering exactly how this sort of effect comes about.

Mind and body pathways

Many of the pathways linking mind and body have yet to be revealed, but two routes are well understood. One lies in the wiring of the nervous system: branches of the peripheral nervous system have been shown to extend right into immune system organs and tissues such as the spleen and bone marrow. Signals sent from the brain to these areas may stimulate or inhibit them directly. The second route is via chemicals and messenger cells that carry information from one part of the body to another. The various types were once firmly assigned to a particular body system: neurotransmitters and endorphins, the chemical messengers in the brain, were associated with the nervous system; hormones with the endocrine system; and cytokines (immune cells) with the immune system. But now they are all revealed to be part of a single family of messenger cells, which mediates between the systems as well as working within them.

The knock-on effect of molecular changes from one system to another explains why a condition such as depression – normally thought of as an illness of the mind – can have profound effects on other parts of the body.

FACT: A recent study found that people who were caring single-handedly for a relative with dementia produced fewer antibodies in response to infection than people whose lives were relatively stress-free.

CORTISOL AND THE BODY'S DEFENCES

The immune system 'army' has an important battalion of natural killer (NK) cells, whose role is to search out and destroy mutant or alien cells. NK cells are activated as part of a sequence of hormonal and chemical changes triggered by injury or disease. The 'alarm signal' that gets them working is a sudden rise in the stress hormone cortisol.

If cortisol levels stay high, however, the NK cells become depleted and are no longer so effective. A study of women with breast cancer found that those whose cortisol levels remained at a high level survived, on average, for three years after diagnosis, while those whose cortisol levels rose and fell in a normal way survived over a year longer. The women with high cortisol levels were also found to have fewer NK cells. Helping to keep stress – and cortisol – down to normal levels may be one reason why relaxation techniques can help cancer patients.

Health through talking The links between the mind and the immune system revealed by PNI, combined with new discoveries about brain processes, have removed much of the mystery and scepticism that used to surround psychological treatments like hypnotherapy, placebos and 'talking therapies'.

A common chemical change in people with depression and dementia is a drop in the levels of noradrenaline, a neurotransmitter in the brain that stimulates brain cells and helps us to generate thoughts and perceptions. A drop in noradrenaline not only causes mental sluggishness but reduces the nerve activity that stimulates tissues to keep certain immune cells circulating. So instead of seeking out and fighting bacteria and viruses, the inactive immune cells allow infections to thrive.

Effects of anxiety and emotion

Anxiety damps down the immune system in a similar way. The brain reacts to anxiety in the same way that it reacts to fear, by telling the adrenal glands (situated above the kidneys) to prepare the body for fight or flight. The adrenals respond by flooding the body with cortisol, which has several useful effects in an emergency: it thickens the blood, helping to reduce catastrophic bleeding in the event of injury; it tenses the muscles in preparation for fighting or fleeing; and it heightens mental alertness.

But while all this is happening, the everyday business of body maintenance is put on hold, such as the tracking down and destruction of foreign or errant cells, including any that won't stop

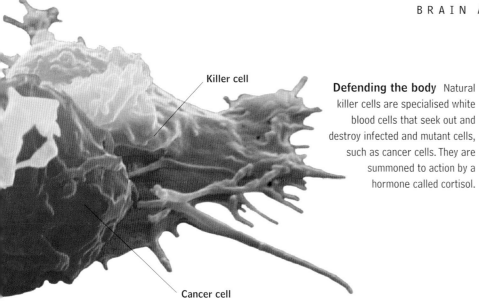

Killer cell

Cancer cell

Defending the body Natural killer cells are specialised white blood cells that seek out and destroy infected and mutant cells, such as cancer cells. They are summoned to action by a hormone called cortisol.

dividing when they should and may therefore produce cancer. Anxiety is certainly not the cause of cancer, but it may in this way allow a tumour to escape destruction at an early stage.

In contrast, positive mental experiences can stimulate the immune system, helping to keep illness at bay. Laughter, for example, brings about profound changes in many parts of the body – it relaxes the muscles, increases bloodflow and stimulates the production of 'feel-good' neuro-transmitters. Anger and hostility, on the other hand, reverse these effects. Anger is thought to have a negative impact on the body because it raises the levels of stress hormones, which damage the linings of blood vessels. This may cause inflammation and the formation of scar tissue, slowing down the passage of blood and encouraging the formation of clots, which can lead to a heart attack. Feeling angry in appropriate situations is not going to cause you harm, but if you can learn to laugh at frustrations rather than get upset about them you may be helping yourself to a longer and healthier life.

The PNI revolution

PNI is helping to bring about a quiet revolution in scientific thinking. In conventional medical research, the fact that many body processes at a mol-ecular level could be reproduced in a test-tube reinforced the idea of the body as a machine. This approach has undoubtedly been very successful in giving rise to drugs and treatments for many diseases. However, the more success doctors have had in curing specific disorders, the more their patients seem to complain of non-specific problems like general tiredness, depression and varieties of vague malaise that do not match the usual text-book descriptions of illnesses that they have been trained to deal with.

The idea that systems in the body and brain are linked to form an inte-grated whole helps us to make sense of this modern epidemic. Treatments that concentrate solely on the part that needs 'fixing' may cure a specific dis-ease but ignore other aspects of mental and physical well-being. Holistic practitioners have always recognised this, and PNI is finally underpinning their approach with a scientific basis.

Real lives

STRESS – STORING UP TROUBLE

Tough people often come off better in stressful situations – in terms of their long-term health as well as at the time. But chronic stress can affect the defences of even the most robust, as the experience of one young woman, Terri, suggests.

'I've always been a bit of a fighter – if someone did anything against me I wouldn't rest until I had turned things round, or got them to apologise. So I wasn't really surprised when my colleagues asked me to represent them in this battle we were having for better work conditions. I put my heart into it for a year – but then management found an excuse to sack me. It was the first time I had ever really lost a battle, and it made me so angry I could hardly think of anything else.

'The odd thing was that, all the time I was in there, fighting, I was healthy – even though it felt really stressful. But after it ended, I went down with one illness after another: first it was flu, then shingles, then my back went . . . it just went on and on. Even now, two years later, I haven't really got my strength back. I think stress gets to you in the end, however tough you think you are.'

3 PERSONALITY AND HEALTH

Speculation on the influence that personality and attitude can have on health crops up regularly in the media. But what are the facts behind the stories? Does stress inevitably make people ill? Are happy, fun-loving people less likely to suffer illness? Are some people condemned to ill health simply through personality? And is it possible to beat an illness through positive thinking?

This chapter surveys the hard evidence on the link between personality and health, and attempts to sort out the reliable facts from rumour and wishful thinking. Along the way, it reveals how certain kinds of thinking can have remarkable healing powers. Cures can and often do start in the mind, it seems, and our behaviour and lifestyle choices – many of which are influenced by personality – have a direct influence on our well-being.

CAN YOUR PERSONALITY AFFECT YOUR HEALTH?

Research has shown that psychological factors play an important role in many diseases, from heart problems to catching a cold. Your physical health is often dependent on your state of mind. And this, in turn, is influenced – at least in part – by your personality.

You might be upset if your doctor told you that your medical problem was psychosomatic, or worse, 'all in the mind'. It would mean that the doctor could not find a physical cause, and assumed a psychological cause. However, psychosomatic illness is quite real, but is often misunderstood – partly because we are used to thinking of mind and body as separate entities. In fact, the word comes from the language of ancient Greece, where doctors understood that mind (psyche) and body (soma) were intrinsically connected.

Emotions and health

Sigmund Freud revived the idea of psychosomatic medicine in the late 19th century. At his practice in Vienna, he treated many patients who had symptoms with no obvious physical origin, and called this condition hysteria. His patients were often young women from wealthy families who exhibited dramatic symptoms, such as paralysis, loss of speech, and even epileptic fits. Freud was able to solve some of these patients' problems through psychoanalysis, revealing and then resolving inner psychological conflicts that had, according to Freud, brought the problems about.

In the 1920s, the American physiologist Walter Cannon (see page 80) carried out research on how emotion affects the body. It was Cannon who coined the term 'fight or flight' for the way the body reacts in response to a threat. His research led, during the 1930s and 40s, to the development of the psychosomatic movement in medicine, led by Helen Dunbar and Franz Alexander. Dunbar believed that psychosomatic medicine could combine the treatment of physical, emotional and spiritual suffering. Meanwhile, Alexander attempted to update Freud's theories with the latest

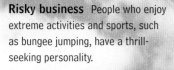

Risky business People who enjoy extreme activities and sports, such as bungee jumping, have a thrill-seeking personality.

Real lives **A TALE OF TWO BROTHERS**

Although they had been extremely close when they were young, brothers Martin and Bill could not have had more different personalities. Martin, 46, was a sales director – ambitious, driven and impatient. He was an exercise fanatic, careful with his diet and a non-smoker.

Bill, 44, was a teacher. He had worked at the same school for 15 years and unlike many colleagues, coped easily with his workload. At weekends, he went fishing or walking. He enjoyed a drink, loved food and was a bit overweight – he even indulged in the odd cigar.

Despite their differences, they got on well, so Bill was devastated when his 'fit' brother was rushed to hospital after a heart attack. Martin recovered and resumed his heavy work schedule, but six months later, he was back in hospital. This time, the consultant warned that he would have to stop driving himself so hard, or he would be dead by 50. With difficulty, and with reminders from Bill and others around him, Martin heeded the warning, and made some major changes to his lifestyle.

developments in physiology. He identified repressed aggression as a particularly important cause of psychosomatic illness.

Hysteria of the type described by Freud is rarely diagnosed nowadays. However, there are still medical conditions, such as chronic fatigue syndrome, for which a physical cause is not evident. Furthermore, doctors are becoming increasingly aware that psychological factors can play an important role in many other diseases, such as asthma, eczema, digestive problems and heart disease.

The personality factor

Your health is affected by how you choose to live – whether or not you smoke, the kinds of food you eat, whether you take regular exercise, or take part in risky activities, such as dangerous sports. Some researchers, including American psychiatrist Robert Cloninger, talk of a specific personality trait called 'novelty-seeking'. People who have an abundance of this trait are easily bored with routine and constantly search for excitement and adventure. They may indulge in risky behaviours, such as taking drugs or driving too fast. They may also take up dangerous sports such as mountaineering or parachuting. A person who has little of this trait will tend to be organised, wedded to a daily routine and likely to stick with the same partner, job and circle of friends. Personality plays an important part in making all these life choices.

Studies show that, beyond these choices, there is probably no such thing as an overall 'disease-prone' personality, just as there is no evidence that happy, well-balanced people live longer or enjoy better physical health

FACT: Some scientists think that novelty-seeking is controlled by the level of a brain chemical called dopamine. The more dopamine you have rushing around your brain, the more of a sensation-seeker you are.

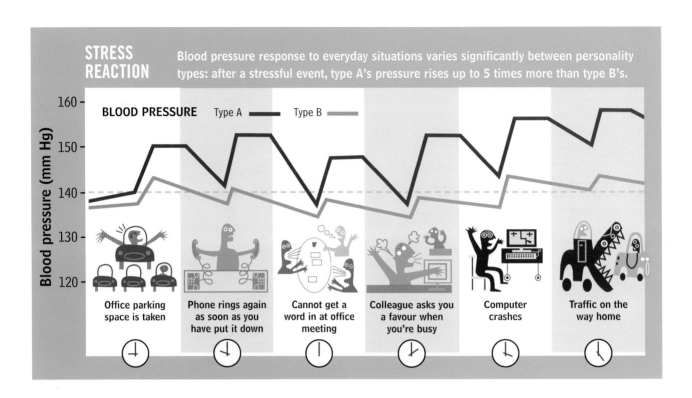

STRESS REACTION

Blood pressure response to everyday situations varies significantly between personality types: after a stressful event, type A's pressure rises up to 5 times more than type B's.

BLOOD PRESSURE — Type A ——— Type B ———

Blood pressure (mm Hg)

160 –
150 –
140 –
130 –
120 –

Office parking space is taken

Phone rings again as soon as you have put it down

Cannot get a word in at office meeting

Colleague asks you a favour when you're busy

Computer crashes

Traffic on the way home

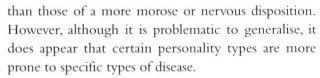

THE DANGERS OF A PERFECT LIFE

Recent research has identified a new personality type that may be vulnerable to stress-related illness. Known as 'repressors', these people seem to have perfect lives: they are hard-working, successful, and never seem anxious or depressed. They pay great attention to detail – their homes are immaculate and they are always well groomed. Their weakness, though, is that they cannot tolerate the uncertainties of everyday life, and see things in all-or-nothing terms.

Tests on responses to emotional experiences show that while non-repressors struggle to express the subtleties and contradictions of their feelings, repressors typically give a simplistic reply. Repressors show the same stressed responses as people with over-anxious personalities, while their immune systems tend to be weak. Studies also show that heart patients who are repressors have a higher risk of complications than non-repressors. It seems that, in health terms, striving to eliminate uncertainty from your life can carry a hefty price tag.

than those of a more morose or nervous disposition. However, although it is problematic to generalise, it does appear that certain personality types are more prone to specific types of disease.

Why is this? The main reason seems to be that your personality can affect how you deal with stress which, in turn, affects both your immune system and your cardiovascular (heart and circulation) system. It is known that in response to stress we produce the hormone cortisol which, if it remains in the body for too long, can trigger the build-up of fatty deposits on the inner walls of the arteries serving the heart.

Type A, type B and heart disease

There is an established relationship between personality and susceptibility to heart disease. You may be familiar with the idea of the type A and type B personalities. Briefly, type A people, who are more prone to heart disease, are typically driven, impatient, ambitious and energetic. In contrast, type B people take life more slowly, are more relaxed and are less likely to develop heart disease.

In the 1950s, two American cardiologists, Friedman and Rosenman, were running a busy practice and wondered why the seats in their waiting room wore out so quickly. An upholsterer came to fix the seating yet again, and commented that it was odd the way the patients would sit on the edge of their seats, clutching at the armrests – as if they were anxious to be off as soon as possible. No wonder the seats kept wearing down in the same place. This throwaway remark about the unusual behaviour of their patients led Friedman and Rosenman to uncover the link between a restless personality and heart problems.

However, the type A personality is composed of several different traits. There is no general agreement on which type of personality is most susceptible to heart disease, but some interesting studies have been done in recent years. A group of men and women were given a frustrating anagram puzzle to solve. When doing the puzzle, those who had admitted in a questionnaire to being more hostile and suspicious showed much higher rises in blood pressure than their more trusting peers. We all know people who get worked up over things that others take easily in their stride, and evidence suggests that reactivity in response to stressors may be significant in the development of hypertension – a major risk factor for heart disease

'Type C' personalities

After heart disease, cancer is the leading cause of death in the developed world. But does your personality affect your chances of getting cancer? There is some evidence to suggest that it might, although the link is not nearly as strong as that between personality type and heart disease. Some psychologists have defined a 'type C' (cancer-prone) personality, which may be characterised as someone who responds to stress with depression and hopelessness, and mutes their negative emotions. Type Cs are also introverted, respectful, eager to please, conforming and compliant. However, the studies that have been done have not taken into account how personality might affect lifestyle – for example, whether a type C person is more likely to smoke, for example, which would increase the chances of developing cancer.

On the other hand, there is evidence to suggest that your personality type can affect the chances of surviving cancer. Those sufferers who deal with the disease either with a 'fighting spirit' or denial seem to do better than those, like the type C personality, who accept their fate passively. David Spiegel of Stanford University in the USA discovered that cancer patients who joined a support group that fostered the fighting spirit survived, on average, 18 months longer than those not in such a group.

However, not only is the data so far inconclusive, there are also pitfalls in over-emphasising the influence of personality on disease. Taken to extreme, it could result in patients feeling they were to blame for their illness, producing feelings of guilt which would only add to their problems. If personality type does influence disease risk, then it probably occurs through a weakening of the immune system via stress. This could undermine the body's defences and in turn make someone more vulnerable to infection. However, much research still needs to be done before the influence of personality on physical health is fully understood.

TRY IT YOURSELF

COPING WITH 'TYPE A' BEHAVIOUR

If you recognise yourself as a type A personality, don't assume you are going to get heart disease. While you cannot expect to transform yourself into a type B, you can at least modify your behaviour to improve your health and reduce your chances of suffering a stress-induced condition.

• The first tip is to choose your battles carefully and stop trying to exert control over minor upsets or events that are beyond your ability to change. If you have been given a parking ticket, for example, just accept it gracefully rather than raging or fuming about your bad luck. Is it really more important than your blood pressure?

• Second, if you are an energetic, driven person, find some way of letting off steam that is easier on your cardiovascular system. Taking part in sport, exercise or regular meditation are all beneficial ways of calming yourself down. However busy you think you are, it is worth spending time on whichever relaxation technique works for you, for the sake of your long-term mental and physical health.

EXTROVERT OR INTROVERT?

		YES	NO
1	Do you become restless when working at something where there is little action?	☐	☐
2	Do you often try to find the underlying motives for the actions of other people?	☐	☐
3	Do you like talking to people so much that you never miss a chance to talk to a stranger?	☐	☐
4	Are you usually among the last to stop clapping at the end of a concert or play?	☐	☐
5	If making a business enquiry would you rather write than discuss it on the telephone?	☐	☐
6	Would you enjoy working on a project that involved a lot of library research?	☐	☐
7	Do you wish that you were able to 'let go' and have a good time more often?	☐	☐
8	Do you often find you've crossed a road ahead of your more careful companions?	☐	☐
9	Do you need to use a lot of self-control to keep out of trouble?	☐	☐
10	Are you always careful to declare everything at customs when travelling abroad?	☐	☐

Do you know what sort of person you are? Our personalities are extremely complex, with many layers and aspects. However, the British psychologist Hans Eysenck identified three major personality dimensions. Use this three-part questionnaire to find out which you are.

DISCOVER YOUR PERSONALITY TYPE

Personality is a collection of individual and relatively enduring patterns of behaviour and interaction with others. Our temperamental and personality characteristics are what make each of us unique. Over a period of several decades, Eysenck developed a model in which he described three main personality dimensions: introversion-extroversion, emotional-stable, and tough-tender. Eysenck saw each of these as a scale on which most people would score somewhere between two extremes, and his three-part model is still commonly used today.

Although your personality tends to remain stable over time, you can change your lifestyle and also alter your behaviour to some degree. An understanding of your personality type could help you to identify particular lifestyle and behaviour tendencies that may have a negative impact on your health.

To discover where you are placed on Eysenck's three personality dimensions, complete the three questionnaires on this page. Then turn to the next page to find out how you scored and what implications this may have for your health. With determination, you may be able to use this awareness to modify your behaviour and improve your mental and physical well-being. One highly revealing way of using the questionnaire is to complete it yourself first, and then have someone who knows you very well to fill it in on your behalf. The differences thrown up can be quite interesting. Write your answers on separate sheets of paper so that your friend's answers are not influenced by your own.

DoyouthinkyouareExtrovertIntro

EMOTIONAL OR STABLE?

YES **NO**

1 Do you often lose sleep over your worries?

2 Are you ever bothered by unimportant thoughts that run through your mind for days?

3 In general, would you say that you are satisfied with your life?

4 Do you see your future as looking quite bright?

5 Do you have a great deal of confidence in your decisions?

6 Are you often afraid of things and people that you know would not really hurt you?

7 Do you often feel ashamed of things that you have done

8 Do you smile and laugh as much as most people?

9 Do you get very upset if someone criticises you?

10 Do you think it's a waste of time going to the doctor with mild complaints such as colds?

TOUGH OR TENDER?

1 Do you set your aspirations low in order to avoid disappointments?

2 If someone does you a bad turn do you feel obliged to do something about it?

3 Do you get angry when you read what certain politicians have said in the papers?

4 Do you often question your own morality and rules of conduct?

5 Do you like scenes of violence and torture in the movies?

6 Do you sometimes do slightly dangerous things just for the thrill of it?

7 Are you turned off by crude and vulgar jokes?

8 Does your blood boil when people stubbornly refuse to admit that they are wrong?

9 Would you put yourself out a great deal to help someone who was suffering emotionally?

10 Do you find it difficult to resist cuddling small furry animals?

See next page for results

tEmotionalStableToughTender?

EXTROVERT OR INTROVERT

HOW TO SCORE

Give yourself one point for each 'yes' to questions 1, 3, 4, 8 and 9 and one point for each 'no' to questions 2, 5, 6, 7 and 10.

A score of 8–10, means that you are outgoing, sociable, active and impulsive – an extrovert.

If you scored 3–7 you are an ambivert, which means that you have some of the characteristics of each type, extrovert and introvert.

A score of 0–2 means that you are quiet, controlled, thoughtful and responsible – in other words, a classic introvert.

Extroverts typically show the following traits: activity, sociability, risk-taking behaviour, impulsiveness, expressiveness, lack of reflection and lack of responsibility.

Introverts, by contrast, exhibit more or less the opposite of all the extrovert's traits to a greater or lesser degree. They are thus more likely to be cautious and reflective, to be reliable, to persevere, to be interested in solitary pursuits and to prefer their own company. Extrovert people may be happier and more fun to be with, but introverts tend to be more independent and reliable.

EMOTIONAL OR STABLE

HOW TO SCORE

Give yourself one point for each 'yes' to questions 1, 2, 6, 7 and 9 and one point for each 'no' to questions 3, 4, 5, 8 and 10.

A score of 8–10 means that you are highly emotional and inclined to be anxious, fearful, guilt-ridden and generally harried by life.

A score of 3–7 indicates fairly average emotionality. You are reasonably well adjusted but not completely immune to anxiety.

A score of 0–2 means that you are unusually stable, confident, secure and untroubled by events.

Stability makes a person content and generally easy to get along with. However, emotional people are often more exciting, creative and artistic than stable people, and they are more likely to sympathise with the problems of others.

Emotionally unstable people are more likely to have personality traits such as low self-esteem, depression, anxiety, obsessiveness, lack of autonomy, hypochondria and feelings of guilt. People of this type are sometimes thought by psychologists to be more at risk of succumbing to physical and mental illness.

TOUGH OR TENDER

HOW TO SCORE

Give yourself one point for each 'yes' to questions 2, 3, 5, 6 and 8 and one point for each 'no' to questions 1, 4, 7, 9 and 10.

A score of 8–10 puts you at the tough end of this dimension – assertive, aggressive, ambitious and sensation-seeking.

A score of 3–7 puts you in the average range – you have a mixture of tough and tender characteristics.

A score of 0–2 means that you are very tender-minded – kind, considerate, nurturing and understanding of others.

Tough people are more likely to get ahead in life and get things done. Tender people provide support, companionship and consolation.

Tough-minded people usually have above-average levels of the following traits: aggressiveness, assertiveness, achievement orientation, manipulation, sensation-seeking behaviour and dogmatism (stubbornness). At its most extreme, somebody of the tough-minded type may have little or no regard for others' feelings. In contrast, tender-minded people are much more focused on other people and their needs.

AreyouExtrovertIntrovertEr

PERSONALITY AND YOUR HEALTH

An enormous amount of research has been carried out to try to establish links between personality and health. Although there is little that anyone can do to change fundamental personality, there is much that can be done to modify self-destructive behavioural traits and reduce health risks, such as poor diet, lack of exercise, high-stress activities, and drinking and smoking. Most people have a mix of attributes, but if the scores in one of the dimensions are very high – or if personality factors are leading to health-affecting behaviours – then making some lifestyle changes may well be beneficial.

EXTROVERT TYPE

Extroverts may need more balance and moderation in their lifestyles. They should be sure to get enough sleep and eat healthily. There may be a tendency to drink in excess, and indulge in too much partying and risk-taking behaviour. Reining in such tendencies could benefit mental and physical health.

INTROVERT TYPE

Introverted people are generally shy and often have less well-developed social skills. They may benefit from some form of social-skills counselling to help them overcome any tendency to excessive shyness. Introverts who live on their own should be careful not to neglect their own physical and emotional needs, in particular by maintaining important social contact with family and friends.

EMOTIONAL TYPE

A very high emotional score may indicate a tendency to suffer from depression, phobias or obsessions. Cognitive behavioural therapy may help to improve mental and physical health. Raising self-esteem, using positive thinking techniques and learning how to deal with anxiety may be priorities for a happier and healthier life.

STABLE TYPE

People with a stable personality tend not to overreact to emotional stimuli, and are not subject to rapid or extreme swings of mood. They are generally seen by others as reliable, although their own lack of emotion may be considered as a sign of detachment. Stable people need to be aware that others do not necessarily share their calm and balanced outlook on life.

TOUGH TYPE

A very high toughness score may indicate a need for anger-management counselling and the curbing of risk-taking behaviours. There is a notable difference in the scores of men and women on this attribute. Men tend to be tougher on average and women more tender, although there is still considerable overlap.

TENDER TYPE

Tender people are generally well-liked by those around them. However, there is a chance that they may be taken advantage of if their tenderness is perceived as a weakness. Behaving in too tender a way can make a person vulnerable to depression when things go wrong or expectations are overturned. Tender people may need to think of others less and themselves more.

tionalStableToughTender?

SYMPTOMS: IN THE MIND OR BODY?

There is a widespread belief that some symptoms are 'physical' while others are 'in the mind'. But mind and body are linked in a single complex system – so, if one part of the system is damaged or malfunctioning, the rest is bound to be adversely affected.

Illness makes itself known in two ways: by signs – physical changes that can be detected by other people – and symptoms, which are only known to the person who has them. For example, if you get a cold, your temperature goes up, your nose runs and you sneeze; these are signs of illness. In addition, however, you may feel feverish, stuffed-up and tired, and these feelings are symptoms.

Symptoms and signs

Most illnesses produce both symptoms and signs: not only do you feel ill but other people can see that you are ill, so the question of whether the illness is 'real' or not does not arise. However, in some illnesses, the signs are either too subtle to be detected or the condition is not yet understood, so doctors do not recognise them. The only way the illness manifests itself is in unpleasant feelings – symptoms, known only to the sufferer. Such conditions are sometimes said to be 'all in the mind', which until recently meant non-physical. But it is now known that there is no such thing as an entirely non-physical sensation: everything we experience – even our thoughts – has a physical basis in the brain.

Take, for example, the condition tinnitus, in which sufferers typically complain of persistent ringing or buzzing in the ear. Not so long ago, tinnitus was often assumed to be 'in the mind', because it had no observable signs that could be detected medically. In recent years, however, imaging equipment has been developed that can show the electrical brain activity of sensations such as hearing. This technology has shown clearly that when tinnitus patients hear a 'phantom' noise, the cells in the brain that register sound display the same physical changes that occur when sound waves hit the ear. The sounds heard by tinnitus sufferers are therefore no more imaginary than any other sounds – it is just that they are produced by a different mechanism.

Real feelings from 'invisible' causes

In the condition known as phantom limb, people report feeling sensation (including pain) in an arm or leg that has been amputated. This phenomenon was once dismissed as some vague psychological attachment to the missing body part. Now, however, research has shown that physical sensations can continue to be produced in the brain's neural 'body maps' even in the absence of input from the body. In other words, if the part of the brain that maps the left leg is activated, a person experiences the sensation even if the leg itself is not present. The feeling is identical to when the brain cells are triggered by messages from nerves in an actual leg. This means there is no difference between 'imaginary' feelings and 'real' ones – they all stem from the same source: physical changes in the brain.

Sometimes symptoms can arise that do not a have a physical cause. Suppose, for example, someone has an accident during which they suffer a whiplash injury, as can often happen when a car decelerates rapidly. Following the incident, nerves in the neck and spine send signals to the brain cells that register pain in that area. This continuous stimulation sensitises these cells, so that even after the injury has healed, they will be inclined to fire at the least stimulation. The slightest jolt may make them flare up, although an examination would show nothing wrong. In effect, the brain has learned to produce neck pain, even when the signals from the original source have ceased.

Feeling the loss
The condition called phantom limb is not an imaginary sensation, but results from nerve cells in the brain's 'body map' continuing to fire.

TRY IT YOURSELF   THE PHANTOM NOSE SENSATION

Phantom limb sensation occurs when the brain 'projects' a feeling on to a limb that is not there. With the help of a couple of friends and a few minutes to spare, you can get some idea of how this feels.

1. Sit in a chair, with one friend sitting in another chair in front of you, facing in the same direction, and the second friend standing on your right.

2. The standing friend should now take your right index finger in their right hand, and use it to stroke and tap the nose of the seated friend in front.

3. At the same time, the standing friend must use their own left index finger to tap and stroke your nose, in precise synchrony with the stroking and tapping using your finger of the person in front of you.

4. Close your eyes and relax. After about 30 or 40 seconds you will find that the feeling of tapping and stroking no longer comes from where your nose is, but has shifted location to where your finger is stroking your friend's nose in front of you. You have 'created' a phantom body part!

Conflicting signals

The illusion arises because the brain is faced with two conflicting streams of information. The hand says that it is stroking a nose some distance in front, but the nose, confirming that it is being stroked, feels that it is happening in the usual place – on your face. The brain has to interpret this information in a way that makes sense. Both messages cannot be right so it chooses between them. Messages from the hands are more credible because the fingers have far more neurons associated with them. So the brain chooses the information given by the finger – that the nose is way out in front.

Expectations of pain

Another way that feelings may be produced without obvious cause is through expectation. Suppose, for instance, that your mother suffered from rheumatism, and as a child you frequently saw her wince when she moved her knee. Furthermore, you heard that this type of rheumatism is hereditary. Now suppose in middle age, when nearly everyone starts to get some joint pain, you feel a slight pain in your knee. Most people would dismiss it as normal wear and tear, but your first thought is likely to be that this is what your mother had. From that moment you are looking out for the next pain, and any sensation in the knee, however slight, gets immediate attention. Attention is known to amplify feeling – it makes the brain cells associated with the sensation fire more strongly – so what might have been a small twinge can become a searing pain. You may have precisely the same degree of wear in your knee as someone else, but your brain reacts more strongly to it because of your expectations.

Similarly, people can become sensitised to body signals. A person who is constantly looking out at the world, rather than inwards, is less likely to pay attention to the incessant buzz of information that the body sends to the brain. Small pains are overlooked, and because they are not noticed, the brain cells that register them do not become sensitised. In contrast, someone who monitors body signals very closely will notice every little sensation, and the brain will react more strongly to any adverse signal.

The simple belief that you have a condition can trigger actual changes in the body that may produce signs of the illness. Just thinking that your blood pressure is rising can cause the blood vessels to constrict, so that

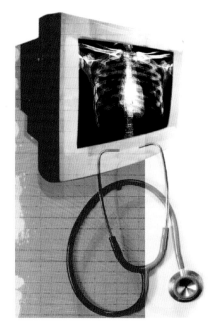

Digital diagnosis Computers can be more accurate than doctors at diagnosis – perhaps because they are not misled by their own prejudices. In one study in a hospital emergency department, the patients' symptoms were fed into a computer, which then made the right diagnosis in 91 per cent of cases; the casualty doctors, by contrast, were right in only 45 per cent of cases.

THINK AGAIN!   DIFFERENT COUNTRY, DIFFERENT DIAGNOSIS

An illness is the same illness wherever you are, right? Wrong. Doctors as well as patients tend to fit signs and symptoms of illness into a disease pattern they are familiar with and expect to see – and expectations differ according to training and speciality.

In Britain, for example, patients complaining of breathlessness, dizziness, tiredness and feelings of panic would probably be diagnosed with hyperventilation, a condition in which blood alkalinity rises as carbon dioxide is reduced through over-breathing. In France the same symptoms would more

usually be attributed to spasmophilia – spontaneous muscle contractions brought on by magnesium deficiency. In Germany, the diagnosis would most likely be vasovegetative syndrome, caused by a nervous system imbalance, while in the United States doctors would probably pronounce 'burn-out'.

when your blood pressure is measured it is indeed raised. The precise mechanisms that cause this are not fully understood, but it seems that the thought of a body change feeds back from the cerebral cortex to the limbic areas of the brain that produce that change. This is an example of 'top-down' brain processing – conscious thoughts influencing unconscious processes. On rare occasions, the body may erupt in spontaneous lesions. A most dramatic example is the religious phenomenon of 'stigmata', in which the person develops sores on the hands and feet in empathy with Jesus' crucifixion wounds (although the causes of this are not fully understood).

Taking control

Just as the brain can produce symptoms of illness, it can also alleviate them. If you can learn to direct your attention away from pain and discomfort and be optimistic about the course of an illness, it will probably cause less distress and clear up more quickly than if you expect it to get worse. Of course, if you have any symptoms that are persistent or could indicate a serious illness, these should always be investigated by a doctor. But if you try to avoid worrying, you may find yourself feeling better without treatment.

FOCUS ON

CHRONIC FATIGUE SYNDROME

Sometimes known as myalgic encephalomyelitis (ME), chronic fatigue syndrome (CFS) is a classic example of a condition that often has profound symptoms but no signs that the medical profession agree on. Sufferers feel perpetually tired, and may be plagued by all manner of uncomfortable feelings, including muscle and joint pain, weakness, stiffness, dizziness, insomnia and noticeable mood changes.

However, doctors have not yet found any clear signs that identify and distinguish the condition. Some experts have found evidence of viral action, others have detected functional differences in the brains of CFS sufferers, and some maintain the disease is caused by a change in the mitochondria – the 'batteries' in body cells that produce energy. Currently, the only diagnostic criterion for CFS is the characteristic bundle of symptoms described by the patient. This leaves the poor CFS sufferer open to the accusation of malingering – because they have no objective, measurable evidence of their illness.

Real lives DELAYED REACTION

Max, a bachelor in his seventies, experienced some strange symptoms upon the death of his mother, whom he had looked after for many years.

'When I was a little boy my mother always insisted that I "pass a motion" before breakfast every day. She always waited until I had done it, and if I was slow she had to wait for her own breakfast and got very irritated. I was scared of mother, but I never dared say anything to her face, even when she was horrible to me. I found, though, that I could annoy her very satisfyingly, just by refusing to open my bowels. I forgot all this until a year ago, when my mother passed away from bowel cancer. I had always looked after mother, and when she went I had very mixed

feelings. I felt lonely, but I also felt resentful that I had given up my life to her – never had a family of my own – and now she had left me alone.

'Shortly after that I started to suffer pains, lose weight, and could feel a hard mass in my abdomen. I had a full medical investigation, but the only thing the doctors could find wrong was chronic constipation, which they said accounted for all the symptoms.

'I didn't believe them, but eventually a psychiatrist got me to talk about things. I realised I was angry with her, though I didn't like to feel that way about her now she was dead. And it occurred to me that I had – in a funny way – been "getting back at her" just like I did

as a child. Then, when I got pains because I wasn't defecating, I assumed it was cancer. The psychiatrist sent me to a hypnotist, who cured my constipation – and now when I get that heavy feeling I reach for the prunes instead of assuming I am dying. It seems crazy that something as physical as a bowel function can be altered by the mind – but it certainly was.'

Hysteria

In the 19th century, hysteria was a common diagnosis, describing a condition in which psychological problems were transformed into dramatic physical symptoms. These curious and debilitating effects are still studied by doctors.

The ancient Greeks thought that the womb *(husterus)* was a free-floating organ that could move around the body creating problems – any mysterious ailments in women were therefore ascribed to 'hysteria'. Although the notion of a wandering womb disappeared, that of hysteria did not. In the 19th century, the condition was held responsible for a host of symptoms in women, including emotional fits, numbness, weakness, sensory dysfunction and fainting.

A Parisian neurologist, Jean-Martin Charcot, studied hundreds of 'hysterical' patients and described how they went through four phases: physical rigidity, muscular spasms, emotional outbursts and delirium. He discovered that he could induce these states in some of his patients, and held demonstrations in which women were taken through the phases, then miraculously cured. Sigmund Freud was fascinated by Charcot's work, and hysteria

Hysteria demonstrated Jean-Martin Charcot (1825–93) held public performances where patients would demonstrate the clinical patterns of hysteria.

became central to his theory of psychoanalysis. He concluded that hysteria was caused by repressed sexual desires and conflicts that were converted into physical symptoms.

Hysteria today – conversion disorder

The term hysteria is rarely used by doctors now; in everyday usage, it usually just means a display of melodramatic emotion. However, the 19th century idea lives on in a set of conditions known as conversion disorders. These are no longer thought to be primarily sexual in origin, or limited to women, but Freud's basic idea – of physical symptoms caused by unconscious conflict or pain – remains fundamental.

Conversion disorder is defined as the appearance of symptoms, usually affecting movement or the senses, which cannot be explained by physical disease and are judged to be associated with some kind of psychological stress. Patients have no

DISSOCIATION – A PROTECTION MECHANISM

Some symptoms of conversion disorder – the modern term for hysteria – may be caused by the 'dissociation' of one part of the brain from another. This type of brain dysfunction is similar to that seen in extreme emotional trauma, when people may 'cut off' the conscious parts of the brain from the parts sensing the outside world. The traumatic event is thus not consciously experienced, and memories of it cannot be recalled in the normal way. They may, however, be triggered in the form of a 'body memory' – a replay of the physical sensations that were present in the trauma. The replay of such memories is thought to

account for many cases of conversion disorder.

Dissociation probably evolved as a survival mechanism – by cutting out damaging sensations, it leaves the rational part of the brain free to work out a response. And when there is nothing to be done, it produces a dreamy, passive, state that would be more useful than panicking. Women and children dissociate into this passive state earlier in the course of trauma than men. Men also dissociate from pain and emotion but act aggressively before becoming passive. Dissociation can thus be useful in extreme situations, protecting the individual from damage.

conscious control over the symptoms, and are usually unaware of the underlying cause. In severe cases, symptoms may include paralysis, blindness, deafness and hallucinations. More often, though, they are vague, and can include dizziness, lack of balance or coordination, headaches, nausea, tics and tremors, and numbness. Conversion symptoms often overlap with another state called derealisation – the sensation that the world is distant, unreal or shifting. Depersonalisation – a feeling of watching oneself from outside – is also common.

Female conversion disorder patients outnumber males by two to one, and the condition seems mainly to affect young people who are naïve about the way their bodies work. The symptoms often mimic popular ideas of how a disease might manifest itself. For example, a patient complaining of chest pain may be unconsciously terrified of lung cancer; however, in real lung cancer cases, chests pains do not appear until the disease is far advanced, usually after a host of other symptoms.

Root causes

The symptoms of conversion disorder are not imagined; they occur because the brain functions abnormally. A brain scan of a woman who was unable to move her left side revealed that when she was asked to lift her left leg, the brain area that plans action became active, showing that she intended to make the movement, but this instruction was not transmitted to the neighbouring motor cortex, which tells the muscles to move.

The only data available to the conscious mind in such cases is that it is trying to move but can't. Not surprisingly, most patients erroneously conclude that there is something wrong with their limbs.

A CASE OF HYSTERICAL BLINDNESS

Hannah was 22 when she experienced blindness following a family tragedy.

'We have a stream running through our farm where the children liked to play. It was quite safe because usually the water was only a foot deep. I used to leave the children there while I took my husband his lunch.

'Last autumn we had a downpour one night, and the next day I saw that the water had risen to about three feet. I left the two older children – aged three and five – on the bank as usual, but told them not to go in the water. Then I went with the baby to see my husband. When I returned a few minutes later the children were nowhere to be seen. I walked back along the bank, then I looked down and saw their bodies in the water. I remember dropping the baby and plunging in – then it all went black.

'When I came round the next day everything was still black. I thought my eyes were bandaged and tried to drag the bandage off, but there wasn't one. I had gone blind.

'I don't remember how long it lasted. In hospital the doctors kept telling me that it was just "nervous shock". Over the next few weeks I started doing things again, slowly. But one day I was with my husband and I said, without thinking, "Pass me that cup". And I realised that I had seen it.'

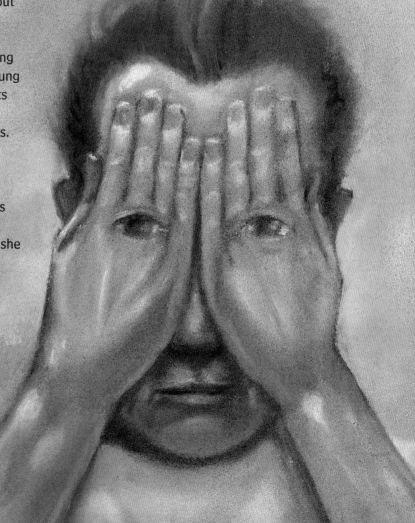

THE PLACEBO EFFECT

The body has remarkable powers of recovery, which can be triggered by the mind to produce a wide range of healing effects. One way of activating this healing potential is to give a patient a 'dummy' treatment that he or she expects to have a curative effect. Such treatment is known as a placebo.

Fifty years ago, one of the most commonly prescribed treatments in general medicine was a sticky, bright pink, strong-smelling mixture called a 'special tonic'. Family doctors handed out this mysterious substance with grave instructions about exactly how and when it should be taken, and encouraged patients to believe that it had powerful healing properties. In fact, the tonic was little more than coloured syrup with no direct curative powers. Yet the doctors were still being truthful when they implied that it could heal. Patients who believed in the special tonic usually showed improvement and reported feeling better.

This placebo effect has been observed since medicine began. Indeed, until the early 20th century, most pills and potions worked in this indirect way. The word 'placebo' is derived from the Latin 'I shall please' – an acknowledgement, probably, that placebos were often employed by doctors to 'please' their patients.

The power of belief

Any form of treatment can be a placebo, and those with the most powerful effects are generally the ones believed by the patient to be the most effective type of treatment. For example, patients who believe in 'natural medicine' are more likely to find that their complaints can be cured by herbs, while people who prefer to trust modern pharmacology may do better with synthetic medicine. Similarly, placebos given by injection are likely to have a greater effect than pills because they are more

Pill or placebo? What is in the medicine may matter less than what you believe is in there. A patient's response to treatment can be driven to a considerable extent by what the patient expects.

F⊙CUS ON DRUG TRIALS

Drugs are tested against a placebo in order to establish how much of a treatment's effectiveness (and side effects) is due to patient expectation, and how much is attributable to the drug's direct medicinal effect. These experiments are known as 'randomised controlled trials' (RCTs), and only drugs that show a benefit in these experiments can be licensed. It is essential that patients do not know whether they are taking the real trial drug or a placebo. Patients who agree to take part in trials are informed in advance that they may be given a placebo, and have the option of refusing to continue.

Trials work by dividing a number of patients with similar symptoms into two groups. One group is given a placebo for a set period while the other is given the treatment.

In order to ensure that patients do not know which treatment they are receiving, where possible the trials are 'double-blind' – that is, the doctor administering the drugs does not know whether the patient is taking the real thing or not. This prevents the doctor from unwittingly influencing the patient.

If it is a pill that is being tested, for example, the placebo will look identical to the real drug. Each pill will carry a code for identification and only at the end of the trial will the allocation of pills to patients be revealed to show who received which treatments. The results can then be analysed and the efficacy of the drug assessed.

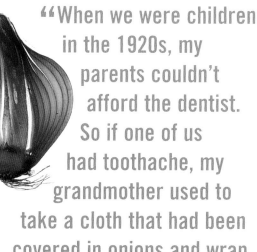

invasive and so are generally perceived to be more powerful.

Probably the most dramatic placebo of all is surgery. In the 1950s, when surgeons were more cavalier about patient rights, a group of people with heart disease were subjected without their knowledge to an experiment intended to test the efficacy of a particular operation. Half the patients had the operation, which involved opening the chest and tying off an artery, while the other half were just cut open and sewn up again. Afterwards, the patients who had undergone the actual operation were found to be in no better or worse health than those who had merely been opened up. The experiment was repeated by different surgeons, and this time the patients who had just been cut open showed even greater improvement than those who had the operation. The improvements were considerable: one patient who had not been operated on was able to run on a treadmill for ten minutes after the treatment, whereas he could barely manage four minutes before. His underlying condition was unchanged, but his ability to function improved enormously, and as functional competence is generally the measure of health it would be true to say that his health had improved.

> **"When we were children in the 1920s, my parents couldn't afford the dentist. So if one of us had toothache, my grandmother used to take a cloth that had been covered in onions and wrap it round your arm on the opposite side to the tooth that was aching. In those days, lots of people believed that onions could cure all sorts of aches and pains."**
>
> Stanley, retired accountant, 85

Real lives RUTH'S PILLS

Ruth McBride, an elderly woman with chronic dyspepsia (indigestion), had first-hand experience of how expectations can influence a drug's effect when her regular prescription was changed.

'A year ago my doctor switched my pills. The new ones were called something else and looked different. As soon as I started them my symptoms came back, so I went back and asked

to be put back on the old ones. My doctor explained that the new ones were identical except that they were called by the generic name instead of the brand name, and were made by a different company. He showed me the book with all the drug names in and I saw he was telling me the truth. I know it sounds funny, but the next day they started to work...'

Placebo-controlled clinical trials

The surgery experiment was an example of a placebo-controlled clinical trial – that is, a study in which the effect of medical treatment is compared to the effect of a placebo treatment on a 'control' group. In this case, previous studies had compared patients who had undergone surgery with others who had received no treatment at all, which had suggested that the operation was useful. However, the placebo-controlled trial showed that the improvement seen after the operation was due to the patients' belief that they had received effective treatment. The surgical procedure was shown to give no additional benefit and so was abandoned.

Surgery is rarely tested against a placebo, but all new drugs must show that they compare favourably to a placebo before they are licensed. Some trials include a third group of patients who receive no treatment at all, and these trials have produced a vast amount of evidence to show just how powerful the placebo effect can be. One large trial, involving nearly 4000 heart-disease patients over a period of five years, found no difference at all in the number of deaths among those who took a real drug and those who took a placebo. However, there was an enormous difference – about 80 per cent – between the health of those who took their pills regularly, whether placebo or real, and those who did not. This strongly suggests that belief in the pills, as demonstrated by keeping to the regime, was more important than any direct effect of the trial drugs. (Effective drugs show a distinct benefit over placebo, and a drug that performed no better than a placebo would not receive a licence.)

The importance of recognition

The placebo effect does not always depend on patients believing they have received effective treatment – simply having symptoms recognised and taken seriously makes an enormous difference. A study of 600 patients who attended their family doctor for sore

RESULTS OF A PLACEBO TRIAL

Placebo trials are used to test all drugs. The graph here shows the results of a typical placebo-controlled trial, in this case to assess the effectiveness of the antidepressant drug paroxetine. Nearly a quarter of patients who took just a placebo showed improved symptoms.

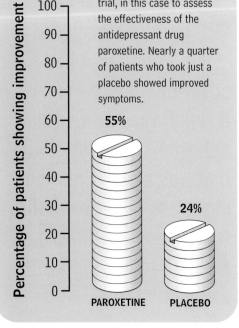

throats found that those who felt they had been treated sympathetically recovered more quickly. A dose of sympathy had generally more effect, it seems, than a course of antibiotics.

Some complementary therapies depend on the placebo effect for their efficacy, but it is difficult to test this because a placebo element is usually built into complementary treatments. A consultation with a complementary therapist will often involve taking a detailed patient history and listening carefully to the patient. It may also involve 'hands-on' treatment, like aromatherapy, massage or body manipulation. These elements are almost certain to have a placebo effect, but if you remove them there may be little of the therapy left to assess. This is why it can be difficult (although not impossible) to test complementary treatments using rigorous scientific measures.

The brain–body response

The placebo effect is brought about by the activation of different physiological mechanisms in the body. Pain can be relieved by the release of natural endorphins – morphine-like substances in the brain. The relief of a problem such as constipation or irritable bowel syndrome may be due to nervous system mechanisms that relax the smooth muscle of the intestine. Infections, and possibly even tumours, may be reduced by the brain activating immune system responses.

However, although physiologically based, the placebo effect is subject to learning and modification. If, for example, you have learned to associate pain relief with taking a small white pill, that association alone can bring about pain relief whenever you take a similar white pill – regardless of what it contains. As long as you believe it is the painkiller, it can have a curative effect. In one experiment, people were given a lozenge that produced heart palpitations. When they were later given an inert but identical-looking lozenge, their heart rates increased to the same extent as with the active substance. The placebo effect is thus not always benign, but tends to produce the effects that the patient expects the treatment to have, which may include unpleasant side effects. Indeed, the high level of side effects reported by many people taking a placebo has prompted some researchers to question the general assumption that placebos are harmless.

Placebos, then, rely heavily on the patient's expectations of the treatment's effectiveness. The body simply 'does what is expected of it' – whatever that is in each case.

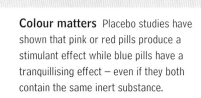

Colour matters Placebo studies have shown that pink or red pills produce a stimulant effect while blue pills have a tranquillising effect – even if they both contain the same inert substance.

THINKING POWER

Your view of the world and what happens to you is coloured by the way that you think. People who are negative thinkers may be more realistic than positive thinkers on some issues, but negative thinking can lead to an unnecessarily gloomy view of life. And when it comes to health, it seems there may be health benefits in adopting a more positive way of thinking.

Events, even stressful ones, are mostly neutral in themselves – it is how we think about them that affects the way we respond. A job may force someone to move away from a place where he or she is happy, but the change may offer the chance to get to know a new area and make new friends. Of course, finding a positive aspect in traumatic circumstances, such as bereavement, is difficult, but there are still differences in the way people cope. A negative thinker is more likely to stay marooned in grief, guilt and anger, while a positive thinker will eventually be able to move on and be thankful for happy memories.

> **"People are disturbed, not by events, but by the view they take of them."**
>
> Epictetus,
> ancient Greek philosopher

Healthy attitudes

The way people perceive everyday events is affected by their thinking style. For example, if a friend does not call when promised, negative thinkers will assume that they have done something wrong and that the friend is angry with them; positive thinkers, in contrast, will probably

 TRY IT YOURSELF **WHAT'S YOUR THINKING STYLE?**

Are you a negative or a positive thinker? To find out, assess your responses in the following situations.

• Is your thinking fixed or changing?
You have had an argument with someone you are close to and just discovered that they were right all along. Do you think 'I always get it wrong' or 'Well, I made a mess of that, but everyone is wrong sometimes'?

The first response is negative, reflecting a rigid mindset. The second is more positive as it acknowledges that each situation is different and that responses can change accordingly.

• Is your thinking global or specific?
Your bank statement arrives and you realise that you are unexpectedly overdrawn and have been charged by the bank. Do you think, 'I can't believe this has happened to me – it's so unfair. I seem to get everything wrong'. Or, do you think, 'Well, finances never were my strong point. I'll have to be more careful in the future.'

A negative thinker will tend to take a global view and assume that if they get one thing wrong, then they always get everything wrong. In contrast, a more positive thinker will realise the specific nature of any failing.

• Is your thinking internal or external?
You have been told that you did not get a promotion you applied for – instead, the company have hired an outside candidate. Do you respond by thinking, 'I wasn't good enough to get that job', or do you think, 'I always thought they would bring in someone new'?

Internal thinkers tend to blame themselves when things go wrong, while external thinkers accept setbacks as being outside their control. So, to enhance your positive thinking, try to see events as changeable, not fixed; specific rather than global; and external rather than internal.

assume that the friend is busy or will ring when they get the chance.

On a more serious level, the way you perceive potential threats governs your stress response, which in turn can affect your health. So does this mean that negative thinking can make you ill? There is no overwhelming evidence for this, but it does seem that a person's thinking style may play some part in their state of health. Conditions such as arthritis, asthma, headaches and heart disease can all be affected by state of mind.

A positive outlook seems to help people to cope better with serious illnesses. For example, psychologists have found that men who had coronary bypass surgery recovered more quickly if they had a positive, rather than negative, outlook on the situation. They returned to normal life more quickly, and when asked about their quality of life six months on, were still doing well.

Breaking down It may feel like letting off steam, but reacting with hostility to the frustrations of everyday life – as the character Basil Fawlty (above) famously did in the classic television comedy series 'Fawlty Towers' – can actually increase the chance of stress-related health problems.

The health cost of hostility

The type of negative thinking that is linked most strongly to ill-health – particularly heart disease – is hostility. People who are hostile complain a lot, are suspicious, get into a lot of arguments and always seem to put the worst interpretation on other people's behaviour. Psychologists at the University of Kansas rated 750 men for hostility then followed their progress over many years. They found that those with high hostility scores were more likely to die prematurely. The same study found that people who are hostile are also more likely to lead unhealthy lifestyles, being prone to smoke, drink or use drugs.

A generally hostile attitude also has a more direct effect on health, as it can lead to more wear and tear on the central nervous system during stress. Psychologists gave a group a frustrating puzzle to solve (a device designed to elicit a measurable stress response). Those who had previously admitted, via a questionnaire, to being more hostile and suspicious in their attitude to others showed bigger increases in blood pressure over the puzzle than those with a more positive attitude. Over a lifetime, these surges in blood pressure in response to normal daily frustrations may well damage the arteries, perhaps setting the scene for heart disease – although this link has not been conclusively proved.

FACT: Norman Vincent Peale, successful author of *The Power of Positive Thinking*, was so disappointed with the first manuscript of his book that he threw it in the waste-paper basket – from where it was rescued by his more positive cleaning lady!

In contrast, positive thinking involves a constructive response to life's problems while keeping a sense of perspective. Positive thinkers are less likely to feel frustrated, helpless or overwhelmed by circumstances, and this can be very helpful in coping with the stresses of everyday life.

STRESS AND HEALTH

Stress is the body's reaction to the challenges and threats of the world around us. Back in our evolutionary past, stress had real survival value, enabling humans to flee from or combat threats from wild animals and enemies. Stress can still be crucial in an emergency, but usually our stress responses merely produce wear and tear on the brain and body.

Stress is often talked about as if it were something outside ourselves, but psychologists use the term to mean our response to something that may threaten our well-being and stability. The external causes of stress are called 'stressors', and practically anything can be one. It could be a truly life-threatening event, such as an out-of-control car coming towards you on the wrong side of the road; or it might be a minor everyday irritation, like a dripping tap or the noise of an electric drill coming from the street. Whatever the disturbance, the brain takes in information from the stressor and, by a complex interplay of the nervous and endocrine systems, produces a bodily response to deal with the threat. The effects of stress are mental, physical and emotional. And if they go on for too long, they can produce ill health. In the short term stress makes the heart race, the palms sweat, and breathing becomes fast and shallow. You may feel fear, anger or even a strange sense of exhilaration. This is all part of the 'fight or flight' response first described by Walter Cannon in the 1930s.

Fight or flight

As the name suggests, the fight or flight response equips you either to run away from a threat or to stay and face it. Either way, you need extra energy, so as soon as the thalamus, the brain's relay station, is made aware of the stressor by the cerebral cortex, it puts the sympathetic nervous system on red alert by sending a message to the adrenal glands. The adrenals pour out two chemicals – adrenaline and noradrenaline – which

(F)OCUS ON   *STRESS IN WORKING LIFE*

Stress can affect you throughout your life: children who are bullied at school suffer enormous stress, and many older people carry the burden of caring for a sick relative. However, it is stress at work that we hear the most about today. The main factors increasing job stress appear to be the rapid pace of change and lack of control over work.

Rapid pace of change
The concept of a 'job for life' is disappearing in today's workplace, with a trend towards temporary and contract work. Some people respond well to the challenge, while others find the lack of security frightening and stressful.

Technological change, with the widespread use of computers, e-mail, and mobile phones, means that opportunities for communication and contact are now limitless. The average office worker is said to be exposed to over 100 digitally transmitted messages a day. This has led to many people experiencing information overload. Also, mastering new technology presents unexpected problems and stresses for people who had managed without these tools for many years.

Lack of control
Dictated to by demanding superiors, busy schedules and long, strict working hours, many people have little control over the work they do. People feel left out of the decision-making process in companies with a hierarchical structure that allows little room for individual input. Often, employees feel they are a mere cog in a big machine, with little personal value beyond their specific task. However, some more enlightened employers are trying to reduce this kind of stress on their workers by offering training, inviting them to meetings, allowing flexible working hours and generally democratising the workplace.

---

increase both your heart and breathing rates to ensure delivery of extra glucose and oxygen to the muscles. Your blood circulation alters too: blood is diverted away from the digestive system, kidneys and skin (which is why you may turn pale), and is channelled towards the muscles.

Cortisol, the stress hormone
The fight or flight response occurs within seconds of being faced with a stressor. It is followed by a second, slower, wave of response that is caused by another stress hormone, cortisol. A brain circuit involving the hypothalamus and the pituitary – the brain's 'master' gland – sends a message to the adrenals, triggering cortisol production. Cortisol provides emergency supplies of glucose fuel for the muscles.

In the short term, this secondary response is useful. However, although the cortisol system is self-regulating, it doesn't always work perfectly, especially under conditions of chronic stress. Canadian researcher Hans Selye, working in the 1930s, showed that laboratory rats exposed to chronic stressors such as overcrowding developed ulcers and impaired immunity. We now know that cortisol is responsible for much of this damage, acting as a slow poison to the body and brain.

FACT: The number of heart attacks among Dutch men increased significantly on the day when the Dutch team was knocked out of the European Football Championship in 1996.

FOUR STRESS MYTHS

1. All stress is bad for you.
No. Without stress, we wouldn't be able to cope with life's problems and challenges. We have to respond to changes in the world and that inevitably involves some stress. Without stress in our lives, we would never feel the satisfaction of overcoming problems and mastering difficult challenges.

2. Everyone gets stressed out by the same things – noise, traffic, overwork.
No. Although these stressors may well cause some annoyance to most people, the extent of the stress each person experiences will be different. We all respond to events in an individual way. Some people adapt to certain kinds of stress and become used to it, while others find even the slightest annoyance too much.

3. People who complain about stress are just weak.
No. Research shows that stress has genuine effects on mental and physical health. Excessive stress should be dealt with promptly before it creates serious health problems.

4. There is a stress epidemic today.
No. Humans have always suffered from stress. In fact, the stressors people faced in the past were probably far greater than they are today – at least in the Western world – including hunger, war, serious overwork, poor health and so on. People today are more conscious of stress as an issue – they hear and read about stress far more, and this has raised awareness.

Identifying stressors

If you made a list of all the things that cause stress in your life, and then compared it with a list made by a friend, it is likely that you would share some stresses, while others would be different. For example, you might both be bothered by transport problems, noise and crowds, but maybe you tend to get stressed by taking on too much at work, whereas your friend might find it difficult to cope with the demands of family life. What is stressful for one person may not be for someone else.

Although it can be hard to predict which situations and events will act as stressors for different individuals, it is clear that events involving major adjustment – such as moving home, getting married, or changing jobs – tend to cause the greatest stress. In the 1960s, the US psychologists Richard Rahe and Thomas Holmes developed the Social Readjustment Rating Scale, in which they assigned different life events a rating depending on how much stress each produced (see page 86). The values were measured in 'life change units' (LCUs). As you might expect, bereavement and divorce were high up the scale, but more surprisingly even positive events such as going on holiday and the birth of a child were rated as stress-producing. Rahe and Holmes argued that people who accumulated a high total of LCUs over a 12-month period were more likely to become ill. Although there has been little hard evidence to support this theory, anyone experiencing a high level of change is certainly likely to feel stressed.

Another way of looking at stressors is in terms of 'hassles' – a term introduced by the US stress expert Richard Lazarus in 1984. Hassles are daily annoyances – such as losing things, or unwanted social obligations – that can, over time, build up and have a corrosive effect on your physical and mental well-being.

Unexpected stressors are often harder to handle than predictable stress. A sense of being out of control makes the body stress circuits go into over-

Staying in control Air-traffic control is one of the most stressful jobs around today. This is probably linked to the pressure of responsibility – a single mistake could be fatal for hundreds of passengers – and to the way a routine situation can suddenly escalate into a crisis.

drive. For example, during the Blitz in World War II, the German air force bombed central London every night. Yet according to a paper published in 1942 in the medical journal *The Lancet*, the incidence of ulcers in central London was lower than in the suburbs, suggesting that the uncertainty of not knowing where the next bomb would drop caused more stress.

While it is widely believed that too much stress has a bad effect on health, it has been hard to prove a direct link between stress and specific illness. But it seems likely that may be that undue stress leads people into unhealthy behaviours like smoking, drinking too much and overeating, and this in turn causes health problems. Research has shown that adolescents who experience a lot of stress are more likely to start smoking, and adults who have given up may lapse during a stressful period.

Managing stress

Whatever the cause, you can learn to lower the stress burden on yourself. Cannon and Selye viewed the brain and body as a machine, responding passively to life's stressors, but the modern view of stress is more dynamic. Richard Lazarus puts great emphasis on the role of appraisal in stress management. First of all, he says, you should assess the stressor to understand what kind of threat it may pose to you. You may learn by experience, for instance, that a noisy neighbour will quieten down after half an hour or so. Then you should assess what resources you have to deal with the stressor. For example, you could move to a part of the house where the noise is less noticeable, or arrange to be out when the disruption is usually at its worst. Whatever response you choose, taking some control over a stressful situation reduces the perceived stress.

Real lives   IN THE AFTERMATH OF TRAUMA

Major stressors, often known as traumas, exact a correspondingly high toll on the mind and body. Situations likely to cause trauma include war, natural disasters, serious accidents and sexual abuse. People respond to trauma with many emotions – revulsion, grief, fear. If recovery is slow, traumatised people may develop post-traumatic stress disorder (PTSD) – a psychological condition marked by nightmares, intrusive thoughts and flashbacks. The effects may last for years.

Dan, now 80, escaped physical injury in World War II, but it took him many years to recover from the psychological stress of seeing comrades killed and wounded. When he returned from the war, his wife complained that he was emotionally distant and, after two years, they separated. He recalls that for at least ten years his sleep was broken by vivid nightmares. People noticed that Dan was easily startled – he would over-react to a sudden noise or unexpected approach. Doctors assessed him as a 'nervous' type, always suffering from problems for which no clear cause could be found.

Despite his problems, Dan managed to keep a modest clerical job and remarried. He and his wife have just celebrated their ruby wedding anniversary. She says that he has finally become more relaxed in the last ten years. Dan was probably suffering from PTSD, but the condition was not recognised until the 1970s. Today, he might have been offered specialist counselling to help him come to terms with the trauma of war.

RESPONDING TO STRESS

It is often said that life is what you make it, and there is some truth in this when it comes to dealing with stressful events. The way we respond to life's ups and downs depends very much on personality and experience, but everyone can learn to respond more successfully to challenging and difficult circumstances.

Often, the stress we experience has more to do with everyday hassles – noise, family disputes, money worries and so on – than with major life events. The mind tends to cope with ongoing 'stressors' (the events or situations that cause us to feel stressed) in different ways. Either people become habituated, or accustomed, to stresses and cease to be affected; or it accumulates to become what psychologists call a state of chronic stress.

Noise is a common cause of stress. If there is long-term building work going on near your home, you probably find it quite stressful for the first few days or so, but then you don't notice it quite so much. This is an example of habituation. But if you go on holiday, and the work is still going on when you return, you will probably need to habituate yourself all over again. Research has shown that most people suffer few long-term health effects from noise, but this isn't true for everyone: older people and children seem to be more vulnerable to the stress effects of noise. One study showed that children who lived in the flight path of an airport performed less well on problem-solving tasks.

Coping styles – confront or avoid?

A useful way of looking at stress responses is to consider the different styles of coping. When things go wrong, do you try to tackle the situation, or do you just hope things will improve? Psychologists agree that, when faced

> ## "If you are in a stressful situation and have the illusion you can control it – even if you can't your stress reaction will be reduced."
> Robert Ornstein, psychologist, and David Sobel, physician

with a stressful event, most people respond by either confronting or avoiding the problem. Doctors have observed this in patients who are diagnosed with a serious illness. 'Avoidant' patients will not seem to take it in – they will not tell their loved ones and may behave as if nothing has happened. By contrast, the patient who adopts a 'confrontative' coping style will want to know all about the illness and the treatment options.

Real lives THE STRESS OF A FLOODED HOME

When Barbara, a 28-year-old divorced mother-of-two, was forced out of her home by severe flooding, she found that much more than just her property was affected.

'When we were flooded out last year, we went to stay with friends. It was supposed to be just until we had cleaned things up. But somehow, I just couldn't face dealing with the mess. I kept putting it off, telling myself it was best to wait till the water went down. Then there was all the paperwork from the insurance company. I still have not filled out the forms. We moved back eventually, but we're living upstairs and we tend to spend every weekend with my Mum. The longer I leave it, the less I feel like sorting all the problems out. The kids are getting pretty upset about the situation and the little one's got a persistent cough because of the damp. I want to sell the house, but I haven't done anything about it. Now reports say that there are more floods coming our way soon.'

Barbara's coping style was avoidant. Although this probably helped at first, as time went on, avoiding her problems and putting things off resulted in many smaller worries accumulating and causing her even more stress.

There is no right or wrong coping style, but one or other may be more effective in certain situations. In general, the avoidant approach might be more successful in dealing with short-term threats: avoiding strangers whose attitude appears threatening may be better than confronting them, for example. When it comes to a long-term threat, however – like a diagnosis of serious illness – then it is probably best to face the problem head-on.

Optimism for health

An optimistic outlook helps people deal better with stress. A study of heart patients undergoing bypass surgery found that the optimistic patients recovered faster, and were back to a normal life sooner than those who were more pessimistic. It seems that optimistic people are more likely to adopt a problem-solving strategy to tackle stressful events and will look out for the positive aspects of the situation, which can help to ease problems. A classic example is the way people react to being made redundant. Of course there are feelings of hurt, rejection and anxiety, but the optimist who sees losing his or her job as an opportunity to do something new probably lowers the risk of developing stress-related ill health. Despite the difficult circumstances, the optimist feels in control because their response gives them hope and forms the basis for future positive action.

FOCUS ON

THE HARDY TYPE

Have you ever wondered how some people seem to breeze through life, seemingly unaffected by stress – even though they have their fair share of problems? Such people are said to have a 'hardy' personality, an idea that was developed by psychologist Suzanne Kobasa and her colleagues from a 1979 study of high-powered US business executives. Those who were never ill, despite their heavy workload, were distinguished from those with poorer health by specific personality traits. Kobasa found three main characteristics that make up hardiness: commitment to what you are involved in; a sense of control – feeling that you are responsible for what happens in your life; and the ability to rise to a challenge. No wonder people with a hardy personality cope so well with what life throws at them.

What stress? Former US president Bill Clinton handled the profound stresses of his position without any apparent health problems.

COPING WITH LIFE'S STRESSES

The causes of stress vary from person to person, but there are certain events that everyone is likely to find stressful. How we respond to such 'objective' stressors depends on personality. Based on psychosocial research, the scale shown below and the questionnaire opposite can help you to evaluate your likely stress level and assess your coping style.

STRESS AND LIFE EVENTS

The 'life change unit scale' was originally devised by American psychologists Thomas Holmes and Richard Rahe in the 1960s. They conducted thousands of interviews, asking respondents to rate specific events in terms of how much change had to be made to cope with the event. The version below gives the top 25 stressful events from a 1995 update of the scale.

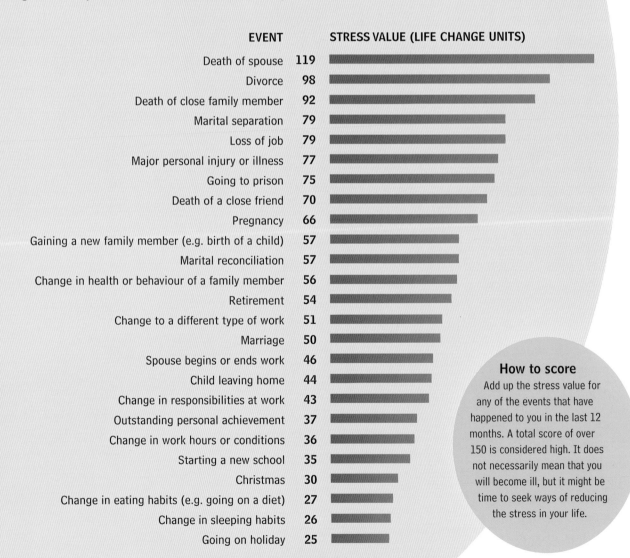

EVENT	STRESS VALUE (LIFE CHANGE UNITS)
Death of spouse	119
Divorce	98
Death of close family member	92
Marital separation	79
Loss of job	79
Major personal injury or illness	77
Going to prison	75
Death of a close friend	70
Pregnancy	66
Gaining a new family member (e.g. birth of a child)	57
Marital reconciliation	57
Change in health or behaviour of a family member	56
Retirement	54
Change to a different type of work	51
Marriage	50
Spouse begins or ends work	46
Child leaving home	44
Change in responsibilities at work	43
Outstanding personal achievement	37
Change in work hours or conditions	36
Starting a new school	35
Christmas	30
Change in eating habits (e.g. going on a diet)	27
Change in sleeping habits	26
Going on holiday	25

How to score

Add up the stress value for any of the events that have happened to you in the last 12 months. A total score of over 150 is considered high. It does not necessarily mean that you will become ill, but it might be time to seek ways of reducing the stress in your life.

HOW DO YOU COPE?

Experts now generally agree that it is not so much the stressful events in life, but how people react to them that has an impact on health. Two commonly used mechanisms for dealing with stress-causing situations are confrontative coping – tackling things 'head-on' – and escape-avoidance, or trying to ignore the problem. Confrontative coping is proactive, involving efforts to change the situation, and implies some degree of risk-taking. Escape-avoidance is passive, involving wishful thinking and efforts to escape or avoid the situation.

To see which of these coping strategies you are more likely to use, think of a stressful event that happened to you recently, then answer 'Yes' or 'No' to the following questions:

YES NO

1 Did you make an effort to alter the situation in some way, even if you felt it wouldn't achieve a great deal? ☐ ☐

2 Did you face up to the people you felt were responsible? ☐ ☐

3 Did you find yourself sleeping more than usual? ☐ ☐

4 Did you try to get the people responsible to change their minds? ☐ ☐

5 Did you eat, drink or smoke more than usual? ☐ ☐

6 Did you wish that the situation would just go away? ☐ ☐

7 Did you do something risky to solve the problem? ☐ ☐

8 Did you try to deny that the situation had happened? ☐ ☐

9 Did you make your feelings known to those around you? ☐ ☐

10 Did you daydream about how things might turn out? ☐ ☐

How to score

If you said 'Yes' to the following questions, you tend to favour confrontative coping: 1, 2, 4, 7, 9.

If you said 'Yes' to these questions, you are more likely to employ escape-avoidance as a coping mechanism: 3, 5, 6, 8, 10.

Most people use a combination of the two strategies, depending on their personality and the nature of the particular stress-causing situation. In general, however, active strategies tend to work better than passive ones in the long run.

HEALTH IN SOCIETY

Health can be very much affected by the social situations we experience and the environment around us, as well as by our individual personalities. In particular, home and work circumstances have a strong influence on whether people are able to maintain healthy lives.

We are all individuals, and it is through our direct associations with one another – whether friends, relatives, neighbours, work colleagues or health professionals – that we can do the most to help everyone maintain the best possible health. But looking at society as a whole can help to reveal sources of health problems and how they can be dealt with by social means. This can contribute, for example, to how new homes are built, how offices and other workplaces are run, and to identifying which groups in society need extra support.

There seems no doubt that relative wealth and status in society has a direct effect on health. In general, people of lower socio-economic status tend to have higher rates of heart disease, and there is much evidence that poverty is stressful. Research on baboon groups carried out by Robert Sapolsky in the USA supports this. Sapolsky found that baboons with a lower rank in the social group had higher levels of the stress hormone cortisol – probably because they were being bossed around by the higher-rank animals. They also had lower levels of HDL (high-density lipoprotein) cholesterol – a state that is linked to heart disease because 'good' HDL cholesterol helps to remove 'bad' (LDL) cholesterol from the blood.

"After my husband died, my friends and neighbours helped enormously. At first, people were embarrassed and didn't know what to say. Some even pretended they hadn't seen me. They didn't need to say anything… just a wave would do, to acknowledge that you still exist."

Eppie, 32, whose husband and both parents all died after long illnesses

▶▶ *CUTTING EDGE* ▶▶   A TALE OF TWO CITIES

There is a large and widening gap in life expectancy and rates of heart disease between the countries of Western and Eastern Europe. A recent Swedish study has assessed the contribution of psychosocial factors in the east-west divide by comparing men in two cities – Linköping in southern Sweden and Vilnius, the capital of Lithuania.

In the study, the Lithuanian men all reported more social isolation, job strain and depression than the men from Sweden – signs that stress was getting to them. Then all the men did a laboratory stress test. The Swedish men all had low levels of the stress hormone cortisol before the test. During the test, the Swedes showed a normal rise of cortisol, which then fell back to normal. Men from Vilnius with a high income had a low baseline cortisol level too, but after the test their cortisol levels took longer to return to normal. However, Lithuanian men with a low income had a high baseline cortisol level which did not even respond to the stress test. These men were already stressed, it seemed, by their circumstances in life and were probably more likely to suffer ill health as a result.

Healthier living Economic conditions can have a significant impact on health. A society where people have time and money for leisure activities is likely to have less stress-related illness.

Conditions in society

The relation between health and social status is not always straightforward, however. For example, a recent UK study showed that middle-ranking civil servants in Britain with little control over their workload run a higher risk of heart disease than their superiors – so far, so predictable. But the study also showed that those ranked below them were less stressed: it seems there may be a position of 'maximum stress' in the work hierarchy. Similarly, several recent studies have shown a higher frequency of eating disorders (such as anorexia nervosa and bulimia) in better-off sections of society. The desire to be thin, it seems, is more common among teenage girls from a wealthy background. Income level is just one part of a complex picture here: the family, ethnic background and media images are all major influences on how people see themselves. The most 'desirable' body shape depends on fashion and culture, and a well-rounded figure has been thought the epitome of beauty in ages and societies other than our own.

The conditions that society imposes on its members can sometimes be positively beneficial. For example, over the last decade, there has been a widespread drive to reduce smoking in public places and to make most offices smoke-free environments. Some employers have introduced programmes to help staff to quit, or at least to cut down their cigarette consumption during working hours. Any initial resentment from smokers usually disappears as people come to appreciate the health advantages both for themselves and others.

Ⓕ*CUS ON*

SUPPORT AND STRESS

In a study to assess whether social support can alleviate the stress response, three groups of volunteers were asked to give a presentation – a standard way of measuring stress. Those in one group brought a friend along for support; people in the second group gave the presentation alone; and the third group had to put up with a critic being present during the experience.

All the volunteers showed a rise in blood pressure, revealing the stress involved. However, those with a friend showed the smallest increase in blood pressure, while those who had to face a critic had the biggest increase. Having support clearly helps to reduce the amount of stress experienced.

4 MIND WAYS TO HEALTH

Few would deny that there are benefits for health and well-being to be found in developing constructive ways of dealing with anxieties, or learning to appreciate the pleasurable experiences that life offers. This may seem like simple common sense, yet it is not always clear how to go about enriching our lives in this way. The key to change is in the mind.

This chapter explores mind-building and relaxation techniques – many of which are used by professional therapists – that can help us to harness the powers of the mind. With these techniques and the will to succeed it is possible to learn how to conquer stress at home or in the workplace, how to diminish pain or cope with chronic illness, and how to face up to and beat an addiction or phobia. The mind is an infinitely versatile tool that can help us to overcome a whole range of difficulties. All we have to do is learn to use it.

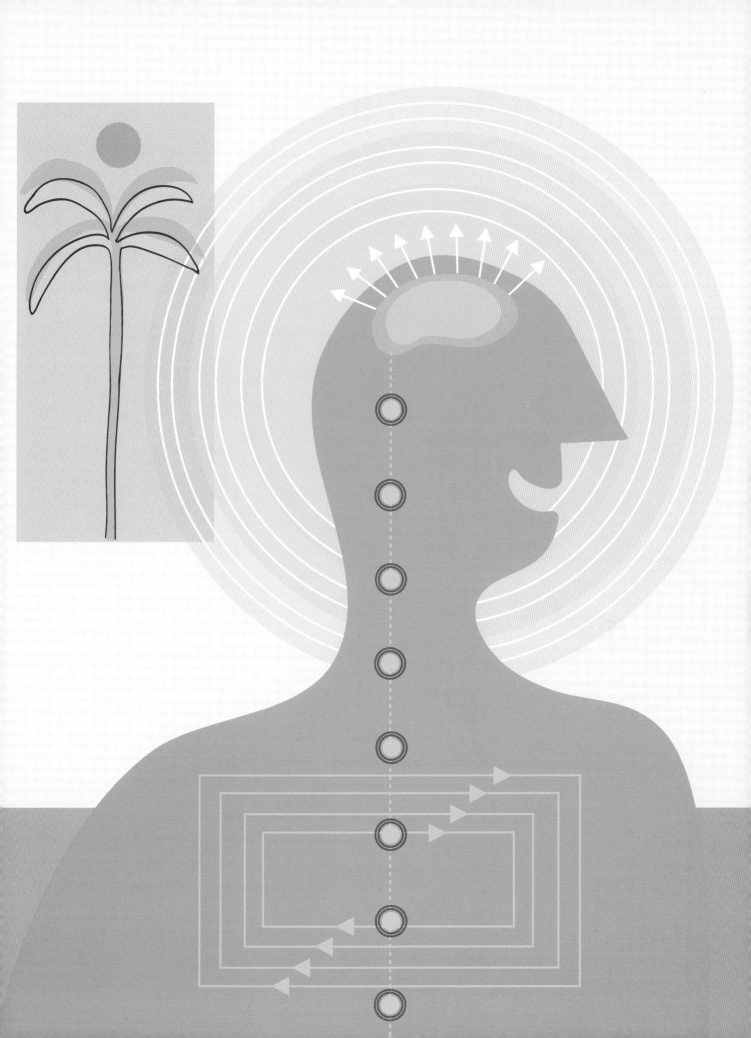

HEALTHY BEHAVIOUR

We are surrounded by information about the health effects of what we do and what we eat. Most foods have nutrition labels, packets of cigarettes carry health warnings, and even a bottle of wine may include a message about the dangers of drinking alcohol. Making reasonable decisions based on such advice is an important way to keep healthy.

Fifty years ago, most doctors thought it was just bad luck if a patient had a heart attack. Today, we know that lifestyle plays a huge role in health problems. Studies show that at least half of all deaths from heart disease, cancer, stroke, and lung disease can be attributed to modifiable risk factors, such as smoking, exercise and diet.

People are now expected to take more responsibility for their own health. Healthy behaviour really starts in childhood, when parents have a chance to instil healthy habits such as brushing teeth, eating well and exercising regularly. By the age of 11 or 12, such habits have often become ingrained. Research also shows that practices in childhood do affect health later in life. For example, dermatologists accept that many cases of skin cancer in middle-aged people are a consequence of over-exposure to harmful UV rays before the age of ten. There is also increasing concern over record levels of obesity in children, as this may cause heart disease in later life.

As children get older, their lifestyles tend to become less healthy. As teenagers, they come under peer pressure to smoke, take drugs, and away from parental direction they may subsist on junk food. They also take more risks. Nearly half of all male deaths between the ages of 15 and 24 are from road accidents, with speeding and alcohol being major contributing factors.

FACT: The number of extra food calories that a person must eat to gain a pound, or burn to lose a pound, is 3500.

Five good health habits

When the signs of age start to make themselves felt – often around 40 to 45 – many people discover a new interest in healthy behaviour, and a landmark study, begun in 1965, suggests that they are wise to do so. Nearly 7000 people in Alameda County in California were

Fruit, glorious fruit Only a small number of people actually manage to eat the five daily portions of fruit and vegetables recommended for a healthy diet. To help you increase your fruit intake, try thinking of it as the ultimate convenience food – it comes in its own packaging, it's ready to eat, and it's good for you. You could also seek out unusual fruits to keep your fruit snacks interesting.

TRY IT YOURSELF   FITTING IN EXERCISE

If you don't like sport, or have little time for physical recreation, you can still improve your fitness by putting more effort into everyday activities.

Keep a diary for a week and see if you can burn up at least 500 extra calories. You might consider making some changes to your daily routine – such as cycling or walking instead of driving the car for short trips, and climbing stairs instead of using the lift – to reach your goal. Minor changes like these can make all the difference. The chart shows how many calories various activities use up (figures are for a person weighing 55kg/8 stone 8lb).

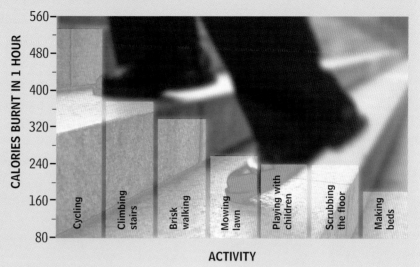

CALORIES BURNT IN 1 HOUR

560 –
480 –
400 –
320 –
240 –
160 –
80 –

Cycling   Climbing stairs   Brisk walking   Mowing lawn   Playing with children   Scrubbing the floor   Making beds

ACTIVITY

asked which of the following five good health habits they practised: (1) sleeping seven to eight hours a night; (2) not smoking; (3) having no more than two alcoholic drinks a day; (4) taking regular exercise; and (5) being no more than 10 per cent overweight. Nine years on, mortality rates were significantly lower for people following all five healthy habits. Those who practised two or less were three times more likely to have died than those who practised four or five. Those who followed all five had far fewer days of illness.

It seems it is definitely worth making an effort to live a healthier lifestyle. However, whether you do so depends on many factors. Some people do not like being told how they should live, particularly when it comes to personal matters like sex, alcohol and diet. Consequently, doctors in the UK have been warned by health campaigners not to nag their patients to stop smoking – one reminder a year is enough, they say.

It is never too late to adopt a healthier lifestyle, and even somebody who has been overweight for many years will benefit from a change of diet and some gentle exercise.

Your own vegetables all the year round ...

if you

DIG FOR VICTORY NOW

Eating for victory Changes in diet forced on the British public in World War II actually produced an improvement in general health. Fat and sugar were rationed, and people were encouraged to grow as many vegetables as possible.

FOCUS ON

EATING FISH FOR A LONGER LIFE

Eating fish reduces your risk of developing a thrombotic stroke (caused by a clot in a blood vessel leading to the brain).

In a US study, researchers assessed 80,000 women (aged between 34 and 59) for 14 years. They found that the more fish they ate, the lower the risk of heart disease. Compared to women who ate fish less than once a month, those who had fish three times a month had a seven per cent lower risk; a weekly fish meal gave a 22 per cent lower risk; two–four meals per week had a 27 per cent lower risk, while five times or more resulted in a 52 per cent reduction.

The beneficial effect derives from the omega-3 fatty acids in fish, which reduce the 'stickiness' of blood platelets, making clotting less likely. Oily fish such as herring, trout, sardines and salmon contain the highest amounts of these fats.

CREATING WELL-BEING

There is more to life than just having your basic survival needs met and more to health than just the absence of illness. A sense of well-being, whatever your personal circumstances, comes from a positive attitude and an appreciation of everyday pleasures.

MUSIC AND WELL-BEING

A growing body of evidence suggests that music has beneficial effects for health. In the 19th century, physicians discovered that music could affect heart rate and blood pressure. In the early 20th century, doctors in the USA used music in hospitals to help alleviate pain. Various scientific studies followed, and these showed that music could influence mood, prolong attention span, relieve stress and stimulate imagination. Music is very much a personal taste, but research suggests that the most natural tempo for a piece of music is 80 beats a minute — about the same as the average human heart rate. This suggests that music appeals by tuning in to our natural body rhythms.

'Quality of life' is a relatively new idea, but it is a concept that doctors and psychologists are beginning to emphasise. Modern medicine has given us more years of life, but often these are marred by chronic illness, loneliness and loss of independence. Quality of life goes beyond physical health – it takes in psychological and emotional factors, too.

Everyone knows at least one person who has had bad luck in life or is in poor health, and yet still seems content. What is their secret? Psychologists have studied such people and attribute their vitality to their ability to nurture their own sense of well-being.

These people are passionate about the things they do, whether it be work, relationships or hobbies. They often have a robust sense of humour, and do not take themselves too seriously. Happy people often look younger than their years, and may even be a little eccentric — according to two studies, eccentric people often live longer than average.

"Pleasure rewards us twice: first in immediate enjoyment and second in improved health."

Robert Ornstein, psychologist

Real lives *A HEALING VIEW*

Marie and Sue were neighbours who found themselves in hospital on the same day for a routine operation. They were admitted to the same ward and were glad of each other's company. Marie's bed was by the window and she could see a big patch of sky and the trees in a nearby park. Sue's bed was close to the corridor, furthest from the window.

The operations were uneventful. Both women had plenty of visitors and they received the same medical care. However, Sue needed more pain medication and sleeping tablets after the operation. Marie was out of bed the following day. 'I don't know why you're doing so much better than I am,' Sue complained as Marie drew up a chair for a chat. 'Must be the view from the window,' Marie joked.

Though she didn't know it, Marie was right. Studies have shown that patients who have a pleasant view from their hospital ward – of a park, for example, with some trees or flowers – recover faster than those who have a view of something less attractive, like a car park or buildings, or those, like Sue, who have no view at all. Some hospitals are now creating gardens in their grounds with this in mind.

Balancing your life

To create a sense of well-being, it is important to live a balanced life. For most people, this means a mixture of work, family and friends, personal time and interests, and service to the wider community. Having different roles in life – as a parent, a manager and a church volunteer, say – contributes to a healthy sense of self. However, it is easy for one role to dominate: if you have a heavy workload, you may find it hard to think of yourself as anything but a worker, while many mothers find that a busy family life makes it difficult for them to be anything other than a parent.

Often, the best way to strengthen your sense of worth and purpose is to help others. Recent research shows that older people who still have an active role in life – as a carer, or as a grandparent, for example – tend to outlive those who no longer feel useful. A study carried out in the USA showed that voluntary work can be very beneficial for health. Psychologists monitored 2700 people for nearly ten years. Men who did regular volunteer work had death rates 2.5 times lower than those who did not. However, there was no difference in rates for women – perhaps because many women already devote much of their time to caring for others.

FACT: Staring at tropical fish in an aquarium for 20 minutes can lower blood pressure by up to ten per cent and produces a state of calm relaxation.

So, does this mean being self-centred is a bad thing? Not at all – in fact, most people have difficulty finding time for themselves to be alone and relax. If we put aside half an hour a day to read, pursue a hobby or just daydream, our general health would probably improve. Finding time to think and develop a more positive mindset can also be beneficial. Some people keep busy because they find their minds churn over with worry and negative thoughts when they are not active. It would be better for them to reflect on their achievements, however ordinary they may seem.

ENRICHING LIFE THROUGH THE SENSES

One way of creating a sense of well-being that is available to everyone is to feed the brain with uplifting, pleasurable thoughts and sensory experiences. It is through our senses that we learn to appreciate the beauty of the world around us, but, too often, we ignore the potential pleasure that the senses can offer. Getting back in touch with your senses can be an important part of promoting well-being. Try some of the ideas here and you will soon be reaping the rewards.

BENEFITS OF TOUCH

Touch is vitally important to babies and children, yet as we get older we often get out of the habit of touching and being touched. We do not always kiss our friends and loved ones in greeting or congratulation. We might neglect to offer a hug or touch on the arm to comfort someone in distress. Often embarrassment, respect for people's personal space or fear of being misunderstood holds people back from touching. Yet touching – of the non-sexual kind – between people can be relaxing and pleasurable. In one study, heart rates were lowered when volunteers were touched lightly on the wrist by a researcher.

Those who live alone and who do not exchange touches regularly should try to get into the habit of touching with friends and family. There are also some other simple and effective solutions. Investing in some form of regular massage – shiatsu, aromatherapy, or reflexology – offers the life-enhancing benefits of touch. If you have a pet, you will probably find that touching, stroking or talking to it lowers feelings of stress.

VISUAL STIMULATION

Giving your eyes something pleasant to focus on enhances the quality of everyday life. In one experiment, people who were shown slides of attractive natural scenes reported higher levels of positive feelings, like friendliness and elation, than when they looked at drab urban scenes. If your office looks out over a car park, or the view from your living room is of a busy main road, try to position your seat so that you can see something natural, like a

tree – and watch it change through the seasons. A few well-chosen pictures or posters can make the inside of your home or your office much more stimulating. Developing your garden, however small, can also be a source of visual pleasure. And you can bring nature into your home with flowers, plants and even pebbles. Walking in your local park or countryside is beneficial too, and many studies have shown that exposure to sunlight improves mood.

USING AROMAS

Smell is probably the most underrated of our senses. Humans can distinguish around 10,000 different odours – and because the part of the brain that analyses odours is intimately connected to emotional centres of the cortex, smell can really affect the way we feel. For instance, peppermint has long been valued as an aid to clear thinking and recent research suggests that a whiff of mint can motivate people before exercise. People often associate lavender with relaxation, but spiced apple has

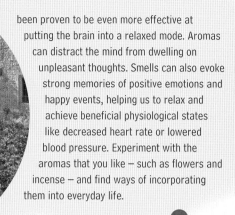

been proven to be even more effective at putting the brain into a relaxed mode. Aromas can distract the mind from dwelling on unpleasant thoughts. Smells can also evoke strong memories of positive emotions and happy events, helping us to relax and achieve beneficial physiological states like decreased heart rate or lowered blood pressure. Experiment with the aromas that you like – such as flowers and incense – and find ways of incorporating them into everyday life.

ENJOYING FLAVOUR

As most people know, food can be a regular source of pleasure and stimulation, and not just a refuelling exercise. There is certainly no harm in treating yourself to some of your favourite foods every now and again. Food and drink can be a great pick-me-up – especially if you have the added satisfaction of having cooked a pleasing dish yourself. As recent changes in British eating habits suggest, curries and other spicy food are enjoyed by many people – chillies, peppers

and other spices produce a feeling of pleasurable sensory stimulation. Chocolate, which is a favourite treat for many people, stimulates endorphins and serotonin production in the brain, which brings on feelings of contentment. Crisp, fresh textures will perk you up, while comforting carbohydrates will make you feel relaxed or sleepy. Whatever your favourite food, it should stimulate your taste buds, creating a sense of enjoyment.

LISTENING FOR PLEASURE

Enjoying everyday sounds can enhance the quality of your life. Natural sounds, such as birdsong or a running stream, can have a soothing effect, as can distant voices or a child's laughter. If you don't have access to a local park or countryside, it is possible to purchase recordings of natural sounds, such as ocean waves, tropical rain, woodland and jungle noises, and rushing streams. Water fountain features for the garden, home or office can provide

soothing background sounds all day. People also find the sound of a cat purring very relaxing – research has suggested that this is because cats purr at the same rhythm as alpha waves in the brain. Obviously music is a great source of comfort, stimulation and energy. Making some time to listen to your favourite music each day can improve your quality of life with the minimum of effort.

COPING WITH A LONG-TERM CONDITION

Many of us will have to cope with chronic illness at some stage in our lives, ranging from high blood pressure or arthritis to hearing loss or physical disability. Whatever the diagnosis, there are ways of adapting mentally.

At any one time, around half of the population is suffering from a chronic illness of some kind. As we live longer, more and more of us are going to have to learn to manage a condition for which there is no cure. Some chronic illnesses have little immediate effect on everyday life – for example, high blood pressure has few obvious symptoms, but must still be regarded as a serious condition because it can cause heart disease and stroke. By contrast, an illness such as Alzheimer's disease will affect a person's ability to live an independent life in quite a short time.

Dealing with a diagnosis

Psychologists have charted a general pattern of response to the diagnosis of chronic illness. Whether the illness is life threatening, like cancer, or not, like arthritis or hearing loss, the response can be similar to that experienced after a bereavement. Perhaps this is not surprising, for a diagnosis of ongoing illness often affects an individual's self-image as a healthy person. In the face of the diagnosis, people may feel shocked or distressed. There might also be a sense of relief – after months of tests and uncertainty, many people say they prefer knowing what they are up against.

Overcoming opposition A determined attitude and ever-improving technology can help people with disability or illness not just to keep active but to excel in their chosen field.

? HOW TO.... BREAK THE NEWS

For those people diagnosed with a serious illness, it can be hard to break the news to family and friends. However, it is best to get family support as early as possible. Anyone diagnosed with a chronic condition might find the following points helpful:

• Be brave, and bring up the subject yourself.
• Make sure you have the person's full attention.

• Begin by saying something like, 'You know I went to the hospital for some tests recently?'
• Try not to deviate from the subject, however uncomfortable you feel.
• Do not be afraid to say how you feel – they will understand that this is a difficult moment.
• Non-verbal contact, such as holding hands, a hug, or sitting together may help you communicate your feelings.

It is difficult to predict how people will respond to the situation. In the long term, they are likely to be resilient and accepting, whatever their initial reaction, but be prepared for those who are not supportive: for example, a friend may find the illness an unwelcome reminder of mortality and start to avoid you. However, most people will care and will want to do all they can to help you through such a difficult time.

Accepting chronic illness

Eventually most people diagnosed with a chronic illness start to accept their condition. Most chronic illness requires patients to do something for themselves: dietary changes and quitting smoking after a heart attack or stroke, keeping to a medication schedule in many illnesses, and with cancer, being watchful for recurrence. Patients who take a realistic and practical attitude are more likely to have a positive outcome.

Other issues affect how people cope with chronic illness. Studies show that patients who believe they can exert some control over their illness – usually, by actively participating in treatment – have a better chance of recovery: cancer patients who feel in control adjust better to the demands of their condition, as do those with rheumatoid arthritis, AIDS, spinal cord injury and patients recovering from a heart attack.

Many people with a chronic illness feel that their sense of self is eroded and that the illness makes them a different person. However difficult it seems, sufferers need to realise that they are still the same person, irrespective of their condition. For example, a man does not cease to be a loving husband because he has a debilitating illness. Some people have even found that chronic illness has some benefits, in that it encouraged them to focus on what is important in life. Many discover that the condition leads them to appreciate each day more and motivates them to do things that they had previously postponed.

Real lives LIVING WITH CANCER

John Diamond, the British journalist and broadcaster who died of throat cancer in March 2001, chronicled the progress of his illness in a newspaper column. He wrote about his experiences of the disease and its effects in an honest and at times humorous way, and in doing so became an inspiration to many people.

Diamond tried to undo some illusions about what it means to be a cancer sufferer, pointing out that undergoing cancer treatment is not really a battle between the patient and the disease: 'I am not fighting cancer,' he said, 'although my doctors are, I hope ...' He wanted to debunk the notion that cancer could be beaten if you tried hard enough. Despite his illness, Diamond's self image did not change because he could continue to do the thing he liked best – writing.

TALKING THERAPY

Most of us find that talking through problems with a friend will help us feel more relaxed and clearer in our minds. The various forms of psychotherapy can be seen as more formal versions of this type of communication offered by experienced professionals.

On the couch In a typical portrayal of psychotherapy, Woody Allen visits his analyst in the film 'Annie Hall'. Some types of psychotherapy can take years, but more recently developed forms can work faster because they focus on tackling present behaviour patterns and thoughts.

Psychotherapy – sometimes known as talking therapy – can be a powerful way of dealing with problems. It can also help people to get to know themselves better so that they can cope better with life's challenges.

Sometimes people feel put off by the very idea of psychotherapy – they may imagine that they will have to lie on a couch and be questioned about their innermost thoughts and feelings. In fact, most talking treatments are not like that at all. There are approximately 200 different types of psychotherapy, of varying degrees of medical and scientific validity. What these therapies have in common is the attempt to establish a relationship – called the therapeutic relationship – between the individual and a trained professional. Whatever the therapy, it is this relationship between patient and therapist that is the crucial factor in resolving psychological problems.

Talking to a professional

It may seem a sad reflection on modern society that many people have to pay someone to talk about their problems. Surely a chat with a good friend, or an older and wiser family member, would be more helpful in a crisis? Social support is vital, of course, and it is known to alleviate stress and keep us healthy. But sometimes a common-sense chat is not enough. Anyone who has suffered from clinical depression or a phobia will know that being told to 'pull yourself together' or 'just do it' by someone close makes them feel worse – however well-meant the advice. Often, friends and family are too close to an individual and their problems to offer objective and useful guidance. A qualified therapist, while he or she may be receptive and friendly, will take a more objective view.

FOCUS ON THERAPY – DOES IT WORK?

Psychologists have investigated the effectiveness of psychotherapy and have come to some broad conclusions based on data from various studies.
• Around 80 per cent of people who have undergone therapy improve in some way, although some therapies are better suited to certain problems.
• Phobias and anxiety are most effectively treated with cognitive and behavioural approaches while humanistic therapies are good for improving self-esteem.
• A study conducted in the US showed that the outcome of most treatment could be predicted by the third or fourth visit to the therapist. By this stage, 30–40 per cent of clients had experienced some kind of progress, while 50–60 per cent had felt some improvement by their seventh visit.
• The same data suggested that the longer a person went without change, the less likely it was for the therapy to be a success. The study suggested that treatment should be brief if there is no improvement within the first seven sessions. However, as long as patients are making some kind of recordable progress, therapy should continue.

Real lives   THAWING AN ICY RELATIONSHIP

Martha and James had been married for 15 years, but had stopped talking to each other. When Martha said she wanted to try marriage guidance, James said he did not want to talk about his private life with a stranger. So she went alone.

At first, Martha was relieved to be able to express her anger at James's coldness to a sympathetic third party, but then Carole, the counsellor, suggested Martha look at her own contribution to the situation. Martha was angry at this and missed the next session. She was surprised when Carole phoned her at home and it was only at this point that she took the therapy seriously. As a result of the sessions, Martha became less irritable.

Martha asked James again to accompany her and, reluctantly, he agreed to go along. Martha felt strange at their first session together – she'd grown used to seeing Carole alone. Having James there changed the patient–therapist relationship. Neither of them liked Carole's insistence that they address their complaints to one another, instead of to her.

However, after four sessions, the ice was broken and within a short time, Martha and James were friends again.

These days, therapy is given by a wide range of professionals: psychiatrists, clinical psychologists, psychotherapists and counsellors (who may or may not have medical qualifications), health visitors and practice nurses. Standards and training vary, so check credentials before you embark on any form of therapy. It is not unknown for a counsellor attached to a general practice to have had only brief training. Such people might be good at helping a client to quit smoking or lose weight, but they may not be equipped to help someone suffering from the psychological problems that come with a serious illness such as cancer.

Two types of psychotherapy

Freud's theory of psychoanalysis, which he developed towards the end of the 19th century, was the origin of the first talking therapy. Freud believed that psychological problems, such as depression, grew out of unconscious conflicts arising during childhood. Some of Freud's patients had physical disorders, such as back pain or speech problems, that were apparently healed by psychoanalysis. In psychoanalysis, the person is made aware of unconscious residues of experience through the analysis of dreams and the free association of thoughts. Once in the conscious realm, any unconscious conflicts lose their stranglehold over the mind.

As psychology and knowledge of the brain progressed during the 20th century, two different schools of psychotherapy emerged, broadly classified

The right route There are many types of psychotherapy and ways of resolving psychological conflicts, and it is important that people choose the method most suited to their problem.

HOW TO.... ?

BE A GOOD LISTENER

It is neither practical nor desirable to use psychotherapy for every problem in life. People can help each other with their problems through sensitive listening. Being a good listener is harder than it sounds, so here are some tips:

• Don't interrupt; if you want to ask for clarification, wait for a natural break.
• Don't just listen to your friend's words – look at the body language to gauge his or her feelings.
• Watch your own responses – do you have a 'blind spot' when it comes to hearing views that differ from your own? Do you, for instance, tense up or switch off when someone says something you disagree with? This can be a huge barrier to being a good listener.
• If you find yourself longing to interrupt, try to re-focus on what is being said.
• Don't offer advice or opinions, unless asked – even then, think carefully before you speak. Try to be open-minded and see the problem from their perspective.

as the psychodynamic therapies and the supportive therapies. The psychodynamic therapies focus on gaining insight into unconscious forces: they include Freudian psychoanalysis, Jungian therapy and humanistic psychotherapy. The supportive therapies – including cognitive therapy, behaviour therapy and counselling – focus more on conscious thoughts and feelings, and often involve an element of helping the patient to learn new behaviour or thought patterns.

In general, the psychodynamic therapies are more patient-centred, with the therapist taking a very non-directive role – some therapists offer very little in the way of comment or advice. Psychodynamic therapy normally lasts years, possibly involving several sessions a week. It is rarely available through health services. People who choose psychodynamic therapies may see themselves as 'psychologically minded', or want to get to the root of a long-standing problem, such as chronic anxiety.

For an acute problem, such as an eating disorder, supportive therapy is usually more appropriate. With supportive therapies, there is far more of a two-way relationship between the patient and therapist. The therapist will ask more questions, may offer opinions and even advice (although no therapist should ever tell a patient what to do – it must always be the patient's decision).

Group therapies

Psychotherapy is not always one-to-one: for certain problems, group therapy is more effective. Sharing experiences in a group can be genuinely beneficial. All too often, people are convinced that no-one understands what it is like to have their problem, so when they discover that others share their feelings, it is often a great relief. People suffering from serious

A problem shared Group therapy has proved very effective in helping people overcome a variety of problems, including addictions and antisocial behaviour.

FACT FILE   TYPES OF TALKING THERAPY

Psychodynamic therapies focus on the unconscious, while supportive therapies concentrate on conscious thought processes. Some of the main forms practised include:

PSYCHODYNAMIC THERAPIES
• **Freudian psychotherapy** (psychoanalysis) seeks to uncover childhood sexual conflicts through the analysis of dreams.
• **Jungian psychotherapy** uses elements of mythology, symbols and dreams to probe the mind.
• **Adlerian psychotherapy** fosters self-confidence by overcoming feelings of inferiority rooted in childhood.
• **Kleinian psychotherapy** focuses on early childhood experiences.
• **Humanistic psychotherapy** concentrates on spiritual growth potential, looking forwards not back.
• **Rogerian psychotherapy** is client-centred and non-judgmental, and assumes the patient is best able to deal with personal problems.

• **Gestalt psychotherapy** emphasises integrating all aspects of experience, encouraging the patient to develop full awareness of the present moment.

SUPPORTIVE THERAPIES
• **Cognitive therapy** aims to replace negative thought patterns with more logical and realistic ones.
• **Behavioural therapy** focuses on the immediate problem and the circumstances surrounding it.
• **Rational-emotive therapy** uses logic, authority and persuasion to help the patient give up irrational ideas or unreasonable expectations.
• **Transactional analysis** examines the different roles a person plays in life (such as 'child', 'parent') and helps the person develop a more realistic, constructive attitude.
• **Counselling** is often directed at specific problems – such as bereavement – and involves listening to clients and helping them to understand their problems.

• **Co-counselling** involves an equal relationship between two people, who take it in turns to talk and listen.

OTHER THERAPIES
• **Group therapy** is valuable where interpersonal difficulties are a key part of the problem.
• **Family therapy** is used where therapy directed at just one member of the family may not resolve matters.
• **Art therapy** involves painting, drawing or sculpture to express emotions associated with a problem.
• **Neurolinguistic programming (NLP)** looks at how we experience the world and applies this knowledge to alter behaviours that limit us.
• **Life coaching** involves a personal coach who will help the individual to tackle specific problems. The coach discusses and monitors progress and sets goals.
• **Eclectic approaches** combine therapies to suit the individual's character, circumstances and problem.

illnesses may meet together under the direction of a nurse or social worker to discuss their concerns. Family therapy is useful in dealing with childhood and adolescent behavioural problems, while couple therapy can help to untangle the complexities of a troubled relationship.

Co-counselling takes place between two people within a group who take turns to be therapist and client. If a person develops an empathy with the co-counselling partner, the technique can be very helpful, without the cost of a personal therapist. But the partners must stick to certain rules – no interrupting while the other person is speaking, no giving advice and no passing judgement – and these can be difficult to follow. Observe yourself when you are next listening to a friend talk about his or her problems. How many times did you interrupt, perhaps to recount a similar experience of your own?

Most people will gain something from a talking therapy. However, for therapy to be successful, it is vital to match the type of therapy to the person and the specific problem.

FACT: Research has shown that cognitive therapy is as effective as antidepressants in relieving depression.

THE POWER OF REASONING

One of our greatest mental gifts is our reasoning ability, which enables us to make decisions and judgements based on the evidence before us. Cognitive therapy can be used to harness our mental powers to improve our health and quality of life.

Psychologists use the term 'cognition' to refer to the information-processing ability of the brain. Cognition enables us to think, remember, analyse, learn and negotiate our way through life. The way we experience physical pain also depends on cognitive factors. If it is a familiar pain, for example, you might decide that it will pass soon, and by assessing the pain in this way reduce your distress. Unproductive ways of thinking are responsible for a great deal of mental suffering and even physical ill health. You may know someone, for example, who always draws negative conclusions: if someone disagrees with them, they always assume it is a personal attack and waste time and energy worrying about it.

Discarding negative thinking

The primary purpose of cognitive therapy is to overcome ingrained negative attitudes of mind, and thereby the ill health that may result from this. The therapy focuses on encouraging new ways of perceiving and thinking about problems, as a means of alleviating symptoms. Aaron T. Beck, who developed cognitive therapy, was originally a Freudian psychoanalyst. After analysing the thoughts and ideas of his patients, he concluded that people affected by anxiety and depression viewed themselves and the world around them in a negative way that was not justified by the reality of their situation.

Beck discovered that the negative mindset of his patients had three main aspects, which he termed 'the cognitive triad'. First, they had a negative view of themselves ('I am no good'). Second, they had a negative view of the world around them ('nothing ever goes right'). Finally, their attitude towards the future was negative ('things will never get better').

The aim of cognitive therapy is to break down these powerful, interlinked beliefs. Rather than attempting to deal with negative attitudes in general, specific elements of negative thinking are tackled by the patient and the therapist together. One of the first things to be confronted is what Beck called 'automatic thinking' – a tendency to jump to negative conclusions without thinking things through. For example, careful analysis might reveal that someone auto-

Role models Socially pervasive images can distort how we think about ourselves. Cognitive therapy helps people to realise that being as slim as Barbie or as fit as Action Man is not necessarily an ideal goal.

matically thinks 'I am useless' whenever things go wrong, although the person may not be aware of making this habitual response. Once exposed in therapy, however, such thoughts lose their power. People with negative belief systems tend to over-generalise – if one thing goes wrong, everything is wrong. So, if they have an argument with a colleague at work, they then assume that no-one in the office likes them. Cognitive therapy teaches them to consider alternative explanations that are less self-centred: if someone is rude at work, it may well be because that person is having a bad day.

Healing through reasoning

Mental health problems fuelled by negative thinking respond very well to cognitive therapy. For example, someone who is depressed will be encouraged to break the constant stream of self-criticism by listing his or her daily successes, however small these may be. The achievements build up, day by day, gradually bringing the person back into the mainstream of life. Cognitive therapy has no set method or approach – often, simple practical exercises are tried first.

Most importantly, cognitive therapy facilitates a reasoned discussion that encourages individuals to assess whether their negative thought patterns are justified. Whereas psychodynamic therapies emphasise past experience and unconscious motivation, cognitive therapy concentrates on present interactions.

Real lives

RECOVERING STEP BY STEP

Cognitive therapy pioneer Aaron Beck described treating a 52-year-old man hospitalised with severe depression who had not moved from his bed for over a year. Beck challenged him to walk the five yards to the door of his room, but the patient said his legs would give way. Beck persisted, and eventually a few steps were achieved.

Next, Beck encouraged the patient to walk to the next room. Each day, Beck built on the previous day's achievement by setting a new goal. Beck decided that the patient should reward himself with a drink from the vending machine once he was walking freely around the ward. For someone who had been in the grip of profound depression for so long, this was a major achievement. By gradually extending his range, the patient was able to walk to the hospital games room. In less than a week, he was enjoying the grounds, and a month later he was able to return home.

►► CUTTING EDGE ►►   REPROGRAMMING BRAIN CIRCUITRY

People with obsessive-compulsive disorder (OCD) are often ideal candidates for cognitive therapy. They are plagued by recurrent, unwanted thoughts (obsessions) that create a state of perpetual nagging anxiety. In attempting to deal with this, they typically carry out various repetitive rituals (compulsions), which can consume so much time and energy that they seriously disrupt everyday life. The most common compulsions are hand-washing and checking rituals, such as checking to see whether the

gas has been turned off, which can be repeated so often they undermine the person's thoughts and actions.

Brain imaging studies have shown that there is a specific brain circuit that is normally active only when we are performing routine tasks, such as having a shower, making a cup of tea or locking the front door. Usually, this circuit is turned on and off as needed, but with OCD sufferers the circuit fires all the time. Treatment with cognitive therapy can calm this overactive circuit down to its normal cycle of activity.

OVERCOMING ADDICTIONS

The common image of an addict is of someone hooked on heroin or cocaine. But most addicts will probably never have seen hard drugs. Alcohol, nicotine and certain prescription drugs, as well as some types of activity, such as gambling and even shopping, can all be addictive. Whatever the substance, addictions can do wide-ranging damage to physical and mental health.

Even when affected by smoking-related diseases, some smokers just cannot overcome their addiction to nicotine. Heavy drinkers can blight their lives – from relationship problems to unfulfilled potential at work – through alcohol abuse. In some people, the drive to keep consuming certain substances or to repeat certain types of behaviour is overwhelming, even when the consequences are disastrous. But what drives this self-destructive behaviour?

The roots of addiction

Addiction – also known as dependence – develops gradually through a complex interaction between the user, the substance (or behaviour) and their environment. Dependence usually arises from increased tolerance of a substance or behaviour: two glasses of wine in the evening becomes four, or the midweek lottery becomes as unmissable as the weekend flutter. Once a craving has set in, behaviour is profoundly influenced by the need for more of the same.

There are a wide range of addictive substances: nicotine and alcohol are two of the most obvious. Others include painkillers, slimming pills, laxatives, and illegal drugs such as cocaine and heroin. Less obvious

"If there was a box of chocolates around, I couldn't stop till I had eaten the lot. After cutting out sugar completely for a month, though, I've just lost the craving for sweet things."

Beryl, 51, who was addicted to sweet things

candidates to add to the list include caffeine, sugar, chocolate and junk food. Gambling is a major behavioural addiction, but there are a host of others arousing concerns among health experts, such as working long hours, surfing the internet, exercise, video games, television and even sex.

Addiction: in the genes?

As knowledge of the brain and of human genetics has developed, addiction has come to be seen as an illness. There does appear to be a genetic factor for alcohol and smoking dependence. One 1960s study looked at the smoking behaviour of 42 pairs of twins who had been raised apart. In 18 pairs, both twins were non-smokers, while 15 pairs smoked. Only in nine of the pairs did the twins not show the same behaviour. This strongly suggests a genetic influence.

Treating addictions

There are various approaches to the treatment of addiction. Medication is sometimes used to treat alcohol, nicotine, shopping and food addictions. Nicotine patches, for example, can help to wean someone off cigarettes, while the drug Antabuse (disulfiram), which is used to treat alcoholism, replaces the sensation of pleasure that the person gets from drinking with nausea. However, fighting the physical addiction is just part of the story; most addicts need to learn new attitudes and patterns of behaviour if they are to succed in the long term. Behavioural therapy can be very effective against addictions. One strategy involves rewarding the individual for reaching certain goals. Above all, people should not be punished for addictions, but encouraged to adopt more positive behaviours that provide the same psychological rewards without indulging the addiction.

Real lives THE SHOPAHOLIC

Barbara died of cancer just before her 80th birthday. At least it had been quick, but she had not stopped smoking – even when she was ill. Barbara had always been a heavy smoker, explained her sister Mary, ever since she was a young woman during World War II. She drank a lot of black coffee too – at least 20 cups a day.

However, what really startled Mary was her discovery when she came to sort out Barbara's flat. There was drawer after drawer of pretty underwear – most of it unworn. In the wardrobe she found over 40 jumpers, still in their carrier bags, and around 60 dresses. She counted 102 pairs of shoes, most of them brand new. There were two more wardrobes in the spare room, both crammed with clothes. The kitchen was full of unused gadgets. There were seven televisions around the flat. Barbara's husband had left her comfortably off but there was not much left for Mary, her only relative. Mary wasn't worried by that – she was just astounded that she had never known about her sister's shopping addiction.

FACT FILE   FIVE STAGES OF RECOVERY

To overcome an addiction successfully, there are a number of stages that must be worked through.

1. Acknowledging the problem Becoming aware of the addiction and acknowledging it is the first step towards recovery.

2. Building awareness A period of honest thinking about the effects of the addiction and ways to beat it.

3. Resolving to stop The decision to give up an addiction demands strong resolution and must come from the addicted person themselves. Joining an appropriate group – from Weightwatchers to Gamblers Anonymous – can help maintain the resolve to beat the addiction.

4. Changing behaviour Establishing different habits and activities to avoid situations associated with the addiction can be crucial in the early stages of overcoming it. In the longer term, a new perspective, attitude and lifestyle should develop.

5. Keeping vigilant For many people, the final stage of recovery is without end. Keeping free from addiction becomes a lifetime process of reinforcing healthy new behaviours.

CONQUERING FEARS

Fear is a part of everyday life. Although it may be unpleasant, it is a perfectly normal and natural response to threats or danger. However, sometimes fear can become uncontrollable and develop into a disabling phobia. Fortunately, many fears and phobias can be effectively treated by psychotherapy and other techniques.

FACT FILE

THE THREE CLASSES OF PHOBIA

Simple phobias

These are fears of specific objects or situations, and include:

• Acrophobia (heights and high places)
• Arachnophobia (spiders)
• Astraphobia (thunder storms)
• Bacillophobia (germs)
• Claustrophobia (enclosed spaces, e.g. small rooms or lifts)
• Haematophobia (the sight of blood)
• Hydrophobia (water, such as rivers and oceans)
• Nyctophobia (the dark or darkness)
• Zoophobia (animals)

Social phobia

This is a feeling of insecurity or fear in specific social situations, coupled with a fear of being publicly embarrassed. Social phobia may include a reluctance to eat or drink if anyone is watching.

Agoraphobia

This is one of the most common phobias, and involves the fear of being alone in public places or in an unfamiliar setting.

If you believe someone is following you down the street at night, your body starts to show the typical fear response: your heart speeds up, you breathe faster, your palms sweat, your mouth becomes dry and blood pressure rises. All of these changes divert blood to the muscles so that you have more energy either to get away from or confront the pursuer. This 'fight or flight' response to danger has obvious survival value in helping us to deal with all manner of threats, not just imagined stalkers on the street. Our emotional and physical response to situations that we fear can also help us to take practical steps. For example, if your home has been burgled, you are more likely to find the time and money to fit secure locks to doors and windows or install a telephone in the bedroom in case you need to call for help. While such practical action can assure, it is natural to feel a sense of anxiety that takes a while to dissipate.

But fear and anxiety can get out of hand. Roughly one person in ten suffers from a phobia – an irrational fear of an object or situation that may be harmless in itself. Phobias are nothing new: the ancient Greek physician Hippocrates described patients disabled by irrational fear more than 2000 years ago. King James I of England was terrified by the sight of unsheathed swords, and Henry III of France was scared of cats.

Sigmund Freud, the founder of psychoanalysis, believed that phobias stemmed from childhood trauma. In some cases, this is true: one woman with a fear of feathers traced the problem back to a large feather in the hat of an unknown woman who leant over her pram when she was a baby, causing her to scream with fear. Fears and phobias vary in severity. Some people just feel mildly uncomfortable when talking about their phobia, and will avoid it if possible. Others will go to any lengths to avoid the object or situation because it produces such intense fear – so bad that they feel they might be about to die. In these cases, a phobia can seriously disrupt everyday life. People with a fear or phobia usually have a clear insight into their problem and know their fear is exaggerated, so in addition they often feel ashamed of their weakness.

Treating fears and phobias

Behaviour therapy can help people overcome most phobias and fears, and sometimes antidepressant drugs can be effective. Behaviour therapy exposes the sufferer to the object or situation they fear. There are two ways of doing this: through fantasy, which is a useful approach in situations that cannot easily be reproduced, such as thunderstorms, or by directly confronting the phobia. Fantasy involves the person imagining the phobia object, or viewing it via video, slides or computer simulations, while being repeatedly told to relax. Fear and relaxation cannot be present in the mind at the same time, so the fear should begin to fade and be replaced by a relaxed feeling.

> **"The more rapidly you confront the worst, the faster your fear will fade."**
>
> Isaac M. Marks, psychiatrist

For direct confrontation, there are two main approaches. Systematic desensitisation exposes a fear gradually. If, for example, a person fears going out at night after being mugged, the victim might begin by going out for short periods with friends, gradually reducing reliance on others until confident enough to walk alone. The alternative approach, called 'flooding', is like jumping straight into the deep end of a swimming pool. The person is exposed to the full extent of their fear – with agoraphobia, for instance, they might go to a shopping centre for a few hours. Flooding demands more of the patient but it yields quicker results. However, the patient must agree to see it through – fleeing halfway would reinforce the phobia.

Healing with hypnosis

Hypnotherapy draws upon our natural ability to enter into a state of mind where we are deeply relaxed, yet focused. Under these conditions, the mind is open to suggestion and ideas that can improve health can be absorbed.

There are many myths about hypnosis. It is often viewed as a stage trick or a type of mind control in which the hypnotist sends someone into a sleep-like trance, before telling them to do embarrassing things. However, although the process of hypnosis remains mysterious to an extent, it is a perfectly natural practice. Hypnosis is a state of awareness that goes beyond deep relaxation. In hypnosis, you are able to concentrate very deeply on certain aspects of your surroundings while others fade into the background. This is a state of mind very similar to becoming absorbed in a book or a film, so reality retreats from the front of your mind.

All hypnosis is in some way self-induced. No-one can be forced into a state of hypnosis unwillingly. The hypnotist is there to help the patient access his or her own unconscious mind. Some people enter a state of hypnosis more easily than others: this is not a sign of weakness, it just means they can easily enter into their own inner world. Generally, younger people are easier to hypnotise than those who are older.

"I was very sceptical at first, but my dentist prepared me for some major work with hypnotherapy. I would strongly recommend it to anyone who dreads the thought of their teeth being drilled."

Kate, 43, who hated visiting the dentist

The power of hypnotherapy

During hypnosis, the mind is more open to suggestion. A hypnotherapist (a therapist who uses hypnosis to treat problems) can use this to help instil positive ideas to improve the patient's health. For example, during hypnosis, it may be easier to accept the idea of giving up smoking, or to release memories of long-buried problems that could be a contributory factor in stress-related ailments like eczema, asthma and psoriasis. Hypnotherapy is a powerful treatment for anxiety, eating disorders and phobias of all kinds.

The hypnosis experience

So what does hypnosis feel like? On a first visit to a hypnotherapist, patients may feel apprehensive, perhaps wondering if they will emerge from the trance. Hypnosis has three main stages – light, moderate and deep. The hypnotherapist begins by asking the patient to focus on a fixed point and breathe slowly. The hypnotherapist will then talk the patient through a routine – perhaps imagining descending in a lift – that will help him or her achieve a hypnotic state, then treatment can begin. If treating someone for a smoking addiction, the therapist may suggest that the next cigarette will make the patient feel sick. In a hypnotic state, such suggestions can make a powerful impression on the mind.

Anyone with a serious medical condition should be wary of hypnotherapists who do not have a detailed knowledge of the illness. As with any form of complementary therapy, people should only consult a properly qualified therapist whom they like and trust.

SELF-HYPNOSIS

You do not need to visit a hypnotherapist to benefit from hypnosis. It is quite easy to put yourself into a relaxed, hypnosis-like state.
• Find a quiet, undisturbed place. Ideally, sit, rather than lie down, to prevent yourself falling asleep. Plan the kinds of suggestions you want to practise – for example, a specific goal, such as giving up smoking, or releasing tension.
• Take three or four slow, deep breaths, holding your breath for a couple of seconds then letting go with the word 'relax'.
• Focus your attention by concentrating on a point on the wall.
• Tell yourself you are going to take three special breaths – the first to relax, the second to move towards hypnosis and the third to be in hypnosis.
• After the breaths, release all tension from your body by systematically relaxing the muscles from your toes to the top of your head.
• Now imagine a staircase with ten steps leading you to a special place. Count down from ten to one as you descend the stairs.
• Visualise your place, and try to experience how it sounds, smells and feels.
• Now begin your positive suggestions relating to the goal of your self-hypnosis.
• When you are finished, count yourself back up from one to ten, telling yourself you have enjoyed a wonderful session of relaxation, and that when you emerge you will feel refreshed.

HYPNOSIS AS ANAESTHETIC

Hypnotherapy can help patients get through painful physical examinations. An American doctor, Michael Nash, reported the experience of a patient who had to have a bladder examination every three months for five years after the removal of a tumour. He refused a general anaesthetic, and an epidural (a spinal anaesthetic) was considered medically dangerous. The first time the patient was examined, he had to be held down as he struggled with the pain, which was a distressing experience for all concerned. Dr Nash decided to teach the patient self-hypnosis. Before the second examination, the patient took 60 seconds to prepare himself. Ten minutes later, the examination was over and the patient reported feeling none of the pain of the previous examination. And the six people waiting to hold him down went for a coffee instead.

CREATE YOUR OWN THERAPY

Professional therapists and counsellors use a wide range of techniques to assist their clients. Many of these can be adapted as self-help tools to help us identify mental and emotional difficulties and work through them towards more constructive ways of feeling, thinking and acting. Try these exercises as the first steps on the road to self-analysis and awareness. Anyone with serious concerns about mental health, should seek professional advice.

COGNITIVE THERAPY

Cognitive psychotherapy can help people to identify and change negative or self-defeating thinking styles. Negative thought drains confidence and creates negative emotions – such as anxiety, depression and anger – which, in turn, prevent us from making the most of our lives, relationships and work opportunities. Change the negative thinking, however, and emotions and behaviour will change too.

Do you have negative attitudes?

If you answer 'no' to any of the following statements, you probably hold negative views about yourself:

- I like myself
- I have a balanced view of my qualities and limitations
- I am a good person
- I do not hold unrealistic expectations of myself
- I believe I have as much right as anyone to the good things in life
- I motivate myself through kindness, not self-criticism
- I value myself

If you indulge in negative thinking, you will probably recognise one or more of the following:

- Mind-reading – acting on assumptions about what other people are thinking or feeling. Do you make statements like: 'He doesn't like me', or 'They probably think I've handled that badly'?
- Black-and-white thinking – is everything either good or bad, right or wrong? Do you think things like: '80 per cent isn't good enough!', or 'I started, so it's bad if I don't finish'?
- Mental filtering – do you 'filter out' positive statements by belittling your achievements? Do you think things like: 'Anyone could do that; they are only being kind'?
- Extremism – do you make sweeping statements like: 'It's always me that has to sort things out', 'I never say the right thing', or 'No one ever thinks of me'?

Overcoming negative thinking

Challenge any negative views and thought patterns by objectively looking for evidence to disprove them:

- Check your facts – ask people what they really think rather than simply acting on your assumptions.
- Think about the times when you 'got things right' – give yourself credit for what you have achieved, even if it is only part of what you set out to do.
- Write down three good things that happen each day.
- Beware of using overgeneralising words like 'never', 'always' and 'nobody' – think of exceptions.

HUMANISTIC THERAPY

Humanistic therapy views every person as a unique individual and aims to involve the client as actively as possible in discovering his or her own ways of feeling and thinking ('client-centred therapy').

The Q-sort method

'Q-sort cards' are used to help people find out which areas of their personality to work on. These cards have personal qualities written on them, such as:

- I am friendly
- I am unfriendly
- My outlook is generally positive
- My outlook is generally negative
- I am usually tense
- I am usually relaxed
- I put myself first
- I put others first
- I am decisive
- I am indecisive
- I am critical
- I am generous
- I have a wide range of interests
- I have few interests
- I often see my friends
- I rarely see my friends
- I am open about my feelings
- I conceal my feelings

Identify your ideal self

In the following Q-sort exercise you should try to be as honest about yourself as you can.

- Make your own set of Q-cards. You could use the qualities listed here or devise your own to create a pack consisting of 20–30 cards. To reduce the possibility of personal bias in your choice of qualities, you could do the exercise together with a friend, making one pack of Q-cards for both of you.
- Shuffle the Q-cards. Sort them into five piles, putting the cards that describe you best into pile 1 and those that describe you least well into pile 5. Grade the others into piles 2–4, using pile 3 as a 'neutral' pile for traits that seem neither characteristic nor uncharacteristic. Note down the qualities that you have placed in each pile. These form a picture of your 'self-concept' – how you see yourself.
- Shuffle the cards again and repeat the exercise, but this time imagine you are your 'ideal self' – the kind of person you would most like to be.

Your self-concept

Compare the two sets of results. The qualities of your ideal self that are lacking from your self-concept represent areas to think about working on. You could begin by looking at those qualities in the first two piles of your ideal self which also appear just one or two piles below that in your self-concept.

DREAM ANALYSIS

Dreams often relate to our present preoccupations. Analysing them can help us to clarify our concerns, desires and fears.

Keeping a dream diary

Keep a daily diary of your dreams for a short period, say two weeks. As soon as possible after you wake in the morning, make a note of:

- The content of your dreams, including the people and places who appear.
- Significant events in your life in the previous 24 hours.
- Significant concerns about your health, job, relationships and so on in the previous 24 hours.

Analyse your dreams

At the end of the two weeks, read through your diary and analyse your dreams as follows.

- Note any dreams that appear to be accounted for by your conscious waking experiences (for example, a dream of water following a visit to the seaside).
- Note any links between your dreams and your personal concerns. These links can be direct (you may dream about being ill or losing your job) or indirect (if you are worried about failing an exam you may dream of falling over). Any such dreams that recur are likely to represent issues you should deal with most urgently.
- Did you have any dreams that cannot be accounted for by your waking experiences or concerns? They may express deep-seated or even unconscious desires or fears – especially if they recur.

BIOFEEDBACK

We are not normally aware of our bodies at work, although physiological factors such as blood pressure, blood flow and heart rate affect our health. The therapeutic technique of biofeedback provides conscious awareness of unconscious body states, and is a powerful tool for learning to control stress-related conditions.

Biofeedback gives people the power to influence some aspects of their bodily functioning that are of benefit to health. For example, it is well known that high blood pressure is a risk factor for heart disease. Blood pressure fluctuates constantly in any 24-hour period, but we are not normally aware of these changes. Using biofeedback, we can learn what it is that raises blood pressure, and what we can do to bring it down again.

In fact, biofeedback is a kind of learning process, consisting of three basic stages. First, the physiological function that you want to control is identified – such as lowering skin temperature or blood pressure. Second, the function needs to be converted into a signal that is easy to recognise – such as a moving needle on a meter, a flashing light or a sound that changes its tone. In order to measure and observe any variation in the signal, you need to be connected to a monitoring machine that has either a visual display (such as a computer screen) or an audible output. For example, a tone may be used to indicate blood pressure. As the pressure falls, so does the pitch of the tone. The third stage is reached when you have learned what it is that makes the signal alter in the direction you want – in other words, how to consciously control your body's response.

Biofeedback training
A patient observes feedback from his brainwaves on a computer screen. Over a number of sessions, he learns to control his brain activity. This can help with problems such as mood disorders and migraine.

"I suffered from cold hands. Using biofeedback, I learned to warm them up by imagining them in a bowl of warm almond oil – lovely! And it really worked."

Shirley, 39

The brainwave data is transformed into a computer game. By playing the game, the patient modifies his brainwave pattern

Sensors on the patient's head pick up brainwave data and feed it into the computer

Real lives OVERCOMING CHRONIC DEPRESSION

Doctors in the USA used biofeedback to cure a woman of persistent depression. She had been treated using psychotherapy and antidepressants for over 12 years, but without success. Biofeedback (by monitoring her brain activity in response to happy or sad film clips) enabled the woman to normalise her brain activity reaction to the clips by means of the 'reward' of a pleasant-sounding tone. After 34 one-hour sessions, her depression had lifted.

A check-up six years later revealed that there had been no recurrences – an impressive result, since many patients with depression do relapse. Since then, a further 20 patients have tried the treatment, 18 of whom have improved.

Thinking of how you felt about your neighbour when he took your parking space, for example, might make your blood-pressure tone rise to a high-pitched squeal. Breathing more slowly and thinking about your forthcoming holiday may alter it to a pleasing hum. Eventually, you will learn what mental tricks work to make these desired changes for you without needing the machine.

How biofeedback works

Biofeedback became popular in the 1960s and since then has been applied to a range of chronic disorders, many of them stress-related. It began with a study conducted at the University of California involving people with epilepsy. Researcher Barry Sterman discovered that the brainwaves of people on the verge of a seizure had an abnormally high level of brain activity. The researchers devised an interactive computer game where the screen image was related to the level of brain activity. By learning how to control the images on screen, patients learned to control and normalise their own brain activity patterns. For example, one patient's image was a rocket and by raising it to the top of the screen – using whatever mental trick worked best – he found he could normalise the electrical activity of his brain when it was highly active and thereby avert a seizure. A variety of similar techniques are in use today.

Using biofeedback

Biofeedback has proved to be successful in treating a wide range of conditions, including high blood pressure, migraine and Raynaud's disease – a circulatory problem in which blood vessels in the hands constrict and cause an aching, cold sensation. Bruxism (teeth-grinding) and temporomandibular joint (TMJ) disorder, where tension in the jaw produces severe facial pain, are two stress-related conditions that respond well to biofeedback. In the USA, biofeedback (or neurofeedback as it is also known) is being used to improve concentration among hyperactive children.

▶▶ CUTTING EDGE ▶▶

IMPROVED PERFORMANCE

There is new evidence that biofeedback may have positive effects even when there is not a specific medical problem. A team at Imperial College London has succeeded in raising the performance of musicians at London's Royal College of Music. The results suggested that enhancing specific brain activity patterns by biofeedback improves attention. After biofeedback training the students made fewer impulsive mistakes when performing, such as playing the wrong note or coming in to the piece too early.

The technique could also be applied to enhance sporting skills. Biofeedback could be used to improve a golfer's swing, for example.

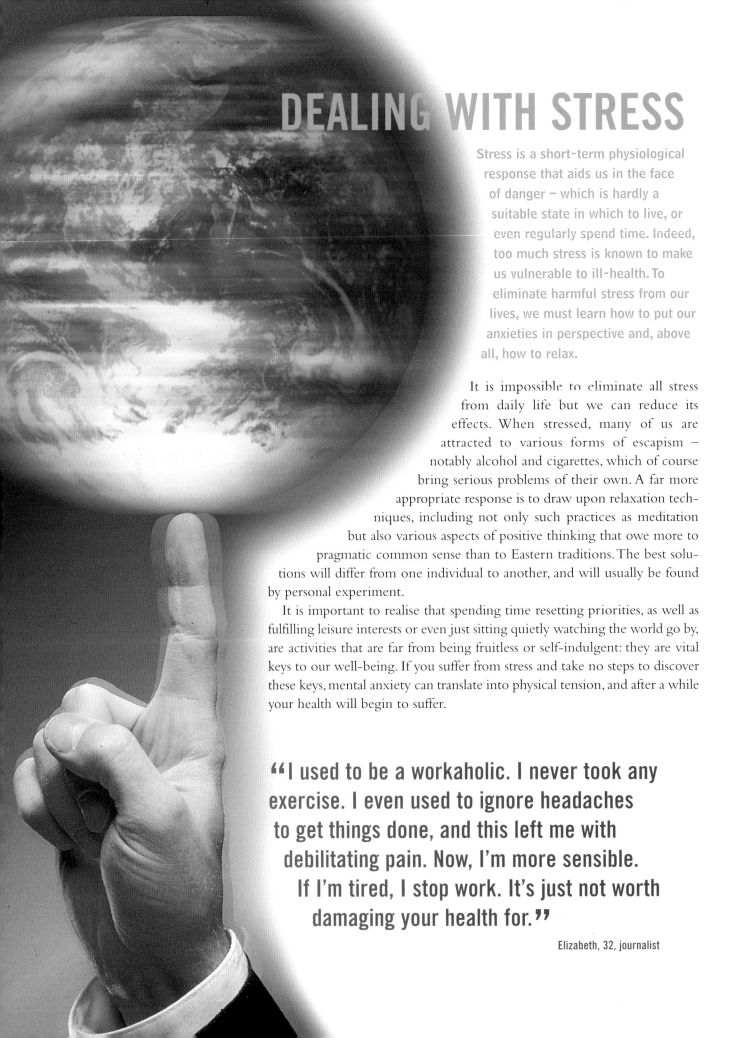

DEALING WITH STRESS

Stress is a short-term physiological response that aids us in the face of danger – which is hardly a suitable state in which to live, or even regularly spend time. Indeed, too much stress is known to make us vulnerable to ill-health. To eliminate harmful stress from our lives, we must learn how to put our anxieties in perspective and, above all, how to relax.

It is impossible to eliminate all stress from daily life but we can reduce its effects. When stressed, many of us are attracted to various forms of escapism – notably alcohol and cigarettes, which of course bring serious problems of their own. A far more appropriate response is to draw upon relaxation techniques, including not only such practices as meditation but also various aspects of positive thinking that owe more to pragmatic common sense than to Eastern traditions. The best solutions will differ from one individual to another, and will usually be found by personal experiment.

It is important to realise that spending time resetting priorities, as well as fulfilling leisure interests or even just sitting quietly watching the world go by, are activities that are far from being fruitless or self-indulgent: they are vital keys to our well-being. If you suffer from stress and take no steps to discover these keys, mental anxiety can translate into physical tension, and after a while your health will begin to suffer.

"I used to be a workaholic. I never took any exercise. I even used to ignore headaches to get things done, and this left me with debilitating pain. Now, I'm more sensible. If I'm tired, I stop work. It's just not worth damaging your health for."

Elizabeth, 32, journalist

FIVE GREAT WAYS TO BEAT WORKLOAD STRESS

Work stresses tend most often to come from workload problems, from feeling insecure or ill-equipped, from work politics, or from inadequate delegation. The first stage in laying such demons to rest is to step back and gain some perspective on the issues, in the context of life as a whole, and then to start working on practical solutions to the problems – *taking them one at a time.* Short-term measures will get you out of a crisis, but they need to be followed by a longer-term review to address the underlying causes of your stress and to make lasting changes.

1 Set yourself realistic targets, in both the short and the long term. Do not feel that you have to achieve all these targets to retain self-esteem. Congratulate yourself on your successes. Do not flagellate yourself for your failures.

2 Create within your schedule time for review and reflection – if possible, have review sessions away from the place where schedule pressures are most acute. Do not get bogged down in detail when what is needed is a fresh look at how things are done.

3 Make your health a priority. The body requires adequate sleep and nutrition to function effectively. Cultivate methods that encourage quality sleep: a hot bath, a milky drink – whatever you find works best for you. Never overlook the fact that physical exercise, as well as family and social life, are vital for emotional and physical well-being.

4 Relaxation is essential. The conditioned fight-or-flight response can act as an obstacle to reducing stress, because the idea of relaxation appears threatening. But you are not letting your guard down by opting to relax – in fact, relaxation is the key to regaining calm. Everyone has their own way to relax, so try different approaches that you can readily fit into your lifestyle. Breathing and stretching exercises, and meditation, are worth considering, as is the Alexander technique.

5 Monitor your use of time and ensure that you are getting the balance right between work and play. Do not neglect holidays or regular leisure commitments. Think of these, if it helps, as ways to refresh your energies for both work and domestic responsibilities. Do not fall into the trap of seeing yourself as indispensable, defending a position against all odds.

Following this five-point plan will help you feel that you have taken charge of your life. It will assist in bolstering feelings of self-mastery and self-worth, and these in themselves will help to reduce stress.

Acceptance and control

When life is not going our way, we might find ourselves using up a great deal of energy in wishing that things were otherwise, perhaps spending energy directing blame towards other people or fate. But it is self-evident that we cannot change what is beyond our control, only what is within it. And what cannot be changed must be accepted. Living according to these facts requires mature, realistic thinking, as well as an accurate assessment of the factors in life that we *can* influence. If we are stressed by the difficulty of selling a house, there is a way through the labyrinth: we cannot conjure a buyer out of nowhere, nor make the kitchen or garden bigger; but we can be patient, and in the meantime enjoy the friendship of our neighbours while we still have it. Issues that only time can resolve must not be allowed to dominate our entire mental landscape.

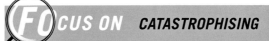

FOCUS ON CATASTROPHISING

Psychologists use the term 'catastrophising' to describe a tendency to feel that a situation is disastrous when, viewed by more objective standards, it is in fact merely negative or unlucky. A psychotherapist will often tackle this syndrome by working on a person's coping skills – the rational ways that are available to us all to deal with life's commonplace anxieties. Catastrophising works by 'snowballing' problems – two or three difficulties, each readily soluble, may appear insurmountable when grouped together. One approach is to train the 'patient' to separate problems into their component parts, and deal with each part individually. Making simple, verifiable statements about the situation can help in this: 'I am sick, but the doctor has said my illness will not affect my lifestyle'; 'I will not see my children for two months, but then we will be spending a two-week vacation together.'

RELAXING MIND AND BODY

Relaxation brings clarity of thought and freedom from stress, and is therefore a route to improved mental and physical health. But we cannot force the process. The best approach is to learn about the classic techniques and apply yourself patiently to the ones that attract you most.

Relaxation is more than just a mood we enjoy when things are going well for us – it is a profound state of mind that ideally should be the mental plateau we inhabit in most of our daily encounters. For many, however, daily life is quite the opposite. The 19th-century American writer Henry Thoreau once said that 'the mass of men lead lives of quiet desperation'. This may be stating things a little strongly, but if you are aware of a background buzz of anxiety as your habitual state, you would probably benefit from practising one or more of the tried-and-tested approaches outlined over the following pages.

Some relaxation techniques can readily be accommodated in virtually any daily routine – even during work breaks you can practise deep breathing, systematic tensing and releasing of your muscles, and stretching exercises. You might be able to take a brisk walk at lunchtime, or by working out in a gym or taking part in a team sport you will gain not only from the exercise but also from the opportunity for your mind to forget its anxieties and expectations and concentrate on the moment. This state of 'mindfulness' – a complete absorption in here-and-now experiences – is greatly valued by Buddhists.

Making time for relaxation

One problem with modern life is that we are so often 'on the go', there is little time left for reflection. Short periods of quiet introspection have been shown to reduce stress. They help you stay in touch with your inner self, and enable you to put the tribulations of your life in perspective. By spending five minutes or more letting your emotions, whatever they are, subside and thinking about what really matters to you, you will come to see that you have choices. You do not have to conform with other people's opinions if you disagree with them. This belief in the 'sovereignty of the self' is a cornerstone of modern approaches to personal fulfilment.

> **" By keeping the body still, you are training the mind to be still and relax. You cannot relax while the mind is jumping around like a monkey from one stressful or stimulating thought form to another. "**
>
> Beryl Bender Birch,
> wellness director and yoga teacher

BREATHING

How we breathe is related to our state of mind. When we are stressed, breathing becomes shallow and rapid; when we are calm, it is deep and slow. Taking a deep breath is an automatic and effective technique for winding down, and deep breathing exercises, from the diaphragm, consciously intensify this natural reaction. They are a good preparation for meditation.

- Breathe in slowly and deeply through the nose to a count of 10, making sure that the abdomen expands but the chest does not rise. Exhale through the nose, slowly and completely, also to a count of 10. Repeat 5–10 times. Counting through each cycle in a concentrated way will help to quieten your mind. You might also imagine yourself inhaling energy and calm, and exhaling worry and tension. Repeat this several times a day.

Some people find singing useful as a way of learning to control breathing – certainly you cannot sing well unless you can breathe well. Also intoning a mantra – a number of (not necessarily meaningful) syllables – is a classic meditation device.

MEDITATION

Deeply rooted in Eastern cultures, meditation is now widely practised in the West. In the words of meditation master David Fontana, it is 'the experience of the limitless nature of the mind when it ceases to be dominated by its usual mental chatter'. Although meditation brings mental peace, this is best achieved in a state of open-mindedness, rather than with any specific goal.

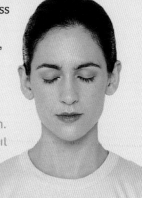

- Wearing loose, comfortable clothing, sit comfortably upright in a pleasant place and close your eyes. Breathe deeply from your abdomen. Then for five minutes – or longer if you wish – imagine a radiating point of light behind your forehead. Think of this as an outpouring of positive energy. Don't worry if thoughts also drift across your mind – just let them pass, without trying to influence them.

The optimum meditation is performed without intention, expectation, impatience or disappointment. But there is no need to be anxious if you do experience such feelings: simply be aware of them.

POSTURE

How we stand, sit and move can have a profound effect on our well-being and energy levels. Many common ailments, such as frequent headaches or low back pain, stem from muscular tension caused by bad posture. The most common failings are slouching, rounded shoulders, arched back and tilted head. More and more people are coming to believe, in line with Eastern thinking, that the body has an optimum flow of energy (the Chinese call this energy 'chi'), and that any blockage in the flow can disturb the harmony of body and mind. Improving posture is the key to eradicating such problems. It can even help to alleviate insomnia and depression.

• Good posture depends on the spine, which should be lengthened and centred. When standing, your weight should be spread evenly over both your feet, and your shoulders level. Viewed from the side, there should be a straight line through your ears, arms, hips and knees to your feet, and a gentle curve in your lower back. When sitting, keep your knees slightly lower than your hips: a wedge-shaped cushion can help. All the following are taboo: slumping in a chair, crossing your legs, and holding a telephone receiver between chin and shoulder.

MUSCLE RELAXATION

Muscle relaxation techniques such as tense-and-relax exercises and stretching are simple to learn and can be practised at any time.

• Tense or clench each muscle tightly for 5–10 seconds, then release it completely, being consciously aware of the muscle relaxing. Start with the toes and move progressively up the body to your face and head. After each tense-and-relax, imagine that the body part has become warm and fluid. Visualise each element as flowing freely. With practice the exercise becomes more effective and will induce relaxation more quickly. It can be particularly useful in getting to sleep.

Loosening tight muscles by stretching is effective for anyone whose job involves sitting for long periods, or continually using the same muscle groups. Stretching increases oxygenation and stimulates lymphatic drainage, which reduces back pain, headaches and indigestion. Reaching your arms high above your head or stretching your legs with a quick walk are enough to get the blood circulating more strongly again, and will reinvigorate you.

VISUALISATION

A classic relaxation technique is to visualise an image or scene that fills you with peace – a bit like running your own stress-busting movie in your mind.

• Find a quiet place and ensure you will not be disturbed for at least 10 minutes. Close your eyes and breathe deeply, then conjure up a favourite or idealised place – perhaps a tropical beach, a city park, even a golf course. Gradually build up the details of the scene in your mind – not only the sights but also the sounds and smells. Be aware of the weather – a cool breeze or warm sun according to your preference. Retreat to this inner sanctuary whenever you need to regain peace of mind.

YOGA

Yoga (a Sanskrit word that means 'yoke' or 'union') is an ancient Indian repertoire of techniques integrating mind, body and spirit. It improves suppleness, digestion, circulation and relaxation. It can also heighten intuition and creativity. At a more profound level it provides a way to achieve enlightenment or self-realisation – in Eastern terms, to forge a union of the individual self with the 'universal self'. The most popular form in the West is Hatha Yoga, which aims first to cultivate physical awareness through classic postures, or 'asanas', and then moves on to develop higher mental awareness. The benefits are physical, emotional and, ultimately, spiritual.

Sleep and health

Most of us take sleep for granted, unless it starts to become elusive. During sleep, your brain and body enter a state quite different from being awake — it is not simply a case of 'switching off'. And when sleep is limited, the impact on health can be significant.

As a society, we probably sleep less now than at any time in the past. Records show that, until the widespread availability of the electric light in the 19th century, people slept for an average of nine hours a night. Today, the average is seven hours, and many people get by on less. But does sleep deprivation have an effect on health? We cannot survive indefinitely without sleep — 11 days is the record (people can go without food for far longer). Sleep, then, would appear to be essential, but there is still no generally agreed account of why this is so. Some scientists think that sleep is necessary because of the body's need to have 'down time' in which to build glucose reserves, or to exercise little-used brain circuits. Other suggestions include the need to conserve energy — but in fact a body asleep continues to use up almost as many calories as it does when awake. Whatever the precise reason for sleeping, it is agreed that it plays an important role in keeping us healthy.

"When I was a student, I'd sleep till midday at the weekends. But it changes as you get older. Now I'm always up by eight — and I don't even have any kids to get me up."

Tracy, 31

SLEEP PROBLEMS

Sometimes we miss out on sleep due to lack of opportunity – the demands of a young family, for example, or an overloaded social life on top of a busy work schedule. But the quality of sleep itself might be deficient and this can indicate another health problem. For example, people suffering from depression may wake up very early in the morning and be unable to get back to sleep. Snoring, too, can be a sign of an underlying problem called sleep apnoea. This is a temporary cessation of breathing, perhaps hundreds of times a night. People who suffer from sleep apnoea are more prone to stroke or heart disease, probably because vital organs (brain and heart) are intermittently deprived of oxygen. They are also prone to daytime sleepiness, which can be dangerous if they need to drive a vehicle.

Of course, insomnia can occur without any obvious cause. But becoming anxious about sleeping will only cause worry and make us less able to sleep. For those people who worry that they are damaging their health through a lack of sleep, laboratory evidence has revealed that insomniacs get more sleep than they think. What seems like only half-an-hour's sleep over the whole night may, in fact, be nearer five hours.

Body changes during sleep

Sleep produces changes in our physiological cycles. Research in sleep laboratories has shown that there is a peak in the levels of growth hormone when people first fall asleep. In adults, this hormone is involved with cell repair, and so maintains the health of skin, bone and muscle. Another hormone produced in early sleep is testosterone, which helps to explain why sleep disorders in men can cause impotence. Sleep also helps the brain to process memories. Studies have shown that it is harder to memorise complex material if sleep is interrupted.

How many hours?

Opinion is divided on how much sleep we really need. Six or seven hours sleep a night may well be fine, although the Canadian psychologist Stanley Coren believes that Western society is sleep-deprived, which leads to accidents and undermines day-to-day efficiency. If you are not sure whether you are actually getting the sleep you need, just experiment with an hour or two more – or less – for a week or so, and see how you feel.

A GOOD NIGHT'S SLEEP

Try the following tips to achieve sufficient quantity and quality of sleep:
• Make sure the bedroom is comfortable – neither too hot, nor too cold, and as dark as it can be made.
• Exercise can help us to wind down, but it should not be taken last thing at night. It will speed up metabolism and make it hard to settle down.
• As with physical exercise, it is important not to work immediately before going to bed, or to get involved in stimulating mental activity.
• Try to choose television programming or reading matter that will not provoke too much thought.
• Try a milky drink, or a soothing herbal tea. A bowl of cereal may also help, because carbohydrates induce sleep.
• The popular belief that cheese causes nightmares is incorrect – it is far more likely to lead to a bout of indigestion.
• If you have real problems, the best way to regulate your sleep–wake cycles is to get up at the same time every day, including weekends.

OVERCOMING PAIN

Pain is simply the way we come to know about damage to the body's tissues, and the feeling it produces differs according to how the brain interprets it. Our brains can present the knowledge as anything from intensely unpleasant to just another piece of sensory information. And we all have the ability to turn the first experience into the second, whether by using drugs or altering our thinking.

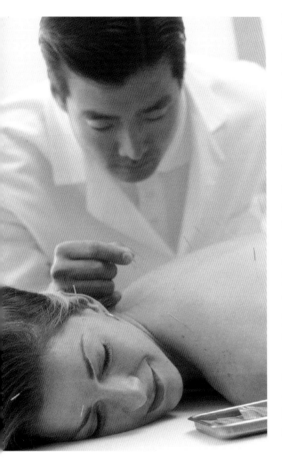

Defeating pain Acupuncture is thought to relieve pain by stimulating nerves that interfere with the transmission of pain signals to the brain – this is the 'pain blockade'. Transcutaneous electrical nerve stimulation (TENS) also exploits this phenomenon.

Nerves distributed around the body run up the spine and into the brain, where they are registered on the somatosensory cortex. It used to be thought that pain information simply travelled up the nerve pathways and was automatically felt as pain once it reached the brain, but now a more complicated picture has emerged.

When you bang your shin, your automatic response is to rub it. 'Rubbing it better' works because the receptors and nerve fibres that transmit pain messages lie close to those carrying sensations such as warmth and pleasant touch. If non-pain fibres next to a pain-carrying fibre are stimulated, the signals from the pain nerves are blocked before they are consciously registered. The pain blockade occurs because only one type of sensation can be felt in the same area of the body at the same time.

The 'competition for consciousness' between painful and pleasant stimuli was first discovered in the 1960s by physiologists Patrick Wall and Ronald Melzack. Their 'gate control' theory of pain proposed that there was a 'gate' in the spinal cord which allowed only one type of sensation to pass through it at a time. However, recent research suggests that the gate effect is in fact provided by the body's attention system.

Attention to pain

An area of the brain called the cingulate cortex, which lies in the groove between the brain's two hemispheres, can turn attention inwards or outwards. If something threatening or exciting is going on, the cingulate cortex switches your attention away from your body and reduces any sensation of pain. This is one reason why soldiers wounded in battle may feel no pain at the time, as their minds are occupied elsewhere. It has even been reported that up to 20 per cent of people who undergo major surgery report feeling little or no pain for hours or days after the operation.

Prolonged severe pain, as may occur in a chronic condition such as sciatica, can have a debilitating effect

FACT: According to a US Gallup poll, 46 per cent of women and 37 per cent of men experience pain on a daily basis, and 89 per cent of all adults experience pain at least once a month. Of those in pain, only half had visited a doctor in the previous three years to seek help.

TRY IT YOURSELF   PAIN MEDITATION

Meditation can help you dissociate yourself from pain. Even if it's there, you don't have to suffer too much. There are many techniques, so experiment to find which works best for you. Here are four options:

1. Concentrate on your breathing. Take long, deep inhalations and focus on the feeling of each one.

2. Focus on a part of the body distant from the pain: if the pain is in your right side, focus on the left; if it's in your head, focus on your feet. This technique works particularly well with migraine: if, for example, your migraine is on the right side, focus on the left side of your body, from the neck down.

3. Close your eyes and imagine you are in some beautiful, peaceful place where there is no pain.

4. If a pain is so overwhelming that you cannot focus on anything else, try a little self-induced dissociation. Close your eyes, and imagine the pain as a physical object. Concentrate on exactly where the pain is, measuring its dimensions and shape. When its form is clear in your mind, imagine wrapping it up in brown paper and tying some string around it. Then imagine taking this 'parcel' out of your body, and placing it a long way away. Place it on the ground. Then walk away from it.

These types of mind control may sound too simple to be effective, but with practice they really can work. If you succeed, you will find that the feeling of pain, although still there, ceases to bother you as much as before.

by reducing a person's mental ability to cope with the continuous discomfort. The sufferer can come to focus increasingly on the pain; this makes it seem more and more severe, as each unpleasant sensation is amplified. Studies have shown that about 70 per cent of people who suffer from chronic lower-back pain do not have any readily detectable injury.

The brain's painkillers

The brain produces its own natural painkillers – a group of chemicals called endorphins. These relieve pain by increasing levels of dopamine, another brain chemical, which enhances feelings of well-being. Other chemicals help to prevent pain from being laid down in the brain. Oxytocin, for example, is a hormone that women produce during labour and one of its functions is to reduce the memory of the pain of childbirth.

Pain thresholds

Sensitivity to pain differs from person to person and culture to culture. You can test your pain threshold by holding your hand in freezing water. How long does it take before it starts to hurt? And when does it become unbearable? Most people cannot manage more than two or three minutes. Such experiments have tended to suggest that women have lower thresholds than men, but the findings are difficult to interpret – it may be that men are socially conditioned to appear brave under such circumstances, so they choose to interpret certain stimuli as discomfort rather than pain. Other studies show that Mediterranean people report pain in response to a stimulus which northern Europeans describe as merely unpleasant. This may reflect a biological difference, or merely demonstrate that some cultures encourage expression while others inhibit it.

Dealing with pain

Hypnosis, relaxation, meditation and behavioural modification can all reduce the experience of pain by turning a person's attention away from it. The effect of attention was dramatically demonstrated in a study in which patients were hypnotised before being operated on without anaesthetic. They were told they would feel no pain, but that a 'hidden observer' in their mind would feel it for them. After surgery, the patients reported feeling nothing. But when the hypnotist addressed the 'observer', they reported excruciating pain. This suggests that, in some conditions, we can dissociate from pain, even though it is laid down in the brain.

Conversely, pain can be made worse by fear and anticipation. If a person has experienced severe pain during a particular procedure in the past – having a tooth filled at the dentist's, say – it can create the expectation (sometimes unconscious) of suffering in the same way again. This will make that person attend more closely to their feelings next time they go to

Breaking the pain barrier
Researchers have found that sports professionals generally have a higher pain threshold than ordinary people. This is because they become so used to experiencing pain while pushing themselves to the limit that they are able to 'tune it out'.

Real lives   *THE PAIN PERFORMER*

American circus entertainer Jim Rose makes his living by subjecting himself to what for most people would be excruciating pain, such as acting as a human dartboard. His secret is to establish a state of mind that enables him to keep pain out of his consciousness. He explains the technique as follows:

'Where I like to go is into a nice warm-watered pool, and I like to be right up to my neck and everything's feeling fine, everything's already nice and warm and relaxed. No, I don't feel the pain. I've worked it out to where it's a mild discomfort.'

But if unprepared, Jim reacts to pain just like anyone else: 'If I stub my toe on the bed at night I'm going to scream just like you, because I didn't expect it and I didn't put myself in the warm water.'

> **"Taking morphine doesn't stop the pain, it just changes your attitude towards it."**
>
> Maureen, 68, recovering from a major operation

the dentist, and the attention will make the new experience even more painful. In cases like this, psychotherapy may help to uncover such unconscious expectations, and give the person the ability to divert their attention from painful stimuli in a future situation.

Refocusing attention away from pain is a technique used by practitioners of yoga, for example, who are able to achieve such feats of endurance as lying on a bed of nails or walking barefoot across red-hot coals. By 'retraining' their brains through meditation, they have managed to reduce the significance of pain signals to a point where they do not experience pain in the same way as an ordinary person.

Pain medication

Although our sensation of pain is very much dependent on our expectation, mental state and psychological make-up, there is much that can be done medically to help people deal with pain, both short and long-term. There is a wide range of pain-killing – or, more accurately, pain-relieving – drugs available, which can be extremely beneficial in many cases. These either act at the site of the pain, or act in the brain by interfering with the pathways that bring pain to conscious attention. The most suitable analgesic will depend on the cause and nature of the pain, but if pain is persistent or severe, a doctor's advice should be sought.

FACT FILE   COMMON PAINKILLERS

Painkillers, or analgesics, are among the most commonly prescribed drugs.

• Analgesics are classified into non-opioid – including over-the-counter remedies such as aspirin and paracetamol – and opioid, such as morphine.
• Generally, non-opioid analgesics are more suited for mild to moderate muscle or joint pain. Opioid analgesics are usually used to combat moderate to severe pain, particularly when it is internal in origin.
• Aspirin is used to treat headache, acute pain, painful menstruation and fever. It is also an effective anti-inflammatory. It may cause stomach irritation, so is best taken after food.
• Paracetamol is similar in effect to aspirin, and is often preferred – especially in older people – as it is less irritating to the stomach.
• Of the opioid analgesics, morphine is the most effective for severe pain, although nausea and vomiting are common side effects.
• Other opioids include codeine, which is effective for the short-term treatment of mild to moderate pain, and diamorphine (heroin), a powerful narcotic drug.

THE PLEASURE RESPONSE

Without pleasure, most of us would feel that our lives were immeasurably impoverished. But did you know that the pursuit and experience of pleasure through mental or physical stimulation can actively enhance health and well-being? For some time scientists have been investigating how our brains respond to pleasurable stimuli.

"... and then my heart with pleasure fills And dances with the daffodils."

William Wordsworth

It is natural to enjoy life and we are born wanting to experience pleasure – it is, and always has been, a powerful motivator for human behaviour. In fact, Sigmund Freud believed that the pursuit of pleasure was all that mattered to babies and young children. As we grow into adults, we tend to be more restrained, but we still spend a great deal of our time – both consciously or unconsciously – seeking out enjoyment.

Society normally places limits on the degree to which the pursuit of pleasure is tolerated. The drive for moderation stems in part from a cultural disapproval of self-indulgence, bolstered by a wealth of evidence of the detrimental effects on health that too much of the 'wrong' sort of pleasure can have on health – lives ruined through alcohol or drug addiction, for example, or physical problems such as heart disease and high blood pressure caused by over-indulgence and smoking.

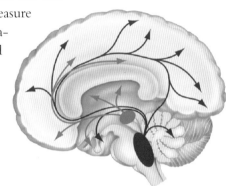

Pleasure pathways Neurotransmitters dopamine (red) and serotonin (blue) link different areas of the brain in the pleasure response.

The pleasure centre

In 1954, the American psychologist James Olds discovered what he believed to be the brain's 'pleasure centre'. Working on laboratory rats, he inserted tiny electrodes into an area of the brain close to the hypothalamus, which regulates hunger, thirst and temperature. By pressing a lever, the rats could electrically stimulate this part of the brain. To Olds' surprise, he found that the rats would press the lever thousands of times – until they fell to the floor, exhausted. They would even ignore food and water in preference to the lever. Stimulating this brain area evidently gave the rats intense pleasure.

We now know that there is no single pleasure centre in the brain, but a number of different areas that are linked together in circuits by means of certain neurotransmitters (brain chemicals). Two of these neurotransmitters are dopamine and serotonin. An intense surge of dopamine – the 'dopamine rush' – is linked to the 'high' experienced when taking drugs

TRY IT YOURSELF   BUILD YOUR OWN REWARD SYSTEM

How often do you treat yourself?
Perhaps your life is built around big, one-off treats, like a meal out on your birthday or an annual holiday. However, a personalised reward system, by which you treat yourself often and seek out small pleasures, can really improve your life. It offers a great way of getting through tedious or difficult chores: you may find it far easier to tackle household tasks, such as ironing or vacuuming, if you link them to a specific reward.

Make a list of 20 small treats which will give you a boost of sensual pleasure – for example:

- Bathing with aromatherapy oils
- A stroll in the park
- Buying fresh flowers
- Having a cup of real coffee rather than instant coffee
- Taking a good break for tea or lunch.

It may not be practical to have a treat after every tedious chore – but you can 'save up' for a reward with a mental points system. For example, if you decide that each completed chore counts as two points, 10 points could buy you some flowers, or you could save up 20 points for a manicure or a massage.

like cocaine; serotonin provides a quieter feeling of contentment – the anti-depressant fluoxetine (Prozac) and other related drugs work by raising levels of serotonin in the brain. Peter Kramer, a psychiatrist in the USA, has found that some people with mild depression experience pleasure for the first time in years after taking Prozac.

Pleasure and health

Pleasure can influence well-being in one of two ways: first, in a preventative way to promote good physical and mental health and to protect against illness; and second, in a curative way to aid the process of unwinding and help repair the harmful mental effects of unpleasant experiences. Research shows that experiencing pleasure leads to a reduction in stress hormones such as cortisol, and contributes to a strengthened immune response and therefore greater resistance to disease. Even simply remembering happy events can give the immune system a boost.

According to the psychologist Robert Ornstein, there are two main channels for tapping into the pleasure circuits of the brain – sensual and mental. Sensual pleasures give immediate gratification, while mental ones are slower-acting and more subtle, and include experiences of loving relationships, or the satisfaction of a job well done. Overall, Ornstein's research has shown that the happiest and healthiest people are those who take pleasure in even the simplest things.

CUTTING EDGE ▶▶ CUTTING EDGE

THE PUZZLE OF ANHEDONIA

Whereas hedonism is the pursuit of pleasure, anhedonia literally means 'loss of pleasure'. Someone with anhedonia gets no pleasure from a baby's smile, cuddling a pet, or eating a wonderful meal; beautiful countryside provokes no more pleasure than a derelict urban environment and a sunny day has much the same impact as a grey rainy one.

Anhedonia was first described in the 1890s, but it was not until 1980 that psychiatrists decided it was evidence of mental disorder (although it can occur in the absence of depression). It is regarded as a key symptom of depression and can be very distressing. Social anhedonia – lack of interest and pleasure in social interaction – may be an early warning sign of schizophrenia.

Targeting anhedonia

Anhedonia is an area of increasing interest, with researchers looking for its origins in changes in the brain. Scans of people with depression have revealed a smaller hippocampus, lesions and a different brain metabolism. At the Institute of Psychiatry in London, volunteers who had been diagnosed as having depression and anhedonia were shown film clips that normally induce pleasure, while undergoing fMRI scans. Comparing the scans with those of healthy people who responded positively to the films revealed different areas of brain activity in those with anhedonia. It is hoped that this will lead to new treatments that target specific parts of the brain.

Life's pleasures

Pleasure is a matter of personal taste, because we all enjoy different things, but it is also an experience we have in common that forms part of the emotional vocabulary of all cultures. A genuinely healthy lifestyle is one which involves embracing pleasure, not rejecting it.

Most people engage in activities that they find pleasurable — such as reading, listening to music, taking holidays, or eating out. Such experiences help people to cope with the stresses of modern life and improve psychological well-being. There are five principal categories of activity that give us pleasure: things that heighten enjoyment; things that counter stress, anxiety or depression; social encounters, such as meeting up to play sport; activities that are a regular feature of everyday life that we might look forward to, such as a tea break; and those regulating arousal or mood changes, such as enjoying an alcoholic drink.

Seeking pleasure

The pursuit of pleasure dictates much of what we do in life. We are attracted to things, people and situations that give us pleasure. For example, we make choices about food and drink primarily for taste rather than nutrition. It is not surprising that the pleasure state is linked with biologically important behaviour, such as eating and sexual activity: it is of evolutionary importance that human experiences involving food and sex should produce feelings of pleasure, which will make us more likely to seek out and repeat the experience. (Of course, not all pleasurable acts are biologically important, and not all biologically important acts are directly pleasurable.)

Regulating pleasure

The level of sensory stimulation at which pleasure is at its peak has been called the 'bliss point' by the Australian psychologist Robert McBride. Rather than overindulging in a state of bliss, we possess in-built regulatory mechanisms that help us to maximise our enjoyment by moderating our consumption of the things we enjoy. These mechanisms should not be confused with conscious and culturally constructed feelings of guilt, which can trigger stress hormones.

This self-regulatory 'pleasure principle' helps us to sustain a balanced diet and prevents us from excessive consumption of pleasure foods, like chocolate. For such substances to remain highly enjoyable, they must be consumed infrequently as 'treats' — if the pleasurable event is experienced too often it becomes repetitive and loses its freshness. Delaying gratification allows for greater expectancy, which enhances the pleasure when it arrives.

Research suggests that feelings of pleasure are caused by the release of endorphins in the brain. Some addictive drugs work by locking on to endorphin receptors in the brain, but it is of course healthier and safer to get an endorphin rush by means other than drugs. The work of psychologist Robert Ornstein has shown that the happiest and healthiest people are those who take pleasure in even the simplest things.

The strengthening of the body's immune responses that occurs as a result of experiencing pleasure suggests that the enjoyment of life's small pleasures may have a cumulative effect over a longer period, which benefits health. Even fantasising about pleasurable things can be useful. Happiness, it seems, really is a state of mind.

THE PLEASURE SURVEY

A 1993 survey in the UK asked people to describe the ten things that gave them pleasure. The age of respondents ranged from 16 to 92, and 74 per cent were women and 26 per cent were men. Approximately 36 different categories of pleasure were mentioned. The top-ranked category for men was food and drink, closely followed by music, reading, and family and children. For women, family and children came top, closely followed by food and drink, nature and scenery, entertainment and reading. Love/sex and sports/exercise were mentioned more often by men, and cosiness, friends and home/garden by women. Some of the selected comments from respondents below confirm the idea that pleasure can be derived from the 'simple things in life'.

FOOD AND DRINK

'Learning about wine on a tasting course has increased the pleasure I take in it.' **(man, 45)**

'The foods that give me most pleasure are: porridge for breakfast, crusty bread and strong Cheddar cheese for lunch, a rich bean stew with lots of vegetables and mashed potatoes for dinner, with lemon meringue pie to follow.' **(woman, 67)**

FAMILY AND CHILDREN

'First and foremost in the ten things that give me pleasure is opening my front door to my family who have travelled a distance to see me. To see their welcoming smiles and giving me that first kiss …' **(woman, 74)**

'When my son was a child, we would spend hours reading together, cycling down country lanes, swimming, camping or walking.' **(man, 49)**

NATURE AND SCENERY

'I love to walk in woods in the autumn, especially after rain.' **(woman, 31)**

'Two pleasures from nature which I cannot explain: the sound of rain falling on a summer garden; and the breeze making shot-silk of a tall green field of barley.' **(man, 64)**

'I never cease to marvel at the miracle of life, even the tiniest insect crawling over a leaf.' **(man, 80)**

FRIENDSHIP AND SOLITUDE

'The pleasure of close friends is probably the most important pleasure to me.' **(man, 33)**

'Being on my own after a busy day, to just stop and think, feel the sun, read a book, sing or do absolutely nothing. I find these times an absolute necessity, and they save my sanity when the going is tough.' **(woman, 38)**

5 HEALING THE BRAIN

The brain possesses a life-long capability to adapt to new challenges and circumstances. This chapter looks at ways of giving the brain its best chance to retain its powers. During adult life, the number of neurons in the brain slowly diminishes. However, the connections between brain cells – which provide the physical basis for everything we know, think, feel and do – are constantly evolving. While these links are made most rapidly when we are young, the brain never stops refining its connections – strengthening old ones and creating new ones as it learns from experience.

Protecting the brain from physical damage, taking regular mental and physical exercise, and avoiding substances and activities that can harm brain tissue are just some of the ways to ensure your brain stays in good condition. Your brain is your most precious possession: by taking good care of it you improve the likelihood of enjoying a long and fulfilling life.

YOUR BRAIN THROUGH LIFE

Although our brains become more complex during the course of our lives – primarily by forming millions of connections between nerve cells – most of the brain's structure is already present at birth. The greatest change, and the most rapid growth, occurs in the first couple of years of our lives.

At birth, after a normal nine-month gestation, there are around the same number of neurons (nerve cells) present in a baby's brain as there will be in adulthood. Most of these cells will not be replaced if they die, although there are a few exceptions. For example, the set of nerve cells involved in smell and taste in the olfactory nerve are continuously replaced through-out life. However, the number of neural connections between brain cells is relatively small at birth and it is not until a child is around six years of age that the density of neural connections will be about the same as in adulthood. In this way, the learning that takes place in early childhood has a chance to shape the growing brain.

During the first years of life, there is a massive increase in the brain's size. By two years of age, the size of the brain and the relative proportions of its parts are basically the same as those of an adult. The brain of a typical full-term infant weighs 350g (12oz) at birth; 1kg (2lb 4oz) at the end of the first year; 1.2kg (2lb 11oz) at age 6; about 1.3kg (3lb) at puberty; and about 1.5kg (3lb 5oz) at adulthood. The virtual trebling of brain weight during the first year is a growth rate unique to humans, owing to the fact that all human babies are born with relatively immature brains – if the brain was any larger, the baby's head would be unable to pass through the mother's birth canal. The rapid increase in size is mainly due to three changes: the growth of pre-existing neurons; production of the many supporting glial cells between the neurons; and a thickening of the sheaths (myelination) around the axons that link neurons together.

Mental development

In early childhood, many important changes occur in the brain that explain the way we behave, remember and think about ourselves. In general, the process of mental maturation starts in the more primitive structures in the middle of the brain and continues upwards and outwards. For example, young babies display simple emotional reactions owing to activity in the limbic system (which is involved in instinct and mood), even though they are not yet conscious of their emotions. Older babies develop the ability to recognise and understand simple spatial relationships, such as when adults play 'peek-a-boo' – hiding an object and surprising the baby

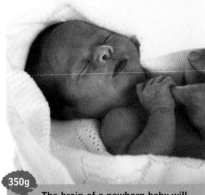

NEWBORN

350g

The brain of a newborn baby will almost treble in weight in the first 12 months of life.

AGE 1

1kg

At one year, babies can control many voluntary movements, thanks to development in the frontal lobes.

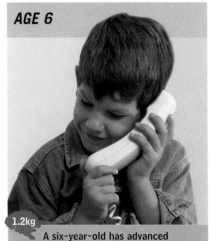

AGE 6

1.2kg

A six-year-old has advanced verbal abilities because the language areas of the brain are well developed.

AGE 13

1.3kg During puberty, hormones play an important role in brain development, as well as altering physical appearance.

AGE 18

1.5kg In young adults, the prefrontal lobes – which are involved in judgment and behaviour – may not be fully mature.

AGE 75

1.35kg By the age of 75, brain weight is declining. However, many cognitive abilities remain as good as ever.

when it reappears. This occurs when the parietal cortex (the outer, side part of the brain) becomes active. The frontal lobes also become active during the first year, so that a baby will start to make simple decisions, such as choosing between two toys.

Language and memory

During the second year, development in Wernicke's area (a part of the cortex on the left side of the brain) enables a child to begin to understand spoken language. Some months later, increasing maturity of Broca's area, which is situated close by, allows the child to start to speak. This is why children are usually able to understand what is said to them before they can speak themselves. It may also partly explain why, around the age of two, toddlers are prone to frustration and even tantrums – they don't yet have the verbal abilities to explain what they want. However, this is usually a brief period of just a few months, and children then go on to develop impressive verbal skills in a very short time: by the age of six they will have a large vocabulary and, even more impressively, be able to understand and use the majority of grammatical rules – such as creating plurals and using past, present and future tenses, without even being aware of what they are doing.

One reason why most of us cannot remember much of our first two or three years of life is because the hippocampus – where the brain stores long-term memories – does not mature until then. However, some emotional experiences from early childhood may be stored in the amygdala, which may be functioning shortly after birth – although these will only ever be recalled as emotional states, rather than explicit memories. The fact that our earliest conscious memories generally date from the age of two or three may also be connected to the development of language and the emergence of a sense of self-awareness, which occurs from around 18 months of age onwards.

FACT FILE

AN AGEING POPULATION

Today, people in the developed world are living longer and retaining their health better than any previous generation. This is demonstrated by the dramatic rise in the proportion of older people in the population in the last few decades:

• The number of people aged 80 or over in the UK:
in 1961: 1 million (1 per cent)
in 1991: 2.2 million (4 per cent)

• The number of people aged 100 or over in the UK:
in 1951: 271
in 1971: 1185
in 1991: 4400
in 1997: over 8000
in 2001 (estimated): 12,000

• The greatest age ever attained by a person that can be verified by reliable records was the 122 years reached by Jeanne-Louise Calment, a French woman, who died in 1997.

Puberty and young adulthood

Puberty is a vital time for brain development, but the hypothalamus (which is central to the body's endocrine and nervous systems) must mature before puberty begins. Although small amounts of sex hormones circulate from the time of birth, during childhood these appear to inhibit the hypothalamus. At puberty the hypothalamic cells become less sensitive to sex hormones and so new hormones – gonadotrophins – are released, which stimulate the production of testosterone by the testes in boys and oestrogen by the ovaries in girls. The sex hormones are then allowed to reach high enough levels to stimulate the growth of secondary sex characteristics and to support mating behaviour.

Certain areas of the brain do not mature for many years. For example, one reason that children often have a short attention span may be due to the fact that the reticular formation (at the base of the brain) does not fully develop until puberty or even later. Similarly, the reason that younger adults are often more emotional and impulsive than older people may be because of the relatively late development of prefrontal lobe areas, where rational processing of emotion takes place.

The older brain

Between the ages of 20 and 75, it is estimated that an average of 50,000 neurons die each day. In a healthy person, this loss adds up to roughly 10 per cent of the original neuronal complement. By the age of 75, the physical weight of the brain is about nine-tenths of its maximum and blood flow through the brain has reduced by almost one-fifth. A loss of neurons does not necessarily mean a comparable loss of function, however – some loss

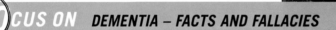

FOCUS ON DEMENTIA – FACTS AND FALLACIES

The term 'dementia' covers a group of diseases that affect the normal functions of the brain, causing memory loss, confusion and personality changes.

• Some degree of dementia is thought to exist in about 10 per cent of people over 65 and 20 per cent of over-75s. Alzheimer's disease – a progressive form of dementia – is diagnosed in 80 per cent of these cases.

• The main symptom of Alzheimer's is intellectual impairment, the first indication being defective short-term memory. Loss of other intellectual functions, such as an inability to concentrate, follows, together with personality changes.

• It is a myth that Alzheimer's disease only affects old people. Although usually diagnosed later in life, particularly over the age of 70, initial signs may appear as early as the mid-30s. Early diagnosis may help prevent further problems and many symptoms can be treated with modern drugs that boost neurotransmitter function.

• Evidence suggests that Alzheimer's patients who keep mentally active can maintain their thinking abilities. Reading, writing and attending adult education classes could all help.

> **"It put Mum under so much stress. It's like having another child to look after. Sometimes though you have to laugh. I mean, Gran really believes I want to steal her underwear!"**
>
> Lizzie, 16, whose grandmother
> has Alzheimer's disease

Mental gymnastics Keeping the brain active throughout life, from youth to old age, is vital. Playing cerebral games such as chess is an ideal way to challenge the brain and maintain healthy neural networks.

may be compensated for by the formation from viable neurons of new branches of nerve fibres and by the production of new synapses. Thus, by learning new things and solving problems we can maintain or even improve brain function – new connections are created whenever we learn something new, but if we do not stimulate our brains the connections will become depleted. As we get older, our brains do become less adaptable, but nevertheless, there are no known limits to the amount of information we can store or the amount of learning we can enjoy through life.

One reason why people sometimes feel less capable as they get older is because, in the West, there is often a belief that ageing causes a decline in intellect. In contrast, elderly Chinese people are held in high esteem, valued for their life-long knowledge and wisdom. A 1994 study found that a group of old people in China performed much better on memory tests than an equivalent US group. The researchers concluded that negative stereotypes about ageing can become self-fulfilling prophecies – in other words, the low expectations of elderly Americans meant that they were not inclined to continue with activities that would help them to maintain good memories.

Differences between the sexes

There are some sex differences in ageing: overall, men lose their brain tissue earlier than women and lose more of it. This particularly applies to the frontal and temporal lobes – areas concerned with thinking and feeling. This could account for some of the personality changes that often characterise older men, such as irritability. Women, on the other hand, tend to lose brain tissue in the hippocampus and parietal areas – where memory and visual-spatial abilities are located. This could explain why some elderly women have difficulty remembering things and finding their way about.

 TRY IT YOURSELF   HOW OLD ARE YOU?

There are many different concepts of age. Try answering the following questions truthfully to see how much variation there is for you:

1. What is your **chronological** age (your actual age in years)?
2. What is your **biological age** (based on your physical appearance)?
3. What is your **subjective** age (based on how old you feel inside)?
4. What is your **functional** age (determined by your lifestyle, interests, family life, status in society and so on)?

5. How old do you think other people believe you are?

You will probably find that you give different ages for some or all of these questions, but this apparent inconsistency is quite normal. Generally, from the age of about 20 onwards, we usually describe ourselves as feeling younger than we actually are – and that applies even to people in their 70s and 80s. This could suggest that chronological age is relatively unimportant when it comes to talking about the well-being of your brain.

When it comes to keeping your brain fit, the adage 'use it or lose it' applies. The questions below are aimed at helping you decide how well your brain functions in seven key areas. Answer them honestly and see what you score in each category.

HOW FIT IS YOUR BRAIN?

If you have only one 'yes' answer in any category (or none at all), you may want to build up your mental fitness in that area – so check the suggestions for activities to help you develop your brain power. But remember, we are all better at some things than others, so don't expect to excel in all areas.

YES NO

VISUAL/SPATIAL SKILLS

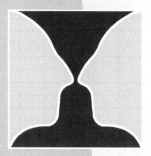

Do you usually see pictures in your mind's eye when you read a book or listen to a piece of music? ☐ ☐

Do you have a good sense of direction? ☐ ☐

Do you find it easy to 'see' visual illusions? ☐ ☐

You can improve your visual and spatial skills by:

• Doing the map reading on a long car journey or to somewhere new – see if you can plan the route and navigate to your destination.
• Joining a sketching or life-drawing class and learning how to represent what you see visually.

VERBAL SKILLS

Are you good at convincing someone of your point of view? ☐ ☐

Is a verbal sense of humour one of your strong points? ☐ ☐

Do you find others ask your advice on grammar, spelling, or the meaning of uncommon words? ☐ ☐

You can improve your verbal skills by:

• Becoming active in a group or society that interests you; having to put across your point of view to a group will make you think how to present it.
• Taking up writing short stories, poetry, or even letters to friends; this will help you to develop ways of expressing your thoughts and feelings in a creative and evocative way.

LOGICAL/MATHS SKILLS

Do you prefer logical ways of looking at life? ☐ ☐

Are you good at working out what legal documents mean? ☐ ☐

Do you quite enjoy doing arithmetic and mathematics? ☐ ☐

You can improve your logical and mathematical skills by:

• Challenging yourself with puzzle and problem-solving books.
• Not always using your calculator but practising your mental arithmetic skills while at home and at work.

YES NO

BODILY/MOVEMENT SKILLS

Can you catch a ball with one hand?

Do you find dance steps easy to learn?

Are you reasonably good at sports?

You can improve your bodily and movement skills by:

• Taking up a game like tennis, badminton or table tennis and playing against partners of a similar standard.

• Joining a keep-fit, line-dancing or other dance class — not only will you get fit but you will also improve your coordination.

MUSICAL SKILLS

Can you tell whether your favourite artists are playing or singing simply from their sound?

Do you find it easy to keep to the rhythm when dancing?

Can you remember the melodies of songs after just one or two hearings?

You can improve your musical and rhythmic skills by:

• Joining a music appreciation class.

• Learning to play a musical instrument, or joining a local choir — it won't matter if your voice is not very strong as it will develop in time.

INTERPERSONAL SKILLS

Do you often find yourself naturally seeing things from other people's points of view?

Are you good at not giving away your feelings?

Do you find you can anticipate what people will say or do?

You can improve your interpersonal skills by:

• Trying to find different ways of understanding why someone has behaved in a particular way — irrespective of its effect on you.

• Considering how your words or actions might affect someone.

INTRAPERSONAL SKILLS

Do you find you can usually explain how your own feelings arise?

Do you find it easy to change yourself when you realise that change is needed?

Do you especially like 'psychological' films or novels that focus on people's motives and emotions?

You can improve your intrapersonal skills by:

• Sharing your reflections about yourself with someone who knows you well — they may have a more objective viewpoint.

• Reading self-help books that focus on emotions such as anger or anxiety that you experience frequently.

LIFE EVENTS

Throughout our lives, we encounter significant 'life events'. While every person is unique, there are certain occurrences that will be experienced by nearly everyone – such as forming close relationships, changing jobs and coming to terms with bereavement. Reactions to such events can have a major bearing on mental well-being.

Research has found that there are widespread similarities in how people rate the upset caused by significant life events, regardless of differences in age, gender and religion. For example, events such as marital separation, divorce and bereavement are all ranked as highly stressful.

Marriage and parenthood

Two significant life events which tend to occur in early adulthood are marriage and parenthood. The vast majority of adults marry at least once, and research shows that marriage has both psychological and physical benefits. A US study found that twice as many married people described themselves as being 'very happy', compared to those who had never married. Sadly, about 40 per cent of marriages in the UK – and even more in the USA – end in divorce, with rates being highest during the first five years of marriage and peaking again after 15–25 years. Of course, for some people, divorce can be a relief from an unbearable situation.

Parenthood usually starts when people are in their 20s or 30s and, in Western societies, is experienced by about 90 per cent of people. Having a child can vary more in personal impact and meaning than any other life

FOCUS ON   *ERIKSON'S EIGHT LIFE STAGES*

According to the US psychoanalyst Erik Erikson, we all go through eight stages of psychosocial development, each stage involving a central personal or social relationship. Erikson believed there is much variation in how people cope with each stage, and that this influences how they cope with subsequent stages.

Age 0–1 Stage 1 is characterised by trust in self and others. Social focus: mother.

Age 2–3 Stage 2 is characterised by increasing independence. Social focus: parents.

Age 4–5 Stage 3 is characterised by showing initiative. Social focus: family.

Age 6–12 Stage 4 is characterised by industry and working hard. Social focuses: school, friends and home.

Childhood: Erikson's stages 1–4

event. The American psychologists Jeffrey Turner and Donald Helms suggest four reasons why many people have children: to experience a sense of achievement; to give and receive love; to fulfil cultural expectations; and to gain a sense of importance.

Unemployment and retirement

Another critical life event is unemployment. This may lead to anxiety and depression, and there can be damage to self-esteem, especially if the reason for unemployment is felt to be personal incompetence, or if redundancy occurs with little or no warning. Another major factor is the reduction in social support owing to the loss of contact with colleagues. To counter such problems, it is important for anyone who is made redundant to keep active and to seek the help of friends and professionals. With positive attitude redundancy can even lead to new and stimulating opportunities, such as moving into another area of work entirely.

Retirement, which usually happens in late adulthood is usually anticipated, and experienced without too much psychological upheaval. There is often an immediate feeling of release and celebration – a 'honeymoon period' – but there is also a danger that this may be followed by emptiness and frustration if positive steps are not taken to adjust. It is important to develop a realistic and flexible view of life's alternatives and to become actively involved in a new lifestyle, by pursuing personal interests, for example, or getting involved with the community.

THINK AGAIN!

THE EMPTY NEST SYNDROME

Some parents, especially mothers, have in the past reported a period of depression when the youngest child grows up and finally leaves home. This may have been due in part to society's view of women primarily as mothers.

However, recent research suggests that most parents today do not find their children's departure from home a distressing time – far from it, in fact. Many report that it is a liberating experience, and they welcome the new opportunities it brings, such as a closer relationship with their partner, returning to education and pursuing hobbies and interests.

Age 13–19 Stage 5 is characterised by the development of identity. Social focus: peer group.

Age 20–30 Stage 6 is characterised by a commitment to intimacy. Social focus: friendship.

Age 30–60 Stage 7 is characterised by productivity (for self and society). Social focus: household.

60+ years Stage 8 is characterised by the gaining of wisdom. Social focus: humanity.

Adolescence and adulthood: Erikson's stages 5–8

PSYCHOLOGICAL DEFENCES

To cope with what life throws at us, we develop 'psychological defences' – patterns of behaviour that can lessen our anxieties in response to what is going on. These defences are often automatic and unconscious, but are vital in allowing us to get on with our lives.

PIONEERS

SIGMUND FREUD

A fundamental part of Freud's approach to the mind was the division of the mind into three parts: id, ego and superego. Freud believed that the ego – the conscious, rational part of the mind – developed defence mechanisms to protect itself and to reduce anxiety. Today, psychologists talk in terms of 'coping strategies' rather than defence mechanisms.

Sigmund Freud (1856–1939)

Sigmund Freud, the father of psychoanalysis, described psychological defence mechanisms which we all employ to protect ourselves from thoughts and experiences that could be psychologically damaging. For example, denial prevents us from thinking about unwanted, threatening or otherwise unpleasant situations or feelings. In everyday life, and in small doses, this can be useful – such as not dwelling on the possible dangers when riding a motorcycle. A reasonable level of denial allows us to remain optimistic and able to cope in most circumstances. Sometimes, however, denial can be unhelpful: for example, when a heavy drinker won't admit that he or she has a problem.

Another defence mechanism is repression – pushing down into the unconscious unacceptable fears or wishes. Again, in moderation, this is necessary for psychological survival. If we were constantly aware of all the traumas and tragedies that we have experienced, then we would find it hard to get on with our lives. Repression allows us to cope, even after traumatic events such as bereavement. As with denial, too

★ FREUDIAN ★ DEFENCES IN ★ ACTION ☆

7:30am: DENIAL John skips breakfast and instead lights up his first cigarette of the day. In refusing to acknowledge the long-term health consequences of his smoking, he doesn't accept the reality of his situation.

8:30am: REGRESSION John is late for work. He feels aggrieved at being told off, but rather than explaining why he was delayed, he reacts by reverting to sullen, childish behaviour.

1.00pm: DISPLACEMENT Still upset by the dressing-down he received earlier on, John snaps at his secretary. He has displaced his bottled-up anger about his boss to a less threatening target.

THINK AGAIN!

JAPANESE WISDOM

Hiroshi Azuma, a Japanese psychologist, has suggested using the advice from old Japanese proverbs to help accept things we cannot change or control. Examples include the following:

• **Willow trees do not get broken by piled up snow** (being flexible prevents us from being 'broken').

• **To lose is to win** (giving in to someone shows the superior traits of self-control, tolerance and generosity).

• **True tolerance is to tolerate the intolerable** (some things that are 'intolerable' are facts of life).

By applying these principles at home, at work or in social situations, we could perhaps protect and improve our relationships with others.

much repression can be harmful, but most of the time, our minds are very good at protecting us, enabling us to forget past events and 'move on'.

Other Freudian defence mechanisms include sublimation, projection, rationalisation and regression. Sublimation is the redirection of unacceptable thoughts or impulses into acceptable actions: for example, going to the gym or digging the garden after an argument rather than venting the frustration on someone else. Projection is the means by which a person attributes their own unpleasant thoughts or impulses to another individual – for example, a parent who is afraid of heights might say to a child 'you won't like that roller coaster, it will make you sick!', thus avoiding the potentially unpleasant experience. In rationalisation, threatening ideas and explanations of behaviour are replaced by non-threatening ones – a persistent gambler might convince himself he is doing it to win money for his family. Finally, regression means reverting to an earlier stage of psychological development when under stress – in other words, becoming more child-like, such as an older child starting to act younger when a new baby arrives in order to get more of the parents' attention.

3:00pm: RATIONALISATION Over coffee John tells a friend why he failed his driving test the previous week. But his apparently rational explanation does not give the real reason: he failed because he was unprepared.

6:00pm: SUBLIMATION After work, John heads for the sports centre. He uses his anger and frustration over his unsatisfactory day at work to convincingly beat his neighbour at squash.

8:30pm: PROJECTION At a drinks party, John feels socially awkward. He projects his own negative feelings onto the other people there, and blames them for not wanting to talk to him.

DAMAGE AND REPAIR

The human brain, like the rest of the body, can be damaged in a variety of ways – through physical injury, or disease, or genetic inheritance. Yet the brain has remarkable powers of self-healing and adaptation, and is often able to regain its function after damage.

As we go through life, our brains can be physically affected by influences from inside and outside the body. While the brain is equipped with protective mechanisms (see page 150), sometimes these are not quite enough. Sometimes, too, brains do not get the best start in life, as certain genetic diseases (those passed on through the genes) can affect the brain. Damage to the brain caused by genetic problems is often apparent at birth or in early childhood. Not all such damage is inherited: it may be caused by chance mutations, or problems in the way the genetic material from sperm and egg combines at conception, such as in Down's syndrome. When genetic diseases are inherited, it may be many years before the symptoms are noticed – as, for example, in Huntington's disease, which often does not appear until the person reaches the 30s or 40s. Some diseases that cause neural damage may have a genetic component but are not directly inherited – for example, multiple sclerosis and Alzheimer's disease.

Damage through life

Over 90 per cent of people over 65 show little deterioration in mental abilities, and even very late in life nerve cells in the brain seem capable of forming new connections with other neurons. This continuous building of connections between brain cells is what happens during lifelong learning, and it is a powerful argument for the importance of education throughout adulthood.

It is true, however, that certain mental abilities, such as being able to solve new problems, seem to collectively decline somewhat later in life. These abilities, referred to by psychologists as 'fluid intelligence', may be affected by a natural process of reduced efficiency in the functioning of brain cells as we get older. There are several theories about why this deterioration occurs in the brain as well as the body. One recent theory focuses on the role of mitochondria. These miniature 'energy generators' exist in most human cells, producing the energy required for general tissue maintenance and specialist usage, such as the needs of muscle cells. It is known that decreased muscle use results in fewer mitochondria in the cells, which in turn leads to a decreased muscle capacity. Future research will perhaps determine whether a similar process of diminishment occurs in the brain. If that proves to be the case, then it may be possible to find ways to stop or even reverse the age-related decline in energy production by exercising the brain.

FOCUS ON BOXING AND BRAIN DAMAGE

Although boxing continues to be popular, many people feel that an activity whose main objective is to injure one's opponent – and if possible render him unconscious – is unacceptable in a civilised society. For these reasons, professional boxing has been banned in some countries, including Sweden, Norway and Iceland.

Despite stricter medical supervision in recent years, professional boxers are still regularly disabled by brain damage sustained in the ring, and the 'punch-

drunk' syndrome (post-traumatic encephalopathy) continues to occur. Amateur boxing also involves repeated blows to the head that can cause short and long-term brain damage, in spite of the widespread use of headguards.

As numerous medical reports from around the world have shown, any severe blow to the head causes concussion and the death of brain cells. There will also be cases when, as a result of head injury, the nerve fibres separate. This leads to dementia, a slow,

shuffling gait and parkinsonism, a syndrome with symptoms and signs resembling those of Parkinson's disease. The former world heavyweight champion Muhammad Ali is the most famous sufferer of this syndrome.

FACT FILE

THE DANGERS OF ALCOHOL

• Short-term harmful effects of alcohol on the brain include dehydration of nerve cells and functional problems such as temporary loss of memory.

• Chronic alcohol abuse may lead to major personality changes including a decline in intellectual abilities and social skills, as well as severe memory loss (amnesia).

• Approximately half of all motor vehicle fatalities in the developed world are alcohol-related. In the UK, 0.8g/litre (80mg/dl) is the maximum permissible blood alcohol level for driving; levels are lower in other countries.

• Alcohol is involved in about 30 per cent of all suicides and plays a particularly significant role in adolescent suicide.

• Excessive drinking in pregnancy can cause foetal alcohol syndrome, leading to problems in newborn babies.

Other sources of brain damage include physical injury; infection; exposure to toxic substances (including drugs and alcohol); and inadequate nutrition, such as vitamin deficiencies. All of these factors can cause different degrees of damage, depending partly on individual susceptibility.

Among neurological diseases, multiple sclerosis (MS) is the most common such disease in young adults, affecting the central nervous system. The main problem is the breakdown of the myelin sheath around nerve fibres. This slows down and interrupts normal signals between nerve cells, typically causing a gradual deterioration of sensory input to the brain – for example, loss of vision owing to optic nerve damage – and movement difficulties. However, the disease is not always progressive, and treatments are available to help with the symptoms, including many complementary therapies. Some people with MS have found cannabis helpful, and research on substances contained in cannabis is continuing with the hope of developing a useful – and eventually legal – drug.

Re-establishing connections

When neurons are destroyed, by whatever means, they cannot be replaced by new nerve cells. However, the human brain is very adaptable and, in the event of damage to some neurons, new connections from other surviving cells can grow, thereby taking over the functions of missing cells and bypassing areas of damage. This is the means by which stroke victims can sometimes overcome, or at least reduce, the physical disabilities that a stroke has caused (see page 148).

The formation of new connections in the brain is achieved by the growth of dendrites and axons from nerve cells. The smaller branches – the dendrites – grow out of the cell body, enabling each neuron to connect to hundreds or even thousands of others. Each neuron also has at least one axon, which can be anything from a fraction of a millimetre in length to a metre or more. Dendrites receive signals from other cells, whereas axons

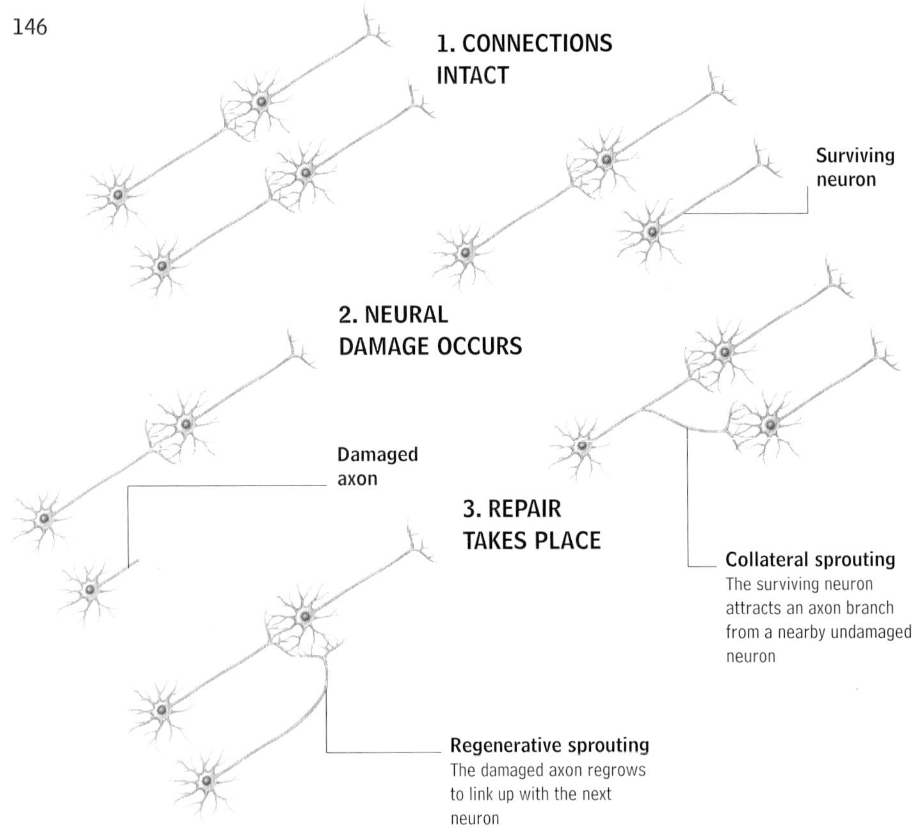

1. CONNECTIONS INTACT

Surviving neuron

2. NEURAL DAMAGE OCCURS

Damaged axon

3. REPAIR TAKES PLACE

Collateral sprouting
The surviving neuron attracts an axon branch from a nearby undamaged neuron

Regenerative sprouting
The damaged axon regrows to link up with the next neuron

Making reconnections After the death or injury of brain cells, new connections can be made in two ways: a neuron can redirect its existing axon to a surviving neuron (regenerative sprouting), or a neuron can grow an additional axon branch (collateral sprouting).

send signals to other cells. When nerve cells are damaged, it is therefore possible for other neurons to take over their functions by establishing new connections. The quality of connections in the brain is crucial. When a nerve cell sends a signal along its axon to another cell, the speed of the signal depends on the diameter of the axon and the thickness of the myelin sheath that surrounds and insulates it. In a healthy person, the speed of nerve conduction can be up to 220 miles per hour (350 km/h). However, when the myelin sheath is damaged, as occurs in MS, then the nerve signals slow down or may be prevented from reaching their destination altogether.

Glial cells: a supporting role

Apart from the neurons, other cells in the brain – particularly the glial cells – have an important supporting role in keeping the brain functioning. There are approximately ten times as many glial cells as neurons, and they are grouped into different types, each with specific functions. One type form the myelin sheath around axons, acting as insulators to speed up nerve signals. Another type, the macrophage, is particularly useful when damage occurs because it helps remove the debris of dead cells. A third type, the astrocytes, help to protect neurons by 'sponging up' any excessive or toxic chemicals, ensuring that neurons have a healthy environment. If a neuron is damaged, astrocytes will increase in size and number and release chemicals to aid neural growth and repair.

CREATING A HEALING GARDEN

The idea of a healing garden is to create a haven of peace and beauty. The benefits of such a garden are becoming increasingly recognised, as people realise that relaxation in a spiritually restful environment can maintain mental well-being and even enhance recovery. The therapeutic effects of plants have been known about for thousands of years, and modern-day healing gardens should be filled with plants and flowers that stimulate the senses with their fragrance and colour. With a little effort, any ordinary garden can be transformed into a healing garden. This is one possible design, incorporating some of the features that are believed to be beneficial.

LIFE AFTER STROKE

Stroke is one of the commonest causes of brain damage. However, the effects of stroke are not, as was once assumed, necessarily irreversible. Brains – even older ones – are incredibly 'plastic' and, with the right encouragement, they can rewire themselves to compensate for the damaged part. Research has shown that the brain can generate new connections after a stroke and recover some of its lost abilities.

Stroke occurs when a major blood vessel in the brain becomes blocked, or ruptures. This reduces the supply of blood and oxygen to the brain tissue, killing brain cells. Even a brief interruption to the blood flow can decrease brain function. If the interruption lasts for more than a few seconds, cells are destroyed, causing permanent damage to that area of the brain.

Varied effects of stroke

The effects of stroke depend on the amount of tissue damaged and the region of the brain in which it occurs. With some strokes, a few moments of dizziness or pain is all that the victim is aware of. But a major stroke can knock out a large part of the brain, producing radical changes in a person's behaviour or abilities. A stroke in the area that controls movement, for example, may paralyse a limb or even one side of the body. A stroke in Broca's area in the left hemisphere will disrupt speech, while one further back in Wernicke's area will cause problems with understanding language. Front-brain damage often results in personality changes, such as depression or, conversely, permanent optimism. Damage to the temporal lobes may remove a very specific type of knowledge, such as names of people and places, while a stroke deep in the limbic system may eradicate personal memories.

> **"The widespread misconception that nothing can be done about stroke is being swept aside as new prospects for prevention, acute treatment and rehabilitation come to the fore."**
>
> Scrip report on stroke, 1998

Recovery and regrowth

Recovery after stroke can be slow, difficult and sometimes only partial. However, it appears that healthy brain tissue can often take over the tasks of damaged adjacent regions. Research using magnetic resonance imaging (MRI) to find out which parts of the brain take over from damaged areas is helping to predict how much recovery is possible and whether rehabilitation is worthwhile. In the right circumstances, and with the right

Real lives

RECOVERING FROM A STROKE

Although stroke is usually associated with old age, it can affect much younger people. David Hinds suffered a stroke at the age of 49. He vividly described how he came to realise one morning what had happened to him.

'When, as if in a dream – or rather a nightmare – I probed myself disbelievingly with a finger that worked, I discovered that one corner of my mouth was an inch higher than the other. I cursed and swore, or rather I tried to, but all that would come out was gibberish! It dawned on me that I was living a nightmare, not dreaming it.'

David went on to make a full recovery. Originally employed as a successful stress-management consultant, he used many of the techniques from his profession to help him in his recovery.

*F*OCUS ON   *RHYTHM THERAPY*

New therapy approaches are helping stroke victims to recover lost abilities. Rhythm therapy involves colour recognition, sound and word enunciation, and physical movements, with an emphasis on rhythmic foundations.

Developed by a jazz drummer, and recognised by the Swedish medical establishment, rhythm therapy has been shown to enhance short-term memory, improve movement control and help impaired speech.

Patients learn sequences of music and movements, beginning with easy sequences and gradually increasing the complexity and speed. The therapist helps them to follow the sequences, using coloured symbols that represent different parts of the body. Patients say what the colour symbol is while performing the corresponding movement in time to the rhythm.

A major advantage of rhythm therapy is that it's fun, allowing the brain to be challenged in an enjoyable way. And it seems to work: the all-round activity stimulates the growth of healthy new connections, creating alternative paths around damaged areas.

FACT FILE

PREVENTING STROKE

Factors known to increase the risk of stroke include high blood pressure, high cholesterol, old age, diabetes, obesity, a previous 'mini-stroke', heart disease, smoking and heavy alcohol use. While some factors (such as age) cannot be changed, there are ways to reduce the risk of other factors:
• Have your blood pressure checked regularly, and take steps to keep it in the normal range.
• If you are diabetic, ensure that your blood sugar is well controlled.
• Don't smoke.
• Lower your cholesterol by reducing your intake of fatty, high-cholesterol foods.
• Exercise regularly (but check with your doctor first).
• Drink only in moderation.

attitude and support, dramatic improvements can be made in quality of life. Wherever the damage occurs, the brain has an in-built capacity for self-repair, and one of the primary ways of triggering this is through therapy. This can be either physical or mental, but the aim of all therapies is to encourage the development of new connections. On a large scale, these new connections lead to whole brain areas taking on tasks previously carried out by damaged areas. In some people with language problems, for example, the brain reorganises itself so that the right hemisphere takes over the task of processing words. This is more likely to happen in women than men because a greater proportion of women already have language abilities in both brain hemispheres, instead of just one.

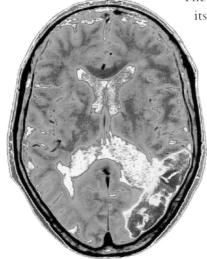

The extent to which the brain can rewire itself depends largely on age: the younger the brain, the more readily it recovers. However, stimulation, practice and novelty can 'excite' even older brains. Whatever your age, the more active you keep your brain, the more chance it has of compensating if it is damaged.

Self-repair The area affected by stroke is vividly shown up on this MRI scan, with affected tissue coloured red. In some cases, the brain is able to re-establish connections and regain abilities that were lost.

PROTECTING YOUR BRAIN

The outer part of the brain – the cerebral cortex – is responsible for the brain's higher functions: consciousness, thinking and interpreting the senses. The delicate tissue of the cortex is extremely vulnerable, so nature has provided protection on three levels: physical, chemical and biological.

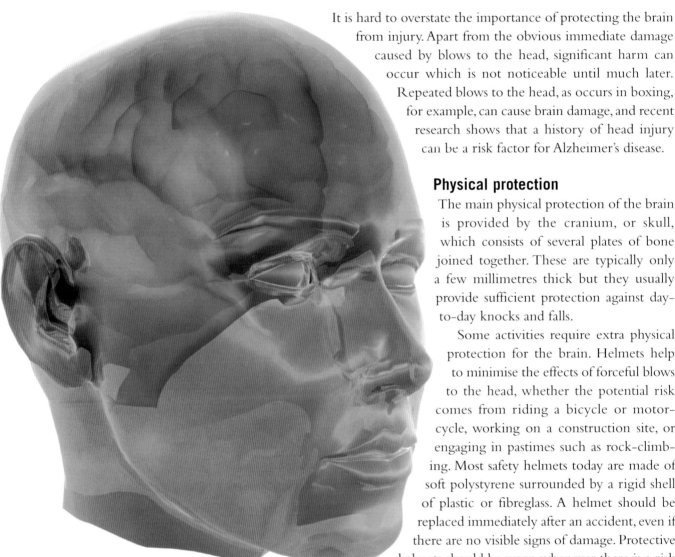

It is hard to overstate the importance of protecting the brain from injury. Apart from the obvious immediate damage caused by blows to the head, significant harm can occur which is not noticeable until much later. Repeated blows to the head, as occurs in boxing, for example, can cause brain damage, and recent research shows that a history of head injury can be a risk factor for Alzheimer's disease.

Physical protection

The main physical protection of the brain is provided by the cranium, or skull, which consists of several plates of bone joined together. These are typically only a few millimetres thick but they usually provide sufficient protection against day-to-day knocks and falls.

Some activities require extra physical protection for the brain. Helmets help to minimise the effects of forceful blows to the head, whether the potential risk comes from riding a bicycle or motor-cycle, working on a construction site, or engaging in pastimes such as rock-climbing. Most safety helmets today are made of soft polystyrene surrounded by a rigid shell of plastic or fibreglass. A helmet should be replaced immediately after an accident, even if there are no visible signs of damage. Protective helmets should be worn whenever there is a risk of physical injury, but there are limits to the protection they provide. Since the brain is fairly fluid in consistency, it can easily be damaged by being shaken within the skull, as often happens in road accidents.

Delicate structure The brain sits within the hard, protective covering of the skull. Other mechanisms that serve to shield the brain from damage include the meninges membranes and cerebrospinal fluid.

Chemical protection

Nature has provided the brain with protection from many poisonous chemicals in the form of the blood-brain barrier. This acts like a filter to keep harmful substances out of the brain and consists of glial cells (which make up the bulk of the brain tissue) wrapped around the tiny blood vessels in the brain. The barrier is so constructed that molecules must effectively pass through two semi-permeable membranes to transfer from the blood to the brain. Useful chemicals – oxygen, carbon dioxide and most fat-soluble molecules – can readily pass through the blood-brain barrier. Alcohol can also pass through, which is why excessive drinking over many years can damage the brain and lead to psychological problems.

The adult blood-brain barrier is permeable to certain substances which the brain needs for health (such as sodium, potassium, and chloride), but is not permeable to large molecules, such as proteins. The blood-brain barrier in children is less well developed, however, so young brains are more sensitive to certain toxic water-soluble compounds, such as those of mercury and lead. This is why the use of lead – for example in paint, water pipes and petrol – has been banned or restricted in many countries.

Biological protection

The brain and spinal cord are completely surrounded by three protective membrane layers called the meninges, which are bathed in a clear watery liquid called cerebrospinal fluid.

Despite the protection offered by the meninges and the blood-brain barrier, the brain can still be infected by bacteria and viruses – the herpes simplex virus, for example. These infections can cause inflammation of the brain (encephalitis), with typical symptoms of headache, fever, seizures, speech difficulties, confusion and even coma. Good hygiene measures – such as careful hand-washing – help to prevent the spread of infection from person to person, and modern drugs can target specific infections once diagnosed. To reduce the risk of such infections arising in the first place, health professionals recommend that all children receive vaccinations for common infections such as measles, mumps and rubella (German measles), all of which carry a risk, albeit small, of brain damage.

Real lives **'MY HELMET SAVED MY LIFE!'**

Lucy, a 15-year-old student, used to hate it when her mother told her to wear a cycle helmet. However, an accident soon changed her mind:

'I didn't like to wear a cycle helmet, because I didn't think it looked… cool. But I'm really glad now! A few months ago, I was cycling along when a car suddenly pulled out in front of me. I couldn't avoid it and went flying over the handlebars into another car. My head hit the door handle before I hit the ground. At first I didn't know what had happened, but when I took my helmet off and saw the huge dent in the top, I realised that could have been my head with a hole in it! At the hospital, the doctor said there's no doubt that the helmet saved my life, or at least saved me from serious brain damage. Now I always wear my helmet, even on short trips.'

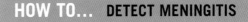

HOW TO… DETECT MENINGITIS ?

Meningitis is an infection by bacteria or viruses of the meninges membranes surrounding the brain. It is potentially fatal and early detection is vital. The main symptoms are:

- High temperature
- Severe headache
- Stiff neck
- Photophobia (extreme sensitivity to light)
- Nausea and vomiting
- A blotchy red skin rash that does not fade when a glass tumbler is pressed against it (in bacterial meningitis only).

Anyone suffering from these symptoms – which can occur in any combination, and are not always all present – should be treated as an emergency, requiring urgent hospital care.

MIND MEDICINES

The brain has a delicate balance of complex chemicals which can be altered by everyday substances, such as caffeine, as well as by over-the-counter and prescribed drugs. Some of these mind medicines are beneficial, but they all need to be taken with due care, whether they are natural or synthetic.

Throughout the world every day, millions of cups of tea and coffee are sipped, and millions of cans of cola are drunk. These drinks all contain caffeine – a mild stimulant that arouses the central nervous system, increasing alertness. While this effect can sometimes be useful, especially if it is necessary to stay awake, many experts argue that people generally consume far more caffeine than is good for them. In some cases, excess caffeine is responsible for psychological problems such as restlessness, nervousness, anxiety and insomnia. Symptoms of too much caffeine include a flushed face and cardiovascular problems, such as a rapid pulse and palpitations. Because caffeine is addictive, people often find that they experience withdrawal effects, including a lack of energy and headaches, if they stop drinking caffeinated drinks. As a general guideline, it is advisable to limit caffeine consumption to two or three cups of coffee a day maximum – with preferably none at all being consumed in the late afternoon or evening to avoid sleep disturbance.

Conventional medicines

Medicines that affect the mind include painkillers (analgesics) and antidepressants. Aspirin (acetylsalicylic acid) was discovered in 1853 in Germany, although similar plant-based substances have been used for centuries. Today, it remains one of the safest and most effective drugs for relieving mild pain, although some people are sensitive to its irritant action on the stomach. Paracetamol is often used as an alternative painkiller to aspirin, mainly because it is less irritating to the stomach. However, its main disadvantage lies in the danger of overdose, which can cause serious irreversible liver damage. Whereas aspirin (and other non-steroidal anti-inflammatory drugs) stops pain

"St John's wort has been shown many times to be more effective than placebo for mild to moderate depression, and as effective as standard antidepressants. However, safety is important."

Edzard Ernst, Professor of Complementary Medicine

impulses travelling from the site of the injury to the brain, paracetamol reduces the perception of pain in the brain itself. Like paracetamol, more potent painkillers such as morphine and other opioid drugs also work by changing the way we think and feel about pain.

Most people become depressed at some time in their lives, especially after bereavement or other loss, and this is considered to be a normal human reaction which will heal in time. However, some people become clinically depressed for no apparent reason, and may benefit from prescribed antidepressants. These drugs relieve the major symptoms of depression, allowing the individual to cope better and perhaps benefit from psychological therapies that may be available in conjunction with the medicine. Other mind medicines include anxiolytics, such as the benzodiazepine drug diazepam (Valium). These widely prescribed drugs can alleviate specific anxiety states, but doses must be kept low in order to reduce the possibility of side effects.

Natural options

The St John's wort plant (*Hypericum perforatum*) has been used as a herbal remedy for depression since the times of the ancient Greeks, who believed that it could drive out evil spirits, and it is once again gaining in popularity. Native to Europe and Asia, the plant has tiny leaves, which contain oil glands, and five-petalled yellow flowers. St John's wort also has antiseptic and anti-inflammatory properties, and is used in both Chinese medicine and homeopathy. However, it should be emphasised that St John's wort is a potent substance: people should always check with their doctor before using it, especially anyone taking other medication and women who are pregnant or breast-feeding.

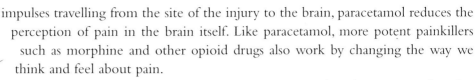

FOCUS ON ANTIDEPRESSANTS

There are three main types of antidepressant drugs in use today:

1. MAOIs (monoamine-oxidase inhibitors)
The first MAOI was discovered in the 1950s, when a tuberculosis drug was found to have antidepressant properties. Research suggested it prevented the breakdown of monoamines (adrenaline, noradrenaline, serotonin and other neurotransmitters) in the brain. Modern MAOIs include phenelzine, iproniazid and tranylcypromine.

2. Tricyclics (and other related drugs)
Tricyclic antidepressants are often preferred to MAOIs as they have fewer side effects. Modern examples include imipramine, which is relatively non-sedating and stimulating, and is used to treat depressed people who are slow and withdrawn. Amitriptyline has more sedative effects and is useful for treating patients who are tense, anxious, irritable and have trouble getting to sleep.

3. SSRIs (selective serotonin re-uptake inhibitors)
As the name suggests, SSRIs work by stopping the re-absorption of serotonin in the nerve cells of the brain, thus allowing more serotonin to be available for longer. This helps because depressed people are thought to have less serotonin than normal. This group includes fluoxetine, marketed as Prozac.

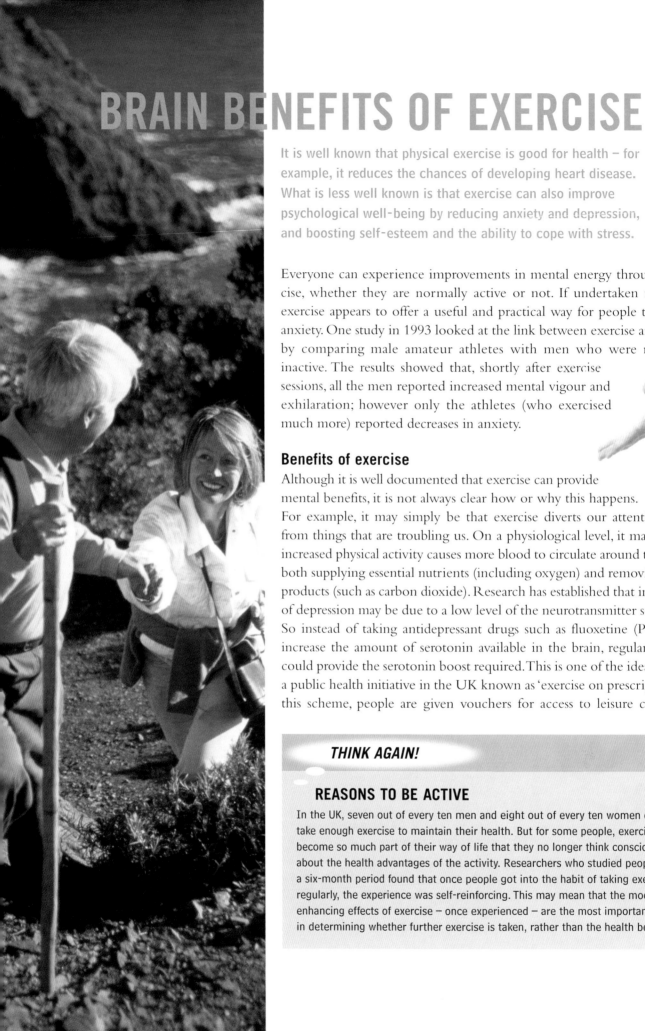

BRAIN BENEFITS OF EXERCISE

It is well known that physical exercise is good for health – for example, it reduces the chances of developing heart disease. What is less well known is that exercise can also improve psychological well-being by reducing anxiety and depression, and boosting self-esteem and the ability to cope with stress.

Everyone can experience improvements in mental energy through exercise, whether they are normally active or not. If undertaken regularly, exercise appears to offer a useful and practical way for people to reduce anxiety. One study in 1993 looked at the link between exercise and mood by comparing male amateur athletes with men who were relatively inactive. The results showed that, shortly after exercise sessions, all the men reported increased mental vigour and exhilaration; however only the athletes (who exercised much more) reported decreases in anxiety.

Benefits of exercise

Although it is well documented that exercise can provide mental benefits, it is not always clear how or why this happens. For example, it may simply be that exercise diverts our attention away from things that are troubling us. On a physiological level, it may be that increased physical activity causes more blood to circulate around the brain, both supplying essential nutrients (including oxygen) and removing waste products (such as carbon dioxide). Research has established that incidences of depression may be due to a low level of the neurotransmitter serotonin. So instead of taking antidepressant drugs such as fluoxetine (Prozac) to increase the amount of serotonin available in the brain, regular exercise could provide the serotonin boost required. This is one of the ideas behind a public health initiative in the UK known as 'exercise on prescription'. In this scheme, people are given vouchers for access to leisure centres or

THINK AGAIN!

REASONS TO BE ACTIVE

In the UK, seven out of every ten men and eight out of every ten women do not take enough exercise to maintain their health. But for some people, exercise has become so much part of their way of life that they no longer think consciously about the health advantages of the activity. Researchers who studied people over a six-month period found that once people got into the habit of taking exercise regularly, the experience was self-reinforcing. This may mean that the mood-enhancing effects of exercise – once experienced – are the most important factor in determining whether further exercise is taken, rather than the health benefits.

appointments with health and fitness advisors. The hope is that more people will be encouraged to exercise regularly and that, in the long term, this will benefit the nation's physical and mental health.

The mental benefits of exercise apply whether the activity is individual or team-based. However, participating in a team sport has the added advantage of social contact. Socialising after the event, and discussing the 'action' afterwards, can provide an added form of relaxation that serves to counter any build-up of stress. Some people, however, prefer to exercise alone or to pursue less formal activities than team sports. Among the most popular pastimes practised today are hill-walking, running and cycling, as well as Eastern disciplines such as yoga and Tai chi.

Exercise addiction?

In addition to health benefits, some forms of exercise can produce a feeling of elation – a 'high'. There is evidence from studies of marathon runners that intense exercise can cause mood-elevating chemicals called endorphins to be released in the brain, and these can remain active for up to three hours. This may help to explain the pleasurable, and possibly even addictive, nature of activities such as running and swimming.

A strong link has even been suggested between physical fitness and sexual energy. A survey by US therapist Linda de Villers of 8000 women aged 18–45 found that after they had exercised three times a week for three months, 80 per cent said they had more sexual confidence, and 25 per cent experienced increased sexual desire. This may be because a workout can stimulate the release of the hormone testosterone, which increases sex drive in both men and women. A general improvement in energy and self-esteem may also be a factor.

TRY IT YOURSELF

FITNESS MADE SIMPLE

• If you are feeling tired or depressed, go for a brisk ten-minute walk. You should find that you feel better and are more able to cope with what you have to do.
• Try to fit in three sessions of moderate physical activity per week of at least 30 minutes each. If possible, space these out throughout the week – every other day, for example. Gradually, the duration and frequency can be increased.
• Find an exercise you enjoy – you are far more likely to stick with it.
• Remember that it is important not to exercise too strenuously or try to do too much too soon. Always check with your doctor or a qualified fitness trainer before starting a new programme of activities.

FACT: People who exercise regularly generally experience less tension, fatigue, anxiety and depression than those who do not.

Brain-enhancing foods

To keep your brain healthy, a good balance of nutrients – proteins, fats and carbohydrates, plus vitamins and minerals – is essential. The right balance in your diet can protect your mental faculties.

Proteins are vital for the brain since neurons, like all our cells, are made from them. Proteins are made from chains of small molecules called amino acids. There are 22 amino acids, of which eight – the essential amino acids – cannot be produced by the body and they must be obtained from food. Good sources of protein include beans, nuts, eggs, milk and cheese, as well as fish and lean meat. Vegetarians and vegans prove it is possible to live healthily without meat or even dairy foods, so long as a varied source of protein is maintained from, for example, pulses and cereals.

Fats insulate nerve cells in the brain and other vital organs – in fact, about one third of the brain is made from fats. The two types of dietary fats, saturated and unsaturated, are classified according to their chemical structure. Vegetable fats are mostly unsaturated, and are particularly important because some of them are used to make essential messenger molecules such as prostaglandins. Animal fats are mainly saturated and, in excess, can contribute to heart disease and other problems. Although fats are a useful source of energy, most experts agree that they should comprise no more than 30 per cent of our calorie intake.

Carbohydrates and the brain

Carbohydrates provide energy and as the brain uses up around a fifth of the body's energy requirements, they are very important for mental functioning. People should try to eat more complex carbohydrates – found in foods such as grains and pulses – and minimise the intake of simple carbohydrates, especially refined sugar. Complex carbohydrates take longer to digest, so they release their energy gradually, providing ongoing energy and stamina. Simple carbohydrates are digested quickly

Packed with energy
Carbohydrates – found in wheat products such as bread – are an important source of energy for the brain

TRYPTOPHAN

Tryptophan is an essential amino acid and it is widely taken as a natural, non-addictive antidepressant sleeping pill. This is because tryptophan – along with vitamins B_3 and B_6, and magnesium – is used to make the important neurotransmitter serotonin, which aids sleep. Tryptophan tablets take about an hour to work, so are often taken in doses of 500mg, along with the other supplements, an hour before bedtime. Natural sources of tryptophan include bananas, dates, peanuts and protein-rich foodstuffs such as eggs, cheese, milk, fish and lean meat. This may be one reason why some people instinctively like milky drinks before they go to bed. Tryptophan is also believed to reduce anxiety, tension and sensitivity to pain.

and can cause too much sugar to be released into the bloodstream. This sudden rise in blood sugar is countered by the release of insulin. The brain is thus alternately flooded and starved of essential glucose, which may lead to unpleasant and potentially dangerous symptoms, including dizziness, anxiety, headaches, thirst, mental confusion and sleepiness.

Benefits of vitamins

Vitamins are essential for many chemical reactions in the body, so vitamin deficiencies can cause illness. While all vitamins are necessary, some are particularly important for mental functions, especially the B vitamins. Vitamin B_1 (thiamine) helps to make the neurotransmitter acetylcholine, making it vital for maintaining an efficient nervous system. Prolonged deficiencies of vitamin B_1 can produce mental disturbances, and there is some evidence of B_1 deficiency being associated with lower levels of intelligence.

Supplements of vitamin B_3 (niacin) can be effective for migraines and headaches, and it has been used to treat schizophrenia. B_5 (pantothenic acid) contributes to acetylcholine production and is believed to boost memory. Vitamin B_5 is also required by the adrenal glands, and so is sometimes known as an 'anti-stress vitamin'. Vitamin B_{12} is needed to make DNA and it helps to form the myelin sheath that insulates nerves; B_{12} deficiency can cause mental disorders.

Dietary minerals

Many minerals are needed for a healthy brain. Minerals are derived from the earth and so, like most vitamins, can be obtained directly from plants or indirectly by eating meat. Calcium, usually associated with healthy bones, is needed by nerves, muscles and blood, as is magnesium. Potassium and sodium work together to maintain water balance and nerve and muscle impulses. Since people often consume too much sodium, they may need more potassium to counterbalance this, from fruit (such as bananas), vegetables and whole grains. Zinc – one of the 'trace elements', minerals that are essential in very small quantities – is necessary for good mental functioning. Extra zinc may be needed if people have too much iron in their diet, or if zinc levels are depleted by stress, alcohol or smoking. Other trace elements needed by the brain include manganese, copper and selenium.

Full of goodness Avocados contain vitamins A, B and C, as well as essential amino acids.

Good fats Oily fish provides essential fatty acids, especially omega-3, which helps prevent strokes.

Healthy nerves Bananas provide potassium, which helps to maintain the activity of the nervous system.

EXERCISING YOUR BRAIN

The brain, like any other organ of the body, needs regular exercise in order to function well and stay healthy. There are many activities in daily life that will keep you mentally fit and boost your brainpower, whatever your age. Four areas of mental activity that are particularly important to all-round mental fitness are language and number skills, reasoning and creativity.

LANGUAGE SKILLS

Do you like adding new words to your vocabulary – or do you stick with familiar words and phrases? Increasing your vocabulary is one of the simplest and most effective ways to keep mentally alert – and it's something that others will notice as a sign of intelligence. If you get into the habit of looking up the meaning of new or unusual words, you'll soon become more precise in your use of language generally.

• Start by treating yourself to a good dictionary, you might like to buy one that gives the derivation of words, as well as their current meanings, as this will show you where their original meaning comes from.

• Check the meaning of words you think you know – you may be surprised! As well as keeping your brain working, thinking more about your choice of words will improve your abilities as a communicator.

• Read books by more literary authors, perhaps from an earlier period, as this will gradually instil an intuitive sense of good grammar.

NUMERICAL SKILLS

Do you regard mental arithmetic as something you gladly left behind with your school days? Everyone can afford a calculator nowadays, but going back to using your head – or pencil and paper – for dealing with figures is a great mental exercise that anyone can do.

• When you next go to the supermarket, keep a running total in your head of what your shopping is going to cost. To make this easier, you can round the cost of items up or down to the nearest pound. Either way, this will help you budget, as well as providing a keep-fit exercise for your brain.

• If you're tempted by some of the points schemes that supermarkets and other businesses use to keep your custom, do a quick calculation to see if you're really saving money. For example, if the supermarket five miles away offers you one point for every pound you spend, and you need 100 points to get a pound back, that means a £15 shopping bill will produce only a 15 pence bonus – hardly worth the petrol.

• If you go abroad on holiday, you'll have ample opportunity to keep your brain fit with mental arithmetic. Try to find a quick and easy way to estimate currency conversions. For example, if you are visiting Spain and there are 250 pesetas to the pound, you can convert from pesetas to pounds by doubling the amount twice, then dividing the result by 1000 (because 1000 divided by 2 twice equals 250). Combining several simple arithmetic operations like this is often easier than carrying out one complex one, so see if you can come up with your own numerical strategies.

REASONING SKILLS

Do you think you are a logical thinker? Are you aware of what makes the difference between a logically valid argument and an invalid one? Sharpening your logical skills will help you to appraise information from all areas of life, and will help you to get your point across in discussions. While you may not always have all the facts at your fingertips, developing a critical way of thinking helps you to spot fallacious reasoning and will keep you – and others – mentally alert.

Many people assume that an argument is logical if the conclusion seems sensible. In fact, all that matters in logic is how the conclusion is reached, not what it is. A logical argument consists of one or more initial statements, or 'premises', followed by a conclusion that follows directly from the premises. For example, if a friend says he thinks Pam Ayres is a good poet because her verses rhyme, and that rhyming verse is the criterion for good poetry, then his argument is logical as the conclusion follows from the premises, even if you don't agree with it. But if you read that genetically modified foods are bad for you because they are produced by multinational companies, the conclusion does not follow from the premise so the argument would not be logically valid.

- Next time you read a newspaper, see if you can analyse which arguments are logically valid and which are not. For invalid arguments, supplying missing premises may make them valid. Looking for these extra premises helps to reveal the hidden assumptions that the article is based on.

CREATIVE SKILLS

Do you think of yourself as a creative person – or do you feel that you are not 'artistic' enough? Everyone has the potential to be creative and millions every day demonstrate it through activities such as cooking or gardening, creating delicious tastes and special places using their imagination and experience.

- Creativity can't really be measured, but psychologists see originality of ideas and the number of possible solutions to a problem as important components. This is the basis of the following exercise: take a simple everyday object, such as a paperclip or a house brick, and write down as many possible uses for it as you can think of. If you do this with a group of people, scores can be allocated on the number of unique ideas each person has (ideas that no one else in the group has thought of). Don't be shy of making wild and wacky suggestions – you're not expected to put them into practice!

- On a more practical level, try applying your imagination to your leisure activities. For example, if you are cooking a special dinner, try including just one dish based on a recipe you have invented. If it's good, you'll have made something new and delicious. If not, it won't spoil the dinner, and you can use your creative powers to improve the recipe for next time. Remember that creativity is a matter of trial and error, as well as leaps of imagination.

2

A GOOD MEMORY

YOUR AMAZING MEMORY

The human memory system is a vast, ever-changing web that reacts to every new experience. Most experiences are too fleeting to leave a noticeable trace on the web, but some alter the shape of the network so that they live on as enduring memories.

RECALLING THE CONTEXT OF AN EVENT IS ALMOST AS EFFECTIVE IN TRIGGERING A MEMORY AS RETURNING TO WHERE THE EVENT OCCURRED

Putting people back in the place where they experienced an event can help them to remember it – but surprisingly, just asking them to recall the surroundings can be almost as helpful.

IT CAN TAKE UP TO TWO YEARS FOR A MEMORY TO BECOME PERMANENT

Experiences that are being processed for storage as long-term memories may be replayed in the mind for up to two years. Once a memory is consolidated in this way, it has the potential to last a lifetime.

THE BRAIN HAS A SPECIAL AREA FOR PROCESSING HUMAN FACES

Faces are important to a social species such as humans, and the brain has evolved to process them quickly. A special area in the cortex extracts detailed information, giving fast knowledge of whom the face belongs to, and its expression.

ACTIONS AS WELL AS THOUGHTS CAN BE INVOLVED IN MEMORISING

Learning is faster if the body as well as the mind is engaged in the task. For example, it is easier to remember the layout of a town by walking the streets than by learning it from a map.

MEMORY MAY BEGIN AT BIRTH – BUT OUR EARLIEST MEMORIES CANNOT BE REACHED

The brain's primitive emotional centre, the amygdala, is fully functional at birth and may be involved in the storage of early memories – but these cannot be accessed at will.

EXCITEMENT ENHANCES MEMORY FORMATION, WHILE DEPRESSION INHIBITS IT

Laying down memories depends on physical processes that are influenced by certain chemical messengers in the brain, which ebb and flow according to mood. The higher the emotional state when a new experience occurs, the more likely we are to remember the experience.

WHEN WE FIRST VIEW A SCENE OR SITUATION, WE RELY ON MEMORY TO HELP US MAKE SENSE OF IT

The eyes see only a tiny part of any visual scene clearly. The eyes dart around taking in more and more information, and memory enables us to assemble this sequence of fragments into a scene.

THE BRAIN HAS A BUILT-IN 'LIE DETECTOR' THAT SHOWS UP FALSE MEMORIES

In everyday life, a person cannot always tell if a recollection is genuine. But brain scans show that an area at the front of the brain tends to be more active when a person accesses a genuine memory than when something that may not have occurred is 'recalled'.

SOME OF OUR MOST EMOTIONAL MEMORIES ARE TRIGGERED BY SCENT

The olfactory system, which processes smells, has direct links to a part of the brain called the amygdala – the seat of our emotions. This may be why unusual scents from the past have such power to evoke vivid personal memories.

MANY OF THE MEMORY METHODS IN USE TODAY WERE FIRST DISCOVERED MORE THAN 2000 YEARS AGO

The ancient Greeks had a clear understanding of the way natural memory could be improved upon. They developed techniques to aid recall of epic stories and speeches that were delivered entirely from memory.

1 WHAT IS MEMORY?

Try to imagine yourself without memory. What would be left of your personal identity? Memory is far more than the sum of past events and knowledge – it is what makes us what we are. The human definition of self rests on this mix of collective and private experience.

Like any human ability, memory does not operate infallibly. Instead of a seamless record of our lives, each of us has a collection of fragments that grows more precious with the advancing years. We accumulate a fantastic body of knowledge, but we do not always have access to the parts we wish to remember.

As we get older, we may wonder if our memory is getting too full to cope. But science tells us that memory capacity is limitless. What we consciously recall is just a fraction of the vast storehouse that our memory comprises, built up from the moment we enter life. And we all have the ability, through technique and practice, to make better use of our natural capacity for remembering.

MEMORY AND IDENTITY

Memories of past experiences, both positive and negative, combine to give us a sense of who we are. Our perceptions of the events we have experienced and emotions we have felt are stored in the memory and help to shape how we see ourselves as individuals.

It is sometimes said that we are what we remember. As we go through life, we acquire layer after layer of memories which inform who we are and help to determine what we will become. Every incident or emotion, whether stored consciously or unconsciously, has the power to create new attitudes and influence patterns of behaviour. Try to imagine having no memories at all – you would be quite lost and unable to understand even your own thoughts. Now try to imagine retaining your existing memories but being unable to make new ones – there would be no personality development and no possibility of emotional or intellectual growth. This was the case for a man known to researchers as 'NA', whose brain was damaged in an accident in 1959. He woke every morning as the same cheerful individual who never changed his haircut and talked about dead film stars as if they were contemporaries.

Importance of first memories

The Austrian psychiatrist Alfred Adler believed that our first memories show our fundamental attitude to life. Adler, who originated the idea of the inferiority complex, claimed that his own earliest recollection was sitting as a sickly child watching the antics of his healthier brother. Fittingly, General Eisenhower's earliest memory was of fighting off a goose, and Albert Einstein's was of staring at a compass needle, trying to work out why it always pointed north. However, if memories shape a personality, it is also true that as adults we selectively remember things that reinforce our ideas of who and what we are. A champion footballer may recollect his first ever goal as a piece of brilliance for which he was highly praised, while an academic may recall the maths lesson when only she knew the answer to the teacher's question.

> **"Every man's memory is his private literature."**
> Aldous Huxley

The archivist and the mythmaker

John Kotre, a psychologist at the University of Michigan, sees autobiographical memory as the result of a struggle between an inner archivist and an inner mythmaker. The archivist tries to construct an objective account of events, while the mythmaker is busy turning us into the protagonists of our own personal adventures. Usually, the mythmaker edits out our blunders and immortalises our victories, but it does not always turn us into

Thoughts of past triumphs and achievements at work can provide confidence for future career building.

Recalling looking great for a special occasion can help to boost self-image during less glamorous times.

Memories of enjoying nature as a child may lead to absorbing interests in adulthood.

heroes. The mythmaker can also make us obsessed with our failures, and doom us to repeating them. But, for good or bad, it helps to make us unique. It exaggerates the differences in experience and perspective between ourselves and others, and contributes to our personal identity.

Creating an alternative past

This process of 'self-making' means that our sense of continuity as individuals may be no more than an illusion. We may never truly have been the children – or the younger selves of any age – that we remember. People who suffer a traumatic event will often create a whole alternative past in light of what has happened. For example, a happily married wife who discovers her husband's affairs may suddenly see her entire marriage as a panorama of suspicion and deceptions. On a less extreme scale, this sort of thing is constantly happening to all of us. Researchers at Stanford University in the USA read a story to a group of people, followed by either a series of depressing homilies or a comic monologue. Later, those who heard the homilies remembered the sad parts of the story; those who heard the comic pieces recalled the happy parts. Despite the apparent continuity provided by memories, and the personality's strong urge to maintain itself, the world forces us to remake ourselves and our pasts every day.

A life of academic achievement can stem from early encouragement and praise.

A memorable first goal might inspire a successful footballing career.

A desire to help others find their place in society could stem from feeling left out as a child.

Real lives IN LOVE WITH THE LIBRARY

Carol, now 47, recalls her first visit to the library as the event that inspired her lifelong love of books.

'I first went to the library on the day after my ninth birthday. I got out two of the Anne of Green Gables books. I was so excited – there were so many books to read. I think my love of reading was born on that afternoon, and I went every Saturday after that.

'Even now, all libraries have for me that same slightly musty scent – a calming smell. I always feel relaxed in a library or a bookshop and I still get the same feeling of excitement – a kind of lift – when I come away with a pile of books to escape into. Recently, I was visiting my home town and couldn't resist popping into the library. It had all changed – there were computers everywhere and they were playing games in the children's section. Everything was different, and yet that Saturday afternoon 38 years ago came flooding back. It was the weirdest feeling.'

MEMORY AND INTELLIGENCE

Memory skills vary widely between one person and the next, as does intellectual capacity. A person with a good memory is not necessarily more intelligent than someone whose memory lets them down, but there is a connection between memory and mental performance.

The Nutty Professor In this classic film, American comedian Jerry Lewis played a bumbling absent-minded professor. Despite the character's genius, he forgot the simplest things.

How would you describe your memory? Good on facts and figures, but heavily reliant on diaries and calendars for appointments? Can you remember all the family's birthdays but find that you are always losing scarves, gloves and other personal possessions? Generally, we tend to categorise ourselves according to the perceived weaknesses in our memories and pay less attention to our memory strengths. Yet memory is as individual as personality – we all have different skills and talents.

The same can be said of intelligence. While a good memory is certainly an asset in mental tasks and tests, the link between memory and intelligence is not straightforward. It is not always the case that a person of high intellect has a good memory in all areas – so the stereotype of the absent-minded professor has some validity. A talented scientist might have developed an advanced theory on how the universe was formed and have superior recall for anything related to the subject, but may be completely unreliable in other areas, losing spectacles and papers, and forgetting appointments. One of the important early predictors of whether information will be held in memory is attention, and many academically brilliant people have very selective attention.

Different kinds of intelligence

Psychologists now talk of multiple intelligences – as many as seven different types – each of which brings at least one aspect of memory into play. A professional footballer or tennis player could be said to have physical intelligence, drawing on body coordination skills that are honed and carved into the memory through practice. Top sportsmen and women

 TRY IT YOURSELF **FIND YOUR INTELLIGENCE TYPES**

Get together with some friends or family members and try these tests to find out your intelligence strengths.

Logical-mathematical intelligence
• Set the clock and get everyone to count backwards in sevens from 100, writing down the numbers – 100, 93, 86 and so on. See who is the fastest and who makes the fewest errors.

• What is the next letter in this sequence, and why? **A C F J O** (See opposite page for answer.)

Linguistic intelligence
• Get everyone to make three lists of words – animals, fruit or vegetables, and countries – each word starting with a different letter. Who makes the fullest alphabetical lists in five minutes?

Social intelligence
• To test who has the best memory for people and personal details, ask everyone to invent a new name, age and home town for themselves. Each person then recites their invented details in turn. Finally, give the group five minutes in which everyone writes down everyone else's details, and see who performs best.

" One individual overflows with poetical reminiscences, another directs symphonies from memory, while numbers and formulae, which come to a third without effort, slip away from the other two as from polished stone. **"**

Hermann Ebbinghaus, psychologist, 1885

Real lives **A MEMORY EXPERT**

Even an expert in memory is not immune to forgetting. Leading UK psychologist Alan Baddeley has described the day he was invited to join two other psychologists on an early morning radio programme. On the appointed day, he was idly looking through the television pages of his morning paper when the realisation dawned that he should at that moment be at the broadcasting studio. He arrived at the studio just in time for the final summing-up – at which point he was asked what tips he would give listeners to help them remember!

teach their bodies to make the right movements in the right situations, and these movements are remembered unconsciously.

A professor of physics or astronomy will score highly in logical or mathematical intelligence and have a memory that can process this type of information rapidly. Architects are likely to excel in spatial memory – in particular, the ability to visualise drawings in three dimensions. People who are able to speak several languages have a high level of linguistic intelligence, supported by a superior memory for words and their sounds, while professional musicians and singers may have an exceptional musical memory as a result of constant practice. One element of high social intelligence is the ability to 'read' others. Leadership and negotiation skills may initially stem from a superior memory for names and personal details, and a sophisticated recognition of behavioural cues exhibited by others.

What is common to all the different forms of intelligence is the ability to concentrate wholly on a task and to make connections between new information and existing knowledge. These are also key strategies in developing a good memory. However high the intelligence, achievement owes as much to interest, dedication and practice as it does to natural memory.

Memory in education Rote learning was once considered a major educational tool. Today, children are encouraged to research material themselves, which not only means they must demonstrate an understanding of what they learn but also increases the chance of it being retained in memory.

The next letter in the sequence is U, which is reached by starting with A and omitting first one letter, then two letters, and so on.

EXPLORE YOUR MEMORY POWER

Most of us have a fairly good sense of how we fare in direct tests of memory such as quizzes and exams, but we usually have a much vaguer notion of the power of our everyday memory. Here are some questions that will help you to explore your personal memory strengths and weaknesses.

Have a look at the images below, which are all taken from news stories in one year. Try to identify which year it is.

• If you don't remember the dates of the individual events, you may find that relating them to something that was happening in your own life will help. Most of us have to make associations of this kind before we can say exactly when events occurred.

NAMES FROM THE PAST

How strong are your memories of schooldays? Most of us can remember close friends but are less sure about other children – even those in the same class. So, how many people can you name from your class when you were ten years old? Try making a list, with first names and surnames if possible.

• Ten or more people is good. You probably had most success with remembering people who went through several years of school with you.

• Now try to describe what your schoolmates looked like. Give yourself bonus points for any details you can remember. Most of us remember hair colour first, followed by general build, and very little else.

Prince Andrew wed Sarah Ferguson.

WHAT YEAR WAS THIS?

Halley's comet made an appearance.

A devastating explosion occurred at Chernobyl nuclear power station.

Mike Tyson became world heavyweight boxing champion.

A MEMORY FOR FACTS?

The Challenger space shuttle launch ended in disaster.

Think back to yesterday's news – whether you read it in a newspaper, heard it on the radio or saw it on television. How many different news stories can you remember?

• If you can come up with three or more topics and a rough outline of the stories, you are doing well.

• Give yourself extra points for memory power if you can remember some names, locations or other details accurately.

PAST PLEASURES

Cast your mind back to a holiday you took about ten years ago – one that you feel you remember well.

• First name the region or country, and say how long the holiday lasted. Even for a holiday that took place some time ago, you'll probably still find that you can remember these basic facts.

• Now try something harder. Can you remember some details – for example, the names of any sights or towns that you visited or any special restaurants and meals? What about some of the people you met on holiday? Give yourself extra points for anything that you can put a name to.

SHOPPING WITHOUT A LIST

How good are you at shopping when you have left your list at home? Read through the following list of 15 foods just once, concentrating hard on each word, but don't take longer than a minute for the whole list.

Onions, Plums, Eggs, Blackberries, Hazelnuts, Shrimps, Tonic Water, Mayonnaise, Basil, Courgettes, Mangoes, Pasta, Ham, Biscuits, Porridge

Now put aside this book and try to write down the items from the list. How many did you remember? See how your score compares with the average score for this task in your age group:

• 18 to 40 year olds – 10 items
• 40 to 60 year olds – 9 items
• 60 to 70 year olds – 8 items
• 70 plus – 7 items.

AN EYE FOR DETAIL?

Test how closely you pay attention to items that you use regularly. List all the objects that you think might be in your bag or briefcase at this moment. Then see how close you were by checking your bag.

• Give yourself a point for every correct item that appears on your list.

• Deduct a point for each object that you wrongly imagined to be there.

What is your final score? An averagely attentive person should get a little more than half of the maximum possible score. Anything higher is excellent.

HOW DID YOU DO?

If you did well in all the tasks, your memory power should come as no surprise to you. You probably find that you can rely on your memory in most real-life situations. However, most people find they fare better on particular types of memory task. For example, you may have performed well on straight facts but have a hazier recollection of events from your past. If you were disappointed with your results in some areas, don't worry – a poor to average memory can be improved dramatically with training. You will find a number of strategies that help with memory tasks like these throughout this book, so you may want to return to these tests later to see how much better you can do.

MEMORY AND GENDER

The brain, like every other part of the body, is moulded partly by sex hormones, which affect its functioning throughout life. These hormones are at least in part responsible for the differing ways in which men and women remember things.

> **"I memorise our route with a body map. I might start at my head, go down my neck, along my left shoulder, right to my pelvis, and so on…"**
>
> Molly, amateur rallying navigator

If a man describes the way to somewhere, the chances are that he provides a verbal route map: road numbers, distances, junctions, left and right turns. A woman, however, is more likely to use landmarks: right at the green gate, carry on to the thatched cottage, left at the little wood…

This difference reflects a general tendency for women to pay attention to, and therefore remember, specific features – a 'what?' rather than a 'where?' approach. In contrast, men are more aware of the lie of the land – a 'where?' rather than a 'what?' approach. These two ways of mapping the world occur because visual information is processed via two different pathways in the brain. There is some evidence that the 'where?' pathway, which distinguishes distance and position, is stronger in the right hemisphere, while the 'what?' pathway is stronger in the left and travels into the region of the brain where long-term memories are stored. This allows new information to be compared with existing knowledge and recognised. The product

of both pathways is brought together in the front of the brain and allows us to be conscious, simultaneously, both of where and what something is.

Every normal brain uses both pathways to arrive at a full picture of the world, but the amount of information fed in from each hemisphere differs according to which side of the brain is most actively engaged. The left hemisphere specialises in processing detailed information, while the right hemisphere takes in the whole picture. Brain studies suggest that when men learn and recall things they tend to use the right hemisphere more, which gives a slight advantage in spatial memory. Women rely more on the left hemisphere pathway, which may account for why they are, on average, better than men at recalling details. For example, studies show women to be faster than men at identifying small changes in tests like 'spot the difference', and faster and more accurate than men at recognising plants.

One theory is that these gender-based abilities may have evolved because early men needed good orientation skills in order to hunt over large areas, whereas women were responsible for foraging, which required close attention to detail to select the right plant. A similar evolutionary pressure perhaps resulted in women being better than men at recalling faces. The face recognition area of the brain is situated along the left hemisphere pathway, and it is possible that the female emphasis on left-brained recollection helped women to develop important social skills in early tribal existence.

The hormone factor

These subtle gender differences in the brain are partly the result of hormone action. Before birth, the periodic doses of testosterone that help to form male characteristics briefly inhibit growth in the left brain hemisphere. As a result, boys tend to have increased activity in the right hemisphere.

While testosterone inhibits left hemisphere processing, the female hormone oestrogen boosts it. In the middle of the menstrual cycle, when oestrogen levels are high, a woman may have a more distinct advantage over a man in detailed memory tasks. Sex hormones also affect general memory. Pregnant women sometimes become startlingly absent-minded owing to the huge fluctuations in their hormone levels, and memory problems are also associated with the drop in oestrogen levels during the menopause.

However, the memory differences between the sexes are tiny compared to the differences between individuals. A good memory depends far more on how we train our memory than on gender. What we remember is what we pay attention to – so to develop memory skills we should observe both the 'where' of things, and the 'what'.

HHHHHHHHHH
HHHHHHHHHH
HHHH
HHHH
HHHHHHHHH
HHHHHHHHH
HHHH
HHHH
HHHHHHHHHH
HHHHHHHHHH

Different views
If you look at this large E formed from small H's, your right brain is more active if you concentrate on the E, while the left brain is busier if you focus on the H's.

TRY IT YOURSELF

SPOT THE DIFFERENCE
In 'spot the difference' tests, women have been shown to be quicker than men to notice small changes. Try this test with friends or family members of both sexes. Time how long it takes to find 15 subtle differences between the pictures and see whether, on average, your male or female friends perform best. (Answers on page 475.)

MEMORY CAPACITY

How much information can the brain hold? The answer seems to be an almost unlimited amount thanks to the brain's dynamic memory-filing system. So why are there times when we feel as if we forget things because our brains are filled to capacity and cannot 'take in' any more?

FACT: Memories are made of neural connections – and the number of possible connections between neurons in the human brain is virtually limitless.

Think of some little incident that happened to you recently – accidentally bumping into someone in the street, perhaps. Now imagine trying to convey every tiny piece of information contained in the recollection: the road you were on, the traffic and people, the colour and texture of the pavement, a dog barking, the slight pain in your shoulder, your own and the stranger's voices apologising simultaneously, the thoughts that went through your mind. You could fill pages just describing that one event, even though it lasted only for a few seconds.

Think of the thousands of similar snapshot recollections you could summon up right now, and the millions more that might pop up if something reminded you of them. Then consider the myriad things you know, from where the Eiffel Tower is to what a polar bear looks like. Then think of all your abilities: how to make a cup of tea, turn on the TV, drive a car. Amazingly, all these billions of 'bits' of knowledge are held in your memory. But this vast array of information cannot be compared to any man-made database because it is not stored in a static way, like images on film or words on a page. We do not replay information from memory; rather, we re-create it each time we use it. A recollection is not an object – like a picture on a wall – that can be revisited and will remain the same. A recollection is a process, producing a slightly different experience each time.

Neural connections

All our experiences are produced by neurons (nerve cells) firing in the brain in response to what we see, hear, touch, smell, taste and feel. Experiences

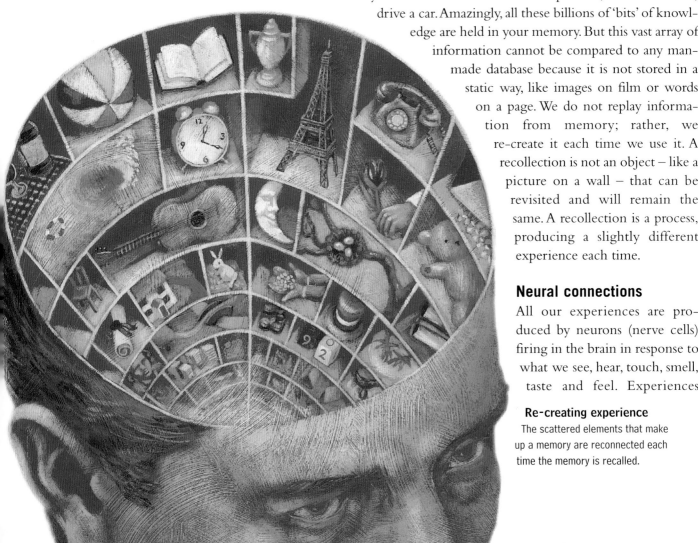

Re-creating experience
The scattered elements that make up a memory are reconnected each time the memory is recalled.

become memories because the neurons that produced the experience form connections with one another. When these neurons are not firing, the memory is merely a potential tendency for them to fire together again in future. When that happens, it creates a faint replay of the original experience and recall of a memory occurs. It is a little like one of those huge illuminated advertising hoardings made up of thousands of different bulbs; different pictures are produced by turning on and off different patterns of bulbs. When one picture is showing, the others exist only as potential patterns – and parts of each picture may be used to create other images.

Each time an event is recalled the neural firing pattern is slightly changed, and this new memory overwrites the previous one. In a sense, memories are 'memories of memories' rather than recollections of events, and the brain can produce an indefinite number of versions.

Memory 'overload'

The vast number of possible connections between neurons means that there is no danger of the brain filling up with long-term memories. So how do we account for the common experience that our memory is unable to cope with what we ask of it?

One factor that contributes to 'memory overload' is that our brains did not evolve to deal with what we ask of them today. As recently as 30 years ago, people did not rush around the way we do now, fitting numerous appointments into each day, meeting deadlines and making complicated holiday itineraries. Perhaps we should regard occasional memory failures as understandable lapses, given the times in which we live.

FACT: The human brain has not changed greatly since early humans lived as hunter-gatherers, but the pace of life – and the demands on memory – have altered beyond recognition.

Real lives **ANGIE'S MEMORY TRIANGLE**

Angie keeps track of a busy work schedule and social life without using a diary. She explains how she does it:

'I used to keep a diary, but then I lost it ... and life just fell into chaos. I never wanted to risk that happening again, so I decided to train myself to hold all my dates in my head.

'I do it by keeping a visual "template" in my head: it's like a triangle with "today" written small at the top and "tomorrow" slightly bigger beneath it and so on. The day that is furthest away is the biggest at the bottom. When I make a date I visualise writing it in under the relevant day and keep that image in mind – repeating it in words as well as looking at it in my mind's eye – for at least one minute.

'During that time I imagine what the occasion will be like, and "tag" the words with images of being there, how I will feel at the time, what I will wear and so on.

'Each night before I go to sleep, I spend about ten minutes "editing". Today is erased, and tomorrow pops up to take its place. I read down through the things I have to do and revisualise each date for at least 30 seconds. The far-off things at the bottom are the biggest and so get the most attention. As they creep up the triangle they get smaller and I spend less time on them. That's OK because by the time something reaches the "today" slot I have been over it so many times that there is no way I can forget it.'

WHAT HAPPENS TO EXPERIENCES?

Every experience leaves a trace in the brain and some traces seem to become permanently etched into its tissue. Yet your brain's event library is highly selective, producing edited highlights rather than a complete recording of your life and experiences to date.

More than half a century ago, the Canadian neuroscientist Wilder Penfield presented remarkable evidence that seemed to show that all our experiences might be recorded somewhere in the brain. Penfield was treating patients for epilepsy and had the opportunity to stimulate their exposed brains just prior to surgery. Because brain tissue does not have pain receptors, brain surgery can be carried out without general anaesthetic: the wide-awake patient can help guide the surgeon to some extent by reporting how he or she feels when various parts of the brain are touched.

Memory 'replays'

Penfield wanted to find out what would happen if an exposed brain was stimulated directly with electrodes, so he asked his patients if they would agree to having their brains touched more than usual. As he probed, he appeared to trigger snatches of memories:

'Yes doctor! Now I hear people laughing… my friends in South Africa…yes they're two cousins, Bessie and Ann.'

'Oh gee, gosh – robbers are coming at me with guns!'

'My nephew and niece… visiting me at home… getting ready to go home, putting on their coats and hats, the dining room. My mother… talking to them. She [is] rushed… in a hurry.'

> **"We do not remember days, we remember moments."**
>
> Cesare Pavese, Italian poet

Penfield found that when he stimulated certain areas of the cortex – especially in the temporal lobes – his patients reported fragmented 'replays' of what seemed like long-forgotten events. This suggested to him that memories might be imprinted in the brain and, if that were the case, everything a person had ever experienced might be laid down and waiting for some stimulation to bring it back to mind.

Reinterpreting Penfield's results

The Penfield experiments have since been replicated many times, but the original interpretation – that memories are stamped into the brain as immutable traces – has changed. Subsequent research has shown that memories are reassembled from many different fragments stored throughout the brain, and that reassembly is always a new version of an event rather than a perfect replay (see page 174). Furthermore, the patients who took part in Penfield's experiments were probably not so much recounting memories as describing dream-like hallucinations made up of past recollections and imaginings, bound together into a familiar-seeming scene. The young boy who reported robbers coming at him had never been attacked by robbers – but he had often fantasised about it. What he reported while he lay on the operating table was a replay of that fantasy, not a memory of a real event.

Faint traces and enduring patterns

Every experience – whether it is a real or perceived event, a thought, a feeling, an act of imagination, or a recollection of a previous experience – involves the activation of a unique neural firing pattern. Each pattern (and there are countless patterns passing through the brain at any one time) leaves a faint trace in that it makes the participating neurons more likely to join together in that pattern again. The vast majority of patterns are so fleeting that their trace disappears almost immediately. So most of what we experience is not available for recall.

However, events that are particularly impressive produce strong and long-lasting patterns, and these tend to pop up again and again. Every time they are reproduced, they become more likely to be reproduced in future, so over time, they become reinforced as 'habits' of mind and firmly established as memories. Those memories that are not replayed in this way fade away and are forgotten.

Experiences, then, are never frozen in memory. Rather, they leave an impression on the brain – like the outline of a body on a feather bed – which may be consolidated by recall, merged into other impressions, or simply left to fade away.

THINK AGAIN!

ALIEN ABDUCTION

Neuroscientist Michael Persinger has devised a 'helmet' that uses magnetic pulses to stimulate the temporal lobes. The effect is similar to that seen in Penfield's experiments – people describe vivid 'memories', such as being abducted by aliens. Persinger suggests that these are not memories but fantasies constructed out of fragmented recollections. The other-worldly feel may be due to the fact that the prefrontal cortex, which has an important role in checking the reality of perceptions, is bypassed.

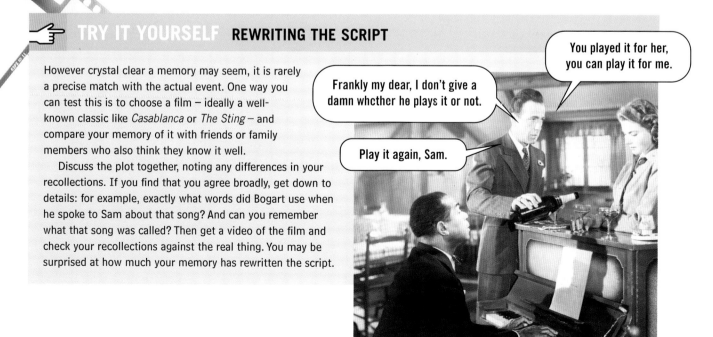

TRY IT YOURSELF   REWRITING THE SCRIPT

However crystal clear a memory may seem, it is rarely a precise match with the actual event. One way you can test this is to choose a film – ideally a well-known classic like *Casablanca* or *The Sting* – and compare your memory of it with friends or family members who also think they know it well.

Discuss the plot together, noting any differences in your recollections. If you find that you agree broadly, get down to details: for example, exactly what words did Bogart use when he spoke to Sam about that song? And can you remember what that song was called? Then get a video of the film and check your recollections against the real thing. You may be surprised at how much your memory has rewritten the script.

Frankly my dear, I don't give a damn whether he plays it or not.

You played it for her, you can play it for me.

Play it again, Sam.

Early memories

What is your earliest memory? However old you are now, it is likely that you can still recall events and brief moments from your early childhood.

Imagine if all memories had to pass a selection process that considered whether they were relevant, useful or important. Most of our early reminiscences would be consigned to oblivion. This is because early memories tend to be an eclectic mix – major and minor events, scraps of conversation, items of clothing, amalgams of school days and family gatherings, all spiked with a full range of emotions.

While we struggle to remember everyday essentials – the items on the shopping list that we left on the kitchen table, for example, or the name of the person we need to introduce to a work colleague – whole incidents or vivid scraps from our distant past seem to be there for the asking, packaged for easy access. We can hook out without effort the memory of a trip to the seaside – the tin bucket decorated with a starfish, the cake wrapped in greaseproof paper, the wave that soaked grandad's sandals, someone saying that sea anemones looked like strawberries from a pot of jam.

These recollections that pop up, often unbidden, some 20, 40, even 80 years after the event are usually among the most cherished of all our memories. Like a piece of antique lace or a faded sepia-tinted photograph, they are made remarkable simply because they have survived.

How far back can you remember?

If you compare, say, your memories of your first year at school with those of the last, the latter are likely to be far richer and more detailed. This isn't just because your last year at school is closer to you in time – although that may play a part if you are still relatively young. It is because far fewer memories seem to be formed in the period from birth to five years. Psychologists have a number of theories about why this might be so (see page 248), and researchers have tried to pinpoint the age at which earliest autobiographical memories are laid down.

One way to investigate this is by asking people if they remember a significant event from childhood. In one study, a group of children and young people were asked what they remembered about a brother or sister being born when they themselves were aged between three and eleven. They were asked questions such as: 'Who looked after you when your

MY BROTHER'S BIRTHDAY

Matt, now 37, recalls a classic childhood memory. 'My first memory is of my younger brother's second birthday. I would have been three weeks short of my fourth birthday. I remember standing in the hall of our house in north London, watching Francis clumsily descending the flight of stairs. As he successfully negotiated the final step, and turned right through the open door of the kitchen, I heard my grandmother's voice cooing "Now you're two". Strange, now, to think that this cameo was played out more than 30 years ago. Equally strange – but oddly comforting – to ponder why this memory of all memories is the one that has stood the test of time.'

mother was in hospital?' and 'Do you remember getting any presents?' The accuracy of the memory could be verified by checking with the parents.

The results showed that, no matter what age the young people were at the time of the study – whether they were aged four, eight, twelve or young adults – what made the difference was how old they had been when their sibling was born. If the birth happened before the child was three, he or she was very unlikely to have a genuine memory of it.

Psychologists have concluded that if you were to write your autobiography entirely from personal recall, it would probably start at around the age of three or four, and even then the memories would be patchy.

Are your early memories really your own?

When people say that they can remember an event from babyhood, do they really remember the actual experience, or has the memory been created subsequently through photographs or other people's accounts? You might like to explore this idea yourself. Try to recall your earliest memory in as much detail as you can. Next time you get the chance, look at some early photographs of yourself. You might be surprised to find one that is a very close representation of your supposed memory. It is often hard to unravel whether seeing a photograph or perhaps hearing a story about yourself repeatedly over the years has reinforced a genuine memory, or instead helped to lay down one that was not yours in the first place.

> " …I go carrying my childhood like a favourite flower that perfumes my hand."
>
> Gabriel Mistral, Chilean poet

COLLECTIVE MEMORIES

We all share with those close to us a pool of collective memories – stories, images and ideas that we agree upon, or at least agree to argue about. Shared memories and records underpin our culture, creating the history of social groups as well as their mythologies and conditions for membership.

Our collective memories – whether shared at the level of a family, a profession, a nation, a faith or an entire culture – provide the context for the making of our personal memories. They can affect what we remember and how we choose to remember it and, to some extent, what we forget. Adopting a new set of collective memories – by joining a religious cult, for example – changes not only our opinions, but can also alter existing memories of events that happened years ago. US psychologist Henry Roediger has shown that it is easy, under laboratory conditions, to make people remember things that never occurred simply by putting them into groups and regularly repeating fictitious stories to them.

Oral traditions

The way in which collective memories are preserved differs from circle to circle. In families or among friends the means tend to be oral – tales and reminiscences are shared directly and transferred from person to person. There are usually pictures, letters and mementoes, but these are often meaningless without a living commentary to put them in context. Home movies and videos share the illusion of being a more complete record, but these are rarely watched in silence: they primarily provide the focus for family discussions.

Collective grief The sea of flowers and tributes outside the gates of Kensington Palace in London after the death of Princess Diana reflected the nation's deep sense of shared loss.

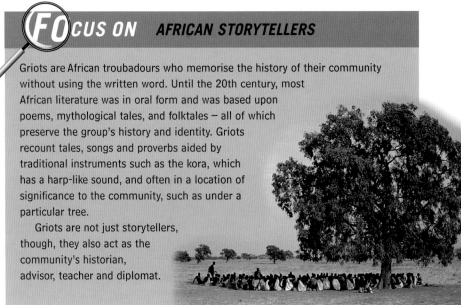

(FO)CUS ON *AFRICAN STORYTELLERS*

Griots are African troubadours who memorise the history of their community without using the written word. Until the 20th century, most African literature was in oral form and was based upon poems, mythological tales, and folktales – all of which preserve the group's history and identity. Griots recount tales, songs and proverbs aided by traditional instruments such as the kora, which has a harp-like sound, and often in a location of significance to the community, such as under a particular tree.

Griots are not just storytellers, though, they also act as the community's historian, advisor, teacher and diplomat.

Real lives ANNE FRANK'S DIARY

One of the most famous personal records to reach a public audience was *The Diary of Anne Frank* – a young girl's account of her life and innermost thoughts during her teenage years. For nearly two years, Anne chronicled the terrible change of fortune for her Jewish family in Amsterdam under Nazi occupation, their life in hiding and their eventual capture.

Anne did not survive but her moving and perceptive account was preserved and published shortly after the war. Since then,

more than 20 million copies in 54 languages have been sold and the book has become a focus for collective remembering, representing as it does the untold stories of millions of other Jewish families who died in the Holocaust.

Anne's diary was published after the war by her father, and it has since become a symbol to oppressed people everywhere. Former South African president Nelson Mandela has said that he drew comfort from it during his years of imprisonment.

Earlier in history, small, non-literate hunting or farming communities preserved their memories in the same way, although in this case there were usually bards, shamans, priests or chieftains who were designated as the guardians of the oral culture. As groups got larger (or, in the case of families, wealthier), there was a need or desire to make more permanent records – from cave paintings and papyrus manuscripts to the audio and video recordings of modern times. Today, in the age of the internet, 24-hour news, spin doctors, digital special effects and lawsuits over intellectual property rights, the collective memory of our culture as a whole has become a battleground where the ideas of different interest groups are constantly at war.

Rituals and commemorations

Within modern society, there are also enduring rituals that preserve the collective memories of particular cultural or ethnic groups. These often act as a link between the experiences of an individual family and those of the larger group. For example, Jewish families celebrate Passover with the Seder meal, at which all the participants have a chance to re-enact the Exodus of the Israelites from Egypt in the days of Moses.

Some such rituals and the events they commemorate can be divisive; others re-create a sense of unity. The traditional marches of the Protestant Orangemen in Ulster celebrate a historic military victory against the Catholics but take place at the expense of local Catholic feelings. Collective memories of Britain in World War II recall hardship and loss, but also solidarity and public-spiritedness in the face of a common enemy. And the public grief following the assassination of President Kennedy or the sudden death of Princess Diana created a vivid sense of having shared in a moment of history – for a while at least, these events evoked a powerful sense of togetherness. Whether through conflict, grief, tradition or conversation, it would seem that our compulsion to share collective memories is the mechanism that ensures their survival.

TRY IT YOURSELF

COLLECTING MEMORIES

Preserving family memories can be as simple as encouraging children to talk to their grandparents and elderly relatives. Old photographs and letters are another good starting point. But there are also more imaginative approaches:

• Research a family tree – this activity often brings to light family stories from previous decades, as well as uncovering previously unsuspected relatives and ancestors.

• Follow the example of the American folk artist Alice Freeman, to create a family 'memory map'. This is a colourful map of a region that is rich in family associations, reconstructed from memory, with a little help from real maps. The map can be studded with relevant quotations, notes, pictures and souvenirs.

• Set up a 'family website', for personal recollections, scanned-in photos, video and speech clips, and interactive letters. Each family member could have a page for his or her own contributions.

2 THE MIND'S MEMORY STORES

The first hundred years or so of psychology has unravelled many of the mysteries of memory. Memory is no longer perceived as a single brain function, but rather as a set of distinct faculties which have different uses and operate over different time scales. A memory can last for anything from a fraction of a second to most of a lifetime.

Studies of how memory skills are lost or retained when the brain is damaged have helped scientists to identify the different areas of the brain involved in different kinds of memory. Recently, imaging techniques have shown remembering in action, revealing memories as enduring patterns of brain activity that re-create experiences.

Only humans seem to have a certain kind of memory: the ability to call up and reflect on previous experiences. This ability may have played a major part in our evolution – and continues to fascinate us in the present day.

WORKING MEMORY: THE MIND'S BLACKBOARD

In our everyday lives, we constantly need to remember little pieces of information – phone numbers, lists of names, a round of drinks – for just a few seconds. This type of temporary memory is known as short-term or 'working' memory.

"I find telephone numbers much easier to remember when they're only seven digits – now that some have an extra number it's much harder."

Ruth, aged 49

Working memory is the mind mechanism that allows you to hold numbers in your head when you are doing mental arithmetic and provides somewhere for you to sketch mental maps when you are giving directions. In fact, you are using your working memory right now: as you read, your working memory holds the beginning of each sentence just long enough for you to reach the end. Without it, nothing you read would ever make sense. This type of memory is often described as the mind's blackboard – like a real blackboard, it provides a space to jot down information needed for the task in hand, and it is 'wiped clean' when you start a new task.

The concept of working memory grew out of the older idea that we have two main types of memory: long-term memory, which stores events, facts and knowledge for anything from a few hours to many years, and short-term memory, which holds information for a matter of moments. Psychologists realised that short-term memory is in constant use as we talk, think and act, so they began to use the term 'working memory' to emphasise its active role.

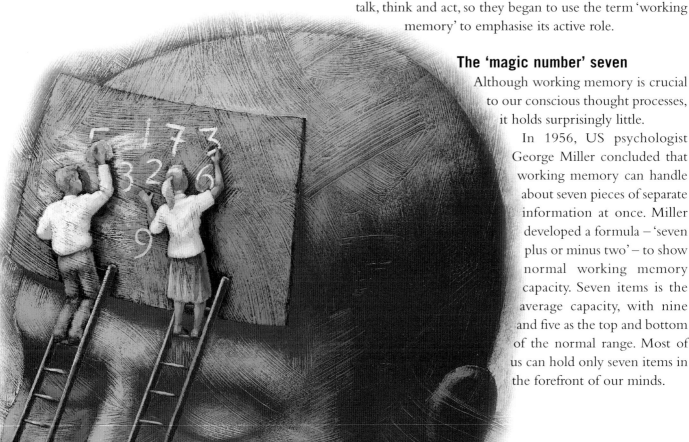

The 'magic number' seven

Although working memory is crucial to our conscious thought processes, it holds surprisingly little.

In 1956, US psychologist George Miller concluded that working memory can handle about seven pieces of separate information at once. Miller developed a formula – 'seven plus or minus two' – to show normal working memory capacity. Seven items is the average capacity, with nine and five as the top and bottom of the normal range. Most of us can hold only seven items in the forefront of our minds.

FOCUS ON *SENSORY AND ICONIC MEMORY*

The most temporary form of memory is known as sensory memory, which holds data from our eyes, ears and other senses for just a split second. Our senses provide us with far more information than we can possibly cope with, so we use sensory memory to hold information briefly while we pick out the important parts.

Sometimes we mishear what someone says and are on the point of asking them to repeat it when we realise that we did hear it after all. This is sensory memory in action. As soon as we realise that we haven't heard properly, we examine our sensory memory and find an exact 'recording' of what entered our ears.

The visual form of sensory memory is called iconic memory. This holds on to visual information taken in a fraction of a second ago. It is this that enables us to make light pictures form in front of our eyes using sparklers, and to see separate images on film as continuous action.

So if you are trying to remember a seven-item shopping list and then think of something else to add to the list, at least one of the original items is likely to be forgotten. If you are distracted briefly, you may forget the entire list. It is this tendency in working memory for new thoughts to push out old ones that sometimes causes us to forget what we were about to say mid-sentence, or arrive upstairs wondering what it was that we were on our way to fetch.

If you need to hold something such as a phone number in your short-term memory for a few seconds, the easiest way to do it is to 'rehearse' it – that is, repeat it over and over again, either out loud, or inside your head. However, if you want to remember the number more permanently, you will need to think about the number and relate it to something you know so that it becomes lodged in your long-term memory store.

The sketchpad and the phonological loop

Two British psychologists, Alan Baddeley and Graham Hitch, first put forward the idea that working memory consists of at least two 'mental blackboards' – the phonological loop, which stores words and numbers briefly in auditory form, and the visuo-spatial sketchpad, which stores images temporarily. It is now known that the phonological loop and the sketchpad use different parts of the brain, which means that both can be used at the same time. This explains why people can normally navigate a car and hold a conversation at the same time. Navigating involves picturing a route and so uses the visuo-spatial sketchpad, while talking involves words and so uses the phonological loop. If, however, you try to carry out two tasks that both use the phonological loop – for example, reading a book while the television or radio is on – you will run into difficulties.

TRY IT YOURSELF

WORD LENGTH
Read the first list of words below just once then close the book. Try to repeat the words in your head to keep them in your working memory, then write down as many as possible in any order.

fish, tree, golf, plant, smile, disc, book, chair, plug, wave

Now try the same procedure with this list of words:

hippopotamus, representative, Yugoslavia, television, ballerina, gladiator, paparazzi, apprehension, radiology, interpretation

Both lists have 10 words, but you probably recalled more from the first than from the second. This is because the words in the first list are shorter and repeating them in working memory takes less time. Longer words are more easily lost because there isn't enough working memory time to rehearse them.

INCREASE YOUR MEMORY SPAN

Your short-term or 'working' memory can store only a tiny amount of information, but it is important because it holds the information that you are actively thinking about – for example, holding on to a telephone number for long enough to find a pen. Given that it is so closely linked to your thinking, working memory capacity is surprisingly small. Most people can keep about seven items in working memory; some people one or two items more, others one or two less. It is rather like being a juggler and having a set number of balls that you are able to keep in the air. If you are thrown one extra ball you are quite likely to drop another one – or possibly lose them all. Fortunately, there are some tricks that can help to boost working memory span.

TEST YOUR WORKING MEMORY SPAN

To find your working memory span, read each of these rows of letters to yourself, one row at a time, at a rate of about one letter per second. As soon as you have read a row, close the book and try to write down the letters in the correct order.

R D H K
L B D S

P W V Q B
M J F H G

X T J B C W
Q K G Y P M

H Q Y J B S P
B K F T L N S

T B S K R Q M W
V J G X S Y P C

M D N W K V R P Z
F P N Y C V K D R

Which was the longest pair of rows that you managed to remember perfectly? Recalling rows of nine letters puts you at the top end of the range, seven is average, and five is still within the normal range. Whatever your score there are ways to improve your performance.

CHUNKING INFORMATION

Read the following list of numbers just once, then close the book and try to write them in the correct order.

2 8 1 4 9 0 4 7 2 8 1 3

The chances are that you did not manage all twelve. Now try again with this list:

1 9 4 5 1 0 6 6 1 8 1 2

How did you do this time? You probably found it as difficult as the first list – unless you noticed that the numbers can be grouped into three famous dates: 1945, 1066 and 1812. At a stroke, this reduces the amount you have to remember from twelve items to

just three, bringing the task well within the range of the average working memory. This process is known as 'chunking' – making things into larger, more meaningful chunks. Chunking also works with lists of words. For example, if you were trying to remember a shopping list of flour, egg and milk you could chunk them into simply 'pancakes', while sausages, bacon, eggs, mushrooms and tomatoes could be chunked into 'cooked breakfast', reducing the amount to hold in memory from eight items to just two.

ADDING MEANING

Chunking numbers into dates is helpful but most numbers do not lend themselves easily to the technique. For example, take this number:

7 0 9 6 3 1 2 5

Trying to say 7096 and 3125 is rather a struggle, and that reduces your chance of keeping them active in working memory. You need to look for alternative ways of relating them to

something you know. For example, the 7th 0f the 9th '63 might be the birthdate of someone you know and 125 the bus you take into town. Birthdays, ages and house numbers all work well, but you may be able to think of a numerical system that has particular relevance for you. One particular athlete much studied by psychologists used his knowledge of running times and distances to remember lists of up to 80 digits after hearing them just once.

USING RHYME AND RHYTHM

Rhythm helps with many memory tasks. Say you have been given the telephone number 619572. As a general rule, repeating the number in threes gives the best results, because this type of grouping resembles the rhythms of speech, something our hearing has specifically evolved to detect. Rhythm and rhyme are much in use in early learning. For example, children at nursery school are taught to divide the 26 letters of the alphabet into groups that rhyme, and then sing them into memory.

LONG-TERM MEMORY

All the facts that you know, all the things you can do, many of the events of your life to date, plus all the surprising things that you are not even aware of knowing – this huge store of knowledge is what makes up your long-term memory.

You can think of your memory as a bit like a library. Close to the entrance is the working memory notice board where transitory items come and go. Inside the labyrinths of the main building is the vast archive of everything you know: your long-term memory collection.

Long-term memory is usually described as having two main divisions: episodic memory and semantic memory. Episodic memories are events and experiences clothed in personal detail – the stories from your life so far. Semantic memories are your store of knowledge and facts.

Psychologists also make a distinction between 'knowing that' and 'knowing how to'. Your episodic and semantic memories fall into the category of 'knowing that'. For example, with a moment's thought you can recount what you did last Sunday (episodic) and can also say with some certainty whether you know the answer to a factual question, such as 'what is the capital of Portugal?' (semantic).

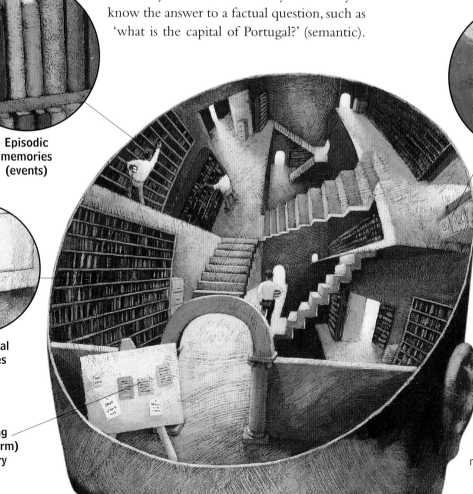

Episodic memories (events)

Semantic memories (facts)

Procedural memories (skills)

Working (short-term) memory

The memory library 'Episodic' memories make up the autobiographical section of the long-term store, while 'semantic' memories are the reference section. Memories for acquired skills ('procedural memory') also find a place in the memory library.

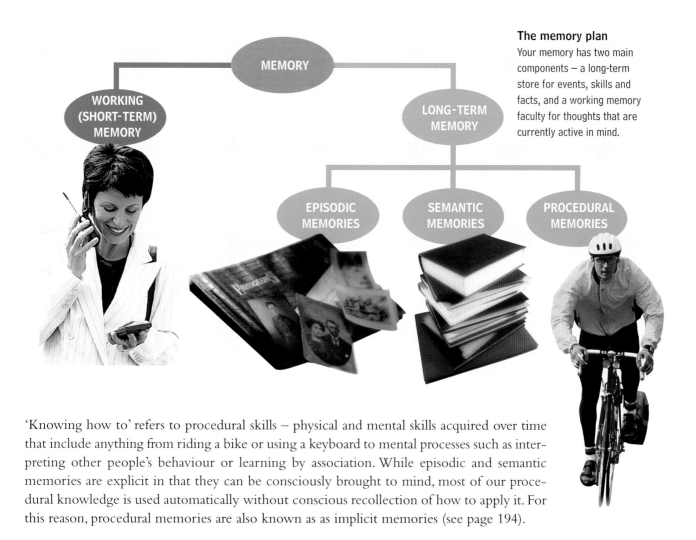

The memory plan
Your memory has two main components – a long-term store for events, skills and facts, and a working memory faculty for thoughts that are currently active in mind.

'Knowing how to' refers to procedural skills – physical and mental skills acquired over time that include anything from riding a bike or using a keyboard to mental processes such as interpreting other people's behaviour or learning by association. While episodic and semantic memories are explicit in that they can be consciously brought to mind, most of our procedural knowledge is used automatically without conscious recollection of how to apply it. For this reason, procedural memories are also known as as implicit memories (see page 194).

Laying down long-term memories

Although we tend to think of long-term memory as our ability to store things that we learned or that happened to us some time ago, the term also applies to items from the last week, day or even hour. Whether these more recent memories become fixed permanently into the long-term store depends on a complex interaction between the world and the brain. Storage in long-term memory is thus a long way removed from a camera recording scenes or a tape recorder laying down sounds.

The first part of the process is attention – the myriad fleeting experiences that pass us by unnoticed are not going to make it into long-term memory. Once our attention is focused, information still needs to be 'encoded' as it arrives – that is, processed so that it can be stored in long-term memory.

Knowledge and experience Episodic memories are personal experiences – such as skating on an icy pond. A semantic memory is something we know irrespective of when we learned it – for example, that water turns into ice at 0°C.

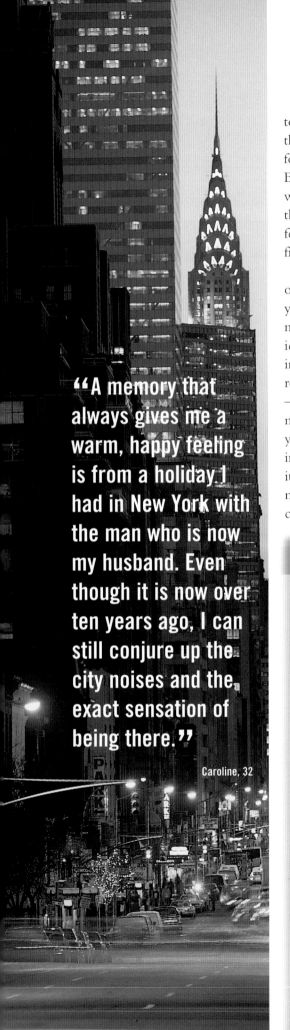

The most effective way to process information for long-term storage is to add meaning. The more we elaborate on meaning, the more established the memory is likely to become. For example, suppose you are told the following information about eels: 'Eels live most of their life in rivers. Before they breed, eels in North America and Europe migrate to the warm waters of the Sargasso Sea. The young eels, called elvers, remain there until they are 30 months old, when they migrate back to the river feeding grounds. There they stay until up to 19 years later, when they finally return to the Sargasso Sea to breed and die.'

After one hearing you might hold on to the gist of this story, but some of the details would almost certainly evade you after a while. However, if you made efforts to elaborate on the key details, you would be much more likely to retrieve them later on. For example, think about geographical locations: picture an eel in a river that you know well and then imagine the journey it would have to make to reach the Sargasso Sea – a region of the Atlantic, south-east of Bermuda. Now think about Bermuda – you may have taken a holiday there or know someone who has. Or you may have heard of or read *Wide Sargasso Sea,* a novel by Jean Rhys. The young eels migrate back at 30 months – think of a child you know starting nursery school at two and a half. This is an exaggerated example, but it demonstrates how processes like these help to incorporate new information into a network of personal experiences and knowledge and so create many routes back to it when you need it.

Real lives ON DIFFERENT DATES?

Even very recent memories of events are prone to distortion, as the experience of Tom and Vivien shows. The couple met through a dating experiment set up by a women's magazine, which paid the bill for new outfits for them both, taxis, drinks and dinner. In return, they each promised to give an account of the evening, which could later be compared to a video film of their date.

Tom said that Vivien was 15 minutes late. She was quiet, which he quite liked, but not a bit nervous. They shared a bottle of champagne before dinner and then they both ordered a salad, duck and cheese to follow. He didn't remember what she was wearing – a black jacket maybe, or was it a suit? Dark, anyway. They didn't leave the restaurant until 11.

Vivien reported that she'd bought a smart black velvet suit by Karen Millen, her favourite designer. She was perhaps a couple of minutes late for her date with Tom, whom she recognised immediately from the photo the magazine had sent her. Tom was

Memory retrieval

The final stage in long-term memory is retrieval. This is when we remember something (or find we have forgotten it). When a memory cannot be accessed, it may be because it was never formed in the first place, or it may be that it simply cannot be accessed at that moment, often because other information in memory is interfering with retrieval.

Most events that lodge in long-term memory are encoded without conscious effort. Episodes that seize our attention and affect us significantly are laid down with a wealth of sensory and emotional details. Yet at other times, this unconscious laying down of memories seems to be infuriatingly random. For example, it is hard to explain why a memory of seeing two strangers having a quarrel on a bus suddenly resurfaces from 25 years ago, or why most of us have to keep looking up how to programme the video recorder but have no problem remembering the names of the characters in a sitcom from years ago.

The answer to such questions may lie in attention and practice. If you never bothered to read the instructions for the video recorder properly and then used it infrequently, programming it is unlikely to have become part of your repertoire of procedural skills. On the other hand, the names of the sitcom characters had your full attention and were given effortless revision once a week, month after month. In summary, it is not the case that everything we ever knew has shelf space in the memory library. Little-used memories usually fade away over time through lack of use.

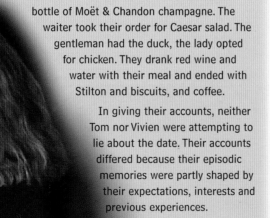

wearing a beige suit and was tall, with fashionably styled hair. They had one glass of champagne each in the bar and then dinner. She wasn't sure what he ate – she had chicken and he may have had a steak – and they had red wine with the meal. They talked about films, his job and her recent trip to Thailand. They left the restaurant in separate taxis at about 10.30.

The restaurant's video camera showed that Vivien arrived at 8.10 – exactly 10 minutes late for her date. Tom had ordered a bottle of Moët & Chandon champagne. The waiter took their order for Caesar salad. The gentleman had the duck, the lady opted for chicken. They drank red wine and water with their meal and ended with Stilton and biscuits, and coffee.

In giving their accounts, neither Tom nor Vivien were attempting to lie about the date. Their accounts differed because their episodic memories were partly shaped by their expectations, interests and previous experiences.

REMEMBERING WORDS

Psychologists have found that even in the simplest memory tasks, words encoded in terms of meaning tend to be easier to remember than those encoded in terms of their sound or by the way they look.

To test this for yourself, look at the words in the left column below and write down yes or no in answer to the question about each word.

WALL	Is it in capital letters?
mat	Does it rhyme with cat?
tulip	Is it a flower?
bottle	Is it in capital letters?
cod	Does it rhyme with man?
Austria	Is it a country?
MOUSE	Is it in small letters?
pin	Does it rhyme with sin?
carrot	Is it a fruit?
rat	Is it in small letters?
saucer	Does it rhyme with cup?
thumb	Is it a part of the hand?

Now do something else for a few minutes to clear your mind. Then write down as many of the 12 words as you can remember in any order.

You will probably find that the ease of recall depends on the way you mentally processed the word in order to answer the question.

Words processed by visual appearance were: **wall, bottle, mouse, rat**

Words processed by sound were: **mat, cod, pin, saucer**

Words processed by meaning were: **tulip, Austria, carrot, thumb**

Most people find words in the third list are better recalled than those in the first or second list.

'HOW-TO' MEMORY

When people think of memory or remembering, what they usually have in mind is conscious recollection. But there is another crucial type of memory that governs all our physical and mental skills: this is procedural or 'how-to' memory. Most procedural memory is called into action with such little effort or conscious planning that we become blind to our own prodigious feats of learning.

In the first hour after waking, most people run through an impressive array of procedural memory tasks – from pushing off the duvet and trawling under the bed for slippers, to showering and making a cup of tea – all accomplished without conscious thought. As the name suggests, procedural memory is our memory of how to do things. Widely shared examples are standing up and walking. However, it takes only a moment watching a toddler striving to master these skills to recognise them for the sophisticated accomplishments they are, achieved only through many hours of intense concentration and with considerable physical courage. And when we attempt some new physical skill, such as learning to skateboard, ski or walk a tightrope, we are returned to something akin to a toddler's state of precarious imbalance.

Acquired skills

For many skills, we can consciously recall the learning process that went into acquiring them. However, more subtle procedural skills, such as communicating in our native language or recognising a friend on the basis of their way of walking, are harder to appreciate. Skills like these are typically gained with little, if any, conscious awareness of what is being learnt or how that knowledge is acquired. Normally, we become aware of having these skills only when they fail us in some way or when we make a mistake – for example, when we struggle to understand a speaker with an unfamiliar accent or rush to greet a stranger who bears a striking resemblance to a friend.

Developing skills
Attempting a challenging new balance trick can remind us of the concentration and practice that goes into first learning to walk and balance.

Our adeptness at acquired physical skills, such as using a phone or a word processor, driving a car, or wallpapering a room, depends on building up packages of small steps that become refined into smooth continuous action. For example, learning to drive involves memorising a complex sequence of instructions and manoeuvres. The learner driver begins by consciously and laboriously checking the mirror, turning on the indicator, releasing the handbrake, letting out the clutch, and controlling the direction of the car. With practice, these are combined into the smooth single action of pulling away from the kerb, all executed automatically while looking for a break in the traffic.

Knowing how and knowing that

Procedural memory relates to 'knowing how', and is quite distinct from 'knowing that', which relates to our memory for events (episodic memory) and for facts (semantic memory). Nevertheless, a great deal of our conscious remembering relies on skills stored in procedural memory. For example, small children have great difficulty remembering information deliberately: they have to learn the skills of committing information to memory and searching their memory for the answers they need. Many of the simple memorisation strategies that adults use, such as grouping similar items together, or reciting them in a fixed order, have had to be learned. Young children and unschooled adults do not use these strategies and so tend to do badly in formal memory tests.

Preserved by practice

Procedural memory is one of the most enduring forms of memory and remains intact even when other types are lost. However, initial mastery of skills must be followed by practice and development – processes that occur quite effortlessly with most skills because we make extensive use of them. Just think how many hours you have spent talking and reading since you learnt how to do so. Although some skills such as riding a bike endure without much practice, others such as speaking a foreign language have a 'use it or lose it' character, and must be kept in regular use to be retained.

TRY IT YOURSELF

INTERPRETING THE SHAPES

When people look at the picture below for the first time, usually all they see is a confusion of black and white blobs. It may take several minutes or even longer to arrive at a recognisable image. Try it for yourself.

If you are still struggling to see anything, being told to look for the head and shoulders of a Christ-like figure might help.

Once you have managed to see the human figure, you will find that whenever you look at the picture again that's what you will see. Without knowing how you did it, you will have learnt the visual procedures for interpreting the picture. This example of perceptual learning is similar to learning to 'read' X-ray images or symbols on an air-traffic controller's screen.

FACT: People with amnesia have intact procedural memory and can be taught new skills, such as using a word processing package. Each time they use the package they think they are trying it for the first time, and are surprised to discover that they know what to do.

UNCONSCIOUS MEMORY

Past events shape our present thinking and behaviour in incalculable ways. Sometimes we try to recall past episodes, while at other times we simply act upon thoughts that seem to have popped into our minds of their own accord. When experiences affect our thinking and behaviour unconsciously, this is called implicit memory.

> **"The memory represents to us not what we choose but what it pleases."**
>
> Michel de Montaigne, French essayist

Unconscious or 'implicit' memory is probably best explained by contrasting it with conscious or 'explicit' memory. For example, if a friend says 'Do you remember the man who sat opposite us on the train on Monday?', you might pause to think for a moment, then consciously experience a series of visual, auditory and other sensory recollections. You may remember making a dash for the train and then squeezing yourself into a seat. Then you may remember the bearded stranger sitting facing you who was engaged in an increasingly frantic pocket-by-pocket search for his ticket. This explicit remembering of a time, place and person fits with our usual understanding of the way memory works.

Inexplicable feelings

But past experiences can have a more subtle influence on our thoughts and behaviour. Imagine you meet a new colleague for the first time and, before learning anything of consequence about him, feel an immediate dislike for him. This might well be a case of implicit memory at work. The new colleague who stirs up unfathomable feelings of antipathy may bear a resemblance to someone else whom you once disliked – perhaps a teacher who had a similar way of speaking. Although you have not made a conscious connection, the resemblance triggers feelings that affect your reactions. Implicit memory is supplying the reason why you feel hostile, but all you experience is the feeling itself.

THINK AGAIN!   UNCONSCIOUS EARLY MEMORIES

Children at junior school are generally poor at recognising photos of former playmates from nursery school because they were only two or three years old when they knew them and most people do not have explicit memories of events before the age of four. However, a study of junior-school children has shown that faces not recognised consciously can still be recognised implicitly. As the children looked at pictures of nursery school friends, the researchers measured their galvanic skin response (GSR) – a measure of skin moisture that is the basis of 'lie-detector' tests. Although the children said they did not recall the faces, their GSR rose indicating that they did recognise their former friends at some unconscious level.

Procedures and priming

Implicit memory also underlies the procedural skills that we develop over a lifetime. For example, when you learn to dance or swim, you find that you know how to do these things without being able to say much about what you actually do. Similarly, most of us can judge whether a sentence is grammatical or not, even if we cannot explicitly state the rules of grammar. We learn them through examples and remember them implicitly.

One way of studying implicit memory is to present people with two apparently unrelated tasks and see whether the first has an unconscious influence on the second. For example, people are given a list of random words to study, such as **miracle**, **violin**, **cataract** and **baggage**, and asked to return for tests a few days later. These tests tend to involve filling in missing letters to make words. Some, such as **m-r--r-m** and **-v-c--o**, may appear too difficult to solve, but the correct answers seem to come to mind quite easily for equally complex words such as **c-ta---t** and **m-r--l-**. This is because the earlier presentation of **cataract** and **miracle** 'primes' people to see these words. People generally do not remember that the words were presented to them in an earlier list.

Priming occurs in many everyday situations. For example, if a person drops an unusual phrase or word into a conversation, there is a good chance that someone else in the group will use it later without being aware of repeating it. Called conversational plagiarism, this is an unconscious form of copying that is an example of implicit memory. Written plagiarism can also have an implicit memory element: writers have been known to reproduce lines of verse and even duplicate entire plots of novels with no conscious memory of acquiring the material from existing works.

Likes and dislikes
When we have a warm or hostile reaction to someone we meet for the first time, an unconscious memory from the past may be affecting our response.

Real lives

PRICKING HER MEMORY

People with amnesia lose their ability to recall information consciously, but they normally retain their implicit memory. In a famous account of this phenomenon, the 19th-century French neuropsychologist Édouard Claparède described an experiment in which a woman with chronic amnesia was shown to retain an implicit memory.

'I pricked her hand forcibly with a pin hidden between my fingers. This little pain was as quickly forgotten as indifferent perception and, shortly after the pricking, she remembered no more of it. However, when I moved my hand near hers again, she pulled her hand back in a reflex way and without knowing why. If, in fact, I demanded the reason for the withdrawal of her hand, she answered in a flurried way, "Isn't it allowed to withdraw one's hand?"… If I insisted, she would say to me "Perhaps there is a pin hidden in your hand."

'To my question, "What can make you expect that I would like to prick you?" she would take up her refrain, "It's an idea that came into my head"… But she never recognised this idea of pricking as a memory.'

The words with the missing letters were marjoram and avocado.

Intuition

When ideas and judgements surface unbidden to offer sudden insights into people and problems, we describe them as intuitions. Although we cannot always rationalise them, intuitions often carry a sense of conviction, suggesting they may be based on memory.

Intuition could be described as a mysterious phenomenon in daily use – our many and varied experiences of it range from a lucky guess in a quiz show to an apparent premonition or paranormal experience. Suppose, for example, a mother has a sudden sense of her son being in danger and then later finds that he was, at that moment, involved in a car accident. She might well interpret the event as evidence of a mysterious intuition at work. She would, of course, be disregarding the many times her flashes of anxiety proved groundless. But while we may question the authenticity of premonitions, the existence of intuition is not in doubt.

Rooted in empathy

Most of our more prosaic experiences of intuition are thought to be based on unconscious memory – skills, abilities and perceptions that are not consciously accessed from memory but that influence much of what we do. For example, one of the most common forms of intuition is empathy, a sense that we know how someone is feeling or even that we are sharing the sensation or emotion. Usually, we are unable to express how we are doing this or point to any obvious clues to the person's emotional state: we are implicitly – rather than explicitly – recognising cues.

An intense form of empathy underlies parental intuition, partly because parents learn to read the fine detail of their children's behaviour, but also because – either through imitation or inheritance – parents and children are likely to share similar forms of emotional expression. As Charles Darwin commented, some expressions of emotion are common to the whole of humanity and our ability to recognise them in others may be innate.

THE CHOICE BETWEEN FACT OR FEELING

Vanilla pods, used in cooking, are fruits containing the seeds of which tropical flower?

• A: Lily
• B: Sweet pea
• C: Honeysuckle
• D: Orchid

A couples version of the popular television quiz show 'Who Wants to be a Millionaire' revealed some interesting differences in the way women and men typically approach quiz questions. Given a question with four possible answers, several of the women seemed happy to base their choice on hunches that 'just felt right', while their husbands were often reluctant to answer unless they knew the facts. Several couples left with half the sum they might have won because they had not acted on the woman's intuition, which turned out to be correct.

The capacity for unconscious memory does not differ between the sexes, so men and women should experience equal feelings of certainty and uncertainty about possible answers. Where they often seem to differ is in their willingness to rely on these feelings. Since intuitions that are based on unconscious memory are often (although certainly not always) correct, it is possible but far from certain that women may be more successful gamblers in circumstances like these.

Darwin observed the reactions of his six-month-old son when his nurse pretended to cry and reported: 'I saw that his face instantly assumed a melancholy expression, with the corners of the mouth strongly depressed... it seems to me that an innate feeling must have told him that the pretended crying of his nurse expressed grief; and this through the instinct of sympathy excited grief in him.'

Experience and expertise

As we gain experience in acting on our natural intuitions, they become further refined through mistakes and successes until we become expert in the activities that we practise the most. An experienced salesperson, for example, closes many more deals than a novice because he or she knows exactly when to apply the pressure, when to walk away leaving the clients to their own thoughts, and when to produce the contract and the pen. Similarly, an accomplished stand-up comedian knows how to 'work' the audience sitting in the half-darkness beyond the footlights and negotiate the risky territory between 'dying' on stage and bringing the house down.

When asked, such experts may describe some conscious strategies that contribute to a successful performance but much of the time they will intuitively know what to do without knowing how or why they do it. Expert performance in any domain is likely to be a combination of conscious tactics that induce a feeling of being in control and intuitions based on implicit memory.

"It's always with excitement that I wake up in the morning, wondering what my intuitor will toss up to me like gifts from the sea."

Jonas Salk, discoverer of the polio vaccine

DISCOVER YOUR MEMORY TYPES

Psychologists have many models and theories to help explain how we form and access our memories, and have discovered a variety of different types of memory. These exercises will help you to discover some of the many different aspects of your own memory.

WORKING MEMORY

Explore the separate audio and visual stores in your working memory.

• Have a go at drawing a picture while listening to the radio. You should find this easy, because the auditory memory and the visual memory do not conflict.
• Now try to hold a conversation with someone else while listening to people talking on the radio. You will find the two sets of auditory information interfere, making comprehension of both at the same time almost impossible.

HOW MEMORY FADES

See how echoic (auditory) memory fades more slowly than iconic (visual) memory.

• Get a partner to write down a string of nine numbers on a card and hold it in front of your eyes just long enough for you to see it clearly. Then try to recall the numbers by visualising. How many numbers can you see in your mind's eye? Try the test three times with three sets of numbers.
• Now ask your partner to recite strings of nine numbers to you and try to access their echo instantly in auditory memory.

You probably won't remember all the numbers in either case, but your accuracy with the spoken numbers will probably be higher.

ICONIC MEMORY

Iconic memory is the way in which the brain holds visual images briefly in your mind's eye before allowing them to fade.

• Draw a dot just beneath the head of a matchstick, then draw an identical dot on the other side of the match just a little further down from the head. Twirl the match between thumb and finger, gradually getting faster and faster.
• At slow speed, you will simply see the two dots succeeding each other. At faster speed, however, it will appear that there is one dot moving up and down the match. This is the optimal movement – the frequency of the twirling equals the speed of fade of the iconic image.

Moving pictures All forms of moving images, from flicker books to film, make use of the brain's fleeting iconic memory to produce the appearance of continuous action.

MEMORY FOR SKILLS

Some skills, like riding a bicycle, endure even if they are not practised for years. Others, such as playing an instrument, quickly become 'rusty' if they are not used.

• Try picking up on some skills that you once had. Check the following list for ideas:

ballroom dancing, solving puzzles, swimming, drawing, knitting, speaking a foreign language, making cakes, rowing, playing the piano

Which ones do you still find easy? Which do you find harder? 'Closed-loop' skills – like riding a bike – in which each action prompts the next, are easier than 'open-loop' skills, in which the nature of the task keeps changing.

ERASING MEMORY

See how distraction can wipe out working (short-term) memory.

• Taking each column below in turn, read the three letters once and then cover them up. Then, as quickly as you can, count in threes downwards from the first number to the second number. Then try to remember the three letters.

TWB	HQM	JBF	QDR
407	106	642	391
377	82	618	367

Having your attention diverted for just a few seconds is usually enough to erase what is in your working memory – even if the amount you are holding is extremely small.

MEMORY FOR EVENTS

Memories are more easily retrieved the more dramatic they are. This comes into play in your episodic memory.

• Search your memory of special events from your life, such as Christmases, holidays and birthdays. How many of the ones that come to mind are best and worst examples?

The chances are that most of the episodes you remember clearly stand out for some exceptional reason. Ordinary examples tend to merge into each other.

MEMORY FOR FACTS

Does your brain record facts accurately or do they become altered in memory? Investigate your semantic memory.

• Find a book of tales from the mythology of a culture you are not familiar with, such as Chinese, Indian or native North American. Read through one story carefully. A few hours later, write down the story as you remember it, then compare it to the original.

You will almost certainly find that your version is shorter and more straightforward than the original. In addition, some of the details, particularly exotic items or magical ideas, may have been unconsciously changed by your mind to fit your own understanding of the world.

LOCATING THE MEMORY STORES

Memory is not one thing but many: there is our store of facts, our skills or 'how to' abilities, personal recollections of events, unconscious knowledge and our continuous monitoring of the immediate past. Each of these memory functions is handled by different parts of the brain.

The human memory system evolved in a rough-and-ready fashion. New skills built onto older ones, taking over and then prompting growth in whichever brain area was most convenient. As a result, various types of memory – although constantly interacting – are located in different regions of the brain.

Apart from instincts, which are genetically encoded memories that arise mostly from a part of the brain called the caudate nucleus, all conscious memory involves the hippocampus. This arching sea-horse-shaped organ is part of the limbic system – the primitive, unconscious area of the brain lying beneath the brain's outer layer, the cortex. When we are paying attention to things that are happening around us, the information we take in through our senses is sent to the hippocampus along nerve pathways from the cortex. Most of it causes a fleeting ripple of activity and then disappears, but memorable events create changes that cause their neural patterns to be retained in the network of hippocampal connections. This process takes about two hours and in the course of a day, millions of these traces are left. Later, we may replay some of them by going over the most important events of the day, and this rehearsing will etch them deeper. At night when we sleep, this process continues. During rapid eye movement (REM) sleep, some of the neural records in the hippocampus are replayed, producing those curious, fractured snatches of past activity that we experience in dreams. This replaying etches them deeper.

Storing events and facts

The replay of hippocampal memories is transmitted to the neurons that lie in the cortex, especially in the temporal lobes on each side of the brain. Events that are particularly exciting or significant tend to be replayed regularly and after up to three years of replay become lodged permanently in both the hippocampus and the cortex. These are our long-term 'episodic' memories – events that we can recall almost as though we are living them all over again. If events are replayed less frequently, usually because they are mundane and unremarkable, the patterns that represent them in the hippocampus eventually fade away and are lost or become inaccessible.

However, even when the memory of an event has disappeared, some of

FACT: If brain function is disturbed in the two or so seconds that it takes for a memory to be encoded in the hippocampus, the event is lost for ever. This is why people who have been concussed can never remember what happened just before the accident.

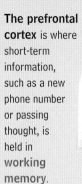

The prefrontal cortex is where short-term information, such as a new phone number or passing thought, is held in **working memory**.

The cortex is the storage location of our **episodic memories.** These records of past experiences are replayed for a period of up to three years in the hippocampus and end up scattered throughout the cortex.

The temporal lobe is where **semantic memories** such as facts and details are stored.

RIGHT HEMISPHERE   THE CEREBRUM   LEFT HEMISPHERE

The amygdala is the brain's emotional centre, and is the storage site for powerful **emotional memories** such as fears and phobias. It may also have a role in facial recognition.

THE LIMBIC SYSTEM

The putamen is where **procedural memories** including acquired skills such as how to ride a bike – are stored.

The hippocampus is the storage site for **spatial memory** – our knowledge of routes and places. This organ of the limbic system also has a major role in consolidating **episodic** and **semantic memories** in the cortex.

its factual elements may remain, encoded in the cortex as semantic memories. For example, long after the hippocampal memory of, say, your first meeting with Mr Jayadeva has disappeared, you may be left with a long-term knowledge of who Mr Jayadeva is but no recollection of when you were first introduced.

The hippocampus plays a crucial role in consolidating long-term memories during the two or three-year period it takes to store them permanently in the cortex. Once firmly lodged there, however, they are no longer dependent on the hippocampus for retrieval. One exception is long-term spatial memory – the cognitive maps of places and spaces that help us to find our way around. These seem to be held permanently in the hippocampus, and people who suffer damage in this part of the brain are often permanently disoriented.

Working memory and unconscious skills

As well as holding long-term knowledge, the brain has a short-term 'noticeboard', or working memory, to keep track of information that needs to be held for just long enough to be acted upon. Regions of the left hemisphere have a larger role in verbal working memory, while the right hemisphere is more involved in spatial working memory tasks. However, the critical area for processing short-term information is the prefrontal cortex, an area of the brain just behind the forehead that expanded greatly during human evolution.

Procedural or 'how to' memories are stored in the putamen. This structure is located above the hippocampus and has close links with the motor cortex, which controls movement. When you access a procedural memory – for example, when you set out to cycle to the shops – the putamen is included in a circuit of activity that runs through the premotor cortex and cerebellum (a structure at the back of the brain concerned with balance,

Real lives STRANDED IN THE PRESENT

Clive Wearing, once a highly accomplished musician, effectively lost his past life when a bout of encephalitis destroyed part of his hippocampus. He emerged from coma unable to recall anything that had happened to him more than about half a minute earlier. His memory for facts – including the fact that he was married and deeply in love with his wife – remains intact, but his memory of events is virtually non-existent. The tragedy of his situation became clear shortly after he woke up. Every time he caught sight of his wife he threw his arms around her and declared his delight in seeing her; when she was not with him, he would phone home every few minutes leaving the same message: 'I'm awake!'

'He cannot remember our wedding, his colleagues, even the nurses who look after him are eternal strangers,' says his wife. 'He constantly feels as though he has just woken up.' Unlike many brain functions, encoding and retrieval of episodic memory is very localised and the loss of hippocampal tissue has permanently deprived Wearing of the ability to lay down new memories. He is aware that something is wrong: 'It's like being dead' he once said. 'Hell on earth – the whole time'.

FOCUS ON   *REVEALING MEMORY IN ACTION*

Today, new methods of brain imaging allow investigators to see the precise brain areas that are activated during recall of different types of information. Although the general areas that process the main types of memory are now well mapped, no two individuals encode information in precisely the same way. Musicians, for example, might store the memory of a piece of music in a different area from someone who is not a musician, because they 'read' the information as a skill memory rather than just a sound. The exact memory 'geography' of every individual brain is unique.

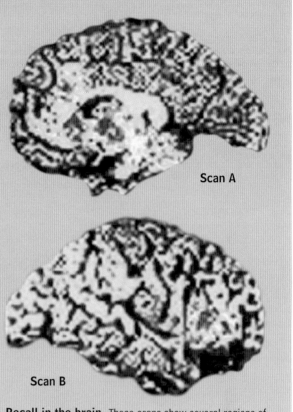

Scan A

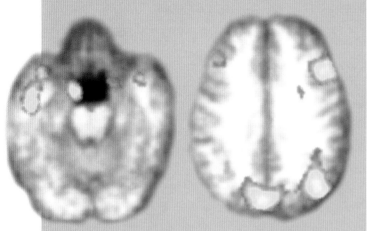

Remembering what   **Remembering when**

These scans show the different areas of the brain that are active when someone is remembering what happened in the past (temporal lobe and areas at the bottom of the brain), compared to remembering when an event happened (frontal and parietal lobes).

Scan B

Recall in the brain These scans show several regions of the right hemisphere that are particularly active during recall. Scan A shows the interior of the brain, revealing activity in the lower parts of the cerebrum, while scan B shows activity on the surface of the brain, especially in the prefrontal cortex.

coordination, timing and incoming sensory information). This circuit integrates all the functions you need to begin pedalling.

Body states such as fear and anxiety are laid down with the emotionally charged events that they accompany and are thought to be stored in the amygdala – the part of the limbic system that registers moods and feelings. Emotional memories cannot be accessed consciously, but may suddenly pop up in the form of panic attacks or flashbacks.

Locating memory in the brain

The brain's memory stores were discovered gradually, largely by observing people who developed memory problems after head injury or stroke, and then comparing the site of the damage with the type of memory lost. For example, the ability to lay down new memories and access recent ones is lost after damage to the hippocampus, while problems with concentration and planning often result from damage to the prefrontal cortex.

EVOLUTION OF MEMORY

Memory is as old as the brain itself. Ever since the first animal nervous systems evolved over five hundred million years ago, creatures have had the ability to learn from experience. But like the brain, human memory has evolved and become more complex.

Memory began in primitive organisms as a simple reflex system. When the body was affected by something nasty, such as a toxic chemical, the nervous system laid down a trace so that next time the chemical was encountered it was recognised and avoided. This capacity to learn from experience forms the basis of all memory. Even the microscopic roundworm has a memory of sorts in that it can learn to avoid certain chemicals. Fruit flies can remember a wider range of danger signals, including odours. More complex animals are able to store information besides danger signals. Bees remember the location of flowering plants, and rats can learn to navigate complex mazes.

Human memory is more complex still, reflecting the larger size of our brains. It is not simply the size of the brain in itself that matters, but the ratio of brain size to body size. In terms of its relation to body size, the human brain is bigger than that of any other animal. Elephants have larger brains than us in absolute terms, but their brains take up a smaller proportion of their body than ours.

Developing memory
As skills evolved, so did different forms of memory – from the procedural memory used by bipedal apes to find food and shelter up to 4.5 million years ago, to the semantic and working forms of memory used by *Homo sapiens*.

BRAIN SIZE 380–450cc

BRAIN SIZE 700cc

BRAIN SIZE 800–1300cc

BRAIN SIZE 1400cc

Australopithecus afarensis	*Homo habilis*	*Homo erectus*	*Homo sapiens*
4.5–2.75 million years ago The bipedal apes, foraging on woodland savannahs in parts of Africa, probably had stored memories of food and other resources in the environment, and procedural memory for skills to find food and shelter.	2.5–1.6 million years ago These were the first species known to make stone tools, thus applying procedural memory to technical skills. They may have had more advanced knowledge of resources, and increased use of vocalisation.	1.8 million–300,000 years ago Migrating into Asia and Europe, *Homo erectus* needed better memory for resources to survive in harsher climates. Episodic memory may have evolved to keep track of social debts and obligations in large social groups.	200,000 years ago onwards Early modern humans applied knowledge broadly. Remembering facts linked with social information may have led to semantic memory. Finally, working memory evolved so different ideas could be held consciously in mind at the same time.

Bigger brains for bigger groups

Scientists are still divided as to why the human brain evolved to be so big. Until the 1970s, most assumed that the expansion of the human brain was driven by adaptation to changes in the physical environment, such as climate change, varying ecological conditions, or changes in diet. However, in 1976, the psychologist Nicholas Humphrey argued that human brains got bigger because of changes in the social environment – the most important being that we started to live in larger and larger groups. This theory is now known as the Machiavellian intelligence hypothesis, after the Italian statesman whose name became synonymous with cunning, manipulative behaviour.

Social bonding Grooming takes place within all primate species. The biologist Robin Dunbar argues that language evolved as a new form of bonding when, as the average human group size increased, grooming became too time-consuming.

The Machiavellian intelligence hypothesis suggests a key role for memory. As group size increased, our ancestors needed to keep track of increasing numbers of people. They needed to remember what they looked like, and what their character was like. Above all, they needed to keep a record of how everyone else in the group had treated them in the past. This, at least, is what is suggested by the theory of reciprocal altruism, which can be summed up as 'you scratch my back and I'll scratch yours'. The biologist Robert Trivers was the first to propose that social behaviour can evolve if animals cooperate only with others who have cooperated with them in the past. Clearly, an animal would need to possess a sophisticated memory to keep track of animals that have been cooperative and others that have not.

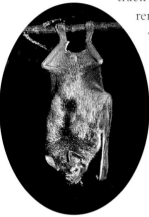

Social bats Like humans, vampire bats have large brains in relation to their body size. They are the only bats to show a rare form of altruistic social behaviour.

Humans and vampire bats

Biologists now think that, among animals generally, reciprocal altruism is quite rare. Most altruism in nature seems to have evolved on the basis of kinship – the drive to bestow favours on family members rather than exchange them with strangers. In evolution, it really does seem that blood is thicker than water.

However, humans may be one of the few species in whose evolution reciprocal altruism has played a large role. Vampire bats are another: they form close friendships, and a bat will regurgitate food to feed a friend (but nobody else) should the friend be unsuccessful at hunting one night. Interestingly, the brains of vampire bats are much bigger, in relation to their bodies, than the brains of other bats. And this expansion has occurred in the cortex (the brain's outer layer), which is also the brain area that expanded most in human evolution. This provides some support for the view that increasing group size, and above all the need for a good social memory, was vital in the evolution of the human brain.

FOCUS ON

MEMORY LAYERS

In brain evolution, new capacities rarely replace old ones; the old ones usually remain and the new ones are simply added on top. This is particularly clear in the evolution of memory.

Humans have evolved complex memories that can store all sorts of information that animals cannot, such as words and abstract concepts. But we also retain the older, primitive kinds of memory that our pre-human ancestors had. Emotional memories, for example, can exist alongside verbal memories, and sometimes the two can point in different directions. Emotional memories are mediated by very old brain structures, such as the amygdala, buried deep beneath the cortex (the outer layer of the brain). The amygdala, the hippocampus and the thalamus are the main components of the limbic system, which is found in even the earliest mammals.

Animal memories

Animals have memories, but do they have human-like memories? Although they can recognise, associate and use memory to understand the world, animals seem to lack the power to recollect – to think about the past in an introspective, autobiographical way.

Animals display surprising powers of memory – none more so than chimpanzees, a species very closely related to our own. Experimenters tested a chimpanzee by leading it around a one-acre compound as they concealed 18 pieces of fruit in different hiding places. Each time they set the chimp free after a few minutes it found, on average, about 12 of the treats – a performance not significantly worse than the average human's. When a mix of foods was concealed, the chimp went straight to whichever morsel it liked best. The chimp appeared to have a pretty clear memory for both where and what had been stored.

Memory for survival

While most animals are not as intelligent as chimpanzees, all show some level of memory. Even a snail learns to avoid a particular smell if it is paired with an electric shock. Goldfish do not seem to

FACT: A trained gorilla called Koko could use and remember over 400 words of sign language.

remember anything for more than about ten seconds, but equally this means that they can remember something for about that long, such as which way to swim to find food or to avoid a shock. Other fish, particularly large varieties, do much better, performing more like lizards. If a lizard is shown food being put behind an obstacle, it will head for the food even if it is held back for two or three minutes. So out of sight is not out of mind, even for reptiles.

Some animals have considerably longer memories. In one study, experimenters fed cats, dogs and baboons in the corner of a particular room. Let loose at the door to this room weeks or even months later, the animals would head straight over to sniff and scratch at the same corner.

Birds show particularly prodigious memories. Every November, the Clark's nutcracker, a North American jay, collects pine seeds and buries them for safe-keeping in thousands of caches to keep it going

NOT SO BIRD-BRAINED

Pigeons have brains 500 times smaller than human brains, but experiments have shown them to have unexpectedly good powers of recognition. Using seed as a reward for correct answers, pigeons were trained to peck at a button whenever they were shown a photograph depicting some chosen feature. The tests revealed that pigeons quickly learn to distinguish photos containing trees from photos without – they could even tell oak leaves from other kinds of leaves.

Next, pigeons were tested on pictures with people and no people, single people or crowds, clothed or unclothed people, and eventually on pictures with or without a particular woman. They learnt to recognise the woman from any angle and were able to distinguish her from pictures of other women dressed in similar clothes. The pigeons' remarkable performance even held up in tests involving pictures of fish and sea creatures – not normally within the experience of the average pigeon.

through the winter and spring. Even after several months, the bird can go straight to each stash – a feat of memory that humans would struggle to match. When the researchers moved rocks and tree stumps around, the birds became confused, which showed that they used visual landmarks to remember their troves.

Absent autobiography?

It seems that animals have no trouble laying down memories that can be mobilised in response to immediate experiences and needs. A particular sight, sound or smell will be instantly recognised and may even spark associations. Hunger pangs and other internal urges can also ring the bells of memory, awakening ideas in an animal about how to respond. The difference with humans is that we seem able to delve into our memory banks at will. We can recall – or at least reconstruct – fairly convincing images of various life events, from what we had for breakfast to a particularly enjoyable concert or party. But it is a consensus among animal psychologists that animal minds seem to lack this kind of introspective recollection.

The difference may lie in language. Speech helps us to categorise memories and also seems to be involved in the organisation of our reminiscences. When we prod our memory banks with a questioning inner voice, words like 'breakfast' and 'birthday party' strike sparks of association. Words act as a stimulus, and recollection of ourselves in another time and place unfolds with a narrative structure.

So animals can display some impressive powers of recollection. But for whatever reason, only humans appear to live autobiographically.

AN ELEPHANT REMEMBERS

The old saying that an elephant never forgets may not be as far-fetched as it sounds. Randall Moore, a Kenyan elephant expert, returned a captive elephant to the wild. Fifteen years later the same elephant was found with an injured foot after an attack by a hippopotamus. The elephant violently resisted all attempts at help until Moore went out and called to it. The elephant seemed to recognise his voice immediately.

An onlooker reported: 'It came up to him and laid down and allowed a vet to examine it. The elephant lifted up his foot and was passive while his rescuers put in syringes and operated.'

3 MEMORY IN ACTION

Sometimes it feels as if our experiences pass directly into memory, but storing the stuff of future remembering is actually an intensely interactive process. Every experience includes elements from a consortium of the senses, and these sights, sounds, scents, tastes and emotions are all part of the memory. However, our minds are not impartial recorders of perceptions and when a picture is less than complete, we use what we expect and what we already know to fill in the gaps. No memory, then, is a perfect replica of the original experience.

Intuitively, we relate new ideas and events to our understanding of the world, and this is reflected in the way information is organised in the mind. New items are woven into a web of existing knowledge. The more time we spend on contemplating and integrating information, the more intricate the web becomes, and the more threads we have to lead us back towards the information we need.

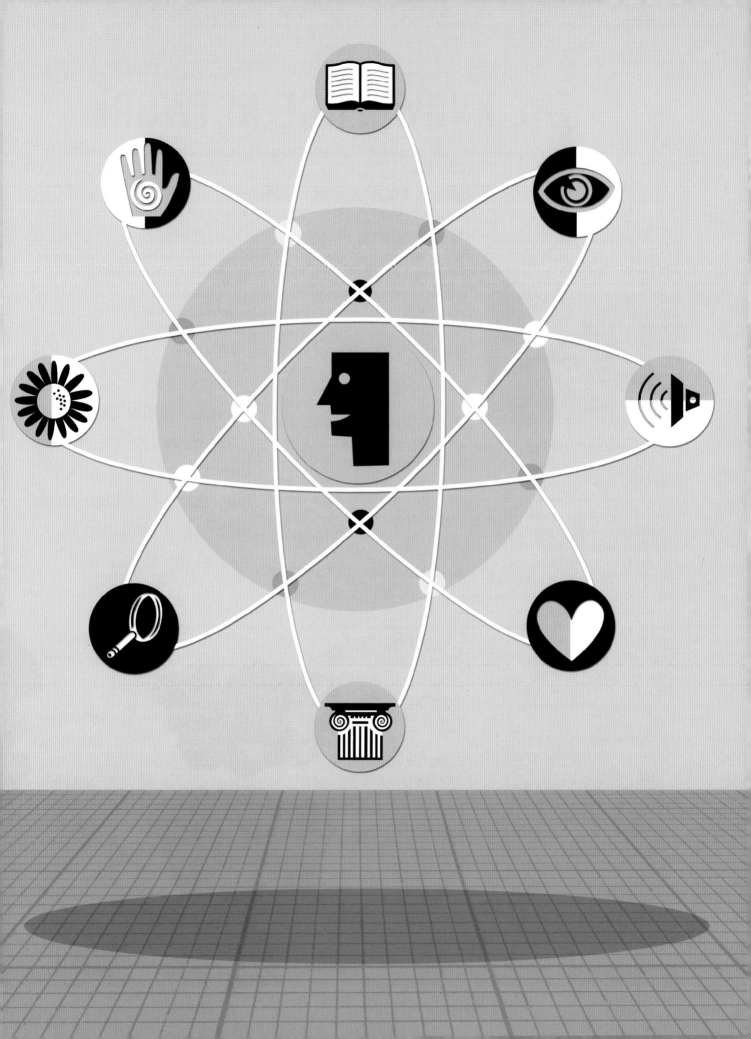

THE KNOWLEDGE NETWORK

Every day brings new information that is absorbed and incorporated into the memory's huge store. Fortunately, new material is not scattered randomly in memory, but linked and organised to help us to find things when we need them.

F *CUS ON*

MENTAL PROTOTYPES

One of the ways we improve the efficiency of learning and recall is by categorising objects into groups. For example, we would say that elephants, badgers and antelopes all belong to the group 'animals'. However, in the human mind, not all members of a group fit in equally well. US psychologist Eleanor Rosch has shown that in the group of things called 'clothes' people feel that shirts fit in better than shoes. Similarly, people see sparrows as a better example of birds than penguins, and carrots as a better example of vegetables than radishes.

Rosch argues that this is because we tend to have a mental image or 'prototype' of the most typical example we know in each category. We then put other things into that group based on how similar they are to this image. This may explain why some people find it hard to think of dolphins as mammals. They are mammals biologically, but they look similar to the mental prototype of a fish.

The main way the brain organises its store of memories is by linking related information together to form a 'knowledge network'. When you are trying to remember something, you may find yourself following these links from one memory to the next until you find the one you want. The more links a memory has to other memories, the more possible ways there are for you to get to it. Imagine travelling around a strange city without a map – you are more likely to end up in a square that has six different streets leading to it than to find yourself in a square with only one street leading to it.

Memory by association

Over time, impressions and information become enmeshed in the network by their association with other pieces of information and events. Memories that have similar connotations form links based on meaning, called semantic links. Take, for example, your knowledge about cows. All the various things

"Lulled in the countless chambers of the brain, Our thoughts are linked by many a hidden chain. Awake but one, and lo, what myriads rise!"

Alexander Pope

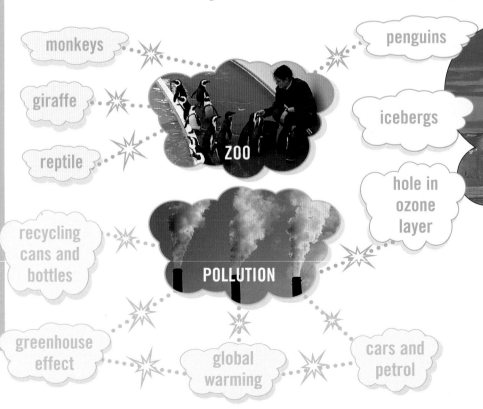

you know about cows – what they look and sound like, that they produce milk and live on farms – are linked because they are related in meaning. Remembering one may lead you to remember the others. Also, your memory of what cows are will be linked to your memory of what sheep are, for example, because these have similar associations. Semantic links act like a cross-referencing system: once you have found a useful piece of information, you can connect with many more that might also be relevant.

Memories that are formed at the same time as one another are linked by association. These associative links are fundamental to our understanding of the world and often allow us to make predictions based on previous experience. For example, we soon form an associative link between seeing rain and getting wet. Less clear-cut but often powerfully evocative associations contribute to episodic memories. When you hear a piece of music and experience a powerful recollection of another time and place, it is because these memories have strong associative links in your mind.

Making links

Most of the time, semantic and associative links work unconsciously: as soon as one concept is activated in memory, activation spreads automatically to other ideas related through meaning or past experience. Experts are able to learn new facts in their chosen field with little effort because they have a rich web of existing knowledge and so can instantly form semantic links between a new fact and many other pieces of information. In a similar way, anyone can improve the efficiency of their knowledge networks by making an effort to relate each new piece of information to something they know already. This helps to form links that otherwise might not have developed.

TRY IT YOURSELF

WORD ASSOCIATIONS

When you hear words, they trigger their own memory traces and also activate the traces of other words (or concepts) with which they are associated. You can test this idea out on your friends or family.

• Read out the following list of words at a rate of one word every two seconds. Tell people that they will later be asked to write down as many as they can remember.

bed, rest, awake, tired, dream, night, eat, wake, comfort, sound, slumber, snore, food

• Wait five or ten minutes, then ask everyone to list all the words that they can remember.

When you look at the lists, you will probably find the words **sleep** and **warm** included in some. This happens because many of the original words are associated with sleep and warmth and so the memory traces for these two words receive some activation too. When people try to recall the list, one or both of these also come to mind.

coldness

explorers

book on explorers bought for my father at Christmas

ANTARCTICA

snow

my only white Christmas

South Pole

FAULTY OVEN AND TURKEY TOOK ALL DAY TO COOK

Spreading ideas Thinking about a concept such as 'Antarctica' activates a host of related items such as penguins, ice and explorers. These in turn trigger chains of associated concepts and knowledge, plus memories of personal experiences.

FORMING MEMORIES

Most experiences float by unrecorded, but some create a more lasting impression. When an experience creates a particularly strong or enduring pattern of neuronal activity, it becomes etched on the brain – and a memory is formed.

Laying down a memory can be a deliberate act, particularly when there is a certainty that the information will be needed again, but most episodes and facts are encoded without any apparent effort. Why is it that some ideas and events become part of the mind's furniture, while millions of others are forgotten or merely submerged in our pool of general knowledge? The durability of an episodic memory depends on how exciting the original experience was or how excited the individual's brain was when it occurred. It also depends, much like the memory of a fact or a piece of information, on how much attention was paid to it and how often it is recalled.

Every experience we have is produced by neurons in the brain firing in a particular pattern. When something is very impressive, or if a person's brain is fired up with excitement, the neurons participating in the experience fire fast and furiously. This encourages the formation of links between the neurons, which makes them more likely to fire together again in future. When they fire again, and the same (or a very similar) pattern recurs, the person experiences a replay of the original experience – in other words, a memory.

A memorable moment Excitement makes experiences more likely to be remembered.

THINK AGAIN!   A MEMORY FULL OF SURPRISES

Researchers have found that people are particularly good at remembering anything that comes as a surprise. In other words, if you experience something that is out of line with your expectations, it can become deeply embedded in your memory.

For example, if you went into a bank and saw all the usual things – clerks, customers, money – it would probably meld with all your other memories of trips to the bank and eventually disappear. But if you went into a bank and saw a walrus waiting in line, this visit would become firmly fixed in your mind. Why? Because queuing up with a walrus totally violates your idea of what should be happening in a bank. This tendency for surprising information to be remembered is sometimes called the Von Restoroff effect, after the psychologist who first described the phenomenon.

FOCUS ON   *CREATING PERMANENT BONDS*

Every time a particular set of neurons fire together, they become more likely to fire together in future. When connections are repeatedly activated, they form even more robust links which bind them into a single unit – a process called long-term potentiation. This is important in forming long-term memories.

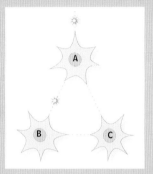 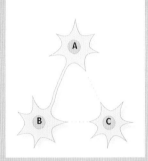 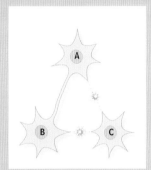 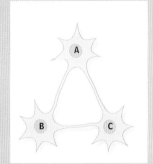

1. If neuron A receives a stimulus that causes it to fire strongly, it will pass the signal to neighbouring neuron B, and in the process cause changes to neuron B that make it more responsive to neuron A in future.

2. Each time the two neurons fire together, the link between them strengthens until they are so closely bonded that they invariably fire together.

3. When neurons A and B fire together, their combined strength is enough to activate another neuron, C, which is weakly linked to both of them.

4. With repeated firing all three cells undergo changes that forge links between them and become bound together in a pattern. A permanent memory has been formed.

Changing contexts

Although recollection involves a replay of experience, the re-run is never precisely the same as the original because each time a memory is triggered, it occurs in a new context – the context of what is happening in the brain when the memory is revived. Imagine that you taste some exotic fruit such as a kumquat for the first time on holiday. The next time you taste a kumquat, it will bring to mind a memory of the holiday, because the kumquat experience is linked to the context in which it occurred. However, your second tasting will also be associated with what is happening then and there – a dinner party, perhaps – and from then onwards, memories of kumquats will have echoes of both experiences. In this way memories are elaborated upon and altered whenever they are recalled.

The ever-changing nature of memories means that no two people ever have the same recollection of a past event – even if they shared the experience at the time. For example, if a couple see a film together, they may leave the cinema with similar memories of it. However, as these recollections become associated in each person's mind with new experiences, they may start to diverge. In a later discussion, there might be disagreement about some of the details from the film – which could be resolved by watching it again. But most experiences are not recorded on celluloid, which is why people who argue about shared events may never resolve the disputes that arise as a result of altered memories.

> **" How it came back to me! That peculiar feeling that we used to call 'Church'… the rustle of Sunday dresses, the wheeze of the organ, the spot of light from the hole in the window creeping slowly up the nave… For a moment I didn't merely remember it, I was in it. "**
>
> George Orwell, *Coming up for Air*

MEMORY AND MACHINES

The average three-pound human brain may lack the speed of a hard drive and microprocessor, but its flexibility outstrips that of the computer every time. Machines that can think and remember are still science fiction, but researchers are developing systems that bring them a step closer.

Computers are often used as an analogy for human memory and there are some basic similarities. People and computers both have a working memory, or processor, that handles information, and a long-term memory, or hard drive, where data is organised and stored. However, even the most basic home PC appears to have advantages in terms of memory capacity, reliability and speed of access to information. It can store complete reference works in tiny folders, and pluck out relevant details on request without the human problems of forgetting or inaccurate recall.

On the other hand, humans have a huge advantage over even the most powerful computers in our memory networking, as limitless and complex links in the brain allow us to make connections that computer designers to date cannot get close to matching. Typically, computer memory – whether in an individual PC or a system such as an internet search engine – is organised in a similar way to a telephone directory: to retrieve a piece of information, such as a name or phrase, the computer searches through the vast amount of data to trawl up matching items. The average computer searches only for the precise item: it cannot make intelligent guesses or generalise on the basis of what it 'knows' in related areas. Nor can it learn from experience as humans can – although new machines are being developed that can do this to some degree.

Expert systems

Programmers can now simulate some human abilities using computer systems that incorporate the facts and rules underpinning the judgement of human experts. Such expert systems use specialised software to apply the criteria to new information and make decisions about it,

Playing games The chess computer Deep Blue eventually defeated world champion Gary Kasparov over a series of matches in 1997, but the machine did not 'remember' strategies like its opponent.

FOCUS ON *A CHAMPION CHESS FORCE*

Even a home computer can challenge a skilled chess player, yet it took many years of development to produce a computer that could beat a world champion. So how did Deep Blue do it?

Humans and machines play chess in very different ways. The major factor in Deep Blue's favour was the sheer brute force of its processing power. An ordinary computer has two or three processors at most, but Deep Blue has more than 250 working in parallel, enabling it to generate up to 200 million possible moves per second. The top human players can evaluate only about three moves per second.

However, as human players become more skilled, they do not consider more moves – they consider better ones. And the reason for this is memory. As they practise and study, players memorise thousands and thousands of board layouts and remember the moves that work in particular situations.

but these can only be used in very specific areas, for example in the diagnosis of blood diseases or the analysis of mineral samples. If the system needs more information to reach a conclusion, it checks other databases or asks the user questions. Deep Blue, one of the most powerful chess computers ever constructed, is in effect an expert system that applies rules and strategies gleaned from master chess players to evaluate outcomes and adapt to new strategies throughout the game.

Neural networks

At the cutting edge of artificial intelligence are computers that use circuitry that simulates the way in which the brain processes information, learns and remembers. Called artificial neural networks, these computers use layers of very simple processing devices, or 'nodes', linked together to form a network that has some similarities to the networks of neurons in the human brain. The network is 'trained' by being presented with examples – for instance, images of male and female faces – and being instructed on which are in which category. Over time, the network will learn to make generalisations based on its experience of the training data, and can then apply this 'knowledge' when presented with new inputs – for example, when asked to judge whether a new face is male or female.

Neural networks have a real advantage in applications where there are no straightforward rules with which a more conventional computer would be programmed. For example, they are already in use in tasks as diverse as recognising speech and analysing financial trends. Although they are still very simple compared to the memory capabilities of the brain, these systems show behaviours that are strikingly similar to human memory and they are opening new avenues for psychological research. It has been found, for example, that when the processing limits of a neural network are exceeded, it does not 'crash' like a conventional computer, but merely performs less well – rather like a person who has too much to cope with.

The electronic nose Neural networks are being incorporated in 'electronic nose' technology, destined for use in food processing and fragrance development industries. Odours are blown over sensors that convert them into digital signals, which can then be compared and identified by the computer.

CONSTRUCTING MEMORIES

It may feel as if our memories are simple records of past events, but all memories are in fact reconstructions of what occurred. Like any thoughts, they are influenced by our personal habits of mind, prejudices and preconceptions about the way the world is.

FACT: People find it easier to remember information that confirms what they already believe than information that challenges their existing ideas.

There are a number of different ways in which people's minds tinker with their memories – whether they are aware of it or not. Think about the last conversation you had. It is unlikely that you can remember exactly what was said word for word; you probably remember just the gist and a few phrases. Your memory preferentially stores the things that seem important at the time, leaving gaps in your recollections. Further gaps appear as time elapses, but when you make a conscious effort to remember the conversation, you tend not to notice them – it feels as if you have a full account. We also tend to infer extra details or draw assumptions from scant information when we cannot make sense of a story or situation; later we may find it difficult to extract the 'real' elements from the added extras. Similarly, our perception of ourselves often leads us to construct, or selectively preserve, those memories that seem to show us in a favourable light.

Memory is not passive: the brain actively constructs and shapes how we remember things according to our understanding of the world. Researchers refer to this as 'top-down' processing, by which previously stored knowledge reaches down to play a role in current thinking. This contrasts with 'bottom-up' processing, in which new sensory information enters the mind and is acted upon. Most long-term memories are heavily influenced by top-down processing, both while they are being laid down and during recall.

Memory 'schemas'

Another major factor in the construction and retrieval of memories is our use of 'schemas' – a term psychologists use to describe how we organise knowledge drawn from previous experience. For example, most of us have a schema about restaurants: when we go into a restaurant we expect to be

Eating habits Past experience helps us to construct a set of expectations for different situations. Each time we go to a restaurant, for example, we know what to expect and what to do.

seated at a table, to look at a menu and order food, which is cooked by chefs in the kitchen and brought to our table by a waiter. Schemas help to guide our actions in new situations. If you go to an unfamiliar restaurant, your restaurant schema will tell you what to expect and how to behave.

Guesses and distortions

Schemas are also useful for filling in gaps in memories. Just as your schemas help to direct your actions in new situations, they also allow you to make educated guesses about things that you have not remembered fully. These organised 'packets' of knowledge are so enmeshed in our general thinking we are largely unaware of them and this can sometimes lead to distortions. Imagine that you visit a friend in hospital. When you later recall the event, you will unconsciously use your hospital schema to fill in missing elements in your memories. This could lead you to 'remember' things that are plausible, but weren't, in fact, there – a bunch of grapes on the bedside table, perhaps, or monitors by the bed – because these correspond with your schema of a hospital.

Schemas that distort our memories in this way can help to explain why we develop stereotypes of people; they also play a part in maintaining our prejudices. When a negative schema dominates a person's view of a particular group in society, it may come into play in each contact with members of that group, casting neutral exchanges and occurrences into an unfavourable light. These constructed negative experiences then serve to strengthen the initial prejudice.

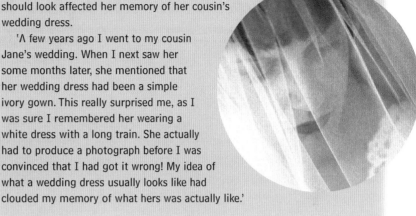

Real lives TRAIN OF THOUGHT

Ellen, 20, recalls how her idea of how a bride should look affected her memory of her cousin's wedding dress.

'A few years ago I went to my cousin Jane's wedding. When I next saw her some months later, she mentioned that her wedding dress had been a simple ivory gown. This really surprised me, as I was sure I remembered her wearing a white dress with a long train. She actually had to produce a photograph before I was convinced that I had got it wrong! My idea of what a wedding dress usually looks like had clouded my memory of what hers was actually like.'

TRY IT YOURSELF A TALE OF TWO SPECIES

Giving a story a title can affect which details are later recalled.

Read the following passage separately to two different people, telling one person it is called 'Watching an ant hill', and the other 'Watching a street from above'.

'I saw the bodies moving around below me. Their legs moved quickly and they all seemed to be walking with something in mind, but not all of them were heading in the same direction. Many were carrying things, although I couldn't see what these

were. None of them seemed to communicate with each other, but I could detect a sense of purpose about the whole moving mass of life.'

Then ask each person if they can recall any phrases or ideas from the passage. You will probably find that they recall different phrases in keeping with the title they have been given.

Finally, try reading the passage to someone without giving it a title. They will probably remember far less, as they have no schema to guide recall.

Eyewitness testimony

When we 'see things with our own eyes', we may feel that our recollection of events cannot be doubted. Yet psychologists have discovered that our openness to suggestion, and confusion about where and when we saw what, can make us unreliable eyewitnesses.

Imagine that you have witnessed a theft, and the police have asked you to look through photographs of known criminals to see if you can identify the thief. You might not be able to spot a familiar face among them, but what if you were called in for an identity parade a week later? You might think that you would spot the thief in the line-up with no trouble – but research has shown that you'd be quite likely to pick someone whose photo you had seen the previous week rather than the real criminal.

Source amnesia

Psychologists use the term 'source amnesia' to describe the uncertainty about where people are remembering something from. We are all prone to

source amnesia, but some of us are more vulnerable than others. Young children can confuse the things they see on television with what they experience in real life, while older people can find it hard to remember who said what. As a result, law courts can sometimes be sceptical about the quality of evidence given by the very young or the very old.

Many legal cases rely heavily on eyewitnesses, and yet it has been estimated that unreliable eyewitness testimony leads to as many as 4500 false convictions a year in the USA alone. Source amnesia could play a part in many of them. For example, imagine what might happen if, during a police interview process or in a court of law, key facts are 'suggested' to an eyewitness, perhaps by using leading questions such as 'did the suspect strike the victim?' Later, it can become genuinely difficult for a witness to keep the new 'suggested memories' separate from the memory of what they actually saw.

Misleading information

The US memory researcher Elizabeth Loftus was one of the first people to explore in detail how witnesses can be influenced by information suggested to them after the event.

In a pioneering series of studies in the 1970s, Loftus showed a group of people a film of a staged car crash, and then asked how fast they thought the cars were travelling when they hit each other. All the volunteers were asked essentially the same question, but for some Loftus used words such as 'contacted', 'bumped', 'collided' or 'smashed' instead of 'hit'. She found that the speeds put forward by the volunteers were directly influenced by the words she used – those who had been told the cars merely 'contacted' estimated lower speeds than those who were told the cars had 'smashed'. A week later, Loftus found

THE SUGGESTIBILITY OF YOUNG CHILDREN

The fact that children tend to be suggestible frequently causes problems when child witnesses or possible victims of child abuse are questioned. It is one reason why in the UK children's evidence is videotaped as soon as possible after the event.

Psychologist Stephen Ceci and his team demonstrated how easy it is to influence young children's memories. They told a story to groups of children between the ages of 3 and 12 and also showed drawings of the major sections of the story. The next day, an adult suggested to half the children details that had not been in the original story.

Two days later, all the children were tested on recognition memory. They were shown pictures that had been presented during the story and pictures of suggested events that were similar to those in the story. One picture showed a girl eating eggs (as in the story), and another showed the girl eating cereal (an adult suggestion). The children were asked to choose a picture to illustrate the story. Ceci found the younger children were much more likely than older ones to pick an image of a girl eating cereal.

that those who had been asked the question with the word 'smashed' in it were also more likely to 'remember' seeing broken glass lying on the road after the accident – although no glass was actually there.

Cognitive interviews

Police forces in countries around the world are responding to research findings on the reliability of eyewitness memory by introducing new interview procedures called cognitive interviews. These are specially designed by psychologists to help witnesses generate more accurate testimonies. Cognitive interviews are successful because they increase the number of cues derived from the context of an event that are available to a witness – for example, the sights, sounds and smells that were present at the time, as well as the feelings of the witnesses themselves. We can remember more about an event if the context is reinstated (see page 230), which is why police often take victims and witnesses back to the scene of a crime.

"Justice would less often miscarry if all who were to weigh evidence were more conscious of the treachery of human memory."

Hugo Munsterberg, psychologist, 1909

PHOTOFIT CHALLENGE

Even if you are generally confident about your memory, it is quite easy to demonstrate to yourself how fallible you might be as an eyewitness.

• Try to generate a full description of someone you see regularly but don't know well – for example, the postman or a local shopkeeper. Write down details such as eye and hair colour, hairstyle, build, any facial hair, whether they wear glasses, and any particular distinguishing features. You could even try to sketch them, like a police artist.

• Keep your notes handy, and next time you see the person, check off the features you remembered correctly, and those you didn't. How accurate was your description?

THE MIND'S EYE

If a picture paints a thousand words, what can we say of the human memory with its remarkable power to store information visually? Most people have an ability to conjure up pictures from memory with extraordinary vividness. We often find that these images endure long after names, dates and circumstantial details have been forgotten.

How many doors do you have in your home? Most people are not able to answer this question straightaway, but have to retrieve an internal image of their house or flat and mentally travel from room to room, counting the doors. In accessing information of this kind, many psychologists would argue that we are using a distinct visual memory system.

According to this idea, long-term memory is housed in two separate systems: a verbal memory system that contains networks of stored facts, and a visual memory system akin to a photographic library where information is stored in the form of images. The visual memory system comes into play when we make visual comparisons between one object and another. For example, is a garden pea a lighter or a darker green than a Christmas tree? To answer this question, you retrieve an image of each object and compare them in your mind's eye.

The capacity of human memory for images is generally far greater than that for words, and

Visual splendour
Our visual memory enables us to conjure up vivid images based on our experiences. Think how many words it would take to describe your memory of a magnificent peacock in full display.

TRY IT YOURSELF   PICTURING WORDS

Memory researcher Alan Paivio argues that easy-to-visualise words can be stored in two memory systems – one for language and the other for images – whereas abstract words can only be stored in the language system. Try this simple experiment:

• Read out this list of 30 words to someone else at a rate of about one word every two seconds. Then ask him or her to write down as many as possible from memory.

house, dress, cold, knife, thing, fruit, meal, similar, challenging, bike, cat, bucket, pain, either, soft, balloon, easy, book, durable, road, middle, faith, spare, castle, plane, earring, key, simple, through

Now take a look at which words were recalled. You will probably find that the list contains more concrete, easy-to-visualise words such as **house**, **dress** and **knife** than abstract words such as **through**, **similar** and **either**. This may be because the easy-to-visualise words are stored in two ways, both visually and verbally, and are therefore easier to remember.

this seems to support the idea of separate visual and verbal memory systems. We are quite poor at recalling all the specifics of a conversation, although we can usually remember the gist of what was said. In contrast, our memory for images is pretty impressive. In tests, it has been shown that people can recognise as many as 10,000 pictures with over 90 per cent accuracy after being shown each picture for just a few seconds. In addition, studies of people with specific problems of visual recognition suggest a separate visual system. For example, people with visual agnosia understand the names of objects but cannot recognise the objects themselves.

Are images stored or constructed?

However, not all researchers agree with this idea. Some think that the images we experience in our mind's eye are not stored but are created as and when we need them. For example, imagine a tiger. Now, are you retrieving an image of a specific tiger from memory? If so (and your mental image is clear), you should be able to see how many stripes the tiger has – but you probably find you cannot. US philosopher Daniel C. Dennett argues that mental images are more like descriptions than pictures: they do not specify every detail. So, to count the stripes on your mental image of a tiger, you would have to construct them.

This raises the question of how we can ever separate 'genuine' images, which stem from actual experience and are retrieved from memory, from the made-up images of our imagination. Although schizophrenics, for example, have difficulty in distinguishing between imagined images and those that relate to real experience, most of us do not have this problem. However, psychologists know from their work on eyewitness testimony (see page 218) that what constitutes a true memory is not always straightforward. One of the current hot topics in psychology is whether retrieved images have fundamentally different properties from constructed images.

FOCUS ON

VISUAL AGNOSIA

This is a fault in visual memory that is brought about by brain damage – caused, for example, by a stroke or an accident. Visual agnosics can see the visual elements of an object, such as the colours and composite shapes, but they cannot put the pieces together to make a meaningful, recognisable 'whole'.

Martha Farah, an American psychologist specialising in visual cognition, recorded one sufferer trying to make sense of the US flag: 'I see a lot of lines. Now I see some stars. When I see things like this, I see a lot of parts. It's like you have one part here and one part there, and you put them together to see what they make.'

THE MIND'S EAR

Hearing plays a special role in remembering because we rely primarily on the spoken word for communicating with each other. Specialised memory systems for sounds have evolved in the brain, enabling us to recognise and respond to different sounds.

Sounds such as brass bands, school bells or the echoing shouts in a swimming pool have a surprising power to take us back to a different time and place. Music is also a startlingly effective trigger for memories – be it a special song that recaptures the early years of a romance or the opening chords of a Rolling Stones track that entices people to the dance floor and erases decades of acquired decorum.

Response to music is partly instinctual. There is some evidence that those spine-tingling riffs that affect nearly everyone mimic the sounds used by animals to convey emotional messages such as affection, loss and danger. Complex melodies, however, have to be learned before they have an effect – hence the constant repetition of certain bars and choruses in most forms of popular music.

Hearing, like every other sensation, is produced by a particular neural firing pattern. Once a tune is learned, we can replay it – albeit faintly – in our heads by re-creating the neuronal pattern produced when we last heard it played. The neurons (nerve cells) that respond to sound are situated mainly in the temporal cortex – the area of brain above and behind the ears. Those in the brain's left hemisphere respond selectively to speech, while those on the right register melody and tone. In addition to the neurons that produce conscious hearing, cells in the limbic system (the primitive, unconscious area deep within the brain) produce an emotional reaction to sound, such as fear or delight.

Learning your name

When someone calls your name, the sound triggers several different types of recognition – each one a form of memory. You recognise the word and that it refers to you. You recognise and interpret the tone, whether it is anxious, urgent or warm. And you may recognise the voice, and connect it to a person. Each element of the message contained in that small sound is encoded in a different part of the brain's memory system.

Just like any other form of knowledge, sounds have to be learned before their full meaning can be recognised. A baby learns the special relevance of its own name by hearing it repeatedly, but repetition alone is not enough to give a word meaning. The word becomes distinguished

The echo of times past Hearing a snippet of sound – a line of a song, the ticking of a grandfather clock, or the sea lapping against the shore – can be enough to transport you back to another time or place.

from other sounds by a context that implies some special personal connection. Parents use the name as they tend to their baby's needs and engage in eye contact, causing the child's sense of self to be activated at the same time as the sound of the name – and the two concepts gradually come to be linked permanently.

Learning the voices that belong to particular people occurs in much the same way. You hear the sound of the voice at the same time as you experience other aspects of the person, such as appearance and details of who they are. Once these links have been made, the mere sound of the voice is enough to hook out memories of the rest of the person. Voice recognition is generally reliable, because the characteristic 'music' of a voice remains similar whether it is loud or soft, at a distance or close up.

Echoic memory and the phonological loop

The brain's briefest memory for sounds is echoic memory – an instant replay that enables us to keep a short string of sounds 'on hold' for a few moments. Fleeting as it is, this type of memory is much in use in some professions: a mechanic listening for a particular knocking noise above the background hum of a car engine uses echoic memory, as does a doctor listening to a patient's heart.

In conversation, words and phrases enter a neural circuit in working memory called the phonological loop (see page 185). Each phrase is held here for up to several seconds and has to be interpreted by the brain before the next one arrives and erases it – which is why listening to a person who speaks very rapidly requires concentrated attention. When we try to hold onto an address or telephone number, it is possible to keep a few words or numbers active in the loop by constantly repeating them, but this information is very vulnerable to interference. For example, being told by a receptionist to 'have a nice day' as an addition to some important information can be counterproductive: it can be just enough to make you forget the vital details that you were repeating in your head.

TRY IT YOURSELF

STOP THE JINGLE
Replaying music in your head can be pleasurable – but not when a song or snippet gets stuck in endless replay. Sometimes the last thing you hear on the radio in the morning (perhaps an infuriating advertisement jingle or a pop song) can go round and round in your head all day. These fragments are similar to obsessive thoughts or flashback visual memories. To get rid of one you need to 'overwrite' it, and the most effective way to do this is to force yourself to recall a different tune until the first one fades.

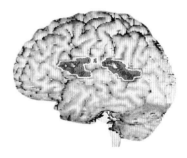

Phonological loop This brain scan taken while someone was repeating words to keep them in memory shows a loop of high activity in the cortical areas involved in this process.

FOCUS ON *LANGUAGE SOUNDS*

Babies are born with the ability to learn any language, but if they are not exposed to particular sounds in a language within the first three years of life they lose the capacity to hear them. The 'r' sound in English, for example, is not used in Chinese, so children who are surrounded only by Chinese speakers in the first few years of life cannot learn to speak English entirely without an accent. However well they learn the language, the 'r' sound will remain

difficult to distinguish from other similar sounds and therefore hard to reproduce in speech. Similarly, certain tones in spoken Chinese are not used in English, so people who do not hear them as young children cannot later learn to pronounce them fully accurately.

Babies lose the ability to hear sounds they are not exposed to because the neural wiring needed to distinguish between language sounds develops during a crucial early period.

SCENTING THE PAST

It is something with which we are all familiar – the way that a simple smell can suddenly bring on a rush of intense memories. It has long been recognised by writers and scientists alike that odours and scents are very potent triggers of memory.

☞ TRY IT YOURSELF

NAMING SMELLS

Identifying smells involves both sides of the brain. Here's a way to test this for yourself. Close your eyes, block your left nostril, then get a friend to give you a whiff of some familiar, strong-smelling substances – like mint, garlic or lemon. Try to name each one as you smell it. However well you know what it is, the chances are that you will not be able to name it. Now unblock your left nostril and try sniffing the substance. Do you find that the name comes back to you?

The reason for this is that smell, unlike other senses, is not automatically processed in both hemispheres. Smells from the right nostril go only to the right side of the brain, and vice versa. As most people have no language-processing ability on the right side, they are unable to link the smell with its name.

One of the greatest literary works of the early 20th century, Marcel Proust's autobiographical novel *A la recherche du temps perdu* (*Remembrance of Things Past*), begins with a famous passage in which Proust encounters the scent of a madeleine – a delicate cake – that has been soaked in lime-blossom tea. The subtle but unmistakable aroma provokes a vivid recollection of a long-forgotten moment from his childhood – the scent providing an unconscious link between entirely different times and places.

Many of the classic elements of a scent-triggered memory can be found in Proust's description: the vividness of the memory and the fact that it was not deliberately recalled; the fact that the triggering scent was an unusual one not encountered every day; and that the memory triggered was a very particular one, drawn from past personal experience. Such powerful scent-evoked memories are now known as Proustian moments.

Where scent seems to be most powerful in triggering memories is in the emotional intensity of the memory evoked. In experiments, people list more associated emotions in response to scents

❝ It's my grandmother. It's the smell of the soap dish… I can see her perfectly, standing there in the kitchen and me helping her to do the dishes the last Christmas we spent together. ❞ Marian, 42

than to triggers from other senses. They also rate the emotions as being more intense, and particular memories as more emotional, when they have been evoked by scent.

Episodic memories

Proustian moments are emotionally intense examples of what psychologists call episodic memory. This is the type of memory you use to remember events, such as what you did yesterday. The reason for the strong link between smell, episodic memory and emotion seems to lie in the structure of the brain. Episodic memories are thought to be stored between the cortex and a relatively primitive area of the human brain called the amygdala–hippocampal complex, which is also the brain's emotional centre. The amygdala–hippocampal complex links directly to the olfactory system, the brain area responsible for smell. Even more remarkably, it is known that during human evolution the amygdala–hippocampal complex developed from the olfactory system. In other words, the ability to experience and express emotion grew directly out of the human brain's ability to process smell. It is therefore not surprising that scent retains such a potent ability to trigger strongly emotional memories, long after they seem forgotten.

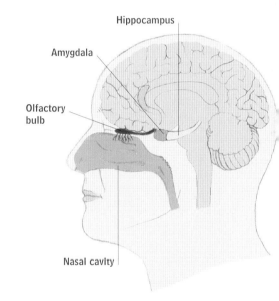

Accessing emotions The olfactory system, which processes smells, is connected directly to the emotional centre of the brain. When we smell something, we take in molecules that trigger scent receptors in the nose. The receptors send messages to the olfactory bulb, which connects to the amygdala-hippocampal complex. These messages set off the emotional memory traces encoded in the amygdala, which in turn triggers the hippocampus to 'hook out' visual and auditory information associated with the recollection.

USE YOUR SENSES FOR A BETTER MEMORY

We tend to talk about memories in terms of hearing and sight, but scent, touch and taste also help recall. When we stimulate more of our senses, more of the brain becomes actively engaged in an experience, increasing our chance of remembering it. Try these sensory exercises and see if they work for you.

TEST YOUR VISUAL MEMORY

Visual memory is particularly strong, and this sometimes leads us to misjudge the accuracy of what we 'see' in memory. Try to visualise something you see every day – perhaps your front door, your street, your desk at work, or the layout of your living room. Now try to draw it, including all the details you can remember, and later check your sketch against the real thing. You may be surprised at how many omissions you make, and the items you add that are not actually there.

TRY THE MOZART EFFECT

Using 'dormant' senses as you read may help you learn and recall. In his book *The Mozart Effect*, the American writer and teacher Don Campbell describes the work of several researchers which suggests that listening to some classical music (especially Mozart and Haydn) improves the ability to learn poetry and foreign languages. Listening to Mozart, even for short periods, has been shown to enhance children's ability to work with mental images in short-term memory – crucial skills for maths and chess.

When you are reading information that you want to remember, you can experiment with different types of background music. Does Mozart do the trick for you? Do you find that pop music makes remembering harder?

SCENT YOUR MEMORIES

The sense of smell is directly linked to the amygdala-hippocampus complex in the limbic system of the brain, often called the 'seat of the emotions' and also important for memory formation. This gives scent a strong power to evoke memories. Use this power to your advantage if you have to learn something for a test or audition by wearing a distinctive scent or body spray that you have not used before. Apply the scent again just before your test, exam or audition – it may help to trigger stored information. Or you could keep the memories of a holiday fresh all year round simply by using a different soap or shower gel while you are away. Afterwards, whenever you feel stressed or tired, washing with the same brand of soap should bring back relaxing memories.

RECAPTURE YOUR TASTES

Now that most foods are available all year round regardless of the season, we have lost some of our most powerful taste cues to remembering. Can you recall how the taste of tangerines used to conjure up Christmas or how strawberries meant June sunshine? And there was the unique cinnamon-and-peel spiciness of hot cross buns at Easter – now on the shelf all the year round.

You could try to recapture the memory power of taste with cookery that reflects the changing seasons: for example, steamed new potatoes and mint in springtime; soft-fruit pudding in summer; blackberry and apple pie in the autumn; chunky winter vegetable soups. Or introduce some unusual delicacies or tastes at picnics and celebrations. The next time you taste them they may bring back the memory of a day by the river or a special birthday.

TRAIN YOUR SENSE OF TOUCH

Put a handful of different British coins in a bag and try to identify them all by touch alone. For a harder task, select a dozen foreign coins left over from trips abroad. Take each one in turn, note the currency and value, then feel its edges – is it milled or smooth? Is the shape round or angled like a 50p piece? Is there a hole in the middle, or a portrait on the front? Once you are familiar with the coins, throw them into a bag and attempt to identify each coin by touch before you pull it out again. You could also try to remember something about the country of origin as you take each one out.

COMBINING SENSES

Try a memory task using just one sense, then two, and then three, and see if your performance improves. Start by writing out three lists of objects around the home, ranging from screwdrivers to teaspoons to towels. Make each list about 10 to 12 items long.

On three separate mornings take one of the lists and spend five minutes learning it. Memorise the first list simply by reading it silently (sense: sight). At the end of the day, try to write out the list and note your score. Learn the second list by reading it out loud to yourself, preferably in a singsong voice (senses: sight and hearing). At the end of the day, you should find you remember more of the items.

For the third list, assemble the objects, sing their names and handle them briefly (senses: sight, hearing and touch). This should be the best-remembered collection of all.

MEMORY AND EMOTION

Every experience is potentially a memory, but in most cases what distinguishes experiences that endure in memory from those that pass without note is that when they occurred they either created, or coincided with, higher than normal levels of emotion.

FACT: Boring facts are memorised more easily if presented to a person immediately after they have watched an emotionally moving film.

Powerful emotion has an important role in the laying down of memories. Emotion is generated in a primitive part of the brain called the limbic system, but its effects radiate to the areas of the brain that process sensations and generate thoughts. One effect of emotional arousal is to direct attention to the events that provoke it, and attention in turn amplifies the brain activation associated with the event. Attention is effectively the first stage of laying down a memory.

For example, if you were lazily surveying a country view, your brain would be registering many different things – the sky, the clouds, the green of the fields, the twittering of the birds. None of these perceptions would be creating a particularly vivid experience – and the impressions of them in your brain would fade into oblivion almost as fast as they arose, leaving only a faint, general impression, like the backdrop to a painting. Later, you might be unable to bring any particular element to mind – the scene would have merged with your general memory of what it is like to be in the countryside. If, however, in the middle of this reverie, a fox ran across your path with a still-flapping bird in its mouth, the sight would provoke

Real lives   THE BIRTH OF A CHILD

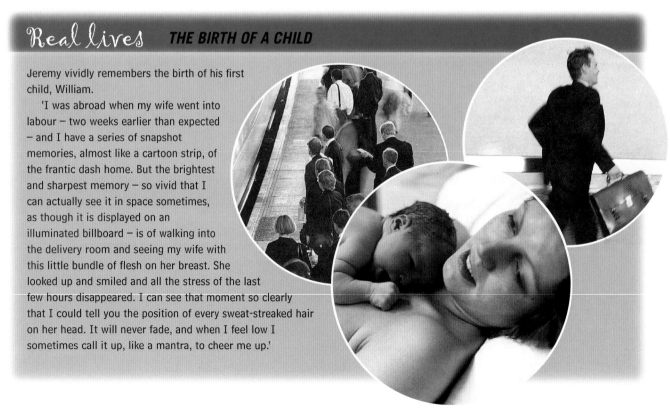

Jeremy vividly remembers the birth of his first child, William.

'I was abroad when my wife went into labour – two weeks earlier than expected – and I have a series of snapshot memories, almost like a cartoon strip, of the frantic dash home. But the brightest and sharpest memory – so vivid that I can actually see it in space sometimes, as though it is displayed on an illuminated billboard – is of walking into the delivery room and seeing my wife with this little bundle of flesh on her breast. She looked up and smiled and all the stress of the last few hours disappeared. I can see that moment so clearly that I could tell you the position of every sweat-streaked hair on her head. It will never fade, and when I feel low I sometimes call it up, like a mantra, to cheer me up.'

a sudden, strong, emotion – horror, perhaps, or excitement, or even pleasure at witnessing nature in the raw. Later, the sight would stand out as a distinct memory. If it made a really strong emotional impression, it might come back from time to time like a scene captured in a flash photograph.

Chemicals in the brain

We understand intuitively that exciting events are more clearly recalled than routine occurrences. One reason for this is that emotion changes the chemical balance of the brain. Excitement, for example, pushes up the levels of brain chemicals acetylcholine and noradrenalin in certain areas of the brain, while pleasure increases production of dopamine and disgust provokes the release of glutamate. These changes help to create links between whatever neurons happen to be firing together at the time. Noradrenalin, for example, encourages the growth of axons – the snake-like tendrils that reach out from one neuron to connect with another, and glutamate triggers the release of adhesion molecules that bind neurons together. Hence emotion helps to preserve the pattern of neural activity associated with an event, making it more likely to be replayed in the future (see page 213).

Emotions in recall

Emotional memories are most easily recalled when a person is again in the emotional state in which the memory was laid down. That is why pleasurable events tend to pop back into memory during similarly enjoyable experiences, and past losses are felt again when a person is grieving for some new loss. Emotional experience itself is laid down as a memory, and the more a particular experience is replayed, the more strongly it becomes engraved into the mind.

There are some clear advantages to a system which automatically preserves emotionally charged events; after all, these are likely to be the more significant events in our lives. From a practical viewpoint, retaining knowledge of such things can help to guide present and future actions. Frightening or dangerous events are likely to be ones that we will wish to avoid in future, and recognition of similar situations in the making acts as a warning. Conversely, memories of pleasurable incidents are likely to guide us to seek out more of them.

☞ TRY IT YOURSELF

FLASHBULB MEMORIES

Exceptional events are recorded in the brain as 'flashbulb memories' – a term used by psychologists to describe moments captured in memory because of the emotional intensity of the event. We all have a private collection of such memories, but we also have individual memories of public news events that made a strong emotional impact on us. In a flashbulb memory, the place we were in when we heard the news, what we were doing, how we reacted, and so on, is usually indelibly recorded, along with the news of the event.

Depending on your age, hearing the news of one or more of the events below is likely to be imprinted in your memory. Can you recall the moment?

WHEN YOU HEARD THAT...

PRESIDENT KENNEDY
HAD BEEN
ASSASSINATED

JOHN LENNON HAD
BEEN SHOT

PRINCESS DIANA
HAD DIED

Where were you?

How did you hear?

Who were you with?

How did you feel?

What were you doing?

Did you tell anyone?

MEMORY AND CONTEXT

Everything that happens to you has a context – not just circumstances and surroundings but also your internal state, emotions and physical feelings as you experience it. If the event is laid down as a memory, some of that context is laid down with it and becomes a hook for remembering.

Imagine you are happily enjoying the sights on holiday when you become aware of a disturbance close by – a man shouting as his camera is snatched from his shoulder. If you were asked to describe what happened, you might begin with your first sighting of the man as he jumped to his feet and perhaps end with a fleeting glimpse of the thief pushing rapidly through the crowds. But no matter how thorough your description of the event might be, your full memory would contain much richer contextual detail.

A richness of experience Our holiday memories are a mix of the sights and sounds that took our attention, together with the characteristic atmosphere that formed the background to any particular event we recall.

Senses and emotions

There are two types of contextual information attached to memories of events. The first is the sensory background. You would have a conscious recollection of the sights and sounds that drew your attention to the camera snatch. Unconsciously, however, you might have taken in the smell of a hamburger being eaten close by, or the background scent of banks of jasmine. And all the time you would have been registering other visual and auditory information – the splash and sparkle of the fountain; a child feeding crumbs to the birds; a clock chiming the half hour. Although peripheral to the main event, these sensations are part of the experience and become part of the memory.

The other type of context is your internal state. If you were feeling happy, these internal feelings would be integrated into the memory along with the peripheral sensations. If you felt uneasy after the theft, your memory will incorporate that shift in mood.

Re-establishing the setting

Contextual elements can be valuable aids to recall because when one part of a memory is retrieved, it often hooks out all the rest. Police make use of this principle in reconstructions of crimes – restaging an event in its original location, using lookalike victims, can help passers-by to recall important details that might have been otherwise forgotten.

Researchers have found that it is easier to recall something learned in a particular setting if you return to the same setting. In one extraordinary experiment, deep-sea divers were asked to learn lists of words under water, while another group learned their lists on the beach. When asked to recall the words, the groups were much more successful when they were tested in the setting in which they learned the words.

This important finding about memory and environmental context can be usefully applied in everyday life. Students have been shown to perform better in exams if they sit them in the classroom where they learned the subject. Similarly, when you are engaged in a frantic search for your keys, it may be infuriating to be asked to think about where you last had them, but recalling the context of when you last used them can be enough to prompt the memory of what you did with them.

Inexplicable feelings

The downside of contextual memory is its power to influence present thoughts. When your mood is low, it can act as a trigger to gloomy recollections, which feed into and deepen your state of unhappiness. This spiral of sad memories is often a feature of depression. By the same token, people in a happy frame of mind are more likely to dwell on pleasant memories.

Contextual links can also prompt idiosyncratic responses. As we get older, we accumulate more and more unconscious links, which is one reason why our reactions to sensations may become increasingly individual. Many of our otherwise inexplicable likes and dislikes may be accounted for by buried context-dependent memories.

TRY IT YOURSELF

IN THE BAG
Using context can help you to recall more than you might think. Revisit the exercise on page 171 and list from memory the contents of your bag or briefcase, but this time ask yourself the following context-related questions to see if they prompt your memory:

• When and where did you last open your bag? What did you put in or take out?

• Imagine yourself back in the same setting – what other items can you 'see' inside?

• Think of other times when you used your bag. When did you last open it at home – and what for?

• Picture the inside of your bag and describe all its compartments one by one. What do you generally keep in them?

Did you recall more items this time? If there were any you failed to remember, the chances are they had not been used for some time.

Real lives UNCOVERING FEELINGS OF SADNESS

Joseph recalls how the smell of rabbits triggered a long-forgotten memory of a sad time in his life:

'When I was three I went to stay with my cousins. I can't remember the house, or the garden, or anything much. I only know about it because my mother mentioned it a few times.

'Then quite recently, I was passing a pet store and there was a white rabbit in a hutch just outside the door. As I passed I caught a whiff of hay, mingled with the smell of rabbit droppings. Suddenly I had an intensely clear memory of helping my cousins to clean out their rabbit. The strange thing was

that at the same time I felt overwhelmingly sad.

'When I got home I called my mother and told her what I had experienced. She confirmed that my cousins did have a rabbit. And she was not surprised that I remembered feeling sad. I had been sent away to my cousins immediately after my father died because my mother was so upset. Until then I had no memory of my feeling about losing my Dad. I can barely remember him and have always told people that I can't remember anything about his death. It took a rabbit – of all things – to bring it back .'

Déjà vu

One of the most peculiar tricks that memory can play, déjà vu is a curious sensation marked by a sudden, intense impression of familiarity – a feeling of 'being here before' or having lived through the moment already.

A sense of déjà vu can occur in any situation. You may be visiting some entirely unfamiliar town, and suddenly feel that you have been right there, in that precise spot, at some other time – even though you know that is impossible. Or you may be talking to friends around the dinner table, and feel that you have had this conversation and lived this moment before. The feeling goes way beyond any vague sense of having seen or done something similar in the past – it is very precise and unmistakable.

Déjà vu can seem more 'real' than a normal recollection, yet it is maddeningly elusive because, unlike flashbacks or 'Proustian' memories (see page 224), it cannot be pinned down to a past event. Usually, the feeling evaporates quickly and cannot be recaptured, however hard you scour your memory.

Ideas and explanations

The sensation of déjà vu is so singular that it has been regarded by some as evidence of reincarnation. Another superstitious explanation is that déjà vu is the memory of a dream in which the person 'lived through' the moment in advance of it happening.

Other more rational explanations have been suggested over the centuries. For example, Freud held that déjà vu occurs when a repressed fantasy of doing or seeing something floats up to consciousness momentarily, but then returns to the unconscious before it is clearly acknowledged.

One speculative explanation for déjà vu is that it may occur as a result of the left and right hemispheres of the brain being slightly out of synchronisation. The slight delay in communication causes the two hemispheres to function, momentarily, as two separate consciousnesses. This may explain why déjà vu is sometimes associated with epilepsy and the aura (forewarning) that precedes migraine.

The latest theory

Current brain research suggests that déjà vu may be the result of a momentary error in the way the brain constructs conscious perception. Everything we experience is processed along many parallel pathways in the brain. Some of these run through areas of the brain's outer layer or cortex and deal with sensory perception. For example, they combine visual information to form complete images and link sensory information to related facts, such as the names of objects and what they are. Other pathways run through the limbic system, the brain's emotional centre, and it is here that information is clothed with emotional significance, including, if appropriate, the

JAMAIS VU

Jamais vu is the converse of déjà vu: instead of something new feeling familiar, something known feels strange. You might, for example, be in your own home when suddenly the furniture and the layout strike you momentarily as utterly unfamiliar. Or you may look at someone you know well and feel fleetingly that he or she is as strange to you as a face in a crowd. Yet intellectually you know that the room or the person are exactly as they have always been.

Like déjà vu, jamais vu is probably caused by a momentary failure of the limbic system to react appropriately – in this case, information that should be recognised as having emotional significance is not, or the emotional 'labelling' does not get through to consciousness.

Although the phenomenon usually lasts for just a few seconds, in rare cases damage to the limbic pathway can produce permanent jamais vu, especially with regard to people. These feelings may become so intense that the sufferer concludes that friends and family have been 'replaced' by impostors or aliens. This conviction, known as Capgras delusion, can have catastrophic consequences. Sufferers often reject their family and may become paranoid and violent.

feeling of familiarity. Normally the information from the limbic and cortical pathways is brought into consciousness at the same time, creating a 'full' picture. Déjà vu is thought to occur when information flowing through the limbic system is tagged with familiarity by mistake. When this incorrectly identified information merges with the information from the rest of the brain, it produces a feeling of familiarity that is at odds with the knowledge produced by the cortex. This leads to the puzzling experience of déjà vu.

"We have all some experience of a feeling – of our being surrounded, dim ages ago, by the same faces, objects and circumstances – of our knowing perfectly what will be said next, as if we suddenly remember it!"

Charles Dickens, *David Copperfield*

REMEMBERING AND FORGETTING

Everyday experience tells us that our conscious attempts to remember are not uniformly successful: some forms of remembering seem to be much easier than others. At times, the sheer randomness of recollection can take us by surprise when buried thoughts seem to surface of their own accord.

The human brain is unsurpassed in its ability to store information – so why do we forget things? Experiments suggest that, with time, items that are rarely used degrade or become overwritten by new thoughts and ideas. We know, too, that diseases and brain damage can cause permanent memory loss, and that there is some decline in brain function as we get older. However, age does not make memory loss inevitable. Much remains to be discovered about remembering and forgetting, but some of the basic mechanisms are clear. These make our forgetting understandable, and in some instances desirable or even essential. Can you imagine how difficult life would be if nothing were ever forgotten?

RECALL AND RECOGNITION

We often talk about remembering as if it is a simple matter of managing to remember or not. But there are a number of different ways to access memories, and the method we use depends on the type of situation.

What is the capital city of Canada? In which year did the Berlin Wall come down? A dromedary has one hump – true or false? Is Nepal in Africa or Asia? These general knowledge questions involve two different types of remembering. The first two questions ask you to *recall* facts, while the second two ask you to *recognise* facts. You may not have thought about it before, but these two processes are rather different. Recall involves searching through your memory for a specific piece of information. In recognition, on the other hand, you are given the information and simply have to decide whether it is familiar or not. The day-to-day demands on our memories tend to include instances of recognition and recall in fairly equal measure.

Everyday experience tells us that recognition is an easier process than recall. For example, it is unlikely that you can remember right now what was on page 36 of this book, but if you turn to that page, you will be able to tell at a glance whether you have read it or not. Similarly, you may have no recollection of the name of a novel or its plot or characters, but as soon as you begin to read it, you remember if you have read it before.

The easier part – recognition

Recognition is what makes a multiple choice question less taxing than an open-ended one. A multiple choice question might ask, for example, whether the capital of Canada is Canberra, Ottawa or Ontario. Getting

Long shots and lucky guesses Researchers comparing answers to recall and recognition questions have to be careful to take into account the element of guesswork. In these questions about the first moon landing, you would be unlikely to get the recall question right unless you actually knew the answer, while the recognition question gives you a 25 per cent chance of simply guessing the answer (c) correctly.

RECALL QUIZ QUESTION

Who was the second person to walk on the moon ?

RECOGNITION QUIZ QUESTION

Who was the second person to walk on the moon ?

A Neil Armstrong   B John Glenn
C Buzz Aldrin   D Jim Lovell

Recognising a distant bird from a fleeting glance is quite an art, but it is one that bird-watchers are particularly adept at. They use the term 'jizz' (adapted from the initial letters of 'general impression of size and shape') to describe the impression of a bird when they first spot it, often from quite a distance. Jizz can refer to a bird's shape, size, colour or flight pattern – in short, anything that helps identification. Here is a way of getting a feel for jizz in everyday life.

• Put yourself in a situation where you are likely to see people who are familiar to you at a distance of about 100 yards – perhaps as you approach your workplace or your children's school in the morning.

• See if you are able to recognise anyone from this distance, even though you cannot see their faces properly.

• If you succeed, think about the particular aspects of each person that made them recognisable. It might be their build, hair colour, clothes, way of walking, gestures, or a combination of all of these characteristics.

the right answer depends simply on recognising it – or eliminating ones you recognise as incorrect. Most people would have a better chance of getting this right than if faced with the recall-based question 'What is the capital of Canada?' – even though the final answer accessed is the same.

One reason why people have greater success with recognition-based questions is that they can take a guess, since the correct answer is in front of them. In the multiple choice question above, there is a 1 in 3 chance of getting the answer right even if you have no idea what the capital of Canada is. In the question 'Ottawa is the capital of Canada – true or false?' the chances of guessing correctly rise to 50 per cent. However, guessing is of little or no value in response to the straightforward recall-based question 'What is the capital of Canada?'

Recognition allows people to get away with partial learning. If you were introduced to 20 new people at a party and were then asked to recall all of their names the following day, that would be a substantial memory task. If, on the other hand, you were given a list of 40 names and asked to tick off the people you had met, you would be able to respond to any name that seemed familiar. Allowing for an element of guesswork, you would probably be fairly good at this task even if your memory of each name was rather vague – a memory that is too weak or incomplete to be recalled can still be used for recognition.

FACT: Simplicity is best for recall. When four different health warnings were introduced on cigarette packets in Australia, half of smokers could not remember more than one.

The form of remembering that we employ in real life depends on the situation. In many types of expertise, from medical diagnosis to archaeological discovery, recognition may be the form of memory that is most in use, albeit backed by reserves of knowledge. Traffic signs are a good example of the use of recognition in everyday experience. It is unlikely that you could draw or describe all the different road signs from memory – but then, why would you need to? What matters with road

THE IMPORTANCE OF FIRST AND LAST

Primacy and recency effects have a powerful influence on memory. Primacy refers to our tendency to recall information more easily from the beginning of a sequence; recency to better recall of information from the end of a sequence. You can try this when watching commercial television.

• During a commercial break, ask someone else to note down the name of the product in each advertisement as a checklist to be used later.

• Wait for about 30 minutes and then write down all the advertisements that you can remember, in any order.

• Now compare what you have remembered with the checklist.

The likelihood is that you will remember more adverts from the beginning and end of the commercial break than from the middle. You can repeat the experiment using different periods of time between watching the adverts and recalling them.

Recognition in animals The fact that usually we find recognition easier than recall is linked to simple associative learning, which we share with animals. For example, a dog's idea of going for a walk can be triggered simply by the sight or sound of a lead, and tapping its bowl is often all it takes for the animal to realise that a meal is on the way.

signs is that you can recognise them instantly and act upon them. It is of no practical use to be able to recall them, and so we do not learn them in a way that enables us to do so.

The harder part – recall

Psychologists suggest that recall may be more difficult than recognition because it involves more stages of memory processing. In recognition, you simply need to make a judgement about whether a particular item fits in relation to the question being asked. In recall, you need to generate in your own head a variety of candidate answers, then use a similar judgement process to decide which is the correct item. According to this view, recognition is easier than recall because it omits the mental generation phase.

If you are having difficulty recalling something, it can help to be given some relevant piece of information as a prompt – perhaps that the capital of Canada begins with 'O', for example. Prompts are particularly useful in situations when you are unable to access information that you are sure you know. Similarly, you may be 'primed' to recall a piece of information because you have heard it mentioned recently.

In one study of remembering, groups of people demonstrated only 38 per cent accuracy for recall tasks, compared to 87 per cent accuracy for recognition. However, subsequent research has shown scores become closer if distractors – confusingly similar items – are used in recognition tests. Distractors are much in use in multiple quiz questions – we might, for example, find it hard to make a choice between Ottawa and Ontario in the earlier quiz question. They are also essential to fair play in real-life recognition situations such as police identity parades. Eyewitness testimony pioneer Elizabeth Loftus cites the example of a witness being asked to identify his 'oriental-looking criminal' from a line-up without distractors (in this instance, men with a similar appearance). Only the suspect was oriental.

Primacy and recency

Not everything we recall is remembered equally distinctly – even events that occurred in close succession. Imagine you are planning to buy a second-hand car and have looked at six or seven promising examples. Memory researchers would predict that you are most likely to settle for either the first or the last car that you saw, because these will be remembered better than the cars you saw in between. The tendency for better recall of things at the beginning of a sequence is called the primacy effect, while the similar effect for items at the end of a list is called the recency effect. Memories of the first and last items — be it speakers on a podium, candidates for an interview, or even diamond rings in a jeweller's shop — tend to be the most distinct and hence enduring. The primacy effect is further enhanced by the fact that the first example you encounter is your basis for judging all those that come afterwards.

Different remembering for different tasks

Researchers have found that we may adopt different learning strategies according to whether we are being asked to remember or recall information. There is evidence that if we learn something expecting to have to remember it one way, we will have difficulty accessing the information if we are asked to remember it another way. One study tested people's memories of a set of pictures using either recall or recognition. Each person was told which type of test they would later receive, but half of them were tested in the way they were expecting and half in the other way. Results showed that recognition was found to be easier overall, but people who received the test they expected performed better than those who were given the unexpected test.

Similarly, the way material is presented can affect whether it is easier to recognise or recall. For example, organising lists of words into categories can improve people's performance in recall tests because it gives them a framework to prompt retrieval. However, organising words has a much smaller effect on success in recognition tests.

THINK AGAIN!

WHAT'S IN A NAME?

Researchers have discovered that we have some strong biases in the type of information we can recall. Most people have experienced being able to remember details about a person while being unable to recall their name. Researchers call this effect the 'baker/Baker' paradox: if you were introduced to someone who was a baker and to a person called Baker, you would be more likely to remember the occupation of the first than the name of the second.

There is some debate over why this should be. Some researchers think that names are stored separately from other knowledge, and so require a whole extra stage of remembering when we see a person we recognise and try to remember their name. Others believe the problem arises from the fact that most names are meaningless in themselves and thus lack links to other memories, which makes them harder to find and recall.

Our special memory for faces

Research has shown that human beings have a special ability to recognise faces. We can often tell at a glance whether the face we are seeing is familiar – even if we can't remember the name or where we have seen the person before.

Faces are the first thing we learn to recognise visually. Newborn babies focus best on objects 20 to 25 cm (8 to 10 inches) away, and that is more or less the distance at which a baby can see its mother's face while nursing. Most young babies love to scrutinise faces – even simple ones drawn on paper. So it is not surprising that, as adults, our memory for faces seems to be generally very good.

Faces from the past If we spend a period of time with the same group of people, their faces may become so familiar that we can still recognise them many years later. At reunions to mark the 50th anniversary of the 1940 Dunkirk evacuation, many veterans recognised comrades they had not seen since the war.

As you walk down the street, you may suddenly pick out one face that you recognise from a sea of strangers – perhaps someone who works in your building or travels on the same train as you each morning. You know nothing about them, yet you recognise their face. In some professions, people could almost be said to be experts in faces. Teachers learn up to 200 or so new faces each year and can recognise former pupils many years later. The Speaker (chair) of the British House of Commons has to be able to recognise the faces of all 650 Members of Parliament.

Testing facial recognition

In studies of facial memory, researchers found that volunteers could recognise 96 out of 100 of the faces shown to them two days earlier. In fact, the length of time between seeing a face and being asked to recognise it seems to have little effect on memory performance – in the tests, the interval ranged from four minutes to one week. In one study, people were 100 per cent accurate in recognising a single face after six months. However, in these early experiments, volunteers were generally shown the same pictures each time. When different images of the same face were used, recognition rates were lower, but still impressive – 76 per cent when either the pose or the facial expression was different, and 60 per cent when both aspects were changed.

Some faces seem 'typical' or normal to us and others quite unusual. For example, studies in the UK showed that people rated the face of British politician David Steel as 'very typical' and that of

WHEN NO-ONE LOOKS FAMILIAR

Prosopagnosia or 'face blindness' results from a specific brain malfunction and causes people to lose the ability to recognise faces – even those of their own family. One sufferer, an eminent professor of psychology, used to recall the time he had met an attractive woman on a theatre trip with friends. When he asked discreetly who she was, his friend had explained it was the professor's own wife! The professor also had problems identifying his students and often had to rely on cues such as voice, physical shape or clothing.

Another sufferer, described in studies as PH, became face-blind after receiving a head injury in a motorcycle accident. In a test he was unable to recognise any of 20 highly familiar faces. Even when presented with pairs of faces, one familiar and one unfamiliar, he was unable to tell which one was familiar. But when he was given the names to put to each pair of faces, he made few mistakes – he clearly knew who each person was but could not access this information just from seeing the person's face. PH could also identify that a series of different views belonged to the same face and could recognise which emotion a face was showing. Only face recognition seemed to be affected.

However, it has been found that people like PH may recognise faces at an unconscious level. When connected to a type of lie detector, they show an involuntary physical reaction whenever they see a familiar face.

Denis Healey, another politician, as 'very distinctive'. Researchers found that people often become confused by a typical face and believe they have seen it before when it had not in fact been shown.

People can avoid being recognised by wearing a wig or false beard, but the best disguise is distortion. A bank robber's stocking over the head makes recognition virtually impossible because it squashes the face. A face also becomes very hard to recognise when it is turned upside-down – it seems that the brain is so thoroughly accustomed to faces being the right way up that it finds it very difficult to process facial features in any other orientation. This is something that apparently does not happen with any other type of object, which means that you would probably recognise an upside-down picture of your car more readily than an upside-down picture of your mother.

Storing faces

To investigate the types of brain processes that might be involved in achieving facial recognition, scientists have created computer models incorporating 'face recognition units', or FRUs. An FRU will respond if it finds a match to an image of a specific face, producing 'recognition'. Other recent research shows that the brain does indeed contain cells that respond to very specific images – perhaps as specific as an individual face.

FACT: Dog breeders are much better than non-experts at recognising the faces of individual dogs. It seems that they process dogs' faces in the same way as we all process human faces.

WHY DO WE FORGET?

Sometimes it seems that, for every occasion when we are able to remember something, there is another frustrating occasion when memory lets us down. Why does this happen?

We frequently forget things, but it can seem baffling why this should happen in some instances and not others. Psychologists have found that forgetting is the result of a number of factors that can affect any stage of the memory process.

Sometimes, forgetting happens because we fail to register a piece of information in the first place. For example, if someone speaks to you while you are reading this page, you might not really take notice of what is being said and so never form a memory of it. In some ways this is the most fundamental form of forgetting – if a memory is never stored then it cannot be remembered later, no matter how hard you try.

After you have taken in a new piece of information, the delay before you come to recall it can be as short as half a second or as long as 50 years, and loss of the information can occur at any stage. However, the exact way in which we forget stored information is controversial. Some researchers think that memories simply decay, while others believe that it takes other memories to disrupt them.

Decay or interference?

The idea that memories decay – in other words, that they fade away over time – was put forward by Hermann Ebbinghaus, a pioneering 19th-century German psychologist. Ebbinghaus made himself the subject of his own memory experiments using lists of made-up words, which he learned and then tested himself on after varying periods of time. He found that soon after reading the lists there was a period of rapid forgetting, and much of what he had learned was lost. Then, as time went on, more forgetting took place, but at a slower rate.

Ebbinghaus came to the conclusion that his memories were fading away over time. It is true that the longer we hold something in memory without actively refreshing its trace in the brain by recalling it, the more likely we are to forget it. However, psychologists cannot tell for certain whether this is simply because memories fade or because other factors also contribute.

Retroactive and proactive interference

Memories can take up to three years to become lodged permanently in the brain, and we do not switch off our minds to other material while we are storing them. We are continually experiencing impressions and thoughts which create new memories that can interfere with existing ones. This is particularly true if we are learning something that is similar to the original material. For example, if you are trying to remember a person's name, you will find it even more difficult if you are told the names of other people in the meantime. This type of interference – in which new information interferes with old

is known as retroactive interference. However, old memories can interfere with new ones, in a form of forgetting known as proactive interference. This type of interference applies in many everyday experiences. For example, previous phone numbers, addresses and car number plates, and even the name of a pet from long ago, can pop up and interfere with recall of more recent information. Some researchers argue that all forgetting may be largely due to some form of interference rather than memory decay.

Problems with retrieval

Forgetting occurs most frequently when we are trying to recall some quite specific information. A typical situation is when you are fairly sure that a piece of information is stored in your memory, but for some reason you cannot quite retrieve it. Often this is only temporary and the relevant snippet seems to surface of its own accord minutes,

F**O**CUS ON   *MEMORY UNDER STRESS*

Our own experiences tell us that we are most prone to forgetting when we are anxious or under stress. Getting ready for a once-a-year holiday, for example, can be extremely stressful because it often involves timetables, erratic postal services and copious lists of things to do and take – all of which make heavy demands on memory. It is unsurprising that each day people turn up at airports without a passport, or tickets, or a vital piece of luggage.

Studies of the effects of stress on memory point to the action of cortisol, one of a group of hormones called glucocorticoids that flood the brain when we are under stress. Cortisol reduces energy supplies to the brain and appears to interfere with its ability to store

information in memory. In one experiment, researchers gave students high doses of cortisol four days before a test and found it significantly reduced their ability to memorise a written passage. After a week without cortisol, the students' memory performance returned to normal – so a two-week holiday should be enough to rectify any memory damage caused by the stress of getting there!

PIONEERS   *HERMANN EBBINGHAUS*

Hermann Ebbinghaus (1850–1909) was born and later went to university in Bonn in Germany. As a young man he became impressed by the rigorous, scientific approach to the study of the human mind that was becoming prevalent in the latter half of the 19th century. Ebbinghaus set about applying these principles to memory, a subject that had for centuries been within the domain of philosophers rather than scientists. He wanted to identify the fundamental laws of memory and, using himself as a subject, began a regulated study of how his memory performed. He began by creating large numbers of nonsense words, so that his prior

knowledge of language could not have an influence on his results. Ebbinghaus plotted the results of his tests of recall over different periods of time in a graph that became known as the 'curve of forgetting'. He also made important discoveries about the relationship between the amount of time spent learning something and how much of it is remembered later.

Later psychologists criticised Ebbinghaus's rigorous and somewhat artificial approach. But in taking memory from the speculations of philosophers into the realm of scientific enquiry, Ebbinghaus established a foundation for future investigation.

Defrost the chicken

Car Service 9 am Tuesday

hours or perhaps days later. The experience might be better described as 'failing to remember' rather than forgetting. The fact that memories can be mislaid in this way and then found again later shows that there is a vast amount more stored in the memory than we can access at any one moment.

Problems with recall occur because memories are inter-linked. We access them by following the links from one to the next until we find what we need, but sometimes these links are temporarily blocked, and we are left with a 'tip-of-the-tongue' effect – the certainty that we know something but it is just beyond reach. At other times, the detail we need is held in check by what psychologists call an 'ugly sister' – a similar word that seems bigger, stronger and more immediate and so gets in the way of the right one. Every time the wrong word is activated, its neural trace is reinforced in memory, and some theorists suggest that nearby competing items are dampened down – among them, the actual word that we want.

The problems of prospective memory

There are some situations where people are particularly prone to forgetting. For instance, have you ever remembered, over breakfast, that you need to buy and send a birthday card when you go into town, then not thought of it again until the evening, when it is too late? This is an example of prospective memory – a term psychologists use for situations in which you must 'remember to remember'. Having remembered the birthday in the first place, you had to remember to do what you planned to do about it (buy a card) later in the day when you were near a shop. This need for 'double remembering' makes prospective memory the most difficult form of memory there is. It is why diaries and organisers are so essential for most of us. They not only make it easier to remember things like addresses and telephone numbers, but they also reduce the strain on prospective memory – provided, of course, that you remember to look at them regularly.

*CHEMIST
SUN-CREAM
PLASTERS
TOOTHPASTE

Washing Machine Customer Services 0800 47321

When we need to forget

For every occasion when we need to remember, there are as many situations where it is helpful to forget. A traumatic event, for example, can leave an indelible imprint on memory and may resurface unprompted for many years afterwards. On a lesser scale, we sometimes become fettered to past mistakes and embarrassments and feel the full force of our original emotions each time we recall them. Any useful lessons from such events will probably have been learned long ago, making rehearsal of them pointless. We should review them calmly in better times, divest them of their emotional heat and then leave them in memory – unrecalled and unregarded.

Forgetting is essential in some occupations where people have to learn large amounts of information rapidly and then use it for only a short period of time. Courtroom lawyers, for example, need to relinquish their grasp of the details of the previous brief each time they take on a new case, and actors in four-episode-a-week soap operas have to learn and then forget scripts at an even faster pace. The repetitiveness of our daily experiences also makes forgetting inevitable and essential. If we make the same journey to work every day, it is pointless to remember each one in perfect detail. For this reason your memory retains only the occasions that were more notable. For example, a month of bus rides may pass in a blur, but the day you were soaked in a downpour and then thrown off the bus because there was 'one too many on board' will stick in your memory. The disadvantage of this type of forgetting is that even enjoyable events such as Christmas holidays and parties tend to become indistinguishable over time.

> **"We forget all too soon the things we thought we could never forget."**
>
> Joan Didion, essayist

ON THE TIP OF YOUR TONGUE

'It's on the tip of my tongue!' – how often have you said this when you can't quite remember the name of something? You can make yourself experience this puzzling phenomenon.

• Using a dictionary, ask someone to read out definitions of words that they think you might know, but would not use very often. Most of the time you will be able to name the word easily, but sometimes you may find yourself in a tip-of-the-tongue state.

• When this happens, think through the following questions. What letter does the word begin with? What sound does it begin with? How many syllables does it

have? If the word has more than one syllable, what is its rhythm?

You'll probably find that you can answer these questions, which shows that you know what the word is but can't quite bring it to the surface. You may also come up with other words that are similar in meaning, especially if they also sound similar. So if you are trying to think of the word 'marzipan', you might think of 'marmalade' and 'macaroon' – both are foodstuffs, and both have the same sound at the beginning, the same number of syllables and a similar rhythm.

HOW TO ESCAPE MENTAL BLOCKS

The most infuriating form of memory failure is a mental block. You feel sure the detail you need is somewhere in memory, but it is as if a brick wall has sprung up to hide it. Memory blocks can strike at any time and range from mildly irritating lapses in mid-conversation to catastrophic memory failures in the middle of an exam. Fortunately, some tricks can help you to overcome them.

DEAL WITH INTRUDERS

When you are struggling to find the right word in conversation or when writing, you may find the wrong word surfaces repeatedly and seems to get in the way of the one you need. Take a closer look at this intruder. It is likely to correspond in a number of ways with the word you want. You will often find that it starts with the same letter, or has the same number of syllables, or is associated by meaning with the word you need. Use these clues to sound out similar words, or say aloud a number of sentences that express the meaning of the word you are looking for. This helps to open up a path to the word you want.

WORK WITH THE ALPHABET

If you are trying to remember a name, getting the initial letter is often enough to bring the whole of it to mind. Say the alphabet slowly to yourself, pausing after each letter to allow time for the process of association to work. Sooner or later you will encounter a letter that 'feels closer' than the rest. Once you think you have hit the right letter, say it out loud. This can help bring the right name or word to mind.

SWITCH YOUR ATTENTION

Sometimes too much effort to remember seems to create a mental block or make one worse. Switch attention to something entirely different — go and make a cup of tea, read the paper or absorb yourself in a crossword. By consciously not trying to remember the piece of information, you may find that the answer surfaces of its own accord. This phenomenon has been called the 'law of reversed effort' and often works well in tip-of-the-tongue situations where you feel the answer is tantalisingly close.

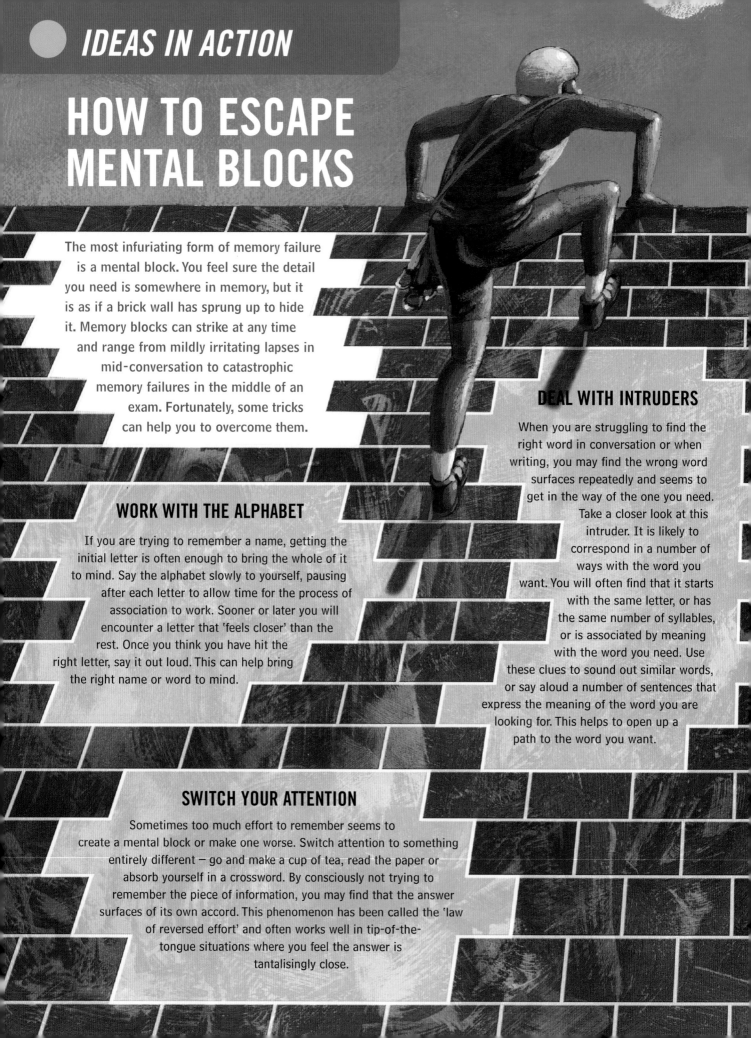

USE FREE ASSOCIATION

Free association of ideas around a topic or word is widely used in psychoanalysis to give an insight into an individual's unconscious mind. You can use a similar technique when you are trying to bring to mind a particular name – perhaps the name of an actor in a film you saw recently. Begin by concentrating hard on what the person looks and sounds like, and describe any distinctive characteristics or physical features. Think about the film and name any other films the actor appeared in. Try to picture any co-stars and remember their names. By focusing on all the associations you have with this person, you may find the name will suddenly slot into place as part of the bigger picture.

SLEEP ON IT

Memory problems occasionally resolve themselves overnight. In these cases, it is rather as if your unconscious mind has been working away at finding the solution while you were asleep. In rare circumstances, you may actually dream the answer to a problem. However, 'sleeping on it' is more likely to be effective because it gives existing memories an opportunity to surface without interference from other thoughts and ideas so that they come to mind more easily the next day.

RE-ESTABLISH CONTEXT

Revisiting the situation in which you experienced something can help to bring back a memory – but just imagining the situation can be almost as effective. If you are trying to remember an address given to you at a party, imagine yourself back there. Whom were you talking to? How did the conversation go? Or if you are searching for the name of a composer of a piece of music you heard on the radio, imagine yourself back in the original setting, the music sweeping over you and then the radio announcer's voice saying who the piece of music was by. Similarly, thinking back to the circumstances in which you first learned something can assist recall in an exam or test – a process known as reintegration.

TRY RELAXATION

Stress is a major factor in mental blocks, and it is easy to panic if the right information does not emerge straightaway, especially in a high-pressure situation such as a job interview. If this happens to you, breathe deeply, reassure yourself and concentrate on one task at a time. Think of the object of your search as a goal to work towards rather than a problem to be overcome. Allow thoughts to surface, but don't try to force the right one to come – it will emerge in its own time.

Childhood amnesia

All of us suffer from a particular kind of forgetting called childhood amnesia. However impressive our memory might be, our ability to remember events from the first three or four years of our lives is extremely poor – no matter how many fascinating things occurred.

The paradox of childhood amnesia is that young children themselves are not amnesic. As all parents know, children under the age of two years have a keen awareness and can quickly and easily learn a tremendous number of things about the world. It is also not the case that everything that is learned early in life is eventually forgotten. Adults have retained a great deal that they learned in early childhood, including the meanings of words and appropriate emotional reactions to objects, smells and sounds. But what they cannot remember is the events that happened to them, even if these were supremely impressive at the time.

Explaining childhood amnesia

The first notable explanation for the phenomenon came from Sigmund Freud. He believed that childhood amnesia resulted when people repressed their infantile sexual impulses, and one of the goals of psychoanalysis was to bring these repressed memories back into consciousness. Although Freud's writings on childhood amnesia and other topics make for fascinating and provocative reading, modern psychologists have not found much support for these ideas.

It is now known that childhood

A QUESTION OF COLOUR

Young children sometimes give surprising answers to seemingly straightforward questions. This is something that researchers have been able to make use of in their investigation of episodic memory in young children.

Children aged three, four and five years were taught to recognise colours with unusual names such as 'chartreuse' and 'taupe'. A few minutes later, all the children were able to identify quickly and confidently the newly learned colours.

Next, the researchers asked 'How long have you known these colours?' While all the five-year-olds were clear that they had just been taught them, all the three-year-olds and many four-year-olds claimed they had always known the colours. It is not until age four or five years that children can reliably remember specific previous events.

Bright lights Babies and young children live in the moment. Sights and sounds such as those at the circus may excite and enchant them, but they form few explicit memories of their experiences.

amnesia results from the relatively slow development of one particular kind of memory, episodic memory. This type of memory allows us to mentally travel back into the past and re-live past events. Episodic memory is not necessary for learning facts about the world, but is needed to relate, for example, that 'last Wednesday, I ate a turkey sandwich and saw a squirrel in the garden'.

The relative immaturity of episodic memory in very young children leads to some curious effects. When children aged three or younger are asked to describe what usually happens at nursery school, they can often give a very impressive general account of the school day and describe a number of activities that they commonly participate in. But when the same children are asked in the evening to describe particular events from that day at school, they are often unable to report even a single thing. This lack of episodic memory in young children means that in later life they will be similarly unable to recollect moments from these first few years.

The maturing brain

There are several factors involved in episodic memories. One is the physical maturation of the brain itself, including the hippocampus and prefrontal cortex. It is not until these areas are relatively mature that children are able to register episodic memories so that they can be recollected later. Also important is a young child's sense of identity, or 'self'. In order to properly organise and retain episodic memories, it is necessary for children to realise that they themselves are enduring entities with a past, a present and a future, and such a realisation is not secure until around the age of three.

"We went to the circus when I was two years old and I don't remember anything about it. But I will never forget putting on my Thomas the Tank Engine boots for the first time on my fourth birthday."

Peter, 20

IS MEMORY LOSS INEVITABLE?

Everyone has moments of absent-mindedness, but as we get older we tend to view these moments as evidence of memory decline. Like the body, the brain slows in later life, but perceived memory loss may be as much to do with our preconceptions about ageing as it is with actual decline in ability.

Memory loss is arguably the decline that people fear most in later life and many believe it to be biologically inevitable. It is true that age-related changes in the brain contribute in a small way to forgetfulness, but they are only part of the story. If a teenager leaves her coat on a bus, for example, she is likely to shrug it off as an irritating episode – her biggest worry is likely to be what her mum will say. But if a 70-year-old woman did the same thing, she is likely to interpret it as as yet another indication of failing memory. Researchers studying memory loss in old age are increasingly looking at factors such as how we perceive forgetting and how other people's expectations influence mental performance later in life.

A good memory in old age
The Labour peer Baroness Castle took an active interest in political life until her death at the age of 91, contributing her valuable experience to discussions of topical issues.

Changes in memory processes

Early research into forgetting suggested that our ability to recognise previously seen information is largely unaffected by age, but that our active recall of information gets worse. This is consistent with the fact that older people tend to have more 'tip-of-the-tongue' experiences in which they feel they know a word but cannot quite bring it to mind.

More recent research suggests that the way we take in information at different stages in life may also be an important factor. Older people are less likely to pay attention to details such as whether something was said

Real lives   *LIVING A FULL LIFE BEYOND 100*

At the age of 104, Lily Hearst still teaches piano, plays in a classical trio and reads *The Wall Street Journal* every day.

Born in Vienna in 1897, Lily moved to the United States in 1938 and can still vividly remember her childhood. She recalls meeting Sigmund Freud, spying on the composer Mahler (who died in 1911), and seeing the renowned cellist Pablo Casals play in Vienna.

What is remarkable is that Lily excels in all forms of mental activity, including memory. She speaks three languages

and continues her lifelong interest in politics, science and the arts. She helps to keep her memory in trim by attending classes at a local centre and maintaining herself in good physical condition by swimming and doing yoga. She only walks with a stick because of a car accident when she was 85. Her sight and hearing are also excellent. Lily organises her life with the aid of a diary and is proud of the fact that she is never late for an appointment. She says 'with a little effort, you can be perfect'.

The Chinese have a traditional saying: 'Never cease to study.' There are more than 110 million people over the age of 60 in China today, and a network of 5000 state-sponsored schools and universities has been developed for them. The majority of the teaching staff are themselves elderly volunteers as it is thought that they have a better understanding of the needs of senior students. Formal education late in life enables retired people to continue to contribute their wisdom to the community. It also provides opportunities for them to further their knowledge, share information and maintain wide-ranging social contacts.

The Chinese institutions are affiliated to the International Association of Universities of the Third Age (AIUTA), founded in France in the early 1970s with the aim of providing life-long learning for older people. There are now 'U3As' in many countries, including Britain, where there are more than 400 local U3A groups with 85,000 members. Courses in a wide range of subjects are offered. No qualifications are required or given, and the atmosphere aims to be informal, enjoyable and stress-free.

by a man or a woman, or what colour an item was. This lack of context creates difficulties when they try to recall what happened on Monday or whether something happened yesterday or the day before. One reason for this may be that the processes that help us to remember context depend to a large extent on the efficiency of short-term or 'working' memory. The elderly are as good as young people at simple short-term memory tests using lists of numbers, but significantly worse at tasks that require more processing, such as repeating a number list in reverse order. One idea is that as we get older, we are susceptible to general cognitive slowing, which affects aspects of memory that depend crucially on fast and efficient processing, such as complex working memory tasks.

However, many other aspects of memory, such as procedural memory for skills, verbal memory, unconscious memory and expertise acquired over a lifetime, show little or no decline. Furthermore, learned strategies can go a long way to compensate for loss of processing speed. The many elderly statesmen and women, scientists, judges and professors who continue to contribute wisdom and to absorb and analyse complex information testify to the enduring power of most forms of memory.

Stereotypes and expectations

One line of research has looked at the effect of culture on memory in old age. In China, the elderly are revered for their wisdom and experience, and age is not necessarily associated with declining memory as it tends to be in the West. In one study, Harvard University researchers compared the memory performance of a group of US volunteers and a group from China. They found little difference between the young people in the two groups. However, the older Chinese outperformed the older Americans, as did those in either group with a positive attitude towards ageing – suggesting that attitude can have a real effect on memory performance.

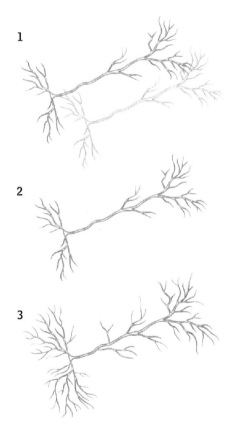

New growth Some of the brain's neurons are lost as part of the ageing process, but neighbouring neurons can compensate. If one neuron from a pair dies **(1)**, the remaining neuron **(2)** sprouts new dendrites (branches) **(3)** with the potential to make many new connections.

AMNESIA

Amnesia can be experienced as anything from a temporary absence of memory to an enduring loss causing severe disruption in a person's life. However, even in prolonged amnesia, the brain is sometimes able to find new ways of remembering information.

Amnesia is defined as the temporary, or permanent, impairment of some part of the memory system. For instance, children who witness a horrific crime – like the murder of a parent – may blank out the experience totally at the time. But skilled questioning by experienced police officers and psychologists, often using models, can often draw out at least some of the story over time. In such cases, amnesia is only a temporary state. Even in its most enduring forms, amnesia is rarely a total wipe-out of memory. For example, people who care for patients with Alzheimer's disease, which is characterised by a gradual decline in memory and other mental skills, are frequently surprised by the level of memory that remains. Sufferers might forget they had breakfast, or how to find their bedroom, yet may be able to name everyone in a family photograph from long ago.

Causes of amnesia

Amnesia is generally caused by some form of brain damage, which may be the result of head injury, stroke, infection or disease. More rarely, psychological trauma leads to a type of memory loss known as fugue, in which people temporarily lose their true identity. Crime writer Agatha Christie suffered from fugue, said to be caused by the stress of marriage breakdown, and disappeared under a false name for several weeks. Like most sufferers, she made a full recovery.

Among younger people, trauma, such as a motorcycle accident, is the major cause of brain damage that leads to amnesia. A sharp jolt to the brain can cause twisting of the meninges – the delicate membrane that protects the brain – and damage the temporal lobes, one of the major areas involved in memory. Afterwards, the victim may suffer a state of disorientation known as post-traumatic amnesia. In a typical scenario, it may take several days before someone who has been knocked down by a car can recognise their own partner. Post-traumatic amnesia may last for hours, days or even months, but complete recovery is usual.

"One of the problems with having such a bad memory is the unbelievable waste of time spent looking for things or having to retrace my steps."

Sheila, in early stage of Alzheimer's disease

Alzheimer's disease and stroke are the main causes of more permanent forms of memory loss in older people. These forms include retrograde amnesia, involving the loss of memories from before the illness, and anterograde amnesia, which affects memory performance after the damage.

Retrograde amnesia

In one famous case of retrograde amnesia, related by Oxford neurologist Ritchie Russell, a 22-year-old man was thrown from his motorcycle. When he recovered consciousness, he insisted that the date was eleven years earlier and that he was still a schoolboy. It was as if the eleven years up to the accident had never happened. As is often the case in retrograde amnesia, as he recovered, the gap between his most recent memory and the traumatic event began to shrink and memories began to return, albeit patchily. Two weeks after the injury, he recalled spending five years in Australia during this lost period. However, a week later, he returned to a village where he had lived for two years and had no recollection of it. Ten weeks after the accident, the memory gap had closed completely, except for the few minutes before the accident.

As with most cases of trauma, the memory of the accident that caused it was extinguished for ever. Research on American foot-ballers who have been knocked out during a game suggests that the injury itself interferes with the brain's ability to lay down a memory of the event.

▶▶ CUTTING EDGE ▶▶

LEARNING FROM AMNESIA
The way some types of memory are selectively impaired as a result of brain damage has taught researchers a lot about how memory might be organised in the brain. In particular, our procedural or 'how-to' memory for skills, such as reading or making a pot of tea, seems to be relatively resistant to damage. Severe amnesics who are unable to lay down any new memories of facts or events, can often still have remarkably effective procedural memory. Clive Wearing was still able to play the piano despite severe amnesia caused by encephalitis (see page 202). In addition, amnesics can often, to their surprise, learn new skills.

Procedural memory involves different brain areas from those needed for conscious, factual memories. Storage and retrieval of procedural memories involve the cerebellum and the putamen – two quite separate brain areas which can remain intact and retain their function even when large areas of the outer parts of the brain are damaged.

Real lives   THE STRANGE WORLD OF 'PHILIP STAUFEN'

Cases of total memory loss are rare, but when it occurs its effects are devastating. The almost complete memory loss of a young man stranded in Canada has robbed him of every part of his identity.

In November 1999, a young man was admitted into the emergency department of a Toronto hospital. He had been mugged and knocked unconscious. He had no form of identification on him, but when he regained consciousness he mentioned the name 'Philip Staufen', which hospital staff took as possibly his own name. He was unable to remember a single detail from his life before the attack and has not regained any memory of it since.

Doctors believe Staufen may be suffering from post-concussion global amnesia, brought about by his head injury. There is no suggestion he is making up his story. He appears to be English, with a trace of a Yorkshire accent, and speaks French and Italian, and reads Latin – suggesting he is well educated. Nearly two years have passed since his injury and no-one has positively identified him – even though his photograph and story have appeared in newspapers in Canada and in the UK. Since he has no papers, he cannot work or travel, or even return to the UK to try to pick up the threads of his life story.

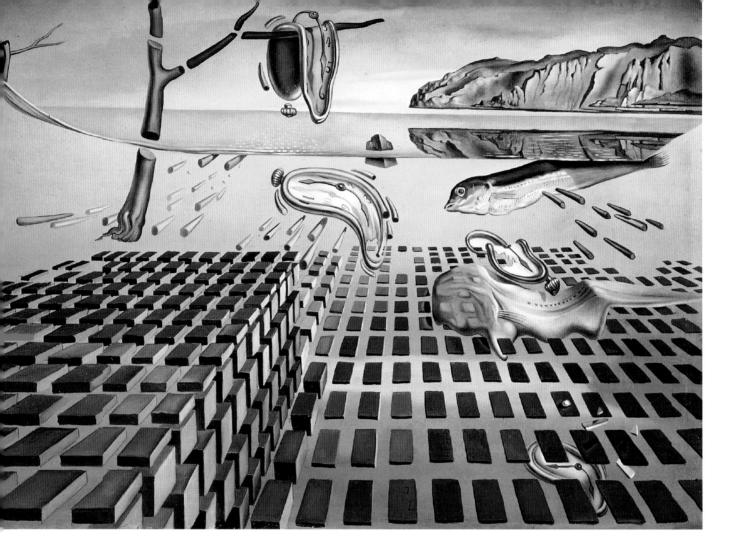

Visualising memory loss In his painting, *The Disintegration of the Persistence of Memory*, Dalí shows a landscape from an earlier work shattered by an atomic bomb. The painting is often used to represent the devastating effects of Alzheimer's disease.

Anterograde amnesia

Anterograde amnesia is the most striking form of memory loss, sometimes occurring alone or with retrograde amnesia. When amnesia affects the ability to store new information in memory this usually has a catastrophic effect on a person's ability to keep track of daily life. In Alzheimer's disease, such memory problems usually develop gradually. For example, one sufferer managed to hide the increasing chaos of her days until she lost her way back to the table during a family meal in a restaurant.

A similar inability to lay down memories occurs in Korsakoff's syndrome, a condition caused by widespread damage to the brain as a result of long-term alcoholism. Typically, Korsakoff's patients fill in the gaps in their memories by confabulation – concocting false details. If the reality-checking frontal lobes of the brain are also affected, they may be unable to distinguish between real and fabricated events.

More rarely, anterograde amnesia results from localized damage to the hippocampus. A person much studied by psychologists, known by his initials HM, had a large chunk of his hippocampus removed surgically in the 1950s as a treatment for epilepsy. Afterwards, he could not remember anything from the previous two years and has never regained the ability to lay down memories. He is now an old man, but still believes he is in his late twenties. When given a mirror he is briefly puzzled by the face that stares back – but within a few minutes he has forgotten it.

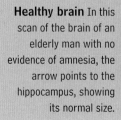

FACT FILE

TESTING FOR AMNESIA

The Rivermead Behavioural Memory test is designed to identify which aspects of amnesia are present that might cause problems in everyday life. Among other tasks, participants are asked to:

• Give the date
• Remember the name of an unfamiliar face
• Remember an appointment
• Recognise a picture shown previously
• Recall a newspaper story – immediately and later
• Remember a new route
• Remember to deliver a message

Recovering memory

Although memory loss can be permanent or continue to worsen, in some cases the brain is able to create new routes to memories. The brain operates as a network of neurons extending over large areas, so if a circuit is disrupted by damage, for example by a stroke, memories can sometimes be retrieved using different pathways. Learning new ways to approach tasks can help this process and outside cues and prompts can also be useful. A timer buzzer that reminds a person to do something at a particular time can be a great help.

Recovery is possible in some cases even when the initial effects are severe. Clinical psychologist Malcolm Meltzer suffered brain damage because of temporary oxygen deprivation when he had a heart attack, aged 44. At first, there were gaps in his personal autobiography and, unusually, some loss of skills – he had to relearn how to operate the stereo and use a razor. His working memory was particularly affected, making planning and organisation of ordinary tasks such as paying bills or going on holiday impossible. He could not remember the plot of a book or a film for long enough to see it through to the end. However, Meltzer's condition improved steadily and eventually he was able to write an article about his amnesia that offered valuable insights into the condition.

FACT: People who fake amnesia are easy for psychologists to spot because they pretend to forget too much. Total amnesia is extremely rare.

FOCUS ON   CRITICAL AREAS FOR MEMORY

Amnesia is generally the result of damage in areas that are important in memory – crucially the temporal lobes, situated near the temples, and the hippocampus, which has a major role in the laying down and retrieval of memory.

The frontal lobes – behind the forehead – are also important. They are large in humans compared to other animals and are thought to be linked with 'higher' mental functions. People with damaged frontal lobes appear normal in many ways, but they are unable to plan and organise their actions, and may have problems with short-term memory. Damage to the frontal lobes also seems to affect a person's ability to distinguish familiar items from similar unfamiliar ones. This may be why many sufferers find it hard to separate memories of real events from imagined ones.

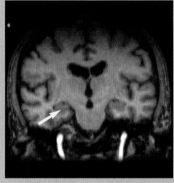

Healthy brain In this scan of the brain of an elderly man with no evidence of amnesia, the arrow points to the hippocampus, showing its normal size.

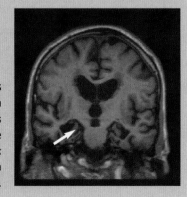

Brain in Alzheimer's Loss of brain tissue in a patient with Alzheimer's disease is revealed by the increased size of the dark cavities (ventricles) and a shrunken hippocampus.

Repressed memories

Not all memories can be accessed at will. According to Freudian theory, some that are too disturbing to contemplate can be repressed so that they are inaccessible to the conscious mind. But whether memories 'recovered' in therapy are reliable is a matter of debate.

The notion of an unconscious mind full of repressed memories and hidden desires originated in the ideas of Sigmund Freud (1856–1939) early in the 20th century. The concept became hugely popular, and went on to dominate Western psychology for more than half a century.

Freud based his theories on his observations of hypnotised patients acting out what seemed to be traumatic events of which they had no conscious memory. He suggested that the memories of the events had been repressed – blocked out of awareness and buried in the unconscious mind. The blockade, however, is not entirely effective, so repressed memories may pop up in dreams or intrude into thoughts in disguised form. Sexual memories and ideas are especially likely to be repressed, so a knife or a stick in a dream, for example, would be held to represent a penis. And unconscious beliefs might be revealed by slips of the tongue – saying, for example, 'you look lonely tonight' instead of 'you look lovely'. Psychoanalytic therapy is largely based on digging up repressed memories so they can be confronted and dealt with consciously.

Freud's theories spread rapidly, with some followers taking his ideas to the point of absurdity. For example, Budapest analyst Sandor Ferenczi once diagnosed 'sexual desire for the coachman' as the cause of a woman's collapse during a drive.

Memories or fantasies?

In the decades that followed, Freudian thinking was gradually replaced in psychology by new approaches to understanding the mind, and today it is no longer

Hidden emotions Psychologists believe that our true feelings are hidden – even from ourselves – beneath the calm face we show to the world.

seen as offering scientifically valid insights. However, repression – or something like it – remains a hot topic of debate: can traumatic events, especially childhood sexual abuse, be buried as unconscious memories and then 'released' by therapy? Or are 'recovered memories' mere fantasies created by the brain or implanted by over-zealous therapists?

The evidence is conflicting. Surveys of children who have undergone a traumatic experience intact suggest that they remember the events only too well. On the other hand, certain emotional memories may indeed be blocked out: a recent study of 129 women who had suffered well-documented abuse as children found that 16 per cent of them seemed to have forgotten all about it – even though it must have affected them dreadfully at the time. One in

THE SNOW-LADEN TREE

Freud recounted the case of a man who could recite an entire poem, apart from one line describing a snow-laden tree 'covered in the white sheet', which he could never recall. To discover why, Freud asked his patient to free-associate (talk freely without forethought) around the phrase from the poem.

The man said it reminded him of a shroud – which he then associated with his brother, who had died of an inherited disease. Eventually, this led to the unearthing of the man's repressed belief that he himself might die of the same thing.

three murderers claims to have no memory of committing the crime. And 'forgotten' emotional memories sometimes resurface after damage to the prefrontal cortex – the brain area that does the things attributed by Freud to the 'super-ego', or the mind's censor.

There are also cases of forgotten traumas being triggered into consciousness by association. A woman who had been raped on a brick path (the incident was recounted by a reliable witness) remembered nothing about it for weeks after the attack. But one day she saw some bricks of the same type – and the whole thing came flooding back.

True or false?

However, there is also evidence that false memories are remarkably easy to create. In one experiment, researchers subjected a group of adults to 'therapy' in which their dreams were interpreted as representing an event where they had either been bullied or lost as toddlers. Two weeks later, half of them claimed that such an event had actually happened. No-one in the 'control' group (which did not have therapy) made any such claim.

Brain scans have shown that a true recollection activates a different area of the brain from one that is false. So eventually the truth of 'recovered memory' cases may be determined not by consulting the memories of the people concerned but by watching those memories being accessed.

ROSE-TINTED MEMORIES

Write down as many events as you can recall from the first eight years of your life. Don't stop until you have come up with at least 20. Then sort them into three categories: pleasant, neutral and nasty, and count up how many there are in each.

Most people list about 50 per cent pleasant memories, 20 per cent neutral and 30 per cent unpleasant. Supporters of the repression theory claim that the preponderance of pleasant over nasty recollections shows that bad memories are repressed. But it may simply be that most of us experience more pleasant events during childhood than unpleasant or neutral ones.

MEMORY AND DREAMS

Many psychologists agree that dreaming is intimately connected to the faculty of memory, but what is less clear is how. Different theories have been put forward to attempt to explain the relationship, and why we find it so difficult to remember our dreams.

Most dreams occur during REM (rapid eye movement) sleep, the stage of the nightly sleep cycle characterised by increased electrical activity in the brain and, as the name suggests, rapid flickering movements of the eyes. Periods of REM sleep happen about five times a night, and it is estimated that most of us spend about two hours every night dreaming. That amounts to some 700 hours – about one whole month – each year. If this figure seems surprising, that is because we remember less than five per cent of our dreams, mostly only those that take place in the last round of REM sleep. It makes sense that we should recall the dreams that we have just prior to waking up, but this does not explain why we forget so many of the others. After all, our brains are highly active every time we dream.

The erasing theory

In 1983, the biologists Francis Crick and Graeme Mitchison speculated that the reason why we forget 95 per cent of our dreams is because our brains are designed not to remember them. They suggested that sleep is a time of 'unlearning', and far from neatly filing in memory everything we have experienced during the day, the brain deletes the vast majority of it as useless. According to this idea, dreaming is a side effect of a nightly review of the vast array of stimuli that bombard the brain via the senses every day. These perceptions are etched into the dense neuron networks of the cortex. The networks can become overloaded with sensory inputs and cease to function properly, so they need to be regularly cleared

> "Dreaming is a kind of remembering, rendered confabulatory and confused by the special conditions of sleep."
>
> Harry T. Hunt, *The Multiplicity of Dreams*

of irrelevant information – for example, the 208 times you glanced at a particular patch of the office wall today, or the 20 times you looked at your watch. In Crick and Mitchison's speculation, dreams arise from the activity of the brainstem in firing neural signals at the cortex to erase unwanted material and thus aid the storage of useful items.

The filing theory

Another speculation, from psychologist Christopher Evans, suggests that sleep has an active role in memory storage. Evans proposes that, during sleep, the brain scans and puts in order all the hundreds of thousands of new sensory experiences we have in the course of the day, filing them in the memory as efficiently as possible. From time to time during REM sleep, the brain becomes briefly conscious of this scanning and cataloguing process and tries to interpret the information in its usual way, as if we were awake and receiving stimuli from the outside world. This often disjointed stream of mental images is what we experience as dreams.

Dreaming and memory performance

The importance of REM sleep to memory performance has been demonstrated by Israeli researchers Avi Karni and Dov Sagi, who trained volunteers to recognise patterns that appeared briefly on a computer screen. Each night, some volunteers were woken up in REM sleep while the others were left to sleep undisturbed. When they were all tested in the morning on the previous night's task, those who had been woken performed less well than those who had not.

There is still much to learn about precisely how dreaming relates to the consolidation of memories, but the process almost certainly involves a melding of new and existing memories. This could explain why our dreams often contain fragments of recent experiences mixed up with old ones.

FOCUS ON   ANIMAL DREAMS AND SURVIVAL

As long ago as the 1950s, researchers in California put forward the idea that that dreaming could have a role in animal memories. They discovered that rabbits, cats and other mammals emitted a previously unknown type of brain rhythm called theta-rhythms from the hippocampus (a brain region) whenever they were exploring new territory or actively on the lookout for predators. The hippocampus emitted the same rhythms during REM sleep – in other words, when the animals were dreaming. The researchers proposed that, during REM sleep, the animals' brains were replaying recent exploratory experiences in order to reinforce in memory the information they yielded – such as new food locations or the territory of a rival.

One Australian mammal, the egg-laying echidna or spiny anteater, shows no sign of dreaming during sleep. On the above theory, this could be because the animal had virtually no predators until relatively recently and therefore did not need to develop enhanced memory faculties.

5 TECHNIQUES TO IMPROVE MEMORY

Most of us know someone with a particularly retentive memory – some people do seem to have a natural gift for remembering – but most memory performers make no secret of the fact that they use techniques to boost their memory power.

Technology provides us with many sophisticated gadgets to keep track of what we need to remember, but none actually improves memory. If we want to work with brainpower alone, we need to learn a method, and this chapter explains how to use the most effective methods known. At first, these memory methods may seem too complicated or even too silly to be useful – why would you want to imagine stuffing a loaf of bread into a shoe, and how is it going to help you remember to buy one? But these techniques are tried and trusted – some have been in use for more than two thousand years. All they require is interest, practice and the determination to improve.

A GOOD MEMORY – BORN OR MADE?

The extraordinary skills of memory experts, who train themselves to remember vast quantities of often random material, seem beyond the reach of ordinary people. While natural talent is certainly an advantage, technique is also vital. With the right training and dedication, could any one of us become a memory maestro?

On a visit to Rome in 1770, the 14-year-old composer Mozart went with his father to hear the Sistine Chapel choir sing the *Miserere*, a famous choral setting of Psalm 51 by the 17th-century composer Gregorio Allegri. This work, which lasts nearly half an hour, was considered so beautiful that its performance and publication outside the Vatican were forbidden. So Mozart had never even heard the piece before – but later that day, he wrote down all the music of the *Miserere* from memory.

Outstanding memory feats like this are often associated with professional expertise. People can acquire a vast amount of specialist knowledge without the need for an exceptional memory simply by working for a long time in a particular field. Virtuoso musicians remember many pieces of music, and actors are able to learn new parts within a short space of time. In such cases, practice has improved the normal processes of comprehension and retention.

Specialist data

Mozart's gifts The famous composer had an extraordinary memory, and not only for music – by the age of eight he could converse in French, Italian and English.

We tend to be most impressed by people who can recall large amounts of material unrelated to their professional knowledge. In the 1930s in Japan, Sigeyuki Isihara showed that he could recall a string of 2500 random digits (numbers) with 99 per cent accuracy. His technique involved converting groups of digits into words and creating a mental image for each word. He then recalled the sequence of word-images using the ancient method of loci (see page 282). Isihara took about two seconds per digit to learn a string of 200 digits and six seconds per digit

The snowflake test Look at these five snowflakes, each for seven seconds, then turn the page and test your memory powers by trying to pick them out from the series of 20 snowflakes shown there.

to learn longer sequences up to 2500 digits. Dominic O'Brien, the World Memory Champion, uses a similar method to learn a random sequence of 3000 binary digits (ones and zeros) in half an hour.

Like Isihara and O'Brien, people who memorise strings of numbers commonly use mnemonic methods to turn them into a more meaningful form that is more suited to the way the mind works. The mind does not make a continuous 'videotape' of experience – if it did, nothing could be retrieved from memory without laborious mental 'rewinding' to the right part of the 'tape'. Instead, the mind is more like a librarian, arranging our vast repository of memories into meaningful categories and going directly to the right 'shelf' to extract what we need from the stored knowledge.

Inherent talents

Dedicated practice and special methods are not the whole story in impressive feats of memory. Studies sometimes bring to light people who can retain and recall large amounts of information without any special training in memory techniques. An unusual musical or visual memory is sometimes associated with autism, although most autistic people are not gifted in this way. There are people with an unusual talent for a particular type of memory task, who can rapidly take in large numbers of words, figures or images and remember them after a substantial delay.

A famous example was Alexander Aitken, a mathematics professor at the University of Edinburgh with an amazing talent for memorising many kinds of material, including number sequences, using his wide knowledge of numerical facts. In 1934 Aitken read an Indian folktale called *War of the Ghosts* twice. Some 26 years later, without seeing it in the meantime, he repeated the tale to researchers, who found that he could recall 58 per cent more than subjects asked to read the story and recall it immediately. In the US, psychologists studied a man known as CJ who could master a new language in just a few weeks. He learned to pronounce the language perfectly with a speed and ease that is normally found only in children, suggesting that he did not learn languages in the way that most adults do.

Using natural abilities

Alexander Aitken seemed to be naturally talented at absorbing and retaining information without the use of any special memory techniques, and both the speed and pattern of CJ's language learning suggested an unusual natural ability. But did they acquire their extraordinary gifts with experience or were they born with them? It seems likely that some people do have innate talent, at least for certain types of information. For example, studies of twins suggest that the ability to remember musical knowledge

---

Real lives

THE MEMORY CHAMPION

With practice, associative memory techniques can produce amazing results. Dominic O'Brien is eight-times winner of the World Memory Championships held annually in London. In this contest, he pits his memory against other national champions in nine events. These include memorising:

- 3000 single-digit numbers in 1 hour
- A 500-word poem in 15 minutes
- 100 names and faces in 15 minutes
- 3000 binary digits in 30 minutes
- 500 unusual words in 15 minutes
- As many single-digit numbers as possible in 5 minutes
- As many digits as possible from a list recited at a rate of one digit every second
- One pack of randomly shuffled cards as quickly as possible
- As many packs of randomly shuffled cards as possible in 1 hour.

At one championship, O'Brien memorised over 19 packs of cards (1026 cards) in an hour. In the latest championships, he competed against 23 other champions and set a new world record, memorising and repeating 128 numbers at a rate of one number spoken per second.

may have a strong genetic basis. So while Mozart's achievements required practice, it is likely that he also had an inherited talent for absorbing musical knowledge – his father and sister were also highly regarded musicians.

Experts versus naturals

Most studies of 'supermemory' have focused on a single expert, but two British psychologists, John Wilding and Elizabeth Valentine, have undertaken extensive studies of people with high memory ability to assess how much is natural and how much is learned. They compared a group of 'normal' people with a good natural memory and a group of acknowledged memory experts – people who had undergone special training in memory techniques. Wilding and Valentine presented each group with a variety of short-term memory tasks, including remembering a story, faces, names, numbers and pictures of snowflakes. A week later, without prior notice, Wilding and Valentine re-tested the participants on the same material. When the results for the various tasks were combined, some of the experts came out very well, but others did less well than some of the 'normal' group.

The most remarkable results came from a 17-year-old schoolgirl known as JR. In the short-term tasks described above, she averaged 84 per cent accuracy, compared with 70 per cent for the memory experts and 56 per cent for the other non-experts. When the two groups were tested without notice on the same tasks a week later, she remembered 80 per cent of the material, compared with 57 per cent achieved by the best of the experts.

JR's memory skills seemed to be a natural gift, since she employed only one simple strategy – making up a story to help her learn a word list. Her talent may have been inherited because, according to JR, one of her grandparents also had a very good memory. Oddly, JR's earliest memory was of something that occurred when she was seven – whereas most people can remember events from about the age of three.

Real lives *A HEAD FOR FIGURES*

Rajan Mahadevan of India became famous in 1981 when he set a world record by reciting 31,811 digits of pi in 150 minutes. The Greek letter pi, or π, is the name given to the ratio of the circumference of a circle to its diameter. The numerical value of π is often expressed as approximately 3.14, but it actually runs to an infinite number of digits. Remembering as many digits of π as possible is thus a favourite challenge for memory experts who like to work with long sequences of numbers.

Mahadevan had an exceptional short-term memory and could retain groups of 13 to 15 numbers in his memory after hearing them once (most people manage only about seven). With lengthy practice, he was able to build up longer and longer sequences of numbers. Mahadevan could even recall specific positions in a sequence (for example, the 3901st digit). His technique, if he had one, was not clear. There was no evidence that he used photographic visual imagery – in fact his visual and spatial memory was generally poor.

Some of Mahadevan's relatives had good memories and he had shown evidence of his talent early in life. He began by learning car number plates as a boy and became so admired for this skill that he went on to develop his other memory feats with numbers.

The strategies used by the memory experts in the Wilding and Valentine tests tended to follow a standard process: first, select one part of the information; second, associate it with something that is easily recalled, such as an image; finally, place this image within a familiar structure, such as a well-known route or a poem. A comparison of the experts and people with good natural memories showed that experts were very good at tasks to which they applied their methods, but unremarkable otherwise, while 'naturals' showed a consistently high success rate at all types of task. The conclusion was that you can supplement an average memory by learning special techniques, but your basic ability remains the same.

While convincing real-life cases of 'photographic' supermemory are hard to find (see page 266), this research shows that memory ability does vary naturally. There are people with an unusual gift for a particular type of memory and others with superior general ability. In another study involving a group of sixth-formers, those who rated their memories most highly tended to perform best at memory tests and examinations. In this case, none of the pupils had exceptional memory ability, but clearly natural variation does produce an occasional memory marvel. For most of us, however, the only way to avoid forgetting or to astonish our friends with memory prowess is to apply ourselves to tried and tested methods.

FOCUS ON

THE KNOWLEDGE

The drivers of London's black taxi cabs spend two years 'doing the Knowledge' – learning every street and route in the city. This special training produces physical changes in the brain. When psychologists scanned the brains of 16 taxi drivers, they found that the area that stores spatial memories at the rear of the hippocampus was about five per cent larger in cabbies than in other drivers, while the front of the hippocampus was smaller. Memorising huge amounts of spatial information apparently caused one part of the brain to grow at the expense of another. The effects were even more marked among more experienced cabbies.

👉 TRY IT YOURSELF   THE SNOWFLAKE TEST

One of the most demanding tests used in memory studies is known as the 'snowflake test'. Participants are shown a series of different snowflake photographs for seven seconds each, and are later asked to try to pick out these originals from among a much larger collection of similar images.

Here is a mini-version to try for yourself. Without studying the snowflakes here, first turn to the five snowflakes on page 263 and look at them for seven seconds each. Then try, from memory, to pick them out from the 20 shown here. How many did you get?

Photographic memory

The concept of a photographic memory has a strong hold on the popular imagination. Many people claim to have known someone with such a memory. But does photographic memory actually exist?

It was not until the first half of the 19th century that the first photographic process was developed. Here was a technique that could freeze moments in time and capture events, scenes and faces in perfect detail, and somehow we ended up with the notion that people with superior memory abilities might be able to capture material photographically – not just the brief after-images experienced in sensory memory (see page 185), but an enduring and complete memory of scenes or whole pages of books.

The discovery of eidetic memory

Modern research provides almost no evidence of photographic memory ability in adults. However, a form of photographic memory called eidetic memory – an ability to hold strong visual images in the mind – may have been found in young children. Two US psychologists, Lyn and Ralph Haber, have claimed that about eight per cent of elementary school-age children possessed eidetic memory. Such children were apparently able to describe a picture previously presented to them in exact detail, as if it were still in front of them. A later study suggested that up to half of all five-year-olds may have some degree of eidetic memory.

Eidetic ability fades as we get older, and it is extremely rare after adolescence, although there are reports of amazing eidetic feats in adults. One such case was an artist referred to as Elizabeth,

Incredible detail
The autistic British artist Stephen Wiltshire has been celebrated for his exceptional memory skills, especially his ability to draw complex architectural structures in fine detail.

who was studied by Harvard psychologists Stromeyer and Psotka in 1970. Elizabeth was able to project detailed mental images onto canvas and to work with them as if they were really there. She could memorise a page of poetry in a foreign language and write it out without hesitation, working from the bottom line to the top.

Elizabeth also successfully passed supremely difficult dot pattern tests (see below). She did, however, require some time scanning the material to achieve this. Following the early reports of her abilities, Elizabeth withdrew from further testing and subsequent attempts to find anyone who could pass the dot tests were unsuccessful.

An eye for detail

Another person with remarkable visual memory is Stephen Wiltshire, an artist whose superior visuo-spatial skill enables him to recall what he has seen in astonishing detail. Stephen can sketch complex scenes after viewing them for only a relatively short time. In one test of his abilities, he was flown over London in a helicopter and a few hours later produced a detailed and accurate aerial view of four square miles of the city.

Stephen is an autistic savant – one of perhaps a few dozen people in the world who possess an extraordinary talent alongside the intellectual disabilities associated with autism. However, although Stephen's savant ability is remarkable, it is not photographic memory. Similar skills might not have been so uncommon in former times: before the age of reprographics, students of art were trained to develop the skills of visual analysis and copying from memory. Driven by his passion for sketching, Stephen Wiltshire has acquired similar skills.

Storybook remembering In a study of eidetic memory in children, young children were shown fleetingly a picture of Alice in Wonderland and the Cheshire cat. Some could later recall the details exactly – such as how many stripes they had seen on the cat.

THE EIDETIC MEMORY TEST

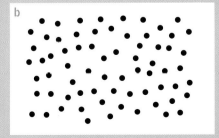

a

b

This test is based on the idea that someone with vivid eidetic memory should be able to fuse an image held in memory with another image and so see a pattern that is visible only in the combination of the two. In the example shown here, when the two dot patterns are superimposed, it is possible to see a number.

To see if you have eidetic memory examine the dot pattern in (a) for as long as you like. When you think you have built up a memory image of the pattern in all

its detail, close your eyes and try to summon it up. If you are not satisfied with your image, continue to examine pattern (a). Once you are satisfied with it, look at pattern (b) and superimpose your image of (a) upon it. When you have fused the two images together are you able to see a number?

Don't be surprised if you don't see a number: one researcher concluded that eidetic ability in the dot superimposition test seems to be a 'none in a million phenomenon'. (The number is given on page 475.)

MEMORY IN THE ANCIENT WORLD

Memory might be regarded as one of the oldest arts. In ancient times, memory was the sole medium by which all history and knowledge could be recorded. The development of good memory skills was not only essential but was also a topic of endless fascination.

The word 'mnemonic' means pertaining to memory, or memory aid. It comes from the ancient Greek word for remember. It is also related to Mnemosyne, the name of the ancient Greek goddess of memory. Mnemosyne was believed to know everything in the past, present and future. As the mother of the nine Muses, who each represented a separate artistic discipline, she was revered as the source of creativity. Greek myth also relates that when the dead entered the Underworld they would drink from Lethe, the river of Forgetting, and instantly all their memories would be obliterated.

These mythic associations reflect the fact that memory was a faculty which the ancient Greeks held in the highest possible esteem. The most venerated literary works in the Greek world were the *Iliad* and the *Odyssey* – two great epics that also form the earliest works of European literature. These epic poems were attributed to the poet Homer. Modern scholars question whether 'Homer' can have been one single person, but it does seem likely that versions of these epics had been composed in preliterate times, and learned and recited for centuries by Greek bards before they were written down in around 750 BC.

> **"Memory is the firm perception, in the soul, of things and words."**
>
> Cicero, 1st century BC

FACT: Mnemosyne, the Greek goddess of memory, was said to be the mother of the Muses, who inspired all aspects of science and the arts.

Natural and artificial memory

Greek thinkers in the 4th century BC began to distinguish between what they called natural memory and artificial memory techniques. The discovery of the importance of visualisation in memory, and the method of loci (see page 282) that makes use of it, is accredited to Simonides, a poet who used superb imagery in his writing. The great philosopher Aristotle also understood the value of the senses, especially sight. He wrote that 'it is impossible even to think without a mental picture', adding that memory belonged to the same part of the soul as imagination, but with mental images conjured up from the past rather than created in the present. Aristotle also recognised that natural memory relies on association.

Cicero tells the story of how Scopas, a nobleman of Thessaly, invited the Greek poet Simonides to sing a lyric poem at a banquet in honour of his host. Moments after the poet had finished his performance and left the banqueting hall, its roof collapsed, killing everyone inside. The bodies were so badly mangled that they were unrecognisable, but Simonides had a clear memory of exactly who had been sitting in each place around the table, and was able to identify them for their distressed relatives.

Simonides realised that this method could be applied as an effective aid to other memory tasks. To remember a list of items, he suggested visualising a sequence of places (an example would be the rooms of a building), and mentally putting an image representing one item to be remembered in each place. The list of items can be recalled later simply by visualising each place and its image in turn. Known as the method of places, or *loci* in Latin, this became one of the most important of all memory techniques.

FOCUS ON

EPIC SONGS

The question of how Homer and other ancient bards memorised lengthy epics perplexed scholars for centuries until the invention of the tape recorder. Epic singers in non-literate societies were recorded singing the same song on separate occasions and it was found that there were large variations in episodes, details and wording. Yet the singers insisted that they always sang the same song with identical words.

The key lies in how 'same' and 'word' are interpreted. For non-literate peoples a 'word' is more like an utterance or idea, and two songs are the 'same' if they convey the same story or set of ideas. Similarly, we would consider two versions of a fairy tale to be telling the 'same' story even though one may be a very short children's book and the other a feature film.

Epic songs also contain natural memory aids such as rhythm, rhyme, narrative and vivid images – elements still used in mnemonic rhymes and in the slogans and jingles devised by advertisers to help us remember their products.

The importance of rhetoric

The main use for memory techniques in ancient Greece was in rhetoric, the art of persuasive public speaking. The ancient Greeks were also the inventors of theatre in the Western tradition, an art form that depends crucially on the memory of the performers.

Roman orators went on to make even greater use of mnemonic techniques. Influential works on Latin oratory by Cicero and Quintilian introduced Greek memory methods to the Roman world, and mnemonics came to be seen as a crucial component of rhetorical technique. The most highly regarded Roman orators were those who spoke convincingly without recourse to written notes. According to Cicero, even a good natural memory such as his own – he could orate non-stop for up to three hours – could be improved by the use of mnemonic techniques.

Our knowledge of ancient memory techniques derives largely from a book on rhetoric written in the 1st century BC called *Ad Herennium* (To Herennius). The anonymous author calls memory 'the treasure house of inventions, the custodian of all the arts of rhetoric' and describes in detail the ancient mnemonic techniques of images and places. His was the only complete guide to rhetoric to survive in either Greek or Latin, and it became the standard textbook for students of classical rhetoric.

Memory through the ages

After the close of the classical period, the arts of memory remained a central part of the educational curriculum well into the Middle Ages. Sometimes, these arts were seen as mysterious and akin to magic. During the Renaissance, progressive thinkers such as Giordano Bruno became fascinated by memory and what it could reveal about the origin of ideas and the supernatural world. However, many such thinkers were persecuted by the church for moving beyond religious teachings.

Over the past hundred years, memory has become a key area of study in the new science of psychology. Today, the memory methods of the Greeks and Romans stand alongside scientific understanding of the mind, remaining as useful today as they were in the ancient world.

PLAN TO REMEMBER

Some things seem to stick in our memories of their own accord. But most information, even material we really would like to retain, seems to slip away. By thinking about what we do remember, we can learn how to remember the things we usually forget.

> **"The one who thinks over his experiences most, and weaves them into systematic relations with each other, will be the one with the best memory."**
>
> William James, 19th-century psychologist

What makes certain facts or events stay in memory? Why, for example, might you clearly recall the time your date failed to show up when you were 17, or the finishing order of the 100 metres final two Olympics ago? Both examples illustrate a simple principle on which much of our remembering is based – many of the things we recall effortlessly have some sort of emotional 'hook'. In the first example, the hook might be feelings of hurt or embarrassment; in the second, a strong interest in athletics.

By contrast, the material we forget is generally unfamiliar and uninteresting to us. We do not remember it because we hardly engaged with it initially. To improve memory performance we need first to address the boredom factor and then to use strategies that anchor material in mind.

Simple strategies

Paying attention is the starting point. Develop the habit of engaging with your current activities – for example, the conversation you are having or the book you are reading – rather than focusing inwards on your thoughts. Then cultivate your curiosity. If the material you have to remember is fundamentally uninteresting to you, ask yourself or others questions about it or try to relate it to something that you do find interesting.

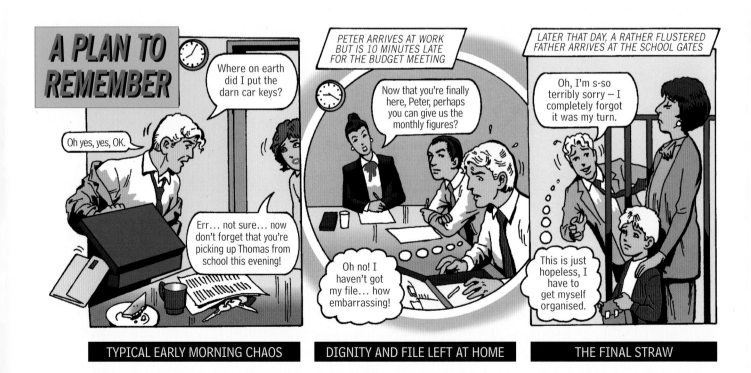

A PLAN TO REMEMBER

Where on earth did I put the darn car keys?

Oh yes, yes, OK.

Err... not sure... now don't forget that you're picking up Thomas from school this evening!

PETER ARRIVES AT WORK BUT IS 10 MINUTES LATE FOR THE BUDGET MEETING

Now that you're finally here, Peter, perhaps you can give us the monthly figures?

Oh no! I haven't got my file... how embarrassing!

LATER THAT DAY, A RATHER FLUSTERED FATHER ARRIVES AT THE SCHOOL GATES

Oh, I'm s-so terribly sorry – I completely forgot it was my turn.

This is just hopeless, I have to get myself organised.

TYPICAL EARLY MORNING CHAOS | DIGNITY AND FILE LEFT AT HOME | THE FINAL STRAW

If you need to remember some important facts or details, select a plan for organising the material in a meaningful way. Give the material a structure or framework to guide your later retrieval of the facts.

One of the most effective strategies to fix material in memory is to keep coming back to it. Start by recalling it very soon after you first learned or experienced it, then recall it again regularly but with longer and longer intervals in between. By frequently reviewing your progress in memorising the material, you also give yourself feedback on how you are doing and where you need to improve.

Avoiding absent-mindedness

Our frustrating everyday memory problems are often to do with absent-mindedness. You may be familiar with the rising irritation that accompanies hunting for something that you had in your hand a minute ago, or finding yourself in the kitchen without quite knowing why you went there. Such cases of absent-mindedness are often seen as poor memory, but they are more to do with attention than memory.

The solution to absent-mindedness is 'present-mindedness' – paying attention to things as you do them – and harnessing the mnemonic power of images. If the phone rings as you enter the house, don't put down your keys and run to answer it. Take the split second required to form a mental image of your hand placing the keys next to the fruit bowl – and the image will lodge in memory. Similarly, if you make it a habit to pause and look at the place you are leaving – your train seat, the office desk – you will be less likely to forget something. Before you leave for work in the morning, visualise yourself at work the previous day to re-establish the context and help you to recall anything you planned to do or take today.

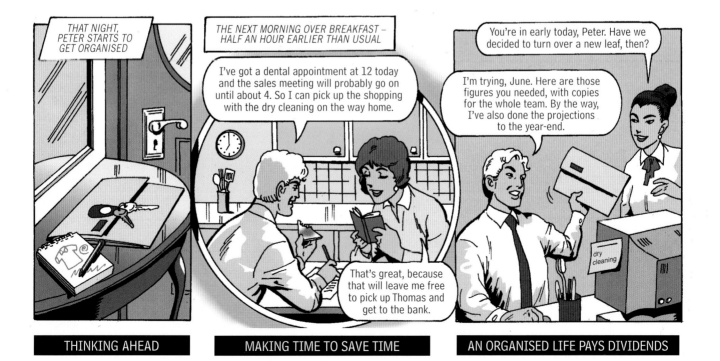

THINKING AHEAD   MAKING TIME TO SAVE TIME   AN ORGANISED LIFE PAYS DIVIDENDS

The mind of a mnemonist

The study of Solomon Shereshevskii, a Russian journalist with an apparently limitless memory, is one of the most famous case histories in psychology. Shereshevskii's extraordinary abilities were recorded over several decades by Aleksandr Luria, a professor at the University of Moscow.

In 1965, psychologist Aleksandr Luria published *The Mind of a Mnemonist*, an astonishing account of his 30 years of memory experiments with a man he referred to simply as 'S'. The man's real name was Solomon Shereshevskii, and he was a young newspaper reporter who had been noticed by his editor because of his uncanny ability to recall highly detailed daily briefings without taking any notes.

Multi-sensory remembering

Luria began memory tests with S and found that he had faultless recall of long and complex series of words or numbers after only a few minutes' study. As the sessions continued, S revealed to Luria that he depended mainly on visual images to remember material. He also appeared to experience a phenomenon called synaesthesia, in which combinations of different senses are triggered by a single stimulus. When S heard words, he saw coloured splashes, smudges and lines, and

Vivid imaginings
Shereshevskii formed vivid visual images of the items he was trying to remember, grafting them onto the familiar streets of Moscow.

THE NEED TO FORGET

Much forgetting is beneficial because experience is repetitive, and all we need to extract from our experiences is a general 'script' to guide us in the future. Only specific events that depart from the general pattern are retained in detail. Shereshevskii apparently could not do this – he recalled everything in detail. This caused problems when lists he had memorised in earlier stage performances interfered with later ones. To make himself forget old lists, he visualised writing them down and burning them, but he could still 'see' traces of writing. One day, however, he realised that, if he didn't want to see an old list, he could simply will himself to put it out of his mind.

experienced taste and touch sensations. On hearing a bell ringing, S said: 'A small round object rolled right before my eyes ... my fingers sensed something rough like a rope ... Then I experienced the taste of salt water ... and something white.' S told Lev Vygotsky, a famous psychologist who worked with Luria, that he had a 'crumbly yellow voice'.

Investigating an infallible memory

Luria realised that it was pointless to attempt to measure S's memory capacity as it effectively had no limits. Instead, he tried to discover how S could retain so much information.

Although S believed he had a form of photographic memory, Luria's accounts of some experiments suggest S may have been using more active memory techniques, but without being taught. In one test, Luria gave S a table of 50 numbers, which he studied for three minutes.

Surprisingly, S took 40 seconds to recall the whole table, but twice as long to recall one column: this suggests he may have been coding each row of numbers to memorise them and then 'unpacking' the codes in turn to recall the table. Using this sytem, he would have to unpack the whole table to recall just one column.

When he was trying to remember lists of objects, S placed images in sequence in locations familiar to him – Gorky Street in Moscow, for example, or his childhood home town of Rezhitsa. To retrieve the list, S mentally 'walked' along the street. Although this is similar to the method of loci (see page 282) – a recognised memory technique – in S's case the process was more intuitive.

S's incredible memory led to his becoming a stage performer, but it was not without disadvantages. He could never overcome the synaesthetic reactions that confused even the simplest situation. The array of images and feelings conjured up by simple words and phrases made it difficult for him to decipher meaning or disregard unimportant details. As a result, he often appeared slow and awkward in his responses to other people, and the memory methods he used were designed as much to control his over-rich mental imagery as to retain things in mind.

ALEKSANDR LURIA

Aleksandr Luria was born in Russia in 1902 and studied both medicine and psychology. In 1924 he began working with the psychologist Lev Vygotsky in Moscow, and from 1937 he focused on the effects of brain injury on mental functioning. He developed great skill in investigating individual cases of brain injury and methods of rehabilitation, and wrote many books on these studies.

One of his best-known accounts is *The Man with the Shattered World*, a description of a soldier who suffered a head injury that destroyed the stability of his perceptual world, producing a constantly changing kaleidoscope of experience. Luria used the soldier's own account of his experience to paint a portrait of the whole person and to reflect on the implications for our understanding of human life. He approached the study of the memory prodigy Solomon Shereshevskii in much the same spirit.

ASSOCIATE TO REMEMBER

The key to memorising something new lies in mentally placing it within a simple and well-defined structure that has already been fixed in the memory. Usually, some kind of association makes this connection permanent – either with the structure itself or with another element conjured up specifically as a 'fixative'.

The number-shape method

A classic way to remember numbers is to translate each digit into an object whose shape resembles the digit. Possible images for the numbers 1 to 10 are illustrated below. Choose whichever associations feel right for you, but be sure to stick to the same ones whenever you follow this system.

1 Sword – or walking stick, candle, index finger

2 Swan – or duck, goose, coathanger

3 Binoculars – or clover leaf, half-moon spectacles, breasts

4 Mast and sail of boat – or golf tee pole and flag

5 Wood clamp – or unicycle, fishhook

6 Golf club – or cherry, yo-yo

7 Hair dryer – or Anglepoise lamp, crane

8 Pasta bow – or hour-glass, fridge-freezer

9 Flag and pole – or balloon and stick, sunflower

10 Pin and bowl – or bat and ball, stick and hoop (use just the bowl, ball or hoop for zero)

Two and a half thousand years ago, Aristotle suggested that all learning and memory are a matter of association. Simple perceptions become associated together to form simple ideas, which are associated with each other to form more complex ideas. Aristotle identified three primary laws of association: contiguity, similarity and contrast. The law of contiguity means that things that occur closely together often become associated. In Ivan Pavlov's famous experiments, dogs that heard a bell when food was presented came to associate the two so that eventually the dogs would salivate at the sound of the bell alone. The law of similarity says that things become associated when they are similar. If you have suffered pain at the hands of one dentist, it is easy to feel afraid in the surgery of another. The law of contrast tells us that the opposite also holds: associations are easily made between opposites such as night and day, up and down, or left and right. For example, people fairly readily transfer skills learned driving on the left to countries where driving on the right is the rule.

Presumably, the law of contrast works because opposites generally belong to the same mental category. Moreover, similarity and contrast are in an important sense dependent on contiguity because it is only possible to discern these qualities when two ideas or events are experienced close together. So, really, contiguity is the basis of all association. Whenever you link items in a unified visual image – the basis of a number of proven memory techniques – contiguity is the principle that you are exploiting.

THE NUMBER-SHAPE METHOD

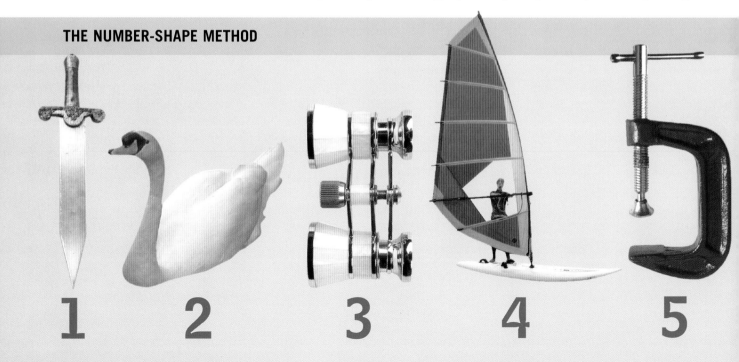

1   **2**   **3**   **4**   **5**

In addition to Aristotle's three primary laws of association, a number of secondary principles have also been proposed. The most important of these in relation to memory is liveliness or vividness. Mnemonic images work best if they are vivid, and are even stronger if they include sound, taste, smell and touch rather than just sight. You will have more chance of remembering to buy coffee if you think of its aroma and flavour than if you merely visualise a jar or packet. Images that are colourful, humorous and exaggerated are also more vivid and hence more memorable. Sexual content can add to the power of an image because most people have a high level of interest in sex. Action is more memorable than inaction, which is one reason why stories can be so effective as memory devices (see page 280).

Peg systems

Imagine that you have memorised the number-shape associations illustrated below. In these images, the shape of the written number forms an association with a familiar object – a sword for 1, a swan for 2, and so on. Now imagine that you want to remember to buy two things, tomatoes and flowers, while you are out to lunch with a friend. Take the object that represents 1, the sword, and combine it in an image with tomatoes – perhaps the sword slicing tomatoes in two. Then take the object that represents 2, the swan, and imagine it swimming amid flowers in a lake. After your lunch, mentally take 1 on your list, translate it into the sword, then ask yourself what the sword was doing in your recent visualization. The answer will spring instantly to mind: cutting tomatoes. Then take 2 on your list, think of the swan and ask yourself what it was doing. The image should come to mind easily and remind you that you need to buy flowers.

What you have been doing here is using numbers as a visual 'peg system'. Such systems use well-known sequences, such as numbers or the

Using numbers as pegs The images below are just two examples of how the number shapes can be used to create memory associations – in this case, as a reminder to buy tomatoes and flowers. The range of different images that you can create is virtually limitless. The more vivid your imagination can make them, the better.

6   7   8   9   10

THE NUMBER-RHYME METHOD

alphabet, like a row of 'pegs' on which we can hang a list of items we need to remember. It might be a shopping list, or a list of ingredients for a recipe, or an agenda for a discussion, a series of tasks you have to perform, or a list of commands for accessing the functions of a new mobile phone. Of course, in such circumstances, one way to make sure that you do not forget the items on your list is to write them down, or to consult a cookery book or instruction manual where someone else has already written down the procedure. But this is not really remembering at all, merely a case of deciding *not* to use your memory.

If you decide you do want to remember for yourself rather than relying on a written list, the first thing you need to do is to organize the pegs. A simple linear sequence is all that is required. The simplest linear sequence that most of us know are the numbers, 1 2 3 4 5 6 and so on. In fact, we know this sequence so well that we have no doubt forgotten the effort of memorising it in the first place. But as children we put in many hours practising the number sequence, and it is now indelibly etched into our memories.

To create a mental list using number pegs, you place the items you want to remember into a sequence and then associate each item with the corresponding number peg, as previously described for the tomatoes and the flowers. The important thing is to combine the number pegs with the items in vivid but coherent visual scenes. Note that in the example already given, you do not merely imagine the sword and the tomatoes side by side, you imagine a positive, even dramatic, act of slicing. The drama of this action fuses the two elements together, so that later, when you think of the peg (the sword), you cannot bring it to mind without immediately thinking of how you imagined the sword.

Another key point is that this method only works if you commit yourself on every occasion to an unvarying set of objects to correspond with the numbers. It is confusing to represent 1 by a sword on one occasion and by a pen on another occasion. Consistency is crucial. Choose your objects now and stick to them whenever you use the number-shape system.

The number-rhyme method

This is another number-based peg system, which is similar to the number-shape system except that each of the numbers 1 to 10 is represented by a word that rhymes with it rather than by an object with a similar shape. One commonly used set of rhymes is shown above:

1 is a bun, 2 is a shoe, 3 is a tree, 4 is a door, 5 is a hive,
6 is sticks, 7 is heaven, 8 is a gate, 9 is wine, 10 is a hen

To use this method, you link each of the items you want to remember to one of the number-rhyme words. So, when compiling your shopping list, you start by creating a mental image linking tomatoes and a bun. It might be an iced bun with a large red tomato on top like a cherry. Or maybe a man with a big red face like a tomato stuffing himself with a huge bun. Next you link flowers to shoes. You might think of a clown's shoes with big yellow flowers on them, or the white silk shoes of a bride holding her bouquet – whatever is most memorable for you. Of course, you can devise your own rhyming sequence.

Extending the system

You may imagine that number peg systems are rather limiting, allowing you to memorise a maximum of only ten items. However, peg systems can be extended almost indefinitely. You can extend the basic ten pegs to a hundred by devising ten scenarios within which your images can be set. For example, the first ten might all be set in an ambulance, the second ten in a bookshop, the third ten in a cinema, and so on. These settings are all alphabetical – their first letters are a, b, c. By using scenarios beginning with the first ten letters of the alphabet, you should have no problem knowing which scenario represents each set of ten numbers, giving you 100 pegs in total. This system can be multiplied by using coloured images: blue for the first hundred, green for the second hundred, and so on. Again, the order of colours can be alphabetical by their first letters.

☞ TRY IT YOURSELF

PEGS IN PRACTICE

The only way to grasp how effective peg systems can be is to try one out for yourself.

Here is a simple shopping list of ten items alongside the memory objects in the number-rhyme system. Take one minute to form the necessary connections. Make your images as vivid as possible. When you have worked your way through the items, test your memory at once: cover the words on the right and go down the rhymes recalling the word you have associated with each one. Your recall is likely to be perfect. How is it when you test yourself again tomorrow? And the day after?

One is a bun	• **Apple**
Two is a shoe	• **Carrot**
Three is a tree	• **Toothbrush**
Four is a door	• **Deodorant**
Five is a hive	• **Cheese**
Six is sticks	• **Eggs**
Seven is heaven	• **Charcoal**
Eight is a gate	• **Bread**
Nine is wine	• **Mustard**
Ten is a hen	• **Bleach**

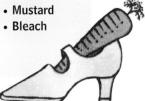

HOW TO REMEMBER NAMES AND FACES

Has this ever happened to you? After a long and interesting conversation with someone you have just met, you turn to introduce them to another person – and find you cannot remember their name. Failing to put a name to a face is something that happens to most of us. Fortunately there are some simple ways to improve your ability to do it.

MAKING THE TASK EASIER

First of all, anticipate the problem. Conferences, job interviews, school events and dinner parties are just a few situations where introductions are likely, so relax and start by taking practical steps to make the task easier.

Make sure you hear clearly

Make sure your host – or the chair of the meeting – takes enough time to introduce people properly. If you don't hear a name clearly, ask for it to be repeated. Don't be embarrassed about doing this: others will probably have missed it too, and will be grateful to hear it again.

Use it or lose it

When you start talking to a new acquaintance, try to use their name at least once or twice. This 'rehearsal' technique helps you to assimilate and store information in memory. The bonus is that most people will feel flattered that you have remembered their name, taking it as a sign that you were interested to meet them.

Pay attention

Although you may be introduced to several people almost simultaneously, try to concentrate on the names as you are hearing them – particularly the ones that you think are important to you or that you are most likely to want to remember.

PUTTING NAMES TO FACES

Now give these methods a try. Here are six faces with their names. Look at the faces, and try memorising the names using one or more of the 'picture a name' association techniques above. Then cover the names, and see how many you can remember.

PICTURE A NAME

One basic memory technique is known to be enormously useful in building the ability to remember names and faces — even allowing people who have suffered brain damage to regain this ability. The idea is to build up a vivid mental image that forms a memorable association between a person and their name.

Build a mental image

The easiest names to remember using this technique are those with a clear meaning. For example, if you meet a man with the surname Fox, first form a mental image of his face. If he has some fox-like aspects to his face — red hair, perhaps — link these to the name. If not, add some fox-like features to the image. When you think of his face later, the foxy aspects will help you recall his name.

A similar approach is to link the new person's image with that of a famous person of the same name. So if you meet someone called Susan, combine her face with Susan Sarandon's.

Add wordplay

Most surnames lack an obvious meaning or connection, so in these cases use your imagination to make word connections. For example, if you meet a woman with the surname Sykes, you might connect this to the word 'socks' and think of her standing in her socks. This technique can help with first names too. For example, if the person's name is Caroline Sykes, you might think of her wearing socks and singing carols in the snow (carolling).

Use characterisation

To help make your memory of a person more vivid, try thinking about what kind of person they look like. Is this a gentle face — or a condescending one? You can then make associations between your observations and their name. However, be careful that this characterisation doesn't influence your true opinion of the person.

Put it all together

When you get used to these methods, try combining them. First, spot resemblances between the new person and someone you know or a famous person. Then build up your name-association image, combining the person you know with the name you want to remember. For example, to remember James French who looks like your uncle, you could imagine your uncle eating some delicious French jam. Or for May Smith who looks like Shirley Bassey, imagine the singer dancing around a maypole watched by a blacksmith.

HELPING RECALL

There will be times when you have not made use of any association techniques but still need to remember a name. In this case, try using some of the general memory methods for helping recall (see page 246). For example, imagining yourself back in the situation where you met the person can help. Similarly, you can prompt recall by focusing on aspects of the name you feel you remember — such as the likely number of syllables or the letter you think it began with. At the very least, such methods get your mind working in the right direction, so you may find the name emerges without effort later on.

Joan Moon

Alexandra Parsons

John Markham

Mark Griffiths

Sarah Kahn

Philip Pascal

RHYMES, STORIES AND SIMPLE MNEMONICS

From our childhood experiences of nursery rhymes and stories we recognise the power of rhyme, rhythm and narrative to hold our interest and make information memorable – these are the elements that underpin many effective memory strategies in later life.

Almost any material becomes more memorable if it is given the form of a story. This approach may be combined with vivid associations that you can readily recapture every time the story is told. Imagine, for example, that you want to remember the names Johnson, Ripley, Appleby, Willmott, and Brown. One story you could spin from this list might be: '**John's son** steals from the orchard, but he **rips** his trousers on the fence and drops his **apple**, which **will** turn **mottled** and **brown** before he gets home'. It does not matter that the story is nonsense, nor that it only gives you clues to the names (you could misremember Appleby as Appleton). There is a framework with a narrative linking the different elements, and often that is enough to jog memories into the light of day.

> **"When summer comes we say 'très bon!' And put our clocks an hour on."**
>
> Traditional rhyme

Using first letters and acronyms

Another technique is to take the initial letters of each item in the list and create a sentence of words beginning with these letters. A well-known example is **Richard Of York Gave Battle In Vain** for the colours in the spectrum (red, orange, yellow, green, blue, indigo, violet). Anyone who did music at school is likely to recall the mnemonic **Every Good Boy Deserves Favour** for the notes on the five lines of the treble stave (the spaces, very conveniently, spell the word **FACE**). The corresponding mnemonics for the bass stave are **Good Boys Deserve Favour Always** for the lines and **All Cows Eat Grass** for the spaces.

Sometimes the initial letters of a sequence of facts can be arranged so that they form a word that serves as a mnemonic. Such words are called acronyms. For example, in chemistry **OILRIG** stands for 'oxidation is loss, reduction is gain'. Inventing your own useful acronyms and mnemonics can be entertaining. If you sometimes forget that Peter and Christine have children called Simon,

Using initials Taking the initial letters of a word sequence you want to remember, and using these as a basis for a sentence, is a simple but effective mnemonic technique.

My Very Educated Mother

Mercury   Venus   Earth   Mars   Jupiter

Elsa and Andrew, you can rearrange all their initials to form an acronym, such as **SPACE**, or another word that contains all the initials, such as **CAPErS**. If you incorporate this mnemonic into a visual image it will be even easier to remember.

Making it rhyme

Before the invention of writing, and in many cultures long afterwards, stories were sung or recited from memory. Rhythm, rhyme and melody were used to provide a framework that aided their memorisation. We see this clearly when someone attempts to recall the lyrics of a song by humming the first few notes of the tune, or recites the first lines of the lyrics to remind them of the tune. In some types of poem, such as a limerick, the powerful effects of rhythm and rhyme can prompt us to 'remember' words we have never actually heard. Try this example:

> There was an old lady of Kent
> Who wobbled wherever she _ _ _ _ _ .
> One leg was long
> And not very _ _ _ _ _
> And the other was little and _ _ _ _ _ .

Rhyme and rhythm figure in a host of verbal memory aids, like the spelling rhyme **i before e except after c** (not to forget its conclusion, 'or when sounded as 'a', as in neighbour and weigh'). The old rhyme that begins **Thirty days hath September, April, June and November** has not been bettered as a way of remembering the number of days in each month, and many people know the weather forecasting rhyme: **Red sky at night, shepherd's delight; Red sky in the morning, shepherd's warning.**

Farmers were once aided by rhymes such as **In May get a weed hook, a crotch and a glove, and weed out such weeds as the corn do not love.** Other popular jingles help to remind us of tricky sequences in history. Try this one for remembering the medieval kings of England: **Willy, Willy, Harry One, Steve and Harry, Dick and John ...**

Or this one for keeping track of what happened to Henry VIII's wives:

> Divorced, beheaded, died;
> Divorced, beheaded, survived.

HOW TO....

MEMORISE THE CALENDAR

Do you know the day of the week your birthday will fall on in 2002? Or the birthdays of your family? By memorising the 12-digit number 744-863-852-742 you can easily work out the answers to questions like this without using a diary.

How does this work? It's actually very simple. These 12 digits give the dates of the first Monday in each month of 2002. The first Monday in January is the 7th, in February the 4th, and so on. So, if your birthday is the 21st of March and the first Monday in March is the 4th, then it is easy to add 7 to get Monday the 11th, and 7 again to get Monday the 18th, and then add 3 days – Tuesday, Wednesday, Thursday. So March 21st will be on a Thursday. Try using this method to work out the day on which your actual birthday or some other event of known date will occur.

Once you have memorised the 12-digit number, you can use it again for 2003 simply by remembering either that each digit will go down by one or that each digit now stands for the first Tuesday in each month. But beware of leap years: after February 29th, the day-numbers go down by 2 rather than by 1.

Saturn   Uranus   Neptune   Pluto

Just Served Us Nine Pickles

PICTURES AND PLACES

Conscious recollection consists of mental reconstructions, involving any of the senses. But for most people, the most powerful aid to memory is a visual image – which is why many mnemonic techniques are based on creating pictures and places in the mind.

A memory house Your own home can provide a framework for recalling items on a shopping list or things to do. Choose some key spots in the rooms of your house and imagine yourself walking from one place to the next in a definite order. Make exaggerated images for the things to be remembered – for example, a giant cotton reel on a kitchen stool for a jacket that needs to be mended, and your neighbour's keys blocking the stairs to remind you to go next door to feed their cat.

The underlying principle of any memory method is to impose a structure on disorganised material that we want to remember. There are two sorts of structure – structure in time and structure in space – but each of these readily transforms into the other. We can arrange a collection of objects spatially by placing them in a straight line, but when we look at each object in turn along the line then we see them in a temporal sequence. One of the best known and most used mnemonic techniques, the method of places, or 'loci', makes use of this space and time structure.

The ancient Greek poet Simonides was the first person to give an explicit account of how to use the method of loci (which means 'places'

Dental appointment

Tea with Lucy

Mend jacket

Neighbour's cat to feed

Golf with Tom

MEMORISING PLAYING CARDS

Memory champion Dominic O'Brien has many methods for memorising packs of cards including this one, which is based on translating cards into well-known faces. You might like to try this method in card tricks or games, or simply to impress your friends.

• First, look at the table which shows you how to convert each card into two letters. For some, the number is converted into its corresponding letter of the alphabet – for example, 5 is E. Others are based on sound (6 is S and 9 is N) or on similarities (10 is O).

• Now look on these pairs of letters as initials and try to think of a famous person or someone you know with the same initials. These faces are now the visual images for your cards. For jacks and kings you can use the initials KH, JH, etc. Queens can be historical figures, storybook characters or celebrities (for example, TV gardener Charlie Dimmock could be the queen of spades.)

• Now turn to page 131 to find out how to remember a sequence of cards by placing your personalities along a familiar route.

1 ♥ Anthony Hopkins   2 ♦ Bob Dylan   5 ♥ Elizabeth Hurley

7 ♦ Gerard Depardieu   9 ♣ Nadia Comaneci   10 ♥ Oliver Hardy

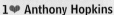
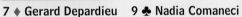

	1	2	3	4	5	6	7	8	9	10
♥	AH	BH	CH	DH	EH	SH	GH	HH	NH	OH
♠	AS	BS	CS	DS	ES	SS	GS	HS	NS	OS
♦	AD	BD	CD	DD	ED	SD	GD	HD	ND	OD
♣	AC	BC	CC	DC	EC	SC	GC	HC	NC	OC

FACT: The ancient Greeks invented the method of places, and used it for remembering speeches and steps in an argument.

in Latin). However, underpinning this method is an organisational system that we all use intuitively. We make use of a simple version of the method of loci in much of our remembering. To demonstrate this for yourself, try answering the following questions:

• Where do the three most helpful people at your place of work sit?
• Which is further north – New York or Tokyo?
• How many of your neighbours have you spoken to in the last month?
• Are all the doors in your house hinged on the same side?

It is highly probable that you used systematic scanning of a visual image in memory to answer at least some, if not all, of these questions. What Simonides did was to point out that by making deliberate use of this natural tendency, we can choose to remember information that we need to. All subsequent developments have been to do with fine-tuning his method of loci, but the basic principles remain unchanged.

Picking your places

The method of loci requires that you choose a number of locations along a route or in a layout that you know well. The places you use should be visually distinctive and sufficiently far apart from one another not to become confused in your mind. They should be without people or objects that are not always in the same place, because change weakens the visual images. Classical authors also advised against using places that are dark or too bright, because that might make it difficult to find images when you want to retrieve them.

You might, for example, choose a series of places along the route you walk from your home to work every morning: 1 - your front gate; 2 - the bridge over the river; 3 – the pedestrian crossing; 4 – the plant stall; 5 – the church; 6 – the station platform; 7 – the newsagent with an awning; 8 – the car showroom; 9 – the supermarket; 10 – the entrance lobby or security gate at your work.

Or you could use the rooms in your home, provided you have enough of them and you can imagine walking round them in a fixed order. Alternatively, your locations might be aspects of a scene in a well-loved picture that you can readily visualise. The important point is that you must be able to visit your locations mentally in a fixed order.

Adding visual images

The next step is to turn the material you are trying to remember into visual images that can be positioned at these fixed points along the route. Imagine you are reviewing the things you need to do during the day as you prepare your breakfast – you want to get a birthday card for your niece and stamps so you can post it; your partner has yet again reminded you to contact the plumber; and the car insurance has to be renewed.

Choosing your route

To create a route to use for the method of loci, pick distinct locations that do not change from day to day. The first six places might be:

1 your front gate
2 the bridge over the river
3 the pedestrian crossing
4 the plant stall
5 the church
6 the station platform.

It is crucial that you settle on an exact number of locations and practise thinking about them until they are entrenched in your memory. Once your route is second nature to you, you will find it surprisingly easy to place visual images along it for things to be remembered.

While you eat your breakfast, picture your niece standing at the front gate (place 1) holding the string of a birthday balloon and fixing you with a look of reproach. Then imagine a huge postage stamp glued to the tarmac of the bridge (place 2); a plumber fitting a tap to the Belisha beacon by the crossing (place 3); and your car ploughing into the racks of plants on the flower stall (place 4). Once you have created these images, run through them again from the start to ensure they are firmly fixed in mind. You do this simply by imagining yourself setting out from home to work. Later in the day, repeat the imaginary journey whenever you want to check if you have any remaining chores to fulfil.

The important thing about memory images is that they should be as vivid and interactive as possible and you should be clear about what they mean to you. For example, if you need to buy strawberries, place a huge red strawberry along your route, or imagine a room full of them in your home. If cheese is on your list, you could visualise your sofa as a huge, smelly wedge and imagine how it would feel to sit on it.

Incorporating extra tasks

If you want to memorise more actions than you have locations, simply associate more than a single action to each one. To do this effectively, you need to combine the different actions into a single image. For example, calling the plumber and insuring the car could be linked to the crossing location by visualising the car in a flood on the crossing, while the plumber struggles to turn off a tap on the Belisha beacon.

HOW TO... ?

REMEMBER YOUR PASSWORDS

Modern life is increasingly about passwords. If you use e-mail or access any personal accounts by phone, you may have several passwords to remember. However, it can take only a few minutes to memorise all your passwords.
• First of all, create an image that links each password to its use. For example, if you use the name of your dog 'Arthur' for entry to your company's financial records, imagine your pet guarding a security box with bared teeth.
• Once you have created your images, deposit them sequentially in the rooms of your house or along your route and then walk your route whenever you need a password. You should never again have difficulty recalling them.

5

6

COMBINING PLAYING CARDS AND PLACES

Depending on your ambitions, you can use the playing card memory method described on page 283 to remember a short sequence of cards in a game or to learn the random order of a whole pack. If you want to try the latter, you need to take time to plan a route with 52 places and run through it regularly to make sure it is firmly set in your mind. Once you have assigned personalities to your cards, practise them regularly too, so they come to mind instantly.

As you go through the pack, place your cast of characters along your route, giving them props and making them interact with their surroundings. For example, if your sixth card is the nine of clubs, imagine Nadia Comaneci in place 6, the station, performing a gymnastic routine.

LEARNING THE LINGO

Your first language is acquired effortlessly when you are very young, but becoming fluent in a second or third language is a laborious task. It relies principally on your ability to store a large number of unfamiliar words and their meanings in long-term memory and retrieve them at will. But there are memory methods that can help to equip you with some useful vocabulary in a short space of time.

One of the most effective uses of memory techniques in solving real-life memory problems has been in foreign language learning. The method most frequently used is the keyword (or 'Linkword') method, which involves linking a word from a foreign language to an English word or phrase that sounds like it, and then adding imagery to visualise and strengthen the link. For example, the French for tablecloth is 'nappe'. Picture yourself having a nap on a tablecloth.

The method was developed by Michael Gruneberg, an expert on memory improvement, and has been used successfully with a wide range of people including many who declared themselves hopeless at language learning. Most people are able to acquire a vocabulary of 400 words and a basic grammar in about 12 hours – which is about half the vocabulary an average schoolchild ends up with after four years of study by traditional methods.

FIRST STEPS

To try out the method, read the examples below and picture each image in your mind's eye as vividly as you can for 10 seconds. Introducing humour helps to fix the images in memory.

The Japanese for **shorts** is **han zubon**. Imagine resting your **hands upon** your **shorts**.

The Russian for **eye** is **glaz**. Imagine you have a **glass eye**.

The Polish for **juice** is **sok**. Imagine drinking **juice** through a **sock**.

The Hebrew for **elephant** is **peel**. Imagine an **elephant** eating orange **peel**.

The Polish for **herring** is **sledz**. Imagine a **herring** sitting on a **sledge**.

The German for **bride** is **braut**. Imagine a **Belgian bride** – a **Brussels braut**.

The Italian for **night** is **notte**. Imagine having a **naughty night** out.

The Portuguese for **bucket** is **balde**. Imagine a **bald**-headed man with his **baldy** head stuck in a **bucket**.

The Spanish for **cow** is **vaca**. Imagine a **cow** with a **vacuum** cleaner, hoovering a field.

The Turkish for **daughter** is **kiz**. Imagine giving a **kiss** to your beautiful **daughter**.

Now what is the English for:

kiz	
vaca	
balde	
notte	
braut	
sledz	
peel	
sok	
glaz	
han zubon	

Don't expect to get them all correct, but if you are getting most of them right, your grasp of the method is good enough for you to move on to learning some more words and how to put them together.

STARTING WITH SPANISH

Here's an exercise that will have you speaking some Spanish in just a few minutes. Learn the words in exactly the same way as you did in the previous exercise.

The Spanish for bread is pan.
Imagine stuffing bread into a pan.

The Spanish for beach is playa.
Imagine a football player playing on the beach.

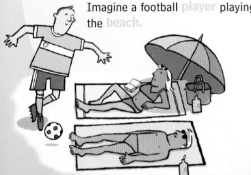

The Spanish for rice is arroz.
Imagine arrows landing in your bowl of rice.

The Spanish for coffee is café.
Imagine drinking coffee in a café.

The Spanish for duck is pato.
Imagine you pat a duck on its head, or imagine duck pâté.

The Spanish for where is dónde.
Imagine asking 'where is Dundee?'

The Spanish for cold is frío.
Imagine finding a trio in the fridge.

One of the words for is is está.
Imagine a star is here.

What is the English for:

está	
frío	
dónde	
café	
pato	
arroz	
playa	
pan	

MAKING SENTENCES

You need to add one more item to make up sentences. The Spanish for the when the noun is masculine is el. Imagine men are hell to live with. The feminine word for the is la. Imagine a woman singing tra la la. All but one of the nouns in the exercise above are masculine, for example, el pato is the duck and el pan is the bread. However, playa is feminine, so la playa is the beach.

So to say the coffee is cold say el café está frío.
To say where is the rice? say dónde está el arroz?

Now translate:
Where is the beach?
The rice is cold.

To learn useful phrases, it is best to learn the individual words first and then put them together.

For example, the Spanish for what is qué.
Imagine you ask what key you need.

The Spanish for you want is quiere.
Imagine that you want to query everything.

So what (do) you want? is simply qué quiere?

Now you have the basics of a method that can be applied to any foreign vocabulary:

1. Select a word or phrase.
2. Find an English word or phrase that is similar.
3. Create a mental image that strengthens the link and incorporates the meaning of the original.
4. String the newly learned words together to make simple sentences.

When time is limited, learn an extended vocabulary of individual words rather than phrases. The right word is often all you need to make yourself understood.

The answers were: Dónde está la playa?
El arroz está frío.

6 MAKING THE MOST OF YOUR MEMORY

From the moment of birth, memory functions as automatically as breathing, responding to and recording our interests and preoccupations throughout life. But perhaps we give memory the attention it deserves only when we believe it is beginning to fail us.

To make the most of your memory throughout life, start with the practicalities of diet, body fitness and sleep, which can all affect mental function. Drugs and alcohol can harm memory, and it is wise to treat with suspicion any chemical 'quick fixes' that claim to boost memory performance. Look for ways to apply what you have learned in this book. Developing good memory habits – paying attention, applying curiosity and reflecting on recent and past experiences – can bring rapid improvement in memory performance. For every occasion when your memory is put to the test, you will find there is a strategy or mnemonic technique to help you fix information in mind. Finally, be confident and believe in your memory ability.

MEMORY THROUGHOUT LIFE

From birth until old age, our memory skills continue to develop. At each stage of life we add new skills, refine established ones and build on our store of experiences and knowledge. The story of our memory throughout life is about change – but not necessarily about decline.

We remember little of what happened in our lives before the age of about three or four. This 'childhood amnesia' is thought to be due to the fact that certain parts of the brain associated with memory are not mature in very young children. However, psychologists have demonstrated in the past few years that babies do have an active memory – although not for events. The mother's voice and smell are immediately familiar, and newborn babies can recognise music that was played regularly to them while they were in the womb.

> **"Time – our youth – it never really goes, does it? It is all held in our minds. "**
>
> Helen Hooven Santmyer,
> bestselling author at the age of 88

The brain develops rapidly in the first few years, increasing the connections that affect memory processes. As well as building up procedural memories for skills, toddlers accumulate a store of knowledge about the way the world works. As children learn, they develop an understanding of their own memory capacities. When asked how many items they will be able to remember from a tray of objects shown to them briefly, five-year-olds typically say that they will recall more than they can in practice, while nine or ten-year-olds usually give a good estimate of their subsequent performance.

Memory at school

During school years, children develop more sophisticated memory skills in response to the demands made on them to learn and remember. They discover that information becomes easier to learn once it is organised, and that repetition and practice strengthen memory for information. They also create associations

Episodic memory – the ability to recall individual events – develops from around the age of three, the time of our earliest memories.

Babies have good recognition memory, and can distinguish a new object from a familiar one as well as recognising mother's voice and smell.

Young children develop procedural skills for increasingly complex activities, and learn the value to memory of practice and repetition.

between new and existing knowledge, which sets up different ways to access a memory and also makes it easier to recall.

A growing interest in the world motivates young adolescents to invest more effort in learning what is important to them. New experiences occur almost every day and they pay attention to nearly everything that comes their way – even if they subsequently lose interest in it. By their teens, most young people will have acquired a strong sense of their own physical and mental strengths and weaknesses and their potential for success in particular areas. As a result, they become more selective about the skills that they wish to improve on and the subjects that interest them most.

Adolescent schoolchildren are faced with the novel demands of studying for formal examinations. At this stage, they begin to acquire strong rote-memory skills and to develop different learning techniques for different memory tasks. The way they learn history or literature, for example, will differ from the way they learn scientific principles.

Young people are often motivated to learn by social goals, such as the desire to feel accepted by their peers or by their immediate seniors. They also want to learn the rules of the adult world so that they can obtain adult privileges. It is at this period, too, that adolescents often learn key skills – for example, how to move with confidence, how to negotiate with others, how to plan and organise their work and social life. Social and physical skills such as these are usually untaught, and teenagers have to work out for themselves how to acquire the necessary knowledge and expertise.

From young adulthood to middle age

Students who go on to higher education are expected to acquire knowledge in a variety of new and often very abstract disciplines. At college, they often learn information for which they may not have a great deal of use in later years unless they choose a career that is directly related to their degree subject. Such information must be applied as early as possible after

PIONEERS

MEASURING MEMORY

Sir Francis Galton, an eminent 19th-century scientist, was a pioneer in the measurement of individual mental capabilities. He devised a technique for testing autobiographical memory in which a person was given a 'cue word', then asked to relate all the recollections that this word brought to mind. These were rated for characteristics such as vividness and level of detail. Galton's findings – that older people typically recalled things from their early life, while younger people recalled much more recent events – still hold true.

Sir Francis Galton (1822–1911)

The demands of exams strengthen semantic memory in teenagers – they learn how to understand different types of information and how to recall it effectively.

By their junior school years, children have honed their physical procedural skills, and are increasingly aware of their individual strengths and weaknesses.

leaving college if it is not to be forgotten. For example, modern language graduates will have to make a special effort to keep up their linguistic skills unless they work in one of the relatively few professions where these are a primary requisite, such as translating or teaching.

Once they have embarked on their chosen career, young adults have to acquire and remember yet another new type of information: the specialist knowledge and skills required for their work. In many careers – even those where some job-related skills are taught on training courses – they are unlikely to face exams and must rely on their day-to-day application of the new knowledge 'on the job' to make it stick. With practice, though, people become better and better at remembering the type of specialist information that goes with their job.

Because they have had more practice, older workers in any given career usually assimilate new specialist information more quickly and in greater quantity than their younger colleagues. The repeated use over many years of information or skills acquired early in one's career also means that employees nearing retirement often show no decline in performance compared with their juniors – older typists, for example, have been found to be just as fast as young ones.

New toys Learning the tricks of a new piece of equipment such as a mobile phone can be a positive joy to a young person but a bit of a chore in later life. Usually, older people need more practise, which is why they may still refer to the manual long after a teenager has mastered the technology.

The later years

Even if retirement involves a complete break from career work, learning is far from over and we continue to build and store information in memory throughout the senior years. With retirement, for example, may come the need to learn numerous practical skills, such as how to manage reduced finances and health. There is also the question of how to organise the increased amount of leisure time without work-centred routines. Many older people pursue interests that they did not have time for before.

Research has shown that people do not generally experience a decline in overall memory function before their fifties or sixties. Past this age, some

Adolescence and young adulthood are full of 'firsts' – new events that are often emotionally charged and become fixed in memory.

The pressure on students to learn complex abstract information is relieved by the pleasures of experiencing the world as a young adult – from which many of our episodic memories are formed.

decline in memory skills is inevitable as a natural part of the ageing process, but some growth may occur as well. As a rule, older people increase those memory skills that they actively use.

Memory changes

Recent studies have led to a better understanding of the complex way in which memory changes with age. Some older people have trouble with memory tasks either because their memory skills have become rusty or because they never acquired them in the first place. Tasks that younger people may find stimulating, such as learning to use a video machine, often present difficulties to older people. It may be that older people encounter novel stimuli less often and are more daunted when faced with something new – a younger person, for whom new stimuli are an almost daily occurrence, is less surprised and so learns readily. Or it may be that an older person is simply less interested.

Other explanations are based on changes in intelligence in older people. One idea is that there are two types of intelligence: 'crystallised intelligence', which is based on acquired knowledge and skills; and 'fluid intelligence', which we use to handle unfamiliar tasks. The theory is that while crystallised intelligence may be enhanced throughout active adulthood, fluid intelligence may deteriorate.

Like most people, older people recall recent events with little difficulty, but they typically find that they can remember their youth better than the intervening years. Childhood and youth are full of new experiences, from a first plane flight and public exams to a first kiss and first day at work – experiences that seize our attention, fix themselves in memory and put their stamp on each passing year. As we get older, the tally of birthdays, holidays and minor successes at work mounts up, each of these events becomes less remarkable to us and less memorable as a result. This is why, as we get older, we sometimes complain that the years seem to 'fly past'.

Real lives

TRACKING MEMORIES

Born and raised on an Indian reservation in California, cognitive psychologist Marigold Linton devised a classic experiment in which she attempted to keep track of her long-term memory over six years during the 1970s. Every day she noted down at least two events on a dated index card. Each month she tested herself on the recorded events and found that, as her diary grew, repeated events such as teaching sessions and meals with friends tended to merge together while one-off events, like the visit of a friend she saw very infrequently, remained distinct.

Linton found that repetition boosted her recall of semantic memories, but repeated episodes tended to merge together and become harder to remember. For example, after she had made the same journey a few times, she could not recall each individual trip. On the other hand, semantic elements such as airport layouts, routes and timetables became firmly lodged in her memory.

Putting knowledge to regular use at work enhances semantic memory and, in turn, our ability to learn further specialist knowledge

The increased demands of work and family life during the mid-life years means people often have to juggle several different memory tasks at once – leading to lapses in memory.

In retirement, people can keep their memory active by pursuing established interests as well as new experiences, such as travel.

COMMITTING TO MEMORY

Even if you left school or university determined never to take another exam, life continues to throw up occasions when you have to rely on your abilities to commit things to memory. Combining what you know about memory processes with mnemonic strategies and techniques can make you equal to the trickiest memory tasks.

FACT: Going straight to bed after studying is effective because while you sleep no new information interferes with what you have learned.

Testing times For most people, the ultimate test of memory is sitting an academic exam. How much you remember largely depends on how you stored the information in the first place.

In any discussion about good or bad memory, people will usually refer back to their performance in examinations. There will be a few who coasted through the school year and then crammed for a few days before the exams, while others slogged away diligently term after term. Some will have found that they went blank as soon as the exam room fell silent. Whichever group you fall into, those early experiences may inform your perception of your memory for much of your life beyond school.

Paradoxically, even when people have experienced little success with learning material in the past, they tend to stick to the flawed methods that failed them. When people are confronted with new procedures to learn for their job, or a driving theory test, or even formal exams, they tend to fall back on reading the material repeatedly and hoping for the best. However, there are better methods – as well as basic overall strategies for memorising – that make use of what is known about the way memory works.

• First, find a quiet place to learn where it is easy to concentrate, and go there each time you try to learn the material. Re-establishing the context helps to put you back in the right frame of mind for remembering.

Real lives   BECOMING A FIRST-CLASS STUDENT

Marie was an extremely able psychology student, but she had a tendency to panic under the stress of exams and forget most of what she knew. She achieved good grades in essays and coursework, but her exam performance was an annual disaster. Then, Marie was encouraged by one of her lecturers to try a first-letter mnemonic strategy. This involved making up words or phrases using the first letters of points she wished to make in exams.

'At first I felt a bit silly using them –

they seemed like a waste of valuable time, but as soon as I turned over the exam paper, I jotted down my mnemonics and the points they represented, and for the first time I felt confident that I had some of the information I needed to answer the questions. That proved to be enough to prevent panic setting in.'

Marie decided to use mnemonics for all her exams, and went from being in a state of despair to getting the results she wanted.

• Make sure you understand the material that you are learning – it is far harder for the mind to encode information that is meaningless because you cannot connect it to what you already know.

• Aim to practise the material for short periods regularly over several days, rather than in long sessions with long periods in between.

• Revise as soon as possible after you have learned something. Material is forgotten most rapidly in the first few hours after learning.

• Once you feel you know the material, go one stage further and learn it all over again. The firmer your grasp on it, the less likely you are to lose some or all of it over time.

Reading to remember

The problem with reading is that it gives the impression that material is being committed to memory when, on average, only a small percentage is retained. You may, for example, have had the experience of picking up a novel that you read recently and realise that you cannot remember a thing about it. Usually this is not a problem – most of us would not find it useful to recall every story that we had ever read. But there are other times when we read something intriguing and later feel infuriated because we can remember very little about it.

One of the most effective ways of improving memory of written material is the PQRST method. This was developed to help students revise but it can be applied to anything that you want to read and remember. The letters stand for **P**review, **Q**uestion, **R**ead, **S**elf-recitation and **T**est. Say, for example, you wanted to make a study of Chapter 2 of this book, 'The Mind's Memory Stores'. You would begin **previewing** the chapter by reading the introduction and then skimming through each topic. Taking one subject at a time, pose **questions** that arise from your preview, for example 'what is sensory memory?' Now **read** through each topic carefully, trying to answer your questions. This is a way of elaborating on

LEARN A POEM

We are all impressed by people who can launch into a perfect rendition of a poem or extract that we only dimly remember from school or college days. But there is no mystery to committing poetry or song lyrics to memory, and it's good exercise for the mind. Try this poem 'He Wishes for the Cloths of Heaven' by W.B. Yeats, or choose some favourite lines of your own:

> Had I the heavens' embroidered cloths,
> Enwrought with golden and silver light,
> The blue and the dim and the dark cloths
> Of night and light and the half-light,
> I would spread the cloths under your feet:
> But I, being poor, have only my dreams;

Poetry is hard to learn if you don't fully understand it, so read through the poem several times, looking up any unfamiliar words.

Then visualise the poem. First, the colours and textures of the cloths and the time of day or night they might represent. Picture each cloth being spread on the ground and the object of the poet's love about to step lightly onto them.

Now read the poem through slowly to establish the rhythm of the lines. Most have nine syllables, but take note of those that have fewer or more and build them into your rhythm. When you can read the poem through smoothly and easily, repeat and test yourself on the first part, which ends naturally at the word 'feet'. Then do the same with the second part. Now keep trying to recite the poem all the way through until it is perfect. Try again an hour later, a day later, and then after a week.

material that helps to fix it in memory. Now for the **self-recitation** stage – try to repeat the main ideas on each topic in your own words, preferably aloud. Finally, the **test**: summarise the whole chapter including as many facts and details from each topic as you can. You may be surprised at the amount you can recall.

Preparing for exams

Many people go into exams armed with some half-memorised facts and only decide how to organise them into answers when they see the questions. It is far better to think about the important points to make on possible topics before the exam. Doing this organises topics in memory so they can be accessed quickly and applied to the questions. Mnemonic systems (memory techniques) can be extremely useful – they help you to hold on to the relevant points in the exam, and using a technique requires you to organise your thoughts. For example, if you decide to use the peg system to remember ten facts to support a particular argument, you first need to select the points that are important, then plan how they will lead on to or link with other ideas. You have to ask yourself 'what evidence will I need to bring in to support my arguments?' and 'how does this lead on to the second point in my peg system?' and so on.

Here is an example of how you might use the peg system to remember to make points about **poverty**, **justice** and **liberty** in an essay on the French Revolution. Abstract words like poverty are not easy to visualise directly, but can be turned into something that is. Picture poverty as a child begging and imagine giving a begging child a **bun** (one). Now, picture a judge in a wig – representing justice – and imagine him banging a **shoe** (two) on a table. For liberty, imagine the Statue of Liberty with a **tree** (three) growing out of the top of it.

Alternatively, you could use the first-letter strategy, which involves taking the first letter of each point to be remembered and making them into a phrase or sentence. Research studies show that supplying the first letter of a word triggers full recall in 50 per cent of cases where the word appears to have been forgotten.

Multiple uses for mnemonics

Mnemonics have a wide range of uses beyond the examination room. They are particularly valuable in situations such as job interviews, where you want to make points or ask questions but it is inappropriate to use notes. The method of loci (see page 282) or the peg system (pages 275–7) can help you to anchor your handful of items into memory. If the points are hard to visualise as images, you could use the initial letters to make an easily remembered sentence. So if you wanted to ask about **prospects**, **training**, **overtime** and **pension** (**PTOP**), you might come up with **Please The Other Person** (which is what you are trying to do in the interview!). You would need to practise the mnemonic so that it brings the information to mind instantly.

Mnemonics can also be useful in job training. Trainee sales people, for example, are sometimes taught the mnemonic **AIDA**. They use this example of first-letter strategy to help them to remember to gain their clients' **Attention**, show **Interest** in their needs, foster **Desire** for an item and then get them to **Act** on it.

Surprisingly, one group of individuals who might be expected to use mnemonics to help them to learn by heart do not usually do so. Actors face a huge memory task when learning lines, but although they pay particular attention to cues from the other actors, most do not use mnemonic techniques. Instead, they try to get involved in their characters and think about why and how they would say the lines in order to help commit them to memory.

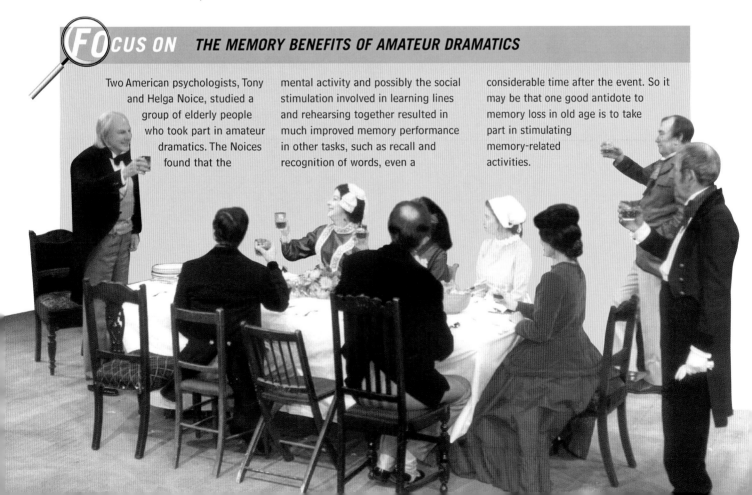

FOCUS ON THE MEMORY BENEFITS OF AMATEUR DRAMATICS

Two American psychologists, Tony and Helga Noice, studied a group of elderly people who took part in amateur dramatics. The Noices found that the mental activity and possibly the social stimulation involved in learning lines and rehearsing together resulted in much improved memory performance in other tasks, such as recall and recognition of words, even a considerable time after the event. So it may be that one good antidote to memory loss in old age is to take part in stimulating memory-related activities.

ADDRESSING AN AUDIENCE

Making a speech, or even just telling a joke, can strike fear into even the most practised performers. But preparation, organisation and a method to keep you on course can do much to reduce your anxiety.

In ancient times, Greek and Roman orators used memory techniques to remember long speeches. A speech was deemed more impressive if the speaker did not resort to notes, and the skill remains impressive today. Speeches given from memory tend to be spontaneous, lively and have an impact on their audience.

However, few people have the confidence to rely on memory alone, and the most effective speakers leave little to chance. Mnemonic techniques can provide a vital, invisible anchor for the points you wish to make.

Preparation and planning

How you prepare and plan your speech depends on the type of content and the occasion. Work-related presentations and speeches tend to follow a simple format – an interesting opening statement, followed by a logical progression of ideas and a succinct summing up. Knowing the material well and putting it in order is often all that is needed, particularly if you are using slides or computer presentations which act as memory cues for each point.

☞ TRY IT YOURSELF THE PEG SYSTEM

Imagine you have to give a speech at a wedding, and there are a number of stories that you wish to tell. The peg system (page 275) is well suited to the task. Suppose, for example, you want to make the following points:

1. You have known the groom since you were both caught stealing apples at the age of seven.
2. You had your first night out on the town together when your parents were away on holiday.
3. You don't hold a grudge against him for telling your parents that you lost all the money they gave you on a horse.
4. You are really pleased that the groom is marrying a girl who can cook.

5. It is remarkable that the happy couple are still so madly in love after knowing each other for so many years.

Choose some keywords for each point, such as:
1. Apples
2. Night out
3. Horses
4. Cook
5. Still madly in love

Now use visual association to attach the keywords to the peg words associated with these numbers:

1. One is a bun
Imagine stuffing an **apple** into a **bun**.
2. Two is a shoe
Imagine a **night out** drinking whisky from a **shoe**.
3. Three is a tree
Imagine **horses** jumping over a **tree**.
4. Four is a door
Imagine a **cook** bringing a meal through your **door**.
5. Five is a hive
Imagine two bees **falling in love** inside a **hive**.

Real lives   *A DISASTROUS PRESENTATION*

It is hard to imagine a worse occasion to make a complete hash of a presentation than while speaking on the subject of memory to a group of high-powered academics.

Professor Jones was giving just such a presentation on his research work when he found, right at the end of his speech, that he had forgotten the point of the entire experiment. In panic, he asked a colleague in the audience to help out, but unfortunately he had not been

listening and couldn't remember the point of the experiment either.

Professor Jones spent many hours analysing where he went wrong. First, he was over-confident about knowing his material and did not imagine that stress might affect his memory. Second, he dispensed with notes – always useful in an emergency. Third, when all else failed, he relied on his colleague – and social prompts, such as asking a partner to remind you of a dental appointment, are notoriously unreliable.

You may be more alarmed at the prospect of speaking at social occasions, such as weddings or retirement presentations. Social speeches are usually a mix of anecdotes, disconnected points, jokes and thanks – the kind of material that is hard to remember if you become nervous – and are usually delivered without the aid of visual props. There is also the added embarrassment factor of facing an audience that knows you well.

Mnemonic techniques can be an invaluable aid in such situations. Begin by thinking about the main points you want to make and then organise them into a coherent and (if possible) entertaining sequence; just by doing this your speech will begin to assume a useful familiarity. Then select a system to fix your ideas in memory in the right order. If you are giving a wedding speech, you could use the 'peg' system (see page 275 and left). Or if you prefer the 'method of loci' (see page 282), think of a journey you associate with the bride or groom – say the walk to your local pub – then turn key words from your points into images to place along the route. If you wish to reveal, for example, that the bride likes to cook curries for her new husband and he has never managed to tell her he prefers the local restaurant, you could visualise a plate of vindaloo on the groom's usual seat at the bar.

"As I was leaving this morning, I said to myself 'The last thing you must do is forget your speech'. And sure enough, as I left the house this morning, the last thing I did was forget my speech."

Rowan Atkinson, actor and comedian

Telling jokes

Most of us hear good jokes from time to time, but may be poor at bringing them to mind later on. Try using the peg system to provide yourself with a ready-to-use list, reviewing it occasionally to keep the jokes anchored in memory. If you enjoy telling long 'shaggy dog' stories but sometimes find yourself approaching a punch line that has become meaningless because you have forgotten to include a vital detail, try using the method of loci. For example, you could incorporate and visualise each stage of the joke inside a different room of your house.

Finally, memory methods are useful, but there is no shame in writing down points as a back-up. If you have memorised your material effectively, the paper is unlikely to leave your pocket.

WAYS TO REMEMBER NUMBERS AND DATES

For almost everything in life there seems to be a number. Examples range from bank codes and account numbers, PINs, national insurance or tax numbers, to telephone numbers, fax numbers and postcodes. We also build our lives around numbers in the form of dates and deadlines for work, appointments and social events.

Although our brains are not naturally well-equipped to deal with these strings of digits, there are ways to help your memory to cope.

THE MAJOR SYSTEM

The digit letter or major system was first used over 300 years ago. The underlying principle is that each number from 0 to 9 is represented by a corresponding consonant. Using these consonants, numbers are translated into sounds, sounds into words, and words into images. Here are the consonants for each symbol together with some simple devices for remembering them.

0 The letters s and z are the first sound in zero.

1 The letters t and d have a single down-stroke.

2 The letter n has two down-strokes.

3 The letter m has three down-strokes.

4 The letter r is the last letter in 'four'.

5 The letter L is the Roman numeral for 50.

6 The letter j is like a reversed 6.

7 The letter k can be made from two 7s.

8 The letter f can be written with two loops like 8.

9 The letter p is a mirror reversal of 9.

The next step is to make a memory image to go with each number you want to be able to remember. For example, to remember the number 10, you first need to think of a word starting with a t or d and

ending in an s or z sound. Any vowel can be used to complete the word because vowels have no set meaning within the system. A word to represent 10 could be doze. The image of your partner dozing with zzzz above his or her head could be your personal mnemonic for the number 10.

The advantage of the major system is that you can use it to convert any string of numbers into a meaningful word or phrase.

Suppose that you want to remember that your holiday is planned for the 14th to the 25th of June. These numbers translate into t-r-n-l which could make the words tour Nile. Alternatively you can make up a phrase with the letters as initials. For example, Take Really Nice Luggage.

REMEMBERING HISTORICAL DATES

You can use the major system to help you remember historical dates. Years are usually four digits in length – but for dates from the last millennium you can take the 1 for granted and convert just three numbers into letters. For example, the Wright brothers made their first flight in 1903. This date becomes p-s-m, which you could remember with the phrase **Powered Sky Machine**.

BIRTH DATES

When filling in official forms, people are often caught out when they try to remember the year of a parent's or child's birth. A rhyme can help, particularly if it has associations with the person or event. For example:

In nineteen hundred and sixty three, Gemma was born in time for tea.

Nineteen hundred and twenty five, The very first year my mum was alive.

See if you can make up some of your own.

KEEPING DATES IN YOUR MEMORY

Keeping a diary is a sensible way to remember next week's appointments – provided, of course, that you always remember to look at your diary.

However, a memory aid such as the method of loci combined with the 'one is a bun' peg system can be effective if you plan and use them consistently. Choose a room or place in your house for each day of the week and then place the people you have to see on each day in the appropriate locations. Suppose you have to meet your sister at 10 on Monday morning and go to the dentist at 3.30 pm; meet a friend for tea on Wednesday; and go to the theatre at 7 pm on Friday night.

First, imagine your **sister** sitting in your bedroom (Monday) clutching a huge **hen** (ten). Beside her, your **dentist** is pinned to the bed by the snapped off half of a **tree** (half three). In the bathroom (Wednesday), your **friend** is sitting in the bath and pouring **tea** into cups on a tray. Entering the sitting room (Friday), you find a stage has been erected and angels are staging a **heavenly** (seven) **play**.

TRYING OUT THE METHODS

Now use one or more of the mnemonic techniques on this page to remember some real dates. In the list below, first complete the details of the personal dates, then memorise the list. Test yourself the next day.

- Day and time next week when you are meeting a friend:
- Your mother's year of birth:
- Your aunt's/niece's birthday:
- The page number of your place in the book you are reading:
- The postcode of someone you send a postcard to on holiday:
- The year of the Russian revolution: 1917
- Execution of Mary Queen of Scots: 1587
- The fall of Rome: 476
- End of World War II in Europe: 8 May 1945
- Year of first manned space flight: 1961

Methods for remembering dates are helpful, but nothing works 100 per cent of the time. All memory methods take practice and may fail if you don't give them your full attention. When you first try out these methods, keep a written list of your appointments, just in case.

DIET AND MEMORY

What we eat can have a role in maintaining a good memory – and can also play a part in diminishing its effectiveness. A diet for a good memory should include an optimum level of beneficial nutrients such as vitamins, minerals and complex carbohydrates, and the minimum amount of potentially harmful substances such as caffeine.

▶▶ CUTTING EDGE ▶▶

GOOD NUTRITION IN PREGNANCY

Fluctuating hormone levels are known to affect memory in pregnancy, but research from the Royal Postgraduate Medical School in London suggests that women's brains may actually shrink during pregnancy. It is not the number of cells that reduces, but the size of the cells. One possible explanation is that the developing fetus uses up essential fats and phospholipids from the mother and this can be crucial if supplies are low. This highlights how important it is for pregnant women to get sufficient essential nutrients.

Modern scientists were not the first to discuss the importance of diet to memory. In 1523, the physician Lorenz Fries wrote that memory could be improved by eating a meal of roasted fowls, small birds or young hares, with apples and nuts for dessert and a good red wine. Eating the petals of particular flowers has also been recommended, as when an apothecary in 18th-century Williamsburg, USA, advised people to consume dandelions to boost their memories.

The right kind of energy

The brain uses large amounts of energy – about 20 per cent of the body's total energy needs – and it must have a constant supply to function, so crash diets will not benefit your memory. Most of this energy is used up in the electrical activity of the brain as neurons continually fire and send signals to each other. The only source of energy the brain can use is glucose, so adequate blood sugar levels are needed if we are to think and remember effectively. However, research over the last 20 years shows that consuming too much refined sugar can be detrimental to memory through causing a sudden rise in blood sugar levels. This triggers the rapid release of insulin from the pancreas to bring levels down again, resulting in the typical sugar 'rush' followed by reduced glucose levels and accompanying feelings of weakness or tiredness.

So how can we maintain the blood sugar levels needed for good memory functioning? The answer is to eat sufficient starchy, complex carbohydrate foods such as wholemeal bread, brown rice, pasta, vegetables, pulses and grains. These are broken down by the body into glucose and other simple sugars, and used at a steady rate or as and when required.

Herbal remedies Research has shown that certain herbs may benefit memory. For example, sage is thought to boost acetylcholine, a brain chemical associated with memory, while rosemary has traditional associations with remembrance.

(F) CUS ON   *THE IMPORTANCE OF TIMING*

Eating too much reduces your memory powers for up to a couple of hours after a meal, so if you have an important memory task ahead – such as a taxing conversation with your boss, a sales presentation or a job interview – don't eat too much beforehand. Large amounts of food make you sleepy. This is because digestion diverts oxygen from the brain, making it difficult to stay alert when you are trying to register or remember information. However, it is also best not to attempt an important memory task when you are hungry, as this will distract you. The best time is after the slow period that immediately follows a meal. Eating at irregular times also has a detrimental effect on memory. If you need energy throughout the day, it is best to keep to a consistent eating schedule.

Acetylcholine boosters

Certain herbal extracts may assist memory and other mental abilities. The ancient Romans recognised the benefits of sage (*Salvia officinalis*), which has been used for centuries as a folk remedy, and has long been thought to aid memory.

A recent study at Middlesex University suggested that rubbing sage oil (which must not be taken internally) into the scalp might protect against dementia. The oil was found to reduce the effects of acetylcholinesterase, an enzyme which breaks down acetylcholine in the brain. Acetylcholine is a neurotransmitter that is important in forming memories, so slowing its breakdown may be beneficial in some circumstances.

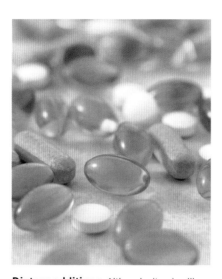

Dietary additions Although vitamin pills and other supplements can help to ensure good nutrition for the brain, they are no guarantee of an improved memory.

Certain herbs and plants are believed to benefit memory. These include gingko biloba, which is said to improve circulation and aid memory and concentration; gotu kola, an ancient Ayurvedic remedy that is known in India as a 'rejuvenator', helping concentration and memory; and rosemary, a herb believed to stimulate the circulation of blood to the head.

Caffeine

There is a myth that caffeine in coffee, tea or cola drinks improves memory and all-round mental performance. While the caffeine in one or two cups of coffee increases alertness and reduces drowsiness, there is no evidence that caffeine does anything more than keep you awake. Indeed, habitual coffee drinkers may need stronger doses to get the same effect. The dehydrating effect of caffeine, which also saps the body of important vitamins and minerals such as B-complex vitamins, zinc and potassium, may in fact result in poorer mental performance.

FACT FILE

MEMORY NUTRIENTS
Several vitamins have come to be regarded as 'memory nutrients', in particular the B-complex vitamins.

• Vitamin B_1 (thiamine, found in peanuts, sunflower seeds and mackerel, for example) and B_5 (pantothenic acid, found in liver, eggs, peas and wheatgerm) also contribute to acetylcholine production.

• Nearly all the B vitamins play a role in brain chemistry. Including plenty of foods such as fish, chicken, oatmeal and whole grains in your regular diet may help your memory to perform better.

• The nutrient believed to be most effective for good memory is choline, which is used in the formation of the 'memory molecule' acetylcholine. Foods rich in choline include eggs, cabbage and caviar.

Remember that vitamins should not be regarded as 'miracle drugs'. Taking supplements is likely to be helpful only if you have a dietary deficiency.

MEMORY AND MIND DRUGS

Are there shortcuts to a good memory? Could simply popping a pill enhance your ability to retain information? For many people, this is an alluring idea – but drugs that target the brain can lead to problems as well as benefits.

Having a good time? Social situations can easily lead people to drinking more than they should – often followed by embarrassment as they find out about behaviour they cannot remember.

In 1972, the first drug with claims to enhance memory was launched. Called piracetam, the drug was developed by a Belgian pharmaceutical company. The lead researcher, C.E. Giurgea, coined the term 'nootropics' (from the Greek word 'nous', meaning 'mind') for the new class of drugs. Since then many extravagant claims have been made for such drugs, but their effectiveness (at least in healthy people) remains unproven.

Often marketed with claims that they revitalise memory and concentration, nootropics aim to enhance specific abilities such as vocabulary skills and mental endurance. However, most of the scientific evidence for such claims comes from studies carried out with animals or with people suffering from a memory-debilitating condition, such as Alzheimer's disease. Transferring results from animal studies is problematic, because the typical memory tasks where people seek enhancement – remembering names, for example – cannot be tested in animals. Similarly, while some drugs have been shown to be genuinely effective in people with dementia, there is no reason to expect this benefit to apply to people without such debilitating conditions. Expecting an anti-Alzheimer's drug to improve your memory is rather like expecting an anti-arthritis drug to improve your tennis, irrespective of whether you have arthritis or not.

Combatting severe problems

The most common cause of severe memory loss is probably dementia arising from Alzheimer's disease. People with dementia are thought to have lowered levels of the neurotransmitter acetylcholine, but early treatments – simply supplying large doses of choline in the diet – were not effective. However, drugs such as donepezil (Aricept) and rivastigmine (Exelon), developed in recent years to treat dementia, do seem to slow memory decline and in some cases even reverse it for a time. These raise levels of acetylcholine in the brain by inhibiting the enzyme that breaks it down.

Substances that damage memory

While some drugs may enhance memory, others – so-called 'recreational' drugs – may cause serious harm. Many such drugs cause memory deficiencies in the short term, followed by apparent recovery when the immediate effects wear off. However, recent evidence shows that more permanent damage is likely. The long-term use of cannabis has been linked to memory loss, paranoia and lethargy, and there is increasing concern that continued use of Ecstasy may lead to permanent memory loss, anxiety and serious depression owing to the loss of neurons that release serotonin.

> ❝It can be positively deleterious to throw chemical spanners into the exquisitely balanced biochemical system that is the human brain.❞
>
> Stephen Rose, memory neuroscientist

The effects on memory of another drug, alcohol, are well known. The 'morning after the night before' kind of memory failure, when you cannot even remember how you got home, is familiar to many people. A drink for 'Dutch courage' before a speech or performance is unwise as it is likely to impair the ability to recall information. More seriously, chronic heavy drinking can lead to a permanent deterioration of the memory – and in extreme cases to the severe and chronic amnesia of Korsakoff's syndrome. There is evidence that even moderate drinking can cause some loss of memory ability in the long term, so it may not be quite as healthy overall as some recent media reports have suggested.

▶▶ CUTTING EDGE ▶▶

HRT MEMORY BOOST

Hormone replacement therapy (HRT) may boost the memory of post-menopausal women. Canadian researcher Barbara Sherwin, of McGill University in Montreal, studied 100 middle-aged women who were plunged into sudden menopause after the surgical removal of their ovaries. Half the group were treated with HRT while the other half received a placebo.

When the women were later given memory tests, those on the hormone treatment performed as well as they had done before the operation, while those on placebo showed a significant decline in memory performance. Sherwin's findings tie in with other studies which suggest that oestrogen (the main female sex hormone) could help prevent memory loss in age-related dementia.

Real lives THE RIGHT MEDICINE

The complexity of brain chemistry can make diagnosis and treatment of mental conditions a hit-and-miss affair, as Marianne's experience of her father's illness shows.

'About ten years ago, my father had a nervous breakdown after a financial crisis. He seemed to recover initially, but he was prone to deep depressions from then on, and ran the gamut of anti-depressant drugs in the hope of finding one that worked. As he aged, he became more and more desperate. Eventually, he began showing signs of dementia – although the doctors denied this – and we decided to try one of the

new drugs aimed at this condition. We didn't expect much, but it was amazingly effective. Not only did my father's memory improve, but his depression lifted at last. He became interested again in all the things he loved doing – reading literature and just talking to people. We had to pay for the drug ourselves, but it didn't matter – it was such a relief to find something that worked. While I guess scientists must know something about the brain to develop these drugs, it seems that doctors often know very little about what's wrong in any individual case – so you just have to keep on trying.'

TAKING CARE OF YOUR MEMORY

Memory is central to our personal and professional lives and is not something we should take for granted. To perform at our best, we need to maintain our psychological and physical well-being.

In recent years, researchers have taken an integrated approach to memory improvement. Mnemonic strategies, repetition and visualisation are valuable memory tools but mental function is also influenced by many factors ranging from our physical and emotional states to our environment and social interactions. We need to be aware of these less obvious influences that can make the difference between memory success and failure.

Health and memory

People who are often ill have significantly more memory problems than those in good health. Serious illnesses such as stroke or Alzheimer's disease can of course cause memory loss, but even the common cold can have an effect, and a particularly bad cold or flu may cause considerable difficulties with recall. High stress levels can also have a significant effect. If you are feeling positive and cheerful, you will generally learn and recall information more readily than if you are depressed or negative. Anxiety and stress reduce your ability to direct attention, so leave room in your day for some relaxation. On the other hand, a moderate amount of stress is better for your memory than none at all. Absence of stress can reduce your sense of urgency to the extent that you fail to pay attention. Routines and repetitive tasks may become so automatic that you barely notice what you are doing and so forget what you have done.

Looking after your physical health can bring positive memory benefits. Exercise boosts the brain's production of endorphins, which are chemical compounds that act as natural antidepressants. The brain needs an abundant supply of oxygen and glucose

to perform at its best, so eating a healthy diet to keep your body well supplied with nutrients is an important step. Getting a good night's sleep is vital for all types of memory performance, so make this a priority. Hearing and eyesight are also important to memory — if we do not hear or see information properly, we cannot register it in memory — so make sure they are checked regularly.

Social pressures

We are more likely to experience memory failure when we are among other people than when we are alone. Sometimes the flow of conversation in a group is too quick, or someone speaks so softly that the effort of hearing distracts us from the task of remembering. We may be distracted by our emotions if the atmosphere is exciting and boisterous, like a party, or tense and formal, like a business meeting. Shyness can hamper our ability to concentrate when people tell us their names and other details. If we recall some event differently from others in a group, their combined scepticism about our version may convince us that we have made a mistake.

But social situations can also provide a great incentive for cultivating a good memory. You may not be aware of it, but you probably have a reputation among your friends or work colleagues for your memory. People keep track of who has a good memory so that they know whom they can depend on in certain situations. It helps if you remain in touch with issues under discussion at work and home. Try to keep up with what you need to know and what others are likely to ask you about. When called upon to remember something, express yourself carefully: overstating or understating what you recall may damage your credibility. It also makes a good impression if you are able to remember people's names and other details. When talking on the phone to friends and family, try to remember some of the details (especially about imminent plans or current concerns) so that you can refer back to these when you talk again.

Competence and expectation

There are many different kinds of memory challenge, and it is not possible to be skilled at all of them. People vary in their competence at everyday memory tasks, as they do at most things. Some people tend to be error-prone, and this will show itself in their memory performance. Others are very careful not to make mistakes and may avoid certain learning and memory tasks unless they are sure they will succeed. Your perception of your own competence will also influence the effort you make to remember certain types of information. It is good to be positive about memory tasks, but you must also be realistic — or you may be led to attempt challenges that you probably should have avoided. Reward and punishment affect memory competence just as they affect other behaviour. For example, we may be highly motivated to remember certain information — such as the details of a potential business contact or a person we are attracted to — because we hope to benefit from knowing it.

Real lives

NELSON MANDELA

Now in his eighties, Nelson Mandela is a celebrated example of someone who has kept his memory powers intact into old age. The former South African president is renowned for his extraordinary memory for names, faces and events. The writer Richard Stengel, who helped Mandela to write his autobiography *A Long Walk to Freedom*, called him 'both camera and calendar: he can picture and re-create a scene in his mind's eye'.

Soon after becoming president, Mandela held a reunion dinner for student friends from his days at Witwatersrand University law school. Guests were astonished when he recognised and greeted them by name — in many cases he had not seen or spoken to them for almost 40 years.

During much of Mandela's gruelling 27 years in prison under apartheid, he was forbidden to write anything down and was refused access to books and other printed matter. He had to rely on memory to keep his existing knowledge intact, to learn from other prisoners, and to ensure that information remained accurate as it was transmitted verbally in secret.

HOW TO KEEP YOUR MEMORY YOUNG

To keep your memory as green as it was in your youth, keep looking at the world as you did then. A curious mind, a thirst for detail and the will to practise are not the sole preserve of the young. These life-long habits are the best possible foundation for keeping your memory sharp.

PLAY MEMORY-BASED GAMES

Playing memory-based games like bridge, scrabble, chess and bingo or doing crosswords is a good way to hone specific memory skills, although it won't necessarily increase your memory powers in other areas. Mnemonic strategies can boost your performance in some games. Try using a peg system or the method of loci to keep track of cards in competitive games, or use techniques to overcome mental blocks (page 246) when you are searching for a word in a crossword or quiz. Try the crossword below to see how many memory words you can remember from this book. (Answers on page 475.)

USE ROUTINE AND NOVELTY

One of the most robust types of memory is unconscious memory, which underlies the effortless carrying out of most of what we do. Many habits are a form of unconscious memory. Developing memory habits – for example, checking your diary as you drink your first cup of tea each morning, or always placing letters to be posted in the same part of your bag – are a way of remembering without conscious memory effort. However, using habits to avoid absent-mindness is not the same as becoming wedded to routines. Encountering new situations helps to encourage the brain into more effortful processing, so take different routes to places, or read a book you would not normally choose.

ACROSS

1 An inability to recognise objects (7)
3 Use this to increase your working memory span (8)
5 Heaven in a peg system (5)
7 Hold a phone number in your phonological —— (4)
8 Techniques to improve memory (9)
9 A peg for number five (4)
11 The most fleeting form of visual memory (6)
12 Can't quite find the right word? (3-2-3-6)
17 Use this to fix a list in mind (3-6)
20 Autobiographical memory (8)
21 Happy and sad memories can depend on your — (4)
22 Make a note in memory (4)
23 What happens to perceptions that fail to impress (4)
25 A pioneer in eyewitness research (6)
27 Use this for number four (4)
28 …and this for number three (4)
29 A mini-plan that helps us make sense of the world (6)
30 The place to go for number seven (6)
31 Five letters to help you commit to memory (5)
33 The opposite of bottom-up processing (3-4)
34 A nerve cell (6)

14 A brain area that is crucial to memory (11)
15 Suffering from memory loss (7)
16 Seen this before? (4-2)
18 Factual memory (8)
19 Ancient Greek inventor of 5 down (9)
24 Re-establishing this may help you remember (7)
26 How a bar of soap might trigger emotional memories (5)
32 What did the hen stand for? (3)

DOWN

1 The first stage of making a memory (9)
2 How most information becomes linked in the mind (11)
4 A picture for number eight (4)
6 …and one to eat (3)
8 Using places to organise a memory (6-2-4)
9 Ten(t) peg? (3)
10 …and a drink for nine (4)
13 Your memory for skills (10)

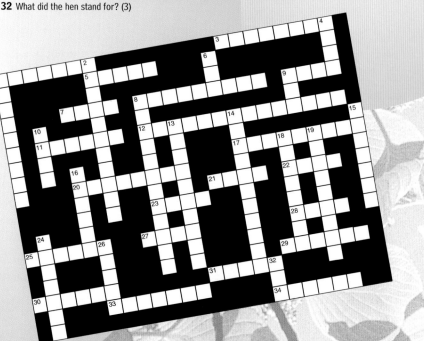

GIVE YOUR INTERESTS EXTRA CONTEXT

Activities that you enjoy can be further enriched by finding out more about them. If you like gardening, learn more about plants and keep a diary of your own garden through the seasons. If you live in an old house, research its history and that of your street or town. Question what you read or hear on the radio and television and follow up areas of interest with some research in the library or on the internet.

MAKE RETIREMENT A NEW BEGINNING

The most remarkable memories in old age usually belong to people who never completely give up their life's work. Most writers, musicians, academics and politicians, for example, continue to work well beyond retirement age. It is only to be expected that abandoning years of challenging mental activity abruptly at the age 65 can leave the brain in need of stimulation. Not everyone can continue their main occupation after retirement, but you can pursue new interests through part-time work or study, or turn your attention to hobbies such as watercolour painting or marquetry that you never had time for previously.

REVIVE AN OLD SKILL OR LEARN A NEW ONE

Relearning is easier than learning for the first time, although it may not always seem to be the case when you first try. Getting back onto a motorcycle or trying out some halting French phrases in a conversation class can be daunting after a 20-year gap. But a few weeks of practice can revive expertise and enjoyment in old skills. Learning a completely new skill is a valuable memory activity at any age, but you need to keep practising to establish it in memory. Once you have learned to master the new microwave without always referring to the instructions, use it regularly and for different types of food. If you have just about grasped word processing, databases and e-mail, use them daily to organise old records, write a daily journal and keep in touch with family and friends.

WRITE INFORMATION DOWN

However adept you become at memory strategies, there is a lot to be said for making notes. Not only is the information there in black and white if you should need to look at the piece of paper, but it also provides another cue for remembering. And as well as 'hearing' the information, it becomes possible to see it written down in your 'mind's eye'.

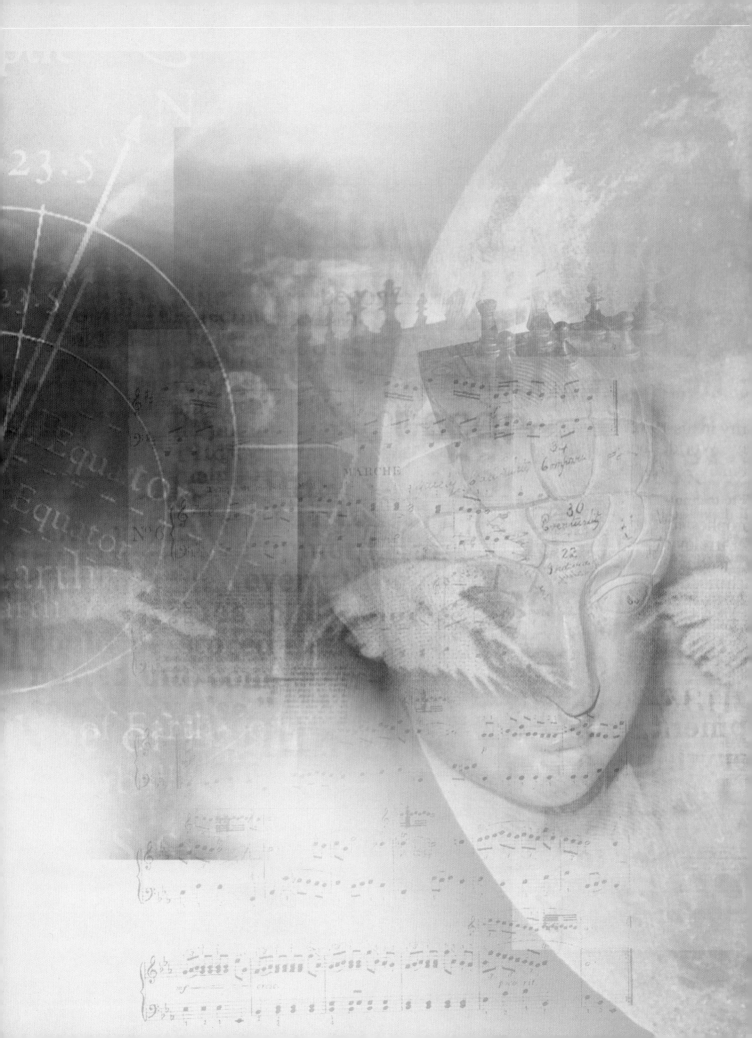

3

THE CONSCIOUS & UNCONSCIOUS BRAIN

THE MIRACLE OF CONSCIOUSNESS

Consciousness is the most remarkable product of the human brain. It is the medium for our thoughts, and gives meaning to our experiences. Without it we could not experience sight or sound, taste, touch or smell; and from it comes our very sense of identity. Consciousness is so multi-faceted that no single definition can do it justice, but we can start by looking at some of its amazing characteristics.

WITHOUT CONSCIOUS PERCEPTION, RAINBOWS WOULD NOT HAVE ANY COLOURS

The colours we see are produced in our eyes and brains. Sunlight is split into different wavelengths when it passes through raindrops – but to see this spectrum of wavelengths as a spectrum of colours requires a conscious mind.

CERTAIN LAWS OF PHYSICS ARE BUILT INTO THE HUMAN BRAIN

Children do not have to learn that physical objects cannot disappear, or that they cannot be in two places at once. This knowledge simply appears in their minds at around the age of eight to ten months, when brain areas related to processing information about the world reach maturity.

CONSCIOUSNESS STEPS IN ONLY WHEN IT IS NEEDED

A skilled tennis player does not consciously work out where to place her racquet or feet when playing a shot. Only when a ball presents a special problem does conscious decision-making come into play.

THE HUMAN BRAIN HAS A BUILT-IN AWARENESS OF OTHER PEOPLE'S THOUGHTS

An intuitive awareness of other people's thinking and their view of situations develops in children at around the age of four. Before this age, children usually assume that others have the same information and feelings as themselves. This 'mind-reading' ability is located in the frontal lobes of the brain.

YOUR BRAIN AUTOMATICALLY 'ZOOMS IN' ON IMPORTANT INFORMATION

If your name is spoken quietly, even amid the loud babble of conversation at a party, you will hear it and be able to tune into the person saying it. The brain accomplishes this by processing incoming information at an unconscious level, and may bring significant information to consciousness.

YOUR BRAIN NEVER STOPS WORKING, EVEN WHEN YOU ARE ASLEEP

Even in deep sleep, there is activity in parts of the brain, including the cortex. Overall, there is practically no difference in total brain activity during a period of sleep and one of wakefulness.

YOU CAN RESPOND TO A STIMULUS BEFORE YOU ARE EVEN CONSCIOUS OF IT

It takes about a fifth of a second for you to become aware of a visual stimulus, such as a ball thrown towards you. But within a tenth of a second your brain has calculated what you need to do to catch it, and started off the process.

THE BRAIN CREATES OUR SENSE OF TIME BY DIVIDING THE FLOW OF EVENTS INTO A SEQUENCE OF FRAMES

A normal brain detects about ten events per second. The brain's 'clock' mechanism is based on the regular rate at which certain brain cells fire. Damage to the brain area involved can make time appear to slow down or speed up.

YOUR BRAIN REMEMBERS A FACE – EVEN IF YOU CLAIM NOT TO HAVE SEEN IT

If a photograph of a face is flashed onto a screen in front of your eyes for about one tenth of a second, it does not have time to enter your conscious awareness. However, if you encounter the same image later, your body will respond to it as though it is familiar.

A CAPACITY FOR SPIRITUAL EXPERIENCE IS WIRED INTO THE HUMAN BRAIN

Certain areas of the brain's temporal and frontal lobes produce feelings of transcendence (like experiences of religious ecstasy) when they are stimulated. This suggests we may be drawn to explore the religious and spiritual dimensions of life because of the way our brains are constructed.

1 WHAT IS CONSCIOUSNESS?

Consciousness is one of those enigmatic words: we use it happily enough in conversation, but as soon as we stop to think about what it really means, it seems impossible to pin it down. Even the experts – philosophers, psychologists, neuroscientists – seem to hit this problem and opinions vary dramatically: some think it may be the fundamental stuff of the universe, the defining characteristic of what it is to be human, while others see it as no more than a fiction, a by-product of the physical interaction of cells.

The quest to understand the nature of consciousness raises some fascinating questions. If consciousness springs from the brain, can we see it in operation in brain scans? Is it a uniquely human attribute, or do animals possess consciousness of a kind? Computers are becoming ever-more powerful, so is it just a matter of time before a machine emerges with a conscious mind?

Astonishing ingenuity has gone into investigating such questions, from many different perspectives. What is clear is that we are still at the beginning of an exciting journey of discovery not just to understand consciousness, but to understand ourselves.

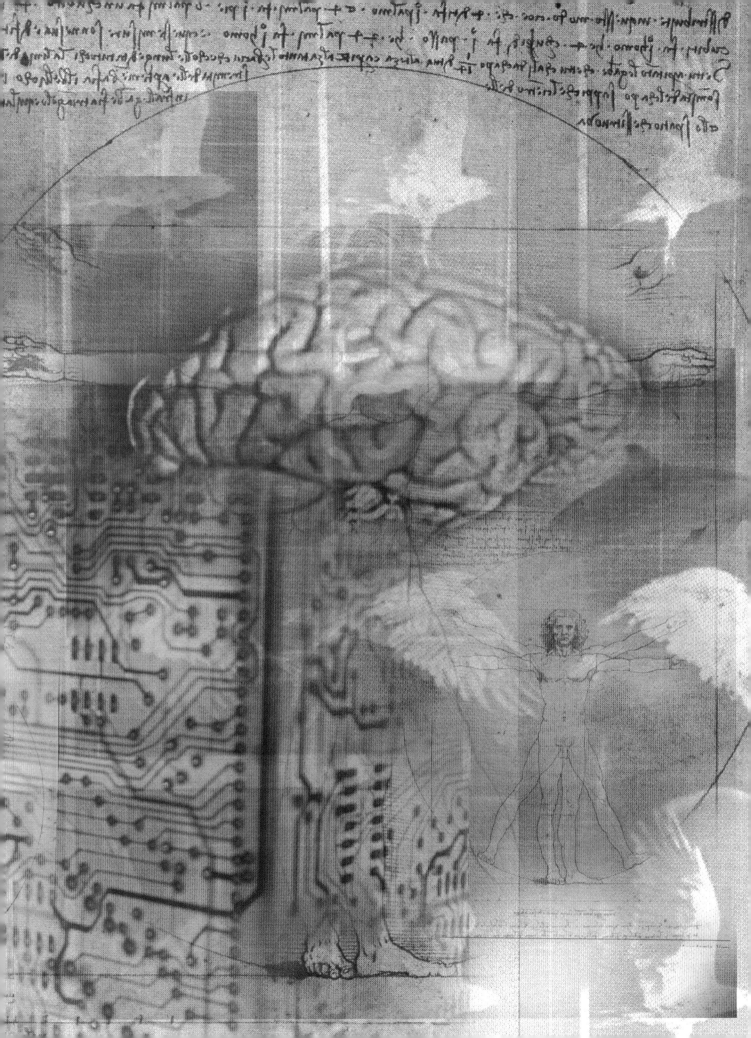

THE ENIGMA OF CONSCIOUSNESS

Although no one knows exactly what **consciousness** is, there are many different theories. Some of them are thousands of years old, while some are new ideas conceived by explorations at the frontiers of philosophy and neuroscience.

Consciousness is a puzzle. For a start, we all use the words 'consciousness' and 'conscious' to mean many different things. For example, we may say that we are conscious of someone or something, meaning that we are aware of that person, idea or object; but this is not the same as simply being conscious. This variety of meanings, and the difficulty of pinning down what we are referring to when we use the word 'conscious', is part of the reason why it is so hard to say exactly what consciousness is.

Even trying to separate the states in which we are conscious from those in which we are not is not straightforward. If you are in a deep, dreamless sleep, you are unconscious – and if you are wide awake and enjoying your experience of the world, you are conscious. This seems clear, but there are borderline cases.

Brain and mind
Smelling and seeing a flower may lead us to think of buying a bouquet for a friend, or remind us of a happy memory. But how do our brain states – which are governed by physical laws – link to our train of thought, which seems to have its own logic? It is not clear that even detailed brain scans could answer this question.

During the process of falling asleep you may be neither fully conscious nor unconscious. And when you are dreaming you seem to be having experiences of some sort, but are you conscious in quite the same way as when you are awake?

Among philosophers and psychologists who study consciousness, there are also many different opinions in answer to the question 'what is consciousness?' One reason why consciousness is so puzzling is that while it certainly depends on the brain, it seems to be a very different sort of thing from what is actually going on in the brain in terms of brain cell activity. For example, when a flower is present in your consciousness, there is nothing remotely like a flower actually in your brain. And the links that your mind makes from one conscious thought or image to another seem to follow a logic that does not correspond to the physical laws that govern brain processes.

Mental and physical realms

This kind of reasoning has led some philosophers to think of consciousness as a non-physical thing – a sort of spiritual container in which your thoughts, emotions, experiences and so on take place. They have argued that you have unique access to your own consciousness-container: only you can look inside it and your knowledge of its contents is infallible. There is no part of the physical world which you have this special access to. For example, a neuroscientist may have much better knowledge of what is going on inside your brain from a physical point of view than you do – but he or she would still have no access to your conscious experiences. It seems to follow, therefore, that your consciousness is not part of the physical world.

René Descartes (1596–1650) was one philosopher who thought of consciousness in this way. The philosophical theory named after him, Cartesian dualism, separates the world into two distinct realms – the physical realm inhabited by atoms, molecules, tables, chairs and human bodies, and the mental realm which souls inhabit and where conscious thoughts and experiences take place.

One major problem with this view is that the two realms cannot be regarded as entirely separate from one another since, as we all know, the body affects the mind and the mind affects the body. When we perceive things, our conscious experiences are affected by events in our sense

> **"Each one of us has only our own thoughts and feelings and no one else's. From the first-person point of view, the great divide is between what is me and what is not me."**
>
> Owen Flanagan, professor of philosophy

FACT FILE

SOME MEANINGS OF 'CONSCIOUS'

• **Being in a state of general awareness**
When you are awake and aware of your surroundings you are said to be conscious. This is perhaps the most standard meaning of being 'conscious'.

• **Perceiving something via the senses**
If you say that you are conscious of a fly buzzing around the room, this means that you believe it is there because you can hear and perhaps see it.

• **Having experiences that we can reflect on**
This normally happens when we are awake, although we can also reflect on our dream experiences.

• **Being aware of something intellectually**
If you say that you are conscious of someone else's opinions, this means that you have understood them and are bearing them in mind.

• **Doing something deliberately**
Saying 'I made a conscious effort' means to make a deliberate effort.

• **Being self-aware**
As humans, we naturally think of being conscious as being conscious of ourselves – that is, being aware of the thoughts that we are thinking and the actions that we are making.

FACT FILE

MODERN THEORIES OF CONSCIOUSNESS

Here are some of the most influential ways in which consciousness has been described by experts. Many other theories lie between and beyond these positions.

• **Idealism**
'Mind' or 'spirit' is the only thing that really exists – the material universe is an illusion produced by it. Consciousness therefore does not need to be explained in physical terms.

• **Functionalism**
Consciousness is not a separate thing, but a way of ordering the physical world. A brain is conscious because it is processing information in a certain way and consciousness is wholly material.

• **Identity**
The physical brain activity associated with consciousness is consciousness. There is no need to explain the link between mind and brain because there is no link – they are one and the same.

• **Eliminativism**
Consciousness does not exist as a 'thing'. We think we are conscious, but it is an illusion. Close scrutiny of what we take to be experience from the senses reveals that it is essentially no different from the knowledge we hold unconsciously.

• **Quantum approaches**
Consciousness is the manifestation of quantum effects in the brain and differs from any other observable part of the natural world because it is not bound by the same physical laws.

organs, and when we decide to act our conscious thoughts affect our muscles and limbs. If the mental realm were totally separate from the physical world and did not even exist in space, how could it interact with and have an effect on the body? And what would happen at the intersection between mind and body, between the non-physical and physical realms? Any process that could cross this intersection – and thus provide the causal link between mind and body that we all experience – would have to be a material process on one side and a non-material process on the other, which seems impossible. Most philosophers today no longer regard Cartesian dualism as a possible solution to the relationship between the mental realm of consciousness and the physical world.

Emerging powers

So what is the alternative? Most thinkers now agree that there is no need to believe that consciousness is in fact something distinct from the activity of the physical brain. Rather, consciousness can be regarded as an 'emergent property' of the brain, a characteristic that arises out of the combined action of its highly complex parts, and occurs only when these parts are functioning together. It is not a feature of the brain that can be observed with a microscope; but nor is it in a realm of its own.

As an analogy, consider a painting of a landscape. The fact that it is a

THINK AGAIN! THE IMPOSSIBLE QUESTION

Some present-day philosophers think that it is impossible to give a valid answer to the question 'What is consciousness?'. Two prominent exponents of such views are Colin McGinn and David Chalmers.

Colin McGinn argues that there must be some natural property of the brain that is responsible for consciousness, but that we are cut off by our own cognitive limitations from ever being able to understand the relationship between the brain and consciousness. We are like five-year-old children faced with the task of understanding relativity theory. We are in this situation because the only way we have of getting access to our conscious experience is by introspection, but introspection is not a faculty that can give us any understanding of the brain. External perception and scientific investigation give us our understanding of brains. But we do not have any faculty that can put introspection and external perception together to give us an understanding of consciousness and brains together.

David Chalmers is less pessimistic. He argues that no theory of consciousness in terms of neuroscience is possible, but that it may be possible to construct a theory that explains the relationship between the brain and consciousness – if we use consciousness, not the brain, as the starting point. This theory would include the concept of experience as a basic term – just as theories in physics use the concepts of mass, charge, and so on as basic – rather than neurons or other brain science concepts. So we would need a new type of science in order to express the relationship between consciousness and brains.

painting of a landscape cannot be observed by studying the microscopic make-up of the painting. We might be able to describe it in detail as a complex array of differently coloured pigments – but we would fail to capture the power of the painting to depict a landscape. This power is a property of the painting as a whole, not of the individual brushstrokes. It is not a separate physical thing, but emerges from the arrangement of the pigments as a distinct quality. In a similar way, although consciousness cannot be fully understood by examining the brain and its component parts, it does not exist as something over and above the brain – just as a separate quality.

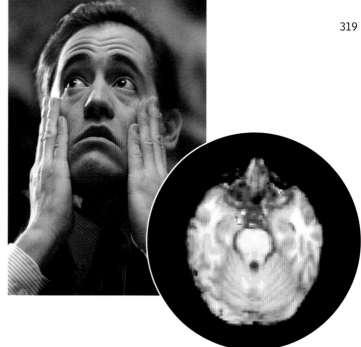

Perspective and allegory

So has the riddle of consciousness now been solved? Not quite. Fundamentally, we understand consciousness through being conscious ourselves, by looking at it from the inside. But when we consider the brain, we must consider that from the outside. The difficulty of understanding consciousness in terms of brain science is in reconciling these two perspectives. Many philosophers think that, while these two perspectives describe exactly the same thing – a physical person, they do so in such different ways and using such different language that it would be impossible ever to completely express one perspective in terms of the other. So, while most thinkers throughout contemporary philosophy and psychology are agreed on a 'materialist' understanding of the mind – that is, that there is no separate mind or soul substance – they are also agreed that we will have to continue talking as if there were a separate mental realm inhabited with motives, suspicions, desires and all the other facets of our own mental experience, as these will not be found directly in the brain.

Finally, where does this leave the soul? Now that the science of the brain has made it more difficult to accept Cartesian dualism, many religious people think the idea of the soul has a mainly allegorical value. The soul may be thought of as a metaphor for what is significant in your life – what makes you special. The idea that the soul lives on after death has largely been superseded by the idea that what is unique about you will not end when you die, even though your conscious mind no longer exists. You will go on living, in a sense, in other people's lives and in what you have done while living and knowing others.

Outside and inside Strong emotions such as anxiety or fear can be read in a person's face and shown in a brain scan. But even if brain science advanced so far that we could tell from a scan exactly what someone was thinking, this would still be quite different from experiencing this from the inside.

The idea of soul This 19th-century painting by Evelyn De Morgan depicts the passing of the soul in a style that is more allegorical than literal.

MIND PUZZLES

When we start to think about our own minds, we encounter puzzles and paradoxes quite apart from the enigmas posed by consciousness itself. For example, have you ever wondered how people make the link between their own minds and the world outside? Or how people can tell what is going on in the minds of others – and whether they experience things in the same way? Throughout the centuries, such puzzles have led leading philosophers into seemingly impossible tangles. But applying some clear thinking can help to resolve these tantalising problems.

COULD YOUR LIFE BE JUST A DREAM?

Tonight you may dream that you are reading this book, and in your dream be completely convinced that this is what you are doing – even though in reality you are fast asleep in bed. This plausible possibility raises the natural question of how do you know right now that you are not in fact in a dream? Even more disturbingly, how do you know that your whole life is not a dream?

One way to answer this question is to consider how well the life you are apparently living hangs together. There may be moments when some things seem not to make much sense, but sooner or later you will find an explanation. In fact, there are explanations for almost everything in your life: if you are in London one day and in Aberdeen the next, there will be an explanation for how you got from one to the other – perhaps a train journey. Things in your life can be investigated to any level of detail, usually without inconsistency – but in a dream, you can be flying over the rooftops one moment and then be in a completely different place the next with no explanation of how you got from one to the other. Real experience is also consistent in a deeper way than in a dream – even if a completely logical dream were possible. In a dream, all the ideas, images and events are derived from what is already in our minds, while in reality our experiences go beyond what we ourselves know about. For example, when Isaac Newton discovered the law of gravity, his new law fitted everyone's previous experience of how objects fell – although no-one had known the law before. So it makes sense to suppose that there is a real world 'out there', beyond our own mind, that is determining our experiences: our minds cannot just be making it all up.

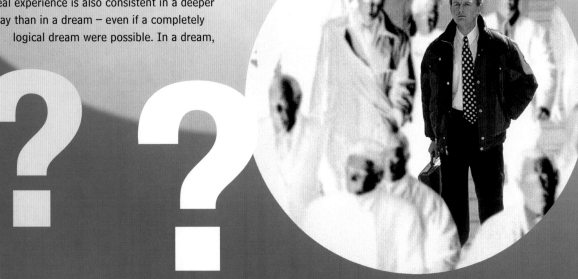

HOW DO YOU KNOW WHETHER YOUR SENSATIONS ARE THE SAME AS OTHER PEOPLE'S?

Have you ever wondered whether other people have the same experiences as you in the same situations? Perhaps you love the taste of marzipan and your friend hates it. Are you both having the same conscious experience but just reacting to it differently? Or does the marzipan taste quite differently to the two of you?

Sometimes it is clear that two people in the same situation do have quite different experiences. For example, someone who is colour blind cannot distinguish certain shades of colour that are visibly different to someone who is not colour blind. If a colour blind person hates a necktie that someone else loves, it is quite possible that this is because they are actually having different experiences of the colours in the tie.

This may apply to the taste of marzipan too. Different people's taste buds have slightly different levels of sensitivity to the various aspects of taste, so marzipan may indeed taste a little different to your friend. But it is also possible that it tastes almost exactly the same to the two of you, but you have different attitudes to it – perhaps through associating it with different experiences in the past. Even though the marzipan tastes the same, however, it is still the case that you have different experiences of the marzipan, because your interpretation of the taste as 'nice' or 'not nice' is part of the overall experience. Your attitudes to an experience cannot really be detached from the experience itself.

So, if someone genuinely seems to have a different reaction to your own, it's likely that at a conscious level this difference is real. But this difference may lie not in your raw sensations, but in how these are interpreted and turned into conscious experiences.

CAN YOU THINK WITHOUT WORDS?

When we think, we certainly seem to use words most of the time. But are words essential for thinking, or could our minds work just as well without language?

A chess player can think through different moves and decide which one to make without putting into words all the reasoning that led to that decision. Visualisation and non-verbal thinking certainly play a part in many activities, from composing a song to cutting a key. But how different would your thinking be if you had no language at all?

Many experts think that language provides the very structure of our thinking. For example, you do not need language to see colours, but whether you perceive a colour as 'red' or 'green' surely depends on having learned these concepts through learning the words. So when you form a mental image of a red bowl, for example, you may do this without words – but your knowledge of language still plays a crucial role in pinning down exactly what you are visualising.

Grammar, too, has a powerful role in thought. It allows us to create statements and questions, and thus to say something specific about objects and events, rather than simply picking them out. A hungry cat waiting to be fed may have a vivid mental image of a plate of food, but this is not the same as having the clear belief expressed by the words 'it's time for dinner!'. Only when we have formed an explicit statement, rather than just an image, can we say – or think – whether it is true or false.

THE CONSCIOUS BRAIN

It is generally agreed today that the workings of the conscious mind – thoughts, perceptions, and awareness of emotions – are linked to physical events in the brain. But neuroscientists are only just beginning to discover how the activity of brain cells translates into the rich and multi-faceted experience of consciousness.

> "The highest activities of consciousness have their origins in physical occurrences of the brain – just as the loveliest melodies are not too sublime to be expressed by notes".
>
> W Somerset Maugham

POINTS OF CONSCIOUSNESS

Some brain cells are responsible for producing awareness of very specific things. Researchers used sensitive electrodes to record the activity of single neurons in the brains of monkeys. They identified one group of cells that became active only when a hand was passed from the right to the left of the animal's visual field. The cells did not respond to the hand alone, nor to any other object moving on the same course. So while consciousness emerges from the activity of the entire brain, some of its contents are due to very localised activity – right down to the level of single cells.

Whenever you are conscious, your brain cells – the neurons – are active, signalling their neighbours with regular electrochemical pulses. But this activity is not enough to explain consciousness in terms of brain activity. Even simple studies of brain activity show that neurons also fire when you are in deep sleep. Conversely, even when you are intensely conscious, most of the neural activity in your brain is linked to unconscious processing.

Imagine, for example, that you are sitting in a room reading a good book. The story is compelling and your conscious mind is filled with the action in the 'virtual' world created by your imagination. You are only dimly aware of your real surroundings – the room you are in, the hum of traffic outside, the feel of the book in your hand. And most remarkably, you are not even conscious of the process of reading. Yet all the time, your brain is processing information about these things. Millions of firing neurons tell your hand how much pressure to exert to hold the book steady. Other nerve cells perceive the shapes of the letters, discern their patterns and extract their symbolic meanings; and others still notice if anything in your environment changes, for example, if someone enters the room.

If your brain works this hard even when you are not conscious, what is so special about the neural activity of the conscious state? To answer this question, we first need to look at how the brain is organised.

Creating conscious perceptions

The human brain is a massive network of interconnected neurons. Each part of the network processes a particular type of information: some sections deal with particular emotions, others with sensory stimuli, memory, language, and so on. And within each of these sub-networks, individual neurons are specialised to deal with even more narrowly focused tasks: for example, in the visual system particular cells respond only to the colour red. The full complexity of human thought and emotion – what we call mind – arises when many of these sub-networks interact.

One theory (put forward by the DNA pioneer Francis Crick) about what happens when information is fed into this network is as follows. Imagine there is an object – say a grapefruit – in the left side of a person's visual field. The neurons concerned with this information begin to fire. These include cells that respond to the colour yellow and cells that respond to a round shape. The person – let's call her Susan – is watching television and not paying attention to the grapefruit. The 'yellow' and 'round' neurons in her brain fire relatively slowly, their activity dies away quickly, and the graprefruit does not contribute to her conscious state. But then the grapefruit captures Susan's attention. The neurons concerned get very excited, firing faster and faster. When they fire at around 40 times a second (40Hz), the 'yellow' neurons detect that the 'round' neurons are, like them, very agitated, and the two groups of neurons pool their information. The result is a perception of a 'grapefruit', rather than just of 'yellow' and 'round'. As long as the grapefruit remains the object of Susan's attention, messages will continue to flow back and forth between the two groups of neurons. If this synchrony lasts for about a fifth of a second, the grapefruit will become a conscious perception. But if the synchrony degenerates in less time, the perception will not reach Susan's consciousness, even though her brain has absorbed the information unconsciously. This sort of perception is known as 'subliminal'.

Attention and consciousness

So to be fully conscious of something – to be able to look back and know that it happened – we need to pay attention to it. Attention is rather like a searchlight: it focuses the brain on a small patch of a vast information field by enhancing activity in the neurons concerned with that patch. When we attend to something, other perceptions drop out of consciousness. The spotlight of attention is never still, so these patches of highlighted activity keep changing: at one moment the grapefruit is privileged, but soon something else takes its place. Other things may be relegated to the half-light of subliminal experience, or go entirely unnoted.

Yellow (colour perception)

40Hz 40Hz

Round (shape perception)

Seeing a grapefruit
When you notice an object like a grapefruit, specialised areas of neurons in your brain are stimulated in response to the colour yellow, while others fire in response to the round shape. Together they create your perception of the grapefruit.

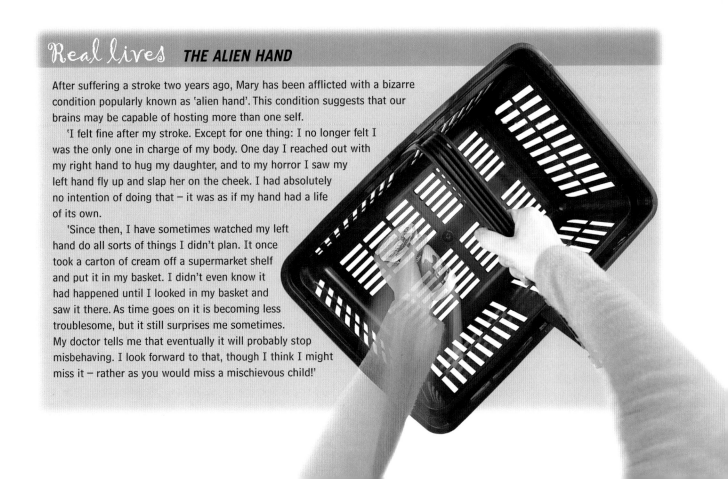

Real lives **THE ALIEN HAND**

After suffering a stroke two years ago, Mary has been afflicted with a bizarre condition popularly known as 'alien hand'. This condition suggests that our brains may be capable of hosting more than one self.

'I felt fine after my stroke. Except for one thing: I no longer felt I was the only one in charge of my body. One day I reached out with my right hand to hug my daughter, and to my horror I saw my left hand fly up and slap her on the cheek. I had absolutely no intention of doing that – it was as if my hand had a life of its own.

'Since then, I have sometimes watched my left hand do all sorts of things I didn't plan. It once took a carton of cream off a supermarket shelf and put it in my basket. I didn't even know it had happened until I looked in my basket and saw it there. As time goes on it is becoming less troublesome, but it still surprises me sometimes. My doctor tells me that eventually it will probably stop misbehaving. I look forward to that, though I think I might miss it – rather as you would miss a mischievous child!'

CONSCIOUSNESS AND THE BRAIN

THE CORTEX

This is the upper layer of the brain, covering each of the hemispheres. At the front are the frontal lobes, containing the prefrontal lobes and the motor cortex, which controls **body movements**. Behind this is the sensory cortex, where information from the body and senses is processed.

Frontal lobes

These are necessary for higher conscious functions, including **language-based thought**. Here, incoming information is combined with existing knowledge and becomes fully conscious. The left motor cortex contains Broca's area, where **speech production** is located. During sleep, activity in the frontal lobes is reduced.

Sensory cortex

This large area includes the primary visual, auditory and somatosensory cortex, which process raw data from the eyes, ears and body; and the sensory association areas, where this data is brought together.

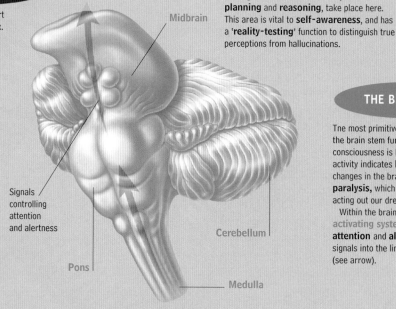

Motor cortex

Thalamus

Amygdala   Hippocampus

Wernicke's area

Broca's area

Somatosensory cortex

Temporal lobes

All auditory processing takes place here. Activity changes in this area are also linked to religious experience. Wernicke's area, where **language comprehension** takes places, is located in the left temporal lobe.

Prefrontal lobes

The highest conscious functions, such as **planning** and **reasoning**, take place here. This area is vital to **self-awareness**, and has a 'reality-testing' function to distinguish true perceptions from hallucinations.

THE LIMBIC SYSTEM

This is a more primitive part of the brain than the cortex. It contains the **amygdala** (where **emotions** such as fear and anger are generated); the **hippocampus** (vital for encoding and retrieving **memories**, and for self-awareness); and the **thalamus,** which directs and modulates activity within the cortex.

Midbrain

Signals controlling attention and alertness

Pons

Cerebellum

Medulla

THE BRAIN STEM

Tne most primitive area of the brain, the brain stem functions even when consciousness is lost; lack of brain stem activity indicates **brain death**. Activity changes in the brain stem cause **sleep paralysis,** which prevents us from acting out our dreams.

Within the brain stem, the reticular activating system (RAS), controls **attention** and **alertness** by sending signals into the limbic system and cortex (see arrow).

FACT: Consciousness occurs when certain brain cells fire in synchrony – but if all brain cells synchronise, consciousness is lost.

The central self

The spotlight of attention flits around, yet our perceptions are bound together into our personal experience of the moment. This sense of a 'me' at the centre of perception is a crucial component of conscious experience. The brain mechanisms responsible for this sense of self are not fully understood, but they seem to reside in a circuit that runs between the frontal lobes of the brain, which deal with abstract ideas, and the language areas of the left hemisphere. This circuit weaves a continual story – the narrative self. As long as the narrative is running, experience can be integrated into the stream of consciousness (see page 406). But when these circuits are inactive, information processing in other areas of the brain ceases to be 'owned' by the individual and therefore cannot be described.

The self system creates such a strong feeling of unity that it is generally assumed that one brain can hold just one consciousness. However, some theorists believe that micro-consciousnesses may exist in every brain, rather like separate individuals. Micro-consciousnesses are, by their nature, impossible to access. If we could examine their contents, they would be brought into the stream of 'owned' consciousness and so would no longer be separate. Only under certain extraordinary circumstances, such as split-brain experiments and the 'alien hand' condition, do they come to light.

(F)OCUS ON   *SPLIT BRAINS*

The human brain has two cerebral hemispheres. The left hemisphere controls the right side of the body and contains the areas involved with language, while the right hemisphere controls the left side. However, research with 'split-brain' patients – where the connections between the hemispheres have been severed for medical reasons (usually the treatment of epilepsy) – has revealed more subtle differences between the hemispheres and led some psychologists to suggest that each hemisphere contains its own separate consciousness.

In this research, the patient faces a screen with a picture on the left or right. The patient fixes their eyes on the centre of the screen, and (because of the normal crossover in the visual pathways) the visual information enters the hemisphere opposite to the side on which the picture is presented. The normal connection between the hemispheres is severed, so the information stays 'stuck' in the receiving hemisphere.

The language centres are in the left hemisphere, so the patient can describe a picture only if the information enters the left hemisphere. If it enters the right hemisphere, the patient will claim to be unaware of the image. However, if asked to select an object matching the image by touching it with the left hand (which is controlled by the right hemisphere), the patient will often succeed. When asked why they selected that object, they cannot explain. What this shows is that, while the right side of the brain appears to be unconscious because it lacks verbal ability, in fact it is capable of sophisticated cognition.

One study bears out this conclusion. Researchers devised a way of 'talking' exclusively to the right brain of a split-brain patient known as PS, by giving his left hand Scrabble letters to spell out messages from the right side of his brain. PS was asked what plans he had for his career. His spoken answer – that he intended to be a draughtsman – was provided by his left hemisphere (where the brain's language capacity is primarily located). In response to the same question, his right hemisphere gave a different answer, spelling out the words: 'automobile drive[r]'. This newly revealed ambition could be the desire of a separate consciousness in the right hemisphere – which, in normal circumstances, was unknown even to the boy himself.

ANIMAL CONSCIOUSNESS

Is a chimpanzee conscious? Or your cat or dog? What about a goldfish, prawn, or wasp? Most of us will only begin to waver with goldfish. But scientists and philosophers have often seemed strangely keen to deny a mental life to any animal.

FACT: Chimpanzees, orang-utans and dolphins are the only animals known to be able to recognise their own reflection in a mirror. Other 'intelligent' animals, such as gorillas, dogs and elephants, fail the test.

René Descartes usually gets the blame for the way we think about animal consciousness. The 17th-century French philosopher lived briefly in St Germain, a suburb of Paris. There he saw the town's famed waterwork statues of characters from Greek myth. Intricate hydraulic machinery would cause a figure of the bathing Diana to hide herself as a visitor approached. A few steps closer, and more hydraulic trickery would reveal a fierce, trident-waving Neptune.

These clever statues inspired Descartes to argue that living animals were also just contrivances. Earlier philosophers, taking their lead from Aristotle, had been quite happy to grant animals a sensitive soul, if not a rational one – consciousness if not cognition. But Descartes said the brain and the body's nervous system were just a hydraulic network and that animal behaviour was purely based on reflexes – there was no mind involved. According to Descartes, only humans possessed the extra component in the midst of all this machinery that could endow the ability to think, speak and reflect. That component was the soul.

Descartes' idea stuck, partly because it fitted in with Church doctrine. And even scientists felt it was justifiable to regard animals as bundles of reflexes, rather than credit them with a consciousness that could not actually be seen or measured.

Inside the animal mind

Descartes' view of animal consciousness has now been largely rejected because it seems obvious that animals think and feel. Anyone can see the light of intelligent awareness in the eyes of a

dolphin, dog or chimpanzee. However, experts still agree that the animal mind is limited. One answer suggested by philosophers as various as Schopenhauer and Locke is that animals are conscious, but their consciousness is locked into the present tense. Or as some psychologists have more recently put it, animals cannot think 'off-line'. All their responses are associative, being connected to the immediate demands and potentials of the moment.

Watch a cat lazing on a sunny lawn. It is conscious of the bees buzzing, the smells wafting on the breeze, the contented feel of a full belly. But you probably do not think it is reflecting on its kittenhood, or planning revenge on the old tom next door, or wondering whether it is having fish or chicken for supper. The cat is vividly aware of life and ready to respond if something disturbs it. But it does not seem to have an inner mechanism for directing its mind away from the moment to ponder the past or ruminate about the future.

However, these off-line capabilities apart, psychologists have found that the thought and memory capacities of animals are remarkably similar to humans. For instance, much has been made of the fact that animals lack insight and have to have lessons drummed in reflexively. But even goldfish and toads prove capable of one-shot learning. Toads only make the mistake of snapping at a bumblebee once, and a single electric shock is enough to make a goldfish reluctant to swim towards a corner of a tank. Chimpanzees were once thought to be exceptional because they were capable of making creative leaps of thought – for example, realising that a crate could be dragged across a floor to serve as a platform to stand on

▶▶ *CUTTING EDGE* ▶▶ ANTS – A COLLECTIVE MIND?

Individually, an ant is a rather limited creature. But collectively, do ants form a group mind? After all, an ant nest is almost one organism genetically, a single queen living with as many as a million daughters. And all those eyes and jaws are linked like brain cells in a network of interactions that can respond to the world with sharp intelligence.

Watch a trail of ants and you will see they are forever bumping into each other, pausing to touch antennae. In every brief meeting they exchange information about what they are doing. Their tiny brains then apply some simple rules. If an ant finds it is rarely meeting another employed in the same task (or too many others doing the same task) it will switch to a different behaviour. So from nest maintenance to foraging, ants spread themselves out across their territory, doing what needs to be done as if the colony were conscious as a whole.

Deborah Gordon of Stanford University studies

Harvester ants in the Arizona desert, and has found that colonies develop more intelligence as they mature. A colony sticks to the same sized territory as it grows in number, thereby creating a web of interactions that becomes ever denser and smarter. When Gordon set problems by blocking foraging trails or messing up the nest site with toothpicks, she found that mature colonies were quicker and more reliable in their response. Younger colonies were erratic in their behaviour as if they had not quite learnt what to do. The older colonies had also discovered how to get along with their neighbours. If foraging trails happened to cross one day, next day the ants would head in the opposite direction. But adolescent colonies always returned looking for a fight.

The evidence suggests that there is a sort of collective intelligence at work in an ant trail. Like a human mind, the trail 'knows' the world.

UNDERSTANDING YOUR PET: FACTS AND FALLACIES

Q: Why is my cat so surprised when a ball drops in front of it?

A: The cat's eye is very sensitive to horizontal motion – try rolling a ball across the floor – but surprisingly blind to vertical motion.

Q: When a bloodhound finds a trail, how does it know which way to head?

A: Its nose is sensitive enough to tell which of two footsteps is a split second fresher.

Q: Why does my cat insist on sitting on the kitchen counter?

A: Some breeds like the Singapura and the Siamese are natural climbers that like to view life from a perch.

Q: Is my dog colour blind?

A: No, just limited in colour sensitivity. Dogs can tell reds from blues, but reds and greens, or blues and purples, look much the same.

Q: Why does my parrot regurgitate on me?

A: In parrots, this is a sign of love! Bonded birds show their affection by feeding each other like they feed their chicks.

Q: What is the smartest – and the dumbest – breed of dog?

A: Collies, poodles and German shepherds are among the brightest – some can learn a new command after just five repetitions. In contrast, some afghans, bulldogs and basenjis may take hundreds.

Q: Why does my cat head straight for a friend who hates cats?

A: Direct eye contact and shrill baby-talk can be threatening to a cat, so they often prefer those who offer a cold shoulder.

Q: What kind of TV do pets like?

A: Golf, or anything with moving balls, is popular with kittens. Dogs like to watch other dogs. And parrots seem to like anything noisy with lots of gunfire.

HOW TO READ A CAT'S TAIL

Cats make more than one hundred different vocal sounds – ten times more than dogs. They also convey a lot of meaning through their swishing tails. Here is how to read some of the signs.

1 Tail raised slightly: cat is interested in something.

2 Tail erect, tip tilted: cat is friendly with slight reservations.

3 Tail fully erect, tip stiff: intense friendly greeting with no reservations.

4 Tail held still, tip twitching: mild irritation.

5 Tail swishing violently: cat about to attack.

6 Tail raised and fluffed out: cat is aggressive.

7

Eagle eye The sensory world of animals is very different to our own. An eagle's eyes are eight times more densely packed with light-detecting cells. It also sees extra colours because its eye samples light at four wavebands rather than just our three.

HOW TO BE TOP DOG IN YOUR OWN HOME

Dogs and humans have a long history – more than 100,000 years compared with less than 10,000 years for other domesticated animals. But as former pack animals, dogs need to know where they rank in your family.

Handing over scraps of your own dinner to a demanding mutt can be a very bad idea, leading it to think that it is actually 'top dog'. So is giving in when your dog decides to sit in your armchair. But a dog that is relegated to the bottom of the bed or a place at your feet will learn to be happy in this subordinate position. At the edge of the human 'camp' is his most natural place.

The natural way to stop a dog barking is to mimic the way a mother wolf silences a noisy cub by grasping its muzzle gently in her jaws and growling a low warning. Wrap a hand over your dog's muzzle and firmly say 'Quiet,' until it gets the message.

7 Tail lowered and fluffed out: cat is afraid.

8 Tail held to one side: sexual invitation of a female cat in heat.

8

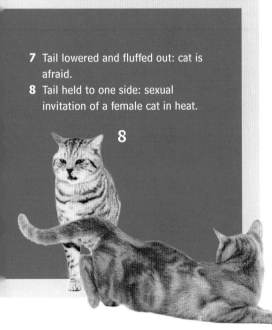

to reach a dangling banana. But then pigeons were found also to be capable of apparently sudden insight on similar set-ups, if they were given appropriate training.

Of course, brain size makes a difference: goldfish can remember which way to swim to reach a reward of food for only about ten seconds; pigeons and lizards can remember such information for minutes; apes for hours. Nevertheless, it seems that the general set of mental skills is much the same across the animal kingdom. Even slugs and insects have some degree of memory or learning ability.

What's it like to be a dolphin?

While the mental abilities of animals are often remarkable, in many respects, animal consciousness is very different from our own. Unlike humans, with their faculties of self-criticism and reflection, animals are thought to live their subjective lives forever in the present, and the present that they inhabit may be very different from human experience. For example, what would it be like to be a dolphin perceiving the world through sonar? Like bats, dolphins emit ultra sonic clicks and build up a picture of their surroundings from the echoes. With their clicks pitched at frequencies of up to 100,000 hertz, dolphins can 'see' right through soft structures as if they had ultrasound scanners. Passing a pregnant swimmer, a dolphin would also see the baby wriggling inside. Or what about being able to feel the pressure of the Earth's magnetic field like a migrating bird? Many birds (as well as mice, dolphins, bees, frogs and even bacteria) seem able to navigate using an inbuilt compass.

The phenomenal worlds of animals – what it is actually like to sense and perceive as another species – may vary remarkably, but confined to our own consciousness we cannot know what it is like to be a dolphin or what it feels like to be a bird.

Evolution of human consciousness

How did the animal mind turn into the self-aware human mind?
What change occurred, freeing us to think objectively and
introspectively? Language, it seems, may have been the key.

Experts agree that the development of human consciousness in all its modern complexity happened astonishingly quickly. For millions of years, early human species had existed as large-brained, bipedal apes. Our direct forebears, *Homo erectus,* could make fires and tools, but these were crude and simple. Then, 150,000 years ago, our own species, *Homo sapiens,* emerged. Just 100,000 years later – a blink of the eye in evolutionary terms – *Homo sapiens* had transfomed itself into the linguistic, highly cultured, fully conscious species we are today.

In this brief time, our tools became finely crafted and technically advanced. We could carve fish hooks and harpoon tips, make ropes and sew clothes, and we mastered fire using hearths, flint lighters and fat-burning lamps. Most significantly, we began using symbols to represent our world. We adorned our bodies, carved statuettes and painted the walls of our caves. Archaeological evidence reveals that our lives became ruled by memories, hopes, beliefs and fears. We had indisputably become modern in our mental abilities.

Willendorf Venus
This statuette symbolising fertility was made about 30,000 years ago.

Better, not bigger
What could explain such a swift transformation? It certainly was not just an increase in brain size: the Neanderthals (*Homo neanderthalensis*), who lived alongside *Homo sapiens* until about 30,000 years ago, had slightly bigger brains but showed little sign of intellectual sophistication. So what did change?

Theorists are divided: some think that an overall change in the organisation of the brain was responsible, while others believe that a single factor – language – holds the key. The overall change theorists suggest that the brains of our apeman ancestors gradually accumulated a range of separate mental skills, such as tool-making, foraging and social behaviour. Then, later, these skills became linked, so whereas before we could employ our tool-using 'module' only to visualise the handling of tools, afterwards, we could use it to manipulate information stored anywhere in the brain.

One drawback of this theory is that there is little evidence that brains are, or ever were, so rigidly

Homo sapiens skull This skull from Ethiopia dates from 100,000 years ago.

150,000 years ago
First *Homo sapiens* appeared

Timeline of culture and consciousness Bipedal ape species date back to 4 or 5 million years ago, but our own species, *Homo sapiens*, first appeared relatively recently (about 150,000 years ago). 100,000 years later, a cultural explosion began: works of art appeared, technology advanced rapidly and complex societies emerged. Language – and through it, consciousness – may have been the key to these crucial steps in the evolution of modern humans.

Ancient cave art This artistically accomplished painting of a horse was discovered in the caves at Lascaux in France, and dates from about 35,000 years ago.

divided into modules. This lends weight to the idea that the power of our brains was unlocked by a single factor – the evolution of language. Anatomical evidence is consistent with this idea. While Neanderthals retained an ape-like vocal tract, early *Homo sapiens* had the arched palate, voice box, and other adaptations needed to speak articulately. But how could our use of language spark the explosive spiral of cultural and technological development that is so evident in the archaeological record of our species?

Talking the talk

The explanation goes like this: while animals have general intelligence, they can direct this intelligence only towards the events of the moment. Words, on the other hand, can bring buried knowledge to mind. Hearing (or saying to yourself) a phrase like 'fat rhinoceros in a pink tutu' will instantly conjure up an image that would otherwise not have been present in your head. And when the symbolic reach of words is combined with the logical engine of grammar, then our thoughts can really begin to go somewhere. So according to some language theorists, there was no great change in our consciousness or intelligence.

Instead, just a minor evolutionary step in the brains of our ancestors – the ability to process grammar – allowed humans to use speech to corral mental images and rouse memories. The result was a step change in our ability to direct our thoughts to wherever we wanted them to go. We became the explorers of our own minds.

But the question that still needs to be answered is what evolutionary advantage did we gain through our ability to examine our own thoughts? Again, answers are speculative, but perhaps one of the most convincing explanations for the evolution of the 'inner eye' was that it allowed us to know what others were thinking. By examining our own thoughts and feelings, we could make informed guesses about the motivations – and therefore the possible actions – of other members of our social group. So consciousness made us all into psychologists, and opened up a whole new arena of human behaviour – sympathy, compassion, jealousy, trust, deviousness, belief and disbelief.

Bone whistle This was carved from a reindeer's toe bone 40,000 years ago.

Flint tool This beautifully worked blade is 20,000 years old.

Pictographic writing This Sumerian clay tablet dates from 3000 BC.

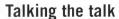

| 60,000 years ago | 40,000 years ago | 35,000 years ago | | 20,000 years ago | 15,000 years ago | | 10,000 years ago | | 5000 years ago |
| First orderly campsites | First lamps, statuettes and shaped bone tools | First cave paintings and spear heads | | First bows and arrows, cloth and sewing needles | First domestic animals | | First villages and crop planting | | First cities and writing |

CONSCIOUSNESS AND MACHINES

Could a machine ever be conscious? Many experts say 'yes, of course', believing that technology will one day be able to produce a machine with a mind of its own. But these experts have been proved wrong in the past – and according to earlier predictions, conscious machines should exist by now.

FACT: If computer power keeps doubling every two years, then the desktop machines of 2050 will be about 15 million times more powerful than today's – surely enough for machine intelligence, if not consciousness?

If you simulated a weather pattern on a computer, would it be real weather? Would its wind ruffle your hair or its rain make you wet? No, of course not, no matter how exact and complete the simulation. So then why would you expect a simulation of your brain processes to be really conscious? On the other hand, think about this. Suppose just one of your brain cells was replaced with a microchip that did exactly the same job. If all the inputs and outputs remained precisely the same, you would never notice the difference. And what if another, then another, cell was replaced, until gradually all 100 billion neurons in your brain had been turned to silicon. Would there ever come a point where you stopped being you? Would you become, in effect, a conscious machine?

These are exactly the kind of questions that cognitive scientists have been throwing at each other since the dawn of the computer era. Even now, science does not seem much closer to answering them.

Applying some logic

Alan Turing, the British mathematician who laid the foundations of modern computing in the 1940s, firmly believed that machines would be able to think for themselves sooner rather than later, and certainly by the

---

PIONEERS   *ALAN TURING*

Alan Turing's life was brilliant and tragic in equal measure. Born in 1912, the son of a civil servant in India, his childhood was a lonely mix of boarding schools and holiday foster homes back in England. In 1937, as a young don at Cambridge University, he published a short paper that at a stroke established the universal mathematical principles behind computers. Then, with the outbreak of World War II, he was recruited to help develop the first code-cracking machines at Bletchley Park, a top-secret intelligence centre in the UK.

After the war, Turing hoped to perfect his designs for a true general-purpose computer. However, this project fell foul of bureaucracy and technical delays, so Turing returned to theoretical visions of future

machines. In 1950, he made his famous forecast that computers would soon think, tickling the public with blithe comments like: 'One day ladies will take their computers for walks in the park and tell each other, "My little computer said such a funny thing this morning!"'

Unfortunately for Turing, when police officers were investigating a robbery at his house in 1952, he accidentally revealed that he was homosexual – which was then illegal. Turing was convicted of gross indecency and only spared a prison sentence on the condition that he took a 'curative' course of female hormone injections. In 1954, aged 41, he committed suicide by eating an apple laced with cyanide.

end of the 20th century. Turing's breakthrough was to prove that, in theory, the simplest computing device – he imagined a single key making or erasing marks in succession on an infinite tape – could carry out any logically defined operation. All computers were therefore identical under the skin, as their workings could always be described in terms of this theoretical device (which became known as a Turing machine). You could build a computer out of anything, even string and old tin cans. While it might not be very efficient or fast, the output of its programs would remain the same. Turing offered mathematical proof that if you could describe the 'programs' being run on the human brain, then the same programs could be run on an artificial brain. He did not think that the technology of his day would have to be scaled up much to run the basic programs of human consciousness at useful speeds.

There was, as Turing himself admitted, a potential problem with this argument, which lay in whether the brain's operations were indeed logical. Could whatever brains did actually be represented as a binary sequence of 0s and 1s? But like most scientists, Turing was optimistic, because brain cells seemed to communicate using on–off patterns of electrical spikes.

So there was a clever intellectual trick at the heart of Turing's argument. He had proved that, in mathematical terms, all computers were essentially the same. Now it was up to others to prove that human brains were not computers. This was, and remains, a very difficult task. Anyone who draws a categorical distinction between the logical workings of a brain and those of a computer can always be undermined – they simply have not considered every last alternative or explored every fact. While you can show that machine consciousness is highly unlikely or impractical, scientifically speaking you cannot remove the doubt about whether it might be done in the future based on some as yet undiscovered fact.

FOCUS ON THE TURING TEST

Working on the principle of that if something walks like a duck and quacks like a duck then it is a duck, Alan Turing once suggested that the only test of consciousness that a computer would have to pass is to convince a human that it is also conscious.

This rather tongue-in-cheek idea has sparked an annual contest in which judges, conversing via a keyboard and screen, have to guess whether they are chatting to an artificial intelligence program or real person. No program has yet duped the judges even though their questions are hardly probing. Would you be fooled by this conversation?

Computer: Hello. My name is Jim. Who are you?
Judge: Charles.
Computer: Charles is a wrestler in As You Like It. Charles is King of France in Henry VI Pt 1.
Judge: Do you like Shakespeare?
Computer: Yeah, sure.
Judge: What do you like about his plays?
Computer: Well, there's a certain je ne sais quoi.
Judge: I think it is great that you like his plays.
Computer: I like phasers.
Judge: Do you mean like those in Star Trek?
Computer: It's possible.
Judge: What's possible?
Computer: Nothing.
Judge: That's a very nihilistic stance.
Computer: Indeed.

Chinese whispers

Philosophers, of course, have made valiant attempts to come up with just such an 'in principle' argument against machine consciousness. The most famous of these is the Chinese Room thought experiment of US philosopher John Searle.

Searle asks us to imagine a man locked in a room. He does not understand Chinese, but he is surrounded by millions of books that give the precise answer to every possible question framed in that language. From time to time, someone shoves a query written in Chinese through a slot. The man's job is to rifle through the books, find a match to the question, then scribble back the prescribed reply. From the outside, the room appears to have an intelligent comprehension of Chinese. And yet we know that inside there is just a man following rules without having the slightest clue about the meaning of either the question or the response. Searle says that exactly the same would be the case with a computer. It might run a program and output realistic behaviour. But there would be no inner light of experience or understanding. A computer has rules, but not semantics – that is, inner knowledge of what in the real world is being manipulated by those rules.

But the computer scientists disagree with this viewpoint. They say that our brains have semantics and true understanding because they manipulate mental representations – broad washes of sensation and memory displayed across millions of brain cells. So the correct way to imagine the Chinese Room is as many little men, each representing points of data in a co-ordinated show. Like individual brain cells, each tiny figure would merely follow local processing rules. But the network as a whole would be conscious. As a system, the Chinese Room really would 'feel' that it understood the questions.

> **"The point is not that the computer gets only to the 40-yard line and not all the way to the goal line. The computer doesn't even get started. It is not playing the game."**
>
> John Searle, professor of philosophy

▶▶ CUTTING EDGE ▶▶ A CONSCIOUS INTERNET?

What if the internet one day grew so connected that it woke up and became conscious? Some experts think this could really happen. Belgian computer scientist Francis Heylighen argues that web pages are like information-containing brain cells, and the hyperlinks between them are like synaptic connections between brain cells. Throw in search engines and other kinds of intelligent programs and perhaps the whole thing could start to come alive.

It's an interesting idea. However, the more sober-minded point out that machines are best seen as amplifiers of human activity. The Industrial Revolution was about the amplification of human muscle power. Today's information revolution is about the amplification of human mental power. So while the internet does promise remarkable things, the real story will not be its emerging consciousness, but how it will extend the reach of our own minds into a global, shareable body of knowledge and culture.

Again, the argument is one that the anti-computer camp seemingly cannot win. Searle has continued to blaze away, objecting that simulated weather will never make you wet and a simulated carburettor will never power a car. Simulations cannot have real effects on the world. But computer scientists reply that a weather model hooked up to your garden sprinkler would certainly make you wet. And in the same way, an artificial brain equipped with eyes to see and hands to act could be just as much a part of the world as you.

On the basis of this line of argument at least, there seems no good reason to rule out the possibility of machine consciousness in principle. On the other hand, 50 years of intensive but largely fruitless research has shown that Turing and many others were wildly optimistic in their forecasts for machine intelligence, let alone machine consciousness.

The unrealised dream

During the 1970s and 1980s, huge amounts of money were ploughed into artificial intelligence (AI) research by governments, industry and especially defence research agencies. Japan, Europe and the US became locked into an intellectual arms race. The reasoning was that if the technocrats failed to deliver the conscious machines they were promising, then even slightly smart ones would have valuable applications. History tells us that the AI movement was largely unproductive. It did give us one or two clever new programming tricks, but the commercial computers of today are much the same as those of yesteryear – the main difference is that they are smaller, cheaper and faster.

There are still die-hards who insist that a major breakthrough is waiting round the corner. They point to the promise of neural networks – computers designed in direct imitation of brain networks. These may have the equivalent of only a few thousand brain cells at present (about enough to power a cockroach), but it might be just 30 or 40 years before such a computer has enough connections to equal a human brain. However, even most computer scientists have grown wary of sweeping pronouncements and some feel that any estimates should be made in terms of decades or centuries rather than years.

The dream of conscious machines will never disappear because science has no way of proving it impossible. Besides, people seem to be too enamoured with the idea to give it up. However, not much faith is being placed on it happening in the near future.

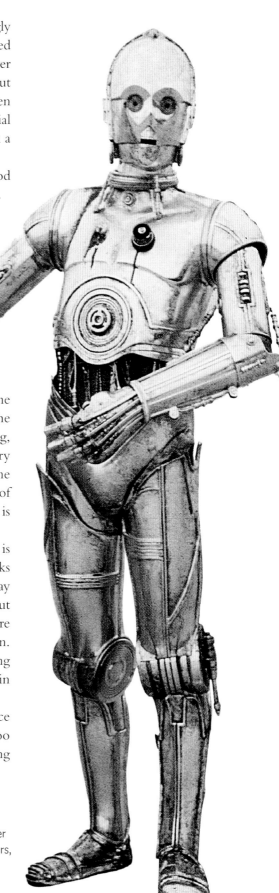

Stranger than fiction The science of artificial intelligence is never far from science fiction. In the imaginations of writers and film makers, robots like *Star Wars'* C3PO are given human characteristics such as reflection, self-awareness and self-interest.

2 STATES OF CONSCIOUSNESS

Have you ever woken to find that the thought 'perhaps I'm just dreaming' occurred to you while you were, indeed, dreaming? Moments like this are when we begin to catch a glimpse of the many-layered, all-pervasive, yet highly changeable nature of consciousness.

A commonsense view of consciousness would seem to say that you must be awake to experience it. Yet did you know that brain activity can be just as busy during sleep? In fact, there are different states of consciousness, and the dividing line between them – and between consciousness and unconsciousness – is by no means hard and fast. Furthermore, we can alter our state of consciousness by various mental and physical means.

Behind all experiences of consciousness lies the mind's remarkable power to construct 'virtual reality' from within. We have all experienced this power in dreams, but even in normal consciousness our thoughts and sensations are to a large extent produced internally by the brain, rather than being direct perceptions of the outside world. This power is the source of illusions and hallucinations – but it is also the gateway to the common reality we share with others.

TYPES OF CONSCIOUSNESS

There is no single 'normal' state of consciousness. Every person experiences a huge range of mental conditions every day as the brain adapts to changing circumstances.

The dividing line between conscious and unconscious states is not sharp. Even within consciousness, there are different degrees. In dreamless sleep you may not be conscious of anything at all, or maybe just of vague thoughts or feelings. When you are daydreaming, you may not be conscious of some of the things in your environment. For example, someone may be talking quite close by and yet you are unaware of it.

A racing driver is acutely conscious of his environment - of the bends in the track, the speed of the car, the position of other cars. But he is probably not very conscious of what is going on in his own mind because he does not have time to notice whether he is feeling afraid or to think about his thoughts. The driver is conscious of his environment but not self-conscious.

Three degrees of awareness

The various states of consciousness can be divided according to the degree of awareness they involve. According to philosopher David Rosenthal from New York, we can describe three main types. The first and most basic state is when we perceive things through our senses, but do not have any thoughts about these perceptions. This happens when you react to, say, a visual stimulus without being consciously aware that you have perceived anything. Think of those times when you carry out familiar routines – driving home from work, for example – without conscious awareness of what you are doing. If something alerts you to your state, you may realise that you have driven through sev-

Real lives

LOST IN REFLECTION

John S. chose to study philosophy at university because he was intensely interested in his own thought processes. His studies encouraged him to concentrate so hard on them that he eventually became dislocated from ordinary life.

'There was a period of my life when I seemed to be permanently stuck on the introspective level of consciousness. Whenever I saw something, I would barely take it in before I found myself thinking about thinking about it. I would look at a flower, and instead of feeling the pleasure of the sight I would think "I am looking at a flower and thinking that I am finding it pretty". Then I would think "But am I really finding it pretty, or am I just thinking that I think it is pretty?" It became such a habit, this sort of reflection, that I stopped feeling anything directly at all – I seemed to be experiencing everything at second-hand. It was as though I was observing my mental processes through a microscope. It was very alienating, and I started to miss having direct feelings. Or, to be precise, I started to think that I should be missing having direct feelings!

'I trained myself to stop thinking about what I was thinking by doing things that were so terrifying they left no room for thought. I took up parachute jumping, and did a bungee-jump, and learned to ride a horse. I was so absorbed in the physical sensations produced by these activities that there was no room for reflection. Gradually I found I could extend that feeling of total immersion to less terrifying pastimes. I still sometimes lose myself in contemplation of my own thought processes. But I try not to – life is too short.'

"By introspection we have access only to a limited amount of what is going on in our brain."

Francis Crick, 1994

eral sets of traffic lights with no memory of their colour. You assume that you noticed the lights because you reacted to them appropriately, but you have no actual memory of it and so cannot be sure. So how did you negotiate the lights safely? The answer is you that reacted quite unconsciously, perceiving the lights without being aware that you were perceiving them. The same unconscious brain mechanisms that allow us to do this also guide our actions in many other activities (see page 374).

The next type of consciousness is the direct awareness of whatever is taking your attention. In this state, you are consciously aware of the contents of your mind – whether these are inner thoughts, such as what to buy for dinner, or more sensory experiences such as trying to walk fast against driving rain. However, you are not reflecting on the thoughts in your mind, so your sense of 'self' is kept in the background. A mountain climber who is completely absorbed in climbing a rock face is intensely conscious in this way. Operating just at this level of awareness, the climber is living in the moment, simply experiencing the flow of the climb and not consciously 'owning' the experience. The loss of self in such 'flow' experiences (and similarly in meditation) appears to produce intense happiness.

Finally, there is the third type known as reflective consciousness, in which you are aware of yourself as having the experience. In this case, you are consciously aware not just of what you are perceiving, but also that it is you perceiving it: your sense of self is brought to the fore. So you do not simply have a thought, you also think about it as though looking at it from outside. We use reflective consciousness in many different ways: in thinking whether we have perceived something correctly or not, or whether we should believe some information, or whether our recall of an event is accurate. This type of consciousness enables us to reflect on our perceptions, beliefs and memories as though they are 'objects' in our minds. Reflective consciousness is also useful in social thinking, such as deciding whether to trust others – or even ourselves – but it can have a downside: thinking too much about what we are doing, such as when giving a talk or making a move in sport, can actually hinder our performance.

KEEPING A CONSCIOUSNESS DIARY

To monitor your own consciousness, set a kitchen timer to ring at intervals of between 30 and 90 minutes. When it rings, note down what is in your mind at that moment. Class it as 'reflective' consciousness if you are thinking about your own thoughts, or as 'aware' consciousness if you are simply aware of what you are thinking or experiencing, without reflecting on it. Do this at intervals for the next eight hours.

Next day, set the timer to ring as before. This time, when it rings, jot down all the thoughts you can recall since it last went off. You will probably find that there are far more introspective thoughts in the recall diary than the one made at the time – an indication of how knowledge of our own consciousness is distorted by memory.

Conscious operations?
We often carry out very familiar routines in a state that is like being on autopilot. Although operating efficiently, we are not consciously aware of what we are doing.

SLEEP AND CONSCIOUSNESS

Every night we shut our eyes, let the mind slip its moorings and enter the blank limbo of sleep. While it is tempting to treat sleep simply as a state of unconsciousness, psychologists tell a very different story in which sleep is really not as far from waking as it first appears.

"All men whilst they are awake are in one common world: but each of them, when he is asleep, is in a world of his own."

Plutarch, Greek biographer, AD 100

Being asleep seems to give us a glimpse of what it would be like to be dead. Sleep undoubtedly appears to extinguish the light of experience, even if our slumber is sometimes fitful or perturbed by the odd dream or nightmare. However, sleep research shows that our repose is a surprisingly active affair in which consciousness is never really switched off.

Brain recordings reveal that we spend each night alternating between two very distinct types of sleep – the deep steady electrical rhythm of slow-wave sleep (SWS) and the frantic buzz of REM sleep (so-called for the rapid eye movements in which the eyeballs seem to chase phantom visions). We begin each night in SWS. At first this is so deep that we are practically comatose. Then, after about

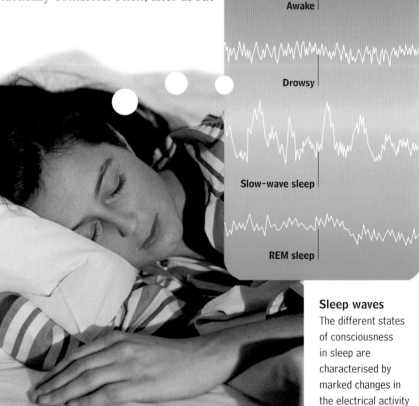

Sleep waves
The different states of consciousness in sleep are characterised by marked changes in the electrical activity of the brain, as shown in this electro-encephalogram (EEG).

Awake

Drowsy

Slow-wave sleep

REM sleep

FACT FILE

CONSCIOUS ASPECTS OF SLEEP

Looking at mental functioning while awake and in REM sleep yields some interesting comparisons:

• While awake, our thoughts and intentions are generally clear and directed, but in REM sleep they are confused and illogical.

• Perception is strong in both states, although in REM sleep it is directed towards internally generated sensations rather than to the external world.

• Memory also is strong in both states, with more distant memories rather than recent ones typically dominant during REM sleep.

• Instinct is a strong influence in REM sleep, whereas in waking it is mediated by rational thinking.

90 minutes, there comes a brief interruption of REM, which lasts about ten minutes. As the night goes on, the switch-over between SWS and REM continues to occur every 90 minutes or so, but the REM periods get much longer and the SWS periods become progressively shallower. On average, we spend about one quarter of every night in REM sleep.

The dreaming brain

When REM sleep was first discovered in the 1950s, it was thought to be the only sleep phase in which dreams occurred. However, it has since been found that mental activity of a sort goes on all night long. Even subjects roused from SWS usually report vague ruminations. US psychologist David Foulkes describes these slow-wave dreams as drowsy thoughts rather than bright images, and, despite their hazy character, their existence shows that the mind muses to itself all through the long hours from dusk to dawn.

Sleep researchers have concluded that the brain never actually shuts down at night. Brain cells have no 'off' switch, and indeed they must fire a few times each second just to stay alive and healthy. So instead of turning its engines off, a better analogy would be that the brain puts itself into neutral when it enters SWS. It puts a block on incoming sensations, preventing external sights and sounds from troubling the mind, and it suspends short-term memory. The resulting state of consciousness is confused and disjointed and any thoughts or images evaporate just as fast as they form.

In REM sleep, the brain switches into quite a different state. Activity in the brainstem is inhibited, temporarily paralysing the body. This essential safety mechanism ensures that dreams are not acted out physically. Then for some reason, the brain erupts into a succession of vivid internally generated imagery. However, the block remains on short-term memory and so the conscious self cannot really fix on what is going on. In a confused way, it tries to make sense of the random images but it never really catches up with them. And any story it spins is usually quickly forgotten on waking.

Functions of sleep

SWS seems to be essential for growth and maintenance, but the purpose of REM sleep is harder to explain. It has been suggested that REM sleep is simply nature's way of keeping us nearly awake, but out of mischief, until morning. It is possible that vivid dreams – the subject of conjecture for centuries – are merely by-products of a slumbering consciousness.

FOCUS ON

SLEEPWALKING

Most of us know someone who walks or talks in their sleep, but some sleepwalking stories are truly bizarre. One woman packed her dogs into her car and drove 20 miles before waking up; another stumbled off the balcony of her holiday hotel, fell 15 feet and did not wake up until she reached hospital. Our capacity to behave unconsciously while asleep is even recognised in law – a number of individuals have been cleared of attempted rape or murder because they were 'asleep' at the time.

Researchers have found there is a clear difference between ordinary sleepwalking and a more specific REM sleep syndrome. Ordinary sleepwalking happens in deep slow-wave sleep. We come awake enough to act on automatic pilot – to get up and do something routine like go to the toilet, or perhaps even take the car for a midnight spin. However, murders and other violent acts must occur in the high arousal of REM sleep, so the usual REM paralysis, the brainstem block on muscular activity that normally prevents us acting out our dreams, is somehow absent in these cases. On closer examination of such people, doctors often find evidence of a degenerative disorder like Parkinson's disease affecting the brainstem.

ALTERED STATES

Most of the time we take consciousness for granted — it is the transparent window through which we view the world. But sometimes the view changes dramatically, as though the window has become distorted or suddenly been flung open. These seemingly mysterious changes are known as altered states.

The contents of our consciousness change from moment to moment. A sensation gives way to an emotion, then a thought, then perhaps a desire or a stab of pain. While no two experiences are exactly alike, the way in which we experience things tends to remain stable. It is rather like watching a film: the action changes from frame to frame, but the screen itself stays the same and is barely noticed.

Sometimes, though, the background 'screen' on which consciousness plays changes and itself becomes the subject of awareness. The change may be profound, as in the extreme distortions caused by hallucinogenic drugs, trance or religious ecstasy; or it may be spontaneous and subtle — the world simply seems different in some undefinable way.

Peaks and troughs

Some altered states are extraordinarily pleasant, but others can be fearful in their unfamiliarity, accompanied by disordered thoughts and terrifying visions. These profound shifts in consciousness are more common than one might think. For example, more than 80 per cent of Americans report having had a 'peak experience' — a sense of being at one with the universe and detached from their normal selves — at some time in their lives.

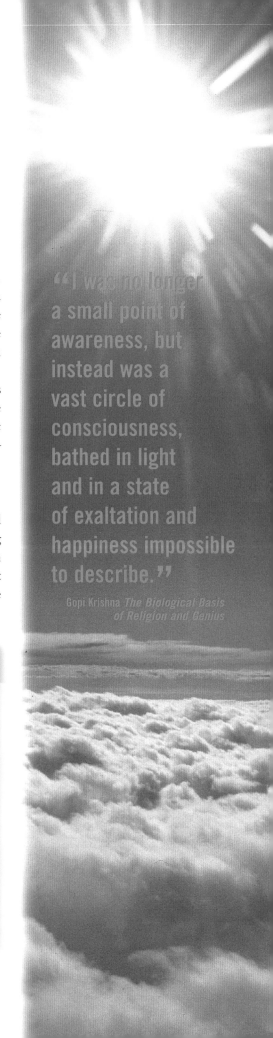

"I was no longer a small point of awareness, but instead was a vast circle of consciousness, bathed in light and in a state of exaltation and happiness impossible to describe."

Gopi Krishna *The Biological Basis of Religion and Genius*

Real lives *A PEAK EXPERIENCE*

Eunice, a 45-year-old advertising executive, has been a churchgoer since having a peak experience.

'I was travelling on business when my car broke down in a strange city. I couldn't get a hotel room, so I asked the emergency repair man if he knew anywhere I could stay. He took me to his own home. His wife showed me to a room, where she had lit a fire in the fireplace. As I watched the flames, they seemed to cast a glow over the room that was far more intense and warm than the fire alone could make it. Then everything was transformed. The room had been tiny, but it seemed to extend into infinity. My gratitude to my hosts became a well of bottomless love for the universe, which seemed to be part of me, not something separate. I recall thinking: "I will never deny the power of the spirit again." Later I found out that this is what people mean by a "peak" experience.'

Peak experiences may happen at any time. One moment the world is a humdrum place; the next it is a glowing universe filled with bliss, beauty and love. People often report being filled with a profound sense of love and gratitude, and ordinary objects and other people seem to radiate beauty. The altered perception may last moments or days, but at the time it seems endless. The person experiencing it is certain that he or she is seeing the world as it really is, and that 'normal' perception is an illusion.

The flip side of peak experience is 'derealisation', in which the normal order of the universe breaks down and the world seems fractured and terrifying. Objects can shrink or become distant; other people seem to be separated by invisible glass shields or vast expanses of space. Individuals experiencing derealisation often report that they feel detached from their own bodies and that their actions seem robotic. Like peak experiences, derealisation can happen at any time – ordinary consciousness suddenly seems uncertain, as though it is a flickering film that may stop at any moment, opening up a chasm of emptiness.

'Recently I had this strange, dreamy feeling for four days without a break,' says Rachel, aged 27. 'I just felt so weird; everything seemed to be far away, voices muffled, and I felt like I was watching myself from the outside. Nothing looked real, I kept forgetting things, staring into space, and all the time this was happening I was thinking "I'm going mad" and trying desperately to get back into my body.' Or as Dale, another regular sufferer from derealisation, explains: 'I see faces, but it is as though I am seeing them in parts – a mouth here, an eyebrow there. I know who they are, but only by piecing the bits together and working it out.'

Fragmented world The experience of 'derealisation' is almost invariably accompanied by an intense feeling of anxiety and restless agitation.

Chemical reality and unreality

Scientists think that altered states occur when different areas of the brain stop interacting in the normal way. Usually, the various information processing systems – sensory, memory, and so on – 'bind' their information to create an integrated perception. However, the integration is not complete – there is always a degree of separation between the components being processed.

A good analogy is to think of a photograph printed in a newspaper. Get too close and all you can see are the individual dots that make up the image: the meaning of the picture is lost. Get too far away and all the picture becomes a blur. In a normal state of consciousness, the picture created by the brain is integrated tightly enough for the individual dots to be invisible, yet it is still close enough to the observer for the whole image to be seen and recognised. A peak experience is like viewing the picture from a great distance – everything seems to be 'one'. In derealisation, the picture is seen too close and so appears fragmented.

The chemistry of consciousness

To create the normal state of consciousness – to allow us to view a complete picture – neurons in different parts of the brain fire in synchrony, and 'pool' their knowledge (see page 323). The synchronisation is mediated by neurochemicals such as dopamine, the so-called 'pleasure chemical'. When levels of dopamine are in the normal range, the emotional processing areas of the limbic system in the brain resonate with parts of the cortex, where memory, thought and perception are located, to unify perceptions. At the same time, other neurotransmitters in the brain inhibit the effect of dopamine; this prevents total synchrony, providing the 'distance' necessary to see the whole picture.

During peak experiences, it seems likely that dopamine, and possibly other chemicals such as serotonin, flood the brain. Activity in the limbic system and frontal lobes becomes hyper-synchronised, producing a feeling of euphoria and seamlessness. In derealisation, it is likely that the opposite happens. Dopamine levels fall, synchrony is lost between various brain areas, and the fragmented activity produces fragmented consciousness.

Causes of altered states

The chemical changes in the brain that cause us to experience altered states may be brought about by extreme psychological or physical stimuli, such as drugs, chanting, dancing, flashing lights and deep meditation. Sometimes, however, the trigger can be more mundane. For example, even small changes in the brain's oxygen balance can affect consciousness. This is why breathing exercises are often used in techniques to induce trance and relaxation. Saturating the brain with oxygen by over-breathing (taking rapid, short breaths) may cause derealisation, while oxygen

---

▶▶ ▶▶ *CUTTING EDGE* ▶▶ ▶▶ *CUTTING EDGE* ▶▶ ▶▶ *CUTTING EDGE* ▶▶ ▶▶

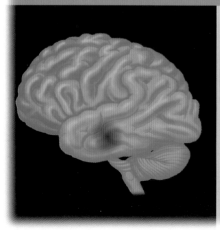

THE 'GOD SPOT'

One of the most impressive types of altered state involves feeling an invisible 'presence' – often interpreted as the awareness of God. Brain studies have found that this feeling comes about due to activity in an area of the temporal lobe. This 'god spot', as it is popularly known, is commonly activated in situations where a period of stress is suddenly brought to an end by a pleasant experience. It can also be stimulated artificially, or induced by transcranial magnetic stimulation (which inhibits activity in specific parts of the brain). The temporal lobes are one of the areas associated with our sense of self. One theory about the mysterious presence felt when the god spot area is inhibited on one side of the brain, is that the equivalent area on the other side floods consciousness with a ghostly self-sense experienced as coming from outside.

FACT: Measurements of electrical activity at 'acupoints' on the body – the places used in Chinese acupuncture – have found a link between reports of peak experiences and changes in the flow of current.

On a high Falls in oxygen supply can cause unexpected changes in conscious state and can lead to fatal errors of judgment. This sometimes happens to climbers at high altitudes, where the atmosphere is lacking in oxygen.

(F)OCUS ON

MEDICINES AND THE MIND

Many drugs used to treat illnesses affect the brain in such a way that consciousness is altered. Some drugs are designed to do this: tranquillisers, anti-depressants and some painkillers work directly on the brain, altering the flow of neurotransmitters to improve mood or stem pain. However, the effects of these drugs cannot be precisely predicted. Sometimes they do not just relieve unpleasant symptoms, but produce experiences like derealisation or euphoria. Other drugs also affect the brain indirectly: antihistamines, for example, can produce drowsiness, and steroids may produce euphoria.

depletion may produce the dreamy 'out-of-the-body' state. Oxygen starvation may account for some of the strange near-death experiences reported by individuals who suffer trauma in accidents or during cardiac arrest (see page 424). Less dramatic falls in oxygen may cause a general downgrading of consciousness – a cotton-woolly feeling in the head, and lapses of memory and judgment. This sometimes happens to climbers at high altitudes, where the atmosphere is thin, and on aircraft where cabin pressure is lower than normal.

Sleep deprivation may also bring about alterations in consciousness. In the short term, lack of sleep tends to produce euphoria – a buzzy 'high' that can verge on mania. The effect is so pronounced that sleep deprivation is sometimes used to treat depression. In the long run, however, it causes severe irritability and even hallucinations. The reasons for these effects are not fully understood.

Alterations in body temperature may also affect consciousness. A fever, for example, makes neural tissue more irritable, and may produce random, spontaneous activity in brain cells, which leads to the rushing thoughts and strange impressions known as delirium. The 'aura' felt by epileptics just before they have a seizure is caused by excessive neuronal activity. When this occurs in the temporal lobes, it often produces transcendent feelings similar to those felt during peak experiences.

INDUCING ALTERED STATES

While altered states of consciousness can be frightening or unpleasant experiences, they can also be intensely pleasurable. Some people claim that they can provide glimpses of a deep reality beyond the reach of everyday thought. It is not surprising that people have developed numerous techniques to explore these states.

Everyone deliberately alters their state of consciousness many times a day. Whenever you take a deep breath to calm yourself down or watch a funny film to cheer yourself up, you are using a mind-altering technique. However, these forms of mind manipulation do not produce a radically different quality of consciousness: they merely intensify or blunt it a little. To achieve the states beyond – of ecstasy, or of the 'no-self' oneness with the universe reported by mystics – most people need extraordinary stimuli or must learn how to make their brains function in an unusual way. Every society, in every age, has had its own methods of doing this.

Altered states result from changes in the workings of the brain. These can be elicited in three main ways: by manipulating neuronal activity directly with drugs; by changing brain state using sensory stimuli, such as dance, breathing exercises or other physical rituals; and by using the mind itself to change its own thought patterns through meditation or other psychological techniques. Sometimes different methods are combined to augment the effect.

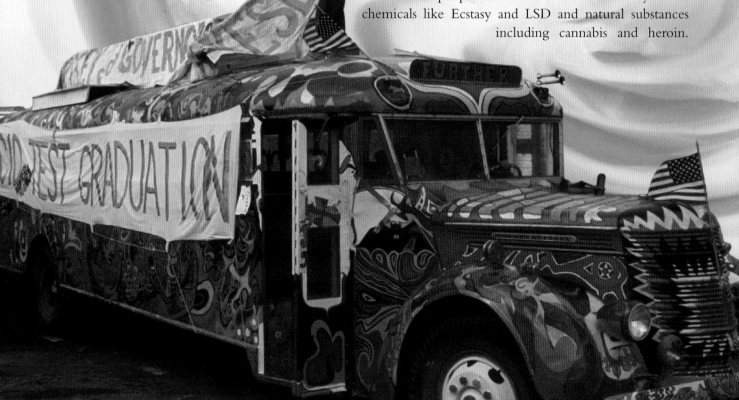

The Magic Bus Writer Ken Kesey's psychedelic bus is prepared for an event in San Francisco in 1966. A significant part of 1960s culture was inspired by drug-induced altered states.

Drug-induced states

Drugs offer the shortest path to a 'visionary' state. Although many mind-altering substances are illegal, vast numbers of people use them. These include synthetic chemicals like Ecstasy and LSD and natural substances including cannabis and heroin.

Inside the opium den Despite the efforts of the Chinese government to ban them, opium dens flourished in 19th century China.

Drug-induced pleasure results from changes to chemical pathways in the brain. The 'high' produced by nearly all recreational drugs results from the release, or increased retention, of the 'pleasure' chemical dopamine. Some drugs also affect other neurotransmitters (brain chemicals): serotonin and endorphins promote feelings of serenity; noradrenaline gives a feeling of excitement; and inhibitory neurotransmitters close down some normal brain processes. Drugs that increase noradrenaline (cocaine, amphetamines) create a feeling of energy and power; those that work on serotonin and endorphins (Ecstasy, heroin) may produce a deep glow of warmth; and those that affect the dopamine system (cannabis, magic mushrooms) may intensify or distort sensory perception.

The precise effects that a drug exerts on consciousness depend on which chemical pathways are affected, on how these changes interact with the subject's mood and expectations, and on the context in which the drug is taken. Certain drugs, especially synthetic prescription drugs such as tranquillisers and antidepressants, target specific groups of brain cells and so have fairly predictable effects. Most, though, work more randomly, altering many different chemical pathways, producing complicated and often unpredictable changes. A little alcohol drunk at a party, for example, produces a feeling of mild euphoria, while the same amount at the end of a stressful day may induce relaxation.

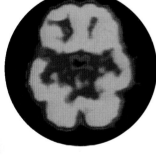

Drug damage Even after four months of abstinence, the brain of a long-term cocaine user (above) shows considerably lower activity compared to a non-user (top). Here, red and yellow indicate the highest levels of brain activity, while blue and mauve show the lowest levels.

FOCUS ON

SPEAKING IN TONGUES

One of the most extraordinary demonstrations of religious ecstasy is 'glossolalia' – speaking in tongues. People affected first become worked up into a state of high excitement, usually as part of a congregation. Then, as though in a trance, they begin to utter sounds in what may seem like a foreign language. Analysis of the sounds shows, however, that they are not words, but strings of repeated noises that lack the structure and variety of true languages. Speaking in tongues was first reported by St Paul at the Church of Corinth in the 1st century and has since cropped up among the French Huguenots in the 17th century, Quakers in the 18th century, Pentecostals in the 19th, and most recently, among charismatic Christians and Mormons.

But drink too much and pleasure may give way to anger, depression or catatonia. Many drugs also have undesirable long-term effects. Ecstasy, for example, can produce 'burn-out' in the neurons it affects, so that users can no longer function normally. The resulting feelings of depression may even lead to a permanent mood disorder.

Dance trance

Altered states can be reached legally, and far more safely, by using sensory or psychological stimuli to change patterns of brain activity. One common technique is dance. Moving the body to a persistent rhythm while shutting out all other thought encourages the release of dopamine in the limbic system, giving a similar effect to certain drugs. Depending on the context and the mental state of the dancer, the result may be heightened awareness of sensory stimuli, which makes the environment seem more vivid and exciting, or a dreamy, euphoric trance.

In the West, dance is primarily a social event. Its cheering effects are more to do with its ability to break down social barriers than to induce altered states. But in other cultures, the purpose of group dance is often spiritual. Shamanic rituals, for example, involve dancing to a repetitive rhythm for hours or sometimes days – long enough for the body to 'know' the music without having to hold it in mind. Movement becomes automatic, leaving the conscious mind free to become aware of messages from the spiritual self. Dancers in this state often experience 'separation' from their bodies and may feel as though they have moved into an alternative reality.

For some people, music alone can produce a similar effect. Most of us have experienced an upwelling of emotion in response to a particularly beautiful or haunting melody. Such a response may be the precursor to feelings of transcendence beyond mere pleasure. Chanting, such as that of Gregorian monks, taps into this channel of experience, with repetitive sounds freeing the mind to tune into spiritual experience.

Ceremony and ritual

Any ritual, even making a cup of tea, calms the mind, because the familiarity of the actions releases consciousness from the task of directing body movements. Some cultures have developed rituals that extend this effect and lead the participants into altered states. The Japanese tea

Ritual dance This Sudanese witch doctor performs a symbolic dance as part of a healing ritual. The repetitive, rhythmic movements of the dance help to induce an altered state of consciousness.

"When I enter a meditative state it is as though the three-dimensional world gives way to one that has many other dimensions."

Shinzen Young, an experienced meditator

The art of ritual Many ceremonies involve purposeful, repetitive actions and movements, which induce altered states of consciousness by quietening the mind and inducing serenity. Chanoyu, the Japanese tea ceremony, developed from Zen Buddhism and combines the four qualities of harmony, respect, cleanliness and tranquillity.

ceremony, for example, is meant to induce relaxation and concentration. Most religious services are deliberately ritualistic and designed to free the mind to take in awareness of God. Some depend on repetitive prayers, actions and sensory stimulation; for example, in Roman Catholicism the 59 beads of the Rosary provide a tactile focus for cycles of prayer. In other traditions, wailing, singing and swaying are encouraged.

The power of thought

Some rituals dispense with physical actions altogether. Instead, the individual goes through a programme of familiar mental behaviours to slow down the frantic rush of thoughts and sensations that typify waking consciousness. This type of practice, known as meditation, takes many forms. It may involve focusing the mind on a thought, an image, a sensation such as breathing, or an imagined sound such as a mantra. The aim of meditation is to rid the mind of content so that only 'pure' awareness remains. It is very difficult to achieve this state because our brains are designed to dart around constantly.

Although meditative states seem to take practitioners outside the everyday mental realm, brain scans show that, like other mind states, they are marked by distinct patterns of brain activity. Compared to brains in a normal state of attentive awareness, the meditating brain has less activity in the sensory cortex – particularly the parietal lobe, which processes information about the body – and it is more active in the parts of the frontal lobes that are concerned with holding attention. Some studies have shown that spiritual experience also activates certain areas of the temporal lobes – the so-called 'god spot' (see page 344).

(see page 344)

Real lives

FINDING THE WAY

Meditation is unlike most endeavours in that the harder you try to do it, the harder it is to achieve, as Abigail discovered.

'I tried and tried to meditate, but nothing happened – I'd dutifully intone my mantra, but all the time I'd be making shopping lists. Then one day I just gave up. It was a group session so I went into the meditative pose and did the breathing exercises. When we stopped twenty minutes later I realised when I opened my eyes that I had been somewhere I had never been before, though I hardly realised it at the time. It was so peaceful, quiet and blissful. I found I had a huge smile on my face that lasted all day. It wasn't that I did anything different – it was what I didn't do that mattered. I didn't try, I didn't worry, I didn't get annoyed that it wasn't working. And that, I realised, is the key – just let go, and it happens.'

HYPNOSIS

Hypnosis is a subject that leaves the experts divided. Some say the trance state produces genuine changes in the brain; others say people are only ever feigning. The truth probably lies in between.

Hypnotism has fascinated people ever since Franz Mesmer wowed 18th-century high society with his displays of control over the minds of others (see pages 372–3). But what is hypnosis? Is it a special level of consciousness, a clever manipulation of normal consciousness, or just quackery? The best answer seems to be that under hypnosis we lose ourselves in vivid imagery and hand over control of this imagery – and so our behaviour – to someone else.

Hypnotic technique

Today's professional hypnotists use a simple conversational technique pioneered in the 1940s by US psychotherapist Milton Erickson. After some small talk to establish a rapport, the hypnotist directs the subject's attention inwards by asking, for example, if his or her hands feel heavy. As the subject becomes absorbed in this thought, the hypnotist starts to assert control, suggesting that one hand is now so light it will rise. Picturing this in mind, some subjects will feel the suggestion to be true and allow their hand to float upwards. The hypnotist can now move on to more elaborate feats of suggestion – such as regressing the person to a past life, or suggesting that an onion is a nice crunchy apple. The person will imagine what the hypnotist asks and respond to the image as if it were authentic.

But is this state of mind real? Studies show that only about one in ten people have mental images so strong they seem like genuine perceptions. For most of us, hypnotic imagery appears fleeting and dull: we cannot shake off the knowledge that the images are 'pro-

An onion a day? People in a hypnotic state have been persuaded to bite into an onion, believing it to be an apple.

FOCUS ON

MINDBENDING SPIES

Recently released CIA files confirm that hypnosis – along with LSD and brain-zapping magnets – was just one of many mind-warping techniques tested out during the Cold War. However, the results were too unreliable to show that hypnotism could be used to force people to do things if they do not want to.

Nonetheless, according to Dr Armen Victorian, author of *Mind Controllers*, the CIA hatched some extraordinary plans. One was to implant a microscopic radio receiver in the ear – or even nostril – of an unsuspecting victim. The idea was that the victim would be cornered and, under hypnosis, have the device inserted, which would then be used for hypnotic control. Later, a whispered radio message could activate them as an assassin, spy or saboteur.

"We are not removing the customer's ability to say no. We are simply increasing their ability to say yes."

Robert Farago, professional hypnotist defending hypnotism courses for car salespeople

duced'. But if we are dragged up on stage, or have paid money to a hypnotherapist, we may feign simply out of embarrassment.

Experiments also show that motivation techniques can match the effect of a supposed hypnotic state. In one test, men were asked to hold a brick at arm's length for as long as they could. Unhypnotised, they lasted barely five minutes; hypnotised, they could stretch to 15 or 20. However, when unhypnotised men were told that women usually managed 20 minutes, suddenly the men found that they could last this long as well.

The 'hidden observer'

One intriguing phenomenon seems to provide evidence on both sides. In a typical study, strongly hypnotised subjects were first told that a small part of their mind – the 'hidden observer' – would always know what was going on during the session. Still under hypnosis, they were given lists of words – along with the suggestion that certain words on the list were not actually there. The subjects duly swore that the words were indeed missing from the lists. But when their 'hidden observer' was addressed, they reported being able to see the 'missing' words after all.

Some researchers say this means that there was always at least a part of the subject's mind that was behaving normally, quite unhypnotised. Others, however, argue that because hypnosis can divide consciousness in this way, with one part of the mind apparently having access to information denied to another part, the hidden observer effect shows that hypnosis involves a real state of dissociation. More recently, brain scanning machines have been used to examine some of the 10 per cent who do have super-strength mental imagery, and it was found that hypnosis could induce a visible change in their brain state. For example, when hypnotised to see a black and white picture as coloured, the scans suggested the subjects really did paint in the sensory impressions of colour. So while hypnosis is a largely self-induced state rather than a helpless trance, some people do have the mental imagery to make it a powerful experience.

Colourful fantasies People strongly suggestible to hypnosis can often be led to see colour in black and white images.

Real lives SURGERY WITHOUT ANAESTHETIC

To prove the power of hypnosis, 58-year-old Bernadine Coady decided to use it as her only anaesthetic during a lengthy operation to reconstruct a misshapen foot. When her hypnotist failed to show up for the operation, she went ahead and hypnotised herself.

Ahmed Shair, surgeon at the Fitzwilliam Hospital in Cambridgeshire, admitted that he felt unusually tentative as his scalpel was poised to make the first incision. The operation involved cutting through muscle and even bone to lengthen some tendons. But Mrs Coady coped by imagining her leg to be an unfeeling iron rod. She turned the waves of pain into ocean waves crashing vainly against a sea wall.

The surgeon said afterwards: 'I have heard of this sort of thing happening but never believed it. When we sawed through the bone she took herself deeper into sleep. She was in absolute control.'

WAYS TO EXPERIENCE ALTERED STATES

Our normal state of consciousness is constructed on the basis of our expectations, which make the world around us a consistent and familiar place. It can be an interesting experiment to try shaking up your expectations deliberately, and through this to induce an alteration in your mental state. The approaches described here will not take you into a kaleidoscopic world of psychedelia, but they can generate subtle and intriguing alterations of consciousness.

ENTERING THE FLOW

Try this exercise the next time you go for a walk. While walking, look straight ahead, but pay attention to your peripheral vision. If you're on a path, pay attention to what lies on either side of the path (such as hedges), rather than the path itself. Stretch your attention as wide as you can – the fields beyond the hedges, for example. Become aware of your other senses – hearing, smell, skin touch and pressure. Soon, you will feel that everything flows more than usual, and you are part of the flow. Your walking is only one action among all the movements in your vicinity; your awareness is part of the awareness that creatures around you are experiencing. Continue until there is only the flow; only the pulse of the world.

LIGHT-HEADEDNESS

In his book *Walden,* Henry Thoreau describes how he induced a dissociated state of consciousness by simply gazing at the reflection of the sun on Walden pond. You can try this for yourself. On a sunny day, sit or lie by a calm lake and watch the reflection of the sun on the surface of the water. Ensure that you won't be disturbed – maybe try this exercise with a friend, taking turns. Just keep gazing, without distraction. Don't hold onto particular thoughts in your mind – allow your attention to drift where it will, but keep your gaze fixed. After a while, you should find yourself moving into a state of consciousness subtly altered from normality. An alternative method of entering this state is to gaze at a bright light reflected in a crystal.

SENSORY DEPRIVATION

To see how your mind responds to a diminishing of sensation, try this route to temporary sensory deprivation. This is not so much a matter of depriving the senses of any input, but of removing any formed, meaningful input. The ideal is to use a flotation tank, since the environment can be carefully controlled. If you have no access to one, you can create similar conditions in your own home. Use a bed in a warm room with dim lighting. Cover your eyes with a bubble wrap mask (you are not trying to blindfold yourself, merely creating a diffuse light). De-tune a radio so you hear a hissing noise and listen to it through headphones. These provide the basics for sensory deprivation, Choose a time of day when you are feeling fairly alert – the object is to stay awake. Try to ensure that there is no air movement or strong smells in the room. Lie down and relax with your eyes open under the mask and the hissing in your ears, and see what happens.

WILD IMAGININGS

The French poet Rimbaud recommended a 'long, tremendous and methodical disturbance' of perceptions and their interpretations in the mind as a way of experiencing an altered state of consciousness. See if you can follow his method. Deliberately imagine that an object that you are seeing is something other than what it is. If it's a book, imagine it's a block of wood; if it's a cat, see it as a mutant fox. So too with sound: label the rustling of leaves as the sound of an animal; the voice of someone in the room as a radio voice. This exercise is hard to start with, and may not be something that you take to, but the method gets easier with practice. Don't worry if it sounds bizarre – that's the point!

CHANGING NAMES

Your name is a key part of your identity. As soon as you hear your name, a host of changes occur in your conscious mind – you pay attention, you become alert, you start questioning what is going on. You will realise how much of your conscious world is centred on your name if you change it. Unless you want to experience a serious sense of dislocation, a total change is not recommended. However, you could make arrangements within a group of close friends. The 'alias' that you choose may reflect aspects of your personality, which may be worth analysing (most people entering internet chat rooms use aliases, which are often revealing). Agree that you will be called by your alias for the course of a weekend. You will discover how de-centred you can become.

TRANCE DANCE

Total absorption in a physical activity can transport you to a trance-like state. You can try this with a group of friends. Clear your biggest room to make a dance-floor. Make sure there is nothing to trip over and that everyone has enough space to turn a full circle with arms outstretched, without touching anyone else. Then – with the exception of one or two trustworthy supervisors – everyone should put on a blindfold and dance for at least 30 minutes. The hypnotic rhythms of African tribal music are particularly good for this exercise. Let the music take over, clear your mind and just let yourself go. To reground yourself afterwards, lie down quietly for 20 minutes.

THE MIND'S VIRTUAL REALITY

The world of our experiences owes as much to our minds as to the world outside. All our experiences – sights, sounds, smells and tastes – are our mind's interpretations of the physical reality that exists around us. Without a mind to perceive it, a sound is just a pattern of vibration in the air. So our perceptions are all in essence an elaborate form of 'virtual reality'.

Imagine that you have landed on a strange planet. You leave your spacecraft but are unable to make out anything at all; you feel nothing, see nothing, hear nothing. Back inside your craft you consult your instruments and discover that there is, in fact, a rich diversity of matter and energy criss-crossing this new world. There are electromagnetic waves, vibrations and molecules – it is just that they are so different from those on Earth that your body has not evolved to be sensitive to them. They are like the high-pitched sound waves that bats use to communicate or the infra-red light-waves that can be seen by night-owls.

> **"The mind is the real instrument of sight and observation."**
>
> Pliny the Elder, 1st century AD

Consulting technical manuals on board, you design a suit that can detect these alien forces. You build in sensors to pick up the vibrations, cells that respond to the electromagnetic waves, and receptors for the molecules that are carried around in the planet's atmosphere. Then you make a transducer that turns the

THINK AGAIN!   THE REALM OF OUR SENSES

Our sensory system has evolved to pick up the type of information that is most useful for our survival. We can see light only in a small part of the electromagnetic spectrum. However, this part includes the wavelengths of light that certain key chemicals in our bodies and environment reflect. For example, haemoglobin and chlorophyll reflect in this range – so we see blood as bright red and plants as bright green. Similarly, the sounds we hear come from a narrow range of vibrational frequencies, so we cannot hear the shrill echolocatory signals of bats, for example – but these are of no benefit or threat to us. If we could redesign our sense organs so that they picked up a different range of stimuli, the world would be very different. We would see different colours, smell many more smells, and hear things that we are usually deaf to.

A world without red Some people's vision is abnormal because the retinal cells are insensitive to red, green or blue. The top picture shows what these red tulips might look like to someone without red vision. Not only are colours changed, but the relative contrasts are different – the blue flowers stand out far more than the red.

TWO-WAY PROCESSING

Conscious perceptions of the outside world are produced in the brain via a combination of bottom-up and top-down processing. Raw visual data from the eyes is sent to an area of the brain at the back of the opposite hemisphere, where 'bottom-up' processing begins. This continues as the perceptual information travels forward, with meaning added at each stage. Meanwhile, conceptual information (such as memories, expectations and verbal labels) is constantly fed back from frontal brain areas. This 'top-down' process integrates the perception into the existing conceptual framework and brings it to consciousness. The final perceptual experience is thus unique to each individual.

Primary visual cortex
Information from the eyes is registered at the back of the brain and sent forward for interpretation.

Visual association areas
These take information from the primary visual cortex and bind it to other relevant information, such as verbal labels.

Frontal lobes
These impose preconceptions on incoming information, fitting it into the web of existing knowledge.

Eyes
Data from each eye crosses to the primary visual cortex on the opposite side of the brain.

suit's responses into stimuli that your body can understand. Wrapped in the suit, you step out again into your new world. This time it is a place filled with objects and resonating with sound, colour, taste, smell and touch.

Our bodies are like that spacesuit. Just as the alien world can only be perceived when we equip ourselves with appropriate sensors, so our own world comes into existence only when its energy forms are translated by the brain and our nervous system into experience. What we think is a view of something 'out there' is in fact a sensation created by the brain from the messages received through the sense organs. In this sense, it is not so much reality itself as 'virtual reality'. The reason why we all perceive the world so similarly is that we all have similar nervous systems – we are all wearing the same type of spacesuit. But how do our brains create conscious experiences from the patterns of energy in the environment?

Constructing experience

A perceptual experience – such as seeing an object, hearing a sound or feeling a texture – occurs when matter or energy in the outside world stimulate our sense organs. For example, when we see something it is because light rays of the correct frequency hit the retina, which then sends signals via the optic nerve to the visual cortex at the back of the brain. Here the information is decoded and turned into a raw sensation. From here, the information passes to the frontal lobes, where it is interpreted conceptually and becomes a conscious visual experience, identified as a familiar – or unfamiliar – object.

THINK YOURSELF FIT

When you imagine moving your body, the 'body map' you carry in your brain springs into action, producing the sensation of movement even if you remain perfectly still. The brain still sends signals that try to activate muscles around the body, and although large movements are inhibited, the muscles nevertheless contract in preparation for the movement. This means you can increase muscle tone in the same way (though not to the same degree) as really carrying out the movement.

When you imagine an object or an event, it may at first seem just as clear and detailed as 'real' experience. But if you test it out, you will usually find the imagined experience is full of gaps and indistinct: its clarity is an illusion.

You can try this by summoning up a familiar image – some patterned curtains in your house, say. Close your eyes and concentrate on one particular part of the image – the pattern near the top, for example. When you have fixed the image clearly in your mind, zoom in on one part of the pattern – say, a flower. Can you see its form in detail?

Can you even state exactly what colours are in it? When you try to capture these details, the haziness of the image becomes apparent – very few people can visualise all the details. This may be because imagination depends more on top-down processing, whereas externally generated images are produced by proportionately more bottom-up activity. Both give the subjective impression of dense sensation, so the experience is very similar. But the actual amount of sensory information contained in imagined experience is relatively sparse – our brains 'fill in' the missing bits.

However, the flow of information is not exclusively from the sensory to the conceptual areas of the brain: the neural pathways run in both directions. When we imagine an experience or call up an image from memory, the flow is reversed. Activity in the frontal region of the brain generates a concept, which passes to the sensory cortices and prompts them to produce appropriate sensory signals. These are then fed forward again, where they are experienced as sensory events rather than just as abstract concepts. En route, they may trigger activity in the limbic system, producing emotions as well. The more the sensory cortex is stimulated, the more vivid the recollection – so imaginary sights may vary from vague impressions to hallucinations so real as to be indistinguishable from the real events.

FACT: The sensory nerves of the body can be trained to 'see', much as the eye does. If electrodes are attached to the skin, and then used to send pulses of electricity that represent the shape of objects, the brain learns to interpret the signals as vision. Using this method, blind people are able to navigate a maze.

For example, if you think of a concept such as 'going swimming tomorrow', the frontal region of the brain stimulates the sensory cortex to produce the neural activity that would normally occur when the body was immersed in water. It may also produce the sort of activity in the visual cortex that would normally be triggered by the sight of water – perhaps a swimming pool or the sea. The image may be very crude – just an impression of water – or highly embellished to include the people you expect to be swimming with, the beach you will be visiting, the feeling of the sun on your skin, the swimming costume you intend to wear. In addition, the thought may trigger dopamine release in the limbic system, which provides a frisson of pleasure – just as though you were experiencing your swimming trip for real.

Time to daydream The fantasies we weave when daydreaming are most easily summoned when we have few distractions. Although they can be very vivid, these inwardly created perceptions are rarely as detailed as ones that we actually experience.

The power of imagination

The detail and vividness of our imagined or remembered imagery depends largely on our ability to focus attention – that is, to limit our brain's activity to the imaginative process. Because many areas of the brain are involved in creating an imagined scenario, any competing cognitive activity will divert resources away from the task. In order to daydream successfully, you must clear your mind of other things and attend to it – just as you have to attend to significant things in the 'real' world.

Internally generated experiences are rarely as rich as those created by outside stimuli because, for very good reasons, the brain is designed to give primary attention to the outside world. If daydreams were as tangible as 'real' experience then we might well fail to notice things that may pose a physical threat, or we might respond physically to events in our own imaginations. So the sensory activity associated with daydreams is easily interrupted by signals coming in from outside: if you are visualising a sunny beach, for example, the image will be shattered if your eye detects a big object moving towards you. This is why daydreaming is difficult in a busy, exciting environment – but seductively easy when there are few distractions.

Real lives **SENSORY DEPRIVATION AND HEIGHTENED IMAGINATION**

Imagined scenarios tend to be more vivid when there are no outside stimuli to compete with the internally generated sensations. Alice, 20, found this when she experimented with a session in a sensory deprivation tank.

'At first I just felt strange and disoriented. There was nothing to fix on, not even the feeling of heat or cool, or where my limbs were, because they were floating in this blood temperature water. But as I relaxed, images started to swim up in front of my eyes. They were much clearer and more detailed than the sights I can usually conjure up. One of them was a girl's face – not a familiar one – and I could actually count her eyelashes and see the pores on her skin. Later I imagined riding my horse, and found that I could actually feel the motion and the slight friction of my seat in the saddle. I've tried to do this since, by shutting my eyes and concentrating – but it is never as clear.'

VISIONS AND HALLUCINATIONS

Many people have experienced false perceptions. They may have heard phantom footsteps on a dark night, felt a touch on their shoulder when they were alone, or glimpsed a figure in an empty corner of a shadowy room. When these experiences are mistaken for reality, they are known as hallucinations.

There is nothing mysterious about hallucinations. They arise from the same brain machinery that is used when we summon up an image from memory or create a new experience from our imagination. In all these cases, the brain produces sensory experiences in the absence of outside stimuli. These 'false' experiences are usually less vivid than those triggered by external stimuli, so we know that they are not 'real'. But in certain circumstances the imagined experiences can be extremely intense, and we lose our ability to perceive them for what they are.

Seeing what you expect to see

There are two types of hallucinations: those produced spontaneously by a normal brain and those triggered by drugs or by disturbances in brain function. Spontaneous hallucinations are created (like all imaginary experience) from memory. A hallucination can be a discrete 'chunk' of memory, such as a familiar face, or it can be assembled from many 'bits' of past experience spliced together to form something apparently new. The sensory component of the hallucination – what is actually seen, heard or felt – is generated by activity in the sensory cortices, just like ordinary perceptions. But the interpretation of this activity also depends on how the sensations are processed by the parts of the brain that deal with beliefs and expectations. So if two observers both see a black shape in the corner of a room, depending on their expectations one might see a coat on a hook, while the other sees a ghostly figure lurking in the shadows.

Ordinary perceptions, too, are open to different interpretations by different observers. But because they are triggered by external stimuli, the 'real' sensory information tends to override the internal imagery generated by expectation and belief. Someone looking at a picture of a cat when she is expecting a picture of a dog, may 'see' a dog if she takes only a brief glimpse. But the longer she looks at the picture, the harder it is to

Ghosts in the shadows Apparitions with a ghostly quality are common because the sensory apparatus for making out forms in semi-darkness is especially sensitive. This is probably because such an adaptation would once have been useful to our forebears, helping them to detect potential physical threats in the dark.

THE SLEEP-WAKE BOUNDARY

Hallucinatory phenomena are often experienced in the twilight state between waking and sleep. These experiences are described as hypnagogic (if they occur as we are falling asleep) or hypnopompic (if they occur as we are waking up).

Hypnagogic hallucinations tend to be visual and often rather alluring. People often report beautiful, dynamic images such as roses unfurling their petals, fascinating landscapes with changing cloud shapes, or colours and kaleidoscopic forms that appear to dance and shimmer.

Hypnopompic phenomena are also primarily visual, but seem to be experienced more fully. People are often convinced that they are awake and therefore find the hallucinations powerful and even frightening. Dreamers may believe that there is an intruder in the room poised to attack them, or that strange creatures are lurking in the darkness. The dreamers may feel even more vulnerable because they are unable to move. This sleep paralysis is a normal feature of REM sleep, and prevents us from acting out our dreams.

sustain the mistaken perception. In other words, the 'bottom-up' content from the senses overrides the signals flowing 'top-down' from the expectations in the conscious brain. Hallucinations, by contrast, contain more 'top-down' content and have little or no outside information to conflict with the self-generated image. For this reason, hallucinations tend, more than ordinary perceptions, to reflect what the mind expects to find.

So people who believe in ghosts are more likely to see them than those who do not. Seeing a dark shadow in a room, they are more likely to notice it, turn their attention to it, and amplify the impression into something that seems very real. By contrast, someone who does not believe in ghosts is unlikely to notice the shadow, and may not even remember seeing it. Similarly, religious believers who expect to see manifestations of gods or saints quite often do. Their visions are wishful embellishments of real perceptions, turning a pattern of currants in a bun into a portrait of Mother Theresa or a cloud formation into an image of the Virgin Mary.

FACT: The Russian composer Dmitri Shostakovitch heard melody hallucinations every time he put his head to one side. He incorporated some of these melodies into his work.

The importance of belief and expectation in shaping visions and hallucinations becomes clear when you compare reports from different cultures. Visions of the Virgin Mary are often reported in Catholic countries, whereas in the USA, where sci-fi movies are a significant influence, sightings of UFOs and aliens are far more common.

Errors of perception

Certain environmental factors predispose us to hallucinations. Many visions occur in semi-darkness because the sensory cells in the eye that detect forms in poor light lie at the periphery of our visual field. This means that when we see objects in the dark, we see them indistinctly – out

'The Nightmare' Henry Fuseli's 1781 painting depicts the demonic figure of an incubus, representing the frightening images experienced in bad dreams. Both nightmares and normal dreams occur during REM sleep, our consciousness producing both terrifying and pleasurable dream narratives.

of the 'corner of the eye'. Darkness also promotes fear, which tends to make our senses more alert. So in scary situations, the visual cortex is more likely to pick up small stimuli that might otherwise be ignored.

We all experience false perceptions from time to time. Usually the error is detected because it does not tally with information from our sense organs or because it does not fit into our belief system. But in some cases, the false perception does tally with our belief system and therefore becomes fixed. Such full-blown hallucinations can be dangerous. For example, an aircraft pilot may misread the position of a needle on a dial, but because the information seems reasonable, he may not examine it closely. Such errors become more common if the pilot is tired or in a situation where information from outside is sparse (when flying through cloud, for example) and they sometimes cause serious accidents.

Dreamscapes

The most familiar way in which our minds produce vivid images and experience without input from the outside world is in dreams. Dreams are the result of activity in the sensory areas at the back of the brain. These become active and produce a stream of sensations, which are woven into a narrative. When we dream, the frontal areas of the brain, which in the waking state select and direct sensory attention according to our wishes, are partially 'turned off'. This means that we have very little control over the content of our dreams – we cannot direct the action in the same way we can in imaginative daydreams.

The frontal areas of the brain are also partly responsible for producing the background sense of self – the awareness of who and where we really are. Because they are underactive in sleep (except in lucid dreaming, see page 362) we are not even aware that we are dreaming, so heightening the reality of the experience.

Hallucination and the damaged mind

People with damaged or diseased brains can suffer severe hallucinations that cannot be distinguished from perceptions triggered by outside stimuli. For example, if a stroke damages the sensory areas of the brain, the

> "In the dream, I raised my arms and began to rise. I rose through black sky that blended to indigo, to deep purple, to lavender, to white, then to a very bright light. All the time I was being lifted there was the most beautiful music I have ever heard."

Andy, of Bay City, Michigan

Real lives VISIONS IN MINIATURE

Doreen has a severe visual impairment, which makes the real world a blur. Yet she sees imagined perceptions as perfectly concrete, clear and vivid.

'One day I watched an entire circus. The clowns came on, then acrobats, then jugglers – I could see every detail of their costumes; the strings of the balloons held by the clowns, the wires that the acrobats performed on. It went on for hours and it was charming and engrossing. What was really strange about it, though, was that it was all in miniature. The entire Big Top was about the size of my thumbnail.'

FOCUS ON   DRUGS AND HALLUCINATIONS

Hallucinations can be generated by a wide range of drugs. Some, including LSD, peyote, mescal and heroin, are used specifically for this purpose, while others may produce hallucinations as side-effects. These include prescription medicines used to treat high blood pressure (clonidine), pain (pentazocine, fentanyl) and depression (Prozac).

The type of hallucination depends on which part of the brain is most affected by the drug. Those that target the visual cortex produce whirling colours, patterns, and altered perception of the size and shape of objects. Those that affect 'higher' brain areas – where sensations are interpreted – may make objects do peculiar things: a spider may suddenly start doing leapfrog with the cat. Drugs that affect the auditory cortex can alter the way that sound is heard, or generate phantom sounds. Some chemicals (including alcohol and steroids) produce tactile sensations such as the feeling of 'bugs' crawling over the skin. Amyl nitrate produces genital sensations that often induce sexual arousal. Drugs that work mainly on the limbic system, such as Ecstasy, may produce emotional hallucinations such as a heightened sense of beauty and love; and those that excite the frontal lobes (amphetamines, cocaine) generate delusions of power and strength.

'Easy Rider' Very much a product of its time, the 1969 cult movie starring Peter Fonda and Dennis Hopper was notorious for the scenes featuring the characters hallucinating on LSD.

reduced sensory information received from outside is constantly over-ridden by 'top-down' processing, so imagined events appear real. Providing the sufferer's thinking is still normal – that is, if the parts of the prefrontal cortex that govern reason and logical thought are still intact, the odd, imagined material will be recognised as false.

It is when damaged sensory brain function is combined with a bizarre belief system or disordered thinking that false perceptions may be really catastrophic. This occurs in people suffering from disorders such as Alzheimer's disease, schizophrenia and severe depression. For example, some forms of schizophrenia are marked by odd and often terrifying hallucinations that make it impossible for sufferers to function in the real world. The most common form of schizophrenic hallucination is auditory – voices, which may be threatening or dictatorial. In extreme cases, the voices may tell the person to commit suicide or murder.

Brain scans of schizophrenics hallucinating voices show that their auditory cortex is activated in just the same way as when voices are actually heard. They also show that the voices are generated by the speech centres of the person's own brain; and sensors that pick up minute movements of the throat muscles reveal that the person even starts the process of articulating them. When normal people generate silent speech, a signal is sent to the auditory cortex to tell it that the speech comes from 'inside', so the person knows that it is imaginary. In schizophrenics, these signals are absent, so they cannot distinguish between imaginary internal speech and actual voices.

FACT FILE

HALLUCINATIONS

• Visual hallucinations affect about 3 per cent of people with sight problems.

• Sleep deprivation produces hallucinations in most people within 48 hours.

• Phantom limbs, in which amputees experience the presence of missing limbs, are a type of tactile hallucination.

• Artists such as Poe, Coleridge, and Baudelaire used hashish and opiates to increase the richness of their visual imagery.

• One of the constituents of cannabis, dronabinol, produces hallucinations in 5 per cent of people who take it.

Lucid dreaming

The world we enter in our dreams is as vivid and eventful as waking reality. Normally, we have no conscious influence on our dream imagery – we are passive observers. But in lucid dreaming, people can control their dream experiences.

When you dream, your brain's conscious 'control centre' shuts down, and you can no longer direct the focus of your attention or rationally examine your perceptions. This means that you accept your dream experiences, no matter how bizarre, as being completely normal. In lucid dreaming, this changes. The brain's control centre 'wakes up' and restores the sense of self. This allows you to direct your dream narratives as you choose. Experienced lucid dreamers do extraordinary things in their dreams. They can fly, chat to long-lost friends, sunbathe on a sunny beach or eat an exquisite meal.

In a lucid dream, you move into a rich dreamscape – seemingly as real as anything experienced in waking life, but with the freedom of being unconstrained by normal physical laws. The key is that you are able to recognise the dream as illusion. For example, you might dream that a lion is chasing you. Becoming lucid, you realise that you are dreaming, and your fear subsides as you remember that you can control what happens. You can turn the lion into a fluffy toy or make it roll over and ask for its tummy to be tickled. Or you can continue the chase just for the thrill of it.

Lucid dreams can occur spontaneously, but many people can train themselves to have lucid dreams by using visualisation techniques (see opposite).

Therapeutic lucid dreaming

Lucid dreaming is not just entertaining – it can be therapeutic. People can overcome phobias, for example, by confronting and controlling them in lucid dreams. Some psychotherapists believe that significant dream symbols can be interrogated in these dreams, providing insights into unconscious motivations.

HOW TO BECOME A LUCID DREAMER

Lucid dreaming is not a particularly 'natural' state because normal brain chemistry tends to produce either sleep (and dreaming) or wakefulness – not a mixture of the two. However, there is no evidence to suggest that training yourself to enter this state has any adverse effects. The following steps, followed every night, should produce lucid dreaming within weeks or months.

1 Go to bed an hour or so earlier than usual, or have a lie-in. Alternatively, set an alarm a couple of hours earlier than usual, get up when it goes off, then return to bed later for a nap. Lucid dreams tend to occur after one has had the normal dose of ordinary REM sleep.

2 In the hours before bedtime, think hard and repeatedly: 'I will have a lucid dream tonight'. The thought will help to 'prime' the brain for lucidity.

3 Select a 'cue' or 'dreamsign' that your brain will recognise when it occurs in a normal dream. Decide that when the dreamsign appears, you will 'know' that you are dreaming. For example, decide that whenever a red object appears in a dream, your brain will latch on to it and recall that this is a dream.

4 Make an effort to become more aware of your ordinary dreams. Keep a notebook by your bed and, on waking, write down everything you can remember. Make a particular note of objects that seem to appear often and select them as dreamsigns.

5 The moment you have a glimmering of awareness in a dream – the thought 'this is too odd to be real' for instance – zoom in on it rather than letting it drift away. This type of awareness is the gateway to lucidity. Most people experience it fleetingly during normal dreams: the trick is to hold on to the thought and elevate it into consciousness without waking up altogether.

6 When lucidity dawns, relax into it. Do not get excited or try to alter the dreamscape immediately. Just relax and enjoy the scenery. Once you have latched on to the thought that you are dreaming, you will find that lucidity floods in. It feels like waking up – except that, instead of becoming sensorily aware of the outside world, your knowledge is purely conceptual. You 'know' you are in bed, because you remember going to sleep, but you don't actually feel the bed. The sights, sounds and feelings you were experiencing when you were ordinarily dreaming continue unchanged – it is just that now you know they are hallucinations.

7 Test the dream. Sometimes it can be quite difficult to distinguish a lucid dream from wakefulness. One way to test it is to try switching on any type of electrical apparatus – in lucid dreams, there is always a delay between throwing the switch and the device coming to life. And electric lights are always very dim in lucid dreams.

8 Slowly start to control the dream. Decide, for example, to change the weather, or the wallpaper of the room you are in. All you need to do is to have the thought 'let it be sunny', or 'walls turn blue'. If you want to conjure up a person, think about seeing them appear, then turn away from the place where you want to see them. When you turn back they will probably be there. If you want to fly, imagine yourself lifting up very gently – when you feel yourself go, do not try to 'help', just let it happen.

9 If you feel yourself waking up and don't want to, try spinning your dream body around in a circle – it helps to maintain the dreamscape.

10 Never panic. Lucid dreams occasionally produce unpleasant experiences, such as a feeling of a charged atmosphere or a sinister presence. And 'false awakenings' are common – you think you have properly woken up, but find that you cannot move. This is because you are still in sleep paralysis. Fighting against the feeling is pointless and may make you feel as though you are suffocating. Instead, relax, remind yourself that this is a false awakening, and float back into your dreamworld.

PERCEPTION AND REALITY

Perception is more than just seeing. Our personal version of reality comes both from the raw material we pick up from our senses and from the beliefs, desires, memories and expectations that we use to interpret this material. For this reason, the way two individuals experience the world may be very different.

Real lives

EROTOMANIA

Erotomania is a curious type of delusion in which people believe that a person they idolise returns their feelings. Jacob – now receiving counselling after being accused of stalking Elisabeth – recalls how he misread her behaviour.

'Elisabeth worked in my office. I was much too shy to talk to her and I realise now that she probably didn't even know I existed until I started to follow her home and generally make a nuisance of myself. But I got the idea into my head that she had fallen in love with me, as I had with her. I would watch her from a distance, and think that she was sending me signals. She had this habit of flicking her hair back, and every time she did it I thought she was flirting with me. Once I got in her way and she said "watch it!" to me. I took this to mean "watch what I signal to you" – it really thrilled me! Of course I realise now that it was all madness – she didn't even know I was looking, let alone that I thought she was sending me messages. But it all seemed obvious at the time – there was no other way of seeing it.'

Most people have much the same sort of sensory equipment; their eyes, ears and other senses work according to the same physical principles, and the sensory pathways in their brains are wired in similar ways. So if two individuals witness the same event, the raw information that they take in will be more or less the same. But no two people will interpret this information in exactly the same way. Those who share a common culture, background and education are most likely to arrive at similar conclusions, but others may form widely variant pictures.

Perceptions can differ on a number of levels, from the purely sensory to the psychologically complex. For example, imagine that you are presented with a neutral tactile sensation, such as a vibration: if you expect it to be painful, you are likely to perceive it as such; but if you are told beforehand that the vibration will be pleasant, then you will probably experience it as pleasant. Similarly, different people's interpretation of a neutral visual stimulus, such as an irregularly shaped inkblot, can vary considerably. At a more complex level, we all interpret other people's behaviour according to the notions we already hold about those people. For example, if someone you know and like ignores you in the street, you will probably assume that they were simply lost in thought and did not see you passing. But if you dislike that person, you may see their action as a deliberate snub.

Cultural distortions

Prejudices like this pervade our every perception. Sometimes the prejudice is individual, but often it is shared by an entire culture. Take our ideas of beauty. Certain qualities are perceived as beautiful by almost everyone because the human brain is wired to see them as such. For example, every known

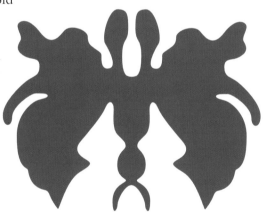

Revealing character The Rorschach inkblot test, used by psychologists to assess personality, exploits our tendency to read meaning into an arbitrary pattern. One person may look at this pattern and see two lovers in an embrace, while another might interpret it as two adversaries locked in combat. The difference depends not on information received through the senses, but on how information is interpreted by memory and other 'higher' cognitive functions.

culture values facial symmetry, probably because it indicates health. But other concepts of beauty are clearly determined by culture: in the West, the 'ideal' female form is slim, but elsewhere a slender build indicates weakness or poverty, and an attractive woman is one with the sort of padding that sends well-heeled Westerners rushing to slimming clinics.

Theory of mind

Everyone's perceptions are private. But in order to communicate and share understanding, we must have some idea of the world that other people construct in their minds. Not surprisingly, humans have evolved sophisticated mechanisms for knowing how other people see things. One such mechanism is actually programmed into the human brain: psychologists call it the theory of mind.

Around the age of four years, normal children suddenly develop the ability to know intuitively that other people have a different point of view to their own. The emergence of this skill can be detected by a test in which the child is invited to watch a play acted out by a couple of dolls,

Points of view Two people can take in the same information, but create quite different perceptions from that information. Here, the painters J.M.W. Turner (1775–1851), left, and Canaletto (1697–1768) offer strikingly different interpretations of the same scene – the Grand Canal in Venice.

(F)OCUS ON   *INEVITABLE ILLUSIONS*

There are certain things that we cannot see as they really are – our brains are 'hard-wired' to distort them. Such inevitable illusions include the mask illustrated here. The brain sees a face as convex, not concave. The picture of the mask on the far right is in fact a concave shape – the inside surface of the mask. But the brain sees it as convex, even re-interpreting the lighting as coming from an unnatural direction to make this possible. Only when the mask is seen side on (middle) can we step aside from our hard-wired prejudice and perceive the shape as it is in reality.

Similar prejudices distort our appreciation of probability. If a tossed coin comes down heads twenty times in a row we are surprised – and may even conclude that some

supernatural force or trickery is at work. But if it comes down H (heads) T (tails) then T H H T H T T T H H H H T T T H T T we are not surprised at all – even though the chances of both sequences are identical.

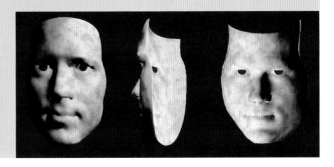

Sally and Ann. At the beginning, Sally is given a sweet, which she places in a box before leaving the room. While she is away, Ann takes the sweet out of the box and places it in a different box. Sally then returns, and the children are asked: 'Which box will Sally think the sweet is in?'

Children under the age of about four usually answer that Sally thinks the sweet is in the second box, because they assume that the doll shares their own view of the world, and are unable to understand that Sally lacks information that they have. Over this age, however, children realise that Sally's view is different – that she did not see the sweet being switched, so she will expect it to be in the box she left it in. The inbuilt theory of mind that allows them to work out another person's perspective is working.

Mirroring emotions

The theory of mind has its physical basis in brain cells known as mirror neurons. When activated, these cells produce a wide range of perceptions, emotions and compulsions to act – just like other brain cells. But what is special about them is the way they are activated. Unlike most other neurons, which respond to a wide range of stimuli, mirror cells become active only when the response they produce in the person is first observed in another. So, for example, when one individual sees another making an expression of disgust, the 'disgust' mirror neurons become active, producing a similar feeling. Mirror neurons give us built-in empathy – an automatic, intuitive sense of what another person is experiencing.

FACT: Perception is altered by mood. Depressed people, for example, see life quite literally as more grey than people in a buoyant state of mind, because the colour areas of their brains are less active.

PIONEERS

R.D. LAING – UNDERSTANDING SCHIZOPHRENIA

The Scottish psychiatrist Ronald David Laing (1927–1989) was one of the most influential and controversial thinkers of the 1960s. He questioned orthodoxy, arguing that the perceptions of people considered to be mentally ill are as valid in their own terms as those of 'normal' individuals. Laing pointed out that almost any behaviour could be taken as a symptom of schizophrenia, allowing psychiatrists to give a medical label to those who simply refused to conform to the expectations of family and society. For Laing, schizophrenia was a way of experiencing the world, not a disease; mental 'illness' could in fact be an existential journey – a cure for misery rooted in childhood and family.

Born in Glasgow in 1927, Laing's own family upbringing was turbulent. After completing his medical training in 1958, he worked in a British Army psychiatric unit. His book *Sanity, Madness and the Family* (1964), which argued that schizophrenia could be caused by communication breakdown within the family, established Laing's international reputation, and he continued high-profile clinical work into the 1970s. Later, Laing's intellectual standing was compromised by his fascination with mysticism and he eventually lost his licence to practise medicine in Britain.

Real lives   THE DELUSIONS OF JOHN NASH

John Nash was a brilliant mathematician, who was awarded the Nobel Prize for Economics in 1994. For many years he was afflicted by schizophrenic delusions, in which he believed that aliens were passing him information.

In 1959, a colleague visiting him asked how, as 'a man devoted to reason and logical proof', he could believe that extraterrestrials were recruiting him to save the world. Nash replied that 'the ideas I had about supernatural beings came to me the same way that my mathematical ideas did. So I took them seriously'.

Contact through conversation

Another, more obvious, way of finding out how another person is perceiving things is by talking. Telling each other about our experiences is important because it allows us to reconcile opposing views. Say, for example, a couple go out to buy a sofa for their home. He wants black leather, she wants red velvet. They could simply state their desires, disagree, and feel mystified at the apparent error of the other's way of thinking. But if he explains that he thinks the black leather is elegant and modern, and she explains that, to her, red velvet is warm and comfortable, they can at least try out the other's point of view and perhaps see its merits.

Most everyday differences in perception that cloud our dealings with other people can be resolved through discussion and compromise. However, some are so fundamental that it is impossible to bridge the chasm between two different perceptions. Sometimes, a person's view of the world is so bizarre that it cannot be shared by others. People with such extreme perceptions are generally regarded as psychotic – dislocated from reality.

Delusions and psychosis

The most extreme psychotic perceptions are held by people who suffer from schizophrenia. To schizophrenics, their perceptions seem to come from the real world, but they are actually made up largely of hallucinations (see page 361). The sufferer cannot detect that the hallucinations are internally generated, but instead seeks a plausible explanation for their origin – perhaps that voices have been beamed into his or her mind by malevolent aliens.

> **"If I don't know I don't know, I think I know. If I don't know I know, I think I don't know."**
>
> R.D. Laing, psychiatrist

Schizophrenic delusions are warped perceptions that can sometimes lead to disaster. But there are many other, more subtle, ways in which non-consensual viewpoints can wreak havoc in society. The distorted world-views of despots like Hitler, egomaniacs like Idi Amin, and cult leaders like Charles Manson are far more threatening than the delusions of schizophrenics because they are combined with a persuasiveness that seduces others into sharing their pathological assumptions. The terrible outcome of such distortions of social values underscores the importance of holding on to one's own sense of reality – and constantly testing beliefs against the widest range of evidence, rather than relying on the opinions of selected others to confirm or deny them.

The doors of perception

Mind-altering drugs have featured in the work of many writers, poets and artists – either as subject matter, or as the means by which they achieved their creative insights.

Psychotropic drugs have influenced the work of countless writers. In a tradition that goes back hundreds of years, many prominent writers have related experiences of drug-induced altered states or have used these states to inspire their work.

The 'stately pleasure dome' in Xanadu, described in Samuel Taylor Coleridge's epic poem *Kubla Khan* (1816), is largely the product of the poet's opium-inspired fantasies. And the near-transcendental appreciation of the natural world and the Gothic fantasies of poets such as Scott, Shelley, Wordsworth, Byron and Poe owe much to the mind-altering effects of drugs. One of the earliest first-person accounts of drug experiences, and the effect of drugs on society, is Thomas de Quincey's *Confessions of an Opium Eater*. Published in 1821, de Quincey's book describes his own and others' attempts to find peace and transcendence in the 'gathering agitation' of the Industrial Revolution, and his discovery that 'some merely physical agencies can and do assist the faculty of dreaming and ... beyond all others is opium'.

Expanding horizons

In the late 19th and early 20th century there were few legal restrictions on

Literary addict Sir Arthur Conan Doyle's detective hero, Sherlock Holmes, was addicted to both laudanum and cocaine. While conceding the damaging physical effects of cocaine, Holmes remarks: 'I find it so transcendentally stimulating and clarifying to the Mind that its secondary action is of small moment.'

drugs: opium, cannabis and, latterly, cocaine were more or less freely available to those who could afford them. Writers of the period were quick to experiment with their possible benefits. In France, Victor Hugo, Alexandre Dumas and Charles Baudelaire, together with other artists and writers, formed 'Le Club de Hachichines' specifically to extol the virtues of cannabis as an aid to creativity.

Many of the strange sequences in Lewis Carroll's *Alice Through the Looking-Glass* (1872) are perfect descriptions of the effects of 'magic' mushrooms, and rumour has it that *The Strange Case of Dr Jekyll and Mr Hyde* (1886), completed by Robert Louis Stevenson in six days and six nights, was written while the author was high on cocaine.

Prohibition and rebellion

In the 20th century, attitudes towards drug use began to change. A spate of books railed about the dangers of drugs – Aldous Huxley's *Brave New World* (1932), for example, characterised the fictional 'soma' as the route to moral degeneracy – and 'dope scandals' in Hollywood revealed that many of the clean-cut heroes of the silver screen were drug addicts. The shock ushered in a new age of prohibition, and the start of the 'war against drugs' that still rages today.

It was not until the 1950s that drugs again started to be used openly by writers as a means of inspiration. Interestingly, it was Huxley himself who helped to reverse the climate with his celebrated investigation of psychedelic drugs. Huxley wrote an essay, titled *The Doors of Perception,* after experimenting with hallucinogens, including mescaline and LSD. Of his first mescaline experience he wrote: 'It was without doubt the most extraordinary and significant experience this side of Beatific vision.' And he described looking at a flower during a drug trip as seeing 'what Adam had seen on the morning of creation – the miracle, moment by moment, of naked existence … words like "grace" and "transfiguration" came to mind'.

This work established Huxley as a propagandist for hallucinogenic drugs, and its publication brought them to wide public attention. It created a storm in literary circles, with some critics hailing it as a major intellectual breakthrough and others as incoherent nonsense. Today it is widely regarded as a classic.

Aldous Huxley

The use of hallucinogens as an expression of rebellion characterised the 'beat generation' of the 1950s, setting the scene for an explosion of drug-related writing in the 1960s. This included the proselytising works of Harvard psychologist Timothy Leary, whose stated ambition was to 'turn on the world'. But Leary went too far for the authorities – he, along with several others of his generation, were hounded by police and finally arrested and imprisoned.

Since then, drugs have continued to feature almost routinely in contemporary fiction and film, though the largely uncritical attitude towards them has given way to a more wary appreciation of their benefits and risks.

> **"What came through that closed door was the realisation … of Love as the primary and fundamental cosmic fact. "**
>
> Aldous Huxley, from *The Doors of Perception*

DRUGS AND THE BEAT GENERATION

The conformity of 1950s America gave birth to a generation of bohemian writers – the 'beats'. The group, which included Jack Kerouac, Allan Ginsberg and William S. Burroughs, created a new vision of art that expressed a bitter disaffection with materialistic post-war society. They teamed drugs like benzedrine, LSD, peyote, morphine, opium and cocaine with Eastern mysticism and elements of Western avant-garde, such as dadaism and jazz, in their search for 'the ancient heavenly connection'. Their work – once derided by the establishment – is now considered to be highly influential, although it was produced at great cost to the authors. Kerouac died a severely depressed alcoholic at the age of 47, while Burroughs spent many years battling his addiction to heroin.

Beat movie A scene from the 1992 film of William Burroughs' 1959 novel, *The Naked Lunch.* The vivid portrayal of drug addiction drew upon the author's own experience.

3 THE UNCONSCIOUS BRAIN

By definition, our unconscious minds are unknown to us: if we could ponder our unconscious mental processes, they would no longer be unconscious. Although we have all experienced the forces that our unconscious can exert on our conscious thinking and behaviour, discovering the exact way in which our minds work beneath our consciousness is not a straightforward matter.

Sigmund Freud famously believed he had discovered what was in the unconscious mind – a dark, seething mass of repressed sexual desires. Other thinkers built on Freud's theories, bringing mysticism and surrealist ideas to bear on the issue. Today, psychologists take perhaps the saner view that, in general, the unconscious is involved in much the same things as the conscious mind. The surprising element is that, in some ways, the unconscious can outsmart the conscious brain. This modern view has given us new routes towards an understanding of the unconscious, and answers are emerging to such questions as: how do our brains work so effectively on autopilot? How powerful is subliminal perception? And is unconscious learning really a possibility?

WHAT IS THE UNCONSCIOUS?

Until a little over a century ago, few people believed in the unconscious: the contents of the mind were, by definition, conscious. But today's psychologists agree with Freud that our lives are ruled by thoughts and feelings of which we are unaware.

When we sink into deep sleep, faint, or have a general anaesthetic, we are unconscious. Being in this state is impossible to describe because it isn't like anything – we are simply unaware of feeling or thinking. It isn't surprising, therefore, that the very idea of an active unconscious was scorned by self-respecting thinkers, from the ancient Greeks onwards. An ancient Greek who had attempted to discuss the unconscious would have been laughed out of the symposium. The contents of your mind were by definition conscious: if you wanted to know what was going on inside your head, all you had to do was look inside with your 'inner eye'.

Even by the 18th century, philosophers such as David Hume and John Locke regarded all mental events – thinking, knowing and feeling – as taking place on the playing field of awareness. As Locke wrote: 'to imprint anything on the mind, without the mind's perceiving it, seems to me hardly intelligible'. Minds were transparent – although you could only know for certain what was going on inside your own.

Towards the unconscious

So what brought us to a belief in the unconscious, and the acknowledgment that our lives are ruled by motivations of which we are unaware? The first steps were taken by the Austrian physician, Franz Anton Mesmer. Experimenting with hypnotism in Paris at the end of the 18th century, Mesmer showed that unconscious thoughts could exert an effect on the body, producing paralysis or insensibility to pain. His work was taken up by French neurologist Jean Martin Charcot, who used hypnosis to induce and study hysteria – a medical condition often involving a mixture of psychological and physical symptoms such as blindness, paralysis and amnesia. Charcot was assisted in these studies by Sigmund Freud, then a brilliant medical student. Together with his mentor, Freud elaborated the theory that the symptoms of hysteria were a disguised means of keeping emotionally charged memories under mental lock and key in the unconscious mind. This led to his development of the technique of psychoanalysis to gain access to the unconscious and effect 'cures'. Freud's theory that unconscious thoughts were responsible for much of human behaviour caused an outrage. Apart from the appalling

> **"Man cannot persist long in a conscious state; he must throw himself back into the Unconscious, for his roots live there."**
>
> Goethe, writer and philosopher (1749–1832)

PIONEERS   *FRANZ ANTON MESMER*

Austrian physician Franz Anton Mesmer (1734–1815) took Paris by storm in the 1780s with his demonstrations of 'magnetic influence'. Mesmer (far left) believed that he could cure diseases using his hands to channel 'animal magnetism', a force he thought related to physical magnetism. Mesmer often gave dramatic public performances of this strange art. The magnetic theory proved to be false – Mesmer in fact was hypnotising his patients by looking, talking and touching.

notion that respectable members of society were all being driven by unthinkable sexual desires, where did that leave notions of free will and responsibility? Nevertheless, Freud's ideas became increasingly accepted and remain highly influential. As post-Freudians, we are all happy to talk about unconscious motives, and ideas like repression and denial have entered the popular vocabulary. In a way, Freud's work has made psychologists of us all.

Modern times

Since Freud's time, scientists have moved away from Freud's model of the unconscious – a potent broth of traumatic memories and repression that only the psychoanalyst could clarify. Today, the more that scientists study the unconscious, the more remarkable it seems. Over the last 40 years, experimental psychologists have found that people constantly engage in all sorts of mental activity that is not simply repressed but is totally beyond the scope of consciousness. All sorts of highly sophisticated mental activities – searching memory, solving problems, making inferences – are carried out at an unconscious level. As the capabilities of the unconscious mind become ever more evident, some researchers have even begun to wonder whether we need consciousness at all.

FACT FILE

WORDS TO DESCRIBE THE UNCONSCIOUS

Different words are used to refer to mental experiences outside consciousness.

• 'Preconscious' and 'subliminal' refer to experiences just below the threshold of consciousness.

• 'Unconscious' and 'subconscious' often indicate a more profound inaccessibility.

• Psychologists also refer to 'implicit' (in contrast with 'explicit') knowledge – that is, knowledge we have without being able to state it.

THE ROBOT WITHIN

When today's psychologists talk about the unconscious, they don't mean the independent force that Freud imagined. Rather, the unconscious is seen more as a network of automatons, each of which controls an aspect of behaviour.

Imagine that you are walking through a wood that you know to be full of venomous snakes. Suddenly you jump backwards. As you are in the air, you become dimly aware of something long, thin and brown that was in your path; you have just avoided treading on a snake. Yet when you started your jump, you weren't aware of anything dangerous at all.

This is an example of an unconscious response initiated not by the cortex – the thinking, judging part of the brain – but by an autonomous processing unit, a subsystem that produces automatic reactions. Your ears detect a signal of danger (the rustling of the snake in the grass), and a signal is sent via the brain's auditory system directly to the amygdala, a structure that controls fear response. Because it bypasses the cortex, the 'danger' signal causes you to move that much faster, gaining you vital milliseconds that may save your life.

FACT: Olympic sprinters leave the starting block one-tenth of a second after the pistol has fired. They don't hear it consciously because it takes about twice as long to become conscious of sensory stimuli.

Unconscious helpers

Countless other subsystems exist in the brain. Moment by moment, this army of unconscious helpers

Automatic skills It takes time and a lot of practice to master complex skills such as touch-typing, but they eventually become automated processes controlled by the unconscious brain.

handles all sorts of complicated processing of which we are not aware. They control blood pressure, build our three-dimensional images of the world from the two-dimensional information coming from the retina, and effortlessly produce grammatical sentences. When we learn a new physical skill – like typing or playing the piano – we are actually training subsystems to carry out sets of complex functions automatically. And even tasks that many people imagine depend on awareness – such as an understanding of speech – are in fact carried out by these unconscious helpers. Each one of the separate processing units is, in the words of one researcher, a 'mindless simpleton' because it can do only one thing – but it does that thing very well and reports its actions back to the central executive of consciousness. So rather than consciousness being seen as the boss, controlling the mind like a general, it looks increasingly like the figurehead of a large organisation – or perhaps a government minister who is backed up by an army of invisible civil servants.

THINK AGAIN!   SPACE GAMES AND REFLEX SKILLS

Experiments carried out on board the space shuttle *Columbia* in 1998 demonstrate how hard it is to override unconscious processing with conscious thought. Astronauts on the shuttle threw balls to one another and attempted to catch them – a straightforward task back on Earth, but not so easy in low-gravity conditions where balls move far more slowly. Even though the astronauts could clearly see the balls drifting toward them, their hands moved far faster than they needed to in anticipation of a ball's trajectory – they were in the right place long before the ball reached them.

The explanation for this is that ball-catching is under the control of unconscious modules in the brain, and these modules have been 'programmed' under conditions of normal gravity. Used inappropriately in the low-gravity environment on board

the shuttle, they cause errors in the judgement of motion.

The experiments also tell us something surprising about the abilities of top cricket and tennis players. The popular view is that good ball players have extra-fast reflexes that enable them to get the bat or racquet to a ball moving at well over 100mph. In fact, their reflexes are often average; what distinguishes a skilled sportsperson is the ability to delay the unconscious response for a fraction of a second. With more time for unconscious processing, the 'intuitive' reaction becomes that much more accurate.

Lunch on the go Astronaut Michael Baker chases a sandwich on the flight deck of shuttle *Atlantis*.

Blind vision

An astonishing demonstration of the abilities of our unconscious pathways comes from studies of a bizarre condition known as blindsight. Graham, a typical sufferer, is totally blind on the right side of his visual field as a result of an accident. Experimenters asked Graham what he could see on the right side; predictably, his reply was 'nothing'. Then the experimenters set up a projector screen in Graham's blind patch. Onto it they projected spots of light, shapes and words and asked Graham to guess what was out there. Remarkably, he could 'guess' with great accuracy. In fact, Graham could see, but he was not conscious of seeing because his vision was being processed by the unconscious helpers alone.

Equally amazing is the fact that the unconscious brain is often better than the conscious mind at interpreting data from our senses. The conscious mind is quite easily fooled by illusion: for example, flat paintings that use perspective often appear to have real depth. But the unconscious is much less likely to be taken in – perhaps because it is designed for fast evaluation and action. The Goodale illusion is a good example. This consists of two circular wooden counters, identical in size and shape, one surrounded by a cluster of smaller counters, the other by bigger ones. The conscious brain cannot help but see an illusion – the counter surrounded by the smaller chips always looks the bigger. But the unconscious robot pathway 'sees' them as identical: if someone is asked to pick up the central counters, careful measurement of the space between their fingers at the moment of contact reveals an identical gap.

The Goodale illusion Psychologist Mel Goodale has used this illusion to demonstrate how the unconscious brain can make better judgements than the conscious mind. Look at the circles in the centre of the two patterns below and try to judge whether the central circle in the left-hand pattern is bigger, smaller, or the same size as the one in the right-hand pattern.

Real lives THE ARTISTIC UNCONSCIOUS

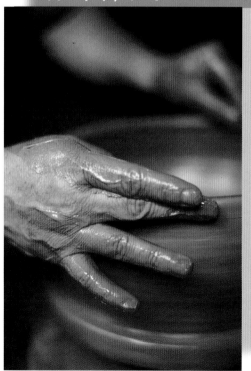

Artist Anthony deliberately 'switches off' his conscious mind when he works to allow his unconscious to take over.

'Several hours of my working week are spent drawing figures from life. There are good days, when every mark on the paper goes just where it should, and bad days when the simplest drawing seems laboured and clumsy. I put this down to being in or out of "the flow". One way I've found to help get into flow is to do the drawing blind – that is, to look at the model while I work, instead of looking at what my hand is doing. When I do this, I usually find the drawing improves.

'Also, when I'm throwing a production run of pots, I need to start with clay pieces of a consistent size. I roll out a long cylinder of clay, then twist off a chunk for each bowl, weigh it, and add or subtract more until it is exactly right. Again, there are good days when I estimate the amount correctly each time, and bad days. Recently I tried turning my head away just at the moment I came to twist off the clay. The result was an immediate improvement. The pieces were within a gram or so of the target weight every time – accurate enough to go right ahead and use it without any adjustments.

'I've come to believe that this sort of instinctive perception plays a crucial role in areas that are often attributed to some mysterious "talent". In fact, artistic talent may just be an ability to let my unconscious get on with the job.'

A new role for consciousness?

Another set of experiments, conducted in the 1960s by the Californian physiologist Benjamin Libet, underlines the extraordinary abilities of the unconscious and challenges our cherished notion of free will.

Libet connected subjects to EEG monitors that recorded their brain waves, in particular one type of electrical pulse known as a 'readiness potential', which signals that the brain is preparing to make a consciously willed movement. The subjects were asked to watch a dot move clockwise on a screen. Libet would then ask them to lift a finger whenever they felt the urge and to note where the dot was at that moment. Remarkably, the EEG readings showed that the readiness potential appeared about half a second before subjects said that they had 'decided' to move. In other words, some combination of the unconscious modules was preparing for a move before the subjects had consciously decided to move.

If the unconscious can do all these things – if it can see, hear and take decisions before we are even aware of them, if it can process language and trigger emotional responses – then what exactly is the role, and indeed the point, of consciousness? In fact, the unconscious and conscious parts of our minds need one another and work in close partnership.

Consciousness – the executive

Brain scans reveal quite different patterns of mental activity when we think consciously about a task (for example, the first time we try to play the piano) and when our unconscious 'simpletons' handle a task unaided (when we can play the piano fluently). When we think consciously, big areas of the brain 'light up' on the scans, as we mobilise our mental resources to deal with an unfamiliar situation. Unconscious activity, in contrast, produces a much fainter trace on a brain scan. So consciousness takes charge of novelty, while commonplace processing takes place unconsciously.

Consciousness also has a crucial 'executive' function in the mind: we have only one body and so consciousness must decide between conflicting unconscious instructions about where to move the legs or turn the head, for example. Consciousness has power of veto over the unconscious – free won't rather than free will – so we are not just slaves to the robot within.

FOCUS ON   UNCONSCIOUS ACCURACY

Consciousness personalises our world. Our conscious perceptions are determined by our beliefs, interests, fears and preoccupations, as well as by what is 'out there'. In contrast, the kind of unconscious processing that we use to make physical (rather than verbal) judgments are less subject to these idiosyncratic influences, and consequently these judgments are often the more reliable.

This effect becomes obvious when people are asked, for example, to estimate the steepness of a hill. Asked for a verbal judgment, almost everyone overestimates the gradient, although younger and fitter people will think the slope is less steep than older or unfit people. But when people are asked simply to tilt their hand to match the slope of the hill, they do so with considerably greater accuracy.

UNCONSCIOUS THINKING

Everything we think and say is informed by unconscious processing. Our emotional reactions, beliefs, opinions – even our most carefully deliberated decisions – are determined to a large extent by mental processes outside our conscious awareness.

FACT: In court cases, 'good-looking' people are assumed to be innocent more often than average.

Conscious perceptions are a bit like takeaway meals. By the time we get them they have been processed, packaged, transported and presented for consumption by a chain of invisible workers. Their original ingredients may no longer even be recognisable.

The 'workers' that produce the contents of consciousness are specialised brain modules that process raw information arriving at our sense organs into sights, sounds, feelings, thoughts, decisions and beliefs. Only some of this processing reaches consciousness, with the vast majority remaining unconscious. This unconscious processing is vitally important, constantly directing our actions by moulding our conscious decisions, or, sometimes, by overriding them.

The chemical unconscious

Consider, for example, what happens when you notice someone looking at you in a restaurant or when queuing for a bus. As soon as you make eye contact, the amount of the neurotransmitter dopamine (sometimes called the brain's pleasure chemical) in your brain is affected. Typically dopamine levels rise if the stranger's face is attractive (symmetrical, young and smiling) and fall if it is unattractive (asymmetrical, aged and frowning). Significantly, this reaction occurs before you have

Real lives

A LIFE IN FREEZE FRAME

Unconscious processing units in the brain control many very specific aspects of everyday actions. When they go wrong, the results can be quite strange.

June can see perfectly well. She can perceive colour and shape, and she has no trouble recognising objects. But a crucial element of her visual world is missing – she has no sense of movement. Everyday scenes appear as if illuminated by strobe lighting – as a sequence of still frames with the intervening bits blotted out. June has difficulty in pouring tea or coffee into a cup because the fluid does not seem to flow, but appears to be frozen. What's more, she

cannot stop pouring at the correct time because she can't see the liquid moving up in the cup. She also finds it hard to follow a conversation because she cannot see other people's faces moving. And being in a room with people walking around is unsettling: they seem to appear suddenly in different places. June cannot cross a street because she is unable to judge the speed of approaching cars: 'When I'm looking at the car first, it seems far away', says June. 'But then, when I want to cross the road, suddenly the car is very near.' June has learned to 'estimate' the distance of moving vehicles from their sound, but her world remains a bizarrely disjointed place.

consciously registered the face, so by the time the image does arrive in consciousness, your unconscious mind has already 'approved' or 'disapproved' of the face. With no way of knowing what is happening to your dopamine levels, you naturally suppose that your first assessment of the person is based on rational deliberation.

It is not hard to see how such unconscious processing feeds into behaviour. For example, candidates for jobs are likely to fare better at interview if they are attractive rather than unattractive; interviewers do not consciously judge by looks, they just know that one candidate makes them feel hopeful and the other disappointed.

Patterns of influence

Every idea, attitude and emotion that we hold in mind is encoded in the patterns of neural firing in our brains. Some of these ideas can be dragged out into consciousness, where they can be moulded and modified by reflection, thought and experience. But others – like the dopamine effect described above – are permanently hidden in the back rooms of the brain and only manifest themselves by their effect on behaviour.

When these patterns are inactive they are 'out of mind' and do not influence our actions. But many patterns fire away at a low rate – not enough to become part of consciousness, but enough to feed into the unconscious information processing that precedes consciousness. These habitual thought processes form a background template of ideas, beliefs and prejudices through which all new information is filtered.

These background, unconscious thought patterns include many of the fixed ideas that we have about the physical world. A good example is the idea of 'object permanence'. We all know that objects do not cease to exist simply because they are hidden from view. This assumption develops in all human infants at the age of about eight months – long before they have enough experience to have arrived at it by deduction. Similarly, we all tend to assign intentions to moving inanimate objects: an observer who sees a small ball rolling along followed by a larger ball will invariably

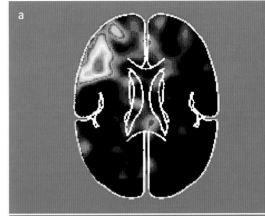

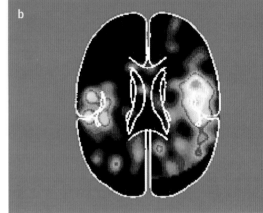

Practice and the brain Different brain areas are used when we are new to a task and need consciously to focus on it, compared to when we are practised at it when less conscious areas take over. Here, a verbal task requiring rapid, conscious thought (a) shows high activity in the left prefrontal cortex. After some practice (b), a less 'conscious' area in the right cortex becomes more active during the task.

THINK AGAIN!   **PROCESSING MEANING**

It's tempting to think that the unconscious modules that process information lack the sophistication of the conscious mind. But studies suggest it is the conscious mind that sometimes makes the clumsier distinctions.

In one experiment, people were shown a sentence with a word missing. It read: 'She looked very (blank) in her new coat'. The subjects wore headphones through which experimenters could relay spoken words. Half of the subjects were played the word 'snug' at normal volume; half were played the same word subliminally – that is, so quietly that

subjects were not conscious of hearing it. The subjects were then asked to 'fill in' the gap, choosing between the words 'smug' and 'cosy'.

The experimenters found that those who could clearly hear the word 'snug' were more likely to choose 'smug', but those who could hear it only subliminally preferred 'cosy'. This means that the conscious mind was being directed more by the sound of the word, while the unconscious concentrated on meaning – an aspect that seems more sophisticated and more useful than mere sound.

UNCONSCIOUS READING

Using a stop watch, time how long it takes you to go through this list, identifying the colour of each 'word'. Say the colour aloud before moving on to the next 'word'.

xxx hhhh ssss
mmmm **hhh**
mmmm ssss
uuuu sss **bbb**
wwww

Now try the same for the following:

green blue
yellow green
red blue red
green yellow
red **blue**

The time taken to read the second list is significantly longer than for the first. The reason is that, when you see a familiar word, like the word 'green' at the top of the second list, your brain starts processing its meaning, even if you try to ignore it. This style of processing conflicts with the ideas – of colour – that you are trying to bring into consciousness. This exercise demonstrates the power of unconscious processing: the brain's language modules cannot help but interpret the meanings of the words, no matter how hard we try to override their influence.

interpret the scene as the large ball 'chasing' the smaller one. And the larger the object, the more 'intentional' it will be perceived to be.

These deep-rooted ideas probably evolved because they were of great survival value to our ancestors: any animal that assumes an object is still present when it is hidden is exercising caution – and is less likely to be eaten by a predator that hides behind a bush. Similarly, it is safer to assume that moving objects have motives – a fast-approaching blur may be a wind-blown branch, but it may also be a vicious animal.

But these quick and easy evaluations are not always useful in a sophisticated environment. The 'folk physics' wired into the brain makes it easy for magicians to fool people, and means that we find it difficult to grasp scientific concepts that conflict with our intuitions. And rules of thumb that were once useful when we lived in small tribes and depended on physical strength for survival are now potentially damaging. For example, the idea that people whom we resemble physically are more likely to be friendly now forms the basis of social pathologies, such as racism and elitist prejudices.

Learning from experience

Many of the things we learn are held in our minds unconsciously. People can be 'primed' to react to something in a particular way by exposing them to an influential stimulus for such a short time that they do not register it consciously – that is, it is presented subliminally. In one laboratory experiment, researchers divided volunteers into two groups. An image was then flashed up in front of the volunteers so quickly – for about 150 milliseconds – that they were not even aware of seeing it. One group was shown an image of a leaf and the other an image of a cup. The two groups were then shown the word 'tea' and asked to add a second word. Most of the group that had been exposed to the image of the leaf wrote 'tea leaf', while most of those who had been shown the cup wrote 'tea cup'. Yet when asked, none of the volunteers were aware that their choice of words had been influenced by a visual image.

Many of our behavioural tendencies are primed by past experience. If a child is bitten by a dog, for example, she is likely to think 'danger' whenever she sees a dog later in life, even if the original incident is long-forgotten and buried in the unconscious. She is also likely to rationalise her fear of dogs – explaining to herself that 'all dogs are vicious and unpredictable' – because her brain seeks an explanation for her irrational fear. Such 'post-rationalisation' of behaviour has been demonstrated by many psychologists. In one experiment, researchers invited women to choose between two pairs of stockings, which, unknown to the subjects, were identical. Nearly all the subjects chose the pair which was presented to their right. This was predictable, because previous studies had already shown that people favour that side in all sorts of ways. But when asked why they had picked that product, the subjects did not mention its placement. Instead they claimed to have detected some superiority of quality such as feel, texture, or colour … imaginary differences that gave spurious reason to what was an entirely unconscious choice.

Another vital unconscious influence on our behaviour is known as implicit learning. We can learn to do something – even something complex, such as playing the piano to an expert level – without consciously knowing or being able to say what we have learned. This also applies to non-physical skills: when we use language – speaking, listening or reading – much of the mental work is in fact carried out at an unconscious level. You can see this when you find yourself unable to describe the complex grammatical reasons behind your choice of a word (such as 'I' or 'me') in conversation, even though your unconscious mind has correctly selected this word in a fraction of a second.

In a laboratory experiment, UK psychologists Diane Berry and Donald Broadbent used a complex 'control task' to study implicit learning. In the task, a simulated factory had to be 'managed' to produce a specific level of output. Some people were given explicit information on the output-related variables, while others were simply left to learn through practice. Remarkably, the explicit information was found not to improve performance at all. At the end of the experiment, those in either group who had learned successfully to control the output were all unable to explain how they did it. This finding has clear consequences for how best to encourage learning: it seems that, even in areas that are more to do with judgment and decision-making, book-learned knowledge is no substitute for hands-on experience.

FOCUS ON

SUBLIMINAL ADVERTISING

In the late 1950s, when paranoia abut brainwashing was at its height, James Vicary, a marketing expert in New Jersey, USA, sparked controversy by experimenting with subliminal advertising in the cinema. Vicary claimed to have flashed the messages 'Eat popcorn' and 'Drink Coca-Cola' between the frames of a film showing at the time, too fast for the messages to be registered consciously. He also reported that this boosted sales of Coca-Cola by 58 per cent and of popcorn by 18 per cent.

Subsequent research failed to verify Vicary's claims, and there are suspicions that he invented his results to publicise his company. Nevertheless, subliminal advertising is now banned in the UK and many other countries.

Unconscious skills
Even when the conscious mind is fully engaged, such as when making decisions, we are in fact constantly tapping into 'implicit' knowledge that we have acquired without being able to express it.

SUGGESTIBILITY

Sometimes we think we have made up our own minds, when in fact they have been made up for us. None of us is immune to the influence of strong ideas forced upon us by other people, and much of our behaviour owes less to free will than it does to the will of others.

Humans are social animals. Many of our higher conscious functions – our ideals, beliefs, standards and even personalities – are products not only of our private experience and genetic make-up but of the influence of other people. Usually these influences are positive: in childhood, our beliefs are shaped by our family members and teachers, and later in life other people present us with new ideas that we can adopt or reject as we choose. But sometimes other people's ideas impinge on our conscious – or on our unconscious – minds with considerable persuasive effect. They change our attitudes and behaviour without our overt consent, as if we have surrendered up part of our consciousness.

Social pressure

Experiments in the 1950s by psychologist Solomon Asch demonstrates how suggestions teamed with social pressure can overwhelm our own thinking. Asch presented groups of eight subjects with a card showing three lines of different length. He then asked the subjects to point out which line on the card best matched the length of a reference line on another card. The answer was obvious, but apart from one person in each group, all the group members were 'plants', briefed to give an incorrect answer. Startlingly, in 75 per cent of the experiments, the one 'innocent' member of the group went along with the others, denying the evidence from his or her own senses.

We are all suggestible in the sense that we yield, to some extent, to social norms. But human suggestibility is also open to deliberate abuse by people who want to persuade or control others – to change not only their behaviour but their

"Half the money spent on advertising is wasted. The problem is in finding out which half."

Lord Leverhulme, industrialist

LEVI STRAUSS OVERALLS

A NEW PAIR FREE IF THEY RIP

NOW! LEVI'S EXCLUSIVE PATENT CONCEALED NON SCRATCH copper RIVETS ON BACK POCKETS

THE RIVETS ARE STILL THERE

WON'T SCRATCH
• SADDLES
• AUTOMOBILES
• FURNITURE

PATRONIZE YOUR HOME TOWN MERCHANT
HE'S YOUR NEIGHBOR

LEVI'S® ENGINEERED JEANS™
TWISTED TO FIT

The power of advertising

Over the last century, there has been a gradual change in the persuasive tactics used to market a product. Earlier advertisements tended to be straightforwardly informative, describing the superior features of a product. Today's advertisements are often more suggestive, creating a desire for products by associating them with glamour and sexual appeal.

FOCUS ON   COERCIVE PERSUASION

Coercive persuasion techniques are well understood by psychologists, and depend on some or all of the following key factors:

1. Physical and emotional stress, especially deprivation of food, sleep and exercise. Social isolation (creating loneliness) is alternated with group sessions that introduce the new beliefs.

2. Simplistic explanations of 'personal problems', together with simplistic 'answers', for example: 'Your parents are giving you a hard time, so reject them completely and join our group.'

3. A leader who appears to offer love, care, acceptance and answers. Cults are typically run by charismatic leaders who demand loyalty and adoration.

4. Influence of other group members, providing praise, emotional support and other reinforcement. Pyramid selling schemes often involve 'introducers' who encourage individuals to join, and talk up their money-making prospects.

5. Some form of entrapment. Often this starts with small things, such as attending a meeting or donating some money. Later these may become more demanding, perhaps involving 'buying in' to a sales organisation or living permanently with a group.

6. Control of information and activities. For example, once a person has become a committed member of a cult, the group will typically dictate what is allowed and whom can be contacted.

underlying beliefs and feelings too. In its most extreme form, the abuse of human suggestibility is called 'brainwashing'. The term was first coined in the 1950s during the Korean War, when Chinese Communists subjected American prisoners of war to various forms of mental and physical torture in an attempt to change their political attitudes. The Koreans 'converted' 7000 POWs to take part in pro-communist broadcasts and other forms of collaboration. Their techniques included food and sleep deprivation, isolation, highly organised group activities, repetitive chanting and forced 'confessions'.

Gentler persuasion?

While brainwashing relies on the use of torture, imprisonment, repetitive music and even drugs, there are less physically aggressive forms of coercion that can be almost as powerful. The use of such techniques – known as 'coercive persuasion' – has been brought to prominence by cults, religious sects and pressure sales organisations over the last 40 years.

The coercive persuasion process typically occurs in steps over a period of weeks or months. Suggestibility expert Philip Zimbardo has found that, while some people are more susceptible to coercive tactics than others, we are all liable to be influenced by such techniques. Those who have succumbed can recover with the help of cognitive-behavioural therapists that can reverse the process. Ironically, the treatment may involve techniques similar to those used in the first place.

In a milder form, coercion is also the basis of everyday advertising. The central aim of advertising is to make you want something that you do not already have. Perhaps the most common technique is the association of the item with pleasant feelings — what psychologists call Pavlovian conditioning. For example, a car will be shown with attractive people in beautiful surroundings, accompanied by evocative music. Your previous satisfaction with your present vehicle and lifestyle may be replaced with a vague hankering for a sleeker new model.

Cult persuasion The 'Children of God' cult is believed to have used coercive persuasion techniques to recruit new members, targeting vulnerable young people and encouraging them to cut off contact with their families. Here, members of the cult sing together before a meal.

UNCONSCIOUS PROBLEM SOLVING

One of the most fascinating aspects of the unconscious mind is the way in which it can solve problems while the conscious mind is occupied with other matters. Many examples of unconscious problem solving come from everyday situations, but there are also well-documented cases where these processes have led to important scientific breakthroughs and artistic inspiration.

We are all familiar with the 'tip of the tongue' phenomenon. We can't remember a name despite thinking hard about it, but the name suddenly springs to mind later on when we are doing something else. Many of us also solve problems when we dream. Consider the following example: Clive moved house, but after unpacking couldn't find his watch anywhere. He kept looking, but without success. One night, he tried an experiment: he visualised the watch in all its detail before falling asleep. That night he had a dream in which he was wearing an old jacket. The next morning he went to his wardrobe and checked the jacket's pockets. Sure enough, the watch was there. His conscious efforts at remembering where the watch was had been fruitless, but his unconscious mind solved the problem for him.

Ring of dreams

Several famous scientists and inventors have solved problems through their dreams. Perhaps the best known case was German chemist Friedrich Kekulé, who attempted to elucidate the chemical structure of the benzene in the 1860s. Kekulé knew that benzene was an organic compound – that is, one made up of linked carbon atoms; he also knew its formula, but its structure – the way the atoms were linked together – remained an enigma. This is Kekulé's story, in his own words:

'I was sitting writing in my textbook, but the work did not progress; my thoughts were elsewhere. I turned my chair to the fire and dozed … the atoms were gambolling before my eyes … My mental eye, rendered more acute by repeated visions of the kind, could now distinguish larger structures of manifold conformation: long rows sometimes more closely fitted together all twining and twisting in snake-like motion. But look! What was that? One of the snakes had seized hold of its own tail, and the form whirled mockingly before my eyes. As if by a flash of lightning I awoke; and this time also I spent the rest of the night in working out the consequences of the hypothesis.'

FAMOUS DREAMERS

It is not only scientists and inventors who have benefited from unconscious problem solving; many artists and musicians have been inspired by dreams too.

• Mendeleyev saw a complete layout of the chemicals in the Periodic Table in a dream.

• Herschel dreamed about the planet now known as Uranus in a dream, before he discovered it.

• Edison, an inventor with more than 1000 patents to his name, sometimes slept at his workbench holding weights in his hands: when the weights fell, they would wake him and he would recall his dreams – often leading to new inventions.

• Salvador Dali produced many of his images from dreams. He used to deliberately deprive himself of sleep in order to induce dream-like states and visions that drew upon his unconscious mind.

• Beethoven, Wagner and Stravinsky all heard music – ranging from fragments to entire canons – in their dreams.

• Bob Dylan wrote songs based on what he heard in his dreams.

Inspired by his dream, Kekulé wondered whether the benzene molecule was ring-shaped – like the snake holding its own tail. When he tested out his idea, he found that it fitted all the known facts about benzene and its chemical nature; his discovery was an enormous step in the development of organic chemistry.

Medical inspiration

Dream inspiration also played a significant part in research in the 1920s on the role of insulin in the human body. The Canadian physician Frederick Banting literally dreamed up the experimental technique that led him to establish the relationship between sugar and insulin. Even more remarkably, another dream led him to the idea that insulin extracted from animals could be used to treat human diabetes. Banting was awarded a Nobel Prize in 1923 for his life-saving achievements in medicine.

Another instance of unconscious problem solving led to a technological breakthrough at the laboratories of industrial giant DuPont. A researcher, Floyd Ragsdale, was developing machines to manufacture Kevlar fibre, used in bullet-proof vests. The equipment then used was unreliable and costly. Ragsdale had a dream about springs inserted into the tubes of the existing machines. He reported this to his boss, who was sceptical about the idea. Nevertheless, Ragsdale persisted and inserted springs into the tubes; the resulting equipment worked much better, and saved his company more than $3 million.

Dreams don't always provide the right answer first time. German physiologist Otto Loewi dreamed about an experiment with frogs that seemed to tell him that nervous impulses had a chemical rather than electrical basis. He awoke in the middle of the night and noted down his idea, but when he read it the next morning it made no sense. Fortunately, the next night the dream recurred; this time, he woke and went straight to the laboratory. The insight helped lead Loewi to the Nobel Prize for Medicine in 1936.

> "Let us learn to dream, gentlemen, then perhaps we shall find the truth. But let us beware of publishing our dreams till they have been tested by the waking understanding."
>
> Friedrich Kekulé, 19th-century chemist

Elias Howe

A new way to sew The development of the automatic sewing machine owes much to a dream had by American inventor Elias Howe (1819–1867). An ordinary sewing needle has its hole at the opposite end to the point, but Howe could not make this work when trying to automate the process. Then one night he dreamed about a tribe who threatened him with spears that had a loop just behind the spear head. He then saw the breakthrough of putting the hole near the tip of the needle.

Hidden abilities

One out of every two hundred people with autism have remarkable abilities. They can perform marvels of mental arithmetic or play accurately a tune they have heard only once. What is more, their abilities can help us to understand our own unconscious minds.

Charles is autistic. He has an IQ of around 58, and the reasoning skills of a four-year-old. He has severe problems dealing with other people, and needs to live in special accommodation. But he can do something few of the rest of us can do. Give him any date in this or the last century, and he can tell you on which day of the week it fell. Psychologist and autism expert Beate Hermelin recalls: 'When I first met Charles he was 13 years old and he immediately asked the date of my birthday. When I told him it was 7 August he said instantly, "That was on a Wednesday in 1940 and in 2004 it will be on a Wednesday again." I was stunned.'

Such 'savant abilities' are intriguing. How can they flourish in minds that otherwise seem so limited? Other autistic savants can accurately draw such complex buildings as London's St. Pancras Station from memory, or play a piece of music note-perfect after hearing it only once or twice. Because such remarkable skills stand out so dramatically, even scientists have tended to marvel at them and leave it at that. Explanations of how savants do it are usually in terms of memorising and constant practice. But it seems that something else is going on that may help us to understand our own minds better.

REMARKABLE ABILITIES

• Someone who is 70 years, 17 days and 12 hours old has been alive for 2,210,500,800 seconds. Peter, who is severely retarded, can work out such sums within half a minute.
• When autistic savant Paul was asked to play a 64-bar piece of music he had only heard twice, his version of the 798 notes was 92 per cent correct.
• The favourite activity of a pair of autistic savant twins, each with a mental age of nine, was to identify prime numbers of up to 20 digits long.

Unknown advantage In the 1988 film *Rainman* Dustin Hoffman plays an autistic savant whose gifts with numbers and playing cards included the ability to memorise phone books.

The unconscious in overdrive

Beate Hermelin suggests that autistic savants provide a glimpse of what happens when someone is totally governed by their unconscious abilities. Autistic savants are severely retarded but have one outstanding skill, which comes from one of the processing units in the unconscious brain working overtime. Hermelin argues that what autistic savants lack is a 'central executive' to pull their abilities together. This idea is backed up by recent research in Australia, which suggests that savants may have access to perceptual processing at a level of detail that, in most of us, is covered up by normal consciousness. Researcher Allan Snyder argues that normal consciousness is rather like the tip of an iceberg. Below the level of awareness are thousands of subsystems that process small units of information, which are in turn patched together to form a conscious perception. As the information is converted into conscious experience, our brains filter out a lot of unnecessary detail. The abilities of autistic savants may come about because their mode of information processing is not so overlaid by the 'higher' conceptual consciousness that most people bring to bear on their perceptions.

Meaning and consciousness

This focus on detail accounts for the problems that autistics encounter, as well as the talents of the savant minority. Typically, autistics have great difficulty seeing the wood for the trees. While the rest of us go for the 'gist' of things and can summarise the central points of something we have heard or seen, autistics concentrate on the details. The result is that they are often good at tasks that involve manipulating the parts of a whole, like the notes in a chord or the factors of large numbers.

A greater understanding of what is going on here comes from Hermelin's work with Christopher, who – although socially inept with a low IQ – knows 16 languages, including Finnish, Greek, Hindi and Welsh. His vocabulary is very impressive: in one test he learned 300 new words in Hebrew in five days after being shown them just once, but he falls down badly on grammar. 'His translations are usually word for word and he will often use English word-order when translating into other languages,' says Hermelin.

The significance of this is that, while we are all genetically programmed to learn grammar from a very early age, when we later learn a new language we have to learn the new grammatical rules consciously. Because Christopher's conscious thinking skills are so poor, he finds this almost impossible. Christopher's abilities are a good example of both the power of our unconscious processing abilities and their limitations. 'He doesn't use language to communicate or impart thoughts, like the rest of us,' says Hermelin. For Christopher, languages are simply a form of acquisition – a kind of linguistic stamp collecting. While the rest of us may lack Christopher's remarkable talents, our consciousness endows us with the precious ability to communicate with others.

"Numbers are friends to me. It doesn't mean the same to you, does it, 3844? For you it is just a 3 and an 8 and a 4 and a 4. But I say hi, 62 squared."

Wim Klein, autistic savant

DISCOVER YOUR HIDDEN THINKING POWERS

Conscious thinking is the surface layer of mind. Beneath it, the unconscious brain stores knowledge which, although it may not be consciously accessible, forms the source of our hunches and intuitions. 'Tuning in' to this knowledge involves circumventing the conscious mind and observing what emerges from the unconscious alone. Sometimes, of course, intuition should be overridden, because it is irrational and therefore can be misleading. It can also be counter-productive, urging us, for example, to flee from challenges. However, learning to interpret your inner voice can help you to sort useful intuitive guidance from beguiling nonsense.

TEST YOUR GUT FEELINGS

You may think that your feelings about future events are a good guide to how they are likely to turn out – but have you ever tested this? By checking the accuracy of your gut feelings, you can increase the value of the information they provide.

• Begin by noting any ordinarily inexplicable sensation, such as a shiver down your back, a 'lump' in the throat or butterflies in your stomach.

• Next, identify the emotion it signifies. Anticipation? Foreboding? Irritation? Try to match the sensation with a specific emotion.

• Work out what event the feeling relates to. This will be easy in some cases, but harder in others.

• Compare the outcome of the event to how you felt about it. If they match, be aware of that intuitive feeling when it next occurs, because it may accurately foretell your experiences. If they do not match, make a note of this. If the feeling recurs in relation to a similar event, you will know not to trust it.

TEASE OUT YOUR HIDDEN KNOWLEDGE

This is not a test of general knowledge or intelligence. Your unconscious mind knows how to decode the cryptic phrases on the right. The task is to let it come up with them. (Example: 4Q in a G means 4 quarts in a gallon.) See how many you can crack, then check the answers on page 475.

1) 7 W of the W
2) 26 L in the A
3) 24 H in a D
4) 12 S of the Z
5) 57 HV
6) 29 D in F in a LY
7) 2 BOTC
8) 10 GB (HOTW)
9) 9L of a C
10) 30 D has S

AVOIDING BAD DECISIONS

Intuition often causes people to make incorrect decisions because they unconsciously accept the way in which a choice is put to them. If this 'framing' is optimistic, they are more likely to accept whatever is being offered. In one study people presented with information framed in a positive way about a new medical drug were twice as likely to say they would take it as those receiving exactly the same information when this had been framed more negatively.

Whenever you are presented with information, to avoid being caught out unconsciously by the framing try turning it round to see if it can be presented in a different way. This is an occasion when the conscious mind should overrule its hidden partner.

GETTING IN THE FLOW

'Flow' is the brain state in which the unconscious mind gets on with the action while the conscious mind sits back and enjoys it. It is especially good for tasks that require integration of sensory skills with physical tasks, such as driving, dancing, painting or sculpting.

• Flow depends on losing awareness of the self, so harness yourself to the moment. If you fantasise about the future or recall the past, you will lose flow.

• Concentrate on what you are doing, not the way you do it. When practising a move in your favourite sport, imagine your limbs moving smoothly and accurately, but do not think about the movements you need to make.

• Relax. You can't work at achieving flow – it comes when you forget to try.

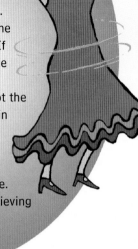

THE PILOT INSIDE

When you travel along a route, or around a town, much of the information you take in is laid down in a way that is not linked to words. If, later, you consciously try to remember the route you took, you might draw a blank.

This is because conscious memory tends to rely heavily on words for recall. However, if you simply head in the general direction of the place you are seeking, and go by 'feel', you might find that you get there without even trying.

RECOGNISING CONFLICT

Sometimes the conscious and unconscious minds give entirely conflicting guidance. When this happens, people often feel a sense of unease – the sense that perhaps something they are about to do is not quite right, or that what seems the 'obvious' choice could have a hidden catch. Once you learn to recognise the feeling of uncertainty that marks such conflicts of information, you can use it as a sign to pause, reflect, and – if possible – delay any decision until more information is available.

EYE TALK

Certain thoughts and feelings produce unconscious eye signals. For example, when a person is visualising something in their mind, their eyes will go up. You can use this knowledge to get on the same wavelength as the person you are talking to. It also gives you some idea of their train of thinking and whether they are tuning into what you are saying, or to their own inner thoughts.

Up and to the right or up and to the left
– visualising an imaginary scene or recalling a visual image. Staring straight ahead into the distance also indicates visualisation.

To the left side
– recalling speech

To the right and down
– feeling emotion

To the left and down
– internal dialogue

FREUD AND THE UNCONSCIOUS MIND

Freud did not invent the idea of the unconscious mind, but he certainly gave it substance and brought it to far wider attention. His work had a profound effect on society and there is no doubting his status as an intellectual giant of the 20th century. But what was it that led Freud to his revolutionary theories?

> "A dream not interpreted is like a letter unread."
>
> The Talmud

Freud's Vienna Freud founded his practice in Vienna in the 1880s. The Viennese bourgeoisie, from whom he drew most of his clients, were shocked by his insistence that sex lay at the root of neuroses.

Sigmund Freud was born in 1856 in the small town of Freiberg, Moravia, which today lies within the Czech Republic. His father, Jacob, was a wool merchant, and his mother, Amalia, was Jacob's second wife and nearly 20 years his junior. Freud grew up with seven younger siblings; he also had two half brothers, almost the same age as his own mother.

As a child, Freud was a voracious reader and was precociously intelligent: 'My Sigmund has more intelligence in his little toe than I have in my whole head,' said his father. Freud was driven to make his mark in the world not only by his innate intelligence but also by his status as a Jew attempting to forge a path into the European intellectual world. His early interest in science led him to medical school in Vienna, where he developed a passion for neurology and physiology, travelling to France to work with some of the foremost psychiatrists of the day.

Freud's early life provides some clues as to how he arrived at his theories of the mind. Freud's interest in family dynamics, which lies at the heart of his revolutionary ideas, was certainly triggered by observations of his own extended family. And his genius to connect diverse sources of information and so reveal hidden connections was strongly influenced by methods, including dream analysis, used in Judaism to interpret the scriptures.

Freud was initially fascinated by the use of hypnosis to treat hysteria and neurosis, and when he returned to Vienna from his studies with Charcot in Paris and Bernheim in Nancy, he opened a private practice in neuro-psychiatry with the help of his friend and collaborator, Josef Breuer.

Studies of hysteria

The seeds of Freud's understanding of the mind are seen in the case of 'Anna O', a woman treated by Breuer in the 1880s. Anna O presented a variety of hysterical symptoms, from minor headaches and lapses of con-centration to hallucinations and paralysis of neck muscles. At one point in her treatment she displayed a fear of water and would not drink from a glass for some six weeks. When encouraged by Breuer to enter a hypnotic state, she recalled an incident in which an acquaintance allowed her dog to drink from a glass, an event Anna found disgusting. Immediately on coming round from the hypnotic state, she was fully able to drink nor-mally. Evidently the memory of the dog episode had remained barred from normal consciousness, yet was responsible for her fear of drinking water. Merely recalling the memory was sufficient to let her overcome her fear. The 'talking cure' – psychoanalysis – was born.

Yet Freud felt there was something missing. Anna O's cure was piece-meal – there seemed more to her case than superficial symptoms, such as her inability to drink. Indeed, at the time that Breuer finished treating Anna, she began writhing with abdominal pain, displaying symptoms of a false pregnancy and declaring, 'Now comes Dr Breuer's child!' Freud sur-mised that Anna O's symptoms were caused by her sexual fantasies and frustrations, and this idea became the lynchpin of his later theories.

Real lives

THE CASE OF DORA

In 1900, an 18-year-old girl Freud referred to as 'Dora' was sent to him suffering from hysteria. Dora's father was having an affair with Frau K, a friend of the family. So that Frau K's husband would put up with this arrangement, Dora's father offered him Dora herself as a bribe. Dora told Freud of two occasions when Herr K had tried to collect on his end of the deal: both times, Dora rebuffed his advances.

In his analysis of Dora – and especially her dream images of a jewel box, which Freud equated with female genitalia – Freud postulated that Dora was unconsciously in love with her father, with Herr K and with Frau K. He read her disgust with Herr K's advances as a hysterical denial of her attraction. One of Dora's symptoms, a cough, was interpreted as an orgasm of the throat, associated with the desire to perform fellatio on her father.

Dora, however, rejected Freud's interpretations and ended the analysis after three months, whereupon Freud decided that she was revenging herself on him.

(F)OCUS ON   *FREUDIAN SLIPS*

We have all experienced unconscious errors like slips of the tongue, mental blocks, or an inability to put a name to a familiar face. And we all make mistakes – indeed, fallibility is part of the human condition. But according to Freud, any slip, no matter how slight, reveals deeper issues in the mind. In his book *The Psychopathology of Everyday Life* (1904), Freud explored these errors, which he called parapraxes. For example, one Viennese gentleman reported to Freud that he had dined with an acquaintance tête à bête (head to fool) instead of tête à tête (head to head). To Freud, this slip was a channel through which the gentleman's real feelings emerged – he clearly thought his acquaintance to be a fool.

FACT: More books have been written on Freud, his ideas and the changes in society brought about by his work than any other 20th-century figure.

FREUD AND RELIGION

Freud saw psychoanalysis as a substitute for the self-cleansing imperative of religion. He referred to religion dismissively as 'the universal obsessional neurosis of humanity' and considered its rituals to be akin to the acts of someone who has not come to terms with an unconscious block.

To Freud, people of religious faith demonstrated a primitive form of thinking in which everything becomes submitted before an all-knowing father figure. He believed that men who had not resolved their Oedipus complex (by accepting the authority of their real father), were more susceptible to the acceptance of a 'super-father' – by which he meant God.

Sex and development

Freud saw all human behaviour as being motivated by unconscious drives to seek out food, water and, principally, sex. The motivational energy for these instincts he called libido (from the Latin for 'I desire'). He asserted (much to the disgust of contemporary society) that children go through several distinct stages of sexual development, and that adult neuroses are linked to repressed memories of these stages.

Freud noted that different parts of our bodies are the focus of tactile and sexual pleasure at different times of life. From birth to about 18 months, the mouth is the focus; from 18 months to 3 years, it is the anus; from 3 to 6 years, it is the genitalia. Freud named these stages oral, anal, and phallic, and recognised that each one included difficult transitions that could become the root of anxieties in later life.

A boy in the phallic stage, for example, seeks an external object for his phallic sexual desire. The obvious choice is his own mother, but there is one big obstacle to his plans – a sexual rival in the form of his father. The boy becomes jealous of his father and wishes him dead, but he feels sure that his father knows about his hostility. He believes that his father hates him, and will punish him by cutting off his penis. The boy's hatred and fear of his father escalates, until eventually he gives up on his mother as an object of desire. He begins to identify with his father, knowing that if he becomes like him, he too will one day enjoy a similar sexual partnership. Freud called this whole process the Oedipus complex after the character in Greek myth who murders his father and marries his mother.

According to Freud, unacceptable or taboo thoughts, memories and wishes (mainly about childhood sexual desires) are repressed or forced out of consciousness, but remain lodged in the unconscious. External events can trigger this material to emerge once more, causing the subject to relive the original anxiety. The thoughts are once again pushed back into the unconscious, resulting in constant conflict at the unconscious level.

Freud's structure of the mind

For Freud, the conflict is played out between three distinct aspects of the personality or foci of the mind – the id, ego and superego. These were famously described in his book *The Ego and the Id* (1925). The id is the source of our instinctive gratification-seeking drives. The ego is our general sense of identity, the 'I', that interacts with the world. The super-ego is a type of conscience, an internal reproduction of authority figures, especially our parents. The ego seeks to balance the demands of the id and the super-ego, while maintaining a healthy orientation to the real world.

In addition to these three foci, the mind comprises three regions: the conscious, the preconscious, and the unconscious. The Freudian unconscious is distinct from the conscious mind because of its sexual content and its illogicality. The preconscious includes material of which we are not

THE REGIONS OF THE MIND

Freud believed that, like an iceberg, most of the mind is submerged and inaccessible. He identified three regions: the conscious, the preconscious (or subconscious) and the unconscious. The regions are separate from, but related to, Freud's three aspects of personality: the id, the ego and the superego.

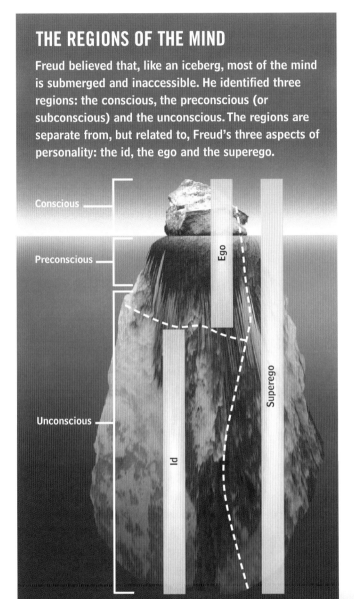

Conscious

Preconscious

Unconscious

Ego

Superego

Id

currently conscious, but that can enter consciousness with no limitations. Unconscious material is repressed – that is, it is actively barred from consciousness, and hence the ego may experience such material only in disguised form.

The talking cure

Perhaps the most important of Freud's assertions was that everything we think, say or do is driven by the unconscious; nothing occurs by chance. Psychoanalysis is a therapy that helps to uncover the hidden causes of our conscious thoughts and behaviour and so allows us to deal with the problems associated with repression. Its goal – according to Freud – is to make the unconscious become conscious. For example, when Anna O recalled the repressed memory of a dog drinking from a glass, it unblocked her own resistance to drinking.

Initially, Freud used hypnosis to examine his patients' unconscious material, but he gradually abandoned the technique because he felt that hypnosis was incapable of penetrating to the deepest – the sexual – aspects of a problem. He favoured the technique of free association, in which the patient would lie in a relaxed position on the famous couch and say whatever came into his or her head. Freud would then analyse what the patient had remembered – paying particular attention to symbols and fragments of dreams, which he considered to be 'the royal road to the unconscious'. The analyst – and only the analyst – could then determine what events in the patient's past had caused his or her current suffering.

Freud in London Freud left Vienna in 1938, following the occupation of the city by the Nazi regime. He and his youngest daughter Anna (an influential psychoanalyst in her own right) sought refuge in London. Freud was already in poor health and he died there in the following year.

Jung and the collective unconscious

Where Freud was the arch-detective of the unconscious, Carl Jung became its high priest. Influenced by myth and religion more than by scientific method, Carl Jung's influential ideas represent the farther reaches of psychology, at the boundary with mysticism.

The art of interpreting the unconscious reached new levels of sophistication in the work of Freud's one-time disciple, Carl Gustav Jung (1875–1961). Born in Switzerland, Jung studied medicine, specialising in the new discipline of psychiatry, and worked with psychotic patients in a mental hospital. Jung listened to his patients, trying to learn from their mental illness, and on reading Freud's great work, *The Interpretation of Dreams,* he recognised a kindred spirit – someone who tried to make sense of the irrational. The two met in 1907 and soon became great friends and intellectual collaborators.

At first, Jung agreed with Freud's theories on the unconscious, but soon he began to question his mentor's opinion that everything could be reduced to the sexual. Jung sought a broader context for the fundamental energy of the psyche, which eventually led him to value the spiritual quest as the primary means to psychic wholeness and general well-being.

To Freud, this was a heresy. Freud considered himself a scientist and even believed that his theories about the unconscious would be eventually substantiated by neurology. He could not countenance Jung's excursion into superstition, religion and spirituality, and the two great psychiatrists argued and became bitterly estranged.

> **"I have known, perhaps, an unusual number of those the world considered to be great, but Carl Gustav Jung is almost the only one of whose greatness I am certain."**
>
> Laurens van der Post

The structure of the unconscious

To Jung, the unconscious had two regions. One, the personal unconscious, was similar to Freud's notion – it was the storehouse of our repressed memories. The second was the collective unconscious, and this was Jung's own idea. This, he believed, contained the collective experience of all humanity – the instinctive behaviours, thoughts and fears inherited from our distant ancestors.

Jung's idea of the collective unconscious came from studying his patients' dreams and the widespread myths and traditions of humankind. He came to believe that certain key themes arose repeatedly in groups so diverse they could not have had direct contact. The ideas must therefore have arisen from some source to which all humans have access – a collective unconscious. One of his

Jung at his desk in 1952 Jung rejected Freud's view that dreams present our disguised sexual wishes, holding instead that they convey messages about what is lacking in our conscious lives.

The Mandala The essential structure of the mandala is a circle surrounding a square with a clearly demarcated centre. To Jung this symbolised the fourfold essence of the self (thinking, feeling, sensing and intuiting) in total balance. The most beautiful mandalas are ornate Tibetan forms that are used to aid meditation. The meditator identifies with the successive layers of the mandala from the outermost, said to represent the fire of mental activity, to the innermost, where the calm and wisdom of true being is found.

FACT: Jung coined the terms 'extravert' and 'introvert' — not to mean 'lively' and 'shy', as we use them today, but to indicate a person's orientation, either mainly to the outside world (extravert) or to the inner world (introvert).

SYNCHRONICITY

Jung led an extraordinary life of visions and seemingly telepathic experiences. In 1913, he had a vision of Europe being covered by a flood, the waters turning gradually to blood. Later, he interpreted this as a premonition of war.

Such events led Jung to argue that events may be connected via a non-causal principle he termed synchronicity. Jung further believed that there was meaning underlying synchronistic events (or coincidences), and understanding this meaning could provide a way to access the unconscious. Accordingly, he became fascinated by divination, astrology and similar practices, which he felt could yield insights into his patients' inner minds.

patients, for example, dreamed of an erect phallus attached to the sun, where in the dream the wind arises. Jung found a similar idea in an ancient Mithraic liturgy, of which the patient could not have had any conscious knowledge.

Archetypes and individuation

Jung's notion of the collective unconscious comprised the archetypes — primary forms that direct the flow of images in the mind (rather like a magnet below a sheet controls an arrangement of iron filings on the surface). Jung maintained that the greatest challenge in our lives is to integrate the ideas welling up from the collective unconscious into our conscious lives. This process, which Jung called individuation, was for him a journey through which we encounter the archetypes. First, the 'shadow' archetype — aspects of ourselves that we unconsciously loathe or fear — must be recognised; second, in a man, the female aspects of the mind (the anima) must be integrated. As the journey continues, the individual encounters the deepest roots of human experience via the archetypes.

Jung also viewed symbols as access points for the archetypes. He considered a whole class of symbols to be 'unitive' — that is, expressing the urge of the psyche to unite opposites, especially its own conscious and unconscious realms. Jung regarded the mandala, which features prominently in Buddhist and Hindu traditions, as the most potent unitive symbol and as representing the self.

Jung's view of individuation was influenced by his study of the medieval practice of alchemy. Jung saw the alchemists' dream of turning base metals to gold as symbolising the quest to bring to fruition the true nature of our personality — the self, our inner gold.

THE PSYCHOANALYTIC LEGACY

Although psychologists now think that Sigmund Freud was wrong about many things, there is no denying that he had a huge influence on Western culture, as have many psychoanalysts who followed him. Without Freud, we might still be living in the buttoned-up world of Victorian values.

"Like an Old Testament prophet, Freud undertook to overthrow false gods, to rip the veils away from a mass of dishonesties and hypocrisies, mercilessly exposing the rottenness of the contemporary psyche."

Carl Jung

Over the past twenty years, scientific psychology has established beyond doubt the key importance of the brain's unconscious processing. We know that conscious experience rests on a base of unconscious processes in perception, memory and emotion. But today's ideas are a long way from Freud. In the words of neuropsychologist John Kihlstrom, Freud's model of the unconscious was 'hot and wet; it seethed with lust and anger; it was hallucinatory, primitive and irrational'. None of these characteristics is evident in the unconscious of scientific psychology today.

Evaluating Freud

Should we, then, cast Freud into the waste-bin? Are his ideas hopelessly outdated? Many have dismissed his work on the grounds that his methods were suspect, his hypotheses were vague and untestable, and he was notoriously selective in what he chose to include in his published work. But Freud deserves a more subtle evaluation; he gave us a way of viewing ourselves that goes beyond consideration of verifiable facts. Freud was a key figure in changing society, and we probably would not want to turn the clock back to the pre-Freudian world of Victorian propriety. He opened the way to us being more conscious of ourselves and exploring our own

FOCUS ON   D.H. LAWRENCE AND THE PSYCHOANALYSTS

Love and sex are the powerful recurring themes in Lawrence's work. In his famous semi-autobiographical novel, *Sons and Lovers*, an almost erotic bond develops between the central character, Paul Morel, and his mother, evoking the Freudian idea of the Oedipus complex.

However, in many ways, Lawrence's understanding of human consciousness was closer to Jung's view than to that of Freud. Like Jung, Lawrence emphasised the joining of opposites in order to realise a higher inner nature. Such a union, he believed, could be achieved through sex. 'Sex is our deepest form of consciousness,' wrote Lawrence. 'It is utterly non-ideal, non-mental. It is pure blood-consciousness.'

By setting these ideas within the lives of powerful, believable characters in his fiction, Lawrence vitalised them as much as, if not more than, any of the analysts.

minds. Without Freud, it is unlikely that the concept of openness, so central to psychotherapy, would have taken such root in our culture.

Freud was also factually correct in regarding the unconscious as much more extensive than consciousness. His view that unconscious mental activity deals with multiple meanings of words or images is quite consistent with modern experimental findings. Indeed, psychologists agree that what differentiates unconscious from conscious activity is the ability of the former to operate in parallel mode, rather than in a serial fashion.

So where was Freud wrong? In a word – sex. There is, for example, no good evidence for the existence of anything remotely like the Oedipus complex (see page 392). Moreover, feminists have correctly argued that his theories are hopelessly male-orientated. Freud's supposed female equivalent of the Oedipus complex – the Electra complex – is poorly thought out and, again, lacking any reasonable evidence. All one can say in Freud's defence is that he so shocked society that he forced a change towards a more liberal stance in which sexual matters could at least be aired.

Evaluating Jung

Jung too exerted a powerful influence on society, especially in the area of religion. Jung felt that the religion of his day had become sterile and largely divorced from people's real experience. Through his concept of individuation, he revitalised what it means to embark on a spiritual journey, but at the cost of 'psychologising' religion. For Jung, God could be understood only as a reality of the psyche – the god within. This is hardly the traditional God that inspires the devotions of the faithful, and some have therefore criticised Jung for creating a self-centred form of religion – religion for the 'me-generation'.

Like Freud, Jung's claims to the scientific validity of his theories are also doubtful, and there is little evidence to back up many of his ideas. For example, the existence of a collective unconscious is claimed from the uniformity of most people's experience with hallucinogenic drugs. Medicine men from a tribe in South America use hallucinogenic plants to enter a visionary world in which they encounter powerful animals, especially snakes and birds of prey. When the drug is given to Westerners with no knowledge of the tribe's customs and expectations, they may experience similar animal hallucinations – evidence, say Jungian researchers, that the images spring from a collective source. Evidence like this is at best equivocal, and hardly a sufficient basis for the theory it is said to support.

Common symbols Cave art from prehistory to recent times shows striking similarities, whether from Europe, Asia or, as this image, from Australia. This lends support to Jung's idea that certain symbols are common to all humanity.

THINK AGAIN!

ARCHETYPAL POPSTARS

The Beatles were loved for their music. But perhaps – just perhaps – their appeal also drew on the archetypes of Jungian theory. Some Jungians maintain that The Beatles represented four archetypes – the philosopher-king, the eternal youth, the mystic and the trickster. By this theory, the Beatles tapped the collective unconscious, releasing its energy to creative effect and empowering us through our own psyches. Or maybe they just wrote good tunes!

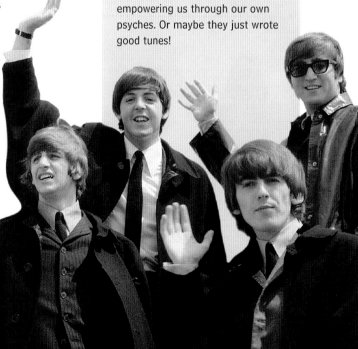

FOCUS ON

HOLLYWOOD AND THE UNCONSCIOUS

In 1957, America was gripped by the case of Ed Gein, a farmer who had murdered some twenty women. Gein dragged their dead bodies home to keep his mother company – his dead mother, that is, whose body he had propped up in a chair in the farmhouse so that he could talk to her. The story inspired Alfred Hitchcock to create *Psycho.* The director also knew his Freud and placed emphasis on the Oedipal aspect of the son–mother relationship. Hitchcock drew on Freud again for the dream sequence in *Spellbound,* which was designed with Salvador Dali's help.

George Lucas in 1977 began the blockbuster *Star Wars* series, shaping characters by Jungian archetypes. For the hero Luke, the shadow archetype is represented by Darth Vader. The fact that he is Luke's father adds an extra emphasis to Luke's battle to overcome his shadow. Princess Leia is an anima figure (the female aspect), and the integration of this archetype occurs when Luke realises that she is his twin sister. And the wise old man archetype is portrayed by Yoda, the Jedi master.

Cultural catalyst

Freud's most important work, *The Interpretation of Dreams,* was published in 1900, the same year that a crucial paper appeared by the physicist Max Planck, which in turn led Einstein to develop his theories. The word 'relativity' could be said to capture the essence of the early 20th century. Freud should be credited with the important role he played in ushering in the new perspective, which allowed ideas of absolute, God-given morality to be challenged, and the rigid roles occupied by men and women in society to be displaced. Although moves in these directions preceded Freud, his view of the mind encouraged their growth.

Freudian ideas fell on ground already prepared, which is why they spread like wildfire in the early years of the new century. Artists and writers were strongly influenced by Freud and the 'discovery' of the unconscious. In his 1924 *Surrealist Manifesto,* André Breton praised him for shining a light into what Breton regarded as the most important part of the mind, the unconscious. Surrealism rejected the logic and rationalism of the conscious, preferring to explore the irrational world legitimised by Freud. Freud himself was sceptical of the surrealist movement but was impressed by Salvador Dali, whose technical mastery he respected. There is no mistaking the Freudian ideas of dream work in Dali's pictures, with their distortion of images, condensation of ideas and blurring of meaning.

The idea of an unconscious hopelessly dominated by base and self-centred needs appears in many literary works of a similar time. Joseph Conrad's *Heart of Darkness* aligns the disturbing colonial world in the African Congo with the evil and corrupting unconscious of man, showing not so much the direct influence of Freud as the effect of his ideas filtering through the cultural world. And D.H. Lawrence drew more explicitly on psychoanalytic ideas in his work; his classic novel *Sons and Lovers* explores the Oedipal attraction between son and mother.

Therapy after Freud

Despite Freud's great influence, his approach to therapy was considered too narrow by many of his followers. First Jung, then the Austrian psychologist Alfred Adler, felt that Freud's insistence on sexual theory was detrimental to analysis. Adler believed that the will to power was a central motive for our actions, and his therapy was directed to understanding how our feelings of inferiority could be overcome. The German-born psychoanalyst and social philosopher Erich Fromm emphasised the social origin of inner conflicts, and felt that understanding the way in which we establish relationships should be a central theme of therapy.

Similar ideas are found in the influential 'object relations' school, which stresses the importance of early relationships. Someone who experiences a problematic childhood, in which secure bonds to early carers are not well established, will suffer not only in their later interactions with other people but also in their involvement with 'objects' in their environment. To cite one example, they may be more likely to become entangled with drug

abuse because the object – the drug – is imbued with the character of a relationship: it is rewarding and damaging at the same time.

Over recent years, therapy and counselling have developed into a huge industry. Freud has been interpreted less rigidly, sometimes with only token adherence to his key notion that unconscious meanings developed in the past can exert critical effects on the present. And the image of the therapist as the sole wise interpreter of hidden motives has waned. In the influential client-centred therapy developed by American psychologist Carl Rogers, the therapist concentrates on creating an aura of trust, in which the 'client' can move towards solving his or her own problems. The therapist does not interrupt and rarely offers advice. While this move away from the authoritarian character of Freudian analysis is generally accepted as an improvement, perhaps a sense of plumbing the full depths of the mind has been lost along the way.

Surrealist influence The work of Salvador Dali, such as *The Metamorphosis of Narcissus* (1937), was strongly influenced by Freud's ideas of the unconscious mind.

PIONEERS   JACQUES LACAN – REINTERPRETING FREUD

The French psychoanalyst Jacques Lacan (1901–1981) was probably the most influential of Freud's reinterpreters. Early in his career he was expelled from the International Psychoanalytic Association for his unorthodox approach. But this probably says more about how most psychoanalysts after Freud had turned his ideas into a dogma than it does about Lacan's supposed errors. Where Freud had argued that the ego strives to relate to the real world (the reality principle), Lacan taught that egohood is a fiction, a construct of language. As such it is the 'human being's mental illness'. The purpose of entering into dialogue with the unconscious is not to bring about healing, but to approach what Lacan calls 'The Real', an ungraspable realm of experience beyond language. Given the unknowability of 'The Real', there is no end to the psychoanalytic process – only the journey.

EXPLORING YOUR UNCONSCIOUS MIND

Just as the stars cannot be seen during the day because they are obscured by the stronger light of the sun, so too with the unconscious mind: it is ever-present, but its activity is obscured by the light of consciousness. Penetrating the unconscious involves learning to be attentive in a defocused way. You must allow what arises simply to be, without rushing to hasty conclusions, and accept that there is a source of knowledge within, for belief in the workings of the unconscious is the key that turns the lock.

FREE ASSOCIATION

Freud believed that free association was a useful way to tap into the unconscious mind. If you have (or can borrow) a tape recorder with a microphone, you can try this for yourself.

Begin by choosing a fragment of material – a word, an idea, a feeling or a picture in your mind. The origin of the fragment is not important: it may have surfaced during a dream or emerged spontaneously from your imagination. When you have chosen a fragment, hold it in mind and talk out loud, recording what you say. Say whatever comes into your head in response to the fragment. Remember there is no right or wrong, only that which flows. If a picture arises in your mind, let visualisation take over as the focus for your associations. If the flow dries up, try to find ways round it: it may feel like a door that won't open – if so, look for an exit to the side.

When you have finished, play back the tape and think about the associations you have made. Try to interpret the words and images in relation to your own life – your parents, your childhood, significant people and events in your life, and your hopes and fears.

FOOD FOR THOUGHT

The role of food in our lives goes far beyond simple nourishment, and our attitudes towards it are deeply significant. This is not surprising, since food does, after all, enter our insides – our inner being. According to Freud, the oral stage of infancy could determine features of our later life. And eating disorders can be especially problematic around adolescence, the time when a person's orientation to the world beyond their family is being established.

So what does food mean to you? Is it something to be savoured or rushed? Then there is the matter of specific foods. Cast your mind back to a meal that has stayed strongly in your memory. Who were you with, or what was the occasion? Which food item really stands out? Free associate around that item, or an item you really don't like. When did you first realise your distaste for it? What is its significance? Honest attention to your associations can be especially revealing in this area.

DREAMING AND KNOWING

Freud said that dreams are the 'royal road to the unconscious'. Using dreams to access the unconscious needs long-term commitment, but can be rewarding. If you want to give it a try, you will need to record your dream life systematically, so keep a diary and a pen next to your bed. When going to sleep, hold the intention in mind that you will write down your dreams; sometimes, it helps to visualise yourself sitting up and writing in the diary. Whenever you awake with a dream fragment in mind – even in the middle of the night – resist the temptation to go back to sleep: sit up and write it down.

Examine your diary daily and at longer intervals, perhaps monthly. In your daily review, identify any content that relates to events that happened in the last few days. Spotting this 'day residue' is not normally too hard, but sometimes the material may be disguised, so you may need to associate around the images to discern their relevance. Mark the day residue passages in your diary, then when you look at it monthly you will be able to see more clearly the patterns that go beyond daily processing. Sometimes these will be recurring themes, sometimes developing patterns or unfolding stories. Don't seek obvious interpretations. The objective is more to develop a close relationship with your unconscious, and trite answers (such as 'the woman with the dark coat is my mother') can block that relationship. Instead, look for ways to amplify the images. For example, if there is a character in your dream diary that you do not immediately recognise, try to visualise them and have imaginary conversations with them. What do they tell you? You may eventually reach a stage where you can consciously engage with the dream content while you are dreaming (see pages 362–3). Again, setting the intention prior to falling sleep is important. You will be surprised what you can achieve.

THE WORD AT THE CENTRE

This exercise uses cues from words in the conscious mind as a way to access material in the unconscious mind. Write eight words across the top of a sheet of paper – they can be any eight words, but they should not make a sentence. Then write another eight words at the bottom. Return to the top and think of a word that somehow connects the first two words on the sheet. For example, if these words were 'tree' and 'mud', you might choose 'root' as the connecting word. Go on to the next two words, and continue making these connections, working row by row alternately from the top and the bottom of the page. Eventually you will end up with one final word in the centre (see the diagram below as a guide). What does that central word mean to you? Spend some time contemplating that word – it will be significant!

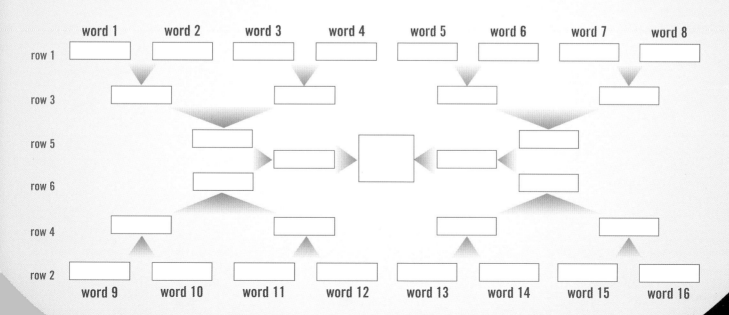

TRUTHFUL SLIPS

Freud believed that any slip of the tongue had meaning and unmasked a hidden motive. Few psychologists today would go so far, but it is true that slips of the tongue can sometimes reveal unconscious thoughts and may be worth examining. When you make a verbal slip, consider how and when it happened. If a word was simply mispronounced, it may not be significant. But if the slip was accompanied by an emotional response – perhaps a rush of energy, or a shiver – no matter how slight, then it could be worth exploring. What significance does the word hold for you? Free associating around this word may help uncover this, and help reveal what your unconscious is trying to tell you.

If you reflect on your verbal slips, you'll also become aware of how ideas that concern you sometimes break out in speech, despite your conscious intentions. This can often be enlightening, but also uncomfortable. Take this case. Daniel meets a friend who has just separated from her husband. He knows about her situation, but decides not to mention it directly. She asks Daniel to light her cigarette, so he tries to strike a match, but presses too hard and snaps it. Without thinking, he exclaims, 'It's a pain when your match breaks, isn't it?' It's likely that his choice of words comes as much from awareness of his friend's problematic private life as from the broken matchstick.

ACTIVE IMAGINATION

Jung used the term 'active imagination' for the process we need to cultivate to understand the unconscious. It involves letting ideas unfold without interference. This sounds easy, but it is probably one of the hardest things for us to achieve because consciousness usually cannot help but interfere. One way to try to engage active imagination is to take some clay or plasticine and mould it in your hands. Let shapes arise spontaneously, rather than deliberately trying to make a particular object. When it feels as if a satisfactory shape has emerged, leave it. Don't even think about it for a day or more. Then return to your shape and consider what it represents. Think especially of creatures or scenes you may have encountered in stories, myths or films. What does it tell you about yourself?

A TUNE IN YOUR HEAD

Whenever you notice that a song is playing in your mind, ask yourself why. If you have just heard the tune on the radio, then it probably has no deep significance. But there are many times when you find yourself humming a tune or holding a song in your head, without any obvious, conscious reason. In these cases, examine your associations to the tune. What is its title? Where did you hear it? Who were you with? What message does it hold for you now? For example, if you find the song 'Strawberry Fields' stuck in your head, you could be remembering a time when you were told off for spilling a bowl of strawberries – and this memory may have been triggered by a current criticism.

PSYCHOLOGICAL TYPES

Jung believed that human behaviour is not random, but follows identifiable patterns that develop from the structure of the human mind. He argued that personality could be classified according to the style of thinking we employ when we perceive and when we judge.

Jung argued that there are basic functions underlying personality – thinking, feeling, perceiving and intuiting – any one of which can be dominant in any individual. He combined these basic functions with his concepts of the introvert and extravert, giving eight basic different types of personality.

To find out which you are, consider how you go about redecorating, for example. Do you think it through, perhaps considering what's in vogue at present (thinking)? Are you mainly influenced by the aesthetics of colour and pattern combinations (perceiving)? Does it have to feel pleasant (feeling)? Or, perhaps, you can't really explain it, but it just 'clicks' when it's right (intuiting). The polar opposite (thinking opposite to feeling; perceiving opposite to intuition) to your dominant function represents an underdeveloped potential, and can help to explain tendencies in behaviour. You may find it irritating, for example, if your partner operates mainly from the opposite function. You may gain insight into your interactions if, instead of merely reacting, you examine the cause of the irritation, and think about the dominant and opposite functions in your and your partner's personalities.

TRUE LIFE DRAMA

Jung believed that the unconscious mind of all human beings contains templates of behaviour called archetypes. According to Jung, these archetypes also appear in the myths and legends of all cultures. Reflecting on mythology can help you to discover which archetypes are most prominent in your unconscious, and thus reveal something of your unconscious motives.

When you read a myth, story or fairytale, ask yourself which ones have most resonance with you. Which characters and situations do you respond to most strongly? The neglected stepchild, the embattled hero, the imprisoned princess?

Another way to find your links to mythology is to try to create a drama from your own life. Write down the details of your childhood, your youth, and your working life. What seems to be the principal direction of your life's journey? You will find that there are crucial moments when major directions were established – it may have been a house move in childhood, the decision of what to study at university, a chance encounter on a holiday, or choosing to change jobs. In retrospect, you will see that there are important moments that shaped the course of your life. Focus on those moments and see which mythic, or perhaps biblical, characters could be related to them. It might be that, like Atlas, you feel you have the weight of the world on your shoulders; or perhaps the occasion when the biblical Joseph is sold into slavery by his brothers has some meaning for you. A myth is an exploration of just these kinds of 'big' human moments. Just as the mythic character is engaged on some form of challenging path, so too are you.

4 CONSCIOUSNESS AND OURSELVES

The sense of self that pervades our consciousness is as natural to us as breathing. Yet unlike the act of breathing, which we know is the function of the lungs, there is no specific part of the body or brain that we can pinpoint as the generator of this sense of personal self. So how does it come about? How is the unending stream of disparate thoughts and impressions that crowd our consciousness distilled into a coherent, enduring sense of self?

Perhaps surprisingly, researchers have found that it is not something we are born with: rather, it is one of the attributes of mind that children develop as they mature. And while the pace of development may slow down, the maturing of personal consciousness is a lifelong process.

Our sense of self at any age depends strongly on our interactions with others, and these can take place at an unconscious as well as conscious level. In many ways these interactions provide the basis of our identity – an identity that lives on, in the minds of those we have known and loved, when our own life comes to an end.

IDENTITY AND THE STREAM OF CONSCIOUSNESS

Consciousness is inherently individual. It is not simply experiencing – there is always a 'me' at the centre doing the feeling, responding and interpreting. But locating this self has proved surprisingly difficult.

Towards the end of the 19th century, pioneering psychologist William James began an exhaustive labour of introspection – a search for the core of his consciousness. But no matter how hard he tried and no matter how complex his mental gymnastics, James could find no centre – no thinker doing the thinking. His thoughts seemed to flicker and play of their own accord, some temporarily illuminated by the spotlight of attention, others dancing on the fringes. And even to observe his thoughts, James realised, was only to have thoughts about thoughts. His mind was an ever-changing play of mental events and, it appeared, his notion of a self was an illusion.

James found a resolution to this existential crisis by likening consciousness to a tumbling stream. The waters of a stream are always in flux, never in precisely the same state twice. For every big eddy – for every distinct thought or clear impression – there are many more background ripples and swirls. But the stream itself has a history, a continuous identity behind the superficial play of the current. Gradually the waters etch out their own banks, creating a landscape that in turn shapes the flows of the water.

The self can be seen in the same way. It is not an inner observer that is a target for mental experiences. Instead, it is the vessel that gives shape to these experiences. From birth, the brain accumulates memories and habits, which in turn shape its circuitry and processing paths, and so guide its response to each subsequent moment. This is what makes every person's consciousness unique and individual. Each brain becomes the product of its own singular history.

> **"As the brain changes are continuous, so do all consciousnesses melt into each other like dissolving views."**
>
> William James, from *Principles of Psychology* (1890)

Shaping the mind

For a long time, James's insight was lost to science. In the middle decades of the 20th century, consciousness was viewed as a software program running on a generalised machine, so the sense of self was merely the sum of many processing events. Memories, for example, were called up by processing – they did not do the processing. But more recent and realistic models of the brain fit well with James's analogy. Today, many scientists view the brain as a neural network, where webs of connections develop through experience, and where the nature of our consciousness arises from our specific history of interactions with the world. And a new generation of computers can also be shaped by their 'life story', with their own unique patterns of processing formed during a 'training' phase.

PIONEERS *WILLIAM JAMES*

Although written over 100 years ago, the works of William James (1842–1910) are still valued for helping to illuminate human thought processes. James, whose brother was the novelist Henry James, had a privileged but odd upbringing, his father trailing the family around the world in pursuit of the perfect education. James gained a degree in medicine from Harvard University in 1869, while also reading widely in psychology and philosophy, and set up the first-ever psychology course there in the 1870s. Although never quite capturing the public imagination like Freud, James's insights were highly influential. Authors such as James Joyce and Virginia Woolf tried to recreate in words James's metaphor of consciousness as a flow of images, urges and snatches of inner speech. Joyce's *Ulysses* became the classic 'stream of consciousness' novel. In this extract, Leopold Bloom listens to a singer in a bar:

'Glorious tone he has still. Cork air softer also their brogue. Silly man! Could have made oceans of money. Singing wrong words. Wore out his wife: now sings. But hard to tell. Only the two themselves. If he doesn't break down. Keep a trot for the avenue. His hands and feet sing too. Drink. Nerves overstrung. Must be abstemious to sing. Jenny Lind soup: stock, sage, raw eggs, half pint of cream.'

A sense of self

So is our sense of self simply the feeling of being the sum of our histories? James realised that our self-sense is not quite this passive. Aspects of our identity are actively constructed. For a start, there is our somatic self – the feeling of what it is like to inhabit our own skins. One of the main tasks of the brain is to draw up the mental boundaries that divide the 'me' from the 'not-me'. Just ponder the feat of being able to chew food in the cramped confines of your mouth. Tongue and dinner move in all directions and yet we manage to keep ourselves separate from our meals and avoid biting ourselves while chewing. The brain's construction of such boundaries is precise, yet also elastic. A racing car driver will feel his tyres gripping on tight corners as if they were an extension of his body, and hammers, pens and paintbrushes can come to feel like part of the hand if used for long periods of time.

Social consciousness

Another aspect of our sense of self derives from the fact that we are social creatures. We must take into account other consciousnesses – the people around us. The more we are aware of the mental existence of others, the more aware we are of our own mental existence. So while the self requires a brain, it has no actual anatomical location. It is rooted in our relationships with our physical space, our social space, and our personal histories.

> **"No man steps into the same river twice."**
>
> Heraclitus (540–480 BC)

FOCUS ON

COGNITIVE DISSONANCE

Consciousness is full of conflicting knowledge and urges, and we often act without fully understanding the reasons why. However, we like to see ourselves as consistent and in control. Psychologists have a term to describe the urge to paper over the cracks in the facade of the self: cognitive dissonance.

If you bought an expensive car and then found that it is uncomfortable on long drives, would you decide to get rid of the car, or console yourself by appreciating its firm, race-bred, handling? Or perhaps you are a smoker and see the latest lung cancer statistics. Do you give up smoking, or tell yourself that as you are only a relatively light smoker you are probably not going to be susceptible to cancer anyway?

Because of the need to see ourselves as unified in mind, most of us become quite skilled at justifying whatever it is that we find our 'selves' deciding to do.

MULTIPLE IDENTITIES

A killer claims he is innocent because his 'alter ego' did it. A woman tells a psychiatric conference she is inhabited by more than 180 different personalities. If these reports are true, then the human mind is – astonishingly – able to host not just one self, but many.

The 19th-century thinker William James argued that our sense of self is glued together by the stream of consciousness (see page 406). Is it possible that, under certain circumstances, the 'glue' could disintegrate and allow two or more selves to inhabit the same mind? Some psychiatrists think so, and label the resulting bizarre state multiple personality disorder; others see it as a fake or delusion. But before examining the arguments, consider the classic case of 'Julia'.

During therapy, Julia described how she had been 'losing' chunks of time since she was a child. She once came round in an unfamiliar classroom and could not account for the last two years. Another time she found herself in a seedy bar talking to a man who seemed to know her much better than she knew him. It emerged that during the 'lost' periods, Julia had been displaced by one of her other selves, and these alternative personalities began to take shape. Among them was George, the burly protector; Joanne, the playful 12-year-old; Sandi, the terrified four-year-old; and Elizabeth, the administrator, who kept some order among the other personalities. In all, Julia had nearly 100 selves.

As therapy progressed, it seemed that the splits in Julia's personality had been caused by a childhood of extreme physical and sexual abuse. Julia had contained her memories of trauma by dividing them among a cast of characters; through therapy she was apparently able to make herself whole again.

Products of therapy?

But can the self really disintegrate under such pressure, or is multiple personality just a product of therapy itself, as patients respond to the suggestions of their counsellors? It is certainly a fact that there had been very few reports of multiple personality until 1973,

> **"They cope with the pain and horror of the abuse they suffered by dividing it up into little pieces and storing it in such a way that it's hard to put back together and hard to remember."**
>
> Frank Putnam, psychiatrist

FACT FILE FAMOUS CASES OF MULTIPLE PERSONALITIES

• An early case of multiple personality emerged in 1906. Christine Beauchamp (real name Clara Fowler) sought help for neurotic symptoms. Under hypnosis, a flirtatious alter ego called Sally emerged first. Later came an angry child-like figure dubbed the Devil or the Idiot.

• In the 1950s, a demure 25-year-old telephonist named Eve White (real name Christine Sizemore) was referred to Dr Corbett Thigpen complaining of headaches, blackouts and hearing voices. Hypnosis revealed Eve Black, a provocative alter ego. Later came Jane, a calm and mature personality, and a further 19 personalities. The case inspired the celebrated book *The Three Faces of Eve*, which was made into a film with Joanne Woodward (right).

• Also in the 1950s, a young student called Sybil Dorsett (real name Shirley Mason) entered therapy, and a tale of abuse by her schizophrenic mother emerged. Under hypnosis, Sybil revealed 16 different personalities.

MULTIPLE PERSONALITY CASES IN COURT

Multiple personality disorder, both faked and apparently real, has featured in several notable court cases. In 1979, Kenneth Bianchi, the 'Hillside Strangler', was charged with the rape and murder of two girls in Los Angeles. Bianchi said that his alter ego, Steve, who emerged during therapy, was to blame, conveniently getting Bianchi off the hook. But when Bianchi was examined by a more critical psychiatrist, Bianchi's apparent symptoms were found to be at odds with clinical knowledge of multiple personality disorder. It was concluded that Bianchi was faking and he was sentenced to life imprisonment.

A case where multiple identities provided a basis for prosecution was heard in 1995. Two women with the disorder had their alter egos sworn in to give evidence against their psychiatrist. The courts upheld their claims that the psychiatrist had sexually abused the alter egos during therapy, swearing them to secrecy.

when the best-selling book *Sybil* related the story of a woman with 16 alter egos. Rates of diagnosis rocketed after its publication, leading doubters to say that this was proof of an imagined syndrome. But those who believe the syndrome is real say that it only shows that therapists now know what to look for.

It is also a fact that there is a consistent pattern to the disorder, which lends weight to the opinion that the multiple personalities are real. Sufferers tend to have a high IQ; there are usually recognisable types among the alter egos; and behind practically every case there lies a tale of extreme and prolonged childhood abuse. Importantly, the abuse has to happen during early childhood – trauma even in teenage years does not produce the disorder.

Open to suggestion?

It is possible that children, who have still-growing brains and incompletely integrated personalities, could be prone to deep-rooted splits in which alternative selves grab a share of the same brain. While doubters concede that most sufferers have been abused, they argue that this fact is significant only because it leads them to seek therapy. Once in therapy, their unstable mental health makes them vulnerable to suggestion. The doubters add that people with multiple personalities almost always score very high for hypnotisability (see page 350). It could be that the hypnosis routinely used to get to the cause of the symptoms is in fact producing them.

It is probably too extreme to claim that all multiple personalities are produced on the therapist's couch. However, people who are highly hypnotisable and who thus have an ability to dissociate (to separate themselves from reality) might be expected to use this skill to escape genuine abuse during childhood. Therapy may contribute to an elaboration of the personalities, but the initial splitting – the act of dissociation – probably takes place at the moment of abuse, just as the sufferers report.

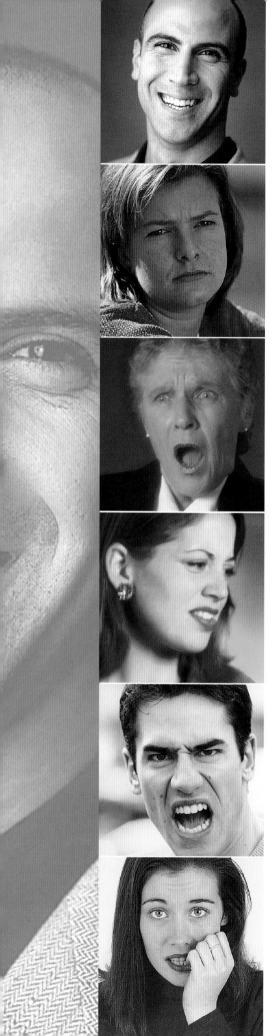

BODY LANGUAGE

When we interact with others, we convey a great deal of information about ourselves through our body language. Such non-verbal signals may be quite unwitting – although the thoughts and attitudes they reflect are often all too conscious.

Much of the information that we get from body language is picked up unconsciously. We are often unable to identify quite why, after being with someone, we have been left with a particular impression of his or her mood. We might just say 'I felt he was upset', without being able to say what has led us to this conclusion. Similarly, we all give out signals that offer clues to our own mood without generally being aware of what we are doing. Some of these signals – such as many facial expressions – are so basic that they go back to a time before humans had language; others simply accompany our verbal utterances, adding to their meaning.

Body movement and speech

As we speak, we cannot help but move. Body movement is closely synchronised with speech – not just our hand gestures, but all parts of the body. Even movements of the legs and the feet have been shown to be co-ordinated with speech.

This language of the body is both highly visible and silent. This can make it extremely useful. We can catch or hold people's attention with flamboyant gestures; we can stress important words or phrases with a movement of the head, a raised eyebrow or an emphatic gesture. Just as a picture may be worth a thousand words, so miming an action may have much greater impact or be more informative than a long verbal description. Some things are too delicate to put into words, but you may be able to express what you mean just with an appropriate hand movement or facial expression. Sometimes we don't want to put something into words for other people to hear, but because body language is silent, it is possible to

> **"Body language adds emphasis to what we say, while the words we use refine the meaning of our body language."**
>
> Peter Bull, psychologist and body language expert

Universal language These six facial expressions are believed to be understood by all humans independent of their culture. From the top: happiness, sadness, surprise, disgust, anger, fear.

catch someone's eye or exchange a meaningful glance so that he or she gets the message.

How we mean others to take our remarks can also be conveyed through body language. What is intended as a joke may be indicated by a smile – and if you say something with a smile, you can get away with almost anything! Conversely, in deadpan humour, nonverbal indicators are withheld; deadpan achieves its effect because we are never quite sure how seriously it should be taken.

Emotions and body language

The 'body language' of the face is of prime importance in communicating emotion. Even newborn babies are capable of producing virtually all the facial movements of an adult. At least six facial expressions of emotion are thought to be universal: happiness, sadness, surprise, disgust, anger and fear are recognised in much the same way by members of different cultures throughout the world. The ability to make and recognise these expressions seems to be genetically programmed into us.

While spontaneous expressions are almost certainly innate – and are a vital source of information about the feelings of others – posed expressions are learned. This idea is supported by the observation that children who are born blind show the same range of spontaneous facial expressions as do sighted children, but they are less able to pose expressions of common emotions. This may be because they lack appropriate feedback on how well they are doing – just as people who are born deaf cannot easily learn to sing.

Once we learn to have some control over our facial expressions, we can conceal what we feel and even fake an expression of the opposite emotion. Some people are much better at this than others. There are those whose faces are an 'open book' and others who conceal emotion behind a 'poker face'. Studies of gender differences show that women tend to express their feelings more openly than men. Cultural differences also affect the display of emotion. Traditionally in Japan there has been a taboo against the expression of negative emotions (such as anger) in public, whereas no such taboo exists in the USA. This can lead to difficulties in communication between people of different cultures if one is more expressive than another.

There are also significant differences between individuals when it comes to picking up signals from facial expressions. Some people are very perceptive, others much less so. Tests have been devised to assess nonverbal perceptiveness: where a gender difference is found, it invariably favours women. This perhaps is the foundation for women's fabled intuition.

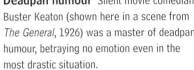

Deadpan humour Silent movie comedian Buster Keaton (shown here in a scene from *The General*, 1926) was a master of deadpan humour, betraying no emotion even in the most drastic situation.

(F)OCUS ON

VOICE MATCHING

Matching your speech style to that of someone you are speaking to is the verbal equivalent of mirroring body language. Its effect is to build harmony between you and the other person. It entails listening carefully to what the other person is saying, noticing the words he or she emphasises and using one or two of them in your own speech in a confirmatory way. This gives the person assurance that he or she is being listened to – and understood. Matching the tone and speed of delivery is also important.

If you want to disengage from a conversation – to end a phone call, for example – try deliberately mismatching your voice. This will give a 'go-away' signal without the person consciously knowing why.

Personal space
In social situations, we unconsciously try to maintain a comfortable 'social' distance between ourselves and others. A closer stance inevitably indicates a more intimate relationship.

Interpersonal relationships

Body language is important in interpersonal relationships. Some people even define the quality of their relationships in terms of body language – by the warmth of a smile, the tenderness of a touch, or the intensity of a kiss. Body language is important at every stage of sexual relationships. People flirt through body language, 'making eyes' at one another, tacitly signalling whether or not an approach is welcome. Happily married couples are better at decoding one another's nonverbal messages than unhappily married couples: in one study, unhappy couples were shown to decode nonverbal messages from total strangers more accurately than from each other. Researchers who study divorce have found that unhappy couples who display facial expressions of contempt or disgust in one another's presence are heading for marital breakdown.

Just as body movement is synchronised with speech, so too is it synchronised with the movements of others. Even strangers who are walking along a crowded pavement co-ordinate their movements – if they did not, they would bump into one another. Body language also provides important clues to the nature of relationships between people. Observers can guess the identity of an unseen conversational partner from the body language of one participant alone. Even very young children are able to do this; for example, they can accurately identify whether their mother is conversing with a friend or a stranger. When people get on well together, they tend to imitate each other's postures. Conversely, if someone wants to dissociate themselves from a certain group, or indicate their superior status, they may do so by using dissimilar postures.

Body language can provide important clues to social status. People of superior status tend to be more relaxed, whereas those of inferior status

FOCUS ON

PUPIL DILATION

The pupils of the eyes dilate in response to loss of light, but they also dilate under the influence of strong emotion. Star-crossed lovers gazing into one another's eyes may have very enlarged pupils, but so too may someone who is enraged or absolutely terrified. Unlike most forms of body language, we cannot directly control the size of our pupils, so they can be an important source of information about emotion. It is said that Chinese jade dealers would gaze into another's eyes in order to see how keen the other was to close a bargain. In this way, they could secure a good price – unless, of course, they were bargaining at dusk, when the fading light could lead them to some mistaken conclusions!

tend to be more tense in the presence of their superiors. In the context of a group, the most important person is often the one who is looked to or at by other group members. Gaze may also be used by a person of superior status as a means of exerting influence on other people – for example, by displaying approval or disapproval.

Practical applications

Interpersonal communication can now be taught, learned and improved through what is known as communication skills training. This typically includes instruction in body language. Such training has been used in many different contexts: as a form of occupational training (with groups such as teachers, doctors, nurses and police officers); in employment interviews; as a therapy for psychiatric patients; and for improving inter-cultural communication. For example, some cultures prefer to converse at close distances, whereas others prefer to keep greater distances between themselves – they are literally 'stand-offish'. Communication between members of different cultures can be difficult if people are unaware of these preferences: there are stories of international gatherings where people virtually chase one another round the room trying to establish a comfortable conversational distance. Training in inter-cultural communication seeks to increase awareness of such differences, and to encourage 'mindfulness' when interacting with people of different nationalities.

Social standing Body language can reveal status within a social hierarchy. Here, the relatively tense stance of the more junior worker on the left contrasts with the typically relaxed posture of her more senior colleague.

However, the practical significance of studying body language goes well beyond such formal instruction. Even reading a short article like this may be influential. By highlighting the fine details of social interaction, it becomes much easier for people to be conscious of and change their behaviour, if they so desire. By heightening awareness of the importance of body language, people may change the way they think about communication. We may not always be conscious of our body language or the clues that we receive from other people's, but it is all around us and its significance is there for those who have the eyes to see it.

Close relations Studies have confirmed that happily married couples are particularly good at reading one another's nonverbal signs. The sympathetic body language of this couple reveals that they probably enjoy a close and happy relationship.

We often feel more confident in 'reading' people's body language than perhaps we should – deception, in particular, is often surprisingly hard to detect.

HOW TO USE BODY LANGUAGE

However, there is no denying that becoming more conscious of the gestures and facial expressions we unconsciously display can improve how we communicate. We can monitor and refine our own nonverbal signals, and become more sensitive to those of others. The examples below illustrate some of the first areas to look at to improve your nonverbal communication skills.

HOW TO READ POSTURE

The face is extremely important in reading emotions, but precisely because of that people are more careful to control their facial expressions. So body movement can also be important. For example, facially someone might try to be attentive to what you are saying, but at the same time support their head on one hand, stretch out their legs and lean back – so the posture conveys a message of boredom. Signs that signal interest include orienting your head towards the other person, sitting reasonably straight and keeping your legs bent at the knee. If you lean forward and draw back your legs, this can suggest great interest.

This man is trying to show interest in his companion's conversation – but his almost sleepy posture reveals that he is actually rather bored.

HOW TO FLIRT

'Giving someone the eye' is all about signalling sexual interest and sexual availability, but timing is everything! The gaze has to be long enough to be perceptible to the other person, but not so long that it seems like an aggressive stare. Repeating the process a few times may do the trick. If the other person keeps avoiding your gaze, you are probably wasting your time, but if the eyes meet and the facial expression shows interest, you may be on your way. For the really shy and reticent, a big smile may also be needed to win them over.

Here the sunglasses are used as a prop to help convey the message – 'I'm interested in you'.

HOW TO MAKE SOMEONE FEEL COMFORTABLE

There are lots of ways of making someone feel comfortable, and body language certainly plays its role. Undoubtedly, bodily relaxation matters. If you are tense, nervous or fidgety, this will make others feel uncomfortable. One useful nonverbal sign that people are getting along is that they tend to imitate each other's postures. See if you can notice how often this occurs in conversation. Try to resist imitating someone else's postures, and you may start to feel you are being really unfriendly! If you wish to create a more positive atmosphere, try to imitate someone's postures (although not too blatantly) – this shows interest and responsiveness to the other person.

The rapport between these two women is clear from the similarity of their postures and gestures.

HOW TO READ FACIAL EXPRESSIONS

Facial expressions can be either posed or spontaneous. So how can we tell the difference? Most revealing is the smile. In a posed smile, often just the corners of the mouth are raised; in a genuine smile, smile wrinkles – 'crow's feet' – may appear at the corner of the eyes. A posed smile may be produced almost as if turning on a light switch, whereas the onset and offset of a spontaneous smile may be more gradual.

Another clue to whether an expression is posed or genuine is its degree of symmetry. An asymmetrical expression is one where the expression on one side of a line drawn vertically through the middle of the face does not match that of the other side. Posed expressions tend to be much less symmetrical than spontaneous ones, so you can use this as a clue to help judge whether someone's facial response is largely genuine, or if it has an element of effort.

In a posed smile, the muscles controlling the mouth are under conscious control as they raise the corners into a conventional smiling expression.

In a genuine smile, many more face muscles come into play, producing raised cheeks and wrinkles around the eyes as well as raised mouth corners.

HOW TO DETECT DECEPTION

Detecting deception from body language is much harder than people often think. There is no 'Pinocchio's nose' that automatically tells you when someone is lying. For example, there is a belief that if someone averts their gaze, he or she may be lying; this may be the case, but the person might also be showing respect or simply be feeling shy.

One useful way to discern deception is to look for very brief expressions, which may occur if someone is surprised, startled, or suddenly influenced by a very strong emotion (such as fear, panic or anger). These expressions may be quickly brought under control, but can be very revealing about someone's underlying emotions. If, for example, you mention an unexpected promotion to a colleague, they might make a fleeting expression of surprise – widened eyes, raised eyebrows – before they regain facial composure and offer their congratulations.

A mixed expression can indicate deception. Here, some surprising news has caused raised eyebrows, which betray the emotions behind the more poised and controlled expression in the rest of the face – and perhaps in contrast with what is being said.

SPOTLIGHT

Mind reading

Can one consciousness directly examine another – and if so, how is this done? When we ask questions like these, we enter the realm of mind readers and psychics.

People are endlessly fascinated by mind readers, psychics and clairvoyants. By offering a mixture of insight, prophecy and sheer entertainment, some have built successful careers and have even been sought out as advisers by politicians and leaders. It is undeniable that the best exponents of mind reading are extremely skilful, leaving even hardened sceptics with the impression that they 'know' more than they should. But how is this done?

Cold reading

Many stage mind readers, psychics, astrologers and palm readers, as well as professional salesmen, use 'cold reading' to convince their subjects that they can get inside their minds. This is not a conjuring trick, but a collection of diverse skills – observation, memory and the ability to lead a conversation – that allow the reader to gather surprisingly accurate information about the subject. Proficient cold readers first scrutinise their subject's appearance, speech and demeanour to gain character clues. They build on this initial profile by making 'predictions' that are likely to be true. For example,

Random choice? Stage mind readers know that, of the shapes above, people are most likely to pick the star, especially if this is in second position – so their chance of guessing someone's choice is considerably higher than 1 in 4.

HOW TO BE A 'MIND READER'

Some acts of apparent mind reading are no more than simple deceptions. Here is an example that makes a good party trick. It relies on the complicity of a 'plant', who needs to be secretly briefed beforehand.

First, tell the assembled group that you are about to read their minds. Pass around identical sheets of paper and envelopes. Ask everyone to write down one phrase that is intensely personal to them, and then to place this in the envelope. Collect the envelopes, but be sure to put the plant's entry at the bottom of the pile. Now take the first envelope from the top of the pile and press it against your forehead in a theatrical way as if you are trying to psychically 'read' the paper inside. Make up any old phrase, and speak it out loud prophetically. This is the plant's cue to shout with amazement 'Those are my words...how could you possibly have known?' Open the envelope and read the words to yourself, as if checking your answer, then discard the paper. You will now have read someone's phrase. Press the next envelope to your forehead as before, and speak the phrase you have read out loud, this time to someone's real amazement. Repeat the sequence until everyone's phrase has been read – or someone cottons on to the trick.

EXTRA-SENSORY EXPERIMENTS

Is it possible to prove the existence of ESP scientifically? In the 1970s, scientists devised an experiment to try just that, and since then the so-called Ganzfeld experiments have been conducted at several reputable institutions.

The idea behind the tests is that by suppressing all normal sensory input (Ganzfeld means 'whole field' in German) the subject becomes more susceptible to picking out the weak signals supposedly involved in ESP. The subject's eyes are covered with semi-opaque material and bathed in red light, while white noise is fed to him or her through headphones. A second person, in another room, then attempts to 'transmit' a visual image from a selection of four, and the subject attempts to identify the image.

In 1994, Daryl Bem and Charles Honorton (of Cornell and Edinburgh universities) analysed the published data from Ganzfeld experiments. On average, they found that subjects identified the right image 35 per cent of the time – a hit rate significantly higher than chance. Many scientists then set about finding flaws in either the experimental technique or the analysis, and in 1999 a rival analysis found that the Ganzfeld tests in fact gave no indication of ESP whatsoever.

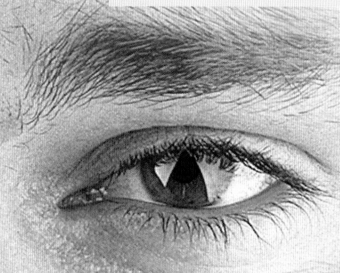

an affluent subject from a cold climate is likely to be planning a holiday in a hot country, so the statement 'I see blue waters and palm trees' is likely to ring true. Responses to such predictions are carefully monitored, allowing the reader to adjust his or her comments and make more accurate predictions, gaining the subject's confidence. This is aided by the fact that people are far more likely to remember correct predictions than incorrect ones, as they seem more significant. In one case study, psychic Peter Hurkos carried out a reading that left a subject stunned by its apparently detailed accuracy. Subsequent viewing of a video recording of the reading, however, showed that Hurkos made 14 incorrect statements for every one that was correct.

Cold readers often exploit our willingness to accept any vague statements about our personality, particularly if they are flattering. This is often called the Barnum effect after the circus showman and trickster P.T. Barnum. In one study, people were so convinced that universally appealing statements such as 'At times you are affable and sociable while at other times you are wary and reserved' were personalised appraisals of themselves that they gave them an average mark of 4.3 out of 5 for accuracy.

Psychic insight?

In a different category are those mind readers who really believe it is possible to reach into another mind through 'psychic' effects such as extra-sensory perception (ESP). But is the skill of such practitioners truly a form of psychic insight – or is it again simply a mix of clever manipulation and mere chance? Studies conducted in the 1950s that 'proved' the existence of ESP have since been exposed as frauds, and much subsequent research in the area has been unreliable, at best. One type of study, the Ganzfeld experiment, has opened up real debate, but the topic remains highly controversial among psychologists.

Seeing the future?
The crystal ball is the classic prop, but fortune tellers are astute judges of their clients' responses, sometimes using touch as well as observation.

CONSCIOUSNESS AND THE DEVELOPING MIND

The brain is a machine that has to build itself. While every newborn baby is born with a set of reflexes, it has to learn how to see, feel and think – that is, how to be conscious – through its interactions with the world.

A baby's brain has to learn how to make sense of its world. Consciousness – in all its sharply focused, meaning-imbued and introspective glory – is not something that we are born with: instead, it is a brain skill that must be mastered in stages.

Learning to be conscious begins in the womb. By 14 weeks, a foetus has a brain. If pricked, stress hormones surge through its body, suggesting that it feels pain. But such responses are just reflexes, as at this age the higher brain is only an unconnected mass of cells. By six months, however, the brain is wired up well enough for the foetus to hear, smell, taste and even blink when bright light shines onto its mother's abdomen. Experiments show that newborns can recognise music and voices that they heard during pregnancy. So significant learning is already taking place in the womb.

> "Children lose in the order of 20 billion synapses per day between early childhood and adolescence. While this may sound harsh, it is generally a very good thing."
>
> Lise Eliot, neurobiologist

Brain growth and early experience

After birth the brain really gets going, growing at a phenomenal rate of around a quarter of a million neurons every minute. Its rampant growth is, however, rather random. The connections established between neurons are chaotic, and nerve traffic flows spasmodically across the jumbled

Child's play According to Piaget, there are clear stages in children's mental development. The 'conservation of numbers' stage occurs around the age of six. If counters are arranged in two rows (a), a child sees that each row has the same number. But if one row is then arranged in a cluster (b), a child under six is likely to think that it now contains fewer counters. Older children realise that the quantities must be the same.

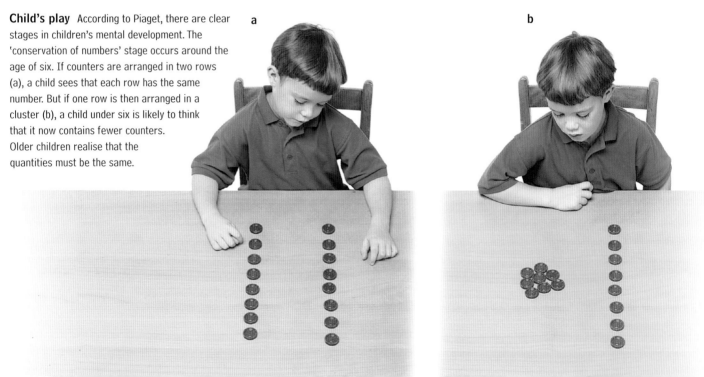

THINK AGAIN!   NEWBORN BRAINS

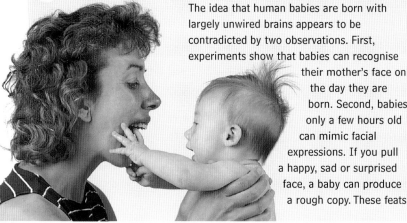

The idea that human babies are born with largely unwired brains appears to be contradicted by two observations. First, experiments show that babies can recognise their mother's face on the day they are born. Second, babies only a few hours old can mimic facial expressions. If you pull a happy, sad or surprised face, a baby can produce a rough copy. These feats should be impossible, because a baby's cortex has hardly any connections at this stage.

The explanation seems to be that newborns are using the midbrain and the amygdala, structures in the more primitive core of the brain that mature in the womb. This early ability to recognise and copy expressions takes place at a reflexive, unthinking level, and only takes on meaning when the cortex develops. This also explains why children develop 'stranger anxiety' at around six months, once they begin to see the world at a more conscious level.

pathways of the immature brain. And studies suggest that a newborn's experience of the world is very different to our own. In one experiment, babies were shown a number of simple patterns; electrical recordings revealed that their brains took in the information very slowly and responded with much the same surge of neural firing to one pattern as to another. So newborns can certainly see, but what they experience – with the likely exception of the mother's face and breast – is little more than an elusive, shifting shape.

But soon the baby begins to acquire the habits of perception – interpreting information from the senses in a way that makes sense of the world and provides the basis for conscious experience. To carry out this wiring, brain growth actually goes into reverse. Links between neurons are severed and some cells die, pruning back the forest of connections into a more efficient network. The brain discovers through experimentation which are the connections that can deliver focused impressions, and the result is a thinking machine that is shaped to fit its world.

Models of development

There have been many attempts to unravel the thinking processes by which children learn and adapt to the world. The two best-known pioneers in this area are Jean Piaget and Lev Vygotsky.

The Swiss psychologist Jean Piaget (1896–1980) was a sharp observer of children, and he noticed that their cognitive development appeared to follow a natural succession of stages. Just as most children learn to crawl before learning to walk, intellectual development takes place in more or less distinct steps. Piaget stressed the role of the individual child in bringing about his or her own intellectual development. Like miniature scientists, children are always experimenting – banging objects, playing around with them – and gradually developing rules that allow them to understand their world.

Real lives

WOLF CHILDREN

The vital influence of other humans on a child's mental development is shown by the story of Amala and Kamala, two Indian girls raised in the wild by wolves. In 1920, a local missionary rescued the girls, then aged three and five, but he was disappointed by their response. They ran on all fours, ate raw meat, showed no facial expressions and preferred the company of his dogs. Their hearing and eyesight seemed unusually sharp, but they never learnt to speak. It seems their brains had already been formed by their early immersion in a wolf's world, and it was too late to develop the self-awareness that characterises human beings.

Their story had no happy ending. The younger died soon after her rescue while the elder died of typhoid at 16, still more wolf than human in mind.

Some researchers believe that adolescence is a life stage unique to humans – unlike most other primate species, which generally go straight from childhood into adulthood.

Anthropologist Barry Bogin believes that this pattern of development evolved to allow young humans time to master the intricacies of adult social relations. According to Bogin, the fact that boys' and girls' physical development follow somewhat different courses bears this out. Boys become fertile and hormone-driven at about 13, yet their bodies stay puny and sexually unappealing to females until muscle development in their late teens. Girls grow a womanly shape at puberty, yet are surprisingly infertile until their late teens.

The theory is that girls needed to look like women before they reached sexual maturity so that they would be included in the routine of baby care, allowing them to pick up the essential skills of mothering. Boys needed the sexual drive and aggression of an adult male while still resembling unthreatening children so that they could learn their roles in society without provoking jealousy and violence from elders.

The child begins by establishing some very general expectations about the world. At about eight months, for example, a child will have learned enough to know that when a toy is hidden by a blanket, the toy still lies underneath it. Later the child masters more sophisticated expectations, learning, for example, that matter is conserved. So when a tall, thin glass of water is poured into a short, fat glass, the child knows that the quantity of water is the same in each, despite the different levels of water in the glasses.

The development of a sense of self characterises another important stage. While most children can recognise themselves in a mirror by the time they are two years old, Piaget considered them to be 'egocentric' until the age of five or six. At this age, children begin to realise that other people may see and feel life from quite a different point of view; they also learn that inner psychological events, such as thoughts and imaginings, are distinct from real events in the outside world. The new ability to put themselves in another's shoes in turn strengthens children's own perception of selfhood – they can be objective about their own subjective existence and have more mature emotional reactions and moral judgments.

Piaget's model of development was incredibly ambitious, because it described the complete transition from birth to adult thinking. Many psychologists have challenged the way Piaget reached his conclusions, and have pointed out that he did not try to account for how or why development occurs; nevertheless, Piaget's ideas remain one of the most prominent influences in developmental psychology.

Social theory

The theories of Russian psychologist Lev Vygotsky (1896–1934) place far more stress on the role played by society and language in shaping the minds of children. Vygotsky pointed out that not only are all children born into the same physical world – and so will learn the same sensory and perceptual lessons – but they are also born into well-defined cultural worlds and so their interactions with other people will be a crucial factor in their mental development. Vygotsky showed how children learn to express their thoughts in words, first through talking out loud, then by internalising their speech as a private monologue – a habit of wrestling ideas from the self. Vygotsky argued that many of the things that we consider to be part of our conscious selves are actually the internalisation of socially evolved ways of thinking. So attitudes like loyalty or rebellion, rather than coming from within, are in fact learned from ideas expressed within our cultures.

Lifelong development

Both Piaget and Vygotsky's theories conform to the common-sense idea that babies are born and then develop increasingly complex minds, each new set of mental skills paving the way for further levels of elaboration. But what has recently astonished psychologists is to find that the human brain seems genetically programmed to develop over a prolonged period. Until relatively recently, psychologists assumed that the brain completed its growth and subsequent pruning in the first few years of life, ending with the language centres, which reach maturity at around six or seven. Yet brain scans have shown that the very highest levels of the brain – those that have most to do with planning, social judgement and emotional control – have a sudden surge of growth just before puberty and then are gradually shaped during the teenage years and even early adulthood.

What this appears to mean is that evolution expects us still to be learning important intellectual lessons at this relatively advanced age. The necessary plasticity has been designed in so that we can assimilate a socialised mindset in a gradual, step-by-step, fashion. If the behaviour of an adolescent seems immature (or interestingly experimental, as a teenager would see it), this is because it quite literally is so. The human mind was meant to develop through a prolonged process of adjustment before finally arriving at a state of well-adjusted fit with its environment.

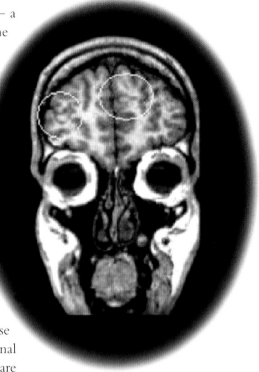

Late development The coloured areas in this image are those in the brain's prefrontal lobes that are specifically active when someone is making a moral judgment. Unlike most brain areas, the prefrontal cortex does not reach maturity until adulthood.

Becoming aware The ability to engage with social and moral issues emerges in the teenage years, as the highest levels of the conscious brain reach maturity.

WHAT IS MATURITY?

In adulthood, we often let our unconscious habits take over our day-to-day life. But there are times – such as when making a difficult decision, or resolving a crisis in our own lives – when we need to fully engage our mature conscious minds.

By the time we reach our late teens, we are in most ways adult. Our bodies are physically mature, and in many respects our thinking skills are at their peak. But at this point most of us will have many years of adult life ahead. So what do the adult years offer in terms of a chance to carry on developing ourselves and our consciousness?

Morality and maturity

Most of us like to think that our ways of judging right and wrong have progressed since we were children, and that developing a realistic yet morally acceptable approach to life is part of becoming a mature, responsible adult. In the 1960s, psychologist Lawrence Kohlberg put forward a theory that is still influential today of how our moral judgment develops. Kohlberg claimed that everyone – irrespective of age or culture – could be placed in one category in a hierarchy of moral development by assessing their response to a hypothetical moral dilemma. At the lowest level was the type of moral reasoning used by children, where right and wrong are judged in relation to whether punishment or reward is the likely result. Next comes the typical adult stage in which 'good behaviour' is determined by what other people, in the social group or society at large, will perceive as such. Finally – and, according to Kohlberg, many adults do not reach this highest stage of moral development – individual conscience becomes the criterion for judgments of right and wrong, and there is an awareness that rules must sometimes be broken for justice to be achieved.

> **"Each individual, to become a mature adult, must develop to a sufficient degree all of the ego qualities, so that a wise Indian, a true gentleman, and a mature peasant share and recognise in one another the final stage of integrity."**
>
> E.H. Erikson, *Childhood and Society*, 1963

FACT FILE   THE CRITERIA OF EMOTIONAL MATURITY

Emotional maturity is associated with the following personality traits:

• Facing reality and dealing with it – tackling problems through finding ways to solve them rather than avoiding them.
• Handling hostility constructively, and looking for a solution to conflict rather than someone to attack.
• Finding as much satisfaction in giving as receiving, and naturally considering the needs of others as well as your own.
• Adapting to change – viewing it as an opportunity rather than a curse and accepting frustration in the short term.

• Being able to learn from experience, and taking responsibility for one's own actions and their consequences.
• Being able to give and receive love, and feeling secure enough to show vulnerability in loving someone.
• Relative freedom from the symptoms of tension and anxiety, such as irritability and pessimism.

Diffusing tension One indicator of emotional maturity is the ability to handle aggression in hostile confrontations.

Real lives   *OVERCOMING THE PAST*

Early traumas can influence feelings in adulthood – but with maturity, a way ahead can often be found, as 23-year-old Jennifer has discovered.

'When I was little, I was very shy and rather unpopular at school. My mother thought the best way to get me over it was to force me to go to lots of parties, and she persuaded the other mothers to invite me to all the birthday parties even when their children didn't really want me there. Little girls can be very cruel, and these events were just torture – I was never invited to be on anyone's team during games, and the other children used to gang up on me and laugh at me until I cried.

'Nowadays I am very confident and I have lots of friends. I love quiet dinner parties, and going out in a group. But whenever I go to a party and see people laughing I always assume that they are laughing at me, however much I try to tell myself this isn't so.'

Life stages

Many psychologists today see the adult years as a succession of key stages, each relating to life events at different ages. On this approach, there may be no specific point at which maturity is reached. Instead, a different mindset is appropriate at each stage, such as ambition in early adulthood, or pride in one's achievements in late adulthood.

One influential life-stage theory that includes a notion of increasing maturity was formulated by psychologist Erik Erikson. He equated maturity in adulthood with the achievement of 'ego integrity' which is achieved cumulatively, through the resolution of specific crises at key stages during adult life. For example, in middle adulthood the crisis of 'generativity' (continuing creative input into work or family life) versus 'stagnation' (loss of interest in life's activities) occurs. According to Erikson, if the outcome of this crisis is positive – that is, stagnation is avoided – a positive outcome at the next stage (old age) is also more likely. Emotional problems lingering from previous stages – even from childhood – can be resolved at later stages, but often with greater difficulty.

Emotional maturity

In recent years, the notion of emotional maturity has become a popular focus for self-improvement books and articles. But what does it mean to be emotionally mature? An ability to take a considered, constructive approach to life is perhaps key, rather than being propelled helplessly by one's enthusiasms or held back by fear of failure or lack of self-worth. Finding a way to 'live well' in relation to oneself and others – recognising the validity of other people's feelings, and accepting the limitations that our past history inevitably places on us – is also important.

The challenge of happy adjustment to the later years of life certainly requires such an approach. Midlife is a point when we become aware of our own mortality and evaluate what we are likely to achieve in our lives as a whole. Bringing our hopes and achievements into line with one another, so that the inevitable frustrations of later years are tempered by a sense of fulfilment, is perhaps the real challenge of maturity.

Maturity in midlife Erikson's theory of life stages suggests that middle-aged people should seek continued active engagement and interest in life. If this is achieved, they are more likely to deal positively with the challenges of later life.

PASSING AWAY

Different philosophies and religions present us with different ideas about death and its spiritual and personal dimensions. In our modern age, while doctors now have precise criteria to decide when death has occurred, there is still debate among medical scientists about exactly what it means to die.

Real lives

MOVING INTO THE LIGHT

Some people who have been close to death report powerful spiritual experiences. This account from a medical practitioner in Kentucky, USA, is typical of what are called near-death experiences (NDEs).

'I knew that I was dying, and I felt completely passive. Suddenly, I was bathed in a brilliant light, far brighter than the sun. At first, the brightness was painful, shocking, but slowly I began to feel safer. The light became reassuring and comforting and it drew me towards its centre. It radiated peace and joy and I wanted nothing more than to merge with it. Then, somebody – I think it was my mother, who died when I was a child – whispered to me "Go back, you haven't finished what you need to do", and the next thing I was back in the emergency room, slammed back into my body.'

Many people maintain that NDEs offer evidence of an afterlife. However, the strange experiences may have a more mundane neurochemical explanation: as the brain is deprived of oxygen and parts of the cortex 'shut down', the irregular firing of neurons may trigger thoughts, sensations and memories. The rush of endorphins produced in response to the stress of the situation may explain the reported feelings of calm and understanding.

The dividing line between life and death would seem to be clear. When someone dies, it means they are no longer an active physical and mental presence. But in reality, the boundary does not seem to be quite so sharp, either in medical terms or in terms of our personal experience.

Most familiarly, perhaps, an individual's identity does not cease to exist when they are no longer around to interact with us. Physical absence often makes little difference to our consciousness of a person. Anyone who has lived through the death of someone they are close to knows that the person's identity lives on vividly in the minds of everyone who knew them. We retain an image of the person as they existed most characteristically in their relations to us. If the person was debilitated by illness or old age, this process of constructing them in memory may begin long before death, as well as extending after it. We prefer to think of the person when they were closer to their prime, rather than in pain and reduced by illness. After the person's death or departure from active life, we are still able to perceive how they would have felt and reacted in certain situations, to imagine their thoughts, to hold conversations with them in our minds and to experience them strongly as a continued presence in our lives.

This is not just something that happens when someone dies. We all at times find ourselves imagining how our best friend, close relative or partner would characteristically respond in a given situation, when they are not currently with us. We carry their existence in our consciousness whether they are alive or dead. Thus we live on in the consciousness of others, as we live in theirs and they in ours in normal life. This is the one sense in which we all can experience a kind of immortality – as a force influencing and affecting those we knew in life.

Medical and legal death

The boundary between life and death in medical and legal terms is also not as clear as one might at first think. Historically, medical science had little difficulty defining death – it was the absence of breathing and heartbeat; when these vital systems closed down irreversibly, so did all the other functions of the body. The patient was dead, with the predictable consequence of physical disintegration to follow.

Today, these old certainties have been obscured by advances in medical technology. Doctors can now keep some body systems functioning long after others have ceased. Bypass machines and respirators can carry out the functions of the heart and lungs in patients who have suffered devastating neurological damage and who will never recover consciousness. In effect, the body can be kept biologically alive – growing, developing, repairing its worn-out cells – although it is capable of existing only at a vegetative level.

The rapid development of intensive care medicine over the past few decades has triggered a complex debate about the nature of death. Not surprisingly, this has been led by the medical and legal professions, which demand definition of death consistent with modern practice, and workable criteria by which to pronounce the end of life. This has legal implications; for example, in determining whether an assault becomes homicide.

Defining death

The move towards drawing up a new definition of death came in 1968 when a committee of distinguished US physicians, theologians, lawyers and philosophers assembled at Harvard Medical School. They concluded that death should be redefined as the irreversible loss of function of the whole brain. A person was to be regarded as legally dead when his or her brain was no longer alive and could not be brought back to life. The so-called Harvard criteria based on this definition were quickly adopted by the medical and legal establishments, and now appear on the statutes of all states in the USA, and in more or less similar form around the world.

The widespread acceptance of the new definition of death owes much to one very practical pressure – the development of transplant medicine. Kidneys were the first organs to be successfully transplanted from one

Celebrating with the dead The Mexican 'Day of the Dead' (1 and 2 November) is a colourful and lively festival. Families gather in graveyards to greet the souls of departed family members. They decorate the tombs with candles, flowers, and gifts of favourite foods such as sweets and cakes, often shaped into skulls, skeletons and coffins. Toys and balloons are brought to the graves of children.

THINK AGAIN!   DEATH IN OTHER CULTURES

While we are accustomed to thinking of death as a clear boundary, this boundary varies surprisingly between different societies. In some cultures, people believe that corpses contain a vital principle long after Western doctors would declare death. For example, Tibetans have a tradition of chanting *The Tibetan Book of the Dead* for 49 days when a person dies – this is believed to be the length of time between death and rebirth in reincarnated form. They chant to the body and its listening spirit for a week

after respiration has stopped, and then continue by a picture of the deceased after the body has been disposed of.

In Islamic belief, death is considered to be the separation of the soul from the body; and because the soul resides in every part of the body a person may be 'alive' even after brain death has been diagnosed. Further back in history, Jewish people at the time of Christ believed that the soul remained in the body until the third day after death (counting the day of death as the first day) – hence the significance of Jesus

being resurrected 'on the third day': any sooner and he would not have been regarded as truly dead.

Many societies invest faith in the continued presence of the dead as members of the social order, with rights and obligations. Conversely, some cultures treat some of the living as if they were dead – for example, if they suffer from a particular disease or have ignored a crucial social taboo. Clearly, death has a social as well as medical dimension – you are dead when your society deems you to be so.

individual to another, but today heart, liver, pancreas and heart-and-lung transplants are performed routinely. Transplant surgery requires the organs to be in good condition, which means that they should be 'harvested' as soon as possible after death. If brain death has been diagnosed, there is no obstacle to the removal of organs while the heart is still beating. Much of today's transplant surgery – and its ability to prolong and improve the life of thousands of patients – would not be possible without the brain death standard.

Between life and death

One of the purposes of the Harvard criteria is to distance doctors from the ethical minefield that now surrounds a diagnosis of death. But there are two conditions – coma and persistent vegetative state (PVS) – that still cloud the issue for clinicians. Coma is a profound state of unconsciousness. It may be caused by a head injury, or a period of oxygen deprivation caused by, for example, a heart attack, smoke inhalation or near drowning. The affected person is alive, but cannot be roused from an apparent 'sleep-like' state and is unable to respond to external stimuli. Recovered patients often report that they were able to see, hear and understand while in the state of coma, which suggests a level of consciousness. However, they had no way of communicating this awareness to other people.

PVS, which sometimes follows coma, is a condition in which the patient loses function of the cerebral cortex – the part of the brain that controls the 'higher' brain activities including perception and conscious thought. However, the brainstem continues to function, maintaining activities such as breathing and heartbeat. The patient may laugh, cry out or make spontaneous movements, and the eyes may even be able to track a moving object.

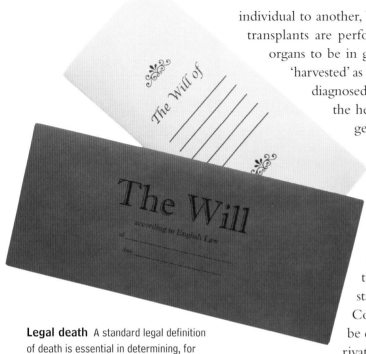

Legal death A standard legal definition of death is essential in determining, for example, when a will should be executed or when life insurance should be paid.

F*O*CUS ON   *DIAGNOSING BRAIN DEATH*

The following criteria must all be met before a doctor can diagnose brain death:

- The patient is unable to take a single breath unaided.
- The pupils of the patient's eyes are fixed open.
- The patient does not respond in any way to painful stimulation, such as a needle prick.
- There is no muscle tone in the arms and legs.
- There are no signs of activity in the brainstem, indicated by the following factors:
- The eyeballs are fixed in their sockets.
- There is no cough or gag reflex when the back of the throat is stimulated.

- There is no corneal reflex – that is, the patient does not move when the surface of the eyeball is stroked.
- There is no response when ice-cold water is poured into the ear (if the person is alive, the person's eyes will move).

After these criteria have been checked, brain death will only be confirmed when the doctor is sure that the patient has not taken opiate or barbiturate drugs within the last 24 hours. In addition, scans must be carried out to confirm that no blood is penetrating into the brain, or EEG measurements made to show no sign of detectable electrical activity in the brain.

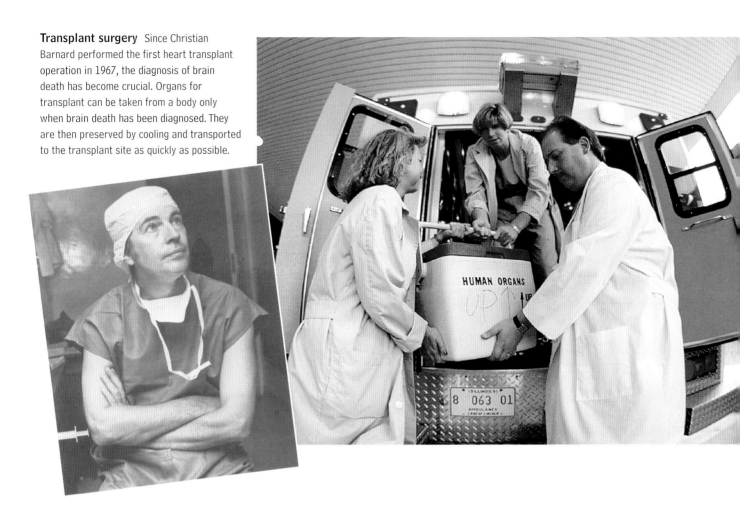

Transplant surgery Since Christian Barnard performed the first heart transplant operation in 1967, the diagnosis of brain death has become crucial. Organs for transplant can be taken from a body only when brain death has been diagnosed. They are then preserved by cooling and transported to the transplant site as quickly as possible.

With intensive physical therapy and medical care, most patients will come out of a coma within four weeks. Many make a full recovery, but some emerge with a range of physical or psychological difficulties. These depend on the severity of the damage to the patient's brain tissue. The prognosis for PVS is far worse. A patient in PVS for more than one month is extremely unlikely ever to regain consciousness, and the few patients who have regained awareness have been severely mentally disabled, blind, deaf or paralysed.

The dilemma raised by PVS is this. Medical science makes it possible to maintain patients in PVS not just for weeks, but for decades. The medical bill for one patient can run into hundreds of thousands of dollars, and today, there are an estimated 14,000 patients in the USA in PVS. Patients in PVS are clearly not dead by current definitions, and yet their prospects for recovery after a few months are negligible. In these cases, should the boundaries of death be widened to include irreversible PVS, and if so, what criteria should be used if we decide to stop feeding and treating patients in this condition?

The matter is still highly controversial, but it is likely that what will follow is a further redefinition of death based on irreversible loss of consciousness – the single characteristic that is most specifically human.

> **"At my age I do what Mark Twain did. I get my daily paper, look at the obituaries page and if I'm not there I carry on as usual."**
>
> Patrick Moore

Consciousness and the soul

The notion of a soul is as old as human civilisation. Its ubiquity across different cultures suggests a powerful desire in the human mind to express the mysteries of life and death, and a yearning to find a basis for immortality.

Beliefs about the soul and immortality reflect the cultures and preoccupations of the societies in which they emerged. Like many potent ideas, they have evolved to maintain their relevance in a changing world. Few scientists today accept the idea of the soul as a separate entity. However, for many people it remains a valuable concept and a cornerstone of religious belief. Even for those who are not religious, the soul provides a metaphor for our conscious and unconscious selves, representing that part of us in which our personality, emotions and free will reside.

Ideas about the soul exist in all the major religions. In Australian Aboriginal and Native American cultures, it was believed that an individual possessed many souls, each of which had its own attributes. For example, the 'life soul' animated the body and departed on death, while the 'free soul' could leave the body during dreams or trances, assuming the form of an animal. If this animal failed to return to the soul's 'owner', the person would die. Similar stories are found in European folklore, where souls are depicted as mice that slip from the mouths of the dead (a red mouse if they have lived a good life, black if not).

The soul in earlier cultures

Many ancient societies believed in an afterlife in which the soul is judged. Such beliefs were held by the Zoroastrians of Persia around 2500 years ago, but were most elaborately developed in ancient Egypt, culminating in their *Book of the Dead*.

The idea of the soul taking on animal form appears in many cultures, reinforcing a common belief in a unitary life force that animates humans and other creatures. Thus, the soul of a Siberian

THE EGYPTIAN CULT OF THE DEAD

The ancient Egyptians held that on death, the soul left the body and entered the underworld – the land of the dead. Here the soul embarked on a perilous journey in search of the god Osiris, who sat in the Hall of Judgement with his retinue of 42 judges. The soul was brought before the judges and the heart of the deceased was weighed in a scale against the feather of Ma'at, goddess of justice. If the heart and feather were in perfect balance, the soul of the deceased merged with Osiris, attaining divine status while retaining an individual human personality. Egyptians believed that the soul was able to return to the world of the living in the form of the *ba*, a human-headed falcon endowed with the individuality of the deceased.

The medieval soul This illustration from a 12th-century manuscript of a text by Hildegard von Bingen depicts the destiny of the Christian soul after death. The person's soul leaves the body, whereupon ranked masses of angels and devils struggle for possession of it.

shaman (holy man) could ride to the spirit world on the back of a reindeer, while in medieval Christian thought, the eagle symbolised a spirit rising to heaven. For the ancient Greeks, the soul left the body on death in the form of a butterfly, which was equated with the breath of life, while in central Asia bodies were fed to dogs to speed their passage to the afterlife.

Chinese myth from the 5th century BC also recognised multiple souls. The *hun* was the spirit of man's vital force, expressed in intelligence and power of breathing, whereas *p'o* was the spirit of man's physical nature expressed in bodily movements. If properly nurtured, these twin souls could attain immortality. On death, rituals were carried out to call the *hun* back into the body so that it did not roam aimlessly but could be nurtured by funerary offerings.

Christian beliefs – in which the soul is a spiritual, immortal entity trapped within a 'lower' physical body – owe much to ancient Egyptian and Greek ideas, especially those of the Greek philosopher Plato (427–347 BC). Plato believed that all higher thought, learning and properties such as virtue belonged to the immortal soul. On death, the soul left the body and entered another person or animal before finally reaching the pure state where it could go on to a higher existence. Platonic ideas of the soul were married with the teachings of the Old Testament and became part of Christian orthodoxy, fiercely protected by a powerful church. It was many centuries before the Christian view of soul and body as separate entities was questioned by the philosophers and scientists of the modern age.

FACT: The word 'psychology' literally means the study of the soul. It takes its name from Psyche – in Greek mythology a beautiful woman who personified the soul and achieved immortality through her love for the god Eros.

5 AWARENESS AND CREATIVITY

We all like to feel and perform at our best – and being alert and 'in the moment' is very much a part of that. While some people seem to have a natural talent for living each moment to the full, most of us need a helpful nudge to remind us not to worry or be distracted unnecessarily. However, there are techniques that can help anyone to achieve a more focused, more conscious awareness in everyday life.

Some of these techniques have come out of what psychologists have discovered about how the human mind processes information – both the limits of our capacity and the conditions under which our minds operate best. Others are based on mind training techniques, such as meditation and mindfulness, derived from Eastern religions, particularly Buddhism. These methods may take a while to master, but the benefits they bring can be profound.

As many who have practised some of these techniques will testify, a heightened awareness can enhance life in countless ways. But perhaps the most satisfying outcome of a fully active consciousness is being able to express ourselves creatively in whatever field of endeavour interests us most.

ACTIVE CONSCIOUSNESS

Being fully conscious means more than just being awake. Engaging your mind fully in whatever you are doing is essential if you are to get the most from each day. You only live your life once, so make sure you're fully 'there' while you're living it.

Many of us live our lives without being as mentally alert as we could be. Instead of being fully engaged in what we are doing, we tend to be easily distracted by those things that catch our attention – whether from the outside environment or from our own passing thoughts. As a result, we may fail to get the most from our experiences.

Modern pressures of living are partly to blame for this. Many of us lead ever-busier lives during which we are expected to juggle multiple responsibilities. Consequently, our minds are pulled away from what we are engaged in towards everyday anxieties and distractions. You can see this for yourself if you close your eyes for one minute, and review the thoughts that run through your head. You will probably find that one thought leads to another, and then another, taking you away from your original point of focus. Memories, ideas, hopes, anxieties, frustrations and reminders of things you mustn't forget to do may all have surfaced during the minute, perhaps with their attendant emotions. Try to gauge how many different thoughts you had during the minute. Multiply this number by 960 – the number of minutes in an average waking day – and you'll get some idea of the extent to which our haphazard thinking impinges on our lives.

Memory and consciousness

We may sometimes be confronted by the lack of awareness of what is going on in our minds. Some mistakes reveal all too clearly our diminished ability to make mental connections because our minds have become over-compartmentalised. Consider this example: Philip arranges to meet a friend for lunch on the following Wednesday; the next day, he agrees to chair a lunchtime meeting at work on the same Wednesday. He holds both of these appointments in mind – but fails to realise that they are incompatible, until too late. You may have had a similar experience, where one part of your consciousness seems to be strangely cut off from another. How can this happen when we are seemingly awake and aware?

It is tempting to put such lapses down to poor memory. And as we get older, the amount we can hold actively in memory may indeed diminish. But in a case like this, where we remember both events and simply fail to bring them together in

HOW TO.... **?**

IMPROVE ACTIVE CONSCIOUSNESS
Have you ever been frustrated by your inability to remember the details of a film or book just a short time after seeing or reading it? A simple solution is to keep notes in a journal. When you finish a book, take 20 minutes to sketch the plot and main characters, and record your feelings about the book. Knowing that you will be doing this will help to keep your attention more engaged while you are actually reading. Mentally highlight key scenes and events, memorable quotes, and descriptions that trigger a particularly strong response in you.

our minds, it seems that more subtle failure is in operation. The answer, in some sense, is a lack of 'active consciousness', where the various parts of mental life – conscious and unconscious, past and present, personal and professional – are not as open to one another as we would like.

Cultivating active consciousness

So how can we achieve a better level of mental integration? Certainly, our minds seem to have no problem becoming fully engaged when we face novel situations that are charged with danger or opportunity. Some individuals deliberately seek out exhilarating situations or take part in dangerous sports – bungie jumping, racing, sky-diving – in order to feel 'wide awake' and 'alive'. But such pursuits do not solve the challenge of maintaining focus and attention in everyday life; this requires a sea change in our way of thinking.

One worthwhile approach is to try to open our minds more to the world we live in. While our lives may revolve around our own material concerns and those of the people closest to us, we can – and perhaps, as fellow human beings, we should – include in our awareness the concerns of those remote from us. Being able to feel emotionally the concerns of those who are not known to us is a rare and great quality, but appreciating these with the mind is something that all civilised people should aspire to and attain. Political or charitable activities are ways to take this further; but even without such practical consequences, a more integrated, rational consciousness will follow from deliberately applying the mind to issues that are beyond its immediate concerns. In addition, there are valuable techniques, such as meditation and mindful contemplation, that aim to enhance awareness of our own inner consciousness. These techniques – some of which are explored in the following pages – can help us to live more in the present moment and less in a tangle of associations, memories and anxieties. They can optimise our mental abilities and enrich our lives with more value and purpose.

> "The perfect man employs his mind as a mirror; it grasps nothing, it refuses nothing, it receives but does not keep."
>
> Suzuki Roshi, Zen master

 TRY IT YOURSELF

INCREASING AWARENESS

Try this exercise in becoming more aware of your surroundings. Go for a walk with a companion in a local park that offers a good variety of sights and activities. Afterwards, each of you write a list of questions to test the the other's alertness. For example, what colour were the flowers in the flowerbed by the tea shop? Were there any geese on the pond? Were the boys on the left playing frisbee or football? What different breeds of dog were being walked? What is the statue next to the bridge?

Try to maintain a level of consciousness in everyday life that would enable you to answer similar questions about any experience. For example, when you are next being driven by car on an unfamiliar route, take more notice of the journey. Not only will you find it easier to navigate yourself another time, but you may notice some intriguing local features you would otherwise miss.

THE ALERT MIND

Alertness is a key aspect of consciousness. When we are not alert, we do not function at the peak of our mental ability. Maximising alertness therefore helps us to function more efficiently. It can also help us to avoid potentially dangerous errors, for example when driving, working with machines or making vital decisions.

The difference between being very sleepy and feeling wide awake is usually obvious, and we can recognise these extremes of alertness both in ourselves and in other people. Less obvious, however, are the different degrees of alertness that occur throughout a normal day.

Many scientists distinguish between two kinds of alertness – tonic and phasic. Tonic alertness is associated with biological rhythms, especially the daily cycle of waking and sleeping. Typically, our alertness is lowest in the very early hours of the morning (3 to 6 am) and highest during the late afternoon and early evening (4 to 7 pm). We also tend to be more alert during mid-morning (10 am to 1 pm) than in the early afternoon (1 to 3 pm).

> **"I believe the greatest asset a head of state can have is the ability to get a good night's sleep."**
>
> Harold Wilson, former British prime minister

Tonic alertness is controlled largely by a part of the brain called the reticular activating system (RAS), which arouses the rest of the brain when it is itself stimulated. Evidence for this comes from studies that have found that damage to the brainstem above the RAS can cause continuous sleep, whereas damage below the RAS does not impair normal cycles of alertness and sleep. Electrical stimulation of the RAS also causes sleeping animals to wake up. Recent research has demon-

Real lives   *A LUCKY ESCAPE*

Jean commutes weekly between London and the north of England. She learned the hard way about the importance of keeping alert while driving.

'We'd had the cottage in the country for a few months, but this was the first time I'd driven back to London on my own. I was a little nervous about finding my way through the country roads, but once I was on the motorway I felt fine. Even though I had only a small city car, I put my foot down and headed south as fast as I could. By the time I was 80 miles or so from London, I had been driving for several hours and knew I was tired, but I felt my destination was within reach and I really wanted to keep going. So I pressed on – and the next thing I knew was when I opened my eyes, with the car drifting into the next lane! I had drifted off to sleep, with the tiredness and monotony of motorway driving. Luckily, it was only for a moment, otherwise I'm sure I would have been killed. Now, I'll pull over to rest as soon as I feel tired or that my attention is drifting. It may take longer to reach your destination – but if you're too tired to drive safely, you're quite likely not to make it at all.'

FOCUS ON *CHOCOLATE AS A STIMULANT*

Chocolate has been used as a stimulant in many cultures. It was revered by the Aztecs and Maya who used it in religious ceremonies and valued it more highly than gold.

Chocolate is made from the seeds of the tropical cacao tree, *Theobroma cacao*, a name derived from two Greek words: 'theos' meaning gods and 'broma' meaning food. Its active ingredients include caffeine and theobromine, both of which are potentially addictive alkaloid stimulants.

Despite its caffeine content, chocolate does not seem to keep people awake at night and is widely used as a bedtime drink. Theobromine has been proven to improve the performance of racehorses, and feeding racehorses chocolate, cocoa beans or theobromine before a race is now illegal. It has not yet been shown that chocolate improves alertness or other performance criteria in humans – but that does not seem to reduce our appetite for this 'food of the gods'.

strated that other parts of the brain, including the thalamus and hypothalamus, are also involved in the sleep–wake cycle and alertness.

The other kind of alertness, known as phasic alertness, is a short-term, temporary arousal, prompted by new and important events around us, particularly potentially threatening ones. Typically, phasic alertness lasts for just a few seconds. For example, if you suddenly hear a loud noise, you will automatically turn to see where it is coming from. Many other bodily changes are also triggered – dilation of pupils, increase of heart-rate and breathing, tensing of muscles, and so on. These are all part of the response to the potential danger or crisis, and prepare your body either to run away from the threat or to stand and fight it. Accordingly, this mechanism is often called the 'fight-or-flight' response.

The impact of environment

Environmental factors are important in maintaining alertness – a fact often overlooked in the design of offices and factories. Many people work in offices where light, temperature and noise levels are optimised for comfort rather than maximum alertness; indeed many places of employment are more conducive to sleep than work. Sitting in an articicially controlled atmosphere, while staring at a computer monitor and lulled by the hum of the fans, it is unsurprising that many of us sometimes find it difficult to concentrate.

It is useful to remember that cool, dry air – especially on the face – can help keep you alert, whereas heat and humidity tend to make you drowsy. Therefore, turning down the thermostat and opening windows are all simple, healthy ways to improve alertness. Another tactic to help maintain alertness, particularly during a difficult or boring task, is to take regular short breaks.

Phasic alertness Any sudden loud noise, such as a balloon bursting, makes us jump. This short-term arousal is known as phasic alertness. This mechanism evolved as a means of allowing us to respond quickly to potential threats in the environment.

NAPS IN FLIGHT

Long-haul flight crews regularly experience extended periods of duty while crossing multiple time zones, which results in disruption of daily cycles and loss of sleep. In a recent study, a group of pilots was monitored to examine the effects of napping on board during off-duty periods of flying 747 aircraft, which have a flight crew of three.

Some pilots were encouraged to nap while off-duty, while others were not allowed to sleep at all on the flight deck. Their performance was then compared over a period of 12 days that involved eight flights. Measurements of alertness were made using both subjective techniques, such as log-books and anecdotal reports, and objective measures, such as physiological recording of brain and eye activity. Of those pilots who were allowed naps, nearly all (93 per cent) went to sleep, with the average sleep session lasting about 26 minutes.

The study found that the 'no nap' pilots showed reduced performance, especially on night flights, whereas the 'nap' pilots had significantly better performance and physiological alertness. Partly as a result of this real-life research, many airlines have now put in place programmes for controlled rest periods for their flight crews.

Food and alertness

Food and drink may have a direct bearing on alertness. People often feel sleepy soon after eating a large meal, because of the diversion of blood and oxygen away from the brain to the digestive areas. In addition, certain foods, including bananas, milk, chicken and turkey, promote sleepiness in certain individuals. Conversely, a simple glass of water can make you feel more awake. Many people use caffeine in the form of coffee, tea and cola drinks to boost alertness temporarily. Reliance on caffeine can be counter-productive because the more you use it, the more you need to produce the same effect. On the other hand, some people are so sensitive to caffeine that just one cup of coffee can disrupt their sleep.

In recent years there have been numerous claims that food supplements can reduce fatigue and increase alertness. Compounds and preparations such as acetyl-L-carnitine, DMAE, ginkgo biloba, ginseng, L-phenyl-alanine, L-tyrosine (the last two being amino acids that are commonly found in high-protein foods) have all been touted as substances that enhance alertness. In most cases, these claims have not been substantiated by scientific evidence.

The role of sleep

The single factor that exerts the strongest effect on alertness is sleep. Experts agree that most adults need to sleep for seven to eight hours every night, while children and adolescents need longer. Less than five hours per night over several days can start to cause noticeable mental impairment including loss of alertness during waking hours; less than three hours per night for a week or more can cause serious health problems. In laboratory experiments on animals, continued sleep deprivation has been found to cause death – chiefly through damage to the immune system. It is there-fore essential to develop regular sleep habits that support rather than conflict with the biological clock in our brains.

The 24-hour society

In today's world, many people work shifts that do not fit in with natural patterns of activity. Some people can cope with changing their patterns of wakefulness more easily than others, but it is vital that all shift workers avoid major sleep loss so they can be alert when they need to be. The dangers of shift workers not being alert, especially in the early morning, may have contributed to major industrial accidents such as those at Three Mile Island and Bhopal, and the *Exxon Valdez* running aground. It is also well documented that road traffic accidents are relatively more common in the small hours.

Part of the reason that alertness drops during the night is that darkness increases the concentration of sleep-inducing melatonin in the brain. So one way of maintaining alertness when working shifts is to make sure that the working area is brightly lit. In the USA, some people take melatonin pills (not licensed for use in the UK because of concerns over its safety) to help them to adjust to a new daily rhythm of work, alertness and sleep.

A useful approach to maintaining alertness throughout the working day, whether you are a shift worker or not, is the judicious use of naps. Your potential for alertness is influenced not only by the amount of sleep you had the previous night but also how long you have been awake. So, for someone who has to work in the morning and evening, an afternoon nap will decrease the number of continuous hours of wakefulness and may help to maintain alertness. Care needs to be taken, however, that the nap does not have the adverse effect. If it is too long, the person may find it hard to get to sleep later on. Also, the period immediately after a nap can be characterised by lack of alertness – often referred to as 'sleep inertia'. Generally, though, studies of strategic napping have demonstrated that they can help to maintain performance and alertness.

FACT: Colour has been shown to have an effect on mood and alertness. Yellow has been suggested as the ideal colour to paint a study, because it helps you feel alert and focused without being overstimulated.

❓ HOW TO... MEASURE YOUR ALERTNESS

Levels of alertness are measured by psychologists using reaction times. A simple measure of how alert you are can be obtained with the help of a friend and a ruler at least 40cm (15in) long.

1. Ask your friend to hold the rule vertically between thumb and finger at the top of the rule. Position the thumb and finger of your preferred hand at the bottom of the rule about 2–3cm (1in) apart, so neither is touching the rule.

2. Your friend should then drop the rule, without warning. As soon as you see the rule falling, grasp it between your thumb and finger. Use the position of your thumb against the rule's markings to see how far it fell before you caught it.

3. Repeat this several times and take an average of the readings. Then try this test at different times of the day or before and after meals and drinks to gauge how much your reaction times vary.

1

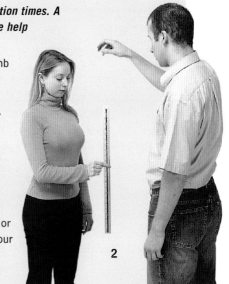

2

HOW TO BE MORE ALERT

There are times when we are less alert than we would like to be. Sometimes these feelings of lethargy can persist, making us feel unfulfilled, and as if we are wasting time. However, there are ways to increase your level of alertness in almost any situation. Here are six simple techniques that you can try.

USE YOUR MUSCLES

Almost any muscle activity will stimulate the nervous system and help to keep you alert. This can involve fine movements of the fingers, hands and feet, or larger movements of the limbs and trunk. Going for a short walk is an excellent way of shaking off lethargy, but if this is not practical, standing up or stretching out your arms or legs can be beneficial.

KNOW YOUR DAILY CYCLE

Throughout the 24-hour cycle of day and night, your body changes rhythmically in temperature, fluid loss, hormonal secretions, and so on. Most people are least alert between midnight and dawn; most alert during late morning; less alert after lunch; and more alert again during late afternoon and early evening. Some people, however, are 'larks' (most alert in the morning) or 'owls' (at their best in the evening). Try to identify your alertness pattern, and use this to decide what time of day is best to tackle certain tasks. Establishing a regular pattern of behaviour will give your body clock a chance to work for you, rather than having to fight against irregularities.

TOUCH AND COMFORT

Massage has been shown to improve alertness and productivity. In one study, workers in one group were given a 15-minute in-chair back massage, while another group spent the same time relaxing. Afterwards, the massaged group completed a set of maths problems in half the time, and with fewer errors, than the other group. Several multinational companies now provide back massages to executives and assembly line workers alike to help efficiency. You can take advantage of this effect by giving a brief shoulder massage to your partner or a friend, or perhaps even offering the same service to a friendly colleague: with luck, your efforts will be appreciated and reciprocated!

A little discomfort is also an excellent way of keeping you more alert. When you sit down at your desk to write that difficult letter or work on those taxing spreadsheets, don't make yourself too comfortable. Instead, find a chair that is comfortable enough to support you, but for which you need to use some muscle power to maintain your posture.

MAKE LIGHT WORK

When it comes to illumination, work with, rather than against, nature. Make sure you receive plenty of light in the daytime, but exclude light at night: this will help to set your internal body clock correctly. And when at work, turn up the lights, as this will make a real difference to your level of alertness. If possible, use 'daylight' bulbs, as these give out light that matches the wavelengths in natural light.

ACTIVE SOUNDS

A quiet environment, or one where there is continuous low-level noise, can be conducive to sleepiness. Any changes in sound level will tend to increase alertness – which is why many people work better when they can converse from time to time or have music playing in the background. Try experimenting with different types of background music to see what benefits they bring; many people claim that Mozart's violin concertos, especially the third and fourth, are particularly effective in boosting alertness.

FOODS AND AROMAS

There is no 'wonder food' that can boost alertness, but a healthy, balanced diet certainly improves overall performance. Food can be eaten at times that complement your natural body rhythms. For example, taking care to have a light but reasonably nutritious lunch can help to minimise the typical early-afternoon drop in alertness. Proteins can help stimulate the production of some neuro-transmitters, so make sure you have plenty of protein-containing foods in your diet. Fluids are important too: keep yourself well hy-drated by drinking lots of water, as dehydration can affect concentration considerably. Certain aromas, such as citrus and peppermint, have a stimulant effect on some people. Try dotting a few drops of essential oil around your working area to see if if works for you.

ATTENTION AND THE FOCUSED MIND

Many everyday tasks require us to pay close attention and concentrate, and most people would like to be able to do this better. There are methods we can all use to help to maintain attention, in ourselves and others, although psychologists have found that there are limits to how much our minds can take in at once.

Whereas alertness is about how awake or sleepy you are, attention is your ability to focus and concentrate on something. Although attention is a familiar concept, it has in the past been surprisingly difficult to define and research. A century ago, pioneer psychologist William James (see page 406) described attention as 'taking possession by the mind, in clear and vivid form, of one of what seem simultaneously possible objects or trains of thought'. Another early US psychologist, Edward Titchener, carried out experiments on attention and discovered the principle of 'prior entry' – that is, when there is more than one thing impinging on our awareness, our attention tends to be taken up by whichever one occurred first.

Studying attention

In the 1920s, attention disappeared from academic psychology for several decades. The subject was dominated by the behaviourist approach, whereby anything not clearly observable or measurable – including the concepts of attention, consciousness and even the mind itself – was dismissed as not open to scientific study. From the 1950s, however, psychologists moved away from behaviourism and began to regard the mind as an information-processing system. Attention and conscious thought became central topics within this 'cognitive' approach.

One of the most important early studies in cognitive psychology was carried out in 1953 by US psychologist Colin Cherry. He was intrigued by the so-called 'cocktail party effect' –

Keeping the thread
Even in a crowded, noisy room, we can keep track of what one person is saying to us because the unconscious mind can pick out that voice and keep our conscious attention focused on it.

FOCUS ON ATTENTION DEFICIT

Some people often find it difficult to pay attention for long periods. In recent years, extreme cases of this problem have been classified as ADD (attention deficit disorder) or ADHD (attention deficit and hyperactivity disorder). Usually, it is children who are diagnosed with the disorder, but adults may suffer from it as well.

Symptoms of ADHD include both inattentive and impulsive behaviour. Typically, a person affected by the disorder may:

• seem not to listen when spoken to directly
• fail to give close attention to details or make careless mistakes
• have difficulty sustaining attention in tasks or play activities
• become easily distracted by extraneous stimuli
• blurt out answers before questions have been completed
• fidget and show other signs of restlessness
• have difficulty waiting for his or her turn
• interrupt or intrude on others, for example by butting into their conversations or games.

It is not known definitely what causes ADHD, although both biological and psychological factors are thought to be involved, and certain foodstuffs – including caffeine and some common food colourings – are thought by some

to make the symptoms worse. Recent research has found that giving affected children magnesium supplements for six months seemed to improve their symptoms significantly. However, further studies are needed to clarify the specific role of magnesium in ADHD.

how we are able to follow just one conversation when many people are talking at once. Using experiments with headphones, Cherry found that we unconsciously use physical characteristics (for example, the gender of the speaker or the direction of their voice) to pick out one voice from the many we are hearing.

Building on the information-processing idea, psychologist and former engineer Donald Broadbent argued that attention is basically a limited-capacity information channel. The brain receives far more information than it can cope with, so incoming material is 'filtered' to select only a small amount for full attention, largely depending – as Cherry had found – on its physical characteristics. The rest of the information is relegated to a much-reduced level of processing, but is not entirely discarded. This is why, for example, you can immediately 'tune in' if someone says your name in a conversation that you are not actually listening to.

Divided attention

More recent theories of attention have addressed the problem of how we can apply our attention to more than one activity. In the 1990s, researchers argued that there is an important distinction between focused and divided attention. In focused attention, you try to select only one thing to attend to, even though two or more activities are going on around you – perhaps if you have to work somewhere that has distractions. Divided attention, on the other hand, is when you are trying to do two things at once – such as driving a car and carrying on a conversation with your passenger. The researchers found three main factors that affect how successfully tasks are achieved under divided attention. First, the more difficult one or both

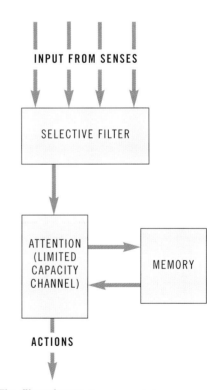

The filter theory As we cannot give our attention to all the information arriving at our senses, Broadbent argued that a 'filter' operates to select which material receives full processing within attention. Once in consciousness, this material can interact with information retrieved from memory.

tasks are, the less successful dual-performance is. Second, practice reduces the amount of attention a task demands – an experienced driver will find it easier to converse with a passenger than will a learner. The third factor is similarity: tasks that are less similar tend to be easier to perform because they interfere with each other less. For example, a person may be able to converse while driving but find it impossible to hold two conversations or read two things at once.

Distractions at work

Background noise and activity can be very detrimental to our ability to keep our attention focused at work. Since the early 1990s, there has been a trend towards open-plan offices. While some staff may thrive on the buzz of frequent interactions, others suffer because they find it so hard to concentrate. Recent research in the USA shows that open-plan offices can significantly reduce both job satisfaction and productivity. A six-year study involving managers and employees in major organisations such as Lockheed, Sun Microsystems and Microsoft showed that the most important factor in job satisfaction and performance is the ability to concentrate on work without distraction. But, while at least half of all professionals' time is spent doing quiet, focused work, about two-thirds of people in open offices are seriously disturbed by the conversations of other people. Mike Brill, who summarised the research, concluded that offices that have no enclosures are 'ludicrous'.

However, not everyone agrees that open-plan offices are a bad idea. For example, Gary Horwitz, vice-president of a California-based internet company, maintains that, from his experience, 'the openness of the space is conducive to a free flow of communication and problem-solving'. The solution to these opposing views may well lie in personality: the introverts among us are likely to work better in quieter environments, while extraverts may be better off in noisier, more stimulating places. Perhaps in the future, therefore, staff will be able to request an environment suited to their temperament – for lower stress and higher productivity all round.

> **"Open-plan offices are big time-wasters. It takes the average person five to ten minutes to get back to a deep level of concentration after being interrupted. Multiply that by ten times a day and you have 50–100 minutes of wasted time."**
>
> Martella Keniry, US workplace consultant

HOW TO PAY ATTENTION

Keep the following advice in mind when you are trying to pay attention to a task that demands concentration, such as studying.

• Get yourself into the right frame of mind when preparing to start the task. Remind yourself of the purpose of the task: relate it to specific short-term or long-term goals.

• Decide on a place and time (for example, a one-hour period) when you will study. If necessary, tell people that you do not want to be disturbed. If you are working at home, perhaps unplug the phone or switch on the answerphone.

• Make sure that your environment is conducive to studying. The study area should be well lit, and the temperature should be comfortable but slightly on the cool side. The work surface and surrounding area should be uncluttered, but everything you need should be easily accessible.

• Try to eliminate obtrusive thoughts that will divert your attention. For example, if you have a lot of pressing things to do, write a list prioritising them before you start studying. If any ideas come while you are studying, add them to the list and tell yourself they can be dealt with after the study period.

• If you are intending to study for longer than an hour, take a break for at least ten minutes between periods. Get up for a drink or go outside for some fresh air.

• If you discover any extra concentration strategies that work for you, note them down.

HOW TO HOLD ATTENTION

While many people need to give talks as part of their work, at some time we are all likely to have to address a group of people – perhaps at a family event or an office party. Afterwards we would all like people to say 'That was interesting!'

There are no foolproof rules for being a good speaker, but keeping your audience engaged is a vital component. To do this, you will need to include some attention-grabbing elements. Bear in mind that people respond to novelty, so try to have lots of variety within your talk. For example:

• Liven up the presentation of factual material by telling a story that illustrates your point, or add some action by holding up a prop or moving around the room.

• Add visual interest – write on a flip chart or board, or project a slide with bullet points, diagrams or other pictures.

• Interact directly with the audience. Ask them questions, or encourage them to comment on what you have said.

You can also use examples to hold the attention of the audience and illustrate your points. When using examples in a talk, keep the following points in mind:

• Be clear and make sure your examples clarify the point you are making. If the connection between your point and the example is weak or tangential, you will lose your audience.

• Be relevant. Don't include jokes simply for the sake of getting a few laughs. Your material also has to be relevant.

• Be brief. If you are giving a ten-minute speech, don't use an eight-minute example.

• Target the audience. Keep the specific interests of your audience in mind. For example: if making a presentation to an audience of gardeners, you might tell a story about Alan Titchmarsh; while to a group of entrepreneurs you might use an anecdote about Richard Branson.

• Use personal experience. Using illustrations of things that happened to you helps to hold an audience's attention. Such examples tend to be more vivid and easier to remember (for you and your audience) than abstract or impersonal ones.

CLEARING THE MIND

At any moment, most of us have many concerns occupying our consciousness – present responsibilities, reflections on past events, and so on. A sense of mental chaos can easily be the result. Mind training techniques can provide an effective way of clarifying our thinking, and can guide us through relaxation to inner peace.

> **"Meditation doesn't teach us anything new. It reminds us what we have forgotten."**
>
> Dhiravamsa, *The Way of Non-Attachment*

There are few of us who do not complain about the stresses of modern living. Much of this stress arises because our thoughts and emotions dominate us, keeping us dwelling on the very things that we would rather not think or feel. Stressful thinking is typically unproductive; it solves nothing, tires us out, and leaves us feeling more worried than ever.

One way that we can take more control over our mental and emotional lives is by using mind training techniques, such as meditation. Meditation teaches us that thoughts and emotions are things that we have, rather than who we are. It can free us from the often oppressive influence of thought by letting us acknowledge that thoughts come and go – and it is up to us how much attention we pay to them.

Eastern religions, such as Hinduism and Buddhism, place great emphasis upon meditation. The mind control that it brings puts practitioners in closer touch with their own being, and clarifies their relationship with the reality outside themselves. However, not all proponents and teachers of meditation come from particular spiritual traditions. For example, transcendental meditation (TM), which became very popular in the 1960s, is essentially a secularised technique borrowed from a respected Indian guru. Stripped of its overtly spiritual dimension, TM is widely practised in the US, and even gained government support.

Meditation has also been approached from a strictly secular and scientific standpoint. For example, Herbert Benson of Harvard University Medical School has developed a meditation technique called 'the relaxation response', which has been shown to be effective in reducing anxiety and slowing heart rate and breathing.

THE BENEFITS OF MEDITATION

DESPITE A FEW ODD GLANCES FROM HIS WORK COLLEAGUES, ROGER TAKES 15 MINUTES AT LUNCH TIME TO MEDITATE

Roger, I just can't cope with this workload! I've got reports to do, orders to despatch, and I need to visit the Birmingham office...

Wait a moment, Tom – you don't need to do all this by tomorrow. Let's sit down and work out the priorities.

BACK HOME BY 11pm, ROGER IS FEELING PLEASANTLY READY FOR A REFRESHING NIGHT'S REST

PHYSICAL RELAXATION Entering a meditative state not only focuses the mind but helps to relax the body.

STRESS REDUCTION Meditation does not eliminate stress, but it does help keep things in perspective.

IMPROVED SLEEP The tranquillity that arises from meditation makes it much easier to get a good night's sleep.

The religious tradition A Buddhist monk in Thailand kneels in meditation by a giant statue of Buddha. Meditation plays a key part in several spiritual traditions.

Meditation for everyone

Anyone can learn to meditate. Many people take up the practice after retirement, or when their children have grown old enough to allow them more freedom. Even the very young can be introduced to meditation. Experiments in the UK have shown the positive effects of meditation in the classroom. Just five minutes of sitting quietly and focusing on breathing at some point in the school day helped children as young as seven to be calmer and more attentive.

Men and women are attracted equally to meditation, and seem to progress at similar rates. Indeed, the main obstacles to successful meditation are not sex or age but impatience and boredom. In the West we have become accustomed to instant results, but meditation demands time and self-discipline. We are also used to a constant diet of entertainment fed to us from outside, and the idea of sitting quietly, doing nothing except experiencing one's own mind, may seem very tame. But the experienced meditator is rarely bored; discovering the serenity and tranquillity of the uncluttered mind gives a unique insight into consciousness itself.

Meditation costs nothing, can be carried out anywhere, requires no apparatus or special clothes, and has many proven physical and psychological benefits, including stress reduction, pain control and even lowering of blood pressure. Meditation is also deeply rewarding as a voyage of self-discovery. Paradoxically, although it is an inward journey, it takes us not away from the world, but more richly and deeply into it.

IMPROVED MEMORY Focusing the mind in meditation helps us to become more focused in our daily lives.

GREATER TOLERANCE The mental and emotional discipline of meditation helps in our relationships with others.

GREATER EFFICIENCY Less wayward thinking means that most tasks requiring ordered thinking are performed more effectively.

Regular meditation, even for a few minutes a day, is physically and psychologically rewarding. There are many meditative techniques to choose from, but they all have one crucial element in common – concentration. Not the sort of hard, determined concentration that we used to learn in lessons at school, but a light, relaxed form, in which you choose a point of focus and fix your attention upon it. Every time thoughts or feelings intrude, you gently steer your mind back to this point of focus. Anyone can meditate: all you need is patience and quiet determination.

LEARN TO MEDITATE

STEP 1: GETTING STARTED

Before starting a session of meditation, it is important to prepare properly. Choose a quiet time when you are unlikely to be interrupted. Most people prefer mornings, just after rising, but evenings just before bedtime are also good. Decide what time is best for you and try to stick to it, incorporating it into your daily routine. Choose a place where you feel comfortable and calm; the corner of a bedroom is often ideal. Wear loose, comfortable clothes (or none at all if you prefer). Ideally, you should sit on the floor cross-legged, with a firm cushion that raises your bottom about four inches from the floor. If you find this difficult or uncomfortable, sit in a straight-backed chair with your feet flat on the floor. Place your hands in your lap palms downwards, with the fingers interlocked or with one hand resting on the other. At first, it is helpful to close your eyes, but as you progress you may like to practise with eyes open.

STEP 2: THE PRACTICE

Once you are comfortable, mentally scan your body for muscle tension. Whenever you find an area of tension, gently let it go. Keep your back straight; it may help to imagine your spine as a stack of coins that has to stay balanced. Now focus your attention on your breathing. Make sure that it is coming from as low down as possible – from your diaphragm, not your chest. Don't take huge breaths, just keep your breathing relaxed and natural, in a gentle, quiet rhythm. Now direct your attention to a point just below your nose – the point where you feel cool air as you breathe in and warm air as you breathe out. The sensation is subtle but clear. Keep your attention fixed on this point at all times, even between breaths.

STEP 3: KEEPING FOCUSED

When you start to meditate, you will almost certainly find that thoughts
bubble up and tug you away from your point of focus. Don't try to push them away. Pay them
no special attention; just let them rise and pass across the surface of your mind in the same way that
clouds gently drift across the sky. If a thought does capture your attention and takes you away from your
breathing, bring your focus gently back. If you find it difficult to stay focused, it is sometimes helpful to count
your breaths. Count from one to ten on each out-breath, then back from ten to one again. Another helpful strategy
is to remind yourself 'I have thoughts, but I am not my thoughts'. If emotions arise, treat them in the same way
as thoughts. Tell yourself 'I have anxieties/fears/anger, but I am not my anxieties/fears/anger'. If your
body feels uncomfortable, treat the discomfort in the same way. Observe these distractions and let
them go, instead of becoming caught up in them.

STEP 4: FINDING TIME

Five minutes of meditation a day is a good start for beginners.
As you become more practised, you will be able to stay focused for longer
and longer – perhaps for 20 or 30 minutes. At the end of your meditation, be
grateful for the time that you have spent quietly. Try to get into the habit
of meditating whenever you have nothing pressing to do – while on a
train journey, waiting for a bus, or before the start of a meeting
(this can be particularly helpful because it
calms the nerves).

STEP 5: PERSEVERING

Some people give up meditation after a short time, protesting that their
minds are so busy that they will never succeed at it. But it is precisely because our minds
are so frantically busy that meditation is of such great value. If we were in control of our minds we
would not need to meditate. The key to meditation is quiet perseverance. Even experienced meditators
have 'off' days when they cannot still their mental chatter. Simply note these good and
bad days, and continue with your practice.

MINDFULNESS

Meditation is a highly effective technique for focusing the mind – and for keeping it focused. With patience and practice, it is possible to apply a similar discipline to everyday activities at home and work. The resulting state of 'mindfulness' can improve memory and help us to operate more effectively across a range of situations.

You put your keys down and moments later you cannot remember where they are. You get to the bottom of the page in a book without registering a single word you have read. These scenarios probably sound very familiar. But the reason for these failures of attention – which nearly all of us experience from time to time – is not so much memory loss as mental chaos. Our minds simply wander away, sparked by thoughts or feelings that are at a tangent to what we are engaged in doing. Surprisingly, the more stimulating the activity, the more likely we are to be distracted; studies have shown that college students actually remember more of a lecture they find boring than they do of an interesting one, because the latter sets them thinking instead of attending.

There is, however, a very effective way of training the mind to pay attention – mindfulness. It is similar to meditation, but instead of focusing on breathing you allow your focus to rest upon the things that you are doing, seeing or hearing. Almost like a camera, you turn to each experience without dwelling on the previous one, and without becoming distracted by the inner world of unproductive thinking.

Mindfulness in practice Hollywood actor Richard Gere has been a practitioner of mindfulness since discovering an interest in Buddhism in the late 1970s. He makes a point of meditating daily, saying 'it helps me set my motivation for the day'.

FOCUS ON **MINDFUL ATTENTION**

In a well-known psychological experiment, participants are shown a short clip of film without being told the purpose, and then asked to answer specific factual questions relating to the content. What colour was the shirt of one of the actors? What did A say to B? What was on the table? Did C have long or short hair? What could be seen through the window? And so on. Not only do many people get the details wrong, they often disagree vehemently with each other over these details.

One of the reasons for the mistakes and disagreements is selective attention. People tend to focus in on the things in which they are interested and to ignore everything else. With the practice of mindfulness, selective attention broadens, so that the conscious mind takes in more of the information being fed to it by the senses. One outcome of this is that our range of interests also widens and we make better use of our eyes and ears.

The mindful arts
Buddhist monks practising kung fu at the Pagoda Forest near the Shaolin monastery in China's Henan Province. Mindfulness is central to kung fu. It enables the practitioner to focus so intently on his opponent that he counters the latter's attack as soon as it is launched.

Open minds

Mindfulness is not the same as concentration, which demands concerted effort and can only be sustained for relatively short periods. Rather, it involves a natural openness to experience – an openness that we all have as young children, but which we lose in the ever-growing torrent of demands, pressures and distractions.

Practising mindfulness brings many benefits. You will probably be far less tired at the end of the day because chaotic thinking often summons up emotions – anger, fear or anxiety – that are energy-draining and that remain with you long after you have started to think about something else. Mindfulness allows you to let go, and so helps you to conserve emotional energy. But far from discouraging thinking, mindfulness helps you to remain alert, fresh and creative, so when productive thinking is required, ideas typically come with a surprising clarity. This is because the practice of mindfulness gives voice to precisely those unconscious thought processes that are the source of creativity. All too often the conscious mind is too busy with its own affairs to remain open to new creative ideas; and like someone failing to be heard above the noise of the room, the unconscious eventually gives up on its unequal task.

There is nothing esoteric or 'way out' about mindfulness. It is simply a way of allowing yourself to remain in the present where you can be fully engaged with your experiences, rather than losing yourself in thoughts about your experiences. Mindfulness is practised by many sports professionals; allowing the mind to wander during a game of tennis, or dwelling too long on the last missed shot can spell disaster. Many sports psychologists acknowledge that the difference between an excellent player and a good one resides more in an ability to remain mindful throughout an arduous match than it does in differences in coordination or athleticism.

> **"Before I learned to practise mindfulness it was as if I went through each day with my eyes shut."**
>
> Michael, an experienced meditator

THINK AGAIN!

THE SOURCE OF ENLIGHTENMENT
Many years ago, a Japanese Zen master was asked for the secret of enlightenment. In reply, he picked up his brush and wrote the symbol for 'attention'. 'Surely there must be more to it than that?' persisted his questioner. The master picked up his brush again and wrote the symbol three times – attention, attention, attention.

CULTIVATING MINDFULNESS

There are many practical ways in which we can encourage mindfulness to develop. They don't demand any extra time – they are simply different ways of carrying out and thinking about everyday tasks. These exercises will help you to recognise that everything around you is part of a continual process of change. Every time you look at a familiar object you see it in a slightly different way, so in a very real sense everything you see is seen for the first time. Mindfulness helps to open you up to the subtlety of each experience and reminds you that you are fully alive.

STAYING IN THE PRESENT

Avoid constantly judging every event, object and environment; don't let your previous experiences get in the way of the present moment. Thoughts like 'I've always hated this dreary old office', 'I wish I'd bought the larger size', or 'I know this is going to be a bore' drag you out of the present and waste emotional energy. Adopt a similar attitude to people: try to see people as who they are now, rather than in ways you remember from previous encounters. And try not to spend so much time in inconsequential chatter. Watching, listening and paying attention can be far more productive in the long run.

WALKING MINDFULLY

Walking is one of the best exercises for cultivating mindfulness. When you next go for a walk, don't get lost in thought, just look around you. Take in the colour of the houses, the shape of the trees, the smell of the city, the sound of your footsteps, and the faces of passers-by. Notice how your mind tries to pull you away from direct experience by thinking about the things you are observing. Resist the temptation to be distracted until you finish your walk, then think back over the experience. Did you notice things that you usually pass over? You'll probably find that your mindful state made the whole walk much more interesting. Mindfulness makes you far more aware of the enchantment of the senses, how the world arranges itself around us, the difference between natural and man-made objects, and the relationship between objects and the space around them.

TAKING A MIND HOLIDAY

Have you ever returned from a holiday more tired than when you left? Many people find this to be true because their minds become even more distracted and chaotic when in a new environment than when at home.

Next time you go away, allow your mind to take a holiday too. Focus on the sights and sounds around you – the blue sky, the waves on the beach, the green trees and the far hills, the feel of the sun and of the wind and the water on your body, the texture of the ground under your feet. Immerse yourself fully in each moment without letting it pass unnoticed and unappreciated.

STOPPING THE FLOW

Ask a friend, partner or colleague to shout 'stop' at some point in the day when you are engaged in routine tasks. Freeze in whatever position you were in, and pay close attention to all the sensations from the body – tensions, tremors, and especially your sense of balance. This exercise will help you to realise just how much of the sensory material constantly coursing through the brain is screened out in your normal state of consciousness.

COMMENTING ON YOURSELF

Set up a silent running commentary of what you are doing at this moment. Some people are rather dismissive when they hear about this exercise, but it can be very helpful, especially if you lead a frantic life. It will fix your experiences in your mind. Aim to keep the commentary going for at least a few minutes several times a day. For example, 'Now I'm reading this letter ... now I'm putting it down on the window ledge as the phone starts to ring. Now I'm answering the phone and listening ... now replying ... now listening. Now I'm putting the phone down and going over to make some coffee'. Later, when you are trying to recall where you put the letter, the memory will return clearly – it's on the window ledge.

REVIEWING THE DAY

Major spiritual traditions such as Buddhism, which lay far greater importance on mindfulness than we in the West, maintain that a review of the day is of incalculable benefit. In the late evening, think back to waking up that morning, and then go systematically through the events of the day. Focus not just on the events that happened but on your thoughts and feelings about them. Alternatively, go through events in reverse order, working back to the moment of waking. Are there any large gaps in your recall of the day's events? Where was your mind during those gaps – what distracted you? Think about how you can avoid such distractions in the future.

CREATIVITY AND THE OPEN MIND

From early childhood, we are encouraged to be creative – to use our imagination and discover innovative solutions. But can creativity be learned at all, or is it one of nature's gifts bestowed on the lucky few? Psychologists who have examined the nature of the creative process may have some answers.

It is often suggested that you can test creativity, like IQ, using standard exercises – such as listing in three minutes as many uses as you can for a brick, or naming as many things as possible that are both white and edible.

These exercises certainly measure your ability to think of alternatives, but this ability is not quite the same as creativity. A more convincing test would be one that assesses inspiration – your ability to solve problems with sudden flashes of insight. A classic exercise of this genre is the hat-rack problem. You are alone in a room with just two poles and a clamp. How do you make a peg steady enough to hang a hat? Try leaning a pole against the wall and it will slip. Snapping the poles to make legs for a tripod is against the rules. And anyway, the clamp could not secure them. But then – eureka! – you look up at the ceiling and realise that if the two poles are clamped together, to make a single, longer pole, they could be wedged between ceiling and floor, leaving the clamp as the peg. This solution is both surprising and apt – the very essence of creativity.

Out of the blue

Geniuses, who can apparently conjure these sideways leaps of thought from thin air, say that they cannot pinpoint their source of inspiration. Picasso said his paintings took him over, controlling his brush strokes. Mozart claimed that whole symphonies sprang to life in an instant, as if he had just heard them played. Einstein joked that he found shaving risky because this was often the time he was seized by a good idea. All remarked on the contrast between the usual hard graft of intellectual labour and the ease and

> "I have no special gift – I am only passionately curious."
>
> Albert Einstein

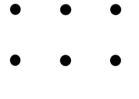

Real lives   *A LEAP OF INSPIRATION*

The role of sudden inspiration in creative thinking is exemplified by the story of Henri Poincaré, the brilliant 19th-century French mathematician, who solved an important algebraic problem while jumping aboard a bus.

Poincaré had just spent 15 fruitless days at his desk slaving over a problem with Fuschian functions – an aspect of multi-dimensional geometry. Then as he was hopping on a bus, the answer struck. 'The idea came to me, without anything in my former thoughts seeming to have paved the way for it,' wrote Poincaré. 'On my return to Caen, for conscience's sake, I verified the result at my leisure.'

completeness of their moments of sudden inspiration. So what goes on in a brain when it makes such jumps? How distinct is inspiration from ordinary problem-solving? Can we learn to tap into this power? The short answer from psychologists is that creativity increases when we relax our grip on established ways of thinking and free our minds to spot offbeat alternatives. And this kind of mental letting go involves a subtle interplay between the two hemispheres of the brain.

Taking sides

Popular belief has it that the brain is divided into a left hemisphere that is logical, verbal and rational, and a right hemisphere that is emotional and holistic. While there is some truth in this simple model, it is more accurate to say that the left hemisphere is specialised for taking a focused, sequential approach, while the right hemisphere looks at the broader context. Some neuroscientists think that the cells of the right hemisphere are rather more widely branched and connected. So when any thought is in mind, the right side rouses a wealth of associated thoughts, feelings and fringe meanings. When we think, the two hemispheres work in a complementary way. The right brain creates a mental backdrop – a sense of the known terrain – which the focused thinking of the left brain can then explore more systematically.

Of course, the problem comes when we want to break fresh ground. If we are faced with a puzzle, such as making the hat-rack, the right brain establishes a general mental picture – an image of the task, an empty room, a clamp and two poles – then the left brain sets to work logically considering the alternatives. However, if no answer is obvious, if no arrangement of the components seems to fit, we need to let go of our existing picture and find a different context within which to continue the search: the right brain has to relax its grip and start again.

So while intelligence can be seen as exploration within an established mental context, creativity is about broadening or changing the context – letting go and allowing your brain to come at a problem from a new angle.

> **"The analysis of data will not by itself produce new ideas."**
>
> Edward de Bono

Creative puzzle-solving A good example of a test of creative thinking is the nine-dot puzzle shown above. Can you join all the dots with four straight lines without lifting your pencil from the paper or going over a line twice? See page 475 for the answer.

Mental reframing

People who are professionally creative seem to have discovered this fact for themselves. When they realise that they have reached a mental cul-de-sac, they step away from their desks, easels or drawing boards and go for a run, meditate, look out of the window, or go to sleep. By engaging in a different activity, a strongly roused set of ideas can fade and a different perspective may form in its place.

Most of us know from experience that holding a thought or image in mind can suppress alternative views of the same thing. For example, when struggling to remember a name that is 'on the tip of your tongue', a similar but wrong name often rises and blocks correct recall. If you stop and forget about the task, the right name often just pops into mind a few minutes later. This happens because the roused brain cells have relaxed enough to let other, weaker-firing, brain cells on the fringe break through with the correct answer.

Just relaxing from a task at regular intervals is an easy way to boost creativity, and there are more systematic techniques that can also help to reframe a problem (see page 458). But relaxation is not the only component. Creative thinking involves sweat as well as inspiration; the sudden snap of insight can only strike a mind that has prepared itself by forming a rich backdrop of knowledge and skill.

> **"Write down the thoughts of the moment. Those that come unsought for are commonly the most valuable."**
>
> Francis Bacon (1561–1626)

A recipe for genius?

This idea is borne out when we look at the lives of geniuses who claimed that their best ideas came out of the blue. Psychologists have shown that most great achievers started early, and usually had a family background that gave them a flying start in their chosen field. They then spent many years patiently learning their trade.

Mozart's father, for example, was a court musician and composer who was ambitious for his son and had him singing scales and tinkling the keyboard at an age when other children were still on nursery rhymes. By the age of 12, Mozart had already spent five years as a performer travelling around Europe and had written his first compositions. Similarly, Picasso had been taught by his father – an art teacher – to paint with classical virtuosity by the age of 15. And Einstein was encouraged to read the works of Euclid and Kant from an early age. Even after these head starts, Mozart,

FACT: Psychologists have calculated that it takes 10,000 hours of practice to become good enough at something – whether it is chess, maths, tennis, or playing the violin – to master a skill enough to be creative in that domain.

The development of genius Creative geniuses usually show a high level of conventional skill before developing innovation. Picasso painted the classical-style *First Communion* (left) in 1896, aged 15. In contrast, *Les Demoiselles D'Avignon* (right) from 1907 demonstrates the bold experimentalism of his maturing style.

Picasso and Einstein took at least ten years before they started to produce original, creative work in their own unique style. They needed to master the complete set of tools of their respective trades before they could begin to experiment within the conventional framework and start producing their unique and innovative work.

As the inventor Thomas Edison famously said: 'Genius is one per cent inspiration and 99 per cent perspiration.' Creative ideas often do strike out of the blue, coming in moments of relaxation or when idly toying with ideas. But behind the ease of the creative flash lies the hard work that is always needed to bring the mind to the brink of inspiration.

FACT FILE   THE FOUR STAGES OF CREATION

British psychologist Graham Wallas has formulated an influential four-stage model of the creative act.

• **Stage 1: preparation** – the intense frontal assault on a problem that familiarises the thinker with all its aspects.

• **Stage 2: incubation** – a period of relaxation that lets established ways of looking at the problem fade so that alternatives can bubble closer to the surface.

• **Stage 3: illumination** – the mental click where some surprise connection suddenly makes sense of the problem: background thoughts finally break through into clear consciousness, or perhaps we idly note a key aspect – such as the ceiling in the hat-rack problem.

• **Stage 4: verification** – Wallas points out that the click of insight usually produces the feeling of suddenly having the right angle on the problem, but logical left-brain work is then needed to prove that the answer really works.

Creative genius

When Igor Stravinsky premiered 'The Rite of Spring' in 1913, he provoked a riot in the Parisian audience. His audacious music was unlike anything they had heard before. What was behind Stravinsky's creative leap – and can such musical genius ever be fully understood?

In its time, Stravinsky's ballet *The Rite of Spring* (*Le Sacre du Printemps*) was truly shocking because it so blatantly challenged musical orthodoxy. Instead of regular, flowing phrases and smooth key progressions, it juxtaposed uneven fragments in unrelated keys over a barbaric, stamping pulse. Yet despite the booing of the majority of the audience, there were some even on that first night who recognised it as a work of genius.

The man and his music
Pictured here in 1958 with the original manuscript of *The Rite of Spring,* Stravinsky (1882–1971) continued to compose innovative and alluring music into the mid-20th century.

Stravinsky's raw materials were the same as those available to any other composer – the instruments of the orchestra. What he did was rewrite the rule book, throwing out all the old certainties and profoundly influencing the composers who came after him.

The elements of genius

The Rite of Spring was undoubtedly the work of an original thinker. Such creative genius relies on drive and ability, and Stravinsky had plenty of both. He was certainly singularly driven – being compelled to write even in the days following his daughter's death. He also had the self-confidence to face the critics. This was earned, at least in part, through his extensive musical training. The son of a leading bass singer at the Imperial Opera, he was initially a self-taught musician. As a blossoming composer in his twenties, he took lessons with the gifted orchestrator Nikolai Rimsky-Korsakov.

The Rite of Spring represented a creative leap – but Stravinsky had leapt from somewhere: his base was the Romantic and nationalistic music of his time. There are many touches of sumptuous orchestration in *The Rite of Spring,* as well as snatches of folk music from Stravinsky's native Russia. Stravinsky also had the good fortune to live in bourgeois Paris at the beginning of the twentieth century where he mixed with avant-garde artists, including Picasso and Cocteau. Replacing Romantic formalism with new forms of expression, these original thinkers both encouraged and influenced Stravinsky's work.

It is clear that Stravinsky possessed the background, the training, the dedication and the inspiration to write splendid, original music. But do these qualities qualify him as genius – or was there another, mysterious ingredient?

> "Instinct is infallible. If it leads us astray, it is no longer instinct."
>
> Igor Stravinsky

Hidden workings

Music is a mathematical art – rhythms, harmony and structure are all based on numbers. When scholars analyse the work of great composers, it is tempting to think they will discover the formula for musical genius hidden within the notes. But genius is not so easy to pin down. Stravinsky's work has been extensively analysed, but attempts to create 'new' Stravinsky by following a set of rules have not convinced the critics. Stravinsky himself claimed that he had no rational formula for writing his music. He said that it came to him instinctively – he used his ear rather than any established musical rules to determine the notes.

In common with many other geniuses, Stravinsky had a restless mind, reinventing himself several times throughout his life. Soon after composing *The Rite of Spring,* he began writing sparse parodies of Baroque dance music. He went through a further metamorphosis in the 1950s, dabbling in the highly structured serial music invented by his rival Arnold Schoenberg.

A century later, *The Rite of Spring* can still move and unsettle an audience. And while we can admire and analyse the work of great composers like Stravinsky, it may still be many years before we discover the basis of musical genius.

ABSOLUTE MUSIC

While some composers work by extemporising – playing with ideas using real instruments – others experiment in their heads. Music that is imagined is free from the constraints imposed by actually playing an instrument, but only the most experienced and gifted musicians are able to work in this way.

Sometimes composers imagine music that is beyond the capability of any human performer. Such work is known as 'absolute music'. Claude Debussy's piano repertoire features impossibly quiet dynamics: in his *Image No 5: And the Moon Descends Over the Temple That Was,* he instructs the pianist to play a chain of nine-note chords that stretch almost six octaves across the keyboard. Chords of this size are difficult to play quietly, but Debussy wants them to start pianissimo (very quietly) then gradually diminuendo (become even softer). And in the early 18th century, JS Bach created absolute music for woodwind: his *Partita for Flute* has long, fast-moving passages without any rests. Players must decide how to break up his imagined, perfect musical line to take a breath.

In the recording studio, however, these limits are removed: today's sound editing technology can make the most challenging piece a reality.

FINDING YOUR OWN CREATIVITY

We all experience occasional bursts of inspiration that give us new insights into old problems. Such creative thinking seems to come naturally to some people, but it is also something that everyone can nurture. The techniques here may not transform us all into artistic geniuses, but they can help to enhance our natural creativity and take us towards successful problem solving at home and at work.

CREATIVE LIVING

• Immerse yourself in your chosen area of creativity, researching or practising as much as possible. Your creativity needs material on which to work.
• Pursue interests in areas well away from your sphere of work and usual occupations. The most creative individuals often have very diverse interests and hobbies.
• Record your dreams, daydreams and doodles. Concepts and feelings arising from the unconscious brain can open up new perspectives.
• Take exercise. Regular exercise increases the amount of nutrients and oxygen available to the brain.
• Experiment with doing routine tasks, such as housework, in completely new ways. Make creative thinking a habit.
• Reward yourself for your creativity, and you will begin to think of yourself as a creative person.

CREATIVE PROBLEM SOLVING

• First, frame the problem. Think of as many ways as you can to express the problem you want to solve, then analyse these to identify the precise question you need to answer.
• Write down any potentially useful thoughts that bear on the question as soon as they arise. Collect them in a notebook and review them regularly to see if they can be applied to any problem in mind.
• Put yourself in a stimulating but comfortable environment, and take regular breaks while thinking about the problem.
• Rhythmic activities, such as walking, swimming, painting, or even washing, can help to tone down conscious thinking and let subliminal ideas emerge from the unconscious.
• Set yourself real targets – for example, a deadline by which a problem must be resolved.
• Get other people to contribute their own ideas. The more ideas you can generate, the better your solution is likely to be.
• Employ creative thinking techniques to generate new ideas – some are described on the opposite page.

MIND MAPPING

If you want to generate creative solutions to complex personal decisions, try this technique derived from mind mapping, as pioneered by Tony Buzan.

- Take a large sheet of paper. In the centre, draw a picture that represents your problem, then use this as the hub to draw out a branching network of associations. Each new thought should be broken down into its components until all possible ideas connected with the central problem are made visible. Hopefully, you will then either spot obvious answers or else gaps where perhaps you need more information.
- Use coloured pens to code different kinds of thoughts – for example, red to highlight drawbacks, yellow to highlight wild possibilities, blue for very obvious connections. Use images rather than words to illustrate your thoughts wherever possible. Go back over the main connections as they start to emerge, making heavy lines that really stand out.
- Once you have made your map, copy it out again in a way that is more organised or that uses some newly discovered idea as the central starting point.

GROUP CREATIVITY

One of the most effective methods of creative problem solving in a group is brainwriting. This technique is often more effective than verbal 'brainstorming' sessions because it avoids social constraints on putting forward ideas to a group, and because more ideas are generated in the given time.

- Begin the session by outlining the problem to be solved. Each participant then writes an idea on a sheet of paper and passes it to the person on his or her left. The recipient can either use this idea as a stimulus for a new idea, which is written on the sheet, or can modify the first idea before passing it on, again to the left.
- After a set period of time, the ideas are organised into groups and evaluated.

RANDOM RESPONSES

If you are simply looking for a new perspective on a problem, abutting incongruous ideas or words can open up new patterns of thought. In the East, this technique has achieved the status of an art form (as in haiku poetry), but it can be adapted into a simple method for triggering creativity.

- Open a dictionary at any page and select a word at random.
- Repeat this procedure until you have a whole list of words, and then apply each to the problem in mind. You will find that almost every word stimulates some ideas on the subject.
- The technique works just as well if you use a phrase as the stimulus: try aphorisms or proverbs like 'a stitch in time saves nine' or 'put the cart before the horse'.

INDEX

PERMISSIONS

The publishers wish to thank the following for their kind permission to reproduce material in this book:

64-7 'Discover Your Personality Type' questionnaire by permission of Dr Glenn Wilson

213 extract *Coming Up For Air* by George Orwell (© George Orwell 1939) by permission of Bill Hamilton as Literary Executor of the Estate of the Late Sonia Brownell Orwell and Secker & Warburg Ltd)

221 extracts from Martha J. Farah, *Visual Agnosia: Disorders of Object Recognition and What They Tell Us About Normal Vision,* Cambridge, Mass., MIT Press, 1990

272 extracts reprinted by permission of the publisher of *The Mind of a Mnemonist* by A.R. Luria, translated by Lynn Solotaroff, Cambridge, Mass., Harvard University Press (© Michael Cole 1968)

286 examples from the Linkword method © Michael Gruneberg/ McGraw Hill Contemporary Books, Lincolnwood, Ill.

296 W.B. Yeats, *He Wishes for the Cloths of Heaven,* A.P. Watt Ltd on behalf of Michael B. Yeats

317 extract from *Consciousness Reconsidered* by Owen Flanagan (© Owen Flanagan 1994), MIT Press

322 extract from *A Writer's Notebook* by W. Somerset Maugham, published by William Heinemann, 1949. Reprinted by permisson of The Random House Group Ltd

332 quote from Alan Turing from the article 'Computer Scientist: Alan Turing' by Paul Gray from 29 March 1999 issue of *Time Magazine* (© 1999 Time Inc.). Reprinted by permission

334 extract from the article 'Is the Brain's Mind a Computer Program?' by John Searle, from January 1990 issue of *Scientific American*. Reprinted by permission of Scientific American Inc.

367 extract from *The Politics of Experience* by R.D. Laing, Penguin Books Ltd, 1967

376 extract from a letter published in 26 September 1998 issue of *New Scientist*. Reproduced by permission of New Scientist

394 extract from *Jung and the Story of Time* by Laurens van der Post, published by The Hogarth Press. Reprinted by permission of The Random House Group Ltd

396 extract from *Memories, Dreams, Reflections* by C.G. Jung, HarperCollins Publishers Ltd, 1967

418 extract from *What's Going on in There?* by Lise Eliot, Penguin Books Ltd, 1999

452 extract from *Albert Einstein: Creator and Rebel* by Banesh Hoffmann and Helen Dukas (© Helen Dukas and Banesh Hoffmann 1972) by permission of Dutton, a division of Penguin Putnam

453 quote from Edward de Bono. For more information on Edward de Bono's seminars and workshops please contact Diane McQuaig at dmcquaig@debono.com or call 001 (416) 488 0008

Every effort has been made to obtain permission for copyright material. The publishers apologise for any omissions, which are wholly unintentional. They will, if informed, make any necessary corrections in future printings of this book.

ANSWERS TO PUZZLES

MEMORY AND GENDER: Page 173 Spot the difference

1: Butter dish lid open
2: No orange flower in vase
3: Different bread roll on plate
4: Different rolls in bread basket
5: White wine bottle instead of red wine bottle
6: Water jug filled with orange juice

7: Red grapes instead of white grapes
8: No tomato on bottom plate
9: Tomato on top plate cut open
10: Dessert spoons reversed
11: Smaller candle in candle stick

12: White wine in one glass instead of red wine
13: Different red wine glass
14: Sugar bowl filled with granulated sugar instead of cubes
15: Different napkin ring

PHOTOGRAPHIC MEMORY:
Page 267
Eidetic memory test

Adding together the dots in the two images yields the pattern shown here – revealing the hidden number 63.

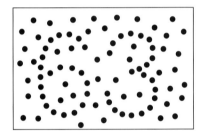

HOW TO KEEP YOUR MEMORY YOUNG: Page 308 Crossword

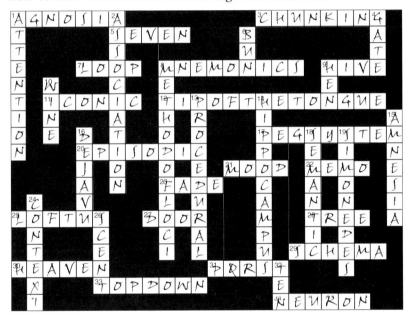

DISCOVER YOUR HIDDEN THINKING POWERS:
Page 388 Tease out your hidden knowledge

1: 7 W of the W = 7 wonders of the world
2: 26 L in the A26 = letters in the alphabet
3: 24 H in a D = 24 hours in a day
4: 12 S of the Z = 12 signs of the zodiac
5: 57 HV = 57 Heinz varieties
6: 29 D in F in a LY = 29 days in February in a leap year
7: 2 BOTC = 2 bites of the cherry
8: 10 GB (HOTW) = 10 green bottles (hanging on the wall)
9: 9L of a C = 9 lives of a cat
10: 30 D has S = 30 days has September

CREATIVITY AND THE OPEN MIND:
Page 453 Creative puzzle-solving

The secret of solving this puzzle lies in extending the lines beyond the confines of the 'box' created by the nine dots: many people assume that they should stay within the lines.

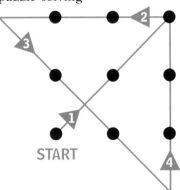

ACKNOWLEDGEMENTS

Throughout these picture credits, the following abbreviations have been used:
t = top; *c* = centre; *b* = bottom;
l = left; *r* = right; *i* = inset;
ca = centre above; *cb* = centre below;
tl = top left; *tc* = top centre;
tr = top right; *bl* = bottom left;
bc = bottom centre; *br* = bottom right;
blc = bottom left centre;
brc = bottom right centre.

12–13 Photonica/Yutaka Iijima;
17*t* Stone/David Allan Brant;
17*b* CorbisStockmarket/John Henley;
18 Stone/David Madison; **19** SPL/Volker Steger; **20** Society of Teachers of the Alexander Technique; **21** A–Z Botanical Collection/H. Thomson; **21***r* Stone/Robert Daly; **22** Stone/Michael Busselle;
23*t* Corbis/Hulton-Deutsch Collection;
23*c* SPL/David Parker; **23***b* Warren Anatomical Museum, Francis A. Countway Library of Medicine, Harvard Medical School; **24***t* © The Nobel Foundation; **24***b* Stone/Joe Polillio;
25*tl* SPL/BSIP EST IOT; **25***tc* SPL;
25*tr* SPL/Tim Beddon; **25***bl* SPL/Hank Morgan; **25***bc* SPL/Alfred Pasieka;
25*br* Stephen M. Smith, Oxford University Centre for Functional MRI of the Brain, John Radcliffe Hospital;
27 Photographer's Library;
32–3 Stone/Chad Slattery;
33 Hulton Archive/Doug McKenzie;
34*t* Corbis/Reuters NewMedia Inc.;
35*r* Corbis/Patsy Lynch;
36 Photonica/Hans Wuryling;
38*t* Stone/Laurence Monneret;
38*b* NHPA/G. I. Bernard; **39** ImageState;
40*t* Photodisc/CMCD; **40***bl* Corbis-Stockmarket/Al France Kevich;
41*t* Stone/Paul Sisul; **41***i* Stone/Tony Latham; **42–3** Stone/Peter Nicholson;
43 Hulton Archive/John Kobal Foundation; **44***t* Robert Harding Picture Library/Cliff Riedinger; **44***bl* ImageState;
44*blc* Stone/Christopher Bissell;
44*brc* Stone/Bob Thomas;
44*br* ImageState; **45***bl* Stone/Stewart Cohen; **45***blc* Stone/Howard Kingsnorth;
45*brc* Stone/Stuart McClymont;
45*br* ImageState; **46***b* Stone/James Darell;

47*t* CorbisStockmarket/K.J. Historical;
47*t* Photodisc/CMCD;
47*b* Moviestore Collection;
47*b* Stone/Edouard Bern; **48***t* Hulton Archive; **48***b* Stone/Colin Hawkins;
50 Stone/Clarissa Leahy; **51***t* Corbis-Stockmarket/Randy M. Ury;
51*b* Stone/David Oliver;
52–3 ImageBank/David Delossy;
55 Stone/James Darell; **56–7** SPL/Eye of Science; **56***b* Stone/Tony Latham;
57*b* Photonica/Charles Gullung;
60 ImageBank/Terje Rakke; **61** Corbis-Stockmarket/H. Armstrong Roberts;
62*b* Stone/Mark Douet; **63** Stone/Ed Horowitz; **69***t* Bridgeman Art Library/Lauros-Giraudon/Louvre, Paris;
72 Corbis/Bettmann; **75***c* Duncan Baird Publishers/Sian Irvine;
76*t* CorbisStockmarket/Tom & Dee McCarthy; **78***t* BBC Picture Archives;
80*t* Corbis-Stockmarket/ Will Ryan;
80*b* Corbis/Bettmann;
81*t* Photonica/Steve Weinberg;
81*b* Photodisc/C Squared Studios;
82–3 Stone/Paul Chesley; **83** Hulton Archive; **85***t* Stone/HMS Group/Doug McKay; **85***b* AP Photo/Beth A. Kieser;
88 Corbis-Stockmarket/LWA/Sharie Kennedy; **89** Greg Balfour Evans;
92 Corbis/Hulton-Deutsch Collection;
93*t* Stone/Mike McQueen; **93***b* Imperial War Museum; **94***l* Photodisc**;** **94***r* Stone/Martin Barraud; **95** Stone/Ronald McKechnie; **96***t* Stone/Christopher Thomas; **96***b* Stone/Val Corbett;
97*t* Stone/Michael Busselle;
97*c* Stone/James Jackson; **97***b* Corbis-Stockmarket/Craig Tuttle; **98** AP Photo/Rick Rycroft; **99** Press Association;
100 Moviestore Collection/United Artists; **101***t* CorbisStockmarket/Susumu Sato; **102***t* Photodisc; **102***b* Stone/David Harry Stewart; **104***l* Rex Features/David White; **104***r* AFP; **105***t* Stone/Terry Vine;
105*b* Photonica/ Benoit Moneca;
106*t* CorbisStockmarket/ Koopman;
108–9 ImageState; **109** Photodisc/Siede Preis; **114** EEG Spectrum;
115 CorbisStockmarket/LWA/Dann Tardif; **116** Photographer's Library;
117 Photodisc/Steve Cole;

118 ImageState; **119***t/b* Duncan Baird Publishers/Matthew Ward; **120–1** *all* Duncan Baird Publishers/Matthew Ward;
124 CorbisStockmarket/Rob Lewine;
126 Corbis/Reuters New Media Inc.;
128*l* NHPA/David Woodfall; **130–1** Stone/Joe Polillio; **131***t* Photodisc/Steve Mason; **131***ca* Stone/Jurgen Reisch;
131*cb* Photodisc/Geostock;
131*b* Stone/Deborah Jaffe;
134*t* Stone/Rosanne Olson;
134*c* Photographer's Library; **134***b* Stone/Michelangelo Gratton; **135***t* Stone/Tony Latham; **135***c* Stone/Donna Day;
135*b* Stone/Terry Vine; **136–7** Pictor;
140*bl* Stone/David Hanover;
140*bcl* Stone/Stewart Cohen;
140*bcr* Stone/Christopher Bissell;
140*br* Stone/Frank Siteman;
141*t* Pictor; **141***bl* Pictor;
141*blc* Photographer's Library;
141*bcr* Stone/Daniel Bosler;
141*br* Photographer's Library;
142*t* Hulton Archive/Leo Baeck Institute;
143*t* Bridgeman Art Library/British Library, London; **145** Rex Features;
148 Photodisc/Steve Mason;
149*b* SPL/Royal Victoria Infirmary, Newcastle upon Tyne/Simon Fraser;
151 Photodisc/C Squared Studios;
152–3 SPL/Maximilian Stock Ltd.;
153 SPL/Custom Medical Stock Photo;
154 Stone/Laurence Monneret;
154–5 Stone/ Richard Fremont;
157*br* Duncan Baird Publishers/William Lingwood; **162–3** Photonica/Makoto Takada; **166***t* Robert Harding Picture Library/The Picture Book;
166*c* FPG International/Gerd George;
166*b* FPG International/David Lees;
167*t* Stone/David Roth; **167***cl* The Image Bank/William R. Sallaz;
167*cr* Photonica/Shin Watanabe;
167*bl* Stone/Zigy Kalunzy;
167*br* Superstock; **168** Moviestore Collection; **169***b* Stone/Zigy Kalunzy;
170*tl* AP Photo; **170***tr* AP Photo/NOAO;
170*c* Press Association; **170***bl* AP Photo/Douglas C. Pizac; **170***br* AP Photo/Bruce Weaver; **171***t* Image State;
171*b* Stone/Nicholas Veasey;
172*cl* Stone/Mark Harris;

172cr Corbis Stockmarket/Ron Lowery; **172**b Stone/Pete Seaward; **175** Stone/Wilhelm Scholz; **176–7** Image State; **177**t Corbis Stockmarket/Dale O'Dell; **177**b Corbis/Bettmann; **178–9** The Image Bank/Colin Molyneux; **178**b Robert Harding Picture Library/International Stock/Camille Tokerud; **180**l Corbis/Peter Tumley; **180**r Hutchison Picture Library; **181** Hulton Archive; **185** Stone/Pauline Cutler; **186** FPG International/Carl Vanderschuit; **187**t DK Images/Dave King; **188**b Photographer's Library; **189**tl Corbis Stockmarket/Ariel Skelley; **189**tlc FPG International/Barry Rosenthal; **189**tr Stone/David Madison; **190** Photographer's Library; **190-1** Pictor; **192**l Superstock; **192**r Corbis Stockmarket/Norbert Schafer; **194**bl Bubbles/Jacqui Farrow; **194**bc Bubbles/Frans Rombout; **194**br Bubbles/Jacqui Farrow; **194–5** Photographer's Library; **196** courtesy of Celador; **196–7** Axiom; **198–9**b SPL/Kingston Museum/Eadweard Muybridge Collection; **200** Corbis Stockmarket/Dale O'Dell; **201**tl Corbis Stockmarket/Ariel Skelley; **201**tc FPG International/Barry Rosenthal; **201**bl Photonica/Gen Nishino; **201**bc Corbis Stockmarket/Ron Lowery; **201**br Stone/David Madison; **202**t SPL/Sidney Moulds; **202**b Rex Features; **203**l Reprinted from Neuron, 19, 1997 pp.863–870 Cabeza, R., Mangels, J., Nyberg, L., Habib, R., Houle, S., McIntosh, A. R., & Tulving, E. (1997). Brain regions differentially involved in remembering what and when: a PET study, with permission from Elsevier Science; **203**r Cabeza, R., Kapur, S., Craik, F. I. M., McIntosh, A. R., Houle, S. & Tulving, E. (1997). Functional neuroanatomy of recall and recognition: a PET study of episodic memory. Journal of Cognitive Neuroscience, 9(2) 254–265; **204**c Natural History Museum, London; **204**b SPL; **205**t Pictor; **205**c NHPA/Haroldo Palo Jr.; **206–7** The Image Bank/GK+ Vikki Hart; **206**b Bruce Coleman/Gordon Langsbury;

207b NHPA/Andy Rouse; **210**t Image State; **210**c Photographer's Library; **210**b Corbis Stockmarket/Lester Lefkowitz; **210–11** Image State; **211**r Corbis Stockmarket/Dennis M. Gottlieb; **212**t Stone/Lori Adamski Peek; **214** AP Photo/H. Rumph, Jr.; **215** courtesy of Pacific Northwest National Laboratory; **216** Impact Photo/Bruce Stephens; **217**b Stone/Anthony Marsland; **218–9** Pictor; **219**b Corbis Stockmarket/CIB Productions; **220–1** Pictor; **221** Pictor; **222** Image State; **223**t SPL/Wellcome Department of Cognitive Neurology; **223**b Stone/Camille Tokerud; **226**l Stone/Rosemary Weller; **226**c Pictor; **227**t Pictor; **228**l Pictor; **228**r Pictor; **228**b Camera Press; **229**t Corbis Stockmarket/Jaime C. Salles; **229**cl Hulton Archive; **229**cr Hulton Archive; **229**b Corbis; **230** Robert Harding Picture Library/Simon Harris; **231**b Stone/Andy Sacks; **236–7** Hulton Archive/NASA; **237** NHPA/Manfred Danegger; **238–9** Warren Photographic/Jane Burton; **239** Corbis Stockmarket/Charles Gupton; **240** Press Association; **240–1** Stone/Bob Thomas; **243**b Wellcome Library, London; **248–9** Photonica/Johner; **249**b Bubbles/Ian West; **250**t Press Association; **250**b Amy Snyder © 1998 Exploratorium, www.exploratorium.edu; **251**t Corbis/Alison Wright; **252** Corbis/Karl Weatherly; **253** Ross-Parry Picture Agency; **254** Bridgeman Art Library/© Salvador Dali, Gala-Salvador Dali Foundation, DACS, London 2001; **255** OPTIMA, Radcliffe Infirmary, Oxford; **256–7** Robert Harding Picture Library/Schuster; **262** Bridgeman Art Library/ British Library, London/Louis Carrogis Carmontelle (1717–1806) Leopold Mozart (1719–87) and his two young children, Wolfgang Amadeus and Maria-Anna; **263**b Linguaphone Institute Ltd.; **264**l Rex Features/Mike Daines; **264**r Rex Features/Tony Larkins; **267** Mary Evans Picture Library; **268** Bridgeman Art Library/Private Collection/Frederic Leighton (1830–96) Mnemosyne, The Mother of the Muses

(oil on canvas); **269** Mary Evans Picture Library; **272-3** World Pictures; **278**t Pictor; **278–9** Pictor; **280–1** FPG International/Space Frontiers; **283**tl Moviestore Collection; **283**tc Press Association; **283**tr Moviestore Collection; **283**cl Moviestore Collection; **2839**cc Corbis/Bettmann; **283**cr Moviestore Collection/Hal Roach; **284**cl Pictor; **284**cr Photographer's Library; **284**bl Photographer's Library; **284**br Hutchison Picture Library; **285**cl Image State; **285**clc Photographer's Library; **285**crc Corbis/Bettmann; **285**bl Photographer's Library; **285**blc Photographer's Library; **285**brc Press Association; **286**t Corbis/Owen Frank; **290**bl Stone/Fiona Alison; **290**bc Pictor; **290**br Stone/Mary Kate Denny; **291**t Corbis/Bettmann; **291**bl Bubbles/Ian West; **291**br Stone/Pauline Cutler; **292**t Stone/Robert Daly; **292**c Bubbles/Lois Joy Thurston; **292**bl Bubbles/Frans Rombout; **292**br Stone/Bob Handelman; **293**bl Photographer's Library; **293**bc Image State; **293**br Stone/David Hanover; **294** Network Photographers/Martin Mayer; **295** Corbis Stockmarket/Roy Morsch; **297** Questor's Theatre, Ealing London 1993 production of Trelawney of the "Wells" by Arthur W. Pinero; **298** Stone/Rick Rusing; **299** Robert Harding Picture Library; **300** The Image Bank/Petrified Collection; **301** Corbis/Bettmann; **302–3** Duncan Baird Archives/William Lingwood; **305** Pictor; **307** Rex Features/Tim Rooke; **308–9** Bruce Coleman/Natural Selections; **309**tl Pictor; **309**tr Pictor; **309**b Pictor; **312–3** Bruce Coleman/Natural Selection Inc.; **316**tl SPL/Wellcome Department of Cognitive Neurology; **316**tr Photographer's Library; **316**bl Stone/Tony Hutchings; **316**br Photographer's Library; **317** Stone/James Cotier; **319**tr SPL/Department of Cognitive Neurology; **319**b Bridgeman Art Library/The De Morgan Foundation, London; **320** SPL/Geoff Tompkinson; **321** Stone/Deborah Jaffe; **326** Pictor; **327**t Pictor; **327**b SPL/Gregory Dimijian; **328–9**t Robert Harding Picture Library;

328bl, bc, br Warren Photographic/Jane Burton; **329**t Frank Lane Picture Agency/Minden Pictures/K. Wothe; **329**bl Warren Photographic/Jane Burton; **330–1** Bridgeman Art Library/Vitlycke Museum, Tanum; **330**t Bridgeman Art Library/Naturhistorisches Museum, Vienna; **330**b Natural History Museum, London; **331**t Robert Harding Picture Library; **331**bl DK Images/Philip Dowell; **331**blc Bridgeman Art Library/Musée des Antiquities Nationales, St. Germaine en Laye; **331**br British Museum, London; **332–3** Corbis/Bob Rowan/Progressive Images; **332**b SPL; **333**b SPL/Colin Cuthbert; **334** Stone/Tim Flach; **335** Ronald Grant Archive; **338** Pictor; **339**b Photographer's Library; **340** Image Bank/David de Lossy; **341** SPL/Oscar Burriel; **342–3** Bruce Coleman/Natural Selections Inc.; **342**b Image Bank/Malcolm Piers; **343**b Photographer's Library; **344–5** Corbis/Robert Holmes; **346–7** Image State; **346**b Corbis/Ted Streshinsky; **347**t Hulton Archive; **347**c SPL/Pascal Goetgheluck; **348** Hutchison Library/Sarah Errington; **349**t Corbis/Michael S. Yamashita; **349**bl Image State; **349**br Pictor; **351** Pictor; **352–3** FPG/Laurance B. Aiuppy; **352**b FPG/Peter Lilja; **353**c Warren Photographic/Jane Burton; **354**b Flowers and Foliage; **356** courtesy of Osborne and Little; **357** Image Bank/Britt J. Erlanson-Messens; **358** Pictor; **359** AKG, London; **361** Moviestore Collection; **365**tl Bridgeman Art Library/Phillips, The International Fine Art Auctioneers, London; **365**tr Bridgeman Art Library/Museum of Fine Arts, Houston; **365**b courtesy of Orion Publishing; **366** Camera Press/Colin Davey; **367** SPL/Gregory Macnicol; **368**cl, cr Mary Evans Picture Library; **369**tl Corbis/Bettmann; **369**b Moviestore Collection; **373**t Mary Evans Picture Library; **374** Photographer's Library; **375**t Corbis/Owen Frank; **375**b SPL/NASA; **377** Corbis/Phil Schemeister; **379** courtesy of Marcus Raichle;

382bl, br Advertising Archives; **383** AP Photo; **385**bl SPL; **386**b Ronald Grant Archive; **390**c, b Hulton Archive; **393**t Corbis Stockmarket/Denis Scott; **393**b Mary Evans Picture Library; **394–5** Art Archive/Musée Guimet, Paris/Dagli Orti; **394** SPL/National Library of Medicine; **396** Ronald Grant Archive; **397**t courtesy of Northern Territories Tourist Commission; **397**b Hulton Archive; **398** Ronald Grant Archive; **399**t Tate Gallery, London/©Salvador Dali, Gala-Salvador Dali Foundation, DACS, London 2001; **399**b Camera Press/G. Botti/Valentin; **400–1** Stone/Tim Brown; **402–3** Stone/Tim Brown; **402**b Image Bank/Daniel E. Arsenault Photography Inc.; **403**t Image Bank/Ghislain and Marie David de Lossy; **403**b Robert Harding Picture Library; **406–7**b Pictor; **407**t AKG, London; **409** Moviestore Collection; **410**l, t, ba Photographer's Library; **410**tb Bubbles/Peter Sylent; **410**b Bubbles/Jacqui Furrow; **411** Ronald Grant Archive; **412** Magnum/Thomas Hoepker; **413**t Photographer's Library; **413**b FPG/David Lees; **417** Corbis Stockmarket/C+B Productions; **419** Bubbles/Loisjoy Thurston; **420** Photographer's Library; **421**t courtesy of the Functional Neuroimaging Group, Department of Neurology, Professor Arno Villringer and Department of Law, Professor Hans-Peter Schwintowski, Humboldt University, Berlin; **421**b Magnum/Martine Frank; **422** Network Photographers/Jeremy Green; **423**t Photographer's Library; **424–5** Bruce Coleman/Natural Selections Inc.; **425** Stone/Michael Townsend; **427**l AKG, London; **427**r SPL/Custom Medical Stock; **428**b Michael Holford; **429** AKG, London/Erich Lessing; **432–3** Corbis/Macduff Everton; **434–5** FPG/Chris Rawlings; **436**b Corbis Stockmarket/Chris Collins; **436** FPG/John McGrail; **438**b Bruce Coleman/Jorg and Petra Wegner; **439**bl, br Pictor; **440**b Stone/Timothy Shonnard;

441t Pictor; **442** Photographer's Library; **444**t Stone/Thomas Del Brase; **445**t Image State; **446–7** Image Bank/Eric Meola; **446**r Stone/Anthony Marsland; **448** Rex Features/Camila Morandi; **449**t Corbis/Keren Su; **449**b Eri Takase; **450** Corbis Stockmarket/Craig Tuttle; **452–3** Hulton Archive; **454** Pictor; **455**l AKG, London/©Succession Picasso/DACS 2001; **455**r Art Archive/Museum of Modern Art, NY/Album/John Martin/©Succession Picasso/DACS 2001; **456**l Performing Arts Library/Ingi; **456**r Bridgeman Art Library/Private Collection; **456–7** Performing Arts Library/Linda Rich.

Studio photography
Matthew Ward **69**b, **74**, **75**bl, **107**, **123**, **156**, **157**tr/bl, **173**, **224**, **227**, **244**, **272–3**, **276–7**t, **282**, **300–1**, **308**, **309**br, **323**b, **339**t, **350**l, **353**tr, **378**l, **414–5**, **418**b, **435**t, **437**b

ILLUSTRATORS
Jamel Akib **73**, **122–3**, **146**, **234**; Jon Berkeley **198**, **199**, **246**, **284**; Stuart Briers **16**, **26**, **68**, **158–9**, **384**; Peter Bull **236**, **276**, **277**, **340**, **364**, **401**; Sue Clarke **87**, **106**; Emma Dodd **189**, **212**, **231**, **245**, **264**, **286**, **287**, **298**, **350**, **355**b, **388**, **389**, **453**, **458**, **459**; Melvyn Evans **2–3**, **10–11**, **15**, **29**, **35**, **59**, **62**, **77**, **91**, **133**; **160–161** Darren Hopes **70**t, **94**, **372**, **408**, **428**; Kevin Jones Associates **149**, **256**; Sally Kindberg **275**, **276**; Debbie Lush **68**b, **111**, **129**, **243**, **296**, **306**; John McFaul **138–9**; Shane McGowan **112**; Deborah Maizels **32**, **37**, **128**, **146**, **212**, **225**, **251**; Sarah Perkins **232**, **258**; John Richardson **142**, **270**, **444**; Matthew Russell **174**, **184**, **100**; Gill Sampson **110**, **125**; Mark Seabrook **310–11**, **314**, **336**, **370**, **404**, **428**; Gill Tomblin **147**; Gary West **54**, **84**, **101**; Ian Whadcock **160–1**, **164**, **182**, **208**, **234**, **260**, **288**; Paul Williams **30**, **344**, **355**t; Philip Wilson **31**, **201**, **402**; Jurgen Ziewe **150**, Jurgen Ziewe **362**, **386**

CREDITS

Making the Most of Your Brain
was created and produced for Reader's Digest, London,
by Duncan Baird Publishers Ltd
Sixth Floor, Castle House, 75–76 Wells Street
London W1T 3QH

Managing Editor Susan Watt
Managing Art Editor Phil Gilderdale
Editors: Part One – Henry Spilberg, **Part Two** – Esther Ripley, **Part Three** – Marek Walisiewicz, Susan Watt
Designers: Part One – Chris Walker, **Part Two** – Chris Walker, Gail Jones, Tim Foster, **Part Three** – Gail Jones,
Sheilagh Noble, Chris Walker
Picture Researcher Ellen Root
Editorial Assistant Kelly Bishop

Academic Consultants: Part One – Claus Vogële, PhD, Dipl Psych, CClinPsychol, Professor of Clinical and
Health Psychology, University of Luton, **Part Two** – Angus R.H. Gellatly, PhD, CPsychol, Professor of Psychology,
Keele University, **Part Three** – Zoltan Dienes, D.Phil. Reader in Experimental Psychology, University of Sussex

CONTRIBUTORS

Part One:
Dr Susan Aldridge
Nigel C. Benson
Rita Carter
Ann Charlish
Jon Evans
Dr Geoff Lowe
Gladeana McMahon
Clare Roberts
Linda Whitney
Paul Wymer

Part Two:
Dr Susan Aldridge
Nigel C. Benson
Dr Pam Briggs
Clifford Bishop
Rita Carter
Dylan Evans
Professor Angus R.H. Gellatly
Dr Michael M. Gruneberg
Dr Steve Kelly
Professor Douglas J. Herrmann
John McCrone
Dr Ian Walker
Dr Mark A. Wheeler
Professor John Wilding

Part Three:
Sarah Angliss
Nigel C. Benson
Dr Peter Bull
Jerome Burne
Rita Carter
Professor David Fontana
Dr Les Lancaster
John McCrone
Dr Rowland Stout
Marek Walisiewicz

ADDITIONAL THANKS
Peter Bently, Tim Foster, Nicola Hodgson, Jude Ledger, Marnie Searchwell, Allan Sommerville, Suzanne Tuhrim,
Christopher Westhorp, Sarah Williams

For the Reader's Digest
Editor Christine Noble
Art Editor Louise Turpin
Editorial Assistant Lucy Murray

Reader's Digest General Books
Editorial Director Cortina Butler
Art Director Nick Clark

*The information in Part One of this book (The Healing Brain) is for interest and reference only; it is not intended as
a substitute for a doctor's diagnosis and care. The editors urge anyone with suspected or ongoing medical problems or
symptoms to consult a doctor.*

Making the Most of Your Brain
was created for Reader's Digest by
Duncan Baird Publishers Limited, London

First edition Copyright © 2002
The Reader's Digest Association Limited,
11 Westferry Circus, Canary Wharf,
London E14 4HE
www.readersdigest.co.uk

Copyright © 2002 Reader's Digest Association Far East Limited
Philippines Copyright © 2002 Reader's Digest Association Far East Limited

The material in this volume was originally published
as three volumes in a series called *Brain Power.*
Copyright © 2001 The Reader's Digest Association Limited, London

Origination: Colour Systems Limited, London
Printing and Binding: Shenzhen Donnelley Bright Sun Printing Co,.Ltd.

ISBN: 962-258-286-9

Reprinted in 2003

PPO/770